Focus on Achievement

LONGMAN KEYSTONE provides explicit, intensive, and focused instruction that maximizes students' academic language proficiency and reading comprehension, giving all learners a *real* chance for academic success.

LONGMAN KEYSTONE:

- Accelerates academic vocabulary acquisition
- Develops transferable cross-curricular academic skills
- Provides an easy-to-use roadmap to academic success

Go to www.LongmanKeystone.com *for the following teaching support:*

Teacher's Area
- *Teacher's eBook*
- *Pacing Guides*
- *Daily Oral Reading Fluency*
- *Daily Writing Fluency Prompts*
- *Assessment Audio*
- *Additional Practice, Reteaching, and Remediation*
- *Lexile™ Information*
- *Professional Development Links*
- *Program Information*

Student Area
- *Project Links*
- *Smithsonian Websites*
- *Academic Word List*
- *Student eBook*

Teacher's Edition
Contents

LONGMAN KEYSTONE

A

Anna Uhl Chamot

John De Mado

Sharroky Hollie

PEARSON

Longman

TEACHER'S EDITION

Pearson Education, 10 Bank Street, White Plains, NY 10606

Staff credits: The people who made up the *Longman Keystone* team, representing editorial, production, design, manufacturing, and marketing, are John Ade, Rhea Banker, Liz Barker, Danielle Belfiore, Don Bensey, Virginia Bernard, Kenna Bourke, Anne Boynton-Trigg, Johnnie Farmer, Maryann Finocchi, Patrice Fraccio, Geraldine Geniusas, Charles Green, Henry Hild, David L. Jones, Lucille M. Kennedy, Ed Lamprich, Emily Lippincott, Tara Maceyak, Maria Pia Marrella, Linda Moser, Laurie Neaman, Sherri Pemberton, Liza Pleva, Joan Poole, Edie Pullman, Monica Rodriguez, Tania Saiz-Sousa, Chris Siley, Lynn Sobotta, Heather St. Clair, Jennifer Stem, Siobhan Sullivan, Jane Townsend, Heather Vomero, Marian Wassner, Lauren Weidenman, Matthew Williams, and Adina Zoltan.

Smithsonian American Art Museum contributors: Project director and writer: Elizabeth K. Eder, Ph.D.; Writer: Mary Collins; Image research assistants: Laurel Fehrenbach, Katherine G. Stilwill, and Sally Otis; Rights and reproductions: Richard H. Sorensen and Leslie G. Green; Building photograph by Tim Hursley.

Text design: Kirchoff/Wohlberg, Inc.
Text composition: TSI Graphics

Text font: 12/14 Minion
Acknowledgments: See page T473.
Illustration and Photo Credits: See page T474.

ISBN-13: 978-0-13-205869-8
ISBN-10: 0-13-205869-3

PEARSON LONGMAN ON THE WEB

Pearsonlongman.com offers online resources for teachers and students. Access our Companion Websites, our online catalog, and our local offices around the world.

Visit us at **www.pearsonlongman.com**.

Printed in the United States of America
3 4 5 6 7 8 9 10 11—CRK—12 11 10 09

About the Authors

Anna Uhl Chamot is a professor of secondary education and a faculty advisor for ESL in George Washington University's Department of Teacher Preparation. She has been a researcher and teacher trainer in content-based second-language learning and language-learning strategies. She co-designed, and has written extensively about, the Cognitive Academic Language Learning Approach (CALLA) and spent seven years implementing the CALLA model in the Arlington Public Schools in Virginia.

John De Mado has been an energetic force in the field of Language Acquisition for several years. He is founder and president of John De Mado Language Seminars, Inc., an educational consulting firm devoted exclusively to language acquisition and literacy issues. John, who speaks a variety of languages, has authored several textbook programs and produced a series of music CD/DVDs designed to help students acquire other languages. John is recognized nationally, as well as internationally, for his insightful workshops, motivating keynote addresses, and humor-filled delivery style.

Sharroky Hollie is an assistant professor in teacher education at California State University, Dominguez Hills. His expertise is in the field of professional development, African-American education, and second-language methodology. He is an urban literacy visiting professor at Webster University, St. Louis. Sharroky is the Executive Director of the Center for Culturally Responsive Teaching and Learning (CCRTL) and the co-founding director of the nationally acclaimed Culture and Language Academy of Success (CLAS).

Can all mysteries be solved?

Thematic Organization
Six thematic units per level are organized around a **Big Question** that provides a starting point for building understanding of key concepts and academic vocabulary. Each reading in the unit asks students to consider different aspects of the **Big Question**, leading to deeper levels of understanding.

Systematic Skills Development
Four readings per unit, half of which are informational text, develop academic skills logically and systematically, in a clear and consistent sequence.

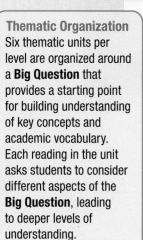

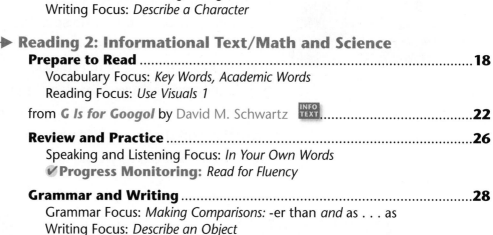

Progress Monitoring
Frequent progress-monitoring checks ensure that students are mastering concepts before moving on to higher-level academic skills.

Evidence of Understanding
Link the Readings provides an opportunity for students to compare and contrast the unit readings as they discuss the **Big Question**, demonstrating their understanding of key concepts and their ability to transfer and apply newly acquired skills to new academic tasks.

Contents

How does growing up change us?

 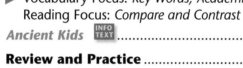

Speaking and Listening
Retelling and **Reader's Theater** exercises allow students to engage and develop key speaking and listening skills, and also provide an opportunity for students to deepen their understanding of the readings.

Cumulative Writing Strand
Writing is developed throughout the unit in a logical, systematic sequence, allowing students to sharpen their writing skills as they build toward the major end-of-unit **Writing Workshop** assignment.

UNIT 3

Contents

Grammar, Usage, and Mechanics
Grammar concepts are taught with each reading. They incorporate extensive use of modeling and provide plenty of practice. Concepts are then applied in the follow-up writing activity, ensuring retention.

Building Visual Literacy
By special arrangement with the **Smithsonian American Art Museum**, *Keystone* provides a unique opportunity for students to develop their visual and cultural literacy. These beautiful end-of-unit features teach students how to "read" works of art for meaning and provide a glimpse into the American experience as seen through the eyes of artists from all walks of life.

Contents

> **Review and Practice**
> Each reading is followed by a comprehension activity that uses the Question/Answer Relationship method: a strategy for building comprehension skills logically and systematically, from factual recall to higher-order critical thinking and classroom discussion.

> **Built-in Differentiated Instruction**
> A variety of differentiated end-of-unit projects allow all learners to demonstrate understanding of concepts according to their abilities.

Contents

 THE BIG QUESTION

How are courage and imagination linked?

Fluency Practice
Frequent opportunities are provided for students to practice reading fluency. These activities offer strategies to help students improve their oral reading and gain confidence in reading and speaking.

Fluency Check
This end-of-unit feature provides a timed activity to help students practice and monitor their fluency development.

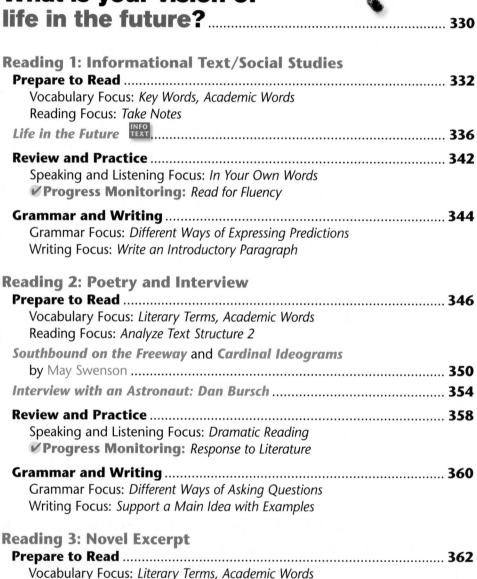

Contents

Handbooks
Features more than fifty pages of additional support in Reading, Writing, Grammar, Technology, Study and Test-Taking Skills, and more. These handbooks provide easy-to-use and easy-to-understand support in the critical academic skills that students need for success.

Keystone Scope & Sequence

SELECTION	VOCABULARY		
	Key Words	**Academic Words**	**Literary Words**
UNIT 1 **Can all mysteries be solved?**	*from* **Chasing Vermeer,** Blue Balliett Novel excerpt *from* **G Is for Googol,** David M. Schwartz Informational text **"Fact or Fiction?"** Informational text **Teenage Detectives,** Carol Farley and Hy Conrad Two mystery short stories	architecture gradual infinity numerals spirals steep archaeologist clues creature disappeared fantasy sacred	identify individual occur physical theory constant illustrate sequence unique accurate create evidence survive aware intelligent motive pursue	characters character traits idioms puns
	Smithsonian American Art Museum: Solving the Puzzle of Letters and Numbers			
UNIT 2 **How does growing up change us?**	**"Ancient Kids"** Informational text *from* **Becoming Naomi León,** Pam Muñoz Ryan Realistic fiction, How-to piece *from* **Later, Gator,** Laurence Yep Realistic fiction **"Amazing Growth Facts"** Informational text **"The Old Grandfather and His Little Grandson,"** Leo Tolstoy Folk tale	ancient ceremony citizen education rights rituals average conversion height length rate weight	classical cultural feature philosophy assist bond conflict process affect author effect perspective benefit category enormous percent	dialogue setting plot point of view narrator
	Smithsonian American Art Museum: Capturing Childhood			
UNIT 3 **How does helping others help us all?**	*from* **Run Away Home,** Patricia C. McKissack Historical fiction **"Extraordinary People: Serving Others"** Informational text *from* **Zlata's Diary,** Zlata Filipović Diary **"Friendship and Cooperation in the Animal Kingdom"** Informational text	assassinated extraordinary founders resistance superintendent tolerance arrangement cooperate damage gigantic intruder tsunami	appropriate communicate period precise achieve alter impact role consist establish method stress attitude comment concept rely on	dialect mood suspense figure of speech hyperbole
	Smithsonian American Art Museum: Respect			

WORD STUDY	READING STRATEGY	LISTENING & SPEAKING	GRAMMAR	WRITING	
				Writing Modes/ Assignments	Writing Elements/ Structure
• Prefixes: *un-, dis-* • Spelling words with *ai, ay, ee,* and *oa* • Same sound, different spellings • Compound nouns	• Predict • Use visuals 1 • Preview • Draw conclusions	• Retell • Reader's Theater • **Listening & speaking workshop:** Description guessing game	• Distinguishing parts of a sentence • Making Comparisons: *-er than* and *as…as* • Passive voice • Subject-verb agreement with indefinite pronouns	**Description** • Describe a character • Describe an object • Describe a place • Describe an event • **Writing workshop:** Descriptive essay	• Include physical traits and character traits • Use sensory details • Use spatial order • Use chronological order
• Spelling words with long vowel sound /ē/ • Suffixes *-ness, -tion,* and *-ation* • Animal verbs and idioms • Spelling words with long vowel sound /ō/	• Compare and contrast • Visualize • Recognize sequence • Use visuals 2	• Retell • Reader's Theater • **Listening & speaking workshop:** Skit	• Showing contrast: transitions and coordinating conjunctions • Non-action verbs • Making comparisons • Simple past: regular and irregular verbs	**Narration** • Write a friendly letter • Write about a character and setting • Write a story from another point of view • Write a personal narrative • **Writing workshop:** Fictional narrative	• Tell a memorable sequence of events in time order, using correct letter format • Use spatial or chronological order, sensory details; describe physical and character traits • Focus on point of view and the effects a shift in perspective has on a narrative • Use chronological order and concrete details; show why an experience or situation was memorable
• Uses of the apostrophe • Spelling words with silent *gh* • Synonyms and antonyms • Greek and Latin roots	• Make inferences • Identify problems and solutions • Distinguish fact from opinion • Identify main idea and details	• Retell • Reader's Theater • **Listening & speaking workshop:** TV talk show	• Simple and compound sentences • Prepositions of time: *in, on,* and *at* • Placement of adjectives • Prepositions of location	**Persuasion** • Write a book review • Use a question-and-answer format • Write a diary entry • Write a critical evaluation • **Writing workshop:** Persuasive speech	• Give an opinion and a recommendation supported by reasons and examples from the book • Ask a question; follow it with a persuasive answer that is supported by facts, details, and examples • Present both sides of an issue; use the first person and a diary format; include figurative expressions and adjectives to persuade • Write topic sentence; examine the topic against a set of standards; make a judgment that is supported by examples

17

Keystone Scope & Sequence

SELECTION	VOCABULARY		
	Key Words	**Academic Words**	**Literary Words**
UNIT 4 **What do we learn through winning and losing?**	"Soccer: The World Sport," Jane Schwartz Informational text "Casey at the Bat," Ernest Lawrence Thayer Poetry "Swift Things Are Beautiful," Elizabeth Coatsworth Poetry "Buffalo Dusk," Carl Sandburg Poetry "The Hare and the Tortoise," Aesop Fable "Orpheus and Eurydice" Myth "Going, Going, Gone?" Informational text "Ivory-billed Woodpeckers Make Noise," Jill Egan Informational text	athletes boundaries professional responsibilities sacrifice uniforms conservationists destruction extinct habitats ornithology predator	element focus positive require brief device final respond sphere structure define instruct objective style environment estimate factors statistics	rhythm repetition rhyme scheme fable moral personification myth
	Smithsonian American Art Museum: Baseball in America		
UNIT 5 **How are courage and imagination linked?**	The Secret Garden, Frances Hodgson Burnett, adapted by David C. Jones Play "Kids' Guernica" Informational text "Hoot," Carl Hiaasen Novel excerpt "A Tree Grows in Kenya: The Story of Wangari Maathai" Informational text "How to Plant a Tree" Informational text	anniversary atomic bomb canvases chaos inspiration mural campaign committee continent democratic natural nutrition	approach convey cooperate drama circumstances construct react region demonstrate deny image site aspect finance resource sustain technology welfare	setting the scene list of characters stage directions humor colorful language
	Smithsonian American Art Museum: Dignity Through Art		
UNIT 6 **What is your vision of life in the future?**	"Life in the Future" Informational text "Southbound on the Freeway" and "Cardinal Ideograms," May Swenson Poetry "Interview with an Astronaut," Dan Bursch Interview from The Time Warp Trio: 2095, Jon Scieszka Science fiction "Genetic Fingerprints" Informational Text	artificial canyons frontier mass-produced robots volcanoes cells defendant forensic genes inherit whorls	function occupation research trend complex interpretation published section shift specific strategies techniques generation legislation medical policy procedure	simile metaphor stanzas science fiction setting
	Smithsonian American Art Museum: Imagining the Future		

WORD STUDY	READING STRATEGY	LISTENING & SPEAKING	GRAMMAR	WRITING	
				Writing Modes/ Assignments	**Writing Elements/ Structure**
• Multiple-meaning words • Spelling long vowel sound /ī/ • Spellings for *r*-controlled vowels • Homophones	• Ask questions • Read for enjoyment • Identify author's purpose • Recognize cause and effect	• Retell • Dramatic Reading • Reader's Theater • **Listening & speaking workshop:** TV sports report	• Present perfect • Simple past: more irregular verbs • Adverbs with *-ly* • Showing cause and effect: *because, because of,* and *so*	**Exposition** • Write a newspaper article • Write a response to literature • Write to compare and contrast • Write a cause-and-effect explanation • **Writing workshop:** Expository essay	• Support a main idea with details that explain *who, where, when, what,* and *why* • Give ideas and opinions about a piece of literature; support the response with examples and details • Compare two topics; tell how they are alike and how they are different • Give an explanation that clearly shows how causes and effects are logically related
• Spelling words with *oo* • Spelling words with *ea* • Prefixes *mega-, tele-, re-* • Suffixes *-ic, -ist, -able*	• Analyzing text structure 1 • Classify • Summarize • Follow steps in a process	• Retell • Reader's Theater • **Listening & speaking workshop:** How-to demonstration	• More adverbs with *-ly* • More uses of the present perfect • Quoted versus reported speech • Imperatives	**Exposition** • Write a formal e-mail • Write a paragraph that classifies something • Write a plot summary • Write how-to instructions • **Writing workshop:** Expository essay	• Use a problem-solution structure and the correct format for a formal e-mail • Organize by category; explain the features of each category • Cover main events of a story: the characters' goals, what they did to achieve them, and whether they succeeded • Put steps in order from first to last; use signal words and imperatives
• Spelling the diphthongs /oi/ and /ou/ • Greek and Latin roots • Schwa spelled *a, e, i, o, u* • Multiple-meaning words	• Take notes • Analyze text structure 2 • Skim • Make generalizations	• Retell • Dramatic Reading • Reader's Theater • **Listening & speaking workshop:** Speech	• Different ways of expressing predictions • Different ways of asking questions • Using punctuation • Using quotation marks	**Research report** • Write an introductory paragraph • Support a main idea with examples • Include quotations and citations • Include paraphrases and citations • **Writing workshop:** Research report	• Select and narrow a topic; ask a question to guide research • Do research and take notes; find specific examples to support the main idea • Support a main idea with quotations; cite sources for quotations • Paraphrase sources; cite them correctly; support the main idea with details

Learner Verification Report

Summary

A yearlong study conducted recently in Santa Ana, California, showed a dramatic improvement in test scores as well as remarkable improvement in English proficiency among students using Pearson Longman materials.

In this district with significantly high ELL enrollments, schools participating in the program piloted the Pearson Longman series in certain ELL classrooms, while other classrooms used an alternative program that was designed for low-level readers and included comprehensive ELL support. While students using both programs showed improvement, the most dramatic results came from those students using the Pearson Longman program.

Methodology and Results

Students were given a benchmark test at the beginning of the study (Pre-Test) and another test at the program's end (Post-Test). Students using the Pearson Longman materials showed a significant improvement in English proficiency.

As the graphs indicate, most learners showed overall improvement in their English proficiencies. (See Figures A and B.) The most dramatic improvement, however, came from classrooms piloting the Pearson Longman program, where a significantly higher number of students who began the study at a Below Basic and Far Below Basic proficiency finished the program at either a Basic or Proficient level. In fact, several students who piloted the alternative program actually lost ground overall in terms of English proficiency, in stark contrast to the Pearson Longman users.

Figure A

GRADE 6 PRE- & POST-TEST RESULTS

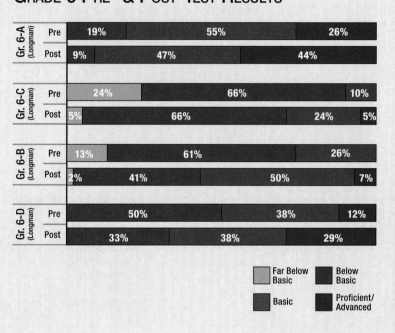

Figure B

GRADE 8 PRE- & POST-TEST RESULTS

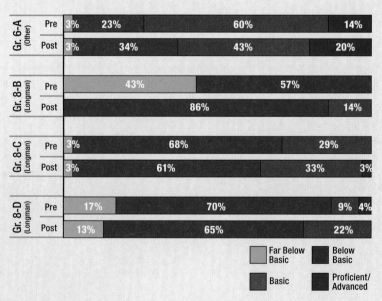

More impressively, an analysis of individual student performance shows that individual gains far outstripped losses in terms of benchmark test scores among students using the Pearson Longman program versus those using the alternative series. (See Figure C.)

Once again, the results showed that a significantly higher percentage of students using the Pearson Longman program saw an increase in test scores when compared to those using the other program. In fact, many more students using the alternative program actually saw their benchmark scores drop rather than increase over the course of the study. (See Figure D.)

Because the overall results of the study were consistent among each of the classes participating in the study and across grade levels, they lend strong support to the argument that English learners benefit more by using complete programs developed specifically for their language acquisition needs, rather than programs designed for low-level readers.

Figure C

PERCENTAGE OF STUDENTS GAINING (DROPPING) 1 OR MORE PROFICIENCY LEVELS

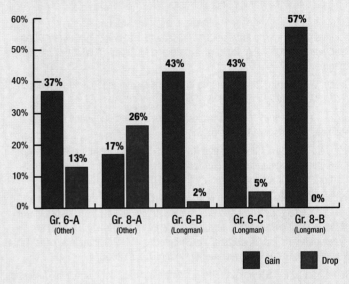

Figure D

PERCENTAGE OF STUDENTS WITH INCREASED (DECREASED) BENCHMARK SCORES

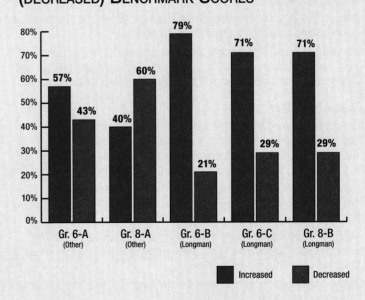

Research Bibliography

READING

Anderson, Neil J. *Exploring Second Language Reading: Issues and Strategies.* Boston, Mass: Heinle & Heinle, 1999.

Anderson, Thomas, and Bonnie Armbruster. "Readable Textbooks (or, Selecting a Textbook is Not Like Buying a Pair of Shoes)." In *Reading Comprehension: From Research to Practice.* Edited by Judith Orasanu (Mahwah, N.J.: Lawrence Erlbaum Associates, 1986), 151–162.

Cummins, Jim. "Language Proficiency, Bilingualism, and Academic Achievement." In *The Multicultural Classroom: Readings for Content-Area Teachers*, edited by P.A. Richard-Amato and M.A. Snow. White Plains, N.Y.: Longman, 1992.

Grabe, W. "Current Developments in Second Language Reading Research." In *TESOL Quarterly* 25 (1991): 375–406.

_____. "Dilemmas for the Development of Second Language Reading Abilities." In *Prospect* 10 (1995): 38–51.

_____. "Reading Research and Its Implications for Reading Assessment." In *Fairness and Validation in Language Assessment*, edited by A. Kunnan (Cambridge: Cambridge University Press, 2000), 226–262.

National Reading Panel of the National Institute of Child Health & Human Development. *Teaching Children to Read: An Evidence-Based Assessment of the Scientific Research Literature on Reading and Its Implications for Reading Instruction. Reports of the Subgroups.* NIH Publication No. 00-4754. Washington, DC: U.S. Government Printing Office, 2000.

Rumelhart, D.E. "Schemata: The Building Blocks of Cognition." In *Theoretical Issues in Reading Comprehension: Perspectives from Cognitive Psychology, Linguistics, Artificial Intelligence, and Education*, edited by R. J. Spiro, B.C. Bruce, and W.F. Brewer. Mahwah, N.J.: Lawrence Erlbaum Associates, 1980.

Spangenberg-Urbschat, Karen, and Robert Pritchard, eds. *Kids Come in All Languages: Reading Instruction for ESL Students.* Newark, Del.: International Reading Association, 1994.

Stanovich, K. *Progress in Understanding Reading: Scientific Foundations and New Frontiers.* New York: Guilford Press, 2000.

Stanovich, P. J., and K. Stanovich. *Using Research and Reason in Education: How Teachers Can Use Scientifically Based Research to Make Curricular and Instructional Decisions.* Washington, DC: National Institute for Literacy, 2003.

VOCABULARY

Chamot, A.U., and O'Malley, J.M. "The Cognitive Academic Language Learning Approach: A Bridge to the Mainstream." In *The Multicultural Classroom: Readings for Content-Area Teachers*, edited by P.A. Richard-Amato and M.A. Snow (New York: Longman, 1992), 39–57.

Fathman, A.K., M.E. Quinn, and C. Kessier. *Teaching Science to English Learners, Grades 4–8.* Program Information Guide Series, No. 11 from the National Clearinghouse for Bilingual Education, 1992.

Miller, G. "How School Children Learn Words." In *Proceedings of the Third Eastern States Conference on Linguistics*, edited by F. Marshall. Columbus, Ohio: The Ohio State University, 1986.

Nation, I.S.P. *Learning Vocabulary in Another Language.* New York: Cambridge University Press, 2001.

Schmitt, Norbert. *Vocabulary in Language Teaching.* New York: Cambridge University Press, 2000.

Schmitt, Norbert, and M. McCarthy, eds. *Vocabulary: Description, Acquisition, and Pedagogy.* New York: Cambridge University Press, 1997.

Short, D.J. "Assessing Integrated Language and Content Instruction." In *TESOL Quarterly* 27 (4), 1993.

Snow, M.A., and D. Brinton. *The Content-Based Classroom: Perspectives on Integrating Language and Content.* White Plains, N.Y.: Longman, 1997.

ENGLISH LEARNERS

Bartlett, F.C. Sir, *Remembering: A Study in Experimental and Social Psychology.* 1932; Reprint. New York: Cambridge University Press, 1995.

Berg, E.C. "Preparing ESL Students for Peer Response." In *TESOL Journal* 8 (2), 1999.

Breen, Michael P., ed. *Learner Contributions to Language Learning: New Directions in Research.* New York: Longman, 2001.

Brinton, Donna M., and Peter Master, eds. *New Ways in Content-Based Instruction.* Alexandria, VA.: Teachers of English to Speakers of Other Languages, 1997.

Chamot, A.U., and J.M. O'Malley. *The CALLA Handbook: Implementing the Cognitive Academic Language Learning Approach.* 2nd edition. White Plains, NY: Longman, 2008.

Chamot, A.U., et al. *The Learning Strategies Handbook.* White Plains, N.Y.: Longman, 1999.

Chamot, A.U., and C. Keatley. *Sailing the 5 Cs with Learning Strategies: A Resource Guide for Secondary Foreign Language Educators.* Washington, DC National Capital Language Resource Center, 2004. http://nclrc.org/sailing/

Cohen, Andrew D. *Strategies in Learning and Using a Second Language.* New York: Longman, 1998.

Cummins, Jim. *Empowering Minority Students.* Sacramento, Calif.: California Association for Bilingual Education, 1989.

_____. "Linguistic Interdependence and the Educational Development of Bilingual Children." In *Review of Educational Research* 49 (1979): 222–251.

_____. *Negotiating Identities: Education for Empowerment in a Diverse Society.* California Association for Bilingual Education, 1996.

Doughty, C., and J. Williams. *Focus on Form in Classroom Second Language Acquisition.* New York: Cambridge University Press, 1998.

Freeman, David E., and Yvonne S. Freeman. *Between Worlds: Access to Second Language Acquisition.* Portsmouth, N.H.: Heinemann, 1994.

Kessler, Carolyn, ed. *Cooperative Language Learning: A Teacher's Resource Book.* Englewood Cliffs, N.J.: Prentice Hall Regents, 1992.

Labov, William, S. Ash, and C. Boberg. *Atlas of North American English: Phonetics, Phonology, and Sound Change.* Berlin: Mouton de Gruyter, 2006.

Larsen-Freeman, Diane, and Michael H. Long. *An Introduction to Second Language Acquisition Research.* New York: Longman, 1991.

Lightbown, Patsy, and Nina Spada. *How Languages Are Learned*, 2nd. ed. New York: Oxford University Press, 1993.

Mccaleb, Sudia P. *Building Communities of Learners: A Collaboration Among Teachers, Students, Families, and Community.* New York: St. Martin's Press, 1994.

O'Malley, J.M., and A.U. Chamot. *Learning Strategies in Second Language Acquisition.* New York: Cambridge University Press, 1990.

O'Malley, J.M., and L. Valdez Pierce. *Authentic Assessment for English Language Learners: Practical Approaches for Teachers.* Reading, Mass.: Addison-Wesley, 1996.

Reid, J. M., ed. *Learning Styles in the ESL/EFL Classroom.* Boston, Mass.: Heinle & Heinle, 1995.

Rubin, J. "A Review of Second Language Listening Comprehension Research." In *Modern Language Journal* 78 (1994): 199–221.

Short, D.J. *New Ways of Teaching English at the Secondary Level*. Alexandria, Va.: Teachers of English to Speakers of Other Languages, 1999.

DIFFERENTIATED INSTRUCTION

Anderson, Thomas, and Bonnie Armbruster. "On Selecting 'Considerate' Content Area Textbooks." In *Remedial and Special Education* (January/February 1988): 9, 47.

Cummins, Jim, and Dennis Sayers. *Brave New Schools: Challenging Cultural Illiteracy Through Global Learning Networks*. New York: St. Martin's Press, 1995.

Dole, J.A., K.J. Brown, and W. Trathen. "The Effects of Strategy Instruction On the Comprehension Performance of At-Risk Students." In *Reading Research Quarterly* 31 (1996): 62–88.

Gardner, Howard. *Frames of Mind: The Theory of Multiple Intelligences*. New York: Basic Books, 1993.

Gay, Geneva. *Culturally Responsive Teaching: Theory, Research, and Practice*. New York: Teachers College Press, 2000.

Gonzalez, Virginia, et al. *Assessment and Instruction of Culturally and Linguistically Diverse Students with or At-Risk of Learning Problems: From Research to Practice*. Boston, Mass.: Allyn & Bacon, 1997.

Ladson-Billings, Gloria. *The Dreamkeepers: Successful Teachers of African American Children*. San Francisco, Calif.: Jossey-Bass Inc., 1994.

Oxford, Rebecca, ed. *Language Learning Strategies Around the World: Cross-Cultural Perspectives*. Honolulu, Hawaii: University of Hawaii Press, 1996.

Pressley, Michael J., and V. Woloshyn, eds. *Cognitive Strategy Instruction That Really Improves Children's Academic Performance*, 2d ed. Cambridge, Mass.: Brookline Books, 1995.

Richard-Amato, Patricia A., and Marguerite Ann Snow, eds. *The Multicultural Classroom: Readings for Content-Area Teachers*. White Plains, N.Y.: Longman, 1992.

Rigg, Pat, and Virginia G. Allen, eds. *When They Don't All Speak English: Integrating the ESL Student into the Regular Classroom*. Urbana, Ill.: National Council of Teachers of English, 1989.

Rong, Xue Lan, and Judith Preissle. *Educating Immigrant Students: What We Need to Know to Meet the Challenges*. Thousand Oaks, Calif.: Corwin Press, 1998.

Scarcella, Robin. *Teaching Language Minority Students in the Multicultural Classroom*. Englewood Cliffs, N.J.: Prentice Hall Regents, 1990.

Sternberg, Robert J. *The Triarchic Mind: A New Theory of Human Intelligence*. New York: Viking Press, 1988.

Wendt, Dirk. "An Experimental Approach to the Improvement of the Typographic Design of Textbooks." In *Visible Language* 13 (2), 1979.

WRITING

Clemmons, J., et al. *Portfolios in the Classroom: A Teacher's Sourcebook*. New York: Scholastic Professional Books, 1993.

Glazer, S.M., and C.S. Brown. *Portfolios and Beyond: Collaborative Assessment in Reading and Writing*. Norwood, Mass.: Christopher-Gordon, 1993.

Hudelson, Sarah. *Write On: Children Writing in ESL*. Englewood Cliffs, N.J.: Prentice Hall Regents, 1989.

Spandel, Vicki. *Creating Writers: Through 6-Trait Writing Assessment and Instruction*, 3d ed. New York: Longman, 2001.

Reviewers

Teaching Learning Strategies

by Anna Uhl Chamot

Many students face challenges to academic achievement. These include English Language Learners (ELLs), Struggling Readers (SRs), and Standard English Learners (SELs). Not only must these students learn standard academic English, but they must do so while also learning content subject matter and skills. In addition, all students are now expected to meet the same national and state standards and assessments as proficient speakers, readers, and writers of standard academic English. *Keystone* provides challenging content-based language development and learning strategies that help students achieve academic goals.

Why teach learning strategies?

Learning strategies accelerate standard academic language learning for all students more effectively and efficiently. Learning strategies are techniques for understanding, remembering, and using information and skills. They are particularly important for students seeking to master academic language and content simultaneously, as they do in *Keystone*.

Learning strategy instruction can help students by:
- showing them techniques for "how to learn,"
- developing their independence as learners,
- increasing their academic motivation, and
- developing their awareness of their own thinking and learning processes.

Research has shown that when students develop metacognition, the awareness of the learning processes and strategies that lead to success, they are more likely to plan how to proceed with a learning task, monitor their own performance, find solutions to problems encountered, and evaluate themselves upon task completion.

All kinds of fiction, poetry, and informational texts provide students with models of academic and literary language. However, to make full use of these models, students need to comprehend what they read. Reading strategies presented in *Keystone* provide detailed instructions on how to apply the strategy to the text they are about to read.

Many of the reading strategies in *Keystone* have broader applications and can be used as learning strategies for listening, speaking, writing, and remembering both vocabulary and content information. Some examples are:

- *Predict*—Anticipate what is coming next during a listening activity.

- *Visualize / Use Visuals*—Make a mental image of the events and characters in a story you are writing; use or draw a visual aid to learn vocabulary.
- *Make Inferences*—Use the context of a listening activity and what you know about the topic to figure out the meaning of new words or ideas.
- *Ask Questions*—Ask the teacher or others to explain what you do not understand; after speaking or writing, ask yourself or others how well you communicated your meaning.
- *Scan / Selective Attention*—Focus on specific content information, academic words, or literary words as you read, listen, speak, and write.
- *Take Notes*—Write down important ideas as you listen and as you prepare to write.
- *Summarize*—Create a mental, oral, or written summary of information you learn.
- *Classify / Sequence*—Classify new words and ideas according to their similarities; sequence events, directions, and steps to solve a problem.

Additional learning strategies that are especially helpful to ELLs, SRs, and SELs in acquiring standard academic English and content are the following three metacognitive strategies and a strategy for using prior knowledge:

- *Plan*—Set goals and identify steps needed to accomplish a learning task.
- *Monitor / Identify Problems*—While working on a learning task, check your comprehension or production and identify any problems you are having.
- *Evaluate*—After completing a learning task, assess how well you have done.
- *Use What You Know*—Use your own knowledge and experiences to understand and learn something new; brainstorm words and ideas; make associations and analogies; explain your prior knowledge about a topic.

Guidelines for teaching learning strategies

Since learning strategies are mental processes with few observable manifestations, it is difficult to tell whether a student is learning how to use them. *Keystone* offers these suggestions to help teachers make strategy instruction more explicit:

- Model the strategy by "thinking aloud" as you perform a task similar to the one students will perform.
- Use the strategy names and refer to them consistently by name.

- Tell students why the strategy is important and how it can help them.
- Remind students to use strategies as they read, listen, brainstorm, write, focus on grammar, learn vocabulary, and work on projects.
- Provide opportunities for students to discuss strategies—how they use them, additional strategies they use, and which strategies they prefer.

The five-phase instructional sequence developed for the Cognitive Academic Language Learning Approach (CALLA) has provided a useful framework for teaching learning strategies. In this approach, highly explicit instruction in applying strategies to learning tasks is gradually faded so that the students can begin to assume greater responsibility in selecting and applying their own preferred learning strategies. An important feature of the CALLA instructional sequence is that the needs and thoughts of students are central to all instruction. The sequence guides students towards increasing levels of independence, thus fostering attitudes of academic self-efficacy. The five phases of the CALLA instructional sequence are:

Preparation Students identify strategies they are already using and develop their metacognitive awareness of the relationship between their own mental processes and effective learning. Activities in the Preparation stage can include class discussions about strategies used for recent learning tasks, group or individual interviews about strategies used for particular tasks, think-aloud sessions in which students describe their thought processes while they work on a task, questionnaires or checklists about strategies used, and diary entries about individual approaches to language and content learning.

Presentation This phase focuses on explaining and modeling the new learning strategy. The teacher describes the characteristics, usefulness, and applications of the strategy. The most effective way to present the new strategy is for teachers to model their own use of the strategy by "thinking aloud" (see above). Teachers can then ask students to name the strategy and explain when and how to use it. Modeling helps students visualize themselves working successfully on a similar learning task.

Practice Students now practice the new learning strategy with an authentic learning task, such as those presented in **Keystone**. For example, a group of students might read a story, then describe the images the story evoked, discuss unfamiliar words encountered and infer meanings through context clues, and take turns summarizing the main points of the story. In a content-based academic language program such as **Keystone**, strategies can be used to understand and remember concepts and skills from curriculum areas such as science, social studies, and language arts.

Self-Evaluation Students evaluate their success in using learning strategies, thus developing metacognitive awareness of their own learning processes. Activities that develop students' ability to evaluate themselves include debriefing discussions after strategy practice, learning logs in which students record the results of their learning strategies applications, checklists of strategies used, and open-ended questionnaires in which students express their opinions about the usefulness of particular strategies.

Expansion Finally, students make personal decisions about the strategies that they find most effective, apply these strategies to new contexts in other classes, and devise their own individual combinations and interpretations of learning strategies. By this stage, the goal of learning strategies instruction has been achieved.

Ongoing monitoring of students' use of both instructed and individually developed strategies is essential if teachers are to scaffold their instruction successfully. In scaffolded instruction, teachers begin with explicit instruction and gradually reduce prompts and cues to students. In this way, students begin to assume responsibility for the regulation of their own learning. Individual students may need greater or lesser amounts of explicit strategies instruction, depending on the degree to which they have already developed strategies independently. When students are able to use instructed strategies without prompting, they are ready to explore new strategies, new applications, and new opportunities for self-regulated learning.

Suggested Reading

Chamot, A.U. *The CALLA Handbook: Implementing the Cognitive Academic Learning Language Approach,* 2d ed. White Plains, N.Y.: Longman, 2008.

Chamot, A.U. "Accelerating Academic Achievement of English Language Learners: A Synthesis of Five Evaluations of the CALLA Model." In *The International Handbook of English Language Learning, Part I,* edited by J. Cummins and C. Davison (Norwell, Mass.: Springer Publications, 2007), 317–331.

Chamot, A.U. "Language Learning Strategy Instruction: Current Issues and Research." In *Annual Review of Applied Linguistics.* New York: Cambridge University Press, 2005.

Where Language Flourishes

by John De Mado

For students learning to read and for students learning English, the importance of vocabulary to general comprehension cannot be overstated. The breadth of a student's vocabulary is an important component of understanding increasingly difficult texts. Without an ample lexicon, reading becomes drudgery; so much so that many students choose to avoid the activity altogether.

Of the five components of reading identified by the National Reading Panel, vocabulary is one that plays a role in all four language skills. Each of us has a Spoken Vocabulary, a Listening Vocabulary, a Reading Vocabulary, and a Writing Vocabulary.

Vocabulary is necessary to students' understanding of what they read. As students begin to read, they recognize that the printed words correspond to words they have encountered in spoken English. While it is not necessary that students know every word they read, as their reading level increases, so does the need for a larger vocabulary.

Writing also enhances vocabulary and plays a role in the literacy process because of the reciprocal relationship it has with reading. When writing, students use the vocabulary they have acquired plus new vocabulary that they have researched in dictionaries and other resources to express their ideas.

Research has shown that vocabulary is learned both indirectly and directly. Direct instruction in vocabulary includes both instruction in the meaning of specific words and instruction in vocabulary learning strategies. Before students read a text, teaching specific difficult words that appear in the text can increase comprehension. Both extended instruction into word meaning and repeated exposure to the word help students "own" the word. Academic vocabulary, in particular, is learned through repeated exposure to a word in a context that explains the meaning. Vocabulary learning strategies include using dictionaries, understanding word roots and word families, and understanding affixes.

The vast majority of vocabulary, though, is learned indirectly. Students can learn vocabulary through everyday oral communication, from listening to others read to them, and by extensive reading on their own.

Research tells us that all output of language, i.e., speaking and writing, is a direct result of *comprehensible input*, i.e., what an individual actually understands. In oral discourse, an individual selects a word to acquire from what he or she understands. Meaning is built for this *self-selected* vocabulary with the help of extra-linguistic cues, such as hand gestures and facial expressions. Therefore, the more oral discourse the student has, the more word meanings the student acquires and can use in speaking and writing.

The use of language is subject to the societies in which it evolves. Students bring with them a great deal of "culturally-nuanced" language. Given the number of words that a student learns through oral discourse, one should consider the influences on this type of vocabulary acquisition.

Sociological Influences: Students interact with one another almost exclusively in an informal register. This register is different from the language of the classroom and textbooks. Our society is one that prefers sound bites and news capsules to a more expansive use of language. This is reflective of a society traveling at hyperspeed.

Technological Influences: Students spend much of their time in silence: headsets donned and wired to their personal music and video devices. Methods of communication, such as e-mail, instant messaging, and text messaging, all invite a minimalist's approach to discourse.

Educational Influences: Under the weight of high stakes testing, classrooms have fallen silent, defaulting instead to the transmission of those facts destined for assessment. Budgetary concerns atrophy courses that enhance language acquisition such as World Languages, Drama, Vocal Music, and Public Speaking.

The combined impact of these influences has a direct result on vocabulary acquisition. Students that spend much of their day in silence have little opportunity to garner new, varied, and substantive vocabulary. We, as educators, must encourage and foster not only explicit instruction in academic language, but also indirect instruction through enhanced opportunity oral discourse.

In a "language-rich" schoolhouse, literacy thrives.

References: National Institute for Literacy, Put Reading First, National Reading Panel Report

Using Culturally and Linguistically Responsive Teaching to Enhance Learning for All Students

by Sharroky Hollie

What is culturally and linguistically responsive teaching? Geneva Gay, in *Culturally Responsive Teaching—Theory, Practice, and Pedagogy* (2004), defines it as the use of cultural knowledge, prior experiences, frames of reference, and performance styles of ethnically diverse students to make learning encounters more relevant to and effective for them. It teaches to and through the strengths of these students. It is culturally validating and affirming. CLR validates and affirms the home language and culture of students through the use of responsive instructional strategies, which act as bridges to acceptance, achievement, and empowerment in academic settings and mainstream culture at large.

Who benefits from CLR? All students is the simple answer. The more precise question is which students benefit *most* from culturally and linguistically responsive teaching? A precise answer delves into who these students are most likely to be. A survey of any recent or past standardized data gives the answer of who is achieving and who is not. In this context, culturally and linguistically responsive teaching would most benefit those students who are termed underserved as opposed to underachieving.

What is a Standard English Learner (SEL)?
A Standard English Learner is a student whose home language differs enough from Standard English and Academic English in these ways: phonologically, morpho-syntactically, syntactically, semantically, pragmatically, and rhetorically. Commonly known as nonstandard languages, African-American Vernacular, Chicano English, Hawaiian Pidgin English, and Native-American dialects represent the languages of many underserved students. Superficially, these students have an apparent proficiency in Standard English and Academic English, but a deep examination of their reading and written skills coupled with the demand of school language posit a different picture. Unfortunately, the students are many times seen as language deficient, not language different, and are skipped over in terms of their linguistic needs.

What are the key strands for culturally and linguistically responsive teaching and learning?

Teaching Using Culturally Relevant Literature
- Purposefully using texts that affirm and validate students' backgrounds, cultures, languages, and experiences

- Using effective literacy and language strategies made culturally responsive

Systematic Teaching of Situational Appropriateness
- Addressing language variation among SELs (Standard English Learners) and ELs (English Learners)
- Using strategies to support Standard English mastery

Cultural Behaviors for a Positive Classroom Community
- Engaging the students in rigorous activities, which tap into the personal learning styles
- Providing protocols for discussion and participation that validate and affirm cultural behaviors and teach situational appropriateness

Academic Vocabulary Through Conceptually Coded Words
- Validating students' knowledge and home vocabulary
- Linking cultural concepts to academic words
- Appling understanding of synonyms/antonyms

A Validating and Affirming Learning Environment
- Accepting, affirmative, risk-free classroom environment
- Including in the room environment images that are reflective of students' cultures from the instructional texts and materials to the instructional activities, from the classroom walls to the classroom library

How do I become culturally responsive?
Some steps to becoming culturally and linguistically responsive:
- Recognize your student population in terms of who is being underserved, who is not being responded to culturally and/or linguistically.
- Assess if these students' underachievement is related to their language proficiency and/or lack of responsiveness on the part of the instruction in relation to engagement, motivation, and/or skills development.
- Use the instructional strands as an umbrella, identify key strategies (labeled like this: (CRI)) that would be culturally and linguistically responsive and act as bridges to achievement.
- Infuse the strategies into your teaching, creating consistent moments for students to connect to what is being taught culturally and linguistically.

Contrastive Analysis
Introduction to Linguistics

How People Speak

All languages have both consonants and vowels. Consonants are made with some obstruction of the vocal tract, either a complete stoppage of air or enough constriction to create friction. Vowels are produced with the vocal tract more open; they have no constriction that might cause friction.

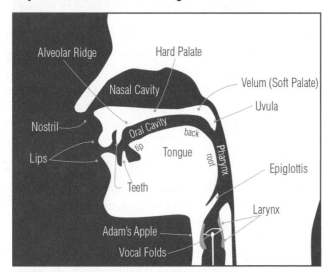

Figure 1: The human vocal tract makes the sounds of speech.

Consonants

Every consonant can be described by noting three characteristics: voicing, place of articulation, and manner of articulation.

Voicing
Many sounds of language, including all vowels, employ vibration of the vocal folds in the larynx. This creates more resonance and energy for the sound. All speech sounds are characterized as either voiced (with vocal fold vibration) or voiceless (with no vocal fold vibration). Feeling the vibration around the Adam's apple can help you understand this difference. If you say "sssss" and then "zzzzz," you can feel the distinction: /s/ is voiceless and /z/ is voiced.

Place of Articulation
This is the location in the vocal tract where the air stream may be constricted. The /s/ sound, for example, is made with the tongue tip close to the alveolar ridge (see Figure 1).

Place of Articulation Terms
Bilabial: using both lips
Glottal: produced at the larynx
Interdental: tongue tip between upper and lower teeth
Labio-dental: upper teeth and lower lip
Labio-velar: rounding of lips; tongue body raised toward velum
Palatal: body of tongue and high part of palate
Palato-alveolar: tongue tip and palate behind alveolar ridge
Velar: body of tongue and velum (soft palate)

Manner of Articulation
This is the type or degree of constriction that occurs in an articulation. For example, the /t/ sound completely stops the airflow with the tongue tip at the alveolar ridge, but /s/ allows air to pass noisily through a small opening.

Manner of Articulation Terms
Alveolar: tongue tip and ridge behind teeth
Affricate: complete constriction followed by slow separation of the articulators resulting in friction
Approximant: close constriction, but not enough for friction
Fricative: narrow constriction; turbulent airflow causing friction
Glottal: produced at the larynx
Lateral: air passes over sides of tongue
Nasal: lowered velum to let air escape through the nose
Stop: complete constriction, closure so that air cannot escape through the oral cavity
Tap: brief contact between tongue tip and alveolar ridge

Vowels

Vowels are open, sonorous sounds. Each vowel can be uniquely described by noting the position of the tongue, the tension of the vocal tract, and the position of the lips. Vowels are described by *height,* where the tongue is relative to the roof of the mouth. They can be high, mid, or low. Tongue backness tells if the tongue articulation is in the front or back of the mouth.

Tense vowels are more common around the world. In English, they are longer and include an expansion of the throat at the pharynx. Lax vowels are shorter with a more neutral pharynx. An example is the tense long *e* as in *meet* versus the lax short *i* as in *mitt.* The lips either can be in a spread or neutral position, or they can be rounded and protrude slightly.

Speaking English

English is the third most widely spoken native language in the world, after Mandarin and Spanish. There are about 330 million native speakers of English and 600 million who speak it as a foreign language.

English Consonant Sounds

The following chart gives the International Phonetic Alphabet (IPA) symbol for each English consonant along with its voicing, place, and manner of articulation. This information can be used to understand and help identify problems that non-native speakers may encounter when learning to speak English.

CONSONANTS OF ENGLISH		
IPA	**Articulation**	**Example**
p	voiceless bilabial stop	**p**it
b	voiced bilabial stop	**b**it
m	voiced bilabial nasal stop	**m**an
w	voiced labio-velar approximant	**w**in
f	voiceless labio-dental fricative	**f**un
v	voiced labio-dental fricative	**v**ery
ɵ	voiceless interdental fricative	**th**ing
ð	voiced interdental fricative	**th**ere
t	voiceless alveolar stop	**t**ime
d	voiced alveolar stop	**d**ime
n	voiced alveolar nasal stop	**n**ame
s	voiceless alveolar fricative	**s**oy
z	voiced alveolar fricative	**z**eal
ɾ	voiced alveolar tap	bu**tt**er
l	voiced alveolar central approximant	**l**oop
ɹ	voiced palato-alveolar affricate	**r**ed
ʃ	voiceless palato-alveolar fricative	**sh**allow
ʒ	voiced palato-alveolar affricate	vi**s**ion
tʃ	voiceless palato-alveolar affricate	**ch**irp
ʤ	voiced palato-alveolar affricate	**j**oy
j	voiced palatal approximant	**y**ou
k	voiceless velar stop	**k**ite
g	voiced velar stop	**g**oat
ŋ	voiced velar nasal stop	ki**ng**
h	voiceless glottal fricative	**h**ope

English Vowel Sounds

Most languages in the world have around five vowel sounds. English has thirteen common vowel sounds, which means that many students of English must learn more vowel distinctions than there are in their native language. The lax vowels are most difficult. Some vowels are diphthongs, meaning the tongue is in one position at the beginning of the sound, and it moves to another position by the end of it.

VOWELS OF ENGLISH		
IPA	**Sound**	**Example**
i	ē	beat
ɪ	ĭ	bit
e	ā	bait
ɛ	ĕ	bet
æ	ă	bat
u	o͞o	boot
ʊ	o͝o	could
o	ō	boat
ɔ	aw	law
ɑ	ŏ	hot
ə	ə	about
ʌ	ŭ	cut
ɝ	er	bird
ɑ ʊ	ow	house
ɔ ɪ	oy	boy
ɑ ɪ	ī	bite

Figure 2 is a schematic of the mouth. The left is the front of the mouth; the right is the back. The top is the roof of the mouth and the bottom is the floor. Placement of the vowel shows where the tongue reaches its maximum in the English articulation.

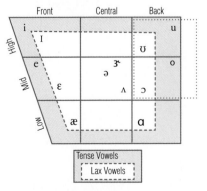

Figure 2: English vowel sounds

Introduction to Linguistics

Transference

Pronunciation

All languages build on the same fundamentals. All languages contrast voiced and voiceless sound, and have stops and fricatives. Many languages use the same places of articulation for consonants as well. The majority of sounds will easily transfer from another language to English.

However, there will always be some sounds that are not found in a person's native language that can pose a challenge to the English language learner. English has a few relatively rare sounds, such as the interdental sounds spelled with *th, /ə/,* and /ð/. The /r/ sound in English is also a very rare type of sound. Most other languages use a tap or trill articulation for an /r/ sound.

In some languages, the /l/ and /r/ sounds belong to one psychological category. This means that they count as the same sound in that language. In this case, it is not the articulation that is difficult, but the perception of the difference and consistent use of one versus the other in any word context. This type of psychological category is called a *phoneme,* and multiple speech sounds all can be categorized as the same phoneme in that language.

This is true for English as well, where, for example, the alveolar lateral /l/ as in *lob* and the velarized lateral /ɫ/ as in *ball* are both counted as the same sound—an *l*—to native speakers of English. It is important to keep in mind that both the phonetic articulation of a sound and its psychological, phonemic category factor into the learning of a new language.

Grammar

Pronouncing English is not the only stumbling block for English learners. The grammar and usage, or syntax, of English may present distinctions that are unique to the language. For example, English syntax requires adjectives to precede the nouns they modify, as in *the tall girl.* In other languages, such as Spanish, Hmong, and Vietnamese, adjectives follow nouns, as in *la chica alta* (literally *the girl tall* in Spanish). This may cause word-order problems, particularly for less advanced English learners.

Other syntactic differences are less obvious and may cause problems even for advanced learners. For example, many East Asian languages (such as Mandarin, Cantonese, and Korean) do not mark agreement between subject and verb. Speakers of these languages may therefore leave out agreement markers such as the *-s* in *The girl like cats.*

The use of articles varies across languages. For instance, Spanish uses the definite article more often than English, while Mandarin and Cantonese do not have articles. A Spanish-speaking English learner might say *The girl likes the cats* instead of *The girl likes cats,* and a Mandarin or Cantonese speaker might say *Girl like cat.*

Plural marking is another potential trouble spot: Vietnamese, Filipino, Cantonese, and Mandarin do not add plural markers to nouns. Learners speaking these languages may have difficulty with English plurals, saying *cat* instead of *cats.*

> **Grammar Hot Spots**
>
> Look for Grammar Hot Spots on the following pages for tips on the most common syntax errors by speakers of languages other than English.

Common First Languages

In the Common First Languages section, you will find details of some common non-English languages spoken in the United States. They are:

- Spanish
- Vietnamese
- Cantonese
- Hmong
- Filipino
- Korean
- Mandarin

You can use the fundamentals of speech articulation already covered to help you understand where the languages differ from English. Differences in the spoken language and in the writing systems are explored as well. These sections pinpoint common trouble spots specific to learners of English.

Culture Clues

Look to Culture Clues for insights into the cultural differences of each language learner as well as ideas for ways to embrace students' diversity.

African-American Vernacular English

While not a non-English language, African-American Vernacular English (AAVE) is spoken commonly in many student populations and can present barriers to success in reading and writing similar to those facing English-language learners. This section provides details on this unique English dialect and suggestions for addressing potential learning problems you may encounter with speakers of AAVE.

Linguistic Contrastive Analysis

The Linguistic Contrastive Analysis Charts provide a quick reference for comparing English sounds with those of other languages. The charts allow you to check at a glance which sounds have equivalents in other languages. For those sounds that don't have equivalents, you can find the closest sound used as a substitute and suggestions for helping someone gain a native English articulation.

In these charts, the sounds are notated using the International Phonetic Alphabet (IPA). This is the most widely recognized and used standard for representing speech sounds in any language. A guiding principle of the IPA across all languages is that each sound is uniquely represented by one symbol, and each symbol represents only one sound.

The chart has columns for each native language with rows corresponding to each English phoneme. Each cell in the chart gives an example word using that sound in the native language, a definition in parenthesis, and transference tips below. If there is no sound equivalent to English, a common substitution used by speakers of that language may be provided.

Transference Tips

Transference Tips give you ideas of how the sound will be produced by the learner. Cells highlighted in yellow note where the English learner will have particular difficulty with the English sound.

Common First Languages

Spanish

Background

Spanish is the second most widely spoken language in the world. There are more than 400 million native Spanish speakers in twenty-plus countries on three continents. Spanish vocabulary and pronunciation differ from country to country. While most dialect differences in English are in vowel sounds, Spanish dialects differ in their consonants.

Spoken

Spanish sounds are similar to those found in English, so there is a strong foundation for the native Spanish speaker learning English. However, there are three key differences between English and Spanish consonants:

1. Most of the alveolar sounds in English, such as /t/, /d/, and /n/, are produced farther forward in the mouth in Spanish. Instead of the tongue touching the alveolar ridge as in English, in Spanish, it touches the back of the teeth.

2. Another difference is that the /r/ sound in English is not found in Spanish. There are two /r/ sounds in Spanish. One is the tap /ɾ/, which occurs in English as the quick sound in the middle of the name *Betty*. Psychologically, this tap sound is a kind of /t/ or /d/ sound in English, while in Spanish it is perceived as an /r/. The other /r/ sound in Spanish is a trill, or series of tongue taps on the alveolar ridge. This does not occur in English.

3. The third key difference between English and Spanish can be found in the English production of the voiceless stops /p/, /t/, and /k/. In English, these sounds are aspirated, with an extra puff of air at the end, when the sound occurs at the beginning of a word or stressed syllable. So, /p/ is aspirated in *pit*. Learners can add a puff of air to such sounds to sound more like native English speakers.

There are five vowels in Spanish, which are a subset of the English vowels. Spanish vowels include tense vowel sounds /a/, /e/, /i/, /o/, and /u/. Lax vowel sounds in English are the problematic ones for native Spanish speakers.

Written

Like English, written Spanish uses the Roman alphabet, so both writing systems are similar. There are a few orthographic differences to note, however.

- The letter *h* in Spanish is silent, but the sound /h/ is written as *j* or *g*.

- A single letter *r* in Spanish represents a tap, while the double *rr* represents a trill.

- Accents are used to show the stress on a syllable when the stress is different from the usual rules. In some cases, words change meaning according to the accents. For example, *el* means *the* while *él* means *he*.

Written Spanish vowels are pronounced like the symbols in the IPA. So, the Spanish "i" is pronounced with the long ē as in the word *beat*. The IPA and Spanish symbol for this letter is the same: /i/.

Vietnamese

Background
Approximately 80 million people in Vietnam speak Vietnamese. The northern dialect is the standard, though central and southern dialects also exist. Most Vietnamese speakers in the United States are from southern Vietnam and speak the southern dialect.

Spoken
Vietnamese is a tonal language, so each syllable is pronounced with a distinctive tone that affects meaning. Vietnamese has a complex vowel system of twelve vowels and twenty-six diphthongs. Its consonants are simpler, but Vietnamese syllable structure allows few possibilities for final consonants.

Students may need help noticing and learning to reproduce final consonant sounds in English words and syllables. Vietnamese syllable structure allows for limited combinations of initial consonants. Students also may need help with the more complex initial consonant clusters of English words and syllables.

Culture Clues

In traditional Vietnamese education, there is a strict division between the roles of student and teacher. Students may be confused if asked to direct a part of their own study, so encourage group work.

Written
Since the 1600s, Vietnamese has used a Romanized alphabet. Many characters written in Vietnamese have sounds different from their English counterparts, such as *d, x, ch, nh, kh, g, tr, r,* and *e.*

Grammar Hot Spots

- Like English, Vietnamese uses Subject-Verb-Object (SVO) syntax, or word order.
- Vietnamese does not use affixes; instead, syntax expresses number, case, and tense.

Cantonese

Background
Cantonese is one of the seven major Chinese languages, not all of which are mutually intelligible. Cantonese is mostly spoken in China's southern provinces, Hong Kong, and Macau by about 66 million people. It is a tonal language, and the same sequence of letters can have different meanings depending on their pitch.

Spoken
Cantonese has six stops, aspirated and nonaspirated /p/, /t/, /k/; three fricatives /f/, /s/, /h/; and two affricates /ts/, /ts^h/. Some sounds that do not exist in Cantonese can be difficult for the English language learner. The /v/ often gets pronounced as /f/ or /w/; the /z/ is often said as /s/, the sounds spelled with *th* are often said as /t/, /d/, or /f/. Cantonese speakers have difficulty distinguishing between /l/ and /r/, since /r/ is not present in their language. They tend to produce an /l/-like sound for both English sounds in words such as *ride* and *lied.*

Cantonese has eleven vowels and ten diphthongs. One of the major problems for Cantonese speakers is distinguishing between English tense and lax vowels, because the distribution of Cantonese short and long vowels is determined by the sound context.

Syllables in Cantonese don't have consonant clusters. English consonant clusters are often deleted or broken up by vowel insertion (e.g., *list* becomes *lis*). This may be especially problematic when producing English simple past (e.g., *baked*).

Culture Clues

"Chinese" isn't a language of its own. There are many regional languages spoken in this large country, including Cantonese. For each language spoken, there may be different cultural traditions and beliefs. Talk about where in China students are from and the celebrations and norms that make them unique.

Written
Cantonese is written with standard Chinese characters known as *Hànzi* where each character represents a syllable and has a meaning. Additional Cantonese-specific characters were also added. Cantonese speakers may have difficulty with sound-letter correspondences in English.

Grammar Hot Spots

- English articles and prepositions are difficult for Cantonese speakers. *In, on,* and *at,* for instance, can be translated as the same preposition in Cantonese.
- Plurals, tenses, and gerund endings are difficult for Cantonese speakers to transfer to English.

Common First Languages

Hmong

Background
Hmong is a group of approximately eighteen languages within the Hmong-Mien family. There are roughly four million speakers of Hmong, including 200,000 in the United States. They are mainly from two groups with mutually intelligible dialects—Hmong Daw and Mong Leng.

Spoken
Hmong vowels are few and simple, but its consonants are complex and differ from those of English. Notable features of Hmong phonology absent from English include consonantal pre-nasalization (the /m/n/ŋ/ sound before a consonant) and the contrast between nasalized and non-nasalized vowels. Hmong is tonal. Each syllable is pronounced with a distinctive pitch.

Culture Clues
In traditional Hmong culture, learning takes place through hands-on experience. Students may find it difficult to adjust to the use of graphics or print media. Competition, personal achievement, and self-directed instruction may be unfamiliar concepts, so students may prefer group work.

Written
The Romanized Popular Alphabet (RPA), developed in the 1950s, is the usual way of transcribing Hmong. Syllable-final consonants are absent in pronunciation but are used to represent orthographically the tonal value of a given syllable. Students may need particular help in identifying and learning to reproduce the final consonant sounds of English words and syllables.

Grammar Hot Spots
- Like English, Hmong is an SVO language. Personal pronouns are marked for number, including inflection for singular, dual, and plural, though they are not marked for case.

- Because Hmong and English prepositions often have different semantic qualities, students may need help mastering uses of English prepositions. For example, it is correct to say "think about [something]" rather than "think on [something]."

Filipino

Background
Filipino and English are the official languages of the Philippines, where 175 languages are spoken. There are about 24 million native speakers of Filipino, and more than 50 million people speak Filipino as a second language. You may hear the terms Filipino and Tagalog being used interchangeably.

Spoken
Filipino has many similar speech sounds to English. The notable exceptions are the lack of the consonant sounds /f/, /v/, and those spelled with *th.* Of these, the English /f/ and /v/ cause the most difficulty for learners. The distinction between long *e* (as in *beat*) and short *i* (as in *bit*) is also a trouble spot. Filipino does not allow consonant clusters at the end of syllables, so *detect* may be simplified to just one consonant (*detec*).

Culture Clues
Most people from the Philippines can speak Filipino, but for many it is not their first language. Ask Filipino students about other languages they speak. Because English is used alongside Filipino as the language of instruction in the Philippines, most Filipinos are familiar with English.

Written
The Filipino alphabet has twenty-eight letters and is based on the Spanish alphabet, so the English writing system poses little problem.

Grammar Hot Spots
- Filipino word order is Verb-Subject-Object (VSO), which does not transfer well to English.

- Inflectional verb endings, such as *-s, -en, -ed,* and *-ing,* do not exist in Filipino, so it is common to leave out the third person singular verb marker (*"He walk,"* not *"He walks"*).

Korean

Background
Korean is spoken by 71 million people in North and South Korea. Standard Korean is based on the speech in and around Seoul.

Spoken
Korean does not have corresponding sounds for English /f/, /v/, /ə/, /ð/, and /ʤ/. In word-initial position, all Korean stops are voiceless. Voiced stops /b/, /d/, and /g/ are only produced between two vowels. Korean speakers may have difficulty producing /s/, /ʃ/, and /z/ in some contexts, in addition to English /r/ and /l/ sounds (e.g., *rock* and *lock*). They may have problems in producing English consonant clusters (e.g., *str-, sk-*). These problems can often be eliminated by vowel insertion or consonant deletion. In addition, the distinction between English tense and lax vowels (e.g., /i/ as in *beat* vs. /ɪ/ as in *bit*) may be problematic for Korean speakers.

Culture Clues
Korean uses a complex system of honorifics, so it is unusual for Korean students to use the pronoun *you* or call their teachers by their first name.

Written
Modern Korean uses the Korean alphabet (*Hangul*) or a mixed script of *Hangul* and Chinese. *Hangul* is an alphabetic script organized into syllabic blocks.

Grammar Hot Spots
- In contrast to English, Korean word order is Subject-Object-Verb (SOV). The verb always comes at the end of a sentence.
- Korean syllable stress is different, so learners may have difficulties with the rhythm of English.

Mandarin

Background
Chinese encompasses a wide range of dialects and is the native language of two-thirds of China. There are approximately 870 million Mandarin speakers worldwide. North Mandarin, as found in Beijing, is the basis of the modern standard language.

Spoken
Mandarin Chinese and English differ substantially in their sound structure. Mandarin lacks voiced obstruent consonants (/b/, /d/, /g/, /ʤ/), causing difficulty for speakers in perceiving and producing English voiced consonants (e.g., *buy* may be pronounced and perceived as *pie*). The sounds spelled with *th* are not present in Mandarin, so they are often substituted with /s/ or /t/ causing, for example, *fourth* to be pronounced as *fours*. Mandarin Chinese has five vowels. Due to the relatively small vowel inventory and contextual effects on vowels in Mandarin, many English vowels and tense/lax distinctions present problems for speakers of Mandarin Chinese. Mandarin allows only a very simple syllable structure, causing problems in producing consonant clusters in English. Speakers may drop consonants or insert vowels between them (e.g., *film* may become /filəm/). The use of tones in Mandarin may result in the rising and falling of pitch when speaking English.

Culture Clues
The use of formal and informal forms of English is hard to master for Mandarin speakers. Chinese speakers will often play down complements they receive.

Written
Chinese is written with characters known as *Hànzi*. Each character represents a syllable and also has a meaning. A Romanized alphabet called *Pinyin* marks pronunciation of characters. Chinese speakers may have problems mastering letter-sound correspondences in written English, especially for sounds that are not present in Mandarin.

Grammar Hot Spots
- The noninflected nature of Chinese causes Mandarin speakers to have problems with plurals, past tense markers, and gerund forms (*-s, -ed, -ing*).
- Mastering English tenses and passive is difficult. Students should be familiarized with correct lexical and syntactic features as well as appropriate situations for the use of various tenses and passives.

African-American Vernacular English in the Classroom

To effectively address AAVE in the classroom, the first and most important step for the teacher is to acknowledge the student's use of home language or AAVE as "language different, not language deficit." To accomplish this, a teacher replaces deficit terminology and phrases such as *correct, fix, make better, proper,* or *say it right* with affirming language such as *translate, code-switch, put it in another way,* or *say it for an academic audience.* The second step involves modifying the instruction, focusing on an established technique for second-language instruction called *contrastive analysis.* With this methodology, teachers have students focus on the rules of the target language through the lens of their home language. The process for doing so is outlined below:

1. **Pre-assessment:** Determine the students' needs for instruction regarding a particular linguistic feature. Use both formal and informal assessments. Listen to students talk; read their writing. In addition, assess the degree to which a student uses a particular linguistic feature. Not all Standard English Learners (SELs) use all Home Language features.

2. **Introduce the AAVE linguistic rule:** For example, explain that multiple negation is the use of multiple negative words in a sentence. The more negative intensifiers in a sentence, the greater the negative sentiment being expressed.

3. **Identify the use of the rule with authentic samples:** For example, explain that the statement *"We don't never have no homework on Friday"* is an example of multiple negation because it contains more than one negative word.

4. **Distinguish between AAVE and the target language:** Give as the SE equivalent *We don't normally have any homework on Friday.* Point out that in Standard English, usage requires one negative word and use of intensifiers (adjectives and adverbs).

5. **Explicitly teach the code switch:** Explain that *We don't never have no homework on Friday. = We don't normally have any homework on Friday.* Point out that Standard English intensifiers *normally* and *any* accurately translate the use of the three negatives in the Home Language sentence.

6. **Address the issue of situational appropriateness:** Emphasize that Standard English is required in many contexts, such as schoolwork, job interviews, and so on.

7. **Assessment:** Assess students to determine their ability to 1) accurately identify the use of AAVE rules, 2) differentiate between home and school language, and 3) code-switch between the two.

AAVE Linguistic Contrastive Analysis Chart

PHONICS	MARKERS	GRAMMAR	VOCABULARY
Digraph /th/ There is no /th/, similar to French as well as other languages. Examples AAVE: *dat* SE: *that* AAVE: *mouf* SE: *mouth*	**Past Tense Marker** /ed/ Markers, such as verb tense, are sometimes indicated by tonality versus a use of a morpheme in Standard English. Examples AAVE: *cook yesterday* SE: *cooked* AAVE: *move last night* SE: *moved*	**Regularization** "Hypercorrection" or over-generalizing of the rule linked to the irregular patterns of Standard English with number agreement and subject/objective pronouns Subject-verb agreement Examples AAVE: *She walk home sometimes.* SE: *She walks home sometimes.* Reflexive pronoun AAVE: *hisself (subject pronoun is regularized object pronoun as well)* SE: *himself*	**Culturally Specific Static Vocabulary** Vocabulary specific to the community that is passed down generation to generation Terms like: *kitchen* (back of the hair) or *tripping* (being bothersome)
Same Voicing Consonant Clusters Voiced Clusters *ld, nd, ng* Unvoiced Clusters *sk, st, ft, kt* Examples AAVE: *col* SE: *cold* AAVE: *des* SE: *desk*	**Possessive Marker** Possession marked by location of possessor and intonation of word when verbalized Examples AAVE: *Bobby toy* SE: *Bobby's toy*	**Use of *Be*** Habitual *Be* The *be* form is durative, referring to an ongoing state. Examples AAVE: *I be talking with them.* SE: *I often talk with them.*	**Dynamic Uses of Slang** Vocabulary of the youth that changes frequently and can be tied to one specific generation Note: terms for money based on the decade 70s—bread 80s—mula 90s—benjimans 2000—cheddar
Vowel Pairs /I/ /i/ Mixing of short and long vowels Examples AAVE: *Ah* SE: *I* AAVE: *Thank* SE: *Think*	**Plural Marker** Unnecessary when numerically defined Examples AAVE: *fifty cent* SE: *fifty cents*	**Topicalization** Subject announced or "topicalized." Examples AAVE: *That teacher she mean.* SE: *That teacher is mean.*	
Reflexive *R* and *L* *R* and *L* before controlled vowels that do not appear; same occurrence in Asian languages Examples AAVE: *Sista', Motha'* SE: *Sister, mother* AAVE: *mi'ion, ye'ow* SE: *million, yellow*	**Negation** Uses of multiple negatives to intensify negative in sentences; not equivalent to double negative in Standard English Examples AAVE: *Don't never do that more.* SE: *Don't do that anymore.*	***Is/Are* Form** *Is/Are* linking verbs and helping verbs not always necessary Examples AAVE: *She going to the game with us.* SE: *She is going to the game with us.*	
Two Syllable Stress Patterns Examples **Po**-lice **Ho**-tel			

Linguistic Contrastive Analysis Chart

The Consonants of English

IPA	ENGLISH	SPANISH	VIETNAMESE	CANTONESE
p	*pit* Aspirated at the start of a word or stressed syllable	*pato* (duck) Never aspirated	*pin* (battery)	*pʰa* (to lie prone) Always aspirated
b	*bit*	*barco* (boat) Substitute voiced bilabial fricative /ɵ/ in between vowels	*ba* (three) Implosive (air moves into the mouth during articulation)	**NO EQUIVALENT** Substitute /p/
m	*man*	*mundo* (world)	*mot* (one)	*ma* (mother)
w	*win*	*agua* (water)	**NO EQUIVALENT** Substitute word-initial /u/	*wa* (frog)
f	*fun*	*flor* (flower)	*phuʾoʾng* (phoenix) Substitute sound made with both lips, rather than with the upper lip and the teeth like English /f/	*fa* (flower) Only occurs at the beginning of syllables
v	*very*	**NO EQUIVALENT** Learners can use correct sound	*Việt Nam* (Vietnam)	**NO EQUIVALENT** Substitute /f/
ɵ	*thing* Rare in other languages. When done correctly, the tongue will stick out between the teeth.	**NO EQUIVALENT** Learners can use correct sound	**NO EQUIVALENT** Substitute /tʰ/ or /f/	**NO EQUIVALENT** Substitute /tʰ/ or /f/
ð	*there* Rare in other languages. When done correctly, the tongue will stick out between the teeth.	*cada* (every) Sound exists in Spanish only between vowels; sometimes substitute voiceless /ɵ/.	**NO EQUIVALENT** Substitute /d/	**NO EQUIVALENT** Substitute /t/ or /f/
t	*time* Aspirated at the start of a word or stressed syllable English tongue-touch. Is a little farther back in the mouth than the other languages.	*tocar* (touch) Never aspirated	*tám* (eight) Distinguishes aspirated and non-aspirated	*tʰa* (he/she) Distinguishes aspirated and non-aspirated
d	*dime* English tongue-touch is a little farther back in the mouth than the other languages.	*dos* (two)	*Đōng* (Dong = unit of currency) Vietnamese /d/ is implosive (air moves into the mouth during articulation)	**NO EQUIVALENT** Substitute /t/
n	*name* English tongue-touch is a little farther back in the mouth than the other languages.	*nube* (cloud)	*nam* (south)	*na* (take)
s	*soy*	*seco* (dry)	*xem* (to see)	*sa* (sand) Substitute *sh*– sound before /u/ Difficult at ends of syllables and words
z	*zeal*	**NO EQUIVALENT** Learners can use correct sound	*ròi* (already) In northern dialect only Southern dialect, substitute /y/	**NO EQUIVALENT** Substitute /s/
ɾ	*butter* Written 't' and 'd' are pronounced with a quick tongue-tip tap.	*rana* (toad) Written as single *r* and thought of as an /r/ sound.	**NO EQUIVALENT** Substitute /t/	**NO EQUIVALENT** Substitute /t/
l	*loop* English tongue-touch is a little farther back in the mouth than the other languages. At the ends of syllables, the /l/ bunches up the back of the tongue, becoming velarized /ɫ/ or dark-l as in the word *ball*.	*libro* (book)	*cú lao* (island) /l/ does not occur at the ends of syllables	*lau* (angry) /l/ does not occur at the ends of syllables

HMONG	FILIPINO	KOREAN	MANDARIN
*p*eb (we/us/our) Distinguishes aspirated and non-aspirated	*p*aalam (goodbye) Never aspirated	*p*al (sucking)	*p*ʰei (cape) Always aspirated
NO EQUIVALENT Substitute /p/	*b*aka (beef)	**NO EQUIVALENT** /b/ said between vowels Substitute /p/ elsewhere	**NO EQUIVALENT**
*m*us (to go)	*m*abuti (good)	*m*al (horse)	*m*ei (rose)
NO EQUIVALENT Substitute word-initial /*u*/	*w*alo (eight)	*gw*e (box)	*w*en (mosquito)
*f*aib (to divide)	**NO EQUIVALENT** Substitute /p/	**NO EQUIVALENT** Substitute /p/	*f*a (issue)
*V*aj ('Vang' clan name)	**NO EQUIVALENT** Substitute /b/	**NO EQUIVALENT** Substitute /b/	**NO EQUIVALENT** Substitute /w/ or /f/
NO EQUIVALENT Substitute /tʰ/ or /f/	**NO EQUIVALENT** Learners can use correct sound, but sometimes mispronounce voiced /ð/.	**NO EQUIVALENT** Substitute /t/	**NO EQUIVALENT** Substitute /t/ or /s/
NO EQUIVALENT Substitute /d/	**NO EQUIVALENT** Learners can use correct sound	**NO EQUIVALENT** Substitute /d/	**NO EQUIVALENT** Substitute /t/ or /s/
*th*em (to pay) Distinguishes aspirated and non-aspirated	*t*akbo (run) Never aspirated	*t*al (daughter)	*t*a (wet) Distinguishes aspirated and non-aspirated
*d*ev (dog)	*d*eretso (straight)	**NO EQUIVALENT** Substitute /d/ when said between vowels and /t/ elsewhere.	**NO EQUIVALENT** Substitute /t/
*n*oj (to eat)	*n*aman (too)	*n*al (day)	*n*i (you) May be confused with /l/
*x*a (to send)	*s*ila (they)	*s*al (rice) Substitute *shi*– sound before /i/ and /z/ after a nasal consonant	*s*an (three)
NO EQUIVALENT Learners can use correct sound	**NO EQUIVALENT** Learners can use correct sound	**NO EQUIVALENT** Learners can use correct sound	**NO EQUIVALENT** Substitute /ts/ or /tsʰ/
NO EQUIVALENT Substitute /t/	*r*in/*d*in (too) Variant of the /d/ sound	Only occurs only between two vowels Considered an /l/ sound	**NO EQUIVALENT**
*l*os (to come) /l/ does not occur at the ends of syllables	sa*l*amat (thank you)	ba*l*am (wind)	*l*an (blue) Can be confused and substituted with /r/

Linguistic Contrastive Analysis Chart

The Consonants of English (continued)

IPA	ENGLISH	SPANISH	VIETNAMESE	CANTONESE
ɹ	*red* Rare sound in the world Includes lip-rounding	**NO EQUIVALENT** Substitute /r/ sound such as the tap /ɾ/ or the trilled /r/	**NO EQUIVALENT** Substitute /l/	**NO EQUIVALENT** Substitute /l/
ʃ	*sh*allow Often said with lip-rounding	**NO EQUIVALENT** Substitute /s/ or /tʃ/	*sieu th*ị (supermarket) southern dialect only	**NO EQUIVALENT** Substitute /s/
ʒ	*vi*s*ion* rare sound in English	**NO EQUIVALENT** Substitute /z/ or /dʒ/	**NO EQUIVALENT** Substitute /s/	**NO EQUIVALENT** Substitute /s/
tʃ	*ch*irp	*ch*ico (boy)	*ch*ính phủ (government) Pronounced harder than English *ch*	**NO EQUIVALENT** Substitute /ts/
dʒ	*j*oy	**NO EQUIVALENT** Sometimes substituted with /ʃ/ sound Some dialects have this sound for the *ll* spelling as in *llamar*	**NO EQUIVALENT** Substitute /c/, the equivalent sound, but voiceless	**NO EQUIVALENT** Substitute /ts/ Only occurs at beginnings of syllables
j	*y*ou	*ci*elo (sky) Often substitute /dʒ/	*y*eu (to love)	*j*au (worry)
k	*k*ite Aspirated at the start of a word or stressed syllable	*c*asa (house) Never aspirated	*c*om (rice) Never aspirated	*k*ʰa (family) Distinguishes aspirated and non-aspirated
g	*g*oat	*g*ato (cat)	**NO EQUIVALENT** Substitute /k/	**NO EQUIVALENT** Substitute /k/
ŋ	ki*ng*	ma*ng*o (mango)	*Ng*ūyen (proper last name)	pha*ŋ* (to cook)
h	*h*ope	*g*ente (people) Sometimes substitute sound with friction higher in the vocal tract as velar /x/ or uvular /χ/	*h*oa (flower)	*h*a (shrimp)

HMONG	FILIPINO	KOREAN	MANDARIN
NO EQUIVALENT Substitute /l/	**NO EQUIVALENT** Substitute the tap /ɾ/	**NO EQUIVALENT** Substitute the tap or /ɾ/ confused with /l/	*r*an (caterpillar) Tongue tip curled further backward than for English /r/
*s*au (to write)	*s*iya (s/he)	Only occurs before /i/; Considered an /s/ sound	*sh*i (wet)
*z*os (village)	**NO EQUIVALENT** Learners can use correct sound	**NO EQUIVALENT**	**NO EQUIVALENT** Substitute palatal affricate /tɕ/
*ch*eb (to sweep)	*ts*a (tea)	*cʰ*al (kicking)	*ch*eng (red)
NO EQUIVALENT Substitute *ch* sound	*D*ios (God)	**NO EQUIVALENT** Substitute *ch* sound	**NO EQUIVALENT** Substitute /ts/
*Y*aj (Yang, clan name)	ta*y*o (we)	je:*z*an (budget)	*y*an (eye)
*K*oo (Kong, clan name) Distinguishes aspirated and non-aspirated	*k*alian (when) Never aspirated	*k*al (spreading)	*k*e (nest) Distinguishes aspirated and non-aspirated
NO EQUIVALENT Substitute /k/	*g*ulay (vegetable)	**NO EQUIVALENT** Substitute /k/ Learners use correct sound between two vowels	**NO EQUIVALENT** Substitute /k/
*g*us (goose)	an*g*aw (one million)	ba*ŋ* (room)	tan*g* (gong) Sometimes add /k/ sound to the end
*h*ais (to speak)	*h*indi (no)	*h*al (doing)	**NO EQUIVALENT** Substitute velar fricative /x/

Linguistic Contrastive Analysis Chart

The Vowels of English

IPA	ENGLISH	SPANISH	VIETNAMESE	CANTONESE
i	*beat*	*hijo* (son)	*di* (to go)	*si* (silk)
ɪ	*bit* Rare in other languages Usually confused with /i/ (*meat* vs. *mit*)	NO EQUIVALENT Substitute /i/	NO EQUIVALENT Substitute /i/	*sik* (color) Only occurs before velars Substitute /i/
e	*bait* End of vowel diphthongized—tongue moves up to /i/ or /ɪ/ position	*eco* (echo)	*kê* (millet)	*se* (to lend)
ɛ	*bet* Rare in other languages Learners may have difficulty distinguishing /e/ and /ɛ/: *pain* vs. *pen*	NO EQUIVALENT Substitute /e/	NO EQUIVALENT Substitute /e/	*seŋ* (sound) Only occurs before velars; difficult to distinguish from /e/ in all positions
æ	*bat* Rare in other languages Learners may have trouble getting the tongue farther forward in the mouth	NO EQUIVALENT Substitute mid central /ʌ/ or low front tense /a/	*ghe* (boat)	NO EQUIVALENT Hard to distinguish between /æ/ and /e/
u	*boot*	*uva* (grape)	*mua* (to buy)	*fu* (husband)
ʊ	*could* Rare in other languages Learners may have difficulty distinguishing /u/ and /ʊ/; *wooed* vs. *wood*	NO EQUIVALENT Substitute /ù/	NO EQUIVALENT Substitute uʼ (high back unrounded)	*suk* (uncle) Only occurs before velars Difficult to distinguish from /u/ in all positions
o	*boat* End of vowel diphthongized – tongue moves up to /u/ or /ʊ/ position	*ojo* (eye)	*cô* (aunt)	*so* (comb)
ɔ	*law*	NO EQUIVALENT Substitute /o/ or /ɑ/ Substituting /o/ will cause confusion (*low* vs. *law*); substituting /ɑ/ will not	*cá* (fish)	*hok* (shell) Only occurs before velars Difficult to distinguish from /o/ in all positions
ɑ	*hot*	*mal* (bad)	*con* (child)	*sa* (sand)
ɑ ʊ	*house* Diphthong starts /ɑ/ and moves to /ʊ/	*pauta*	*dao* (knife)	*sau* (basket)
ɔ ɪ	*boy* Diphthong starts at /ɔ/ and moves to /ɪ/	*hoy* (today)	*ròi* (already)	*soi* (grill)
ɑ ɪ	*bite* Diphthong starts at /ɑ/ and moves to /ɪ/	*baile* (dance)	*hai* (two)	*sai* (to waste)
ə	*about* Most common vowel in English; only in unstressed syllables Learners may have difficulty keeping it very short	NO EQUIVALENT Substitute /ʌ/ or the full vowel from the word's spelling	*mua* (to buy)	NO EQUIVALENT
ʌ	*cut* very similar to schwa /ə/	NO EQUIVALENT Substitute /a/	*giòʼ* (time)	*san* (new)
ɝ	*bird* Difficult articulation, unusual in the world but common in American English Learners must bunch the tongue and constrict the throat	NO EQUIVALENT Substitute /ʌ/ or /eɾ/ with trill	NO EQUIVALENT Substitute /ɨ/	*hæ* (boot)

HMONG	FILIPINO	KOREAN	MANDARIN
ib (one)	zɪːʃaŋ (market)	zɪːʃaŋ (market)	*ti* (ladder) Sometimes English /i/ can be produced shorter
NO EQUIVALENT Substitute /i/	*límampu* (fifty) This vowel is interchangeable with /i/; hard for speakers to distinguish these	**NO EQUIVALENT** Substitute /i/	**NO EQUIVALENT**
tes (hand)	*sero* (zero)	*beːda* (to cut)	*te* (nervous) Sometimes substitute English schwa /ə/
NO EQUIVALENT Substitute /e/	*sero* (zero) This vowel interchanges with /e/ like *bait*; not difficult for speakers to learn	*thɛːdo* (attitude)	**NO EQUIVALENT**
NO EQUIVALENT Substitute /ɛ/	**NO EQUIVALENT** Substitute /ɑ/ as in *hot*	**NO EQUIVALENT**	**NO EQUIVALENT** Substitute /ə/ or /ʌ/
kub (hot or gold)	*tunay* (actual) This vowel interchanges with /ʊ/ like *could*; not difficult for speakers to learn	*zuːbag* (watermelon)	*lu* (hut) Sometimes English /u/ can be produced shorter
NO EQUIVALENT Substitute /ɨ/ (mid central with lips slightly rounded)	*gumawa* (act) This vowel interchanges with /u/ like *boot*; not difficult for speakers to learn	**NO EQUIVALENT**	**NO EQUIVALENT**
NO EQUIVALENT	*ubo* (cough)	*boːzu* (salary)	*mo* (sword) This vowel is a little lower than English vowel
Yaj (Yang clan name)	**NO EQUIVALENT** Spoken as /ɑ/ as in *hot*	**NO EQUIVALENT**	**NO EQUIVALENT** Substitute /o/
mov (cooked rice)	*ikaw* (you)	*maːl* (speech)	*ta* (he/she) Sometimes substitute back /o/ or /u/
plaub (four)	*apoy* (fire)	**NO EQUIVALENT**	**NO EQUIVALENT**
NO EQUIVALENT	*himatay* (faint)	**NO EQUIVALENT**	**NO EQUIVALENT**
qaib (chicken)	**NO EQUIVALENT** Spoken as /ɑ/ as in *hot*	**NO EQUIVALENT**	**NO EQUIVALENT**
NO EQUIVALENT	*rin/din* (too) Variant of the /d/ sound	**NO EQUIVALENT** Difficult sound for learners	**NO EQUIVALENT**
NO EQUIVALENT	**NO EQUIVALENT** Spoken as /ɑ/ as in *hot*	**NO EQUIVALENT**	**NO EQUIVALENT**
NO EQUIVALENT Substitute diphthong /əi/	**NO EQUIVALENT** Spoken as many different vowels (depending on English spelling) plus tongue tap /ɾ/	**NO EQUIVALENT**	**NO EQUIVALENT**

How to Use *Keystone*

Keystone is a research-based, standards-aligned program that ensures that students will master the academic skills necessary to be successful across the curriculum. The many resources of the program have been carefully designed to make lesson planning, pacing, teaching, and assessment easier.

Teaching the Unit

Each of the six units in a level focuses on a theme and is organized around a Big Question, which serves as the focal point for building students' understanding of concepts and helping them to develop their skills. The four readings in each unit were carefully chosen to give students experience reading informational texts balanced with classic and contemporary literature.

Use the *Unit Opener* to prepare your students to learn about the theme and to activate prior knowledge as they explore the Big Question. Within each reading, students think about and discuss the Big Question from different points of view.

 Technology

Capture student interest with the engaging **Video Program DVD**, featuring background information about the theme.

At the end of each unit, students get assessment practice and a fluency check in *Link the Readings*. Next, they recombine, practice, and apply the skills they have learned in a *Listening and Speaking Workshop* and a *Writing Workshop*.

Finally, students develop cultural and visual literacy through authentic art presented by the *Smithsonian American Art Museum*. These pages explore the theme of the unit and the Big Question through artistic expression.

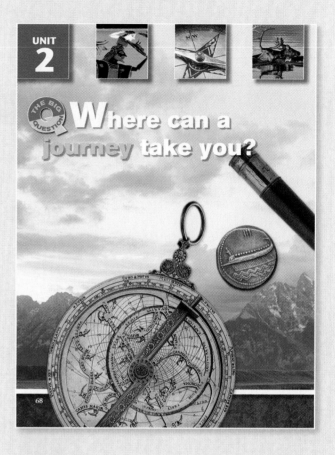

UNIT 2

THE BIG QUESTION

Where can a journey take you?

68

Learn about Art with the
Smithsonian American Art Museum

Capturing the Power of Contrasts

Sometimes life is easier if we can put things in categories: black or white, light or shadow, good or evil. Such clean dividing lines often help us make decisions. Artists often use strong contrasts in their work to create a mood or make a point. They appeal to the viewer's need for simple, bold storylines.

Edward Hopper, *Ryder's House* (1933)

In *Ryder's House*, Edward Hopper painted outdoors and captured a typical New England house in a natural landscape. Hopper chose to paint a particular view of the two-story structure that emphasized the house's massiveness. The sharp horizontal lines of the rectangular building are repeated in the small hills of grass in the foreground and the sky and clouds above. This contrast gives the viewer the feeling that the house stands firmly in the field.

▲ Edward Hopper, *Ryder's House*, 1933, oil, 36⅛ x 50 in., Smithsonian American Art Museum

The simple, sun-washed, white building projects a feeling of stability that Americans appreciated in the 1930s, when the country was in a terrible economic depression. Hopper's use of light and shadow in *Ryder's House* creates a dramatic effect where many of us might see none.

68

44

Planning and Preparing to Teach

Start your planning with the **Teacher's Edition**. The *Longman Keystone Teacher's Edition* was specifically designed to provide easy-to-use, step-by-step lesson planning tools and includes a list of available teaching resources for every lesson. The program is organized in six-week instructional blocks so that the thorough skills coverage is presented in manageable chunks. A benchmark test is provided at the conclusion of each block so that you can effectively monitor student progress. This systematic, logical organization with built-in progress monitoring allows you to make sound instructional choices. The standards covered in each lesson are listed on the bottom left-hand pages throughout each lesson so that you and your students know what specific skills are being taught at any given point.

Technology

Use the **Teacher eBook and CD-ROM** with **ExamView™ Test Generator** to make lesson planning and testing easier. The eBook includes the entire teacher's edition as well as all other print components made available at the click of a mouse. The **ExamView™** electronic test generator lets you customize assessment to meet ever-changing classroom needs, while its powerful reporting functions let you get the most from your teaching.

Use the **Teacher's Resource Book** for lesson plans, standards correlations, graphic organizers, selection summaries in multiple languages, and Parent/Guardian letters.

Preview the Unit

UNIT 2

STEP 1: Introduce

Unit Content

Tell students that they will read several selections about journeys. Lead students in a discussion about how life is like a journey. Tell students that this unit contains both fiction and nonfiction selections, including an epic poem, a novel excerpt, and two articles. The readings are grouped to help students understand the literal and figurative meanings of journeys. Students practice reading strategies and comprehension skills. They apply vocabulary strategies such as using context and analyzing word structure.

The Big Question

Explain to students that the Big Question of the unit is "Where can a journey take you?" Then ask students to talk about journeys of their own. Use questions to stimulate the discussion:

* Do all journeys involve actual physical travel? Why or why not?
* What is the difference between a journey and a trip?
* What are some ways you can grow as a person while on a journey?
* Is life a journey or a destination?

STEP 2: Teach

Visual Literacy

Have students describe some journeys they have taken and what they learned as a result. Then preview the selections in this unit with the students. Discuss the fact that many of the photos and illustrations show images that relate to the theme of journeys. Have volunteers select a visual and explain how it relates to journeys.

Teaching Resources

* *Resources*, Unit 2 Lesson Plans, pp. 15–26
* *Transparencies*, Unit 2 Daily Language Practice
* CD-ROM/e-book, Big Question
* Video, Segment 2
* *Resources*, Letters Home, pp. 111–112

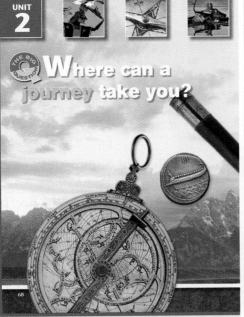

THE BIG QUESTION

Where can a journey take you?

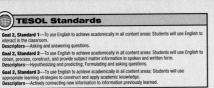

TESOL Standards

Goal 2, Standard 1—To use English to achieve academically in all content areas: Students will use English to interact in the classroom.
Descriptors—Asking and answering questions.
Goal 2, Standard 2—To use English to achieve academically in all content areas: Students will use English to obtain, process, construct, and provide subject matter information in spoken and written form.
Descriptors—Hypothesizing and predicting; Formulating and asking questions.
Goal 2, Standard 3—To use English to achieve academically in all content areas: Students will use appropriate learning strategies to construct and apply academic knowledge.
Descriptors—Actively connecting new information to information previously learned.

This unit is about journeys. You will read literature, science, and social studies texts about exploring, migrating, leaving home, and trying to return home. Learning about these topics will help you become a better student. It will also help you practice the language you need to use in school.

READING 1: Myth
■ From *Tales from the Odyssey*, retold by Mary Pope Osborne

READING 2: Social Studies Article
■ "Early Explorers"

READING 3: Science Articles
■ "Migrating Caribou"
■ "Magnets in Animals" by Darlene R. Stille

READING 4: Novel Excerpt
■ From *The Journal of Wong Ming-Chung* by Laurence Yep

Listening and Speaking

At the end of this unit, you will relate a **personal narrative**. In your personal narrative you will tell about a journey you took.

Writing

In this unit you will practice **narrative writing**. This type of writing tells a story. After each reading you will learn a skill to help you write a narrative paragraph. At the end of the unit, you will use these skills to help you write a fictional narrative.

QuickWrite
Make a list of places you have been to or places you would like to visit.

Visit *LongmanKeystone.com*

68   69

STEP 3: Practice

QuickWrite

Ask students to list places they have visited and places they want to visit using a T-chart. Help them get started by suggesting examples. On the board, list different types of places such as a new country, a new city, or someone's house. Include natural places such as a rain forest or a desert. As students complete their T-charts, have them refer to the categories on the board.

STEP 4: Extend

Go over the titles of the readings and ask students to predict how each reading might relate to places journeys take us.

Teaching a Reading

Introduce each reading with a refocus on the *Big Question* to activate prior knowledge. *Build Background* fills in knowledge gaps about the reading, while the *Vocabulary* feature introduces key terms and academic vocabulary. A *Reading Strategy* is also introduced at the beginning of each reading to further aid student comprehension.

 Technology

Use the interactive **Student eBook and CD-ROM** to make selections and activities come alive with audio support and interactivities for each section.

Use the **Audio CD** to model oral reading fluency and to give additional support to English learners and struggling readers.

Use the *Review and Practice* that follows the reading to monitor progress, check comprehension, practice oral reading fluency, and deepen students' understanding of the unit theme and the Big Question.

Students learn and practice *Grammar and Writing* skills at the end of each reading. Each writing assignment includes a model written by a real student, and builds essential writing skills that culminate in the end-of-unit *Writing Workshop*. Use the graphic organizers from your **Teacher's Resource Book** to help students gather and organize ideas for their writing. The *Writing Checklist* provided with each assignment will help students focus their attention on the Six Traits of Writing to improve their writing skills.

Each unit of *Keystone* teaches different aspects of a single mode of writing, and each reading gives students a variety of opportunities to learn the grammar and language structures necessary for written academic communication.

For additional support, use the *Handbooks* in the back of the Student Edition to give students practice in language learning, grammar, reading, using visuals, writing, and technology.

Resources to Support Learning

Workbook
Graphic Organizers
Reading Summaries
Reader's Companion Workbook
Daily Language Practice Transparencies
Penguin Library
Assessment Package
Audio CD
Video Program
Student eBook and CD-ROM
Teacher eBook and CD-ROM

Monitoring Progress

Keystone makes it easy to monitor your students' progress with frequent opportunities to assess mastery and reteach material.

- Use the **Placement Test** before students begin using the program to ensure they are starting at the correct program level.

- Use the *Pre-test* in the **Assessment Package** to determine student readiness. You will find frequent checks and suggestions in the Teacher's Edition for monitoring student progress throughout each lesson.

- Use the *Reading Test* to assess comprehension and mastery of the vocabulary, grammar, and skills taught with the Reading.

- Use the *Unit Exam* to assess student competency in vocabulary, oral reading fluency, word study, spelling, grammar, and writing.

- Use the student score sheets in the **Assessment Package** to identify skills that have been mastered, and those that need to be retaught.

- Use the Exam*View*™ electronic test generator to customize assessment. Use the reporting tools to help tailor instruction to individual needs.

- Use the *Exit Exam* to determine whether students are ready to tackle mainstream coursework or continue to the next level of the program.

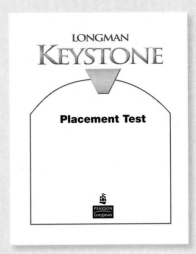

Built-in Differentiated Instruction

Keystone gives unprecedented opportunities for reaching all students.

- **Teacher's Edition:** Use the strategies and techniques geared toward English learners (including Standard English Learners) and struggling readers. The *Culturally Responsive Instruction* icon (CRI) denotes suggestions that are particularly appropriate for SELs.

- **Reader's Companion:** This workbook gives students extra reading support and helps them develop active reading habits.

- **Transparencies:** *Daily Language Practice* applies skills students learned in the previous lesson. *Graphic organizers* give struggling readers and English learners a toolkit to organize their thinking and writing.

- **Teacher's Resource Book:** *Reading Summaries* in English, Chinese, Cambodian, Hmong, Spanish, and Vietnamese give students a preview of each reading in their home language.

Differentiated Instruction	
Beginning	Ask students what Julia saw the caterpillar doing first (spinning a cocoon).
Early Intermediate	Have students put the life cycle of a silkworm in the correct order. (Egg, worm, cocoon, moth).
Intermediate	Ask students to recreate the story in a manner of their choosing—either as a poster, a letter, or a reactment. Encourage them to share their version of the story with the class.
Standard English Learners (CRI)	Explain the word *jostling* to students. Tell them that the verb is *to jostle*. Ask students to describe this action in their own words, or to give an example of when this might happen.

Using *Longman Keystone* with SIOP®

The Sheltered Instruction Observation Protocol, developed by Drs. Echevarria, Short, and Vogt, is a research-based model consisting of eight components and thirty features. This model has been proved effective in meeting the needs of English learners and struggling readers.

Longman Keystone is designed to help English language learners develop English language skills and succeed in all content areas of academic studies. The recursive structure of the program aligns clearly with the components and features of the SIOP model.

Preparation			
The Big Question (content objectives)		What You Will Learn (language objectives)	
Building Background			
QuickWrite	Reading Focus	Vocabulary Focus	Word Study
Comprehensible Input			
Photos, Pictures, Captions	Glossed Words (pronunciation)	Diagrams, Charts, Graphic Organizers	Smithsonian American Art
Strategies			
Listening and Speaking Tips	Reading Strategy Boxes	Read for Fluency	Word Study
Interaction			
Work with a Partner	Dramatic Reading	Discuss in Pairs or Small Groups	Reader's Theater
Practice and Application			
Listening and Speaking Workshop	Writing • Grammar Focus • Writing Focus		Projects and Further Reading
Lesson Delivery			
The Big Question	What You Will Learn	Vocabulary Focus	Reading Focus
Review and Assessment			
Assessment Practice — Before You Go On — Review and Practice — Apply What You Learned — Fluency Checks — The Big Question Wrap-Up			

For more information visit **www.LongmanKeystone.com**.

LONGMAN
KEYSTONE
A

Anna Uhl Chamot

John De Mado

Sharroky Hollie

PEARSON
Longman

LONGMAN
KEYSTONE A

Pearson Education, 10 Bank Street, White Plains, NY 10606

Staff credits: The people who made up the Longman Keystone team, representing editorial, production, design, manufacturing, and marketing, are John Ade, Rhea Banker, Liz Barker, Danielle Belfiore, Don Bensey, Virginia Bernard, Kenna Bourke, Anne Boynton-Trigg, Johnnie Farmer, Maryann Finocchi, Patrice Fraccio, Geraldine Geniusas, Charles Green, Henry Hild, David L. Jones, Lucille M. Kennedy, Ed Lamprich, Emily Lippincott, Tara Maceyak, Maria Pia Marrella, Linda Moser, Laurie Neaman, Sherri Pemberton, Liza Pleva, Joan Poole, Edie Pullman, Monica Rodriguez, Tania Saiz-Sousa, Donna Schaffer, Chris Siley, Lynn Sobotta, Heather St. Clair, Jennifer Stem, Siobhan Sullivan, Jane Townsend, Heather Vomero, Marian Wassner, Lauren Weidenman, Matthew Williams, and Adina Zoltan.

Smithsonian American Art Museum contributors: Project director and writer: Elizabeth K. Eder, Ph.D.; Writer: Mary Collins; Image research assistants: Laurel Fehrenbach, Katherine G. Stilwill, and Sally Otis; Rights and reproductions: Richard H. Sorensen and Leslie G. Green; Building photograph by Tim Hursley.

Text design and composition: Kirchoff/Wohlberg, Inc.

Text font: 11.5/14 Minion
Acknowledgments: See page 473.
Illustration and Photo Credits: See page 474.

Library of Congress Cataloging-in-Publication Data
Chamot, Anna Uhl.
  Longman keystone / Anna Uhl Chamot, John De Mado, Sharroky Hollie.
    p. cm. -- (Longman keystone ; A)
  Includes index.
  ISBN 0-13-239442-1 (v. A)
  1. Language arts (Middle school)--United States. 2. Language arts (Middle school)--Activity programs. 3. Language arts (Secondary)--United States. 4. English language--Study and teaching. I. Demado, John II. Hollie, Sharroky III. Title.
  LB1631.C4466 2008
  428.0071'2--dc22
                                        2007049279

ISBN-13: 978-0-13-239442-0
ISBN-10: 0-13-239442-1

PEARSON LONGMAN ON THE WEB

Pearsonlongman.com offers online resources for teachers and students. Access our Companion Websites, our online catalog, and our local offices around the world.

Visit us at **www.pearsonlongman.com**.

Printed in the United States of America
3 4 5 6 7 8 9 10 11 12—DWL—12 11 10 09 08

Dear Student,

Welcome to LONGMAN

KEYSTONE

Longman Keystone has been specially designed to help you succeed in all areas of your school studies. This program will help you develop the English language skills you need for language arts, social studies, math, and science. You will discover new ways to use and build upon your language skills through your interactions with classmates, friends, teachers, and family members.

Keystone includes a mix of many subjects. Each unit has four different reading selections that include literary excerpts, poems, and nonfiction articles about science, math, and social studies. These selections will help you understand the vocabulary and organization of different types of texts. They will also give you the tools you need to approach the content of the different subjects you take in school.

As you use this program, you will discover new words, use your background knowledge of the subjects presented, relate your knowledge to the new information, and take part in creative activities. You will learn strategies to help you understand readings better. You will work on activities that help you improve your English skills in grammar, word study, and spelling. Finally, you will be asked to demonstrate the listening, speaking, and writing skills you have learned through fun projects that are incorporated throughout the program.

Learning a language takes time, but just like learning to skateboard or learning to swim, it is fun! Whether you are learning English for the first time, or increasing your knowledge of English by adding academic or literary language to your vocabulary, you are giving yourself new choices for the future, and a better chance of succeeding in both your studies and in everyday life.

We hope you enjoy *Longman Keystone* as much as we enjoyed writing it for you!

Good luck!

Anna Uhl Chamot
John De Mado
Sharroky Hollie

v

Dear Student,

At the end of each unit in this book, you will learn about some artists and artworks that relate to the theme you have just read about. These artworks are all in the Smithsonian American Art Museum in Washington, D.C. That means they belong to you, because the Smithsonian is America's collection. The artworks were created over a period of 300 years by artists who responded to their experiences in personal ways. Their world lives on through their artworks and, as viewers, we can understand them and ourselves in new ways. We discover that many of the things that concerned these artists still engage us today.

Looking at an artwork is different from reading a written history. Artists present few facts or dates. Instead, they offer emotional insights that come from their own lives and experiences. They make their own decisions about what matters, without worrying if others agree or disagree. This is a rare and useful kind of knowledge that we can all learn from. Artists inspire us to respond to our own lives with deeper insight.

There are two ways to approach art. One way is through the mind—studying the artist, learning about the subject, exploring the context in which the artwork was made, and forming a personal view. This way is deeply rewarding and expands your understanding of the world. The second way is through the senses—letting your imagination roam as you look at an artwork, losing yourself in colors and shapes, absorbing the meaning through your eyes. This way is called "aesthetic." The great thing about art is that an artwork may have many different meanings. You can decide what it means to you.

This brief introduction to American art will, I hope, lead to a lifetime of enjoyment and appreciation of art.

Elizabeth Broun
The Margaret and Terry Stent Director
Smithsonian American Art Museum

Glossary of Terms

You will find the following words useful when reading, writing, and talking about art.

abstract a style of art that does not represent things, animals, or people realistically

acrylic a type of paint that is made from ground pigments and certain chemicals

background part of the artwork that looks furthest away from the viewer

brushstroke the paint or ink left on the surface of an artwork by the paintbrush

canvas a type of heavy woven fabric used as a support for painting; another word for a painting

composition the way in which the different parts of an artwork are arranged

detail a small part of an artwork

evoke to produce a strong feeling or memory

figure the representation of a person or animal in an artwork

foreground part of the artwork that looks closest to the viewer

geometric a type of pattern that has straight lines or shapes such as squares, circles, etc.

mixed media different kinds of materials such as paint, fabric, objects, etc. that are used in a single artwork

oil a type of paint that is made from ground pigments and linseed oil

paintbrush a special brush used for painting

perception the way you understand something you see

pigment a finely powdered material (natural or man-made) that gives color to paint, ink, or dye

portrait an artwork that shows a specific person, group of people, or animal

print an artwork that has been made from a sheet of metal or a block of wood covered with a wet color and then pressed onto a flat surface like paper. Types of prints include lithographs, etchings, aquatints, etc.

symbol an image, shape, or object in an artwork that represents an idea

texture the way that a surface or material feels and how smooth or rough it looks

tone the shade of a particular color; the effect of light and shade with color

watercolor a type of paint that is made from ground pigments, gum, and glycerin and/or honey; another word for a painting done with this medium

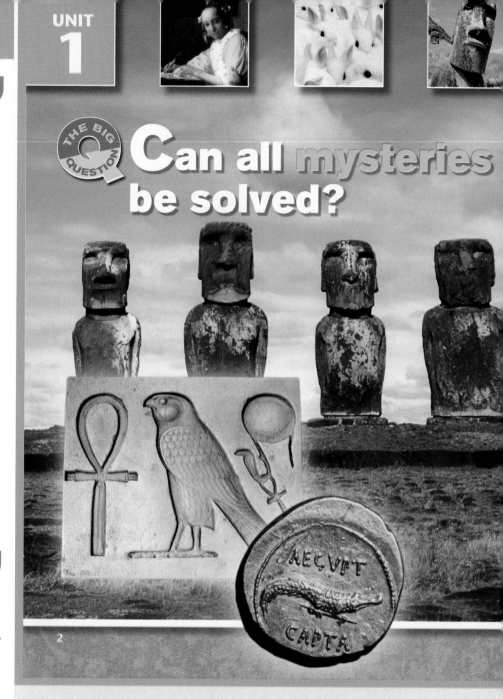

Can all mysteries be solved?

STEP 1: Introduce

Unit Content

Tell students that in this unit they will learn about a variety of mysteries, from ancient times to today. The two fiction and two nonfiction readings are grouped together to help them explore these unsolved mysteries. Students will practice reading and comprehension skills, such as predicting and using visuals. They will study words and apply strategies to learn new vocabulary. Throughout, they will use writing and grammar skills.

The Big Question

Introduce the Big Question, "Can all mysteries be solved?" Encourage students to give some potential answers to the question and probe their thinking. Emphasize that there is no right or wrong answer to the question. To facilitate class discussion, ask the following:

- Do you believe that all mysteries can be solved? Why or why not?
- How are mysteries usually solved?
- What mysteries do you know of that have been solved?
- What mysteries do you know of that have not been solved?
- What are your favorite kinds of mysteries?

STEP 2: Teach

Visual Literacy

Discuss that to solve a mystery, people need to look for clues, observe them closely, and record the information they find. With students, preview the unit for illustrations and photos that show how mysteries are solved. Some questions to ask are:

- *In the picture on page 11, what is this girl doing to figure out a mystery?*
- *On page 37, who is the man in the photo, and what is he doing to solve the mystery of this mummy?*
- *On page 49, how can these footprints help solve a mystery?*

Teaching Resources

- *Resources*, Unit 1 Lesson Plans, pp. 3–14
- *Transparencies*, Unit 1 Daily Language Practice
- CD-ROM/e-book, Big Question
- Video, Segment 1
- *Resources*, Letters Home, pp. 109–110

TESOL Standards

Goal 2, Standard 1—To use English to achieve academically in all content areas: Students will use English to interact in the classroom.
Descriptors—Asking and answering questions.

Goal 2, Standard 2—To use English to achieve academically in all content areas: Students will use English to obtain, process, construct, and provide subject matter information in spoken and written form.
Descriptors—Hypothesizing and predicting; Formulating and asking questions.

Goal 2, Standard 3—To use English to achieve academically in all content areas: Students will use appropriate learning strategies to construct and apply academic knowledge.
Descriptors—Actively connecting new information to information previously learned.

This unit is about real-life and make-believe mysteries. You'll read about crimes, strange events, unusual number patterns, mysterious cities, and monster-like creatures. Exploring these mysteries will help you become a better reader. It will also help you practice the academic and literary language you need to use in school.

READING 1: Novel Excerpt

■ From *Chasing Vermeer* by Blue Balliett

READING 2: Math/Science Article

■ From *G Is for Googol* by David M. Schwartz

READING 3: Social Studies Article

■ "Fact or Fiction?"

READING 4: Two Short Stories

■ *Teenage Detectives* by Carol Farley and Hy Conrad

Listening and Speaking

At the end of this unit, you and your classmates will play a **description guessing game**.

Writing

In this unit you will practice **descriptive writing**. This type of writing tells what things look, sound, feel, smell, or taste like. After each reading you will learn a skill to help you write a descriptive paragraph. At the end of the unit, you will use these skills to help you write a descriptive essay.

QuickWrite

In your notebook, write the words *look*, *sound*, and *feel*. Look around your classroom. What do you see, hear, and feel? Write for five minutes.

3

QuickWrite

Review the five senses with students and explain the roles of sight, sound, touch, taste, and smell in solving mysteries. Then ask students to write three words in their notebooks: *look*, *sound*, *feel*, and to generate a quick list of classroom items they can see, hear, and touch. Help students get started with examples of each.

STEP 4: Extend

Go over the titles of the readings, and ask students to predict how each title might relate to solving mysteries. **SAY:** *The excerpt from* Chasing Vermeer *is part of a novel, a work of fiction. What kind of mystery do you think it might be?* (Perhaps it's a story of a mysterious chase for Vermeer's paintings.) **SAY:** *From* G Is for Googol *is a math and science article. It is nonfiction. From the title and subtitles, what unsolved mysteries might you be reading about?* (a different unsolved mystery for each letter of the alphabet) **SAY:** *"Fact or Fiction?" is a social studies article. It is also nonfiction. From the subtitles, what kind of mysteries might these be?* (They might be about ancient secrets, mysterious cities, a huge circle of stones, and an island of giant statues.) **SAY:** Teenage Detectives *is a work of fiction. It contains two short stories. From the title and subtitles, what kind of mystery do you think it might be?* (Teenagers probably act like detectives and solve crimes. The subtitles describe two of their cases.)

T3

STEP 1: Introduce

Objectives

With students, read the list of objectives in the What You Will Learn section. Tell students that this reading will be about an art mystery. Have students work in pairs to restate the list of things they will learn.

The Big Question

Remind students that the Big Question is "Can all mysteries be solved?" Point out that some people think a work of art is a mystery. **SAY:** *In many paintings, it's hard to know what the artist is trying to tell us. I've been to modern art museums where most of the paintings are just lines and boxes. It's a mystery. What makes an object a work of art?* (It's personal. Everyone has a different point of view.) *Besides paintings, what else do you think can be works of art?* (sculptures, monuments, buildings, illustrations, books, ballet, and so on)

Build Background

Point out that *Chasing Vermeer* is an art mystery story. **SAY:** *Name some mystery stories you have read or seen on TV. How are most mystery stories alike?* (They are filled with suspense, have lots of plot twists, are exciting, are full of surprises, and have many unexpected events.)

Create an idea web on chart paper with the words *Mystery Stories* in the center circle. Place student responses in the outer circles. Post the web for easy reference as students work on the unit.

STEP 2: Teach

Understanding the Genre:
Novel Excerpt

Point out that a novel is a long work of fiction. Novels contain elements such as characters, plot, setting, and conflict, although they are not about real people and events.

Explain that the excerpt from *Chasing Vermeer* is part of a mystery novel. A mystery novel contains a puzzle to be solved and clues that help readers guess the outcome.

Teaching Resources

- CD-ROM/e-book, Literary Words
- Audio CD 1, track 2
- *Workbook,* p. 1

What You Will Learn

Reading
- Vocabulary building: *Literary terms, dictionary skills, word study*
- Reading strategy: *Predict*
- Text type: *Literature (novel excerpt)*

Grammar, Usage, and Mechanics
Distinguishing parts of speech

Writing
Describe a character

THE BIG QUESTION

Can all mysteries be solved? Have you ever wondered about what makes something a work of art? Some people think that the nature of art is a mystery. Think about a painting that you know and love. What makes it a work of art? Does it have to be in a museum? Does it have to be created by a famous person? Do you have to like it?

Work with a partner. Study the painting below by the seventeenth-century Dutch painter Johannes Vermeer. It is called *A Lady Writing.* Describe what you see and feel when you look at the picture. Jot down your ideas. Do you think the picture is a work of art? Why or why not?

BUILD BACKGROUND

Chasing Vermeer is a mystery novel about a painting by Vermeer. In real life, there are many mysteries surrounding Vermeer's life and work. For example, one of his paintings was stolen from a museum in Boston, Massachusetts, and it has never been found.

Mysteries are about puzzles and strange events. The people in a mystery novel try to use clues to solve a puzzle. Mysteries are very popular because they are exciting and full of suspense. As the people in the story try to solve the puzzle, so do you.

Vermeer painted *A Lady Writing* around 1665–1666.

4

🌐 TESOL Standards

Goal 1, Standard 3—To use English to communicate in social settings: Students will use learning strategies to extend their communicative competence.
Descriptors—Listening to and imitating how others use English; Exploring alternative ways of saying things; Focusing attention selectively.

Goal 2, Standard 1—To use English to achieve academically in all content areas: Students will use English to interact in the classroom.
Descriptors—Requesting and providing clarification; Participating in full-class, group, and pair discussions; Negotiating and managing interaction to accomplish tasks.

Goal 2, Standard 2—To use English to achieve academically in all content areas: Students will use English to obtain, process, construct, and provide subject matter information in spoken and written form.
Descriptors—Selecting, connecting, and explaining information; Understanding and producing technical vocabulary and text features according to content area.

VOCABULARY

Learn Literary Words

Novels, short stories, and poems are all types of literature. The people or animals in a novel or short story are called characters. Like people in real life, the characters in a story have certain qualities, or character traits. You can learn about characters and their traits through what the characters say and do and by what happens to them in the story. You can also get to know the characters' personalities, or traits, by paying attention to what other characters say about them.

In the excerpt you are about to read, you will meet several characters, including Petra Andalee and Calder Pillay. You will learn about their traits by the way they speak, act, dress, and think and by what they say about each other. Read this short section from the beginning of the book. What do you learn about Petra and Calder?

Literary Words

characters
character traits

> Calder, at that moment, looked out his front window to see Petra walking by holding a leaf several inches from her nose. He knew he was kind of weird, but she was *exceptionally* weird. She was always by herself at school, and didn't seem to care. She was quiet when other kids were loud. Plus, she had a fierce triangle of hair that made her look like one of those Egyptian queens.
>
> Calder wondered if he was becoming just as much of an oddball. No one had asked him what he was doing after class that day. No one had told him to wait. . . .

Practice Workbook Page 1

Think of a character from a movie or television show whose character traits you know well. In your notebook, make a copy of the character-traits web below. Fill in the web with traits and examples. Then describe this character to a classmate.

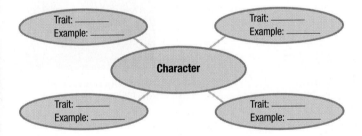

5

Differentiated Instruction

Beginning	Ask students when Vermeer painted, "A Lady Writing," as seen on page 4. (1665–1666)
Early Intermediate	Ask students to tell what the girl in the painting is doing.
Intermediate	Have students look at the painting on page 4 and try to describe the character traits of the girl in the painting.
Struggling Readers	Ask students to name some characters they know from other books they've read. Ask them to describe the character and tell why they like the character.

Vocabulary

Learn Literary Words Play the CD. Have students listen and repeat. If you are not using the CD, direct students to the Literary Words at the top of the page and read them aloud. Ask students what comes to mind when they hear each word. Write down student responses. **SAY:** *These words are called Literary Words because in a discussion of literature, they have a unique meaning. Read the paragraph in your book that defines* characters *and* character traits.

Write the following definitions of *characters* and *character traits* on the board or an overhead transparency to reinforce learning.

- **characters:** people or animals in a novel or short story
- **character traits:** the qualities or traits of the characters in a story

Provide examples of characters and character traits. **SAY:** *The characters in the famous children's story "Cinderella" are Cinderella, her stepmother, her stepsisters, and the prince. Cinderella's character traits are sadness and sweetness. The stepmother's and stepsisters' character traits are meanness and laziness. The prince's character trait is charm.*

Ask students to use the words *characters* and *character traits* in new sentences. For extra practice, have students use the corresponding Workbook page.

Encourage students to keep a personal vocabulary list called a Word Book.

STEP 3: Practice

Read aloud the instructions for this practice exercise. Then model how to use the character traits web. On the board, draw an empty web, and ask students to name a TV or movie character they all know. Write that person's name in the center oval. Discuss what the character says and does on TV or in a movie, what happens to the character, and what others say about him or her. Using that information, decide together what character traits the character has, and write them in the outer ovals on the web. For example, if the character says he's a great singer, students might say that he is *egotistical* or *confident*. If the character gets into trouble but manages to get out of it, students might say he's *cunning* or *mischievous*.

STEP 1: Teach

CD1 T3–T4

Vocabulary

Learn Academic Words Play the CD. Have students listen and repeat. If you are not using the CD, read the academic words aloud. **SAY:** *Look at the Academic Words chart. The definition for each word is on the left side. On the right side, each word is used in a sentence. Work with a partner to write an additional sentence for each academic word. Write each word, its definition, and the sentence in your personal Word Book.*

STEP 2: Practice

Write the following question on the board, and underline the words as shown: How do <u>you identify the artist of an unsigned painting</u>? **SAY:** *When you are asked a question, try to include words from the question in your answer. Look at the question on the board. Think of an answer, using the underlined words. Possible answer:* <u>You identify the artist of an unsigned painting</u> *by recognizing the artist's style of painting.*

ANSWERS

Possible responses:
1. You identify the artist by recognizing the artist's style of painting.
2. An individual might go to a museum to study a work of art.
3. A mystery about a stolen painting might occur in an old, abandoned warehouse.
4. Artists have to be in good physical shape because they need to stand all day and concentrate without becoming distracted.
5. Detectives find evidence to prove the theory of a crime.

Teaching Resources

- Audio CD 1, tracks 3–4
- *Workbook*, pp. 2–4
- CD-ROM/e-book, Academic Words, Word Study

Learn Academic Words

Study the red words and their meanings. You will find these words useful when talking and writing about literature. Write each word and its meaning in your notebook. After you read the excerpt from *Chasing Vermeer,* try to use these words to respond to the text.

Academic Words

identify
individual
occur
physical
theory

identify = recognize and name someone or something	➡	The teacher has her students **identify** different examples by pointing at them.
individual = a person, not a group	➡	Petra Andalee is an **individual** in *Chasing Vermeer*. She is one of the characters you will read about.
occur = happen	➡	The main events in *Chasing Vermeer* **occur** in a big city in the United States.
physical = relating to the body or to other things you can see, touch, smell, feel, or taste	➡	Being an artist takes a lot of **physical** effort. The painter is tired from standing and painting all day.
theory = an explanation that may or may not be true	➡	Everyone has a different **theory** about what makes something art. In my opinion, movies are a form of art.

Practice Workbook Page 2

Work with a partner to answer these questions. Try to include the red word in your answer. Write the answers in your notebook.

1. How do you **identify** the artist of an unsigned painting?
2. Where might an **individual** go to study a work of art?
3. Where might a mystery about a stolen painting **occur**?
4. Why do artists have to be in good **physical** shape?
5. What do detectives do to prove a **theory** about a crime?

▲ Petra Andalee is an individual who likes art.

6

🌐 TESOL Standards

Goal 1, Standard 3—To use English to communicate in social settings: Students will use learning strategies to extend their communicative competence.
Descriptors—Self-monitoring and self-evaluating language development; Learning and using language "chunks"; Practicing new language.

Goal 2, Standard 3—To use English to achieve academically in all content areas: Students will use appropriate learning strategies to construct and apply academic knowledge.
Descriptors—Focusing attention selectively; Applying basic reading comprehension skills such as skimming, scanning, previewing, and reviewing text; Planning how and when to use cognitive strategies and applying them appropriately to a learning task.

Goal 3, Standard 3—To use English in socially and culturally appropriate ways: Students will use appropriate learning strategies to extend their sociolinguistic and sociocultural competence.
Descriptors—Analyzing the social context to determine appropriate language use.

Word Study: Prefixes *un-*, *dis-*

A prefix is a word part added to the beginning of a word that changes the word's meaning. Knowing the meanings of prefixes can help you figure out the meanings of many words you read and hear.

The prefixes *un-* and *dis-* occur often in English. *Un-* can mean "not" or "the opposite of." *Dis-* can mean "not," "outside of," or "the opposite of." Look at the examples below. Notice how the meaning of the prefix changes the meaning of each base word.

Prefix	Base Word	New Word
un- +	certain	uncertain ("not certain")
un- +	explained	unexplained ("not explained")
dis- +	approved	disapproved ("opposite of approved")
dis- +	appeared	disappeared ("opposite of appeared")

Practice Workbook Page 3

Work with a partner. Use what you have learned about prefixes to figure out the meanings of the words below. Then check the meanings in a dictionary. Write the words and definitions in your notebook. Then use each word in a sentence.

| disagree | disoriented | unfair | unkind | unknown |

READING STRATEGY | **PREDICT**

Predicting helps you become a better reader. Before you read, predict (or guess) what the story will be about. To predict, follow these steps:

- Stop after each paragraph. Ask yourself, "What will happen next?"
- Look for clues in the story and illustrations.
- Use the clues from the story and what you already know to predict what will happen.

After you read the first two pages of the excerpt from *Chasing Vermeer*, predict what will happen next. See if you are right.

 Workbook Page 4

7

Linguistic Note

Usage of *un-*, *dis-*, and *in-*

English learners may have difficulty knowing when to use *un-* and when to use *dis-*, because of the prefix, *in-*. There are no hard and fast rules that dictate usage, but there are a few rules of thumb: *un-* is used before a word of Germanic origin, *in-* is used before a word of Latin origin. Example: *Unbelievable* versus *incredible,* or *uneaten* versus *inedible.* Point out that *dis-* has a slightly different meaning from *un-/in-.* While *un-* and *in-* simply mean *not, dis-* implies change. For example, an *uncolored* shirt has no color, whereas a *discolored* shirt used to have a certain color, but lost/changed that color. Other examples are *unclaimed/ disclaimed* and *unproven/disproven.*

STEP 1: Teach

Word Study

Prefixes Read aloud the opening paragraphs in the student book, and ask students what the prefixes *un-* and *dis-* mean (*not, the opposite of, outside of*). Review that prefixes create new words when added to a base word. Go over the examples on the chart, and model several more, such as *acceptable/unacceptable, appear/disappear, repair/disrepair,* and *known/unknown.*

STEP 2: Practice

To figure out the meaning of a word in the box, ask students to cover the word's prefix with a finger and read the base word. If they're unsure of its meaning, they can look it up in a dictionary. Students then think of the opposite of the base word. **SAY:** *The word* agree *means to have the same opinion. The opposite will be to have a different opinion.*

ANSWERS

disagree: not agree; to have a different opinion
disoriented: not oriented; confused.
unfair: not fair; not just.
unkind: not kind; not friendly.
unknown: not known; not aware of.

STEP 3: Teach

Reading Strategy

Predict Read aloud and discuss the bulleted steps for predicting. Model how predicting is used in the story of "Cinderella." **SAY:** *Which clues in the story give you hints about what will happen? (Although Cinderella has no ball gown, a fairy godmother appears to provide her with clothes to attend the ball.) From what you already know about people like the stepmother and the stepsisters, how will they treat her? (They'll be mean to her and make her do all the work.) Predict what will happen in the story. (Cinderella will get to the ball, and Prince Charming will fall in love with her.) To see if your prediction is correct, what do you have to do? (Read on.)*

For extra practice or homework, assign the corresponding workbook page.

Read

STEP 1: Introduce

Reading Summary

Students at a famous private school have been told to bring in something from home that is like a work of art. Petra brings in an old book she has found, creating a mystery about where the book came from and why it had been thrown away.

 The Big Question

Point out that some mysteries have been around for a long time. For example, the life of the artist Vermeer is riddled with mysteries. One of his paintings was stolen and has never been found. Others have been copied and sold as his work. Have students search the Internet for other mysteries that surround Vermeer's life and art.

STEP 2: Teach

Set a Purpose for Reading

Tell students that when they read from *Chasing Vermeer*, they should think about Petra. Explain that her character traits may help her solve an art mystery. **SAY:** *Certain character traits are helpful in solving mysteries. What do you think they are?*

Preteaching Highlighted Words

With students, preview the highlighted words on pages 8–9. Write the words on the board, and point out that they are defined in the gloss at the bottom of each page. **SAY:** *Some of the vocabulary words in this reading are idioms, such as "all ears."*

Ask volunteers to read the definitions. Model how to use the words in original sentences. For example, *I was all ears when my favorite actress began to speak.* Then ask volunteers to create a word book in which they define each word and copy the sentence from the text in which it occurs.

CD1 T5 **Scaffolding:**
Listen and Read

Have students read along as you play the CD recording of the reading. Pause the recording at the end of each page to answer questions.

Teaching Resources

- *Resources*, Summaries, pp. 123–124
- Audio CD 1, track 5

READING 1 — **LITERATURE** / **NOVEL**

Set a purpose for reading What kind of individual is Petra? How would you describe her? What puzzling object does she find? Read to find out why this object is so appealing to her.

from
CHASING VERMEER

Blue Balliett

Ms. Hussey isn't your typical teacher. She asks her students to do unusual projects and investigate mysterious ideas and events. Petra Andalee and Calder Pillay like being in her sixth-grade class. They are about to receive a new assignment from Ms. Hussey that will lead to a mysterious discovery.

By the sixth week of sixth grade, Ms. Hussey still wasn't a disappointment. She had announced on the first day of school that she had no idea what they were going to work on that year, or how. "It all depends on what we get interested in—or what gets interested in us," she had added, as if this was obvious. Calder Pillay was all ears. He had never heard a teacher admit that she didn't know what she was doing. Even better, she was excited about it.

Ms. Hussey's classroom was in the middle school building at the University School, in the neighborhood known as Hyde Park. The school sat on the edge of the University of Chicago campus. John Dewey, an unusual professor, had started it a century earlier as an experiment. Dewey believed in doing, in working on relevant projects in order to learn how to think. Calder had always liked the man's appropriate name. Not all teachers at the U., as it was called, still agreed with Dewey's ideas, but Ms. Hussey obviously did.

They began the year by arguing about whether writing was the most accurate way to communicate. Petra Andalee, who loved to write, said it was. Kids like Calder, who hated it, said it wasn't. What about numbers? What about pictures? What about plain old talking?

Ms. Hussey had told them to investigate. They took piles of books out of the library. They found out about cave art in France, about papyrus scrolls in Egypt, about Mayan petroglyphs in Mexico, and about stone tablets from

---

all ears, very interested in listening to someone
papyrus scrolls, rolls of paper that are made from a plant
petroglyphs, pictures or sets of marks cut into rock
tablets, flat pieces of hard clay or stone that have words cut into them

8

 TESOL Standards

Goal 1, Standard 3—To use English to communicate in social settings: Students will use learning strategies to extend their communicative competence.
Descriptors—Using the primary language to ask for clarification; Using context to construct meaning.

Goal 2, Standard 1—To use English to achieve academically in all content areas: Students will use English to interact in the classroom.
Descriptors—Asking and answering questions.

Goal 2, Standard 2—To use English to achieve academically in all content areas: Students will use English to obtain, process, construct, and provide subject matter information in spoken and written form.
Descriptors—Analyzing, synthesizing, and inferring from information; Hypothesizing and predicting; Formulating and asking questions.

the Middle East. They tried things. They made stamps out of raw potatoes and covered the walls with symbols. They invented a sign language for hands and feet. They communicated for one whole day using nothing but drawings. Now it was almost mid-October. Would they ever study regular subjects, like the other classes did? Calder didn't care. What they were doing was real exploration, real thinking—not just finding out about what a bunch of dead, famous grown-ups believed. Ms. Hussey was cool. . . .

Petra, like Calder, was fascinated by their new teacher. She loved Ms. Hussey's questions and her long ponytail and the three rings in each ear. One earring had a small pearl dangling from a moon, another a high-heeled shoe the size of a grain of rice, another a tiny key. Petra loved how Ms. Hussey listened carefully to the kids' ideas and didn't care about right and wrong answers. She was honest and unpredictable. She was close to perfect. . . .

One day Ms. Hussey brought up the nature of art.

"You know," Ms. Hussey said finally, "Picasso said that art is a lie, but a lie that tells the truth." She was pacing now. "Lies and art . . . it's an ancient problem. So if we work with art," she said slowly, "we'll have to figure out something else first: What makes an object a piece of art?"

Denise rolled her eyes but stayed quiet.

---

brought up, mentioned a subject or started to talk about it

✔ **LITERARY CHECK**

Which of Ms. Hussey's **character traits** *does Petra admire?*

BEFORE YOU GO ON

1 Who is John Dewey and how does Ms. Hussey feel about him?

2 What does Ms. Hussey's class argue about first?

💡 **On Your Own**
What do you think is the most accurate way to communicate? Why?

9

✔ **LITERARY CHECK**

Point out the Literary Check box, and read the question aloud. If students need help remembering the meaning of *character traits*, have them go back to page 5. Answer: Petra admires Ms. Hussey's honesty, unpredictability, and respect for kids' ideas.

STEP 3: Monitor Progress

Ask students to check what they have understood in the reading. If you are using the Audio CD, pause the recording.

Before You Go On

Point out the Before You Go On box, and have students read and answer the questions. Remind them to go back to the text if they don't know the answers to the first two questions. Explain that the On Your Own question asks for your opinion. Any thoughtful answer is correct.

ANSWERS
1. John Dewey, a professor at the University of Chicago, started the University School a century ago. Ms. Hussey admires him. She agrees with his way of teaching.
2. At first, the class argues about whether writing is the best form of communication.

On Your Own Have students write an answer to the On Your Own question on a separate sheet of paper. Encourage volunteers to share their responses with the class. Then collect student responses to monitor their comprehension, writing skills, and fluency.

Differentiated Instruction

Beginning	Have students draw a picture of one of the strange events from Petra's book, *Lo!*
Early Intermediate	Have students name some of the strange events mentioned in Petra's book, *Lo!*
Intermediate	Have students write a short paragraph describing one of the strange events mentioned in Petra's book, *Lo!*.
Standard English Learners (CRI)	Point to the glossed expressions, *get a grip* and *bent over backward* on page 12. Ask them to think of other ways of expressing these phrases.

Preteaching Highlighted Words

Before reading this spread, review the highlighted words and terms to students. Define each one, pointing out the location of the definition in the gloss at the bottom of the student book page. Make sure that students understand each word. If appropriate, ask students to generate original sentences using the words. When correcting original sentences, focus on usage instead of mechanics.

✔ LITERARY CHECK

Point out the Literary Check box, and read the sentences aloud. Ask partners to look back over the reading to find out what kind of character Petra is. Have them discuss her character traits. They can review the meaning of *character* on page 5. Answer: Petra is a curious character. She thinks deeply and has strong opinions.

Across the Curriculum: Math and Science

Calder says that he might become a cross between Einstein and Ramanujan. Point out that these men were among the greatest geniuses of the 20th century. Albert Einstein (1879–1955) was a mathematician and physicist who discovered the theory of relativity, for which he received the Nobel Prize in physics in 1921. Srinivasa Ramanujan Iyengar (1887–1920) was a mathematician who, with almost no formal training in pure mathematics, made substantial contributions in the areas of mathematical analysis, number theory, infinite series, and continued fractions.

"Here's what I want you to do: Start by choosing one item at home that feels like a work of art to you. It can be anything. Don't ask anyone for advice—this has to be your own thinking. Describe this object for us without saying what it is. And this time, I won't let you off the hook." She grinned. "We'll read some of your ideas aloud."

Calder wondered what Picasso had meant. Was it that art wasn't exactly the real world, but it said something real?

He began thinking up other combinations of art, a lie, and the truth that made sense. It worked almost like the logical arrangements of five squares that made up each piece of his set of pentominoes. How about: Art is the truth that tells a lie? Maybe all of life was about rearranging a few simple ideas. Calder, smiling at the chalkboard, now squirmed in his chair with excitement at the thought. If he could just get to those simple ideas, with a little practice, he'd be a cross between Einstein and the mathematician Ramanujan—or maybe Ben Franklin—. . .

There was nothing at home that felt like a piece of art.

Petra considered an embroidered pillow, but it had a big tear in it; she found a silk caterpillar kite, but it had lost one eye; she thought of the stick her mom used to make a bun for her hair, the one with amber on it, but it had been missing for days.

What *was* art anyway? The more she thought about it, the stranger it seemed. What made an invented object special? Why were some manmade things pleasing and others not? Why wasn't a regular mixing bowl or a spoon or a light bulb a piece of art? What made certain objects land in museums and others in the trash?

She guessed that most people who went to museums didn't ask that question. They just believed that they were looking at something valuable or beautiful or interesting. They didn't do any hard thinking about it.

She wasn't going to be that kind of person—*ever*.

She thought about pictures at the Art Institute that made her feel as if she could leave everything predictable behind. She always felt that way when she stood in front of Caillebotte's *Rainy Day* painting—the wet cobblestones underfoot, the people going places in their long skirts and top hats, the inviting turn of the street. This was art that was an adventure. It let her into another world. It made familiar stuff seem mysterious. It sent her back to her life feeling a little different, at least for a few minutes.

✔ LITERARY CHECK

What kind of character is Petra? Describe some of her traits.

set of pentominoes, math tool containing twelve pieces, each of which is made up of five squares
embroidered, having beautiful patterns that have been sewed on
amber, a yellowish-brown stone used to make jewelry
Caillebotte, a French painter whose picture *Rainy Day* hangs in the Art Institute of Chicago

10

TESOL Standards

Goal 1, Standard 2—To use English to communicate in social settings: Students will interact in, through, and with spoken and written English for personal expression and enjoyment.
Descriptors—Sharing social and cultural traditions and values.

Goal 2, Standard 3—To use English to achieve academically in all content areas: Students will use appropriate learning strategies to construct and apply academic knowledge.
Descriptors—Using context to construct meaning; Applying self-monitoring and self-corrective strategies to build and expand a knowledge base.

Goal 3, Standard 3—To use English in socially and culturally appropriate ways: Students will use appropriate learning strategies to extend their sociolinguistic and sociocultural competence.
Descriptors—Experimenting with variations of language in social and academic settings.

She was still thinking about Caillebotte's Paris street on her way to the grocery store. If he had painted Harper Avenue, would it have looked just as intriguing? As she approached the corner, she noticed a man with suspenders . . . step out the front door of Powell's, look around, and drop a book into the giveaway box outside. She sped up.

The book had a cloth cover with several dark stains, and the paper was thick and creamy, soft at the edges. The title jumped out at her: *Lo!* The illustrations were done in black and white—distorted, rubbery figures clutched each other or screamed.

She read a few paragraphs:

TERRIFIED HORSES, UP ON THEIR HIND LEGS, HOOFING A STORM OF FROGS.

FRENZIED SPRINGBOKS, CAPERING THEIR EXASPERATIONS AGAINST FROGS THAT WERE TICKLING THEM.

STOREKEEPERS, IN LONDON, GAPING AT FROGS THAT WERE TAPPING ON THEIR WINDOW PANES.

WE SHALL PICK UP AN EXISTENCE BY ITS FROGS.

WISE MEN HAVE TRIED OTHER WAYS. THEY HAVE TRIED TO UNDERSTAND OUR STATE OF BEING, BY GRASPING AT ITS STARS, OR ITS ARTS, OR ITS ECONOMICS. BUT, IF THERE IS AN UNDERLYING ONENESS OF ALL THINGS, IT DOES NOT MATTER WHERE WE BEGIN, WHETHER WITH STARS, OR LAWS OF SUPPLY AND DEMAND, OR FROGS, OR NAPOLEON BONAPARTE. ONE MEASURES A CIRCLE, BEGINNING ANYWHERE.

I HAVE COLLECTED 294 RECORDS OF SHOWERS OF LIVING THINGS.

What? Petra flipped back to the front and saw that the book had been written in 1931, by a man named Charles Fort.

She tucked it under her arm.

---

suspenders, two cloth or leather bands that go over the shoulders and are attached to pants to hold them up
springboks, small African deer that can run very fast
Napoleon Bonaparte, the emperor of France (1804–1815) whose armies took control of most of Europe until they were defeated in 1815

BEFORE YOU GO ON

1 Why doesn't Petra want to be like most people who go to museums?

2 What does Petra find in the giveaway box?

On Your Own
If you were in Ms. Hussey's class, what would you choose as a work of art?

11

Read

Preteaching Highlighted Words

Before reading this spread, point out the highlighted words and terms to students. Define each one, pointing out the definitions at the bottom of the page. Make sure that students understand each highlighted word or term. If appropriate, ask students to generate original sentences using the words.

Model the
READING STRATEGY

Predict

Have students go back to page 7 and review the steps for predicting what this story would be about. Use these questions to stimulate class discussion:

- Which clues at the beginning of the story gave you hints about what would happen at the end?

- From what you already know about people like Petra and Ms. Hussey, what kinds of things could you predict they would do?

- How did your original prediction about what would happen in the story turn out?

That night, flipping around in *Lo!*, Petra was more and more amazed. She had never seen a book like this. It was, first of all, peppered with quotes from journals and newspapers around the world—there was the *London Times*, the *Quebec Daily Mercury*, the *New Zealand Times*, the *Woodbury Daily Times*, the *New York American*, *The Gentleman's Magazine*, the *Ceylon Observer . . .* the list went on and on.

There were hundreds of stories of bizarre happenings, many of them similar. Venomous snakes dropped into backyards in Oxfordshire, England; red and brown worms fell with snowflakes in Sweden; bushels of periwinkles fell from the sky on Cromer Gardens Road, outside Worcester, England; luminous, floating lights traveled slowly over open land in North Carolina and in Norfolk, England. Wild animals turned up where they shouldn't have. People disappeared and then were found far away, disoriented and confused. There were crashes and explosions that no one could explain.

Fort had apparently spent twenty-seven years going through old newspapers in libraries. He had copied out thousands of articles about unexplained goings-on. . . .

Rereading each sentence in pieces, she began to get a grip on what Fort was saying: Depending on how you looked at things, your world could change completely. His thought was that most people bent over backward to fit everything that happened to them into something they could understand. In other words, people sometimes twisted what was actually in front of them to fit what they thought should

---

bizarre, very unusual and strange
venomous, poisonous
periwinkles, small ocean creatures that live in shells
goings-on, activities or events that are strange or interesting
get a grip on, understand
bent over backward, did as much as possible

12

 TESOL Standards

Goal 1, Standard 3—To use English to communicate in social settings: Students will use learning strategies to extend their communicative competence.
Descriptors—Testing hypotheses about language.

Goal 2, Standard 1—To use English to achieve academically in all content areas: Students will use English to interact in the classroom.
Descriptors—Explaining actions.

Goal 2, Standard 2—To use English to achieve academically in all content areas: Students will use English to obtain, process, construct, and provide subject matter information in spoken and written form.
Descriptors—Retelling information.

be there, never even realizing they were doing it. People liked to see what they were supposed to see, and find what they were supposed to find. It was quite an idea. . . .

Why wasn't more time in school spent studying things that were unknown or not understood instead of things that had already been discovered and explained? Ms. Hussey always asked for their ideas. Wouldn't it be great to go digging for weird facts like Charles Fort did? To try to piece together a meaning behind events that didn't seem to fit?

And why wasn't this book a piece of art? She grabbed her notebook and began to write:

This object is hard on the outside and bendable on the inside. It is the color of an unripe raspberry, and it weighs about as much as a pair of blue jeans. It smells like a closet in an old house, and it is an ancient shape. It holds things that are hard to believe. There are living creatures falling like rain and objects that float by themselves. People vanish and reappear.

It is made of substances that once grew, that once bent in the wind and felt the night air. It is older than trips to the moon or computers or stereo systems or television. Our grandparents might have seen it new when they were young.

There was a woman's name in faded brown ink inside the cover. Petra wondered who else had loved this book and why it had ended up outside Powell's. Why had it been thrown away?

She would never lose it. Not ever.

---

substances, materials

ABOUT THE **AUTHOR**

Blue Balliett, like Ms. Hussey, loves mysteries and unexplained happenings. She was a teacher in Hyde Park, Chicago, for ten years. Many of the ideas and characters in *Chasing Vermeer* come from her experiences as a teacher and mother. Balliett spends a lot of time in museums, too. One of the goals of *Chasing Vermeer* and its sequel, *The Wright 3,* is to encourage students to solve mysteries, love art, and think for themselves. *Chasing Vermeer* was on the children's bestseller list and won the 2004 Chicago Tribune Prize for Young Adult Fiction.

✔ **LITERARY CHECK**
What character traits do Petra and Ms. Hussey share?

BEFORE YOU GO ON

1 How does Petra feel as she reads *Lo!*?

2 Who wrote *Lo!* and where did the information in it come from?

💡 **On Your Own**
Do you think that some of the mysterious events described in *Lo!* could actually have happened? Explain.

13

✔ **LITERARY CHECK**

Explain that the traits Petra and Ms. Hussey share are not directly stated in the text. Suggest that to get the answer, they will have to think about the things both Petra and Ms. Hussey say and do and what we know about them. Remind students they can review the definition of *character traits* on page 5. Answer: Petra and Ms. Hussey are both curious, have strong opinions, and think for themselves.

Study Skills: Internet

Point out that Blue Balliett, the author of *Chasing Vermeer*, wrote another book about Petra and Calder. In *The Wright 3*, they take action to save a historic landmark, but ghostly sounds and moving shadows from within make them think there may be something strange about the special house. Have students use the Internet to find out more about this novel.

STEP 7: Monitor Progress

Ask students to check what they have understood in the reading.

Before You Go On

Remind students that these questions will help them monitor their progress. Put students in pairs to answer the questions. Encourage them to share their answers with the class.

ANSWERS
1. Petra is fascinated as she reads *Lo!*
2. Charles Fort wrote *Lo!* The information in the book came from journals and newspapers.

On Your Own Have students write an answer to the On Your Own question on a separate sheet of paper. Encourage volunteers to share their responses with the class. Then collect student responses to monitor their comprehension, writing skills, and fluency.

Review the Purpose for Reading

Elicit responses to the Set a Purpose for Reading questions at the beginning of this reading. Remind students to relate their responses to the Big Question.

STEP 1: Introduce

Speaking Tip

Point out that punctuation marks help us speak slowly and with feeling. A comma tells us when to pause in the middle of a sentence. A question mark tells us that our voice should go up toward the end of a sentence. An exclamation mark tells us to speak with extra feeling.

Reader's Theater

Performing by reading aloud is excellent practice for students. It gives them a reason to rehearse their reading several times, to increase fluency, and to improve expression and intonation.

Have students work with a partner and decide who will play the roles of Calder and Petra. Students should practice pronouncing their dialogue clearly. Suggest that they think about how their character feels at this point in the story.

Students should find a quiet corner in which to rehearse. When they are ready, ask volunteers to perform before the class.

STEP 2: Practice

Comprehension

Have students work individually or in small groups to write answers to the questions. Encourage students to answer in complete sentences.

ANSWERS

1. Ms. Hussey's classroom is at the University School.
2. She asks the class to find an object of art.
3. The three main characters are Ms. Hussey, the teacher who encourages her class to look for a work of art at home, Petra, the main character who finds the book *Lo!*, and Calder, her friend and classmate.
4. Fort's theory is that people try to fit odd events into our reality rather than accept them and understand them.
5. Curiosity will help her solve mysteries.
6. Possible response: Calder thinks he is not a good writer. He likes a different way of communicating.
7. Answers will vary.
8. Answers will vary.

Teaching Resources

• *Workbook*, p. 5
• CD-ROM/e-book, Reader's Theater, Comprehension, Response to Literature

---

READER'S THEATER

Act out the following scene between Petra and Calder.

Calder: Did you find something to bring in for Ms. Hussey's assignment?

Petra: Yes, I did, but it was hard. At first, I couldn't find anything that seemed like art.

Calder: Me, too. What did you end up choosing?

Petra: I found a cool old book published in 1931 called *Lo!*

Calder: Where did you find it?

Petra: Well, this man was leaving Powell's bookstore. I saw him look around in a mysterious way, and then he dropped the book in the giveaway box.

Calder: That's strange! What's the book about?

Petra: The author, Charles Fort, spent years going through newspapers and finding things that were hard to explain.

Calder: Like what?

Petra: Like snakes and periwinkles falling from the sky!

Calder: Wow! I want to see this book.

COMPREHENSION

Workbook Page 5

Right There

1. Where is Ms. Hussey's classroom?
2. What does Ms. Hussey ask the class to find?

Think and Search

3. Who are the three main characters? Briefly describe each one.
4. What is Fort's theory about how we look at things?

Author and You

5. Which of Petra's traits will help her solve mysteries?
6. Why do you think that Calder enjoys physical activities such as making stamps and using sign language?

14

🌐 TESOL Standards

Goal 1, Standard 1—To use English to communicate in social settings: Students will use English to participate in social interactions.
Descriptors—Sharing and requesting information; Engaging in conversations.

Goal 1, Standard 2—To use English to communicate in social settings: Students will interact in, through, and with spoken and written English for personal expression and enjoyment.
Descriptors—Participating in popular culture.

On Your Own

7. In your opinion, what character traits make the individuals in a novel seem like real people even though they are not?

8. Think about what Petra says about school. Should more time be spent studying things that are unknown or not understood instead of things that have already been discovered and explained? Why?

DISCUSSION

Discuss in pairs or small groups.

 Listening TIP

Listen carefully to other classmates' ideas. Compare them to your own.

1. Ms. Hussey tells the class: "Picasso said that art is a lie, but a lie that tells the truth." Picasso was a famous twentieth-century artist. What did he mean by this statement? How can art lie and tell the truth at the same time?

2. What objects in Petra's home does she consider when she is looking for a work of art? Choose one, and explain why Petra doesn't select it.

3. The book *Lo!* tells of strange events. What is the strangest event you have ever heard about? What made this event so strange?

Q **Can all mysteries be solved?** Ms. Hussey's students have a chance to explore many unsolved mysteries. Would you enjoy being in Ms. Hussey's class? Why or why not?

RESPONSE TO LITERATURE

Workbook Page 5

Imagine that you are in Ms. Hussey's class. Find an object in your home that you think is a work of art. In your notebook, explain why you think the object is art. Then write a paragraph-long description of the object. Use Petra's description of *Lo!* as a model. Include details the way Petra did. For example, you might write about the object's color, texture, shape, and size. Share your description with a classmate.

This vase by Picasso is in the shape of a dove. Do you think it's a work of art? Why? ▶

15

Differentiated Instruction

Beginning	Have students name the characters seen in the illustration on page 9. (Ms. Hussey, Petra, Calder)
Early Intermediate	Have students share with the class reasons why they think the vase on page 15 is a work of art or not.
Intermediate	Ask students to describe in their own words, what happened in the scene illustrated on page 11.
Greater Challenge	Have students act it out for the class. Encourage them to act rather than just read. Ask students to choose another scene from the story.

Listening Tip

Remind students that listening carefully to other classmates' ideas will help them better understand the reading.

(CRI) Discussion

Congratulate students on successfully completing the reading. **SAY:** *We've learned a lot about the Big Question from the reading. Now let's discuss a few questions.*

Model a discussion starter for each question. **SAY:** *For the first question, do you agree that a lie can tell a truth about something? Why, or why not? What book, movie, or TV show do you know of where a lie helped to tell the truth? How did it help?* **SAY:** *For the second question, think of a work of art that other people might not consider art. Explain why you think it is art.* **SAY:** *For the third question, do you think that "strange events" are really strange, or are there explanations for everything? Explain your point of view to the group.*

Q **Can all mysteries be solved? SAY:** *Now that you have read the excerpt from* Chasing Vermeer, *how does it affect the way you would answer the Big Question? Think of a teacher who reminds you of Ms. Hussey. How is this person like her?*

Response to Literature

Read aloud the instructions for creating the paragraph-long description of an object. Then model the activity with an object, such as a classroom globe. On the board, list headings to describe the globe, such as *Color, Shape, Size,* and *Texture.* Ask students for words to describe the globe, such as *round, smooth, blue,* and *green,* and write them on the board below the correct headings. Then, with students, create a paragraph describing the globe, using the listed words. Students use the same headings for their own object.

STEP 1: Introduce

Tell students that writers use several parts of speech to make interesting sentences. Explain that you will be reviewing how to distinguish the different parts of speech.

STEP 2: Teach

Grammar and Writing

Parts of Speech Read aloud and discuss the information about different parts of a sentence (subject, verb, object, and prepositional phrase). On the board, draw a four-column chart to display this information. Find additional sentences, and with students, decide which words are the subject, verb, object, and prepositional phrase. Place them in the correct column in the chart. Example: *The hikers (subject) carried (verb) their backpacks (object) on their shoulders (prepositional phrase).*

STEP 3: Practice

Write the first sentence on the board. **SAY:** *Notice the parts of speech written above different words in this sentence.* <u>The classroom</u> *is marked as the subject because that is what the sentence is about.* <u>Was</u> *is marked as a verb. It comes from the verb* to be, *and it describes a state or fact.* <u>In a tall building</u> *is marked as a prepositional phase. It shows location.*

Pair English learners with proficient English speakers, and have them work on the rest of the sentences.

ANSWERS

Subject	Verb	Object	Prepositional Phrase
The classroom	was		in a tall building.
They	invented	a sign language.	
She	tucked	the book	under her arm.
Venomous snakes	dropped		into backyards.

Teaching Resources

- *Workbook*, pp. 6–7
- CD-ROM/e-book, Grammar, Writing
- *Transparencies*, Writing Model 21
- *Transparencies, Resources*, Graphic Organizer 4
- *Assessment*, Reading 1 Test, pp. 35–38

Distinguishing Parts of Speech

Studying parts of speech will help you with your writing. A complete sentence must contain a subject and a verb. The subject can be a noun, pronoun, or noun phrase that performs, or does, the action. The verb is the action word in a sentence or a word that describes a fact or state.

Many sentences also contain an object—the noun, pronoun, or noun phrase that receives the action of a verb. Other parts of speech include *prepositions* and *adjectives*.

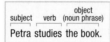

Objects often follow a preposition. Prepositions show location and time, such as *at, on,* and *in.* A preposition plus an object is called a *prepositional phrase.* An adjective describes a noun, pronoun, or noun phrase. It usually comes before the noun it modifies, or describes.

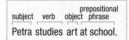
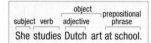

Practice **Workbook** Page 6

Copy the sentences below into your notebook. Work with a partner. Label the parts of speech in each sentence, as in the example.

subject   verb prepositional phrase
1. The classroom was in a tall building.
2. They invented a sign language.
3. She tucked the book under her arm.
4. Venomous snakes dropped into backyards.

16

🌐 TESOL Standards

Goal 2, Standard 1—To use English to achieve academically in all content areas: Students will use English to interact in the classroom.
Descriptors—Following oral and written directions, implicit and explicit; Elaborating and extending other people's ideas and words.

Goal 2, Standard 2—To use English to achieve academically in all content areas: Students will use English to obtain, process, construct, and provide subject matter information in spoken and written form.
Descriptors—Listening to, speaking, reading, and writing about subject matter information; Gathering information orally and in writing; Responding to the work of peers and others.

Goal 3, Standard 1—To use English in socially and culturally appropriate ways: Students will use the appropriate language variety, register, and genre according to audience, purpose, and setting.
Descriptors—Using a variety of writing styles appropriate for different audiences, purposes, and settings.

WRITING a DESCRIPTIVE PARAGRAPH

Describe a Character

Before you write a descriptive essay, you need to learn some of the skills writers use to describe people, places, and things. On this page, you'll learn how to describe a character. You'll use a graphic organizer like the one at the right to help you write a descriptive paragraph.

When writers describe a character, they usually include both physical traits and character traits. To describe a character's physical traits, you use words to create a picture of how the character looks. For example, you might describe the character's height, clothing, and hair color. Writers also describe a character's traits. To do this, you show how the character speaks, acts, and thinks.

Here is a model of a descriptive paragraph about Ms. Hussey. Notice the different traits the writer includes. Also, notice the way the writer *shows* you what Ms. Hussey is like, instead of just *telling* you.

Physical traits	Character traits

> Andrew C. Dubin
>
> Ms. Hussey
>
> Ms. Hussey is a sixth-grade teacher. She has a long ponytail and wears three earrings in each ear. The middle school she teaches at is located on the University of Chicago campus, in the Hyde Park neighborhood of Chicago. Ms. Hussey is a different kind of teacher. She wants her students to work on projects that make them think instead of just reading books. Ms. Hussey is fascinating to her students. She is honest and unpredictable. She once even admitted that she didn't know what she was doing, but seemed excited about that. Her students like the way she listens carefully to their ideas and doesn't care if their answers are right or wrong. To Petra and Calder, she is a perfect teacher.

Practice  Workbook Page 7

Write a paragraph describing Petra. Use words to "paint a picture" of her physical traits and her character traits. Copy the T-chart above into your notebook. List your ideas on the chart. Decide on a logical order for presenting your ideas. Be sure to use parts of speech correctly.

Writing Checklist

WORD CHOICE:
- ☑ I chose my words carefully to create a clear description of a character.

ORGANIZATION:
- ☑ I put physical details and character traits in a logical order.

CONVENTIONS:
- ☑ I put adjectives in the right place.

17

Accelerate Language Development

The Verb *be*

Dialects that students speak reflect their culture and should be treated with respect. In some students' dialect, the use of the verb *be* differs from that of Standard English. The verb *be* is used in verb phrases to indicate habitual occurrence. (*They be very intelligent.*) or is omitted as an auxiliary in verb phrases. (*This object small.*) As students prepare questions for their descriptive guessing game, monitor the use of verbs and focus students' attention on the appropriate verb form in each question.

STEP 1: Introduce

Tell students that a descriptive paragraph that describes a person can include both physical traits and character traits.

STEP 2: Teach

Writing a Descriptive Paragraph

Describe a Character Review the difference between physical traits (height, weight, hair and eye color, and so on) and character traits (how pleasant, trustworthy, honest, and so on, the person is). Then explain that students will be creating a paragraph with physical and character traits to describe Petra.

Model Writing Skill Point out the T-chart on the student page, and draw it on the board. Label the columns *Physical Traits* and *Character Traits*. Then ask a volunteer to read aloud the model descriptive paragraph about Ms. Hussey, and with students, fill in the traits described in the paragraph on the T-chart. **SAY:** *I know Ms. Hussey's physical traits—how she looks. The paragraph says she has a long ponytail and wears three earrings in each ear. I will write those words under* Physical Traits. *I know Ms. Hussey's character traits—how she acts and thinks. The paragraph says she's honest, unpredictable, excited about learning, and she listens to her students' ideas. I will write that under* Character Traits.

Now have students create a T-chart for Petra, listing her physical and character traits. Encourage students to create complete sentences from the list and write them in logical order for their paragraphs.

STEP 3: Assess

Writing Checklist Note

Word choice Check that students used words that help us see what Petra looks like and the kind of person she is.

Organization Check that students' paragraphs are presented in an orderly way, with details about Petra's appearance, then details about her character traits.

Conventions Check that students placed adjectives before nouns in their sentences.

STEP 1: Introduce

Objectives

Read the list of objectives in the What You Will Learn section, encouraging students to join in. Tell students that this reading will be about math mysteries. Have pairs of students work together to restate the list of things they will learn.

 The Big Question

Read the Big Question aloud. Ask students to list words that come to mind when they think of patterns, such as *design*, *plan*, *arrangement*, *repetition*, *series*, and *sequence*. Explain that this reading discusses the mystery of some mysterious number patterns in nature. **SAY:** *Which patterns can you see every day in nature?*

Build Background

Invite students to bring in a math text or library book that tells more about Fibonacci. Elicit that Fibonacci was also known as Leonardo of Pisa or Leonardo Pisano, meaning he was from the town of Pisa in Italy. He lived from about 1170 to 1250, and many consider him the most talented mathematician of the Middle Ages. As a young boy he traveled with his father throughout the Mediterranean world and learned about the Arabic number system. He recognized that arithmetic with Arabic numerals is simpler and more efficient than with Roman numerals. Fibonacci later published a book about this topic and thereby introduced Arabic numerals to Europe.

STEP 2: Teach

Understanding the Genre:
Science/Math Article

A science and math article is a non-fiction text. Its purpose is to present science and math facts and other information about real people, events, places, and situations. This article looks at some categories of fascinating facts.

Teaching Resources

- CD-ROM/e-book, Key Words
- Audio CD 1, tracks 6–7
- *Workbook*, p. 8

What You Will Learn

Reading
- Vocabulary building: *Context, dictionary skills, word study*
- Reading strategy: *Use visuals 1*
- Text type: *Informational text (math/science)*

Grammar, Usage, and Mechanics
Making comparisons: *-er than* and *as . . . as*

Writing
Describe an object

THE BIG QUESTION

Can all mysteries be solved? Have you ever seen any interesting and unusual patterns in nature? Look at the photograph below of the head of a sunflower. Study it closely. What shapes and patterns do you see? Describe them in your notebook. Now look at the following series of numbers. Can you guess the next number in the series? Can you figure out what the numbers have to do with the sunflower? Don't worry if you can't. This number puzzle will be solved when you read the next selection.

| 1, 1, 2, 3, 5, 8, 13 |

The spirals at the center of this sunflower are an example of a mysterious pattern. ▶

BUILD BACKGROUND

People who study numbers are called mathematicians. Many great mathematicians have studied objects in nature in order to develop mathematical ideas. *G Is for Googol* is an informational text about an Italian mathematician named Fibonacci. He discovered a mysterious number pattern through his study of nature. This pattern is called the Fibonacci sequence. It appears in many living things, such as flowers, plants, and snail shells. In fact, the sunflower you just wrote about contains the Fibonacci sequence.

▲ Fibonacci discovered an intriguing pattern in nature.

18

⊕ TESOL Standards

Goal 2, Standard 2—To use English to achieve academically in all content areas: Students will use English to obtain, process, construct, and provide subject matter information in spoken and written form.
Descriptors—Demonstrating knowledge through application in a variety of contexts.

Goal 3, Standard 1—To use English in socially and culturally appropriate ways: Students will use the appropriate language variety, register, and genre according to audience, purpose, and setting.
Descriptors—Using a variety of writing styles appropriate for different audiences, purposes, and settings.

Goal 3, Standard 3—To use English in socially and culturally appropriate ways: Students will use appropriate learning strategies to extend their sociolinguistic and sociocultural competence.
Descriptors—Observing and modeling how others speak and behave in a particular situation or setting; Rehearsing variations of language use in different social and academic settings.

VOCABULARY

Learn Key Words

Read these sentences. Use the context to figure out the meaning of the red words. Use a dictionary to check your answers. Then write each word and its meaning in your notebook.

1. The architecture of our city is very varied. All the buildings have different styles and designs.

2. I didn't notice the gradual growth of the oak tree outside. It occurred very slowly.

3. The pattern of numbers continued to infinity. It never ended.

4. Sometimes we use Roman numerals to write numbers: IV (4), X (10), III (3).

5. You can see spirals in the head of a sunflower. Some of these curves go clockwise, and some go counterclockwise.

6. The steps are very steep. Each one is over a foot high.

Practice Workbook Page 8

Write the sentences in your notebook. Choose a key word to complete each sentence. Then take turns reading the sentences aloud with a partner.

1. In class, we use Roman _____ when we make an outline.
   a. spirals   b. numerals

2. Many patterns end, while others go on and on to _____.
   a. infinity   b. architecture

3. Seashells form _____, not straight lines.
   a. spirals   b. numerals

4. A _____ increase occurs bit by bit, and not all at once.
   a. gradual   b. steep

5. Because the trail was so _____, it was hard to climb.
   a. gradual   b. steep

6. People who study _____ learn all about buildings.
   a. infinity   b. architecture

▲ Many clocks and watches still use Roman numerals.

19

CD1 T6–T7

 Vocabulary

Learn Key Words Play the CD. Have students listen and repeat. If you are not using the CD, read aloud the Key Words at the top of the page. **SAY:** *These words are called* Key Words *because they are important in the text we are reading.* On the board, write the Key Words below and their definitions.

- **architecture:** the style and design of buildings
- **gradual:** happening or changing slowly over a long time
- **infinity:** space or distance that has no limits or end
- **numerals:** written signs that represent numbers
- **spirals:** shapes that go around and around as they go up
- **steep:** rising or falling sharply

Have students copy the definitions into their Word Books or notebooks and generate original sentences for them. For extra practice, assign Workbook page 8.

STEP 3: Practice

Have students work with partners to complete the activity. Model the first one. **SAY:** *The first sentence says, "In class, we use Roman _____ when we make an outline." I know that outlines use Roman numerals, and I've never heard of Roman spirals, so I am going to select answer **b**.*

Have students take turns reading the sentences aloud with a partner. As they work, remind them to think about the Key Word that makes the most sense in that sentence. Once they decide, they write the completed sentence in their notebooks.

ANSWERS

1. b; 2. a; 3. a;
4. a; 5. b; 6. b

Differentiated Instruction

Beginning	Ask students to list some words that describe the photo on the top of page 18.
Early Intermediate	Have students look at the photo on page 19. Ask them if they prefer Roman numerals or Arabic numerals and why.
Intermediate	Have students write alternative example sentences for two of the Academic Words on page 20.
Struggling Readers	Ask students to choose one of the key words and write a paragraph using it.

STEP 1: Teach

CD1 T8–T9

Vocabulary

Learn Academic Words Play the CD. Have students listen and repeat. If you are not using the CD, read the Academic Words aloud. Then model how to use the chart. **SAY:** *Notice that the chart on this page contains two parts: academic words and their definitions are on the left and sentences containing the words on the right. What other sentence can we create with the word* constant? *(Possible response: There is a constant stream of cars on the freeway.)*

Partners work together to add another sentence for each Academic Word. They write each word, its definition, and the sentence in their personal Word Book.

STEP 2: Practice

To model the exercise, write the following question on the board, as shown: *Each person has _____ physical traits and character traits.* **SAY:** *This is a fill-in-the-blank question. I need to look at the list of words at the top of the page to see which one best fits in the blank. At first I thought the answer was both, but that word isn't on the list. The word* unique *fits with the traits of a person and with this sentence. I think this is the correct answer.* Have students complete the activity with a partner.

ANSWERS

1. unique
2. constant
3. sequence
4. illustrate

Teaching Resources

- Audio CD 1, tracks 8–9
- *Workbook*, pp. 9–11
- CD-ROM/e-book, Academic Words, Word Study

Learn Academic Words

Study the **red** words and their meanings. You will find these words useful when talking and writing about informational texts. Write each word and its meaning in your notebook. After you read the excerpt from *G Is for Googol,* try to use these words to respond to the text.

Academic Words
constant
illustrate
sequence
unique

constant = happening regularly or all the time	Light travels at a **constant** speed of 299,792,458 meters (186,282 mi.) per second.
illustrate = explain or make something clear by giving examples	Photographs of plants help to **illustrate** patterns in nature.
sequence = a series of related events, actions, or numbers that have a particular order	Fibonacci discovered a **sequence** of numbers with a regular pattern: 1, 1, 2, 3, 5, 8, and so on.
unique = the only one of its type	Each tiger has a **unique** pattern of stripes on its coat. No two tigers have exactly the same markings.

◀ Each tiger's coat is unique.

Practice Workbook Page 9

Write the sentences in your notebook. Choose a **red** word from the box above to complete each sentence. Then take turns reading the sentences aloud with a partner.

1. Each person has _____ physical traits and character traits.
2. The _____ crying of the baby kept the family awake all night.
3. Each morning I go through the same _____ of steps.
4. The student drew a picture to _____ the shape of a snail.

20

Word Study: Spelling Words with *ai*, *ay*, *ee*, and *oa*

Learning to identify sound-spelling patterns will help you read and spell words correctly. Vowel digraphs, or vowel teams, are two letters that work as a team to stand for one vowel sound. For example, in the word *pail*, the digraph *ai* stands for one sound: the /ā/ sound. In English, the digraphs *ai*, *ay*, *ee*, or *oa* often stand for a long vowel sound. The first letter in these digraphs usually tells you what the long vowel sound will be. Look at the chart below. Take turns reading the words aloud with a partner. Notice the digraphs in each word and the vowel sounds they stand for.

/ā/ spelled *ai*	/ā/ spelled *ay*	/ē/ spelled *ee*	/ō/ spelled *oa*
painter	say	seed	oak
snail	tray	knee	float
aim	spray	feel	soap

Practice Workbook Page 10

Work with a partner. Copy the chart above into your notebook. Say a word from the chart, and ask your partner to spell it aloud. Then have your partner say the next word. Continue until you can spell all of the words correctly. Now work with your partner to spell these words: *toad, always, steeply, pairs, coast, maintains, okay, needles*. Add them to the chart under the correct headings.

READING STRATEGY   USE VISUALS 1

Using visuals helps you understand the text better. Visuals include art, photographs, diagrams (labeled pictures), and charts. Many informational texts include visuals. To use visuals, follow these steps:

- Look at the visual. Ask yourself, "What does the visual show? How does it help me understand the reading?"
- Read any titles, headings, labels, or captions carefully.

As you read *G Is for Googol*, pay close attention to the visuals. Think about how they help you understand the text.

Workbook Page 11

21

Workbook Page 10

STEP 1: Teach

Word Study

Spelling Words with *ai*, *ay*, *ee*, and *oa*
Read aloud the information about digraphs, and review its meaning. (two vowels that stand for one vowel sound) Explain that two vowel teams that stand for /ā/ are *ai* and *ay*. Two vowels that stand for /ē/ are *ee*, and two vowels that stand for /ō/ are *oa*. Point out the words on the student page, and ask for other examples. For example, the word for a bucket (*pail*), the month after April (*May*), a round, turning object (*wheel*), and the sound a frog makes (*croak*).

STEP 2: Practice

Write the chart and headings on the board. Help students sound out the practice words, and write them on the chart.

ANSWERS

/ā/ spelled *ai*	/ā/ spelled *ay*	/ē/ spelled *ee*	/ō/ spelled *oa*
pairs maintains	always okay	steeply needles	toad coast

STEP 3: Teach

Reading Strategy

Use Visuals With students, read the bulleted items for using visuals. Then have the class preview "G Is for Googol" for its visuals. Encourage students to read all labels and captions as well. Discuss what each visual shows. **SAY:** *What can we learn from the chart on page 23?* (It tells the number of rabbit pairs we'll have after 1–11 months.) *What does the diagram and caption on page 24 tell us about pinecones?* (You get a Fibonacci number by counting the spirals on the bottom of them.)

Linguistic Note

The *th* Sound

The word *theory* begins with one of the most difficult sounds in the English language: *th*. English distinguishes between the voiced (*the*) and the voiceless (*theory*) *th*. Demonstrate the difference. Then explain the voiceless *th*: Put your tongue between your teeth so that the tip of your tongue is touching the tips of your top teeth. Blow air through your teeth without using your voice. English learners may confuse the voiceless *th* and *s*. Demonstrate the difference: *thin/sin, thick/sick, think/sink*. Mention that the voiceless *th* can appear at the beginning (*theory*), in the middle (*pathway*) and at the end of a word (*faith*). Examples: *through thick and thin, thesis, further, parentheses, mathematics, health, wealth, tooth*. To pronounce the voiced *th*, position your tongue as described before, then add your voice to the mix when blowing air through your teeth. Demonstrate the difference: *thick* versus *the*. Examples are: this, that, there, the, feather, and weather.

Read

STEP 1: Introduce

Reading Summary

These two sections from a math/science alphabet book introduce students to Fibonacci's sequences as they appear in rabbit populations, pinecones, and other natural phenomena.

 The Big Question

Explain that nature is full of interesting mysteries that are studied by scientists. Discuss whether students think a person as knowledgeable as a scientist can solve all the mysteries of nature? Why or why not? Point out that an unsolved mystery of nature was discovered and documented by a mathematician known as Fibonacci. Have students read and learn more about the Fibonacci sequence.

STEP 2: Teach

Set a Purpose for Reading

SAY: *Many clues to mysteries can be better understood if you see them in a photo, a chart, or a diagram. As you read "G Is for Googol," try to figure out the Fibonacci sequence, using the visuals.*

Previewing Highlighted Words

With students, preview the highlighted words on student book pages 22–23. Write the words on the board, and point out that they are defined in the gloss at the bottom of each page. Ask volunteers to find and read the definitions. Model how to use the words in original sentences. For example, "She used a calculator to figure out the sum of many large numbers." Then ask for volunteers to do the same.

CD1 T10 ### Scaffolding: Listen and Read

Have students read along as you play the CD recording of the reading. Pause the recording at the end of each page to answer students' questions.

Teaching Resources

- *Resources, Summaries,* pp. 125–126
- *Audio CD 1, track 10*
- *Reader's Companion Workbook,* pp. 1–7

Set a purpose for reading What mysterious number pattern occurs in pinecones, flowers, and seashells? Read to find out who Fibonacci was and what he discovered about nature.

from

G Is for Googol

David M. Schwartz

Did you know that a googol is a 1 followed by 100 zeros? G Is for Googol is a math alphabet book that explains many unusual mathematical words and facts. Read two sections from this amazing book. Both are about a mysterious number sequence.

F Is for Fibonacci

In the 1200s, an Italian mathematician named Leonardo of Pisa wrote a book about numbers. He signed his name *Fibonacci* (pronounced fib-o-NOTCH-ee).

In his book, Fibonacci said that the people of Europe should stop using Roman numerals. He wanted everyone to switch to the numerals used in the Arabic world. Instead of writing LXXVIII, they could write 78. Isn't 78 easier to write than LXXVIII? Well, Fibonacci thought so, and because of him, we use Arabic numerals today.

Fibonacci's book also included story problems. One was about rabbits: How many pairs of rabbits will there be each month if you start with one pair of newborn rabbits, and that pair produces a pair of babies every month? The rabbits start **producing** babies when they are two months old, and their babies also have their first babies when they become two months old.

---

producing, having

22

1 2 3 5 8 13 21 34 55 89

 ## TESOL Standards

Goal 1, Standard 2—To use English to communicate in social settings: Students will interact in, through, and with spoken and written English for personal expression and enjoyment.
Descriptors—Expressing personal needs, feelings, and ideas.

Goal 2, Standard 3—To use English to achieve academically in all content areas: Students will use appropriate learning strategies to construct and apply academic knowledge.
Descriptors—Taking notes to record important information and aid one's own learning; Actively connecting new information to information previously learned.

Here's one way to look at it:

After How Long?	How Many Rabbits?
Starting point	1 pair
After 1 month	1 pair
After 2 months	2 pairs
After 3 months	3 pairs
After 4 months	5 pairs
After 5 months	8 pairs
After 6 months	13 pairs
After 7 months	21 pairs
After 8 months	34 pairs
After 9 months	55 pairs
After 10 months	89 pairs
After 11 months	144 pairs

Let's look at the answers another way:

| 1 | 1 | 2 | 3 | 5 | 8 | 13 | 21 | 34 | 55 | 89 | 144 |

These are the first 12 numbers in the famous *Fibonacci sequence* of numbers.

See if you can figure out what's so special about the Fibonacci sequence. After the first two numbers, how can the others be made? Think about it before you read on.

Whenever you add one number to the next, you get the following number in the sequence. Try it. Add 2 and 3. What do you get? Now add 5 and 8. Got it? Okay, now what number comes after 144 in the Fibonacci sequence?

Fibonacci numbers are interesting, but what's *amazing* about them is how often they appear. You can find Fibonacci numbers in art, architecture, music, poetry, and nature. Read **N is for Nature**. Get ready to be amazed.

---

figure out, think about a problem or situation until you find the answer or understand what has happened

▼ Within eleven months one pair of rabbits and their offspring will produce 144 pairs of rabbits.

BEFORE YOU GO ON

1 Where and when did Fibonacci live?

2 What number comes after 144 in the Fibonacci sequence?

On Your Own
Where do you think Fibonacci numbers will show up in nature? Use the visuals on pages 24–25 to make predictions about the text.

23

Study Skills: Index

To find out more about a googol, have students look in the index of their math books. The index, at the back of the book, lists all topics in the book, in alphabetical order. Students might find some of the following: A googol is 10^{100}, that is, the digit 1 followed by one hundred zeros. The term was coined in 1920 by the nine-year-old nephew of American mathematician Edward Kasner. Googol is of no particular significance in mathematics, but it is useful when comparing other incredibly large quantities such as the number of subatomic particles in the visible universe.

STEP 3: Monitor Progress

Ask students to check what they have understood in the reading. If you are using the Audio CD, pause the recording.

Before You Go On

Remind students that the Reading Strategy they are practicing is using visuals. Point out that using visuals can be especially helpful when trying to understand new math concepts or large numbers. **SAY:** *What impression do you get when you look at the picture of the rabbits on this page?*

ANSWERS

1. Fibonacci lived in the 1200s in Italy.
2. 233

On Your Own Have students write an answer to the On Your Own question on a separate sheet of paper. Encourage volunteers to share their responses with the class. Then collect student responses to monitor their comprehension, writing skills, and fluency.

Differentiated Instruction

Beginning	Ask students what the tenth number in the Fibonacci sequence is. (55)
Early Intermediate	Ask students what number is represented by the word "googol." (1 followed by 100 zeros)
Intermediate	Ask students what kind of numerals were used in Europe in the 1200s. What kind did Fibonacci want to switch to? Why?
Special Needs	Select five words from the reading that you feel students may have difficulty spelling. Explain spelling rules as necessary and have students copy the words into their notebooks.

STEP 4: Teach

Preteaching Highlighted Words

Before reading this spread, point out the highlighted words and terms to students. Define each one, pointing out the location of the definition in the gloss at the bottom of the student book page. Make sure that students understand each highlighted word. If appropriate, ask students to generate original sentences using the highlighted words. When correcting original sentences, focus on usage of the highlighted word. Do not explicitly correct other errors. Model correct usage and grammar by repeating the student's current version of the sentence.

Model the
READING STRATEGY

Use Visuals 1

Review the bulleted list for using visuals on page 21. Then ask students to study the diagram of the pinecones on page 24.

SAY: *This diagram has numbers on it. What do the numbers show you?* (The numbers show the clockwise and counter clockwise spirals on the bottom of a pinecone.) *Does this diagram show how the spirals on the bottom of a pinecone work, or does it illustrate the parts of the pinecone?* (It shows how the spirals work.)

N Is for Nature

There are numbers in *nature*. Lots. Do you remember the Fibonacci sequence of numbers? Here are the first twelve numbers of the Fibonacci sequence:

1	1	2	3	5	8	13	21	34	55	89	144

Fibonacci discovered this number sequence, but he did not invent it. Nature invented it. If each page of this book stated one way that Fibonacci numbers appear in nature, we'd need a book so heavy you couldn't lift it. Here are just a few.

The number of petals in a flower is usually a Fibonacci number. Some flowers, like daisies, don't have true petals, but petal-like parts called *florets*. Florets come in Fibonacci numbers, too.

---

petals, the brightly colored parts of a flower

Pine needles come in groups, or *bundles*. The bundles almost always have 1, 2, 3, or 5 needles. Do these numbers look familiar?

But pine needles aren't nearly as interesting as pinecones. Find a pinecone. The hard little knobby parts are called *bracts*. (Make sure your pinecone is in good condition, with no missing bracts.) Turn the cone so you're looking at its base. Can you see how the bracts make spirals? There are clockwise spirals, and there are counterclockwise spirals. Follow one spiral as it winds all the way around the cone to the pointy end. Dab a little paint on each bract in that spiral. Now dab a different color on a spiral going in the other direction. You'll see that one spiral winds gradually, and the other one winds more steeply. How many of each type are there? Count them. Remember, it's not the number of bracts that you're counting; it's the number of spirals.

The petal-like parts of a daisy come in Fibonacci numbers. ▶

If you count the clockwise or counterclockwise spirals on the bottom of a pinecone, you will get a Fibonacci number. ▼

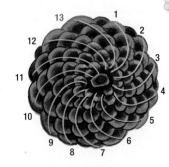

24

🌐 TESOL Standards

Goal 1, Standard 1—To use English to communicate in social settings: Students will use English to participate in social interactions.
Descriptors—Expressing needs, feelings, and ideas.

Goal 1, Standard 3—To use English to communicate in social settings: Students will use learning strategies to extend their communicative competence.
Descriptors—Using the primary language to ask for clarification; Using context to construct meaning.

Goal 2, Standard 1—To use English to achieve academically in all content areas: Students will use English to interact in the classroom.
Descriptors—Requesting information and assistance.

Some pinecones have 3 gradual spirals and 5 steep spirals. Some have 5 gradual and 8 steep. Or 8 and 13. Or 13 and 21. A pinecone's spirals come in Fibonacci numbers. In fact, Fibonacci numbers are sometimes called "pinecone numbers."

Fibonacci numbers could also be called "sunflower numbers," "artichoke numbers," or "pineapple numbers" because you will find the numbers in spirals formed by a sunflower's seeds, an artichoke's leaves, and a pineapple's scales (the diamond-shaped markings on the outside).

Fibonacci strikes again!

No one really understands why Fibonacci numbers show up so much in nature. It's a mystery!

Here's another way that Fibonacci numbers are found in nature: They make a spiral that maintains a constant proportion all the way to infinity. To find that spiral, take a rectangle that has "Fibonacci" proportions, say 3" x 5", then repeat that same proportioned rectangle, smaller and smaller . . .

---

maintains, continues in the same way
proportion, the amount of something compared to something else

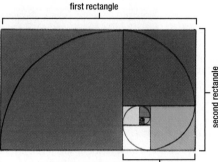

first rectangle

second rectangle

third rectangle, and so on

▲ These seashells have spirals that follow the Fibonacci sequence.

ABOUT THE **AUTHOR**

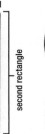

David M. Schwartz enjoys all things mathematical. In addition to *G Is for Googol*, he has written other award-winning books, including *How Much Is a Million?* and *If You Made a Million.* Each year, Schwartz visits more than fifty schools and conferences to spread his enthusiasm about numbers. He is also fascinated by the stars in the night sky, birds in the rain forest, and other natural wonders.

BEFORE YOU GO ON

1 Which part of a pinecone comes in Fibonacci numbers?

2 Where do Fibonacci numbers show up in a sunflower, an artichoke, and a pineapple?

💡 On Your Own
Do you think that scientists will ever be able to explain why Fibonacci numbers show up throughout nature? Explain.

25

Study Skills: Internet

Point out that David M. Schwartz, the author of "G Is for Googol," has done many exciting things in his life in addition to writing whimsical math and science books. Students can use the Internet to find out more about his childhood, his other books, his presentations, his traveling adventures, and how to get in touch with him.

STEP 5: Monitor Progress

Ask students to check what they have understood in the reading.

Before You Go On

Tell students that when they answer each question, they should look for the place on the page that substantiates that information.

ANSWERS

1. the bracts
2. Fibonacci's numbers show up in the spirals formed by a sunflower's seeds, an artichoke's leaves, and a pineapple's scales.

On Your Own Have students write an answer to the On Your Own question on a separate sheet of paper. Encourage volunteers to share their responses with the class. Then collect student responses to monitor their comprehension, writing skills, and fluency.

Review the Purpose for Reading

Elicit responses to the Set a Purpose for Reading questions at the beginning of this reading. Remind students to relate their responses to the Big Question.

STEP 1: Practice

Comprehension

Ask students to complete the questions either independently or in groups. They can respond orally or in writing. Model the first question with the class so they can see how to answer in a complete sentence.

ANSWERS

1. Fibonacci wanted people to use Arabic numerals.
2. The first twelve numbers in the Fibonacci sequence are 1, 1, 2, 3, 5, 8, 13, 21, 34, 55, 89, and 144.
3. The Fibonacci sequence is special because it appears in many places in nature.
4. The spirals at the bottom of a pinecone give the Fibonacci sequence whether you count them clockwise or counter clockwise.
5. Fibonacci didn't invent the sequence. Nature did. Fibonacci discovered the sequence.
6. The author used a pinecone to show the Fibonacci sequence. This made it easier to understand than a long paragraph with many numbers.
7. Answers will vary.
8. Answers will vary.

Speaking Tip

Brainstorm words and phrases that use the five senses to help make Fibonacci's sequence clearer to classmates, such as *yellow petals on a flower, a book so heavy you couldn't lift it, hard little knobby parts of pinecones.*

In Your Own Words

Read aloud the instructions for this activity, and help partners find five important facts to share with each other. Remind students of the 5Ws: *Who, What, Where, When,* and *Why.* Discuss the possibility of bringing in actual pine cones, pineapples, or sunflowers.

Teaching Resources

• *Workbook,* p. 12
• CD-ROM/e-book, Comprehension, Extension
• *Reader's Companion Workbook,* pp. 8–12

COMPREHENSION

Workbook Page 12

Right There

1. Which type of numerals did Fibonacci want people to use?
2. What are the first twelve numbers in the Fibonacci sequence?

Think and Search

3. What is so special about the Fibonacci sequence?
4. How do the numbers of spirals on the bottom of a pinecone illustrate the Fibonacci sequence?

Author and You

5. Why does the author say that Fibonacci did not invent the Fibonacci sequence?
6. How did the author use visuals to explain the Fibonacci sequence? Did this help you understand the author's ideas? Why?

On Your Own

7. Think about nature. Have you ever noticed an interesting pattern on an animal or in a plant, flower, or body of water? Describe the pattern and why it attracted your attention.
8. Think about what you have learned in your math classes. What is something you find interesting about numbers or number patterns? Why?

▲ This sequence of nine photographs shows different kinds of water patterns.

IN YOUR OWN WORDS

Work with a partner. Imagine that you are teaching a younger student about Fibonacci and his discovery. Tell your partner five important facts that you learned in the reading. You may want to use actual objects or visuals, such as diagrams and photographs, to help explain some of the facts. Take turns telling your partner about Fibonacci and the number sequence he discovered. Then, in your notebook, describe one example of the Fibonacci sequence.

Speaking TIP
Use words that help your partner visualize and understand facts about Fibonacci and the Fibonacci sequence.

26

TESOL Standards

Goal 1, Standard 1—To use English to communicate in social settings: Students will use English to participate in social interactions.
Descriptors—Using nonverbal communication in social interactions; Conducting transactions.

Goal 1, Standard 3—To use English to communicate in social settings: Students will use learning strategies to extend their communicative competence.
Descriptors—Selecting different media to help understand language.

Goal 2, Standard 3—To use English to achieve academically in all content areas: Students will use appropriate learning strategies to construct and apply academic knowledge.
Descriptors—Determining and establishing the conditions that help one become an effective learner (e.g., when, where, how to study); Recognizing the need for and seeking assistance appropriately from others (e.g., teachers, peers, specialists, community members); Knowing when to use native language resources (human and material) to promote understanding.

DISCUSSION

Discuss in pairs or small groups.

1. How do daisies, seashells, and rabbits illustrate the Fibonacci sequence?

2. Fibonacci made life easier by having people use Arabic numerals rather than Roman numerals. What would happen if we suddenly had to use Roman numerals again? How would our lives change?

Q Can all mysteries be solved? What is mysterious about the Fibonacci sequence? Does knowing about the Fibonacci sequence help you understand other mysteries in nature? Explain.

Listening TIP

If you don't understand something a classmate says, wait until the next speaker has finished and then ask your question.

READ FOR FLUENCY

It is often easier to read a text if you understand the difficult words and phrases. Work with a partner. Choose a paragraph from the reading. Identify the words and phrases you do not know or have trouble pronouncing. Look up the difficult words in a dictionary.

Take turns pronouncing the words and phrases with your partner. If necessary, ask your teacher to model the correct pronunciation. Then take turns reading the paragraph aloud. Give each other feedback on your reading.

EXTENSION

Workbook
Page 12

Fibonacci was a famous mathematician. Many other people made important contributions to mathematics. Go to the library or do research on the Internet to find information about another famous mathematician, for example, Archimedes, Descartes, Pascal, or Pythagoras. Then write a brief report on the mathematician. Explain why the person is important. Tell what you learned about math from your research. Use this chart to organize your research:

Who?	
Where?	
When?	
What?	
Why?	

27

Differentiated Instruction

Beginning	Ask students what Fibonacci's real name was. (Leonardo of Pisa)
Early Intermediate	Ask students what the story problem was that Fibonacci addressed in his book.
Intermediate	Have students share with the class a pattern in nature that they may know of that wasn't mentioned in the reading.
Greater Challenge	Have students present their reports on other famous mathematicians to the class.

Listening Tip

Explain that the polite way to let a speaker know that you don't understand something is to say, "Excuse me, could you please explain what that means?" These words show respect.

(CRI) Discussion

Congratulate students on successfully completing the reading. **SAY:** *We've learned a lot about the Big Question from this reading. Now let's discuss a few questions about it.* Model a discussion starter for each question. For the first question, **SAY:** *Let's review the Fibonacci sequence. How is it formed?* (When you add one number to the next, you get the following number in the sequence.) **For the second question, SAY:** *How do you use Roman numerals in your life?* (in outlines for writing assignments) *Where might you see Roman numerals?* (on old monuments and buildings)

Q Can all mysteries be solved? SAY: *Now that you have read "G Is for Googol," how does it affect the way you would answer the Big Question? Have you changed your ideas? How so?*

Read for Fluency

Guide students in selecting a paragraph. For best results, students should select a paragraph for oral reading that they enjoyed reading silently. Point out that paragraphs with words in parentheses, words in quotes, and long Roman numerals present more of a reading challenge.

Extension

Model how to use the chart. For example, provide information about Archimedes, and ask students where they would record it on the chart. The chart may look like this:

Who?	Archimedes
Where?	Syracuse
When?	287 BCE–212 BCE
What?	Made discoveries in mathematics and geometry; made first-known summation of an infinite series of numbers
Why?	Advanced our knowledge of mathematics, physics, and engineering

STEP 1: Introduce

Review the meaning of an adjective (a word that describes a noun), and introduce the term *comparative adjectives*. Explain that these adjectives compare two things. They usually end in *-er* or are used in the expression *as . . . as*. Tell students they will be reviewing comparative adjectives.

STEP 2: Teach

Grammar and Writing

Making Comparisons Read aloud the information and examples of comparative adjectives on this page, and ask students to find other examples from the student book.

Then draw a four-column chart on the board with the following heads: *Add -er, Add -r, Double the last letter + -er,* and *Change y to i + -er*. Ask students to help fill in the chart with adjectives that follow each of the four patterns when they become comparative adjectives. Students can start with the examples from the student book.

STEP 3: Practice

Read aloud the instructions for this exercise, and model the first sentence. **SAY:** The sentence is *"Cats are ___ than rabbits when they have babies. (old)" The adjective is* old. *In order to compare cats and rabbits, I need to add -er and say: "Cats are <u>older</u> than rabbits when they have babies."*

ANSWERS
1. Cats are older than rabbits when they have babies.
2. Arabic numerals aren't as difficult as Roman numerals.
3. A book about Fibonacci numbers would be heavier than this textbook.
4. The number 144 is larger than 89.
5. The Fibonacci sequence is as mysterious today as it was in the 1200s.

Teaching Resources
- *Workbook,* pp. 13–14
- *CD-ROM/e-book,* Grammar, Writing
- *Transparencies,* Writing Model 22
- *Transparencies, Resources,* Graphic Organizer 3 or 9
- *Assessment,* Reading 2 Test, pp. 39–42

GRAMMAR, USAGE, AND MECHANICS

Making Comparisons: *-er than* and *as . . . as*

Certain kinds of words are useful when you want to describe how two things are the same or different. An adjective is a word that describes a noun. Comparative adjectives compare two things.

For most one-syllable adjectives, you add *-r* or *-er* to form a comparative adjective. For two-syllable adjectives ending in *y*, you change *y* to *i* and add *-er*. The word *than* usually follows a comparative. Study the chart. Notice the spelling changes that occur in comparatives.

small (+ *-er*)	This rectangle is smaller **than** the others.
large (+ *-r*)	Sunflowers are larger **than** daisies.
big (double the last letter + *-er*)	A bear is bigger **than** a cat.
easy (change *y* to *i* + *-er*)	Isn't 78 easier to write **than** LXXVIII?

Another way to compare two things is to use the expression *as . . . as*. Use *as . . . as* to show that the two things being compared are equal. Use *not as . . . as* to show that the two things being compared are not equal.

> The oak tree is **as tall as** our house.
> Pine needles are **not as interesting as** pinecones.

Practice **Workbook Page 13**

Copy the sentences below into your notebook. Complete each sentence by forming the comparative adjective of the word in parentheses.

1. Cats are _____ than rabbits when they have babies. (old)
2. Arabic numerals aren't as _____ as Roman numerals. (difficult)
3. A book about Fibonacci numbers would be _____ than this textbook. (heavy)
4. The number 144 is _____ than the number 89. (large)
5. The Fibonacci sequence is as _____ today as it was in the 1200s. (mysterious)

28

TESOL Standards

Goal 2, Standard 1—To use English to achieve academically in all content areas: Students will use English to interact in the classroom.
Descriptors—Following oral and written directions, implicit and explicit.

Goal 2, Standard 2—To use English to achieve academically in all content areas: Students will use English to obtain, process, construct, and provide subject matter information in spoken and written form.
Descriptors—Gathering information orally and in writing; Representing information visually and interpreting information presented visually; Demonstrating knowledge through application in a variety of contexts.

Goal 2, Standard 3—To use English to achieve academically in all content areas: Students will use appropriate learning strategies to construct and apply academic knowledge.
Descriptors—Evaluating one's own success in a completed learning task.

WRITING A DESCRIPTIVE PARAGRAPH

Describe an Object

You have already described a person's traits. Now you will describe an object using a graphic organizer like the one at the right. When writers describe something, they often use words that appeal to the five senses: sight, hearing, touch, taste, and smell. Using words that appeal to the senses, or sensory details, makes writing come alive.

Here is a model of a descriptive paragraph about a pineapple. Notice the sensory details the writer includes to illustrate what the object looks, sounds, feels, tastes, and smells like.

Wendy Willner

The Pineapple

The pineapple is dark, hard, and elongated in shape. Its stiff dark-green leaves stand silently on the table. The pineapple seems as if it wants to tell you something, but it doesn't want to tell you too much. When you pick the fruit up, the coarse skin scratches your hands. The scales form three sets of spirals. A set of five spirals goes gradually up to the right. A set of eight spirals goes more steeply down to the left, and a set of thirteen spirals goes very steeply up to the right. These are Fibonacci numbers. When you slice the pineapple open, it is as bright and yellow as the sun at noon. Put a slice in your mouth, and it tastes sweet and juicy. The fresh-cut pineapple fills any room with a refreshing smell. When you eat it with your hands (you shouldn't but I do), it feels as if you are touching liquid gold.

Practice **Workbook** Page 14

Write a paragraph describing a fruit or vegetable. Use a sensory-details web like the one above to gather and organize details. Include at least one detail for each sense: sight, hearing, touch, taste, and smell. If the feel or scent of the object reminds you of something else, use comparatives and other expressions to compare.

> **Writing Checklist**
>
> **VOICE:**
> ☑ I included many sensory details so that my reader can feel what I felt.
>
> **IDEAS AND CONTENT:**
> ☑ I used details and comparisons to make my description fun to read.

29

Accelerate Language Development

Than versus *then*

English language learners often have difficulty distinguishing the word *than*, associated with the comparison structure, and the word *then*, associated with time expressions. Example: *My house is bigger than yours./First you need to do your homework, then you can watch TV.* Point out the different spellings of *then*/*than*, and demonstrate the different pronunciation. Then write a few sentences on the board, leaving blanks for *than* and *then*, respectively. Ask for volunteers to fill in the blanks.

STEP 1: Introduce

Tell students that a descriptive paragraph can describe an object. This kind of paragraph includes sensory details that appeal to the five senses: sight, sound, touch, taste, and smell.

STEP 2: Teach

Describe an Object With students, brainstorm examples of sensory words (Sight: *colorful, shiny, lustrous, snowy*; Sound: *loud, high-pitched, soft, musical*; Touch: *velvety, furry, scratchy, itchy*; Taste: *bitter, sweet, salty, peppery*: Smell: *refreshing, smoky*.) Explain that students will create a paragraph with sensory words to describe a fruit or vegetable.

Model Writing Skill Point out the sensory-details web on the student page, and draw it on the board. Write *The Pineapple* in the center oval. Above each outer oval, write: *Tastes, Sounds, Feels, Looks,* or *Smells*. Then read aloud the "The Pineapple," and with students, fill in the outer ovals. **SAY:** *In the first sentence, I read that the pineapple is dark, hard, and elongated. I can see something dark and elongated, so I'll put those words in the Looks oval. I can feel something hard, so I'll write that word in the Feels oval.*

With students, continue analyzing each sentence for sensory words and phrases, and complete the web. Then have students work together to create a sensory-details web for a different fruit or vegetable. It should contain words and phrases that appeal to sight, hearing, touch, taste, and smell.

STEP 3: Assess

Have students evaluate their work, using the Writing Checklist.

Writing Checklist Note

Voice Check that students use words that appeal to the five senses in describing their fruit or vegetable.

Ideas and Content Check that students compare a fruit or vegetable to something else, and to use expressions that make the description fun to read.

Teach

STEP 1: Introduce

Objectives

Read the list of objectives in the What You Will Learn section, encouraging students to join in. Tell students that this reading will be about world mysteries. Have pairs of students work together to restate the list of things they will learn.

The Big Question

Remind students that the Big Question is "Can all mysteries be solved?"

Create a three-column KWL chart for the pyramids of Egypt, and ask students to complete the first two columns with what they already know about pyramids and what they want to learn about them. Point out that after they read, they can fill in the third column.

Build Background

Discuss how to tell whether something is a fact. (A fact hinges on evidence—something you can actually prove.) Explain that although the pyramids still seem mysterious, scientists today have many tools, such as carbon dating and electron microscopes, to help get facts about their strange shape and the mummies in them. In the future, some mysteries we now think of as "fiction" may be solved by fact-finding.

STEP 2: Teach

Understanding the Genre:
Social Studies Article

A social studies articles is a type of informational text. Its purpose is to present facts and other data about real people, events, places, and situations. The format of this social studies article is a series of short segments about old mysteries from different cultures.

Teaching Resources

- CD-ROM/e-book, Key Words
- Audio CD 1, tracks 11–12
- *Workbook*, p. 15

What You Will Learn

Reading
- Vocabulary building: *Context, dictionary skills, word study*
- Reading strategy: *Preview*
- Text type: *Informational text (social studies)*

Grammar, Usage, and Mechanics
Passive voice

Writing
Describe a place

THE BIG QUESTION

Can all mysteries be solved? You are going to read about a series of real-life mysteries. The first concerns the Egyptian pyramids. Work with a partner to explore everything you know about pyramids. What do they look like? Where, when, and how were they built? In your notebook, record what you already know.

Now look at the picture below. Read the facts about the Great Pyramid at Giza in Egypt. Discuss the picture and facts with your partner.

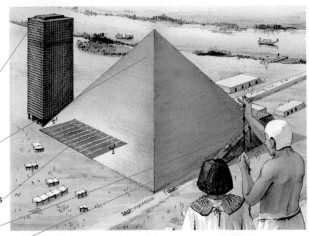

The pyramid is as tall as a forty-story building. It took 20,000 workers twenty years to build it.

It is made up of more than 2 million blocks of stone. Each block weighs about 2,200 kilograms (5,000 lb.).

The bottom of the pyramid is as big as eight football fields.

Workers used a knotted string as a measurement tool.

Workers used logs and ramps.

BUILD BACKGROUND

"Fact or Fiction?" explores mysterious places, creatures, and events from the past. First, this nonfiction article focuses on the pyramids of Egypt, one of the most puzzling of mysteries. Then it goes on to explore other historical puzzles: *What happened to the people of Machu Picchu? Is there really a curse on King Tutankhamen's tomb? What mysterious creatures live in the depths of the sea? Is there a monster in a lake in Scotland?* As you read, think about how you would try to solve one of these mysteries.

30

TESOL Standards

Goal 1, Standard 3—To use English to communicate in social settings: Students will use learning strategies to extend their communicative competence.
Descriptors—Selecting different media to help understand language; Using context to construct meaning.

Goal 2, Standard 3—To use English to achieve academically in all content areas: Students will use appropriate learning strategies to construct and apply academic knowledge.
Descriptors—Focusing attention selectively; Applying basic reading comprehension skills such as skimming, scanning, previewing, and reviewing text; Using context to construct meaning.

VOCABULARY

Learn Key Words

Read these sentences. Use the context to figure out the meaning of the red words. Use a dictionary to check your answers. Then write each word and its meaning in your notebook.

Key Words

archaeologist
clues
creature
disappeared
fantasy
sacred

1. The **archaeologist** tried to understand the past by digging through the ruins of old buildings.

2. To understand the mysterious ruins, scientists used **clues** from the soil, statues, and ancient scrolls.

3. A mysterious **creature** lived in the forest. People believed it was part human and part horse.

4. The first English colony in America **disappeared** mysteriously. One day, all the people were gone.

5. The unicorn is a **fantasy**. It is an unreal animal that lives only in the imagination.

6. A church, a temple, and a mosque are three kinds of **sacred** buildings.

Practice

 Workbook Page 15

Work with a partner to answer these questions. Try to include the red word in your answer. Write the sentences in your notebook.

1. What does an **archaeologist** do?

2. What **clues** would the police use to track a bank robber?

3. Which **creature** scares you the most? Why?

4. Why do you think dinosaurs **disappeared** millions of years ago?

5. Why do people sometimes like **fantasy** better than reality?

6. What is something that is **sacred** to you or someone you know?

▲ The unicorn was a popular fantasy during the middle ages.

31

 Vocabulary

Learn Key Words Play the CD. Have students listen and repeat. If you are not using the CD, direct students to the Key Words at the top of the page and read them aloud. **SAY:** *These words are called* Key Words *because they are words that are important in the text we are reading.* On the board or an overhead transparency, write the Key Words and their definitions. Definitions can be found in the Glossary at the back of the student book.

Have students copy the definitions into their Word Books or notebooks and generate original sentences for them. For extra practice, assign Workbook page 31.

STEP 3: Practice

Have students work with partners to complete the practice activity. Model the first one. **SAY:** *The first question asks:* What does an archaeologist do? *I know from the sentences above that this kind of person digs through the ruins of old buildings. I could write:* An archaeologist digs through the ruins of old buildings.

ANSWERS

Possible responses:

1. An archaeologist digs through the ruins of old buildings.

2. Police would use surveillance photos, tire tracks, fingerprints, and DNA clues to track a bank robber.

3. A snake is the creature that scares me the most because it slithers so fast, it can bite me before I can escape.

4. I think dinosaurs disappeared millions of years ago because the Earth got too hot.

5. People sometimes like fantasy better than reality because it distracts them from their problems.

6. The Virgin of Guadalupe is sacred to me.

Differentiated Instruction

Beginning	Have students point out the pyramid, office building, and river in the illustration on page 30.
Early Intermediate	Ask students to identify and describe what type of text "Fact or Fiction" is.
Intermediate	Write some of the key words on the board. Ask students what they associate with these words. Create a word web on the board using students' responses.
Struggling Readers	Ask students to identify other creatures they may have seen in movies or read about in books.

Teach

STEP 1: Teach

CD1 T13–T14

Vocabulary

Learn Academic Words Play the CD. Have students listen and repeat. If you are not using the CD, read the Academic Words at the top of the page aloud. **SAY:** *Look at the Academic Word chart. The definition for each word is on the left side. On the right side, each word is used in a sentence. Work with a partner to write an additional sentence for each academic word.* (Example: The attendance report for our class must be accurate.) *Write each word, its definition, and the sentence in your personal word book.*

STEP 2: Practice

Write the following question on the board, and underline the words, as shown: *Where could you find accurate information about Egypt?* **SAY:** *When you are asked a question, try to include words from the question in your answer. Notice the underlined words in the question on the board.*

Then write this answer on the board: *You could find accurate information about Egypt at the Smithsonian Institution.* Point out the underlined words in the answer that also appear in the question. Have partners work together to answer the other questions.

ANSWERS
Possible responses:
1. You could find accurate information about Egypt at the Smithsonian Institution.
2. You could create a model of a pyramid by piling up sugar cubes.
3. Archaeologists might use surviving written records to figure out why a group of people suddenly vanished.
4. In order to survive, human beings need air, water, food, and shelter.

Teaching Resources

- Audio CD 1, tracks 13–14
- *Workbook*, pp. 16–18
- CD-ROM/e-book, Academic Words, Word Study

Learn Academic Words

Study the red words and their meanings. You will find these words useful when talking and writing about informational texts. Write each word and its meaning in your notebook. After you read "Fact or Fiction?" try to use these words to respond to the text.

Academic Words

accurate
create
evidence
survive

accurate = correct or exact	➡	Archaeologists must collect **accurate** information when they try to solve mysteries from the past.
create = make something exist	➡	The scientist wanted to **create** a model pyramid to see how it was made.
evidence = facts, objects, or signs that make you believe that something exists or is true	➡	The scientist looked for **evidence** to prove when the building had been constructed.
survive = continue to live or exist	➡	No one knows why the animals did not **survive** after the storm; all of them died.

Practice Workbook Page 16

Work with a partner to answer these questions. Try to include the red word in your answer. Write the answers in your notebook.

1. Where could you find accurate information about ancient Egypt?
2. How could you create a model of a pyramid? What materials would you use to make the model?
3. What types of evidence might archaeologists use to figure out why a group of people suddenly died out or vanished?
4. What kinds of things do human beings need in order to survive?

▲ Although the Inca people died out, they left behind evidence of what their culture was like. One example is this counting necklace.

32

Word Study: Same Sound, Different Spellings

In English, sometimes the same sound can be spelled in different ways. The only way to figure out the correct spelling is to check the word in a dictionary and memorize it. When you read "Fact or Fiction?" you will come across the words *calendar, together, calculator*. Say each word aloud with a partner. What sound do you hear in the final syllable of each word? Notice that the final sound /ər/ is the same, though the spellings are different.

The sound /ər/ can be spelled in different ways when it comes at the end of a word in an unstressed syllable. Study the chart for more examples.

ar	er	or
sug**ar**	feath**er**	auth**or**
cell**ar**	Decemb**er**	mirr**or**
regul**ar**	pitch**er**	neighb**or**

Practice **Workbook** Page 17

Work with a partner. Copy the chart above into your notebook. Say a word from the chart, and ask your partner to spell it aloud. Then have your partner say the next word. Continue until you can spell all of these words correctly. Then work with your partner to spell the following words: *beggar, cracker, doctor, dollar, hammer,* and *tractor*. Add them to the chart under the correct headings.

READING STRATEGY | **PREVIEW**

Previewing a text helps you understand the content more quickly. When you preview a text, you prepare yourself for the information you are about to learn. To preview, follow these steps:

- Read the title and headings (section titles).
- Try to turn the headings into questions.
- Look at the visuals and read the captions or labels.
- Think about what you already know about the subject.

Before you read "Fact or Fiction?" look at the title, headings, visuals, and captions. Think about what you already know about these subjects. What more would you like to know?

 Workbook Page 18

33

Linguistic Note

ent/ence versus *ant/ance*

Many students have difficulty deciding when to use the suffix *ence* and when to use *ance*. There are no easy or helpful rules that distinguish the ending in the words *evidence, consequence* and *existence* from that in the words *resistance, tolerance,* or *radiance*. The same is true for the suffixes *ent* and *ant* in adjectives such as *tolerant* and *evident*. The reason for the different spelling lies in their Lain origin: *ance/ant* is added to Latin verbs that end in *-are* while *ent/ence* is added to verbs that end in *-ere*. Encourage your students to learn the spelling of a word ending in *ent/ence* or *ant/ance* along with its meaning.

Word Study

Same Sound, Different Spellings Read aloud the information about the different spellings of the sound /ər/. Explain that this sound can be spelled *ar, er,* and *or,* as shown in the words on the chart. Ask students for other examples of words with these spellings, such as *scholar, copper,* and *predator*.

Read aloud the instructions for this exercise and write the chart and headings on the board. Help students sound out the practice words, and write them on the chart. Check the ANSWERS below for help sorting these words into the right category.

ANSWERS

ar	er	or
beggar dollar	cracker hammer	doctor tractor

Reading Strategy

Preview With students, read the bulleted items for previewing. Then preview "Fact or Fiction?" Read the title and all the headings. **SAY:** *What can we learn from previewing these headings? What question can you make from the first heading on page 35?* (What is the secret of the great Sphinx?) *What can we learn about pyramids from the diagram on page 34?* (There's a shaft inside it.) *What can we learn from the caption below the photo of the Sphinx?* (It's half man, half lion.) For extra practice or homework, assign Workbook page 18.

Read

STEP 1: Introduce

Reading Summary

Some mysteries have been solved about the pyramids, the Great Sphinx, Machu Picchu, Stonehenge, Easter Island, the pharaohs' curse, giant squids, the Loch Ness monster, Bigfoot, and Yeti.

Q The Big Question

Remind students that the Big Question is *Can all mysteries be solved?* Point out that in recent years, many ancient mysteries have been solved, while others still remain a mystery. Ask students what mysteries they would like answered? (For example, Is there human-like life on other planets?)

STEP 2: Teach

Set a Purpose for Reading

Tell students that as they read, they should use the information they've already learned through previewing to learn more about the mysteries.

Preteaching Highlighted Words

With students, preview the highlighted words on student book pages 34–35. Write the words on the board, and point out that they are defined in the gloss at the bottom of each page. Ask volunteers to read the definitions. Then model how to use the words in original sentences. For example, *The pharaoh had a pyramid built for his afterlife.* Ask volunteers to do the same. Students should write the definition for each word and copy the sentence from the text in which it occurs in their notebooks.

CD1 T15 Scaffolding: Listen and Read

Have students read along as you play the CD recording of the reading. Pause the recording at the end of each page to ask and answer questions students may have.

Teaching Resources

- *Resources*, Summaries, pp. 127–128
- Audio CD 1, track 15
- *Reader's Companion Workbook*, pp. 14–21

Set a purpose for reading Preview the text. What kinds of mysteries do you think the text will present? Read to find out why some mysteries are so hard to solve.

Fact or Fiction?

Path to the Stars?

About 4,500 years ago, the pharaoh Cheops and his son and grandson built the three Pyramids of Giza in Egypt. These pyramids were tombs, or places to bury the dead. For thousands of years, people didn't understand why these three pyramids were grouped together.

Then Belgian engineer Robert Bauval noticed that the shape of the three pyramids was the same as part of a group of stars in the sky called Orion's Belt. The whole group of stars—Orion—was sacred to the Egyptians. When Cheops died, he was buried in the Great Pyramid of Giza. The Egyptians made a shaft—or hole—in this pyramid. The shaft led from Cheops's tomb to the sky and the three stars of Orion's Belt. Scientists believe that the Egyptians built this shaft so that Cheops could fly from the pyramid to Orion. There, he would become a god.

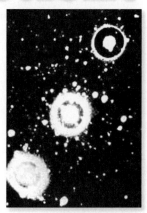

▲ The three stars in Orion's belt

---

pharaoh, ancient Egyptian ruler
engineer, person who plans how to build machines, roads, and so on

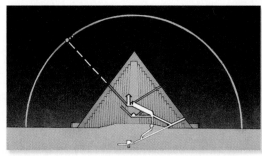

▲ This diagram shows the shaft in the pyramid.

34

▲ The three Pyramids of Giza from high above

🌐 TESOL Standards

Goal 1, Standard 1—To use English to communicate in social settings: Students will use English to participate in social interactions.
Descriptors—Sharing and requesting information; Expressing needs, feelings, and ideas.

Goal 2, Standard 1—To use English to achieve academically in all content areas: Students will use English to interact in the classroom.
Descriptors—Asking and answering questions; Requesting information and assistance.

Goal 2, Standard 2—To use English to achieve academically in all content areas: Students will use English to obtain, process, construct, and provide subject matter information in spoken and written form.
Descriptors—Selecting, connecting, and explaining information; Analyzing, synthesizing, and inferring from information.

The Secret of the Great Sphinx

A huge statue with the head of a man and the body of a lion stands in Giza, Egypt. Known as the Great Sphinx, it seems to defend the pyramids behind it. Like the pyramids, the Sphinx is made from limestone, which is very common in Egypt. The exact age of the Sphinx remains one of the world's great mysteries. For thousands of years, wind and sand have eroded this enormous sculpture. Some archaeologists believe that water also damaged the Sphinx many centuries ago. Was the Sphinx once buried at the bottom of the sea? No one knows for sure.

Mysterious Cities

Some ancient cities were abandoned and no one knows why. One of these cities is Machu Picchu, located about 2,440 meters (8,000 ft.) high in the Andes Mountains of Peru. The Inca built Machu Picchu from about 1460 to 1470 C.E. They lived in parts of South America, including what is now Peru. They used stone blocks to make most of the buildings. The blocks fit together perfectly.

In the early 1500s, everyone left the city. No one knows why. Perhaps people died or left because of smallpox, a deadly disease that was brought to the Americas by European explorers and colonists. Machu Picchu was forgotten for hundreds of years. Then, in 1911, the American explorer Hiram Bingham rediscovered it. Today, tourists from all over the world visit this unique city.

▲ The Sphinx has the head of a man and the body of a lion.

---

statue, shape of a person or animal made of stone, metal, or wood
limestone, a type of rock that contains calcium, often used to make buildings
eroded, slowly destroyed
centuries, periods of 100 years
abandoned, left completely behind and not used anymore
colonists, people who settle in a new country or area

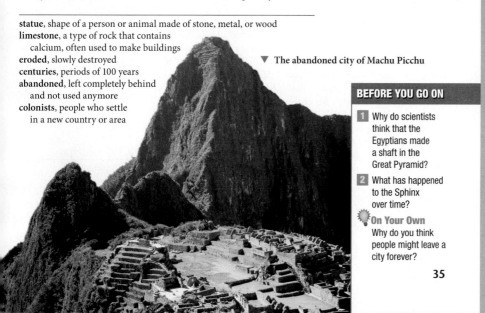

▼ The abandoned city of Machu Picchu

BEFORE YOU GO ON

1. Why do scientists think that the Egyptians made a shaft in the Great Pyramid?

2. What has happened to the Sphinx over time?

On Your Own
Why do you think people might leave a city forever?

35

STEP 3: Monitor Progress

Ask students to check what they have understood in the reading. If you are using the Audio CD, pause the recording.

Before You Go On

Remind students that reading the questions before reading the text can help them understand the text. Preview these questions with students before they read the page so they know what to look for.

ANSWERS

1. Scientists think that the Egyptians made a shaft in the Great Pyramid so the pharaoh, Cheops, could fly to the stars and become a god.
2. Over time, wind and sand have eroded the Sphinx's features.

On Your Own Have students write an answer to the On Your Own question on separate sheets of paper. Encourage volunteers to share their responses with the class. Then collect student responses to monitor their comprehension, writing skills, and fluency.

Differentiated Instruction	
Beginning	Ask students to name the group of stars that was sacred to the Egyptians. (Orion)
Early Intermediate	Ask students which of the discoveries in the article they find the most interesting. Have them give reasons for their answers.
Intermediate	Ask students to explain in their own words why the Egyptians built a shaft in Cheops's tomb.
Standard English Learners (CRI)	Have students work in pairs to find other words with a similar meaning to *abandoned*. Tell them to look up the antonym of each word in a dictionary.

Preteaching Highlighted Words

Before reading this spread, point out the highlighted words and terms to students. Define each one, pointing out the location of the definition in the gloss at the bottom of the student book page. Make sure that students understand each highlighted word. If appropriate, ask students to generate original sentences using the highlighted words.

Model the
READING STRATEGY

Preview

Remind students that previewing visuals and captions will help them understand what they are reading. **SAY:** *The photo of Stonehenge on this page shows a huge stone circle. What does the caption reveal about the photo?* (The stones came from 300 miles away. We don't know for sure how people got them here.) *What does the photo of Easter Island tell us?* (There are huge stone statues there.) *What more does the caption reveal?* (The statues are about 13 feet tall.)

Stonehenge

Stonehenge is a mysterious monument of huge stones in England. Ancient peoples built Stonehenge about 5,000 years ago. No one really knows who these people were or why they built this strange circle of rocks.

Some people believe that Stonehenge was a temple to the sun. Other people believe that Stonehenge was a great stone calendar or calculator. They think that the stones were arranged to measure the sun's movements. For example, the stones may have been used to measure the summer and winter solstices—the longest and shortest days of the year. Perhaps Stonehenge was created to mark the rise of the sun and moon throughout the centuries. How will we ever know for sure?

Island of Giants

Easter Island is a tiny island in the Pacific Ocean, 3,620 kilometers (2,250 mi.) off the coast of Chile. It was named by Dutch explorers who arrived there on Easter Sunday, 1722. The island is covered with nearly 900 large statues, called "moai." Scientists believe the statues are the gods of the ancient people of Easter Island—the Rapa Nui people. But no one knows for sure. Another mystery is how the Rapa Nui people moved the heavy stones as far as 23 kilometers (14 mi.).

Archaeologists have found wooden tablets with the ancient language of the Rapa Nui people on them. No one knows how to read this language today. So the history of the Rapa Nui people is still a puzzle. Only the great stone statues remain to watch over the island.

 Some stones at Stonehenge came from 480 kilometers (300 mi.) away. How people moved them is a mystery.

▲ The Moai have an average height of 4 meters (13 ft.).

---

monument, something that is built to help people to remember an important person or event
temple, holy building
calculator, instrument used to figure out mathematical problems
Easter Sunday, a special Sunday in March or April when Christians remember Christ's death and his return to life

36

Curse of the Pharaoh

Tutankhamen was a pharaoh in ancient Egypt from 1333 to 1324 B.C.E. When he died, Tutankhamen was buried in a tomb with gold and other treasures.

In 1922, a group led by British archaeologists Howard Carter and Lord Carnarvon opened the tomb of Tutankhamen. They found many treasures, including a beautiful gold mask. Some people believed that a message carved in the tomb wall said, "Death will slay with his wings whoever disturbs the peace of the pharaoh." Lord Carnarvon died soon after opening the tomb. According to one story, Carnarvon's dog died at the same time at his home in England. Then, five months after Carnarvon died, his younger brother died suddenly.

According to one report, six of the twenty-six people at the opening of Tutankhamen's tomb died within ten years. However, many other people who were there when the tomb was opened lived to be very old. Was there really a curse? What do you think?

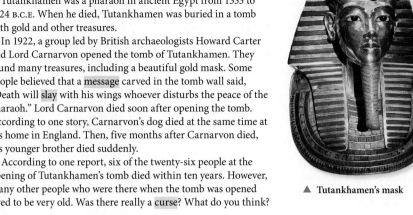

▲ Tutankhamen's mask

---

message, piece of information that is communicated in words or signals
slay, kill
curse, wish that something bad would happen to someone

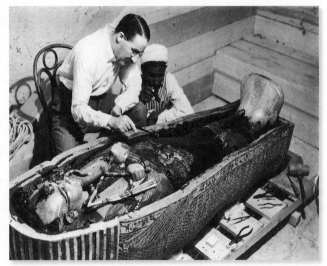

◀ Howard Carter and Tutankhamen's mummy

BEFORE YOU GO ON

1. What is mysterious about Stonehenge and Easter Island?

2. What is the "curse of the pharaoh"?

💡 **On Your Own**
How do you think Howard Carter and Lord Carnarvon felt when they opened the tomb of Tutankhamen? Would you have liked to be there? Why or why not?

37

Preteaching Highlighted Words

Before reading this spread, point out the highlighted words and terms to students. Define each one, pointing out the location of the definition in the gloss at the bottom of the student book page. Make sure that students understand each highlighted word. If appropriate, ask students to generate original sentences using the highlighted words.

Across the Curriculum:
Science

Giant squid are mollusks—animals similar to clams, snails, and octopus. Males are smaller in size than females, which can reach up to 43 feet long. Giant squid live in all of the world's oceans. They are believed to be solitary hunters, as only individual giant squid have ever been caught in fishing nets. Fish such as the Hoki are among the giant squid's diet. An adult giant squid's only known predators are sperm whales and Pacific sleeper sharks, found off Antarctica.

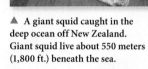

Terrifying Tentacles

Scientists say that we know more about Mars than we do about the mysteries at the bottom of the ocean. For instance, little is known about giant octopuses and squid. These sea creatures are usually only about 60 to 90 centimeters (2–3 ft.) long. However, there have been reports of giant octopuses and squid with tentacles long enough to pull a ship underwater. In 1753, a man in Norway described seeing a huge sea monster "full of arms." The man said that the monster looked big enough to crush a large ship. More recently, giant squid have been discovered with tentacles 10 meters (33 ft.) long. Imagine eating calamari rings the size of truck tires!

Scary Monsters

Most people believe that dinosaurs disappeared millions of years ago. However, a few dinosaurs may have survived. The famous Loch Ness monster may be a living dinosaur-like reptile called a plesiosaur.

People first reported seeing the Loch Ness monster in April 1933 when a new road was built on the north shore of Loch Ness, a lake in Scotland. A man and woman saw a huge creature with two black humps swimming across the lake. Then two more people saw a strange animal crossing the road with a sheep in its mouth. There is now a Loch Ness Investigation Bureau, but most scientists believe that the Loch Ness monster is a creature of fantasy.

---

tentacles, long, thin arm-like parts
calamari rings, sliced squid, often served fried or in a salad
reptile, type of animal, such as a snake or lizard, whose blood
    changes temperature according to the temperature around it
humps, raised parts on the back of an animal

▲ A giant squid caught in the deep ocean off New Zealand. Giant squid live about 550 meters (1,800 ft.) beneath the sea.

This famous photograph of the Loch Ness monster is not authentic. The photographer tied a plastic head to a toy submarine. ▶

38

Bigfoot and the Yeti

In various parts of the world, people have told stories about seeing large ape-like creatures. Different cultures give the creature different names. In the United States, for example, this creature is called Bigfoot or Sasquatch. In Tibet, it is called the yeti.

The first reports of Bigfoot date back to 1811. At that time, a man reported seeing footprints 36 centimeters (14 in.) long. In 1924, another man claimed that Bigfoot had kidnapped him. Each year many people in the United States claim to see Bigfoot. They often report seeing the creature in the forests of the Northwest.

Reports of a huge creature frightened the first European travelers in Tibet. (In Tibet, the word *yeti* means "man-like creature.") In 1951, a Mount Everest explorer found giant footprints in the snow.

Do creatures like the yeti and Bigfoot really exist, or are they figments of the imagination? Bernard Heuvelmans (1916–2001), a famous zoologist, believed that the world is full of creatures still unknown to science. What do you think?

◀ Bigfoot (above) and the Yeti (below) look like giant apes. ▼

---

various, different
figments of the imagination, things imagined to be real that do not exist
zoologist, scientist who studies animals

BEFORE YOU GO ON

1. Do most scientists believe that the Loch Ness monster is real or a fantasy?

2. In the United States, where is Bigfoot usually seen?

💡 **On Your Own**
Do you believe that mysterious animals like the yeti or the Loch Ness monster exist? What is your opinion?

39

Study Skills: World Map

After students have read this page, encourage them to find places on a world map where the large ape-like creatures have been cited. (Tibet, Mount Everest in Nepal, and the forests of the northwestern part of the United States) Ask on which two continents these two places are found (Asia and North America.) Point out that on a world map, Asia is usually found at the right side and North America is at the left side. Using the map's compass rose, ask students to determine which continent is in the east and which is in the west.

STEP 7: Monitor Progress

Ask students to check what they have understood in the reading.

Before You Go On

Invite volunteers to read the questions aloud after listening to the CD recording of pages 38–39. Or have students preview the questions before reading so they will know what information to look for as they read.

ANSWERS

1. Most scientists believe that the Loch Ness monster is a fantasy.
2. In the United States, Bigfoot is usually seen in the forests of the Northwest.

On Your Own Answers with vary.

Review the Purpose for Reading

Elicit responses to the Set a Purpose for Reading questions at the beginning of this reading. Remind students to relate their responses to the Big Question.

Teach & Apply

Comprehension

Students can answer these questions independently or in groups. They can respond orally or in writing. Model the first question with the class so they can see how to answer in a complete sentence.

ANSWERS

1. The Egyptian pharaoh, Cheops, his son, and his grandson built the three pyramids of Giza.
2. Archaeologists found nearly 900 huge stone statues on Easter Island.
3. The pyramids are huge tombs that were built for pharaohs. They are geometric in shape. The Sphinx is a huge piece of stone sculpture that was probably built to protect the pyramids. The shape of the Sphinx is a lion's body and a human head.
4. The mysteries of Easter Island and Machu Picchu are similar in that civilizations with large numbers of people seem to have vanished without a trace.
5. **Possible response:** No, I don't think the author believes in Bigfoot or the Loch Ness Monster because he always gives an explanation of what it probably is.
6. **Possible responses:** The author probably believes there are logical answers to the mysteries in "Fact or Fiction?," but we'll never be sure. The pyramids were probably constructed to align with three stars in Orion's belt. The Great Sphinx was probably built to guard the pyramids. Stonehenge was probably built to mark the rise of the sun and the moon throughout the centuries. Giant squid were probably what sailors saw rather than strange sea creatures that could crush ships.
7. Answers will vary.
8. Answers will vary.

Teaching Resources

- *Workbook*, p. 19
- CD-ROM/e-book, Comprehension, Extension
- *Reader's Companion Workbook*, pp. 22–26

READING 3 — Review and Practice

COMPREHENSION Workbook Page 19

Right There

1. Who built the three Pyramids of Giza?
2. What did archaeologists find on Easter Island?

Think and Search

3. In what ways are the pyramids and the Sphinx different?
4. How are the mysteries of Machu Picchu and Easter Island similar?

Author and You

5. Do you think that the author believes in the Loch Ness monster or Bigfoot? Explain.
6. How do you think the author feels about the mysteries described in "Fact or Fiction?" Give examples that reveal the author's feelings about four of the subjects.

On Your Own

7. Would you like to be part of the Loch Ness Investigation Bureau? Why?
8. Do you believe that there are still many creatures unknown to science? Why or why not?

The dragon shown in this tile is a creature of fantasy. Or is it? ▶

40

🌐 TESOL Standards

Goal 3, Standard 1—To use English in socially and culturally appropriate ways: Students will use the appropriate language variety, register, and genre according to audience, purpose, and setting.
Descriptors—Using the appropriate degree of formality with different audiences and settings; Determining when it is appropriate to use a language other than English; Determining appropriate topics for interaction.

Goal 3, Standard 2—To use English in socially and culturally appropriate ways: Students will use nonverbal communication appropriate to audience, purpose, and setting.
Descriptors—Interpreting and responding appropriately to nonverbal cues and body language; Using acceptable tone, volume, stress, and intonation, in various social settings; Recognizing and adjusting behavior in response to nonverbal cues.

IN YOUR OWN WORDS

Work with a partner. Imagine that you are telling a younger student about "Fact or Fiction?" First make a list of the key topics and main ideas in the article. You may want to use the headings in the article as a guide. Then take turns explaining the information you remember from the article. Try to use some of these words: *pharaoh, engineer, centuries, eroded, survive, disappeared, sacred, temple, clues, statues, archaeologists, message, unique, accurate, evidence, humps, creature,* and *fantasy.*

 Speaking TIP

Write your important ideas on note cards. Write just a few words in big letters on each card. Use the cards to help you remember your main ideas.

DISCUSSION

Discuss in pairs or small groups.

1. What might have caused the people of Machu Picchu to disappear?
2. Which place described in "Fact or Fiction?" would you most like to visit? Explain.

Q Can all mysteries be solved? Which of the mysteries in the selection do you predict will be solved first? Explain.

 Listening TIP

Be quiet and pay attention while others are speaking. Open your eyes and ears.

READ FOR FLUENCY

Reading with feeling helps make what you read more interesting. Work with a partner. Choose a paragraph from the reading. Read the paragraph to yourselves. Ask each other how you felt after reading the paragraph. Did you feel happy or sad?

Take turns reading the paragraph aloud to each other with a tone of voice that represents how you felt when you read it the first time. Give each other feedback.

EXTENSION Workbook Page 19

Archaeologists and scientists examine information and data to learn more about mysteries. Imagine that you are an archaeologist. Go to the library or do research on the Internet to find more information about one of the mysteries from "Fact or Fiction?" Then present the new information to the class.

41

Differentiated Instruction

Beginning	Ask students what the two names are for the mysterious, large ape-like creature discussed in the reading. (Bigfoot, yeti)
Early Intermediate	Ask students to write a short paragraph summarizing the similarities between Machu Picchu and Easter Island. Encourage students to read their paragraphs to the class.
Intermediate	In small groups, have students discuss some possible explanations to the mysteries in the reading.
Greater Challenge	Ask students to consider how the reading relates to their social studies or science classes. Invite students to share their thoughts with the class.

Speaking Tip

When you tell your partner your important ideas, first look at the note card, try to memorize it, and then look up to explain your ideas.

CRI In Your Own Words

Help pairs of students find the headings in the article, and list them on the board. Then list the italicized words, too. As you point to each heading, ask volunteers to circle the words that relate to the information. Students can copy headings and words onto note cards.

STEP 2: Extend

Listening Tip

Remind students to show the same kind of respect to speakers as they would like when they speak. They should listen quietly and carefully.

CRI Discussion

Congratulate students on successfully completing the reading. **SAY:** *Let's discuss a few questions about the reading.* For the first question, *Who are historians, and why might they know the answer to the mystery of the disappearance of people from Machu Picchu?* (Historians are people who are authorities, or specialists, in history.) For the second question, *Why do people like to visit places? What kind of places do you like to visit?*

Q Can all mysteries be solved? Answers will vary. Make sure students support their answers with reasons.

STEP 3: Assess

Read for Fluency

Guide students in selecting a paragraph. For best results, students should pick a paragraph for oral reading that they enjoyed reading silently. Point out that paragraphs with words in parentheses, abbreviations, dates, and long numbers, present more of a reading challenge.

Extension

Read aloud the instructions for this activity. Then have students fill in a two-column chart labeled *Information from "Fact or Fiction?"* and *New Information.*

They can present the new information to the class.

STEP 1: Introduce

Tell students that in the passive voice, the focus is on the receiver of the action. It is the opposite of the active voice, in which the focus is on who or what does the action. Explain that you will be reviewing how to distinguish between these voices in both the present and past tenses.

STEP 2: Teach

Grammar and Writing

Passive Voice Point to the examples of active and passive voices in the chart. **SAY:** *In the first Passive Voice sentence,* "The Pyramids of Giza were built by the pharaoh," *I see that a form of* be + *the past participle is used. The words* were built *tell me that this sentence is in the passive voice.*

STEP 3: Practice

Before students complete this exercise, model how to use the passive voice in a sentence. On the board, write "The bird watchers observed the geese." **SAY:** *Let's change this sentence to the passive voice. We'll need a form of* be + *the past participle to take the place of the verb* saw. *The focus of the action will be on the receiver* (the geese). *We could say,* "The geese were observed by bird watchers."

ANSWERS

1. The pyramids were built by the Egyptians.
2. Nearly 900 statues were discovered by explorers.
3. Sightings of the Loch Ness monster were reported by many people.
4. Last year, Machu Picchu was visited by thousands of tourists.
5. The dead were respected by the ancient Egyptians.
6. The stones were arranged by ancient peoples.

Teaching Resources

- *Workbook*, pp. 20–21
- CD-ROM/e-book, Grammar, Writing
- *Transparencies*, Writing Model 23
- *Transparencies*, *Resources*, Graphic Organizer 11
- *Assessment*, Reading 3 Test, pp. 43–46

Grammar and Writing

GRAMMAR, USAGE, AND MECHANICS

Passive Voice

When you read, you will see text in both the active voice and the passive voice. The active voice is used when the focus is on who or what does the action, also called the performer. The passive voice is used when the focus is on the receiver of the action. Form the passive voice with a form of the verb *be* + the past participle. A *by*-phrase identifies the performer.

Active Voice	Passive Voice
The pharaoh **built** the Pyramids of Giza. [focus is on the pharaoh]	The Pyramids of Giza **were built** by the pharaoh. [focus is on the Pyramids of Giza]
The Inca **abandoned** Machu Picchu. [focus is on the Inca]	Machu Picchu **was abandoned** by the Inca. [focus is on Machu Picchu]
Dutch explorers **discovered** Easter Island. [focus is on the Dutch explorers]	Easter Island **was discovered** by Dutch explorers. [focus is on Easter Island]
A huge creature **frightened** the travelers in Tibet. [focus is on a huge creature]	The travelers in Tibet **were frightened** by a huge creature. [focus is on the travelers in Tibet]

Practice **Workbook Page 20**

Rewrite the sentences below in your notebook, changing each from the active to the passive voice. The first one has been done for you. Discuss each answer with a partner. Does the sentence sound better in the active or passive voice? Why?

1. The Egyptians built the pyramids.

   The pyramids were built by the Egyptians.

2. Explorers discovered nearly 900 statues.
3. Many people reported sightings of the Loch Ness monster.
4. Last year, thousands of tourists visited Machu Picchu.
5. The ancient Egyptians respected the dead.
6. Ancient peoples arranged the stones.

42

TESOL Standards

Goal 1, Standard 2—To use English to communicate in social settings: Students will interact in, through, and with spoken and written English for personal expression and enjoyment.
Descriptors—Describing, reading about, or participating in a favorite activity.

Goal 3, Standard 1—To use English in socially and culturally appropriate ways: Students will use the appropriate language variety, register, and genre according to audience, purpose, and setting.
Descriptors—Responding to and using slang appropriately; Responding to and using idioms appropriately.

Goal 3, Standard 3—To use English in socially and culturally appropriate ways: Students will use appropriate learning strategies to extend their sociolinguistic and sociocultural competence.
Descriptors—Experimenting with variations of language in social and academic settings.

WRITING A DESCRIPTIVE PARAGRAPH

Describe a Place

You described a character and an object. Now you will describe a place, using a graphic organizer like the one on the right.

First, gather sensory details to show readers the physical qualities and mood of the place. Next, put the details in a logical order. One way to arrange the details is to put them in spatial order. This means arranging details from *near to far, left to right, large to small,* or some other spatial way. Pretend to be a movie camera. Use signal words to guide your reader's "eye" from one part of the place to another. Use words such as *close up, in the distance, to the right, above,* and *below.*

Here is a model of a descriptive paragraph that describes a pyramid at Chichén Itzá, Mexico. Notice how the writer uses spatial order to guide your eye from one part of this place to another.

Top
Middle
Bottom

Angelina Xing

Chichén Itzá

The ruins of Chichén Itzá are located on the Yucatan Peninsula of Mexico. As you approach the site, the tallest pyramid, Kukulkan, looks intimidating. It is seventy-nine feet high. When you get closer, you can see the ninety-one original steps that you must climb to get to the top. Before climbing, you can enter an inner temple through a narrow passageway on the north side of the pyramid. Inside is a statue of a scarlet jaguar with eyes made of jade that glow green. Then you can go outside and climb up to the top for a spectacular view of the surrounding ruins. When there is an equinox, crowds of people gather below to see a serpent crawling down the pyramid, an illusion created by the shadow of the sun.

Practice

Workbook Page 21

Write a paragraph that describes a mysterious place. Use a sensory details web like the one on page 29 to gather details. Then use a spatial-order chart to arrange the details. Use the passive voice if you focus on the place as a receiver of an action, for example: *The house was torn down a long time ago.*

Writing Checklist

WORD CHOICE:
- ☑ I included details to guide readers from one part of the place to another.

ORGANIZATION:
- ☑ I put my ideas and details in spatial order.

43

Accelerate Language Development

Subject/Object Change

When an active sentence is transformed into a passive sentence, the subject and object change grammatical roles. Point out that in English the change from active to passive does not result in any change to the nouns, because subject and object do not have different grammatical forms. English nouns do not have declensions, and the noun remains the same whether it is the subject of an active sentence or the object of the preposition *by* in a passive sentence. The only sentence part that does change during the transformation from active to passive is the verb. Write an example on the board, and ask volunteers to draw a line below the changes. Example: *Many tourists <u>visit</u> the Sphinx. The Sphinx <u>is visited</u> by many tourists.*

STEP 1: Introduce

Tell students that a descriptive paragraph can describe a place. This kind of paragraph includes sensory details that are written in spatial order.

STEP 2: Teach

Writing a Descriptive Paragraph

Describe a Place With students, brainstorm ways to arrange things in spatial order, such as near to far, left to right, large to small, top to bottom, and inside to outside. Explain that students will be using spatial order to create a paragraph with sensory words to describe a mysterious place.

Model Writing Skill On the board, draw the sensory-details web from page 29, and review how to use it. Then draw the spatial-order chart on this page. Ask a volunteer to read aloud "Chichén Itzá," and with students, first fill in the sensory-details web, and then the spatial-order chart. **SAY:** *First let's find sensory details in this paragraph. The second sentence says that the tallest pyramid looks intimidating. I'll write this sensory detail under "Looks" on the sensory-details web.* With students, continue analyzing where sensory details are placed on the sensory-details web, and complete it. Partners then fill in the sensory-details chart to arrange the details from Top to Middle to Bottom. **SAY:** *The "tallest pyramid looks intimidating" goes in the box marked Top.*

STEP 3: Assess

Have students evaluate their work, using the Writing Checklist.

Writing Checklist Note

Word Choice Check that students use sensory words to describe their mysterious place and the passive voice.

Organization Check that ideas and details are written in spatial order.

Teach

STEP 1: Introduce

Objectives

Read the list of objectives in the What You Will Learn section, encouraging students to join in. Tell students that this reading will be about teenage detectives who solve crimes in their town. Have pairs of students work together to restate the list of things they will learn.

The Big Question

Read aloud the Big Question. Point out that detectives, like the ones in this story, solve mysteries. They know how to look for details, and they try to connect them to the clues of a mystery.

Build Background

Brainstorm mystery stories that students know. Ask if they've heard of the famous fictional detective, Sherlock Holmes. A creation of Sir Arthur Conan Doyle, Holmes is known for his intelligence, use of deductive reasoning, and astute observation to solve difficult cases. Point out that fans of mystery stories are good at predicting what will happen next because they pay close attention to the clues. Ask students if they think people can be taught to be detectives, or or if they think it is an inborn talent.

STEP 2: Teach

Understanding the Genre:
Short Story

A short story is a work of fiction that is shorter and less complex than a novel. It usually has fewer characters and a simpler plot. As in a novel, the characters experience a problem or conflict. *Teenage Detectives* is a pair of short stories about the experiences of two young sleuths.

Teaching Resources

- CD-ROM/e-book, Literary Words
- Audio CD 1, track 16
- *Workbook*, p. 22

What You Will Learn

Reading
- Vocabulary building: *Literary terms, word study, dictionary skills*
- Reading strategy: *Draw conclusions*
- Text type: *Literature (short stories)*

Grammar, Usage, and Mechanics
Subject-verb agreement with indefinite pronouns

Writing
Describe an event

THE BIG QUESTION

Can all mysteries be solved? A detective is someone who solves mysteries for a living. A detective's most important tool is his or her brain. That's because detectives are problem solvers. But what other tools do they use? Work with a partner. How do detectives solve crimes? In your opinion, what is the most important tool they use? Share what you know with the class.

BUILD BACKGROUND

Teenage Detectives contains two short stories about two young detectives who are cousins. Their names are Max and Nina. These characters are fictional, or make-believe, but they act like real detectives. They use realistic tools and clues to solve mysteries.

People read mystery stories like these because they enjoy trying to figure out the mystery. Mystery stories are often called "whodunit" stories. *Whodunit* is a made-up word. Look at it carefully. It really says, "Who done it?" It means, "Who did the crime?" Readers want to find out who committed the crime. How did the detectives solve the mystery? What clues did they use? Read *Teenage Detectives* to discover "whodunit"!

▲ Tools detectives use to find fingerprints

44

Learn Literary Words

Writers often use words in new and exciting ways. The authors of *Teenage Detectives* use idioms and puns to make their stories funny and interesting to read. Idioms are expressions that have a meaning that is different from the meanings of the individual words that make them up.

In one of the mystery stories in *Teenage Detectives*, the writer says that a character "mopped his brow." The word *brow* means a person's forehead, the part of the head immediately above the eyes. The character didn't really wipe his forehead with a mop. The writer uses this idiom to create a picture.

Like many writers, the authors of *Teenage Detectives* also make jokes with words. To do this, they use a literary tool called a pun. Puns can be formed in two ways. First, a writer can make a pun by using a word that has two meanings. Second, a writer can make a pun by using words that have the same sound but different meanings.

Here's an example of a pun from one of the stories in *Teenage Detectives*. It's the last line of the first story: "'I had *concrete* evidence,' Nina answered." The pun is on the word *concrete*. The word has two meanings. As a noun, *concrete* refers to the material used to make sidewalks. As an adjective, *concrete* means "real." As you read *Teenage Detectives*, look for puns.

Literary Words

idioms

puns

▲ What does the idiom "a fork in the road" mean?

Practice

Workbook Page 22

Take turns reading these idioms and puns with a partner. Identify what each idiom means. Explain the humor in the puns.

Idioms
Bees in her bonnet
Flew off the handle
It's a whole new ballgame

Puns
What did the triangle say to the circle? You're so pointless.
The baker stopped making donuts after he got tired of the hole thing.
When a clock is hungry, it goes back for seconds.

45

Differentiated Instruction

Beginning	Ask students which idiom or pun on page 45 they find the most humorous. Have them explain why it is humorous.
Early Intermediate	Point to the picture on page 44. Ask students to predict what this reading will be about.
Intermediate	Have students find some common idioms and/or puns by looking on the Internet or checking in a dictionary. Ask students to share their findings with the class.
Struggling Readers	With students' participation, build a word web on the board starting with the word *concrete*. Encourage students to make associations with the word to build meaning.

CD1 T16

 Vocabulary

Learn Literary Words Play the CD. Have students listen and repeat. If you are not using the CD, read the Literary Words aloud. Ask students what comes to mind when they hear each word. Write down student responses. Point to the words on the page, and **SAY:** *These words are called* Literary Words *because in literature, they have a unique meaning. Read the paragraphs in your book that define* idioms *and* puns.

Write down key points on the board or an overhead transparency to reinforce learning. Write the following key elements of idioms and puns.

- **idioms:** expressions that have a meaning that is different from the meanings of the individual words that make them up
- **puns:** jokes with words. They can be formed in two ways: by using a word that has two meanings or by using words that have the same sound but different meanings.

Provide examples of idioms and puns. **SAY:** *"She got it straight from the horse's mouth" is an idiom. It means she got some information directly from the source. "The restaurant name "Dewdrop Inn" has a pun in it. Dew and do have the same sound but different spellings and meanings. Dewdrop Inn sounds like "Do drop in" or "come by."* Ask students to use the words *idioms* and *puns* in new sentences. Have them use the Workbook page 22 for extra practice.

STEP 3: Practice

Read the instructions for this practice exercise, and ask partners to talk through these examples. Review the meanings of *idioms* and *puns*.

ANSWERS

Idioms

- *Bees in her bonnet* means there is something she is so obsessed about, she can't stop thinking about it.
- *Flew off the handle* means lost your temper.
- *It's a whole new ballgame* means it's a different situation.

Puns

- A circle has no angles. It has no points; it is pointless. *Pointless* also means not having a reason to exist. The pun is funny because it can mean that the circle has no reason to exist.
- This pun is funny because *hole* and *whole* sound alike but have different meanings. The *hole thing* refers to the donuts. The *whole thing* refers to the entire project of making donuts.
- A clock measures time in hours, minutes, and seconds. *Seconds* also means getting more food. The expression *it goes back for seconds* is funny because it can mean that the clock wants to eat more.

T45

Teach

STEP 1: Teach

CD1 T17–T18

 Vocabulary

Learn Academic Words Play the CD. Have students listen and repeat. If you are not using the CD, read the Academic Words aloud. **SAY:** *Look at the Academic Words chart. It contains two parts: the definition on the left and a sentence containing the word on the right. Work with a partner to add another sentence using the Academic Word. Write each word, its definition, and the sentence in your personal Word Book. Then add a context sentence that you create. For example:* I was not aware that my fish was sick before it died.

STEP 2: Practice

Write the following question on the board, and underline the words, as shown: How do you become aware of world events? **SAY:** *When you are asked a question, try to include words from the question in your answer. Think of an answer, using the underlined words.* (Possible response: You become aware of world events by reading the newspaper.)

ANSWERS

Possible responses:
1. You become aware of world events by reading the newspaper.
2. Archaeologists and detectives have to be intelligent to observe and piece together the clues in a case.
3. A motive a criminal could have for committing a murder might be to hide another crime.
4. It is easier for the police to pursue a suspect by foot because cars cannot go everywhere.

Teaching Resources

- Audio CD 1, tracks 17–18
- *Workbook*, pp. 23–25
- CD-ROM/e-book, Academic Words, Word Study

Learn Academic Words

Study the red words and their meanings. You will find these words useful when talking and writing about literature. Write each word and its meaning in your notebook. After you read *Teenage Detectives*, try to use these words to respond to the text.

aware = realizing that something is true, exists, or is happening	➡	Detectives are **aware** of how criminals act, and they know which clues will help them solve a case.
intelligent = having a high ability to learn, understand, and think about things	➡	Detectives are **intelligent**, which makes them good problem-solvers.
motive = the reason that makes someone do something, especially when this reason is kept hidden	➡	The man's **motive** for stealing was that he didn't have any money for food.
pursue = chase or follow someone or something to catch him, her, or it	➡	The detective had to **pursue** the criminal from one city to another in order to catch him.

Practice Workbook Page 23

Work with a partner to answer these questions. Try to include the red word in your answer. Write the answers in your notebook.

1. How do you become **aware** of world events?
2. Why do archaeologists and detectives both have to be **intelligent**?
3. What **motive** could a criminal have for committing a murder?
4. Is it easier for the police to **pursue** a suspect by car or on foot? Why?

▲ What motive might this man have for hiding in the shadows?

46

🌐 TESOL Standards

Goal 1, Standard 3—To use English to communicate in social settings: Students will use learning strategies to extend their communicative competence.
Descriptors—Testing hypotheses about language.

Goal 2, Standard 2—To use English to achieve academically in all content areas: Students will use English to obtain, process, construct, and provide subject matter information in spoken and written form.
Descriptors—Hypothesizing and predicting; Formulating and asking questions.

Goal 2, Standard 3—To use English to achieve academically in all content areas: Students will use appropriate learning strategies to construct and apply academic knowledge.
Descriptors—Applying basic reading comprehension skills such as skimming, scanning, previewing, and reviewing text.

Word Study: Compound Nouns

A compound noun is made up of more than one word. Some are written as one word, as in *airplane* or *courthouse*. Some are written as two words, as in *bubble bath*. Some are written with hyphens between the words, as in *sister-in-law*. Study the examples in the chart below.

One Word	With a Hyphen (-)	Two Words
footprints	take-off	tree house
shortcut	mix-up	boarding pass

New compound nouns are formed in English all the time. Knowing how to divide compound words into their parts helps you spell them and understand what they mean. If you are not sure how to spell a compound noun, check a dictionary. If the compound noun you are looking for is not in a large dictionary, it is spelled as two words.

Practice **Workbook** Page 24

Work with a partner. Write two headings in your notebook: *Nouns* and *Compound Nouns*. Copy these words into the Nouns column: *fire, sun, eye, news*. See how many compound words you can form using these nouns (for example, *firefly, sunshine, eyelash, newspaper*). Write them in the Compound Noun column.

READING STRATEGY | **DRAW CONCLUSIONS**

Drawing conclusions helps you figure out the meanings of clues and events in a text. Good readers are like detectives. They put together the clues until they can draw a conclusion. To draw a conclusion, follow these steps:

- Read until you come to a passage that is hard to understand.
- Ask yourself, "What do I think the author means?"
- Look for clues in the text, and think about what you already know from similar situations that you have read about or experienced.
- Add the clues and what you know together, in order to draw a conclusion about what is happening in the text.

Read the first part of "The Case of the Defaced Sidewalk" on pages 48–49. Stop before you come to the heading "How did Nina figure it out?" Draw a conclusion. Finish reading the story. Was your conclusion correct?

Workbook Page 25

47

Linguistic Note

Compound Nouns

Point out that English compound nouns can consist of two words of different word categories. For example, a compound noun could be made up of two nouns, a noun and an adjective, a noun and a verb, a noun and a preposition, a verb and a preposition, or a verb and an adjective.

noun+noun	adjective+noun	verb+noun	noun+preposition	verb+preposition	verb+adjective
hotel guest	hotplate	swimming pool	underground	intake	dry run
toothpaste	greenhouse	cooking apron	beforehand	output	public speaking

---

STEP 1: Teach

Word Study

Compound Nouns Read aloud the first paragraph in the student book, and discuss the three types of compound nouns on the chart: one word, with a hyphen, and two words. Ask students to name additional compound words and tell which kind they are. (i.e. *handcuffs* [one word], *slow-motion* [with a hyphen], *boxing gloves* [two words])

STEP 2: Practice

Model how to complete this exercise. On the board write *Nouns* and *Compound Nouns*. Then write *fire, sun, eyes,* and *news* below *Nouns*. **SAY:** *I'll write* firefly *in the* Compound Nouns *column, next to* fire, *because* firefly *is a compound word made up of* fire *and* fly. Sunshine *goes in the* Compound Nouns *column, next to* sun, *because* sunshine *is a compound word made up of* sun *and* shine. *Where shall we place the words* eyelash *and* newspaper?

ANSWERS

fire: firefly, fireplace, firehouse, firefighter, fireproof, fireworks, fire drill, fire engine, fire sale, fire escape, fire-eater; sun: sunshine, sunset, sunblock, sunburn, sunscreen, Sunday, sun roof, sunglasses, sun bath; eye: eyelash, eyebrow, eyeglasses, eye-opener, eye shadow, eye chart; news: newspaper, newsletter, newsroom, newsstand, news agency, news conference

STEP 3: Teach

Reading Strategy

Draw Conclusions With students, read the bulleted items for the reading strategy. **SAY:** *People draw conclusions by combining new information with what they already know. For example, if I get an invitation to a piñata party that's set for 9 o'clock, I can draw the conclusion that it will be held at 9 PM rather than 9 AM and that we'll be eating Mexican food. I know this because most parties are given at night, and piñatas come from Mexico. I combined the clues to draw a conclusion.*

T47

Read

Reading Summary

In the first of two cases, Max and Nina find the person who stepped in wet cement and left footprints in the sidewalk. In the second case, they track down the person who removed a sign.

The Big Question

SAY: *The teens in this story use common sense. They ask questions, observe, and check out leads to solve mysteries. How do you use common sense to figure out mysteries?*

STEP 2: Teach

Set a Purpose for Reading

SAY: *Many mysteries are solved by drawing conclusions. Use information you already know and clues in the first story to try to solve this mystery. Before you read "How did Nina figure it out?" draw a conclusion about who is guilty.*

Preteaching Highlighted Words

With students, preview the words on student book pages 48–49. Write the words on the board, and point out that they are defined in the gloss at the bottom of each page. **SAY:** *Some vocabulary words in this reading are idioms, such as* slow going *and* hot tip. Ask volunteers to read the definitions, and model using the words in original sentences. For example: *His torn sandal was a clue in solving the mystery.* Then ask students to write the definition for each word and the sentence from the text in which it occurs, in their notebooks.

CD1 T19 Scaffolding:
Listen and Read

Have students read along as you play the CD recording of the reading. Pause the recording at the end of each page to answer questions.

✔ LITERARY CHECK

Tell students to read the question before reading the text. They can review idioms on page 45. Answer: *Taking a shortcut* means to take a path that is shorter and quicker.

Teaching Resources

• *Resources*, Summaries, pp. 129–130
• Audio CD 1, track 19

Set a purpose for reading How do Max and Nina solve two detective cases? Look for the types of detective tools they use.

Teenage Detectives
The Case of the Defaced Sidewalk

Carol Farley

Teenage cousins Max and Nina love solving crimes in their town, Harborville. In these short stories, they solve two different cases. See if you notice the same clues the detectives do.

One Saturday morning, Nina saw the three musketeers in the mall. Jenny, Brittany, and Mitzi called themselves the three musketeers because they were always together.

"I've been shopping for sandals," Jenny told Nina. "But I have such a wide foot nothing seems to fit. We've been looking everywhere."

"And it's been slow going," Mitzi added. "On account of Brittany's—"

"I know," Nina said, looking at Brittany. "I heard you sprained your ankle in gym yesterday. Does it still hurt a lot?"

"It's okay as long as I move really slowly," Brittany told her. "We're going to get ice cream at the Just Desserts Shop now. Want to join us?"

"Better not. Max is meeting me at home. See you later."

Nina was taking a shortcut through Harborville's city park when she saw Mr. Hansen kneeling beside a new sidewalk. The city maintenance man frowned as she drew closer.

---

three musketeers, characters from the novel *The Three Musketeers* about a group of adventurous young soldiers
sandals, open shoes worn in warm weather
slow going, not happening quickly
sprained, hurt but didn't break
maintenance man, man who fixes and cleans things

48

✔ LITERARY CHECK

What does the **idiom** *"taking a shortcut" mean? Use your own words to define it.*

🌐 TESOL Standards

Goal 2, Standard 2—To use English to achieve academically in all content areas: Students will use English to obtain, process, construct, and provide subject matter information in spoken and written form.
Descriptors—Comparing and contrasting information; Retelling information; Selecting, connecting, and explaining information; Analyzing, synthesizing, and inferring from information; Understanding and producing technical vocabulary and text features according to content; Formulating and asking questions.

"Somebody jumped right in the middle here while the cement was still wet," he said, pointing at two narrow footprints embedded in the concrete. "Now I'll have to rip out this section and redo it. I sure can't leave the sidewalk looking like this!"

"Any idea of who did it?" Nina asked.

"A kid over there on the slide said that three girls named Brittany, Mitzi, and Jenny were the only ones near here. But he doesn't know which one ruined my sidewalk."

"I know who did it," Nina declared.

How did Nina figure it out?

The footprints were narrow. Jenny has wide feet. Brittany couldn't have jumped because of her sprained ankle. So Mitzi had to be the guilty one.

"You were able to walk into a quick solution for this case," Max told Nina later. "I sure am glad that I'm on your side."

"I had concrete evidence," Nina answered.

BEFORE YOU GO ON

1 What happened to Brittany in gym class?

2 Why is Mr. Hansen frowning?

On Your Own
What conclusion did you draw about the three girls and "whodunit"?

49

STEP 3: Monitor Progress

Ask students to check what they have understood in the reading. If you are using the Audio CD, pause the recording.

Before You Go On

Point out the Before You Go On box, and have students read and answer the questions. Remind them to reread the text if they don't know the answers to the first two questions. Explain that the On Your Own question asks for an opinion. Any thoughtful answer is correct.

ANSWERS

1. Brittany sprains her ankle in the gym.
2. Mr. Hansen is frowning because the sidewalk cement has dried with footprints in it.

On Your Own Have students write an answer to the On Your Own question on separate sheets of paper. Encourage volunteers to share their responses with the class. Then collect student responses to monitor their comprehension, writing skills, and fluency.

Differentiated Instruction

Beginning	Have students identify the title of each story. Then ask them who the author of each story is.
Early Intermediate	Ask students where Max and Nina live and how they know each other.
Intermediate	Have students describe what a detective does.
Special Needs	Allow students extra time to read the text. Monitor frequently, giving assistance as necessary with unfamiliar words and structures.

Preteaching Highlighted Words

Before reading this spread, point out the highlighted words and terms to students. Define each one, pointing out the location of the definition in the gloss at the bottom of the student book page. Make sure that students understand each highlighted word. If appropriate, ask students to generate original sentences using the highlighted words. When correcting original sentences, focus on usage of the highlighted word. Do not explicitly correct other errors. Model correct usage and grammar by repeating the student's current version of the sentence.

Model the
READING STRATEGY

Draw Conclusions

Have students turn to page 47 and review how to draw conclusions. **SAY:** *I can draw a conclusion about who may have something to do with the missing sign. The story says Mrs. Stearns is old and lives in one of only two houses on the block. I know that some older people do not like change. I can draw the conclusion that she has something to do with this mystery.*

The Case of the Disappearing Signs

Hy Conrad

Nina was eating cold pizza for lunch at Max's house one hot July day. Max's mom, Mrs. Decker, a real-estate agent, came in looking warm and weary.

"I'm so disgusted," she said. "Remember that old house over on Norton Drive that I listed? I put a FOR SALE sign up in the yard early this morning. I just drove by now and it's gone. This is the third sign this month that has disappeared."

"Why would anyone steal a realtor's signs?" Nina asked. "What would anybody do with them?"

"Who knows?" Mrs. Decker poured herself a glass of lemonade. "Probably some kids with nothing better to do. I suppose they could use the signs to build something. They were the wooden ones."

Max nudged Nina. "Want to bike over and see what we can find out?"

"Not much there to see," his mother told him. "Only two houses on that whole street. An old lady—Mrs. Stearns—lives in the house next to the empty one."

"Maybe she saw something," Nina said. "Let's go ask."

Half an hour later, the two were biking toward the end of Norton Drive. A pick-up truck was parked in front of the empty house. A man was standing on the sidewalk looking in all directions.

---

real-estate agent, person who sells houses
disgusted, upset or angry
listed, advertised; put on a list of items for sale
realtor's signs, signs that advertise that a house is for sale
nudged, pushed someone in a gentle way, using your elbow
pick-up truck, vehicle with an open part at the back, used for carrying things

50

"Do you kids know anything about this place?" he asked. "I'm from out of town, and my nephew, Paul, has been checking houses for me this past month. He thought I might like the one at the end of Norton Drive, so he let me borrow his truck to drive over here. But I don't know if this is the house he meant. There aren't any signs."

"This house is for sale," Max told him. "My mom is the real-estate agent."

"Great! Then can you tell me her name and company? I'd like to ask about this property. Paul tells me that houses in this part of town sell fast. He says this one has been on the market for quite some time. I'm glad I got here before it was sold! I just couldn't get over here any sooner."

As soon as Max gave him the information, the man drove off.

Nina stared after the truck. "Know what? His nephew, Paul, might have taken the signs. Maybe he didn't want people to see that the house was for sale until his uncle had a chance to look at it. You can put lots of things in the back of a truck."

Max nodded. "Let's ask Mrs. Stearns if she saw anything this morning."

Mrs. Stearns came to the door as soon as they knocked. She was gray-haired, but she stood straight and tall. "Oh, I think I know who might have taken those signs," she told them. "Freddie Swanson. He lives a block away, and he's always up to mischief."

---

on the market, for sale
mischief, bad behavior, especially by children

BEFORE YOU GO ON

1 Who does Mrs. Decker think stole the signs?

2 Why does Nina think that Paul might have stolen the signs?

On Your Own
What motive do you think someone might have for stealing a FOR SALE sign?

51

Study Skills: Dictionary

The word *sign* is used in this story as something put up in a yard to advertise a house for sale. Point out to students that in English this word has over 25 meanings. Have them look up the noun *sign* in a dictionary and list some of the definitions on the board. Some commonly used synonyms for *sign* are *mark*, *token*, *note*, and *symptom*.

STEP 5: Monitor Progress

Ask students to check what they have understood in the reading. If you are using the Audio CD, pause the recording.

Before You Go On

Answering questions before you go on to the next page in the text is one way to help predict what may happen next. When students answer each question, have them find the source of the information on that page.

ANSWERS
1. Mrs. Decker thinks some kids in the neighborhood stole the signs.
2. Nina thinks that Paul might have stolen the signs because he's been hoping no one would see the house before his uncle sees it.

On Your Own Have students write an answer to the On Your Own question on a separate sheet of paper. Encourage volunteers to share their responses with the class. Then collect student responses to monitor their comprehension, writing skills, and fluency.

Read

STEP 6: Teach

Preteaching Highlighted Words

Before reading this spread, point out the highlighted words and terms to students. Define each one, pointing out the location of the definition in the gloss at the bottom of the student book page. Make sure that students understand each highlighted word. If appropriate, ask students to generate original sentences using the highlighted words.

Across the Curriculum:
Science

One of the clues in "The Case of the Disappearing Signs" is the old and worn boards on the tree house. Explain that these boards were weathered. Weathering is erosion of wood from the sun, wind, and moisture. If wood is not protected by paint or stain, the weathering process removes about 1/4 inch of wood per century.

She held the door open as she talked, and Nina peeked inside. She liked the cozy living room. The sofa and chairs were velvet-covered antiques. Lace doilies covered the end tables. A large painting hung over the intricately carved fireplace mantel, and a cheerful fire crackled below.

"I know Freddie," Max said. "And I know where he lives. Let's go see him."

Freddie was putting a lawn mower in the garage when they reached his house. He mopped his brow as he talked to them. "Why would I take a dumb old sign?" he asked. "Besides, I've been out here doing yard work all morning."

---

antiques, very old, valuable objects
doilies, small circular mats or napkins
crackled, made popping sounds

52

TESOL Standards

Goal 3, Standard 3—To use English in socially and culturally appropriate ways: Students will use appropriate learning strategies to extend their sociolinguistic and sociocultural competence.
Descriptors—Experimenting with variations of language in social and academic settings; Seeking information about appropriate language use and behavior; Analyzing the social context to determine appropriate language use.

Nina stared past him at the garage. Her parents could hardly get their car in her garage at home because of all the stuff in it, but this one was practically bare. Then she noticed a crudely built tree house in the yard. The boards were gray and weather-beaten.

She and Max talked as they biked back to his house. Mrs. Decker was washing the lunch dishes when they ran into the house.

"We think we know who took the signs," Nina told her.

How did Nina and Max figure it out?

There was no evidence to show that Paul had used his truck to transport the signs. The boards in Freddie's tree house were too old and worn to have been made with the signs. Mrs. Stearns had a fire in her fireplace on a hot July day. She didn't want neighbors moving in next door, so she took the signs and burned them in her fireplace so nobody would know the house was for sale.

"That fire was a hot tip," Nina said later as she joined Max and Mrs. Decker for a cold drink of lemonade.

✔ **LITERARY CHECK**
*In this story, why is the phrase "a hot tip" a **pun**?*

---

practically bare, nearly empty
crudely built, not carefully made
transport, move or carry goods or people from one place to another
a hot tip, a good clue

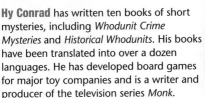

ABOUT THE **AUTHORS**

Carol Farley has always loved mysteries. Her first book, *Mystery of the Fog Man*, came from an idea she had in the sixth grade. She has written many books for children, including *The Case of the Vanishing Villain* and *The Case of the Lost Look-Alike*.

Hy Conrad has written ten books of short mysteries, including *Whodunit Crime Mysteries* and *Historical Whodunits*. His books have been translated into over a dozen languages. He has developed board games for major toy companies and is a writer and producer of the television series *Monk*.

BEFORE YOU GO ON

1 What does Nina like about Mrs. Stearns's house?

2 What does Nina notice about Freddie's garage and backyard?

💡 **On Your Own**
Do you think that fictional mysteries like these two short stories are easier or harder to solve than real-life mysteries? Explain.

53

Study Skills: Internet

Point out that Hy Conrad, the author of "The Case of the Disappearing Signs," not only writes mystery books, he is also a writer of a popular TV mystery show. Have students use the Internet to find out more about Hy Conrad.

✔ **LITERARY CHECK**

Read aloud the Literary Question, and remind students that they learned the meaning of *pun* on page 45. Answer: The word *hot* has many meanings. Among them are *very warm* and *very new and interesting*. The pun *A hot tip* is funny because the fire was not only very hot, it was very important in solving the mystery.

STEP 7: Monitor Progress

Ask students to check what they have understood in the reading.

Before You Go On

Remind students that these questions will help them monitor their progress. Put students in pairs to answer the questions. Encourage them to share their answers with the class.

ANSWERS
1. What Nina likes about Mrs. Stearn's house is her cozy living room.
2. Nina notices that there is a crudely built tree house in Freddie's backyard, and his garage is practically bare.

On Your Own Have students write an answer to the On Your Own question on separate sheets of paper. Encourage volunteers to share their responses with the class. Then collect student responses to monitor their comprehension, writing skills, and fluency.

Review the Purpose for Reading

Elicit responses to the Set a Purpose for Reading questions at the beginning of this reading. Remind students to relate their responses to the Big Question.

Teach & Apply

STEP 1: Introduce

Speaking Tip

Point out that gestures are body movements that help express or emphasize ideas and feelings. Discuss different gestures the actors could use in this scene. (moving arms and hands, pointing at each other, stepping forward at the mention of the cement)

 ### Reader's Theater

Performing by reading aloud is excellent practice for students. It gives them a reason to rehearse their reading several times, increase fluency, and improve expression and intonation.

Have students work with partners and decide who will play the roles of Nina and Max. Have students practice pronouncing their dialogue clearly. Suggest that they think about how their character feels at this point in the story.

Have partners rehearse in a quiet corner of the room. When ready, ask them to perform before the class.

STEP 2: Practice

Comprehension

Have students work individually or in small groups. They can respond orally or in writing.

ANSWERS

1. Mitzi
2. Mrs. Stearns
3. Nina knew that Brittany had hurt her ankle, and Jenny had wide feet, and the footprints are narrow. So the culprit must be Mitzi.
4. Mrs. Stearns's motive for taking the signs was that she didn't want anyone to buy the house and move in near her.
5. The author presents three suspects because it makes the mystery more intriguing than when there is only one.
6. I can tell that the authors have a sense of humor because they use puns.
7. Answers will vary.
8. Answers will vary.

Teaching Resources

- *Workbook*, p. 26
- CD-ROM/e-book, Reader's Theater, Comprehension, Response to Literature

---

READING 4 — Review and Practice

READER'S THEATER

Act out the following scene between Max and Nina.

Nina: Which of our cases did you like the best?

Max: Well, I really enjoyed solving the case of the missing signs. It was fun because the clues were difficult to find. This made the mystery more exciting for me. What about your favorite case?

Nina: I liked that case a lot, too. I like how we figured out that it wasn't Freddie. I wouldn't have wanted him to get the blame for something he didn't do.

Max: Being a detective is a lot of fun, especially when we have a chance to help people.

Nina: I enjoyed figuring out who stepped in the cement. This time, we got to protect property rather than people.

Max: That's true. Now people who visit the city park will have a smooth sidewalk to walk on. Being detectives lets us help people in so many ways.

 ### COMPREHENSION Workbook Page 26

Right There

1. Who jumped in the wet concrete?
2. Who stole the FOR SALE signs?

Think and Search

3. What clues did Nina use to solve "The Case of the Defaced Sidewalk"?
4. What motive did Mrs. Stearns have for her actions?

Author and You

5. Why does the author present three possible suspects for each crime? Why do mystery writers make readers suspect more than one character?
6. How can you tell that the authors of *Teenage Detectives* have a sense of humor?

54

> **Speaking TIP**
>
> Use gestures to help express your character's thoughts and feelings.

TESOL Standards

Goal 2, Standard 3—To use English to achieve academically in all content areas: Students will use appropriate learning strategies to construct and apply academic knowledge.
Descriptors—Applying self-monitoring and self-corrective strategies to build and expand a knowledge base; Determining and establishing the conditions that help one become an effective learner (e.g., when, where, how to study).

Goal 3, Standard 1—To use English in socially and culturally appropriate ways: Students will use the appropriate language variety, register, and genre according to audience, purpose, and setting.
Descriptors—Responding to and using humor appropriately; Using the appropriate degree of formality with different audiences and settings; Recognizing and using Standard English and vernacular dialects appropriately.

Goal 3, Standard 3—To use English in socially and culturally appropriate ways: Students will use appropriate learning strategies to extend their sociolinguistic and sociocultural competence.
Descriptors—Deciding when use of slang is appropriate.

T54

On Your Own

7. Would you like to pursue a career as a detective when you grow up? Why or why not?

8. Some people enjoy puns, while other people think they are silly. What is your opinion of puns? Do you find them funny? Explain.

DISCUSSION

Discuss in pairs or small groups.

1. Do you think Mitzi should have to fix the sidewalk? Why?

2. Can you think of a better way that Mrs. Stearns could have prevented people from moving in next door to her?

3. Mrs. Stearns does not want neighbors. A poet once said: "Good fences make good neighbors." He did not think neighbors should be too friendly. Explain what makes someone a good neighbor. Should neighbors be friendly or not?

Q Can all mysteries be solved? Were serious crimes committed in these stories? What is the difference between a minor crime and a serious one? Give examples of each.

Listening TIP

Do not interrupt your classmates when they are speaking. Save your questions until the speaker is finished.

RESPONSE TO LITERATURE

Workbook
Page 26

Max and Nina solved two mysteries. They used clues and what they already knew. Take one of these stories and change a few of the clues so that the outcome is different. You may want to use a chart like the one below:

Story title:	
Original Clue 1:	New Clue 1:
Original Clue 2:	New Clue 2:
Original Clue 3:	New Clue 3:
Original outcome:	New outcome:

When you are done writing, share your story with a partner. Don't read the ending! See if your partner can figure out the new ending.

55

Differentiated Instruction

Beginning	Ask students which of the two short stories they liked best.
Early Intermediate	Have students explain why they liked one short story better than the other.
Intermediate	Have students explain the clues in the illustrations on page 49 and page 52. Tell them that using visuals will help them understand more.
Greater Challenge	Have students read their stories with the new endings to the class. Ask the class which ending he or she liked better, theirs or the original.

STEP 3: Extend

Listening Tip

Remind students to show each other respect during a class discussion by listening without interruption. Students can jot down questions and ask them at the end of the presentation.

(CRI) Discussion

Congratulate students on successfully completing the reading. **SAY:** *We've learned a lot about the Big Question from the reading we've just completed. Now let's discuss a few questions about it.*

Model a discussion starter for each question. For the first question, **SAY:** *Do you think people should always have to pay for their crimes? Why or why not?*

For the second question, **SAY:** *What kind of person is Mrs. Stearns? Do you think she was always that way? Explain.*

For the third question, **SAY:** *What reasons do you think Mrs. Stearns had for not wanting neighbors? What might you say to her to persuade her that neighbors would be a good idea?*

Q Can all mysteries be solved? **SAY:** *Now that you've read* Teenage Detectives, *how does it affect the way you would answer the Big Question? Have you changed your ideas? How so?*

STEP 4: Assess

Response to Literature

Have students decide which story they want to change, and then copy the chart on this page to record their ideas. Together, fill in the original clues and outcome, and then brainstorm how to change them. **SAY:** *Here's an example. If there was no fire in Mrs. Stearn's fireplace, and Freddie said he went to a friend's house all morning but his tree house was made of new wood, I would draw the conclusion that Freddie stole the signs. Would you?*

STEP 1: Introduce

Review the definitions of a subject, a verb, and an indefinite pronoun. (Remind students that an indefinite pronoun does not name a specific person, place, or thing.) Point out that the subject and verb in a sentence agree, even when the subject is an indefinite pronoun. Tell students you will be reviewing subject-verb agreement with indefinite pronouns.

STEP 2: Teach

Grammar and Writing

Indefinite Pronouns Read aloud the information and examples of indefinite pronouns on this page. Ask students to find other examples from the story. Write the sentences on the board and underline the subject and verb in each. (i.e. p. 48, "But I have such a wide foot, <u>nothing seems</u> to fit"; p. 49, "<u>Somebody jumped</u> right in the middle here…"; p. 51, "Do you kids <u>know anything</u> about this place?") **SAY:** *Notice that in each sentence, the subject (indefinite pronoun) and verb agree. If the indefinite pronoun is singular, the verb is singular, whether it's in the present or the past.*

STEP 3: Practice

Write the first Practice sentence on the board: "Each (thinks/think) Freddie stole the signs." Model how to complete it. **SAY:** *I know that the indefinite pronoun in this sentence is the word* each. *It is a singular subject. Therefore I need a singular verb to agree with it. I will choose* thinks, *because it is the singular form of the verb.* Pair English learners with proficient English speakers to work on the rest of the sentences. Have volunteers write their answers on the board.

ANSWERS

1. thinks; 2. is; 3. was;
4. love; 5. use; 6. was

Teaching Resources

- *Workbook*, pp. 27–28
- CD-ROM/e-book, Grammar, Writing
- *Transparencies*, Writing Model 24
- *Transparencies*, *Resources*, Graphic Organizer 7
- *Assessment*, Reading 4 Test, pp. 47–50

Grammar and Writing

GRAMMAR, USAGE, AND MECHANICS

Subject-Verb Agreement with Indefinite Pronouns

Indefinite pronouns are words that don't name a specific person, place, or thing. In the mystery stories you just read, the authors use indefinite pronouns to make generalizations or to refer to a previously used noun.

> Generalization:
> Why would **anyone** steal a realtor's sign? [non-specific person]

> Previously used noun:
> Brittany, Mitzi, and Jenny were the only **ones** near here. But he doesn't know which **one** ruined my sidewalk. [*ones* refers to Brittany, Mitzi, AND Jenny; *one* refers to Brittany, Mitzi, OR Jenny]

An indefinite pronoun must agree with the verb in the sentence. An indefinite pronoun is either singular (one person or thing) or plural (more than one person or thing). If the indefinite pronoun is singular, the verb must be singular; if it is plural, the verb must be plural.

Singular				Plural
anybody	somebody	everybody	nobody	both
anyone	someone	everyone	no one	few
anything	something	everything	nothing	many
each	one			ones

Practice **Workbook Page 27**

Copy the sentences into your notebook. Work with a partner. Circle the verb in each sentence that agrees with the indefinite pronoun.

1. Each (thinks / think) Freddie stole the signs.
2. Everything in the story (is / are) interesting.
3. Someone (was / were) guilty of stepping in the cement.
4. Both (loves / love) solving mysteries.
5. Which ones (uses / use) clues to solve mysteries?
6. No one (was / were) in the house.

56

TESOL Standards

Goal 1, Standard 1—To use English to communicate in social settings: Students will use English to participate in social interactions.
Descriptors—Sharing and requesting information; Expressing needs, feelings, and ideas.

Goal 1, Standard 2—To use English to communicate in social settings: Students will interact in, through, and with spoken and written English for personal expression and enjoyment.
Descriptors—Describing, reading about, or participating in a favorite activity; Expressing personal needs, feelings, and ideas.

Goal 3, Standard 1—To use English in socially and culturally appropriate ways: Students will use the appropriate language variety, register, and genre according to audience, purpose, and setting.
Descriptors—Using a variety of writing styles appropriate for different audiences, purposes, and settings; Responding to and using idioms appropriately; Responding to and using humor appropriately; Determining when it is appropriate to use a language other than English; Determining appropriate topics for interaction.

WRITING A DESCRIPTIVE PARAGRAPH

Describe an Event

On this page, you will describe a mysterious event using a graphic organizer like the one at the right. Think about the four readings in Unit 1. How did each writer describe puzzling events? Write three headings in your notebook: *Event, People, Place.* Jot down ideas and details under the headings.

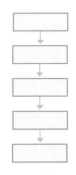

One of the simplest ways to organize a description of an event is to put the ideas and details in chronological, or time, order. This means putting the events in the order in which they occurred, from first to last. Use words that help your reader follow each step in the sequence of what happened. These words include *first, second, last, next, then, finally, today,* and *yesterday.*

Here is a model of a descriptive paragraph about a mysterious event. Notice that the writer puts her details in chronological order and includes a pun.

> *Anna Espínola*
>
> The Case of the Missing Hoop
> I'm a good detective, but even I had trouble with one case. I bought my sister Sue a striped hula hoop for her birthday this year. First, I hid it in a shopping bag under a pile of old clothes in the closet. Then I decided not to tell anybody because I wanted it to be a big surprise. When Sue's big day came, Mom asked Sue to take some old clothes to our local thrift shop. Finally, I had a chance to wrap the gift, but the hoop had vanished. I looked everywhere but couldn't find it. A week later, I solved the mystery. I was passing the thrift store and saw the hoop in the window for $5. When Sue had dropped off the clothes, she had given away the hoop, too, without knowing it. I bought the hoop again, and gave it to her. Boy did I have to jump through hoops for my sister this year.

Practice

Workbook
Page 28

Write a descriptive paragraph about a made-up event that puzzled you. Try to include some humor, puns, and idioms. Use a sequence-of-events chart to organize your ideas and details. Check your subject-verb agreement.

Writing Checklist

VOICE:
☑ My paragraph describes an event in a unique way; it is humorous and includes puns and idioms.

ORGANIZATION:
☑ My paragraph presents details in a clear chronological order.

57

Accelerate Language Development

Indefinite Pronouns that Can Be Singular or Plural

Point out that there are a few indefinite pronouns that can be both singular and plural: *all, most, none, some.* Depending on whether the indefinite pronoun is referring to or replacing a singular or a plural noun, the verb is either singular or plural. Example: *You have a lot of money in your pocket.* *Some* *of it* *is* *mine.* *Some* in this case is referring to the singular noun *money,* and therefore the verb has to be singular. Example: *Many people have seen this movie.* *Some of them* *are* *children.* In this case *some* is referring to *children,* a plural noun, and the verb therefore has to be in the plural. Write other examples on the board, leaving a blank for the verb form, and ask for volunteers to fill in the blanks.

STEP 1: Introduce

Tell students that a descriptive paragraph can describe an event. This kind of paragraph is often organized in chronological, or time, order.

STEP 2: Teach

Writing a Descriptive Paragraph

Describe an Event With students, brainstorm words and phrases that show chronological order. (i.e. *first, second, third, next, then, when that happened, in the meantime, at last,* and *finally.*) Then explain that students will be creating a paragraph in chronological order to describe a made-up event. Students should try to make it funny, using puns or idioms.

Model Writing Skill Point out the sequence-of-events chart on the student page, and draw it on the board. Do not write the words in the chart. Then ask a volunteer to read aloud "The Case of the Missing Hoop," and with students, fill in the chart. **SAY:** *When I read this paragraph, I was looking for words that show chronological order. The third sentence starts with "First," so I'll write the sentence "First I hid it in a huge shopping bag…" in the first box. I'll write the sentence "Then I decided not tell anybody…" in the second box, because that's the next sequence word I found. Try to find two more sentences with sequence words and write them on the chart.*

STEP 3: Assess

Have students evaluate their work, using the Writing Checklist.

Writing Checklist Note

Voice Check that students use a humorous voice that includes puns or idioms.

Organization Check that details in the paragraph are presented in chronological order.

Unit Wrap-Up

Link the Readings

Critical Thinking Ask students how the readings in the unit are the same (they're mysteries) and different (they have different purposes, and the content relates to the mysteries differently).

Write the words *entertain*, *inform*, and *persuade*, on the board, and explain the meanings of these purposes for writing. Then write the Big Question and model how to use the chart on this page. Have partners work together to complete it.

ANSWERS

Title of Reading	Purpose	Big Question Link
From *Chasing Vermeer*	to entertain	The origin of the book that Petra found was mysterious.
From *G Is for Googol*	to inform	The Fibonacci sequence in nature is still a mystery.
"Fact or Fiction?"	to inform	We still cannot solve some of these mysteries.
Teenage Detectives	to entertain	The characters solve mysteries.

 Discussion

Remind students to refer to the charts they created to find information for their discussion. Point out that *Chasing Vermeer* is different from *G Is for Googol* in that it is a work of fiction. It was written to entertain. *G Is for Googol* is nonfiction and was written to inform. Both readings concern mysteries that haven't been solved.

Q Can all mysteries be solved? SAY: *Now that you've read the entire unit, how does it affect the way you would answer the Big Question? How have you changed your ideas about natural and fictional mysteries?*

Fluency Check

Review with students how to use a stopwatch or a clock's second hand. Then have them draw the fluency chart, and show them how to write minutes and seconds (i.e. 1:15). If students don't improve after several readings, look closely at their comprehension of English and the passage vocabulary. Remind students that reading quickly is important, but above all, they need to understand what they are reading.

Teaching Resources

• *Assessment*, Unit 1 Test, pp. 133–142
• CD-ROM/e-book, Fluency Check, Projects

Link the Readings

Critical Thinking

Look back at the readings in this unit. Think about what they have in common. They all tell about mysteries. Yet they do not all have the same purpose. The purpose of one reading might be to inform, while the purpose of another might be to entertain or persuade. In addition, the content of each reading relates to mysteries differently. Now copy the chart below into your notebook and complete it.

Title of Reading	Purpose	Big Question Link
From *Chasing Vermeer*		
From *G Is for Googol*	*to inform*	
"Fact or Fiction?"		
Teenage Detectives		*The characters solve mysteries.*

Discussion

Discuss in pairs or small groups.
- How is the excerpt from *Chasing Vermeer* different from the excerpt from *G Is for Googol*? How do both readings concern mysteries?
- **Can all mysteries be solved?** What conclusion can you draw about mysteries in nature, based on what you read in "Fact or Fiction?" and *G Is for Googol*? How are these mysteries the same as fictional mysteries such as the ones in *Teenage Detectives*? How are they different?

Fluency Check

Work with a partner. Choose a paragraph from one of the readings. Take turns reading it for one minute. Count the total number of words you read. Practice saying the words you had trouble reading. Take turns reading the paragraph three more times. Did you read more words each time? Copy the chart below into your notebook and record your speeds.

	1st Speed	2nd Speed	3rd Speed	4th Speed
Words Per Minute				

TESOL Standards

Goal 1, Standard 1—To use English to communicate in social settings: Students will use English to participate in social interactions.
Descriptors—Engaging in conversations; Conducting transactions.

Goal 1, Standard 3—To use English to communicate in social settings: Students will use learning strategies to extend their communicative competence.
Descriptors—Seeking support and feedback from others; Using the primary language to ask for clarification; Selecting different media to help understand language.

Goal 2, Standard 2—To use English to achieve academically in all content areas: Students will use English to obtain, process, construct, and provide subject matter information in spoken and written form.
Descriptors—Listening to, speaking, reading, and writing about subject matter information; Gathering information orally and in writing; Selecting, connecting, and explaining information; Analyzing, synthesizing, and inferring from information; Responding to the work of peers and others; Representing information visually and interpreting information presented visually; Understanding and producing technical vocabulary and text features according to content area; Demonstrating knowledge through application in a variety of contexts.

Projects

Work in pairs or small groups. Choose one of these projects.

1 Create a skit based on *Teenage Detectives*. Choose one of the stories and perform it as a play for the class. You may wish to include simple costumes and music, too.

2 Create a scale model of one of the real-life places described in "Fact or Fiction?" For example, you might construct a model of the Great Pyramid at Giza, Stonehenge, or Machu Picchu. Start by establishing your scale (for example, 1 centimeter equals 5 meters or 1 inch equals 10 feet). Then choose a building material and create your model. Write a description of the mystery on an index card to put with the model.

3 What do you think happens in the next chapter of *Chasing Vermeer*? Tell a classmate what you think will happen in the next chapter. Then read the book to see if your prediction is correct.

4 Draw a picture of something from nature that shows the Fibonacci sequence. You may choose a sunflower or pinecone, for instance. Explain the number sequence to your classmates.

Further Reading

To find out more about the theme of this unit, choose from these reading suggestions.

Stranger than Fiction Urban Myths, Phil Healey and Rick Glanvill
This Penguin Reader® is full of strange, funny, and sometimes unbelievable myths.

The Wright 3, Blue Balliett
In this sequel to *Chasing Vermeer*, Petra, Calder, and a new member of the detective team join forces to save Frank Lloyd Wright's Robie House.

From the Mixed-Up Files of Mrs. Basil E. Frankweiler,
E.L. Konigsburg
Hiding in New York's Museum of Metropolitan Art, a sister and brother spot a beautiful angel statue. Could it be a work by Michelangelo? Mrs. Frankweiler, the statue's previous owner, holds the key to the mystery.

59

(CRI) Home-School Connection

These projects provide students several ways to practice and apply what they have learned in this unit. The projects can be completed independently, with partners, or in small groups. Students can complete the projects either in the classroom or at home.

Further Reading

Each book listed on this page pertains to the Big Question. Encourage students to peruse them in their free time or read them for extra-credit book reports. The first book on the list is easily accessible, the second is accessible, and the third is challenging.

Websites

Log onto www.LongmanKeystone.com for links to other interesting websites about solving mysteries.

Differentiated Instruction

Beginning	Ask students to identify which readings were nonfiction. Ask them how they know.
Early Intermediate	Have students explain why they enjoyed a particular reading.
Intermediate	When doing the Discussion activity, remind students to listen attentively to what other students are saying.
Struggling Readers	Ask students to think about the readings in this unit and choose one that they would like to know more about. Ask them to give reasons for their choice.

Listening & Speaking Workshop

STEP 1: Introduce

CRI Begin this workshop by discussing what a guessing game is. Model how to play a guessing game, such as Twenty Questions. Ask a contestant to select a place, such as an abandoned cabin, an old warehouse, a pirate ship, or the Louvre Museum, and tell no one what was selected. Remind the other students to take turns asking the contestant "Yes/No" questions, such as *Is the mystery place in a city? Is it a big place?* Students get twenty chances to figure out the name of the place.

Think About It Help students brainstorm topic ideas that would make good descriptions for the guessing game. As they brainstorm, students can list their ideas under one of two categories: Objects or Places. Encourage students to select the idea they think would be most fun to describe.

STEP 2: Teach

Gather and Organize Information Draw the sensory-details web on the board. Model how to use it by asking students what a place like an old, abandoned cabin looks, sounds, smells, and feels like. Fill in their answers on the web. Then write on the board the organizational steps that appear on this page: *Research, Order Your Notes*, and *Use Visuals*. Go over the directions, and clarify any questions. Point out that *Order Your Notes* tells you to put the note cards in the order they will be used in the presentation. The word *visuals* is used to describe things you can see, like drawings.

Teaching Resources
- CD-ROM/e-book, Gather and Organize Information

Put It All Together

LISTENING & SPEAKING WORKSHOP
Description Guessing Game

You will describe an object or place and let your classmates guess what it is.

1 THINK ABOUT IT In this unit, you've learned about all kinds of solved and unsolved mysteries. You've also learned how to write descriptions. Now you are going to play a guessing game in which you will describe an object or place related to a crime. Your classmates will act as detectives and try to guess what your object or place is.

In small groups, discuss some of the objects and places discussed in the unit readings. Think of other objects and places that might be related to a crime. Write down your ideas.

Work on your own to make a list of objects and places you could describe in this guessing game. Choose one, and don't tell anyone what it is.

2 GATHER AND ORGANIZE INFORMATION
Brainstorm details about the object or place you have chosen. Organize them in a sensory details web.

Research Go to the library, look at pictures, or use the Internet to get more information about your object or place. Add the new details to your web.

Order Your Notes Think about how you will describe your object or place to the class. Which details will you include? Write them on separate note cards. Do you want to begin with the most important detail and end with the least important one? Do you want to use spatial order, such as top to bottom or left to right? Select the method of organization that works best with your topic. Put your note cards in that order.

Use Visuals Find or draw a picture of your object or place. You will show it to the class after someone guesses your object or place. Do not show it to anyone now!

▲ Alfred Hitchcock was famous for making mysterious movies.

60

🌐 **TESOL Standards**

Goal 3, Standard 2—To use English in socially and culturally appropriate ways: Students will use nonverbal communication appropriate to audience, purpose, and setting.
Descriptors—Interpreting and responding appropriately to nonverbal cues and body language; Demonstrating knowledge of acceptable nonverbal classroom behaviors; Using acceptable tone, volume, stress, and intonation in various social settings; Recognizing and adjusting behavior in response to nonverbal cues.

Goal 3, Standard 3—To use English in socially and culturally appropriate ways: Students will use appropriate learning strategies to extend their sociolinguistic and sociocultural competence.
Descriptors—Experimenting with variations of language in social and academic settings; Seeking information about appropriate language use and behavior; Analyzing the social context to determine appropriate language use; Rehearsing variations of language use in different social and academic settings.

3 PRACTICE AND PRESENT Use your note cards as an outline, but practice describing your object or place without reading them. Ask a friend or family member to listen to your presentation, or tape-record yourself and listen to the tape. Find the places where you need more work. Keep practicing until you can present your description smoothly and confidently. Try to include enough details so that the audience can guess your object or place, but not so many that you give away the answer too easily. Remember not to let anyone see your visual.

Deliver Your Description Speak loudly enough so that everyone can hear you. Look at people as you speak. Emphasize key details with your voice and gestures. When you're finished, invite students to guess your topic. After someone guesses correctly, or if no one guesses correctly, show your picture of the object or place.

4 EVALUATE THE PRESENTATION
A good way to improve your skills as a speaker and listener is by evaluating each presentation you give and hear. Use this checklist to help you judge your presentation and the presentations of your classmates.

- ☑ Did the description include lots of sensory details?
- ☑ Could you picture the object or place that was being described?
- ☑ Could you hear and understand what the speaker was saying?
- ☑ Did the speaker seem to be having fun?
- ☑ What suggestions do you have for improving the presentation?

🔊 *Speaking* TIPS

Be sure you are speaking slowly and clearly. Ask your listeners for feedback. Can they understand all of your words?

Try to stay relaxed and have fun as you give your description. Remember, this is a game!

🔈 *Listening* TIPS

Listen for clues to the speaker's topic. Try to figure out right away if the topic is an object or a place. Then you can get more specific.

Write down key details as you listen. Think about how they relate to objects and places you know.

61

STEP 3: Practice

Practice and Present With students, read the information about preparing for their presentations. Point out that practicing will help them feel confident and more relaxed. Explain that another way to practice is to face a mirror and present to yourself. In addition, remind students to review the Speaking and Listening Tips.

Speaking Tip

Review with students that just before they present, they should remind themselves to speak slowly and clearly, take a long, deep breath, and then begin. Point out that the better prepared they are, the more relaxed they'll be when they speak.

Listening Tip

Be sure students know exactly what they will be listening for. If appropriate, review the purpose of the speeches. Encourage students to keep a pencil and paper ready as they listen. Jotting down a few key points will help them remember what they want to say after the speech is delivered.

STEP 4: Assess

Evaluate the Presentation Suggest that students use the Listening and Speaking Checklist on this page to evaluate the presentations. On a sheet of paper, have students number 1 to 5 for each presentation. After they listen to a speaker, they read the five questions on the checklist and write *Yes* or *No* next to the first four. For the fifth question, they offer specific examples taken directly from the presentation. Remind students that feedback should be given in a kind, helpful way.

Differentiated Instruction

Beginning	Have students find a visual or draw a picture of the object or place to present to the class once someone has guessed what it is.
Early Intermediate	Have students take notes during presentations. Remind them that paying attention to details like sounds, sights, smells, etc., will help them guess the object or place.
Intermediate	Have students come up with questions to ask the presenter if they still cannot guess the object or place when the presentation is finished.
Greater Challenge	In addition to making the presentation, ask students to act out the object like in the game of charades.

Writing Workshop

In this workshop, students will use the steps of the writing process. They will apply each of the steps and the characteristics of descriptive writing to write a descriptive essay.

STEP 2: Teach

Prewrite Review the steps in the writing process with students: Prewrite, Draft, Revise, Edit and Proofread, and Publish. Point out that these steps will help make the job of writing their descriptive essays easier and more orderly. Write the words *descriptive essay* on the board, and review with students that an essay usually includes an introduction, two or more body paragraphs, and a conclusion. **SAY:** *The key to descriptive writing is to describe the topic in a way that the reader can imagine it. Remember to use your five senses, and write in an organized way.*

Have students read the Prewrite instructions on this page and brainstorm essay topics. List possible topics on the board. Then model how to use a word web to develop one of them. **SAY:** *The name of the topic goes in the center oval. Ideas and details about the topic go in the outer ovals.*

Once students have selected a topic, have them complete a word web about it.

Draft Explain that a draft is a work in progress and that it does not have to be perfect. Students can make further changes later on. Review the parts of a descriptive essay and the draft of Talia's essay on page 63. Ask students to identify the introductory paragraph, the three body paragraphs, and the concluding paragraph.

Teaching Resources

- *Transparencies, Resources,* Graphic Organizer 3
- *Transparencies,* Writing Model 25, Proofreader's Marks 51
- CD-ROM/e-book, Writing Workshop
- *Workbook,* pp. 29–30

WRITING WORKSHOP
Descriptive Essay

In this workshop you will write a descriptive essay. An essay is a group of paragraphs that develops a specific idea. Most essays include an introduction, two or more body paragraphs, and a conclusion. In a descriptive essay, the writer describes a person, place, thing, event, or experience. Sensory details help create a vivid picture of the topic in readers' minds. Information is presented in an order that makes sense: chronological order, spatial order, or order of importance.

Your assignment for this workshop is to write a five-paragraph descriptive essay about a mysterious and memorable scene that amazed you.

1 **PREWRITE** Brainstorm possible topics for your essay in your notebook. Choose a topic that is full of sensory details. You might want to describe a spectacular dinosaur exhibit or the best July 4th fireworks display you ever experienced. Or you might want to describe an amusement park or a wax museum.

Carlsbad Caverns ▼

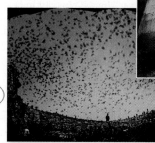

List and Organize Ideas and Details After you choose a topic, use a graphic organizer such as a sensory details chart or a word web to develop your essay. A student named Talia wrote about what she saw during a visit to Carlsbad Caverns, New Mexico. She used a word web to gather her ideas and details.

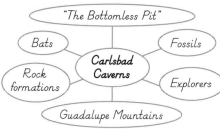

2 **DRAFT** Use the model on page 65 and your graphic organizer to help you write a first draft. Remember to include an introductory paragraph, three body paragraphs, and a concluding paragraph.

62

---

3 REVISE Read over your draft. As you do so, ask yourself the questions in the writing checklist. Use the questions to help you revise your essay.

SIX TRAITS OF WRITING CHECKLIST

- ☑ **IDEAS:** Does my essay describe a memorable and mysterious scene?
- ☑ **ORGANIZATION:** Are my ideas presented in an order that makes sense?
- ☑ **VOICE:** Does my writing express who I am?
- ☑ **WORD CHOICE:** Do I include vivid sensory details?
- ☑ **SENTENCE FLUENCY:** Do my sentences flow smoothly?
- ☑ **CONVENTIONS:** Does my writing follow the rules of grammar, usage, and mechanics?

Here are the changes Talia plans to make when she revises her first draft:

> Carlsbad Caverns
>
> Imagine ~~you are~~ taking an elevator down into another world—a world where there are stalagmites sticking up in front of you and stalactites hanging from above. Inside this place, It's ~~more~~ cold*er* and damp*er* than the world you just left. Bats swoop fly all around and, if you look hard enough, you might even find the fossil of an ancient sea snail. These are examples of what a traveler might discover on a trip into Carlsbad Caverns.
>
> Although you can find different rock formations in all caves, the ones in Carlsbad Caverns are particularly special. People have given very funny-sounding names to these different formations, because the rocks sometimes look like everyday objects. "Cave Popcorn,"

63

Revise Point out that the revising step focuses on improving the content and wording of a draft. It is not the same thing as editing. Have students look over Talia's first draft and notice the kinds of changes she made. (She deleted unnecessary words, replaced uninteresting verbs for more descriptive ones, added more details, and moved around text.) Ask students to look at their own drafts and make changes in content or wording. Be sure they review the Six Traits of Writing Checklist and answer each of the questions.

STEP 3: Assess

Writing Checklist Note

Read aloud the Six Traits of Writing Checklist with students, and go over each entry.

Ideas *Check that the scene you are describing sounds interesting, mysterious, or memorable.*

Organization *Check that your essay makes sense to readers. Your first paragraph introduces your topic. The next three paragraphs develop the topic with interesting details. The last paragraph ties up your ideas.*

Voice *Check that your writing sounds like you and is in your own style.*

Word Choice *Check that you include words that awaken the senses, capture your readers' attention, and make your essay memorable.*

Sentence Fluency *Check that your essay flows smoothly from one sentence to another. Use linking words to start some sentences, such as First, Then, At that time, Therefore, So, The next time, and so on.*

Conventions *Check that you use complete sentences, with a subject and a verb. Use objects and prepositional phrases correctly.*

Differentiated Instruction

Beginning	Before students start writing, brainstorm ideas with the class. Write students' suggestions of mysterious places or scenes on the board.
Early Intermediate	Refer students to the Writing Handbook at the end of their books for additional help in writing their first draft.
Intermediate	Tell students to study Talia's first draft. Ask them to explain to you why she made the changes she did.
Special Needs	Have students read Talia's draft carefully. Review the changes Talia made with them, providing explanations as necessary.

Edit and Proofread Pair English learners with English-proficient students. Review with students the kinds of edits Talia made on her final draft. (She deleted a comma, added quotation marks, added a period, and capitalized a word.) Discuss why you think each edit was made. Keep dictionaries nearby to check spelling.

"Limestone Curtain," and "Bent Straw," are just a few of the oddly shaped rocks in these caves.

All the different "rooms" of the caves also have unique names, like "Mystery Room, "Chocolate High," and "Ballroom Bedroom." The Bottomless Pit got its name when early explorers tossed stones down the hole to see how deep it was. They never heard a sound. Later

Since the explorers   ∧*they figured the pit didn't have a bottom*

exploration proved that the pit was only 140 feet deep, but the ∧*soft* dirt at the bottom muffled the sound of the falling rocks.

Nowadays, lots of bats live in Carlsbad caverns. In addition to rock formations, there are living things and traces of other living things found in the caves The presence of ocean fossils reveals that around 250 million years ago the area was a coastline that eventually turned into a limestone layer of rock. In fact, there are sixteen species of bats, but most are Mexican Free-tailed bats.

Carlsbad Caverns are located in the Guadalupe Mountains in Southeast New Mexico. If you are ever in that area, you will definitely want to check out Carlsbad Caverns. They are ∧*as* mysterious

as a strange land in an amazing dream
and memorable.
         ∧

 4 EDIT AND PROOFREAD Workbook Page 29

Copy your revised essay onto a clean sheet of paper. Read it again. Correct any errors in grammar, word usage, mechanics, and spelling. Here are the additional changes Talia plans to make when she prepares her final draft.

TESOL Standards

Goal 3, Standard 1—To use English in socially and culturally appropriate ways: Students will use the appropriate language variety, register, and genre according to audience, purpose, and setting.
Descriptors—Using the appropriate degree of formality with different audiences and settings; Recognizing and using Standard English and vernacular dialects appropriately; Using a variety of writing styles appropriate for different audiences, purposes, and settings; Determining appropriate topics for interaction.

Talia Marcus

Carlsbad Caverns

Imagine taking an elevator down into another world—a world where there are stalagmites sticking up in front of you and stalactites hanging from above. Inside this place, it's colder and damper than the world you just left. Bats swoop all around and, if you look hard enough, you might even find the fossil of an ancient sea snail. These are examples of what a traveler might discover on a trip into Carlsbad Caverns.

Although you can find different rock formations in all caves, the ones in Carlsbad Caverns are particularly special. People have given very funny-sounding names to these different formations, because the rocks sometimes look like everyday objects. "Cave Popcorn," "Limestone Curtain," and "Bent Straw," are just a few of the oddly shaped rocks in these caves.

All the different "rooms" of the caves also have unique names, like "Mystery Room," "Chocolate High," and "Ballroom Bedroom." The Bottomless Pit got its name when early explorers tossed stones down the hole to see how deep it was. Since the explorers never heard a sound, they figured the pit didn't have a bottom. Later exploration proved that the pit was only 140 feet deep, but the soft dirt at the bottom muffled the sound of the falling rocks.

In addition to rock formations, there are living things and traces of other living things found in the caves. The presence of ocean fossils reveals that around 250 million years ago the area was a coastline that eventually turned into a limestone layer of rock. Nowadays, lots of bats live in Carlsbad caverns. In fact, there are sixteen species of bats, but most are Mexican Free-tailed bats.

Carlsbad Caverns are located in the Guadalupe Mountains in Southeast New Mexico. If you are ever in that area, you will definitely want to check out Carlsbad Caverns. They are as mysterious and memorable as a strange land in an amazing dream.

5 PUBLISH Prepare your final draft. Share your essay with your teacher and classmates.

Workbook
Page 30

65

Publish Have students look at their own final drafts, and discuss their options for publishing. Explain that to publish means to share your writing with others, or to make it public. **SAY:** *Think about how best to publish your piece of writing. Does your essay need illustrations? Photos? Colored paper? Before you copy your final changes, plan how you will show your writing, such as in a class book or on a bulletin board. The computer may have some clip art or other illustrations for you to add.*

Career Connection

Detective Explain that a large part of the job of a detective is looking for clues and solving puzzles and mysteries. Some detectives work for the police force, solving crimes. Others work as scientists, solving medical mysteries or questions. A detective needs to be a keen observer, a logical thinker, and a systematic note taker. A detective writes many reports and must organize records so others can use the findings at investigations and court trials.

Accelerate Language Development

Capitalization

Not all languages distinguish between upper and lower case. Arabic uses only one letter size, and Chinese and Japanese do not have letters to capitalize. European lanuages did not introduce capitalization until the 13th century. The rules vary from language to language. For example German capitalizes all nouns; French does not capitalize the days of the week. Tell students to refer to the Handbook at the back of their book to review the rules of English capitalization.

STEP 1: Introduce

Remind students that the Big Question is *Can all mysteries be solved?* **SAY:** *You have read about some mysteries in this unit.* Explain that some artists enjoy working with codes and rebuses (pictures or symbols, often presented as a puzzle) in their artworks. These works show that art can be fun as well as serious.

STEP 2: Teach

Visual Literacy

Mike Wilkins Point out the image on page 66. Explain that Wilkins used license plates from all fifty states and the District of Columbia in *Preamble*. To learn more about how the automobile impacted living patterns in the United States, go to the Smithsonian National Museum of History online exhibition "America on the Move" and look at the Classroom Activity Guide (www.LongmanKeystone.com). Click on "Unit Four: 1950s and 1960s" and use this lesson to look at photographs that show new sprawling suburban neighborhoods, commuters catching a train, and other images that reflect the growing exodus of people from the inner city to the suburbs, due partly to car ownership and new roads. **ASK:** *What kind of community do you live in—urban, suburban, or rural? Does a major highway go through your city/town? If so, how does that highway affect the way people live in your area?*

Have students create their own rebuses to make a personal statement. They can use cardboard to cut out letter-and-number stencils, and/or paint or heavy markers. Have students present their rebuses to the class to see if their classmates can interpret them.

Robert Indiana Point to the sculpture on page 67. Explain that Indiana enjoyed working with numbers and letters as symbols in his art. Go to the Smithsonian American Art Museum website feature "Bottlecaps to Brushes" (www.LongmanKeystone.com) for a Lesson Plan on how students can use letters and numbers to create their own artworks. Have students make a sign for a room using numbers and letters that hold a special meaning to them, such as a birth date or address. Students must decide what shape and color they want their sign to be; they can trace a plate or even place one shape on top of another using glue. Have them share their signs with the class and see if other students can decipher their meaning.

Teaching Resources

• *Workbook*, pp. 31–32
• CD-ROM/e-book, Smithsonian

Solving the PUZZLE of Letters and NUMBERS

M*ost of us have seen movies in which someone must figure out a code. Sometimes the character has to find a treasure. Other times he or she might have to use the code to save a friend. Often the code uses letters. We can recognize the letters but not the words they spell. They make no sense until we figure out the pattern of the code.*

Some American artists even hide coded messages or stories in their work. They like to use them because the codes add a little mystery and fun!

Mike Wilkins, *Preamble* (1987)

When you look at them one by one, none of the license plates in Mike Wilkins's *Preamble* makes much sense. The trick is to read the license plates from left to right, starting in the top left corner. By the end of the first line, you realize that Wilkins is composing the preamble to the United States Constitution. The letters on the first two license plates, WE TH and P PUL, stand for the words "We the People . . ." LIBBER is part of the word "Liberty."

The plates are listed in alphabetical order by state, with Alabama first and Wyoming last. Wilkins put the license plates against a large square background.

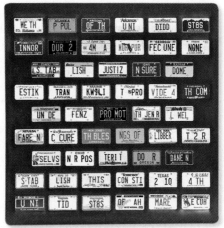

▲ Mike Wilkins, *Preamble*, 1987, metal, 96 x 96 in., Smithsonian American Art Museum

66

TESOL Standards

Goal 2, Standard 2—To use English to achieve academically in all content areas: Students will use English to obtain, process, construct, and provide subject matter information in spoken and written form.
Descriptors—Analyzing, synthesizing, and inferring from information; Hypothesizing and predicting; Formulating and asking questions.

Goal 2, Standard 2—To use English to achieve academically in all content areas: Students will use English to obtain, process, construct, and provide subject matter information in spoken and written form.
Descriptors—Representing information visually and interpreting information presented visually.

Goal 2, Standard 3—To use English to achieve academically in all content areas: Students will use appropriate learning strategies to construct and apply academic knowledge.
Descriptors—Focusing attention selectively; Applying basic reading comprehension skills such as skimming, scanning, previewing, and reviewing text; Planning how and when to use cognitive strategies and applying them appropriately to a learning task.

The background brings all the license plates together into one work of art. It also highlights the differences in color between the plates.

It took a year for Wilkins to get license plates from all fifty states and the District of Columbia. He had to figure out word and number combinations that worked together to form the preamble. Each state has different laws about the number of letters and numbers that could be used on a plate. Eventually, Wilkins put this rebus (a puzzle that uses letters and numbers) together. This artwork celebrates the way the fifty states and the capital work together to form the United States.

Robert Indiana, *Five* (1984)

The artist Robert Indiana based *Five* on a poem called "The Great Figure," which is about a fire truck. He used objects that people had thrown away, like an old wood beam from a house. He also used a wooden dowel (the pole running through the beam) and two metal wheels to make the sculpture. At the top of the beam, he painted a small number 5 and a larger 5 over a red five-point star. They all come together to form one image.

Indiana's color choices seem bright when seen against the dull wood beam. He liked to use letters and numbers to make the printed portions of his work look as though they were part of a commercial sign. The red letter *L* on the very top adds to the idea that there is some mystery or story going on that we must figure out. In the same way that we would read a road sign, we must study how all of the various shapes and colors work with each other to create a "story" or message.

As a boy, Indiana spent a lot of time on the highway. He loved the way road signs play with numbers, letters, and bright colors to capture people's attention. Think about some of the signs you see every day on streets and highways: STOP, 55 MPH, YIELD.

The best codes and rebuses force you to use old images in new ways. They celebrate the mystery and beauty of shapes and the way those shapes work together when placed in unexpected patterns.

▲ Robert Indiana, *Five*, 1984, wood beam, 69⅛ x 26¾ x 18½ in., Smithsonian American Art Museum

Apply What You Learned

1 How do both Mike Wilkins and Robert Indiana use codes in their artworks?

2 In what way are both of these artworks related to cars and other kinds of vehicles?

Big Question

How would you make artwork with a mystery or puzzle? Would you want viewers to be able to solve the mystery or puzzle? Why?

Workbook Pages 31–32

67

Explain that Indiana's *Five* was inspired by the poem, "The Great Figure," by William Carlos Williams. Read the poem to the class:

> Among the rain
> and lights
> I saw the figure 5
> in gold
> on a red
> firetruck
> moving
> tense
> unheeded
> to gong clangs
> siren howls
> and wheels rumbling
> through the dark city.

Explain that Williams believed that the object of writing is "to set a thing up against the moment and have it escape banality" [the commonplace]. **ASK:** *Do you think the artist would agree with this statement?* (Yes, because he makes us see commonplace objects in a new way in his artwork.)

STEP 3: Apply

Apply What You Learned

Have volunteers read the questions aloud, and be sure students understand the meaning of difficult words and concepts. Encourage students to carefully study the artworks, and if necessary, reread the text to help them. Explain that there are often no right or wrong answers when responding to art.

ANSWERS

1. Both Mike Wilkins and Robert Indiana use letters and numbers in codes to express an idea we must decipher.
2. *Preamble* is related to cars and other vehicles in that the artwork is made up of license plates. *Five* is related to cars and other vehicles in that the sculpture was based on a poem about a firetruck.

Q Possible response: I'd create an artwork with different shapes and colors. I'd provide a key at the bottom to help people figure out my secret code. I'd want viewers to be able to solve my mystery so they would know why I made it.

Differentiated Instruction

Beginning	Ask students to identify the names of the artists whose work appears on this spread.
Early Intermediate	Have students list similarities and differences between the two artworks.
Intermediate	Have students tell whether they like these artworks. Ask them to explain their position.
Struggling Readers	Have students identify when the works on art on this spread were created. Have them scan for the information.

STEP 1: Introduce

Unit Content

Lead students in a discussion about how people, animals, and plants grow. Tell students that this unit contains both fiction and nonfiction selections. They are grouped together to help students understand the concrete and emotional experiences of growing up. Students will also learn skills, such as comparing and contrasting, and visualizing.

 The Big Question

Ask students the Big Question, making it clear that there are no right or wrong answers. Let students know that they will be exploring answers to the Big Question throughout the unit. To stimulate discussion, ask:

- Do boys and girls have different experiences of growing up?
- What are some of the positive things about growing up? What are some of the difficult things?

STEP 2: Teach

Visual Literacy

Tell students that a publisher often includes pictures, maps, and charts with a reading. In groups of two or three, have students preview the pictures in this unit. Ask them to make a list of what the pictures show people doing.

[For example: Celebrating as a family, p. 68, playing a game, p. 70, reading and studying, pp. 74–75, carving, pp. 86, 90, holding a dog, p. 98]

Teaching Resources

- *Resources*, Unit 2 Lesson Plans, pp. 15–26
- *Transparencies*, Unit 2 Daily Language Practice
- CD-ROM/e-book, Big Question
- Video, Segment 2
- *Resources*, Letters Home, pp. 111–112

 How does growing up change us?

68

TESOL Standards

Goal 2, Standard 1—To use English to achieve academically in all content areas: Students will use English to interact in the classroom.
Descriptors—Asking and answering questions.

Goal 2, Standard 2—To use English to achieve academically in all content areas: Students will use English to obtain, process, construct, and provide subject matter information in spoken and written form.
Descriptors—Hypothesizing and predicting; Formulating and asking questions.

Goal 2, Standard 3—To use English to achieve academically in all content areas: Students will use appropriate learning strategies to construct and apply academic knowledge.
Descriptors—Actively connecting new information to information previously learned.

This unit is about what happens to people, plants, and animals as they grow and change. You will read about growing up in three ancient cultures and fun facts about plant and animal growth. You will read novel excerpts and a folk tale about conflicts within families and lessons family members teach one another. As you explore growing up, you will grow as a reader and practice the academic and literary language you need to use in school.

READING 1: Social Studies Article

■ "Ancient Kids"

READING 2: Novel Excerpt

■ From *Becoming Naomi León* by Pam Muñoz Ryan

READING 3: Novel Excerpt

■ From *Later, Gator* by Laurence Yep

READING 4: Science Article and Folk Tale

■ "Amazing Growth Facts"

■ "The Old Grandfather and His Little Grandson" by Leo Tolstoy

Listening and Speaking

At the end of this unit, you will perform a skit about ancient kids.

Writing

In this unit you will practice **narrative writing**. This type of writing tells a story. After each reading you will learn a skill to help you write a narrative paragraph. At the end of this unit, you will write an essay-length fictional narrative.

QuickWrite

In your notebook, write several sentences about your first day in school. Who was your teacher? What happened?

STEP 3: Practice

QuickWrite

This QuickWrite asks students to write in the simple past. Write the topic on the board, and give students a few minutes to compose. Help them by giving them an example. The purpose of a QuickWrite is to practice generating on-the-spot writing and help writers begin by getting something down on paper.

STEP 4: Extend

Ask students if they have read any books about growing up. Review the titles of the readings with students. Ask students how they think each reading will relate to the Big Question.

● What do you think "Ancient Kids" will tell you about growing up?

● Do you think the cultural background of the children in *Becoming Naomi León* and *Later, Gator* will influence their experiences growing up?

● What do you think "Amazing Growth Facts" will be about?

● What do you think "The Old Grandfather and His Little Grandson" will tell you about growing up?

Teach

Objectives

Read the list of objectives in the What You Will Learn section, encouraging students to join in. Tell students that this reading will be about growing up in different cultures in ancient times. Have students work in pairs to restate the list of things they will learn.

The Big Question

Remind students that the Big Question is "How does growing up change us?" To stimulate discussion, **SAY:** *What is daily life like for children growing up in America today? Do you think children in ancient times had a similar childhood to ours? How might childhood in ancient times have been different from one culture to another?* Point out that Ancient Kids is about what daily life was like for children in the past.

Build Background

Show students a world map, pointing out where ancient Greece, ancient Rome, and the Maya civilization (in present-day Mexico and Central America) were located. Explain that ancient Greece strongly influenced the development of ancient Rome, but that the Maya, being so far away, were not influenced by either culture. In fact, ancient Greeks and Romans were not even aware that the Americas existed. Ask the class to predict three similarities between their lives and the ways children in each of these cultures lived.

STEP 2: Teach

Understanding the Genre:
Informational Text

Point out that "Ancient Kids" is an informational article that focuses on an important social studies topic. An informational text, or an informational article, is a piece of nonfiction writing that might appear in a magazine, an academic journal, or on the Internet. It focuses on facts rather than opinions. It is often written in sections that address different aspects of the topic. "Ancient Kids" has different sections about childhood in ancient Greece, ancient Rome, and among the ancient Maya.

Teaching Resources

- CD-ROM/e-book, Key Words
- Audio CD 2, tracks 1–2
- *Workbook*, p. 33

READING 1

Prepare to Read

What You Will Learn

Reading
- Vocabulary building: *Context, dictionary skills, word study*
- Reading strategy: *Compare and contrast*
- Text type: *Informational text (social studies)*

Grammar, Usage, and Mechanics
Showing contrast: transitions and coordinating conjunctions

Writing
Write a friendly letter

THE BIG QUESTION

How does growing up change us? What is daily life like for children growing up today? How do children get an education? What sports do they play and watch? What games and toys do they like to play with? Which animals do they keep as pets? Work with a partner. Copy these headings: *Education, Sports, Games,* and *Pets* into your notebook. List your ideas under each heading. Then share what you know with the class.

BUILD BACKGROUND

"Ancient Kids" describes children's lives thousands of years ago in three different cultures. It tells about growing up among the ancient Greeks, Romans, and Maya. Ancient Greece was a great civilization from around 2000 to 146 B.C.E. The Greeks created the first democracy, or government by the people. They left behind beautiful architecture, sculptures, and vase paintings. They also wrote works of literature and philosophy that are still read today.

Rome became powerful after Greece (and remained so up to 476 C.E.). The Romans made important contributions in the areas of building, medicine, and government. They built more than 80 million meters (50,000 mi.) of roads. Many are still used to this day. They also had a government with three branches.

The ancient Maya established a great civilization in southern Mexico and Central America from 1000 B.C.E. to 1550 C.E. They made accurate studies of the stars, planets, sun, and moon. They had their own calendar, mathematical system, and form of writing. They built remarkable stone temples that are still standing.

Knucklebones was a popular ancient game, played with five small objects made from ankle joints of small animals. ▶

70

TESOL Standards

Goal 1, Standard 3—To use English to communicate in social settings: Students will use learning strategies to extend their communicative competence.
Descriptors—Listening to and imitating how others use English; Exploring alternative ways of saying things; Focusing attention selectively.

Goal 2, Standard 1—To use English to achieve academically in all content areas: Students will use English to interact in the classroom.
Descriptors—Requesting and providing clarification; Participating in full-class, group, and pair discussions; Negotiating and managing interaction to accomplish tasks.

Goal 2, Standard 2—To use English to achieve academically in all content areas: Students will use English to obtain, process, construct, and provide subject matter information in spoken and written form.
Descriptors—Selecting, connecting, and explaining information; Understanding and producing technical vocabulary and text features according to content area.

Learn Key Words

Read these sentences. Use the context to figure out the meaning of the red words. Use a dictionary to check your answers. Then write each word and its meaning in your notebook.

1. Studying **ancient** cultures, or cultures from thousands of years ago, helps us learn about ourselves.

2. At a wedding **ceremony**, people celebrate a marriage.

3. The girl learned what was expected of her and became a good **citizen**.

4. Long ago, boys and girls did not get the same type of **education**. They learned different things.

5. In the past, women did not have many **rights**. They could not vote or own property.

6. People long ago had **rituals**, including specific songs and dances, to celebrate important events.

Key Words
ancient
ceremony
citizen
education
rights
rituals

Practice 📖 **Workbook Page 33**

Work with a partner to answer these questions. Try to include the red word in your answer. Write the sentences in your notebook.

1. What are three objects that we use today that **ancient** people didn't have?

2. What would you expect to happen at a graduation **ceremony**?

3. What are some rules a **citizen** has to follow in the United States?

4. Which subjects are important to your **education** at school?

5. What **rights** do you think are most important? Why?

6. What **rituals** does your family perform to celebrate a birthday?

This ancient Greek vase shows a ceremony honoring an important man. ▶

71

CD2 T1–T2

 Vocabulary

Learn Key Words Play the CD. Have students listen and repeat. Direct students to the Key Words, and read them aloud. **SAY:** *These words are called key words because they are words that are important in the text we are reading.* On the board write the key words and their definitions:

Ancient: happening or existing very far back in history

Ceremony: formal event that happens in public on special occasions

Citizen: someone who lives in a particular town, state, or country

Education: the process of learning in a school or other program of study

Rights: something that you are allowed to do according to law or moral ideas

Rituals: ceremonies that are always done the same way

Have students copy the definitions into their word books and write original sentences for them. For extra practice, assign Workbook page 33.

STEP 3: Practice

Read and clarify the list of key words with students. Have students complete the practice exercise with a partner.

ANSWERS
Possible responses:

1. Three things we use today that ancient people didn't have are cars, computers, and phones.

2. At a graduation ceremony, graduates receive their diplomas.

3. Some rules a citizen has to follow are paying taxes, obeying laws, and serving on juries.

4. All subjects are important to my education.

5. I think the rights of free speech and equality before the law are our most important rights.

6. Family birthday rituals include cake and gifts.

Differentiated Instruction

Beginning	Have students draw a "growing up timeline" of the key dates and events in their lives so far.
Early Intermediate	Have students draw a "growing up timeline" of the key dates and events in their lives so far. Have them compare their timeline with a partner's.
Intermediate	Have students draw a "growing up timeline" of the key dates and events in their lives so far. Have students choose one event and tell the class about it.
Struggling Readers	Ask students to tell the date when they were born, when any siblings were born, when they moved to a new home, or any other event important to them.

Teach

STEP 1: Teach

CD2 T3–T4

 Vocabulary

Learn Academic Words Play the CD. Have students listen and repeat. Have students read the Academic Words on page 72 of the student book. Explain that academic words can help the class discuss the informational text and learn new concepts. Ask students to use each word in a sentence. Some of these words may be familiar to English learners, but in a different context. If this is the case, model sensitive ways to correct wrong usage. Then divide the class into pairs. Have the partners write original sentences that show the meaning of each academic word.

STEP 2: Practice

Model how to answer the questions on page 72 by completing the first one with the whole group. **SAY:** *The first question says: "Where might you look to see classical art from long ago?" I know that the question "Where?" means a place. The word* classical *is defined in the chart as belonging to the culture of ancient Greece or ancient Rome. My answer is "You might see classical art from long ago in a museum."*

ANSWERS
Possible responses:
1. You might see classical art from long ago in a museum.
2. The part of American cultural life I know the most about is music.
3. A unique feature of our school is that everyone learns two languages. Most other schools don't have that.
4. I think people study philosophy to better understand themselves and others.

Teaching Resources

- Audio CD 2, tracks 3–4
- *Workbook*, pp. 34–36
- CD-ROM/e-book, Academic Words, Word Study

Learn Academic Words

Study the red words and their meanings. You will find these words useful when talking and writing about informational texts. Write each word and its meaning in your notebook. After you read "Ancient Kids," try to use these words to respond to the text.

Academic Words
classical
cultural
feature
philosophy

classical = belonging to the culture of ancient Greece or ancient Rome	➡	**Classical** plays from thousands of years ago are still performed in large, outdoor theaters in Greece and Rome.
cultural = relating to a particular society and its way of life	➡	Creating art, music, and literature are **cultural** activities.
feature = quality, element, or characteristic of something that seems important, interesting, or typical	➡	A special **feature** of Maya culture is its system of writing.
philosophy = the study of what it means to exist, what good and evil are, what knowledge is, or how people should live	➡	People still read ancient Greek **philosophy** today. They learn how people thought and what they valued.

Practice **Workbook Page 34**

Work with a partner to answer these questions. Try to include the red word in your answer. Write the sentences in your notebook.

1. Where might you look to see classical art from long ago?
2. What part of American cultural life do you know most about? Do you know about music, art, or literature?
3. What is a unique feature of your school? What makes it different from other schools?
4. Why do you think people study philosophy?

Classical plays were performed in theaters like this one. ▼

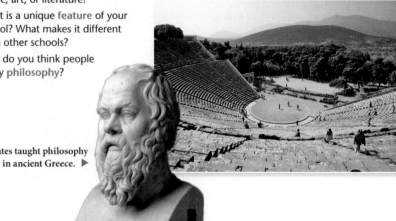

Socrates taught philosophy in ancient Greece. ▶

72

TESOL Standards

Goal 1, Standard 3—To use English to communicate in social settings: Students will use learning strategies to extend their communicative competence.
Descriptors—Self-monitoring and self-evaluating language development; Learning and using language "chunks"; Practicing new language.

Goal 2, Standard 3—To use English to achieve academically in all content areas: Students will use appropriate learning strategies to construct and apply academic knowledge.
Descriptors—Focusing attention selectively; Applying basic reading comprehension skills such as skimming, scanning, previewing, and reviewing text; Planning how and when to use cognitive strategies and applying them appropriately to a learning task.

Goal 3, Standard 3—To use English in socially and culturally appropriate ways: Students will use appropriate learning strategies to extend their sociolinguistic and sociocultural competence.
Descriptors—Analyzing the social context to determine appropriate language use.

Word Study: Spelling Words with Long Vowel Sound /ē/

In English, the long vowel sound /ē/ can be spelled in many different ways. For example, when you read "Ancient Kids," you will read the words in the first row of the chart below. Say each word with a partner. Notice the /ē/ sound and its spelling. Study the rest of the chart for more examples.

e	ee	ea	ie	y	ey
evil	Greece	wreaths	married	baby	journey
he	free	treat	fields	lady	honey
redo	wheels	leave	buried	ceremony	money

Practice  Workbook Page 35

Work with a partner. Copy the chart above into your notebook. Say a word from the chart, and ask your partner to spell it aloud. Then have your partner say the next word. Continue until you can spell all of these words correctly. Now spell the words in the box below and add them to the chart under the correct headings. Circle the letters that stand for /ē/.

bead	families	philosophy	studied	valley
even	geese	response	treat	vary

READING STRATEGY | **COMPARE AND CONTRAST**

Comparing and contrasting helps you to understand what you read more clearly. When you compare, you see how things are similar. When you contrast, you see how things are different. To compare and contrast, follow these steps:

- Look for words the author uses to show that things are similar, such as *alike, also, too, in the same way,* and *likewise.*
- Look for words the author uses to show that things are different, such as *one main difference, but, however, yet, unlike,* and *opposite.*
- Use a graphic organizer to list your comparisons and contrasts.

As you read "Ancient Kids," compare and contrast the Greek, Roman, and Maya cultures.

 Workbook Page 36

73

Linguistic Note

Homophones

The English writing system uses letters to represent sounds. Not all languages are based on an alphabet. Chinese characters represent an entire word (logographic writing system), and Japanese kana characters represent a syllable (syllabic writing system). English learners from these language backgrounds may have difficulty with English spelling rules because English is not spelled phonetically. This means that one sound can be spelled with several different letters and one letter can have different sounds. This is the reason for the many homophones in English. Homophones are words that contain the same sound but have different spellings and meanings, like, for example, *be* and *bee*. Write some of the homophones containing the long /ē/ sound on the board, and discuss their different meanings. Examples are: deer/dear, meat/meet, Greece/grease, piece/peace, see/sea, seem/seam, and week/weak.

STEP 1: Teach

Word Study

/ē/ Spelled in Different Ways Read the information about the spellings of the vowel sound /ē/. Say aloud each word in the chart, modeling pronunciation, and note the spelling of the vowel sound /ē/. Give students more examples, such as *cheese, heal, we, funny, shield,* and *money,* and ask them to write them in the chart.

STEP 2: Practice

Read aloud the instructions for this practice exercise. Model the first few. Have students search the reading for additional examples.

e	ee	ea	ie	y	ey
even	geese	bead	families	philosophy	money
response	need	treat	studied	vary	abbey

STEP 3: Teach

Reading Strategy

Compare and Contrast Go over the Reading Strategy with students. To, **SAY:** *I'll compare and contrast my desk and chair as examples. My desk has four legs. My chair has four legs, too. Words like* too *signal sameness. However, my chair is shorter than my desk. Words such as* however *signal difference.*

Have students write a paragraph that compares and contrasts two objects, using the Reading Strategy. Assign the corresponding Reading Strategy workbook page for extra practice or homework.

Read

Reading Summary

This informational article tells about the lives of children in three ancient cultures. By comparing childhood experiences in three civilizations, we see commonalities of play, school, and rites of passage.

 ## The Big Question

Remind students of the Big Question: "How does growing up change us?" Draw a three-column chart on the board and write *play*, *school*, and *rites of passage* as the three categories. Fill in the chart with examples from students' lives. Tell students they'll be learning about the lives of children in ancient times.

STEP 2: Teach

Set a Purpose for Reading

SAY: *We are reading "Ancient Kids" to compare and contrast the way that children in ancient times lived with the way that you live today.* Refer students to the three-column chart to help them compare and contrast.

Previewing Highlighted Words

Preview the highlighted words on student book pages 74–75. Write the words on the board, and point out that they are defined in the glosses at the bottom of each page. Ask volunteers to find and read the definitions. Model using the words in an original sentence. For example, *The girl learned how to play the lyre.* Then ask for volunteers to do the same and create a word book including the definition, a sentence using the word, and perhaps a picture.

CD2 T5 ## Scaffolding:
Listen and Read

Have students read along as you play the audio CD recording of the reading. Pause the recording at the end of each page to ask and answer any questions students may have.

Teaching Resources

- *Resources,* Summaries, pp. 131–132
- Audio CD 2, track 5
- *Reader's Companion Workbook,* pp. 27–33

T74

READING 1 **INFORMATIONAL TEXT** **SOCIAL STUDIES**

Set a purpose for reading Compare and contrast what it was like growing up among the ancient Greeks, Romans, and Maya. How did each culture treat children differently? What is different about growing up today?

ANCIENT KIDS

Growing Up in Ancient Greece

ANCIENT GREECE

2000 B.C.E.   146 B.C.E.   0   2000 C.E.

When a baby was born in ancient Greece, the father performed a ritual. He did a dance, holding the newborn baby. For boy babies, the family decorated the house with wreaths of olives. For girl babies, the family decorated the house with wreaths made of wool.

There were many differences in the lives of boys and girls as they grew up. One main difference was that girls did not go to school and boys did. Some girls learned to play musical instruments.

Mostly, girls helped their mothers with chores in the house or in the fields. They didn't leave their houses very often. Sometimes they went to festivals or funerals. They also visited neighbors.

Girls stayed home with their parents until they got married. Girls' fathers usually decided whom the girls would marry.

---

decorated, made it look more attractive by adding things to it
wreaths, circles made from flowers, plants, or leaves
instruments, objects used for making music
chores, small jobs

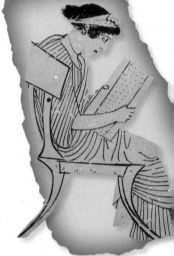

▲ Some girls learned to read and write at home.

74

 ## TESOL Standards

Goal 1, Standard 3—To use English to communicate in social settings: Students will use learning strategies to extend their communicative competence.
Descriptors—Using the primary language to ask for clarification; Using context to construct meaning.

Goal 2, Standard 1—To use English to achieve academically in all content areas: Students will use English to interact in the classroom.
Descriptors—Asking and answering questions.

Goal 2, Standard 2—To use English to achieve academically in all content areas: Students will use English to obtain, process, construct, and provide subject matter information in spoken and written form.
Descriptors—Analyzing, synthesizing, and inferring from information; Hypothesizing and predicting; Formulating and asking questions.

Boys stayed home until they were six or seven years old. They helped grow crops in the fields, and they learned to sail boats and to fish.

When boys were about seven years old, they started their formal education. They went to school and learned reading, writing, and mathematics. They had to memorize everything because there were no school books! They memorized the poetry of Homer, a famous poet. They also learned to play a musical instrument, such as the lyre.

At school, boys learned about the arts and war. They also learned how to be good citizens. At the age of eighteen, boys went to military school for two years.

Children played with many toys, such as rattles, clay animals, pull-toys on four wheels, yo-yos, and terra-cotta dolls. Children also had pets, such as birds, dogs, goats, tortoises, and mice.

▲ A student and his teacher working together

crops, wheat, corn, fruit, and so on, that a farmer grows
formal education, education in a subject or skill that you get in school rather than by practical experience
lyre, ancient instrument, similar to a guitar
military school, school where students learn to fight in wars
terra-cotta, baked red clay
tortoises, land animals that move very slowly, with a hard shell covering their bodies

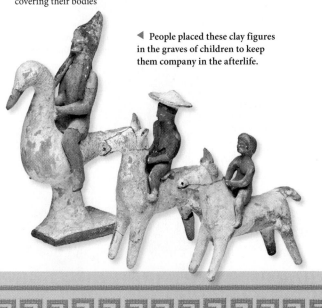

◄ People placed these clay figures in the graves of children to keep them company in the afterlife.

BEFORE YOU GO ON

1. How were boys' lives different from girls' lives in ancient Greece?
2. What toys did children play with?

☀ **On Your Own**
Did your family have any special ceremonies when you were born? Describe them.

75

Study Skills: Encyclopedia

After they finish reading about ancient Greece, have students look it up in an encyclopedia. It will probably be a subsection of the article on Greece. They can also look up the Roman Empire and the Maya. Compare the size of the Maya Empire to ancient Greece. Ask students to create a chart comparing the different civilizations. On a map, they can also compare the borders of the ancient empires to those of modern day countries.

STEP 3: Monitor Progress

Ask students to check what they have understood in the reading. If you are using the Audio CD, pause the recording.

Before You Go On

Tell students that answering questions before going on to the next page is one way to make sure they understand. When students answer each question, they should look for the place on the page that gives them that information.

ANSWERS

1. Boys went to school and got a formal education. Girls stayed home and learned how to take care of the house.
2. Children played with toy rattles, clay animals, pull-toys, yo-yos, and terra-cotta dolls.

On Your Own Have students write an answer to the On Your Own question on a separate sheet of paper. Encourage volunteers to share their responses with the class. Then collect student responses to monitor their comprehension, writing skills, and fluency.

Differentiated Instruction	
Beginning	Have students identify when the ancient Greek civilization began and ended. (2000 B.C.E.–146 C.E.)
Early Intermediate	Have students list examples of how ancient Greek boys' and girls' lives were different.
Intermediate	Have students pick a photo from pages 74–75 and rewrite the caption in their own words.
Standard English Learners (CRI)	Have students do some basic research to find out reasons why the Ancient Greek, Roman, or Maya civilization ended. Have students share the facts they found with the class.

Read

Preteaching Highlighted Words

Before reading this spread, point out the highlighted words and terms to students. Define each one, pointing out the definition in the gloss at the bottom of the student book page. Make sure that students understand each highlighted word. Ask students to generate original sentences, using the highlighted words. When correcting original sentences, focus on usage of the highlighted word. Do not explicitly correct other errors. Model correct usage and grammar by repeating a correct version of the student's sentence.

Across the Curriculum:
Math

The Maya, ancient Romans, and ancient Greeks each had a mathematical system that was different from the one we use today. The Maya used three symbols: a shell represented zero, a dot represented one, and a bar represented five. The ancient Greeks and Romans did not have the concept of zero in their numerical system. Romans used Roman numerals. In this system, for example, *V* meant five and *X* meant 10. This numerical system continued to be used in Europe after the Romans, but was later discarded in favor of Arabic numbers, which we use today. Before the Romans, ancient Greeks used a variety of numerical systems, such as writing the first letter of the number.

Model the
READING STRATEGY

Compare and Contrast
Model the compare and contrast reading strategy after reading and listening to each page. You may want to refer students back to the chart on the board about their daily lives. Or you may want to encourage students to compare and contrast the three cultures about which they are reading.

Growing Up in Ancient Rome

ANCIENT ROME

| 753 B.C.E. | 0 | 476 C.E. | 2000 C.E. |

ANCIENT GREECE

| 2000 B.C.E. | 146 B.C.E. | 0 | 2000 C.E. |

When a Roman baby was born, a relative put the baby at the feet of the father. The father picked up the baby to accept it into the family. The baby was named nine days after birth.

The oldest man in a family—the father, the grandfather, or an uncle—was the "head of the family." However, women were also important to family life. They managed the house and household finances. In the early years of ancient Rome, women did not have many rights. In later years, they had more rights. They were allowed to own land and to have some types of jobs. They could manage some businesses, but they were still not allowed to hold jobs in the government or to become lawyers or teachers.

Girls and boys wore a special locket, called a *bulla*, around their necks. The bulla protected them from evil. A girl wore the bulla until her wedding day. A boy wore the bulla until he became a citizen. A boy became a citizen at age sixteen or seventeen. The family had a big celebration on this day.

Some Greeks lived in southern Italy and Sicily. The ancient Greeks had a cultural influence on the Romans. Greek teachers introduced the Romans to the Greek gods and goddesses and to Greek literature and philosophy.

▲ Roman children dressed like their parents. They wore long shirts called tunics.

Marble heads of a
▼ Roman girl and boy

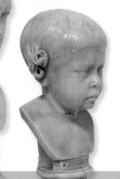

---

head of the family, person who is in charge of the family
managed, controlled or directed
finances, money matters
locket, piece of jewelry like a small round box in which you put a picture of someone
influence, effect

76

TESOL Standards

Goal 1, Standard 2—To use English to communicate in social settings: Students will interact in, through, and with spoken and written English for personal expression and enjoyment.
Descriptors—Sharing social and cultural traditions and values.

Goal 2, Standard 3—To use English to achieve academically in all content areas: Students will use appropriate learning strategies to construct and apply academic knowledge.
Descriptors—Using context to construct meaning; Applying self-monitoring and self-corrective strategies to build and expand a knowledge base.

Goal 3, Standard 3—To use English in socially and culturally appropriate ways: Students will use appropriate learning strategies to extend their sociolinguistic and sociocultural competence.
Descriptors—Experimenting with variations of language in social and academic settings.

▲ Glass and clay marbles

School was not free. Most children in ancient Rome were not from rich families. They were poor. In poor families, parents taught their children at home. Many poor children did not learn to read or write.

Rich families sent their children to school at age seven to learn basic subjects. Girls did not continue in school after they learned the basic subjects. They stayed at home, where their mothers taught them how to be good wives and mothers.

Boys from rich families continued their education in formal schools or with tutors. They became lawyers or worked in government.

What did children do after school? They played with friends, pets, or toys. Toys included balls, hobbyhorses, kites, models of people and animals, hoops, stilts, marbles, and knucklebones. War games were popular with boys. Girls played with dolls. They also played board games, tic-tac-toe, and ball games.

What kind of pets did children play with in ancient Rome? Dogs were the favorite pets. Roman children also kept birds—pigeons, ducks, quail, and geese—as pets. Some children even had pet monkeys.

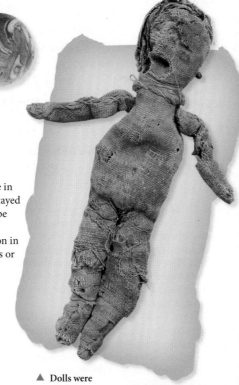

▲ Dolls were popular toys.

---

tutors, teachers of one student or a small group of students
models, small copies
stilts, a pair of poles to stand on, used for walking high above the ground
quail, small fat birds that are hunted and shot for food and sport

BEFORE YOU GO ON

1 What did Roman girls do when they grew up?

2 What kind of work did Roman boys from rich families do?

On Your Own
How is what you do after school different from what Roman children did?

77

Study Skills: Dictionary

Looking up unfamiliar words is invaluable for students seeking to understand a text in any subject. Students looking up a word may discover that it has several possible meanings. Students should first identify the part of speech of the word as it is used in the text. They can use context to determine if a word is a noun, verb, adjective, etc. A word in a dictionary may contain definitions for usage as both a noun and a verb in different contexts. Then students should carefully read the definitions for the right part of speech and consider which one is most likely to apply in this situation.

STEP 5: Monitor Progress

Ask students to check what they have understood in the reading. If you are using the Audio CD, pause the recording.

Before You Go On

Tell students that when they answer each question, they should look for the place on the page that substantiates that information.

ANSWERS

1. Roman girls became mothers and wives and managed the house and household finances.
2. Roman boys from rich families became lawyers or worked for the government.

On Your Own Have students write an answer to the On Your Own question on a separate sheet of paper. Encourage volunteers to share their responses with the class. Then collect student responses to monitor their comprehension, writing skills, and fluency.

STEP 6: Teach

Preteaching Highlighted Words

Before reading this spread, review the highlighted words and terms with students. Define each one, pointing out the location of the definition in the gloss at the bottom of the student book page. Make sure that students understand each highlighted word. If appropriate, ask students to generate original sentences using the highlighted words. When correcting original sentences, focus on usage of the highlighted word.

Across the Curriculum:
Social Studies

At its most powerful, the Maya civilization had over forty cities in Mexico and Guatemala. No one is certain what caused the Maya civilization to decline. Some scientists believe that war and famine were the two key factors. That does not mean, however, that Maya people do not exist today—they do! The Maya continue to live mainly in Mexico, with small populations in Guatemala. They work mostly as farmers, growing corn, beans, and squash. Most Maya today observe a mixture of Christianity and their indigenous religion.

Model the
READING STRATEGY

Compare and Contrast

Return to the reading strategy exercise on page 73 of the student book. Ask questions of students to prompt them to use the skill.
SAY: *Remember that when we compare, we look for sameness. When we contrast, we look for differences. Key words that signal sameness are* like, also, too, in the same way, *and* likewise. *What sentences signal sameness? Key words that signal difference are* one main difference, differences, but, however, yet, unlike, *and* opposite. *What sentences signal difference?*

Growing Up in the Ancient Maya Culture

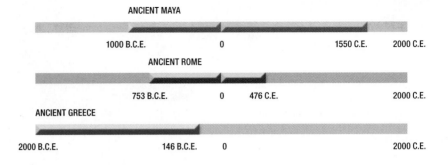

ANCIENT MAYA

| 1000 B.C.E. | 0 | 1550 C.E. | 2000 C.E. |

ANCIENT ROME

| 753 B.C.E. | 0 | 476 C.E. | 2000 C.E. |

ANCIENT GREECE

| 2000 B.C.E. | 146 B.C.E. | 0 | 2000 C.E. |

The Maya lived throughout parts of southern Mexico and Central America, including Belize and Guatemala. They built large cities and created extraordinary art and architecture. You can visit the ruins of some ancient Maya cities, such as Chichén Itzá in Mexico's Yucatan region.

In Maya culture, the father was the head of the family. Maya men worked hard to support their families, and they paid taxes to the government. Women in Maya society cooked, made cloth, sewed clothing, and took care of the children.

When a boy was about five years old, the Maya tied a small white bead to the top of his head. When a girl was about five, the Maya tied a red shell around her waist. When boys and girls were twelve or thirteen years old, the village had a big ceremony that marked the end of childhood. During the ceremony, a priest cut the beads from the boys' heads. Mothers removed the red shells from the girls' waists. After the ceremony, boys and girls could get married. Young men painted themselves black until they were married.

Maya boys and girls, unlike Roman children, did not have to pay to go to school. They learned from their parents, too. Girls learned

---

ruins, parts of buildings that are left after other parts have been destroyed
taxes, money that must be given

All women did some weaving and spinning. They made things for their families and to sell.

78

◀ This Maya vase shows a jaguar.

▲ A toy dog on wheels

how to weave and cook. Boys learned to hunt and fish. Children also learned how to grow crops, such as corn. At age seventeen, boys joined the army to learn about war and fighting.

Children played games and they played with toys. Some of their toys had wheels. Surprisingly, the Maya did not use wheels in their work or transportation. However, toys, such as animal pull-toys, had wheels.

Animals were important in everyday life and religion. The Maya used animals in their art. They decorated various items with pictures of foxes, owls, jaguars, hummingbirds, eagles, and other animals. The Maya sometimes ate dogs, but they mainly used dogs for hunting. The Maya thought that dogs could guide people on the journey to the afterlife. This is why they buried dogs with their owners.

jaguars, large wild cats with black spots
guide, show the way to
afterlife, life that some people believe you have after death

BEFORE YOU GO ON

1. What are three modern-day countries where the ancient Maya lived?

2. Why did Maya boys and girls have a special ceremony when they turned twelve or thirteen?

💡 **On Your Own**
What would you have enjoyed about growing up among the Maya?

79

Teach & Apply

Comprehension

Students can answer these questions independently or in groups, responding orally or in writing. Model the first question with the class so they can see how to answer in a complete sentence.

ANSWERS

1. The pets the children of ancient Greece had were birds, dogs, goats, tortoises, and mice.
2. They introduced Greek gods and goddesses, Greek literature, and philosophy to the Romans.
3. The mothers of ancient Maya girls taught them to weave and cook.
4. Six-year-old boys and girls in ancient Greece stayed home with their parents.
5. **Possible response:** All three cultures had toys for their children because children love to play with toys.
6. **Possible response:** The most important feature of education in ancient Rome was that boys and girls got to learn basic skills.
7. Answers will vary.
8. Answers will vary.

Speaking Tip

Tell students to begin each topic with an opening statement. For example, *I am going to compare the ancient Greeks and the ancient Romans.* This will help the speaker organize his or her thoughts and let the listeners know what to expect from the presentation.

 In Your Own Words

Read aloud the instructions for this activity and model the first one for students. Remind students that *summarizing* means to focus on the most important main ideas, use their own words, and be concise.

Teaching Resources

- *Workbook*, p. 37
- CD-ROM/e-book, Comprehension, Extension
- *Reader's Companion Workbook*, pp. 34–38

READING 1 — Review and Practice

COMPREHENSION
Workbook Page 37

Right There

1. What pets did the children of ancient Greece have?
2. What did Greek teachers introduce to the Romans?

Think and Search

3. Who taught ancient Maya girls how to weave and cook?
4. What did both six-year-old girls and boys in ancient Greece do?

Author and You

5. Why do you think grown-ups in all three cultures had toys for their children?
6. What do you think was the most important feature of education in ancient Rome?

On Your Own

7. Do you think that cultural activities are as important today as they were in ancient times? Why?
8. What do you think makes a person well educated? What do you think people should learn in school?

IN YOUR OWN WORDS

Summarize the reading. Use the topics and vocabulary below to tell a partner about growing up among the Greeks, Romans, and Maya.

 Speaking TIP

Present each topic clearly.

Ancient Greeks	Ancient Romans	Ancient Maya
The Birth of a Baby	The Birth of a Baby	Life for Men and Women
Education for Boys	Women's Rights	Ceremonies
Education for Girls	Education for Boys	Education for Boys
Learning to Play Music	Education for Girls	Education for Girls
Toys	Toys	Toys
Pets	Pets	Animals

80

TESOL Standards

Goal 1, Standard 1—To use English to communicate in social settings: Students will use English to participate in social interactions.
Descriptors—Sharing and requesting information; Engaging in conversations.

Goal 1, Standard 2—To use English to communicate in social settings: Students will interact in, through, and with spoken and written English for personal expression and enjoyment.
Descriptors—Participating in popular culture.

DISCUSSION

Discuss in pairs or small groups.

1. What are some examples of ceremonies in "Ancient Kids"? What ceremonies are important to family life today?

2. Which ancient society would you have wanted to grow up in—the Greek, Roman, or Maya culture? Why?

3. Why do you think education is important for children?

Q **How does growing up change us?** Compare and contrast what it was like growing up in ancient cultures to growing up today. What is different for kids today? What is similar?

> »)) *Listening* TIP
>
> Respect each speaker. Listen politely, even if you disagree with the speaker's ideas.

READ FOR FLUENCY

When we read aloud to communicate meaning, we group words into phrases, pause or slow down to make important points, and emphasize important words. Pause for a short time when you reach a comma and for a longer time when you reach a period. Pay attention to rising and falling intonation at the end of sentences.

Work with a partner. Choose a paragraph from the reading. Discuss which words seem important for communicating meaning. Practice pronouncing difficult words. Give each other feedback.

EXTENSION

Workbook Page 37

In "Ancient Kids" you learned about growing up long ago. Choose any one of the three cultures you read about. Think about what features of the culture you would like to research. For example, you could read more about ancient Greek games like knucklebones or find out about an ancient Maya ballgame called pok-a-tok. Select a cultural feature to research. Then use encyclopedias, books, and the Internet to find the information. Share the information with your classmates.

▲ The ancient Maya played pok-a-tok on large ball courts.

81

STEP 2: Extend

Listening Tip

Tell students that when they give a presentation, people will have questions. When people ask questions, they should listen quietly until the questioner has finished speaking.

(CRI) Discussion

Model some approaches to the questions to initiate discussion. For the first question, **SAY:** *Maya children had a ceremony for the end of childhood. Today, we have graduation ceremonies.* For the second question, **SAY:** *If I were a boy, I would have wanted to grow up in Roman society. Why might my answer be different if I were a girl?*

Q **How does growing up change us?** Remind students that the Big Question is "How does growing up change us?" Guide students in a discussion about the similarities and differences between growing up in an ancient culture and growing up today. **SAY:** *How can our culture change how we grow up?*

STEP 3: Assess

Read for Fluency

Have students time their reading. Emphasize that precise timing is important to getting accurate scores. If students report that they are having trouble comprehending the words, suggest that students listen to the CD recording of this passage.

Extension

Read aloud the instructions for this extension activity. Model the example of ancient toys and games, and brainstorm other topics. Write ideas on the board for easy reference. Have students partner or work in small groups.

Differentiated Instruction

Beginning	Ask students which one of these ancient cultures existed for the longest time. (Maya)
Early Intermediate	Have students tell the class which ancient society they'd rather grow up in and why.
Intermediate	Have students present their research from the Extension assignment to the class.
Greater Challenge	Have students make a presentation to the class in which they compare and contrast growing up in the United States to the three ancient cultures.

STEP 1: Introduce

Tell students that showing contrast by using transitions and coordinating conjunctions can help them point out differences when they are writing. Tell them you will be reviewing ways to contrast ideas by using transitions and coordinating conjunctions.

STEP 2: Teach

Grammar and Writing

Showing Contrast Review with students the meaning of *contrast*. Read the information on page 82 of the student book. Be sure to enunciate the transitions and coordinating clauses. Sound out the pauses after the transitions, and be sure to tell students that there are no commas (i.e., pauses) after coordinating conjunctions. Write the rules and examples on chart paper for easy reference.

STEP 3: Practice

Review with students how to show contrast. Ask students to make statements, using the transitions and coordinating conjunctions they have learned.

ANSWERS

Column A	Column B
1. The father was the head of the family, yet	women were also important.
2. Animals were kept as pets, however,	they were also eaten.
3. Children worked hard in school, but	they still had time for fun.
4. A girl learned to weave and cook, but a	boy learned to hunt and fish.
5. Greek boys went to school. However,	Greek girls did not.

Teaching Resources

- *Workbook*, pp. 38–39
- CD-ROM/e-book, Grammar, Writing
- *Transparencies*, Writing Model 26
- *Transparencies, Resources*, Graphic Organizer 17
- *Assessment*, Reading 1 Test, pp. 51–54

Grammar and Writing

Showing Contrast: Transitions and Coordinating Conjunctions

When you want to contrast two things in your writing, transitions and coordinating conjunctions can help you. Certain transitions and coordinating conjunctions point out differences.

Study the charts and explanations below. Notice that transitions begin the sentences, but coordinating conjunctions join two sentences. Use a comma (,) after a transition and before a coordinating conjunction.

Transitions	Coordinating Conjunctions
The oldest man was the "head of the family." **However,** women were also important to family life.	The Maya sometimes ate some dogs**, but** they used most dogs for hunting.
The Maya did not use wheels in their work or transportation. **On the other hand,** toys, such as animal pull-toys, had wheels.	Women could manage some businesses**, yet** they were still not allowed to hold jobs in the government.

Practice **Workbook** Page 38

Work with a partner. Copy the sentence starters in Column A into your notebook. Find the contrasting idea in Column B that best completes each sentence. Finish writing each sentence in your notebook.

Column A	Column B
1. The father was the head of the family, yet	they were also eaten.
2. Animals were kept as pets. However,	they still had time for fun.
3. Children worked hard in school, but	women had some rights.
4. A girl learned to weave and cook, but	Greek girls did not.
5. Greek boys went to school. However,	a boy learned to hunt and fish.

▲ A statue of a Roman guard dog

82

WRITING A NARRATIVE PARAGRAPH

Write a Friendly Letter

On this page, you'll write a narrative paragraph in the form of a friendly letter. You'll use a graphic organizer like the one at the right to help you put your narrative paragraph into a letter format.

A narrative is a real or make-believe story that describes characters and events. When writers tell stories, they include ideas, memories, and sensory details to make the story interesting. Sometimes people tell a memorable story in a friendly letter. A friendly letter has five parts: the date, the greeting (or salutation), the body, the closing, and the signature.

Here is a model of a friendly letter written by a student named Tyler Welsh. Notice how the writer tells his grandfather a sequence of events in time order.

Salutation (or greeting)	Date
Body	
	Closing, Signature

July 23, 2009

Dear Grandpa,
   Did I ever tell you how being in my school play helped me overcome stage fright? I was only six years old, and I didn't really enjoy performing in front of others. All week, my class and I practiced hard, but I couldn't get over my fear. Then, on the night of the play, I was so nervous! When I walked on stage, I had the urge to run away. The heat from the stage lighting was almost unbearable. During the performance, I felt as if the eyes of everyone in the audience were glaring at me. Yet I performed well, even though I was really nervous. Afterwards, I felt an amazing sense of accomplishment. Since you saw the play, I wanted to share my memory of that night with you.
                              Love,
                              Tyler

Practice
Workbook Page 39

Write a friendly letter to an older family member. Tell a story about an event that occurred when you were younger. Use the "parts of a letter" organizer to put your story into the correct format. Tell your story in time order. Use transitions and coordinating conjunctions if you want to contrast two things.

Writing Checklist

WORD CHOICE:
☑ I included vivid sensory details and memories in my narrative.

ORGANIZATION:
☑ I put my narrative in time order.

83

STEP 1: Introduce

In this age of e-mail, letters are usually used for more formal occasions. Read with students the information about the parts of a letter. Model where these parts go by drawing on the board.

STEP 2: Teach

Writing an Expository Paragraph

Write a Friendly Letter Read aloud the instructions for this practice exercise. Ask a student to read the model letter aloud, and have students note the order of events.

Model Writing Skill Have students first summarize the event they plan to write about. Then have them use a sequence chart to put the event in time order. **SAY:** *Break the event into parts so that you are sure to write about what happened first, next, and last.* When students have completed the chart, they should write the letter. Have students exchange letters with a partner and read each other's letter.

STEP 3: Assess

Have students evaluate their work using the Writing Checklist on page 83.

Writing Checklist Note

Word Choice Check that the words students used in their paragraphs offer vivid language and help us visualize the details and memories.

Organization Check that students' narratives are presented in an orderly way, starting with the earliest event and ending with the latest.

Accelerate Language Development

Yet

Point out that the word *yet* can be used as a coordinating conjunction and as an adverb. When used as a coordinating conjunction, it means *however, nevertheless.* Example: *He said he'd be on time, yet he arrived over an hour late.* *Yet* can also be an adverb of time and mean *still.* Examples: *He may change his mind yet.* As an adverb of time, *yet* is frequently used in combination with *not.* Example: *He has not yet arrived.* Or: *Your order isn't ready yet.*

Teach

STEP 1: Introduce

Objectives

Read aloud the list of objectives in the What You Will Learn section, encouraging students to join in. Tell students that they will be reading an excerpt from a novel about growing up. Have students work in pairs to restate the list of things they will learn.

The Big Question

Review the exercise students completed on page 84 for the Big Question: "How does growing up change us?" To stimulate discussion, talk about your own family growing up. Ask students about their own families. You may want to use the discussion of how our families influence who we become to lead into the excerpt from *Becoming Naomi León*, which is about a girl's divided family.

Build Background

On a map, locate the state of California and the state of Oaxaca, Mexico. The town of Lemon Tree, California, is a fictional town, but Oaxaca is a real city in the state of Oaxaca, Mexico. A key element in the story that links Naomi to her father is the artistic carving of objects. Artistic talents such as singing, painting, and music often run in families. Ask students what talents are common in their families.

STEP 2: Teach

Understanding the Genre:
Novel Excerpt

Tell students that a novel is a long work of fiction. Novels contain such elements as characters, plot, conflict, and setting. The writer of the novel creates these elements. This reading is an excerpt. An *excerpt* is a short reading from a novel containing an episode or an event. This excerpt from *Becoming Naomi León* is about a girl finding her family heritage.

Teaching Resources

- CD-ROM/e-book, Literary Words
- Audio CD 2, track 6
- *Workbook*, p. 40

READING 2 — Prepare to Read

What You Will Learn

Reading
- Vocabulary building: *Literary terms, dictionary skills, word study*
- Reading strategy: *Visualize*
- Text type: *Literature (novel excerpt)*

Grammar, Usage, and Mechanics
Non-action verbs

Writing
Write about a character and setting

THE BIG QUESTION

How does growing up change us? What kinds of families do children grow up in? Some grow up in large families, with two parents, a grandparent, and many children. Others grow up in small families, with one parent and one or two children. Sometimes children are raised by their grandparents, aunts, or uncles.

Work with a partner. Talk about the kinds of families you know about from your own experience and from stories in books and on TV. In your notebook, draw a picture of a family from a TV show or a book. Label the members of the family using words such as *mother, father, sister, brother, aunt, uncle, grandmother, grandfather, stepmother,* or *stepfather*. Discuss how our families influence who we become.

BUILD BACKGROUND

Becoming Naomi León is a realistic novel—a fictional narrative about events that could happen in everyday life. The main character, Naomi Soledad León Outlaw, lives in Lemon Tree, California—in a whale-like trailer called Baby Beluga. She and her younger brother, Owen, have been well cared for by Gram, their great-grandmother, ever since their mother left them seven years ago. Despite Gram's loving care, Naomi often feels unhappy. To cheer herself up, she writes lists and carves beautiful objects out of soap. In the novel excerpt, you will read about Naomi's reunion with her father in Oaxaca, Mexico.

Oaxaca is a city in southern Mexico. The people there hold a radish-carving festival every year in which they make many lovely sculptures out of radishes. After reading the novel excerpt, you may want to try carving, too. A how-to piece called "Soap Carving" will tell you how.

A radish carving ▶

84

TESOL Standards

Goal 2, Standard 2—To use English to achieve academically in all content areas: Students will use English to obtain, process, construct, and provide subject matter information in spoken and written form.
Descriptors—Demonstrating knowledge through application in a variety of contexts.

Goal 3, Standard 1—To use English in socially and culturally appropriate ways: Students will use the appropriate language variety, register, and genre according to audience, purpose, and setting.
Descriptors—Using a variety of writing styles appropriate for different audiences, purposes, and settings.

Goal 3, Standard 3—To use English in socially and culturally appropriate ways: Students will use appropriate learning strategies to extend their sociolinguistic and sociocultural competence.
Descriptors—Observing and modeling how others speak and behave in a particular situation or setting; Rehearsing variations of language use in different social and academic settings.

VOCABULARY

Learn Literary Words

In fiction, you can learn a lot about a character by paying attention to what the character says. Dialogue is the exact words spoken by two or more characters. Writers use dialogue to reveal what the characters in a story are like. Often, dialogue makes the characters seem like real people.

Read the examples of dialogue below. They are from *Becoming Naomi León*. Notice that each bit of dialogue begins and ends with quotation marks ("—").

Literary Words
dialogue
setting

> "I will go with you," said Santiago, and they headed towards the garden.
> "Do not be sad," he whispered.

Another important part of a story is the setting—the time and place where the narrative occurs. Identifying the setting will help you better understand what is happening in a story. Sometimes writers state the setting directly. In other cases, you must use clues to figure out where the narrative takes place. Clues might include details about the type of clothing, houses, land, weather, time of day, and transportation.

Practice
Workbook Page 40

Work with a partner. Take turns reading each setting aloud. First, identify the time—past, present, or future—of the setting. Then identify the place.

Type of Literature	Setting
Mystery story	Joe walked down a dark road on the edge of town. It was raining hard and flashes of lightning lit up the deserted house at the end of the street. Joe heard a clock strike midnight and a dog howl in the distance. He took out his cell phone, but the battery was dead.
Science fiction novel	In the year 3050, a strange yellow aircraft landed on Earth. Two huge insect-like creatures stepped out. They waved their many legs in the air but did not speak.
Historical novel	In the 1850s, I met a woman who ran a big cattle ranch in Texas. She used to ride into town on a palomino pony, wearing a big leather hat and a long cotton skirt.

85

Differentiated Instruction

Beginning	Ask students the name of the town that Naomi Leon lives in. (Lemon Tree, California)
Early Intermediate	Ask students to locate Oaxaca on a map of Mexico.
Intermediate	Ask students to describe the setting of today's class. (town, school, room number, students in class, time, weather, etc.)
Standard English Learners	Have students write a short paragraph that includes dialogue and present it to the class.

Vocabulary

Learn Literary Words Play the CD. Have students listen and repeat. Direct students to the Literary Words and read them aloud. **SAY:** *These are called* literary words *because we use these words when we discuss literature.* Read the words aloud. **SAY:** *Read the paragraph in your book that defines these words.* Write down the following key points on the board in order to reinforce learning. Have students give examples of what the words mean. Ask students to write each word in an original sentence.

Dialogue: the exact words spoken by two or more characters

Setting: the time and place where a narrative occurs

SAY: *An example of dialogue is, "'Where is the spaceship, Mr. Norida?' Alice asked. 'We don't see any sign of it.'" An example of setting is, "It was a dark and stormy night at the McBriar mansion. The only sound was the rumble of thunder."*

STEP 3: Practice

Draw a three-column chart on the board. Write in the headings *Type of Literature, Time, Place.* Model the first example, then have students work with partners to fill in the chart.

Type of Literature	Time	Place
Mystery story	midnight	On a dark road at the edge of town
Science fiction novel	Year 3050	Earth
Historical novel	1850s	Cattle ranch in Texas

Teach

STEP 1: Teach

CD2 T7–T8

Vocabulary

Learn Academic Words Play the CD. Have students listen and repeat. Read aloud each of the academic words and discuss their meaning. **SAY:** *Look at the academic word chart. The definition for each word is on the left side. On the right side, each word is used in a sentence. Work with a partner to write an additional sentence for each academic word. Write each word, its definition, and the sentence in your Word Book.*

STEP 2: Practice

SAY: *When you read a sentence, you can understand a word's meaning from context. For example, in the example sentence for the word "conflict," the word disagreement gives us context for understanding what a "conflict" is. You can use this information to understand words and help with filling in the blank exercises.*

Read aloud the instructions for the practice exercise. Review with students that this is a fill in the blank exercise, which means they should read the sentence and then find the word on the academic word list that best completes it. Model the first one for students.

ANSWERS
1. conflict
2. bond
3. process
4. assist

Teaching Resources

- Audio CD 2, tracks 7–8
- *Workbook*, pp. 41–43
- CD-ROM/e-book, Academic Words, Word Study

Learn Academic Words

Study the red words and their meanings. You will find these words useful when talking and writing about literature and informational texts. Write each word and its meaning in your notebook. After you read the excerpt from *Becoming Naomi León*, try to use these words to respond to the text.

Academic Words

assist
bond
conflict
process

assist = help someone do something	➡	Grandparents sometimes **assist** parents with child care.
bond = a feeling or interest that unites two or more people or groups	➡	Children usually feel a strong **bond** with their parents.
conflict = disagreement	➡	The two friends solved their **conflict** by discussing their disagreement openly.
process = a series of actions that someone does in order to achieve a particular result	➡	There are many steps in the **process** of writing a story.

Practice **Workbook** Page 41

Write the sentences in your notebook. Choose a red word from the box above to complete each sentence. Then take turns reading the sentences aloud with a partner.

1. We want this _____ between the two countries to be settled right away. Otherwise, the two countries may go to war.
2. Brothers and sisters often have a close _____. They feel attached to each other.
3. My friend from Oaxaca explained the steps involved in the _____ of carving radishes.
4. I often _____ my aunt when she is caring for her son. I help her make his lunch.

A young girl in the process of carving radishes ▶

86

🌐 TESOL Standards

Goal 1, Standard 3—To use English to communicate in social settings: Students will use learning strategies to extend their communicative competence.
Descriptors—Comparing nonverbal and verbal cues.

Goal 2, Standard 2—To use English to achieve academically in all content areas: Students will use English to obtain, process, construct, and provide subject matter information in spoken and written form.
Descriptors—Representing information visually and interpreting information presented visually.

Goal 2, Standard 3—To use English to achieve academically in all content areas: Students will use appropriate learning strategies to construct and apply academic knowledge.
Descriptors—Imitating the behaviors of native English speakers to complete tasks successfully.

T86

Word Study: Suffixes -ness, -tion, and -ation

A suffix is a letter or a group of letters placed at the end of a base word. A suffix can change a word's part of speech and its meaning. Sometimes when a suffix that begins with a vowel is added to a base word that ends in a vowel, the last letter is dropped from the base word. Study the examples in the chart below. The letter *e* in the verb *admire* is dropped before adding the suffix *-ation*.

Word	Suffix	New Word
fierce (adjective)	-ness	fierceness (noun)
admire (verb)	-ation	admiration (noun)
consider (verb)	-ation	consideration (noun)

Practice **Workbook** Page 42

Copy the chart below into your notebook. Work with a partner. Add the suffix to the end of the word to create a new word. Check the dictionary to make sure that you have written the word correctly. Write the word in the chart.

Word	Suffix	New Word
good (adjective)	-ness	(noun)
imagine (verb)	-ation	(noun)
transport (verb)	-ation	(noun)

READING STRATEGY   VISUALIZE

Visualizing helps you understand what the author wants you to see. When you visualize, you make pictures in your mind. To visualize what you are reading, follow these steps:

- Read the text, such as these sentences from *Becoming Naomi León*:

  Tied to the branches with transparent fishing line, the carved wooden animals appeared suspended. When a warm breeze tickled the dragons, reptiles, birds, and lions, they twirled and swayed.

- Now, close your eyes and visualize what you read. What do you see?
- As you read, look for descriptive words the author uses.

  As you read the excerpt from *Becoming Naomi León*, ask yourself, "What words help me create a picture of what things look like and what is happening?"

Workbook Page 43

87

Workbook Page 42

Workbook Page 43

Word Study

Read aloud the information from the student book, and ask students how the suffixes *-ness* and *-ation* change the part of speech of each word (adjective to noun, verb to noun, verb to noun). Clarify pronunciation of the *sh* sound in *-ation*, and where it occurs. Review the examples on the student book chart, and model several more, such as *kind/kindness* and *adore/adoration*.

Model the first example for students. **SAY:**
When I combine the adjective good *with the suffix* -ness, *I get the new word* goodness. *It is a noun.*

Have partners copy and complete the Practice chart.

Reading Strategy

Visualize Read aloud the first paragraph and discuss what it means to *visualize*. **SAY:** *Close your eyes. Think of your favorite person. Can you see that person in your mind? What does the person look like? Where is the person in your mind? Can you describe the place?*

Point out that good writers help us visualize the setting, characters, and events by using lots of description. **SAY:** *Let's read the paragraph from* Becoming Naomi León. *What interesting description does the author use to help the reader visualize the setting?*

Linguistic Note

Suffixes Provide Meaning

Point out that English suffixes and prefixes give clues to the meaning and the function of words. For instance there are suffixes are used only for nouns and others that are used for verbs, adjectives, and adverbs. For example, *-ness*, *-tion* and *-ation* are used to create nouns. A suffix can also help to give meaning to a word. For example, *competition* and *competitor* are both nouns from the verb *compete*. However, *-or* indicates that there is a person performing the action, whereas *-tion* indicates a condition or state of being. Ask for other examples with different suffixes that change meaning. Possible answers are: *admiration/admirer, transportation/transporter, legislation/legislator, creation/creator/creativeness*.

STEP 1: Introduce

Reading Summary

The main character, Naomi León, is eleven years old and lives with her grandmother. Gram and the children have gone to Mexico to find Naomi's father and ask him to help make Gram Naomi's legal guardian.

The Big Question

Discuss the meaning of *legal custody,* which is the legal right to make decisions about a child, care for them and have them live with you. Ask how a change in custody might bring changes in the life of a family.

STEP 2: Teach

Set a Purpose for Reading

Tell students that as they read, they should visualize the places and things described. **SAY:**
When Naomi describes things vividly, it shows how she feels about these things. Visualization can help you to know how she feels.

LITERARY CHECK

Remind students that the meaning of the word *setting* appears on page 85. Answer:
The setting is Christmas morning in Oaxaca, Mexico. There are bright-colored carvings on the branches and below the jacaranda tree.

Preteaching Highlighted Words

With students, preview the highlighted selection vocabulary on pages 88–89. Write the words on the board, and point out that they are defined at the bottom of each page. Ask students to find and read the definitions. Model how to use the words in original sentences. For example, **SAY:**
The gorgeous decorations made the party quite a spectacle.

CD2 T9

Scaffolding:
Listen and Read

Have students read along as you play the audio CD recording of the reading. Pause the recording at the end of each page to ask and answer any questions students may have.

Teaching Resources

- *Resources,* Summaries, pp. 133–134
- Audio CD 2, track 9

Set a purpose for reading Naomi is reunited with her father in Oaxaca after many years. How does the experience change her?

from
Becoming Naomi León

Pam Muñoz Ryan

Life changes when eleven-year-old Naomi's mother, Skyla, comes back and tries to obtain custody of Naomi. Gram and the children flee in their trailer, Baby Beluga, to Oaxaca in search of the children's father, hoping that he will make Gram the children's legal guardian. They arrive just in time for Oaxaca's radish-carving festival. Naomi finally finds her father and discovers that he loves carving, too.

    On Christmas morning Owen and I stood in the yard and looked up. I had to pinch myself to make sure I was not dreaming. A jungle of painted beasts floated beneath the jacaranda tree, the leaves and purple flowers like a canopy above them. Tied to the branches with transparent fishing line, the carved wooden animals appeared suspended. When a warm breeze tickled the dragons, reptiles, birds, and lions, they twirled and swayed.

    Owen and I lay down on the ground and watched them. A few minutes later Santiago came out from behind the trailer, where he had been waiting. He lay down next to us and we watched the spectacle to the music of Owen's raspy laughter.

    Later in the afternoon I sat outside, carving with Santiago. He was an expert on wood and had brought some of the special copal branches from the trees in the mountains. I loved watching him carve.

    He held up a curved branch. "Each piece has a personality. Sometimes you can look at the wood and see exactly what it might be. The promise

LITERARY CHECK
*Describe the **setting** at the beginning of the excerpt.*

---

custody of, the right to legally care for
jacaranda, type of tropical American tree with purple flowers
canopy, cover attached above a bed or seat, used as decoration or as a shelter
transparent, clear and easy to see through
spectacle, public scene or show that is very impressive
raspy, rough sounding

88

TESOL Standards

Goal 1, Standard 2—To use English to communicate in social settings: Students will interact in, through, and with spoken and written English for personal expression and enjoyment.
Descriptors—Expressing personal needs, feelings, and ideas.

Goal 2, Standard 3—To use English to achieve academically in all content areas: Students will use appropriate learning strategies to construct and apply academic knowledge.
Descriptors—Taking notes to record important information and aid one's own learning; Actively connecting new information to information previously learned.

reveals itself early. Other times you must let your imagination dictate what you will find. How do you see your soap today? It is a dog, right?"

I nodded. I had been working on it for several days. "This end will be the tail. And here"—I pointed to the bottom corner—"will be one of its legs, running."

Santiago nodded.

Almost done, I pulled my knife across the soap but dug a little too deep and a large piece crumbled to the ground. With one slip of the knife, I had accidentally carved off the running leg.

I gasped.

"No, do not be sad," said Santiago. "There is still some magic left inside. Let us say that the missing leg is *simbólico* of a tragedy or something the dog has lost. Or that its destiny was to be a dog with three legs." He picked up my carving, and with a few strokes of the knife smoothed the ragged piece into a perfect three-legged dog. "You must carve so that what is inside can become what it is meant to be. When you are finished, the magic will show itself for what it really is."

---

dictate, influence or control

simbólico, Spanish for "symbolic"; standing for a particular event, process, or situation

tragedy, event that is extremely sad, especially one that involves death

---

BEFORE YOU GO ON

1 How do Owen and Naomi spend Christmas morning?

2 What is Naomi carving out of her bar of soap?

On Your Own
Have you ever created something and in the process allowed your imagination to "dictate what you find"? Describe the experience.

89

Study Skills: Internet

Learning to use the Internet as a research tool will give students access to a wide variety of useful information.

In the story, Naomi and Gram arrive in time for the radish-carving festival. Students can find images of radishes and learn about the festival by using search engines.

- Use a search engine to do an image search and find images of radishes from around the world.
- Use a search engine to research *La fiesta de los rábanos*. This radish-carving festival has been held on December 23 in Oaxaca, Mexico, for over 100 years. The governor of the state of Oaxaca judges the final results. An image search will find pictures of the final results.

STEP 3: Monitor Progress

Ask students to check what they have understood in the reading. If you are using the Audio CD, pause the recording.

Before You Go On

Point out the Before You Go On box, and have students read and answer the questions. Remind them to go back to the text if they don't know the answers. Explain that the On Your Own question asks for your opinion. Any thoughtful answer is correct.

ANSWERS

1. They spend the morning watching the carvings in the tree.
2. A dog.

On Your Own Have students write an answer to the On Your Own question. Encourage volunteers to share their responses with the class. Collect student responses to check their comprehension, writing skills, and fluency.

Differentiated Instruction	
Beginning	Have students name the two characters in the illustration on page 89. (Owen, Naomi)
Early Intermediate	Ask students what they think Naomi said when she first saw her father.
Intermediate	Have students describe a hobby that they share with a family member or close friend.
Special Needs	Have students listen to the audio recording. Encourage them as far as possible to read along as they listen.

Read

Preteaching Highlighted Words

Before reading this spread, review the highlighted words and terms with students. Define each one, pointing out the location of the definition in the gloss at the bottom of the student book page. Make sure that students understand each highlighted word. If appropriate, ask students to generate original sentences using the highlighted words. When correcting original sentences, focus on usage of the highlighted word.

Model the
READING STRATEGY

Visualize

Ask students to turn back to page 87 and review the steps for visualizing. **SAY:** *I can visualize the carvings Santiago describes on page 90, like the parrot with a fish tail. What other descriptions on this page help you to see images in your mind from the story? What do the other carvings he describes look like?* Help the students to identify the most descriptive words.

✔ LITERARY CHECK

Point out the Literary Check box, and read the question aloud. Remind students that *dialogue* is defined on page 85. Answer: The dialogue suggests that Santiago feels carving is imaginative, magical, unpredictable.

Santiago considered an odd-shaped piece of wood. "When the promise does not reveal itself early, your imagination must dictate your intentions. Then the wood, or the soap, it will become what you least expect. Sometimes the wood fools me. I think I am carving a parrot, and when I am finished it has a fish tail. Or I begin a tiger, and in the end it has the body of a dancer."

With the small machete, he scraped at the layers of the bark that had built up over time, exposing the innards of what used to be a tree branch and revealing the unprotected heart meat. He traded the machete for a knife and chaffed at the wood with quick strokes. Soon he handed me a rough figure.

I held it up in the air. I could see that is was a lion's body with a human's head, maybe that of a girl.

As I turned it around, admiring it, Gram came out of the house and slowly sat down in one of the chairs. She stared at her folded hands and cleared her throat. "I just checked in with [our neighbor] Mrs. Maloney [in Lemon Tree]. The mediator, a young woman, showed up at Avocado Acres yesterday to interview her. Imagine showing up on Christmas Eve! The woman asked Mrs. Maloney where we were because she needs to talk to all of us by Friday, January third. Mrs. Maloney told her we'd return from our family vacation in time for the interview, which is what I had told her to say if anybody asked. That's in nine days, and what with four or five days' driving ahead of us . . . I'm sorry, Naomi, but we should leave the day after tomorrow."

---

machete, knife with a broad, heavy blade, used as a cutting tool
innards, inside parts
mediator, person who tries to help two groups to stop arguing and make an agreement

✔ LITERARY CHECK

How does the dialogue reveal Santiago's feelings about carving?

90

 TESOL Standards

Goal 1, Standard 3—To use English to communicate in social settings: Students will use learning strategies to extend their communicative competence.
Descriptors—Using the primary language to ask for clarification; Using context to construct meaning.

Goal 2, Standard 1—To use English to achieve academically in all content areas: Students will use English to interact in the classroom.
Descriptors—Requesting information and assistance.

I took a deep breath and looked around the yard. "Can't we just stay here?" I asked, my hands suddenly quivering. "You like it here. You said so yourself." I heard Owen's and Rubén's giggles coming from the garden. "Owen loves it and we could . . . we could go to school here. We're learning Spanish real good. Or . . . or we could go to Puerto Escondido and live in the little house and help sell the carvings. . . . I could learn to paint them, like Aunt Teresa . . . and . . ."

Santiago pulled me from my chair to his side on a small wooden bench. He put his arm around me.

"Naomi, I would love for you to come to my house, but right now your life is in California. I have written the letter for the judge. I told the truth about your mother and that my wishes are for you and Owen to live with María [Gram]. I told that I want to be a part of your life and see you . . . maybe in the summer for vacations if that is all right with you and Owen. More, if it is possible."

My lips trembled. I stared at the ground.

"I did not fight for you when you were little," said Santiago. "It is something for which I am sorry. I should not have believed your mother when she said I would never be able to see you. If I had been stronger, maybe things could have been different, but maybe they would not have been so different. . . . How will we ever know?"

I looked at him. "But why can't you come with us?"

"For that to happen," he said, "I would have to prepare. Much would need to be done. Sell my house. My boat. Much of my money comes from my carvings, which are sold only in Oaxaca. My work, it is here."

"But what if the judge—"

"Naomi," said Gram, "we are not going to consider the worst that could happen. Thinking that way does not help self-prophecies."

Since we'd found Santiago, Gram was wearing her fierceness again. At least on the outside.

"I guess I better tell Owen," said Gram.

"I will go with you," said Santiago, and they headed toward the garden.

Alone, beneath the jacaranda, I stared at the three-legged dog and the lion girl in my lap.

We rode home to Lemon Tree silently. The truck and Baby Beluga seemed to drag along the highway. We traveled with less than we had brought. . . . So why did we seem to plod along? Did the weight of our memories slow us down?

---

quivering, shaking slightly because of nervousness or worry
Puerto Escondido, Spanish for "Hidden Port," a port city in the state of Oaxaca, Mexico
trembled, shook because of fear
self-prophecies, predictions about yourself that could come true

✔ **LITERARY CHECK**

*What does the **dialogue** between Gram and Naomi show about Gram's character?*

BEFORE YOU GO ON

1 What does Santiago carve out of the tree branch?

2 Where does Santiago sell his carvings?

💡 **On Your Own**
How would you feel if you were Naomi? Would you want to stay in Oaxaca? Why?

91

Study Skills: Map

Naomi mentions places in Oaxaca, such as Puerto Escondido, and Gram says it is four or five days back to Lemon Tree. Students can use a map of Mexico to find distances. Have students find Oaxaca, and Puerto Escondido. Find the border of Mexico and California. Driving 500–600 miles a day, four or five days of driving would take them around 2500 miles. That means that Santiago is that far away from Naomi, and Lemon Tree is somewhere in Southern California. San Diego is about 1700 miles from Oaxaca.

✔ **LITERARY CHECK**

Have students read the questions in the margin before they read the story. This preview strategy is used by good readers and test takers so that they know what to look for while they read. If students need help remembering the meaning of *dialogue,* refer back to page 85. **SAY:** *Is Gram very emotional when she speaks?*

STEP 5: Monitor Progress

Ask students to check what they have understood in the reading. If you are using the Audio CD, pause the recording.

Before You Go On

Remind students that when they answer each question, they should look for the place on the page that gives them that information.

ANSWERS
1. Santiago carves a lion girl for Naomi.
2. Santiago can only sell his work in Oaxaca.

On Your Own Have students write an answer to the On Your Own question on a separate sheet of paper. Encourage volunteers to share their responses with the class. Then collect student responses to monitor their comprehension, writing skills, and fluency.

STEP 6: Teach

Preteaching Highlighted Words

Before reading this spread, review the highlighted words and terms with students. Define each one, pointing out the location of the definition in the gloss at the bottom of the student book page. Make sure that students understand each highlighted word. If appropriate, ask students to generate original sentences using the highlighted words. When correcting original sentences, focus on usage of the highlighted word.

Across the Curriculum:
Science

Explain to students that the jacaranda and copal trees mentioned in the story are both native to Oaxaca. Jacaranda trees are famous for their large, beautiful purple-blue flowers. Copal tree wood is used for carving and to make incense, because it is very fragrant and produces resin. Carvers like the wood because it is soft, and sands to a smooth finish.

For hundreds of kilometers, I held the lion girl and thought about all that I wanted to tell [my friend] Blanca, especially about my father.

On our last days in Oaxaca, Owen and I had gone everywhere with Santiago: to visit Aunt Teresa, to *el zócalo*, to *el Mercado* for pineapple-coconut ice cream. And to admire the statue of Soledad in *la basilica*.

I would never forget that day. The statue with the long robe, a crown of gold, the sparkling stained-glass windows. Our footsteps echoing on the floor. Holding Santiago's hand and listening to his adoration.

"*Our Lady of Solitude* is loved by sailors and fisherman," he said. "She protects us at sea: when our boats are rocking in a storm, when it is foggy and we cannot see the way, when we need to get home and our motor fails us. Then we ask for her assistance. She is part of Oaxaca. And since you have her name and have been here to see the wonder of this city, Oaxaca is part of you."

The morning we left, Santiago came early to help load the last of the luggage. He cut down all the animals hanging from the jacaranda and gave them to Owen and me.

It was a long good-bye . . . the kind of good-bye where everyone hugged and kissed every single person, then stood around talking and looking at each other, then all of a sudden started hugging and kissing everyone again, crying a little each time.

When we were finally ready to climb into the truck, Santiago hugged me and said, "Be brave, Naomi León."

I nodded, but when he took me in his arms one more time and rocked me back and forth, I didn't pretend to be brave.

"Do not be sad," he whispered. "We have found each other. I will write. You will write. We have much for which to be thankful and everything will be the way it was meant to be. You will see. I promise. I promise. Now you must promise."

"I promise." . . .

Oaxaca had long disappeared from our view. I opened my notebook to make a list of all that I hoped to remember, but I closed it. My pen seemed too heavy to lift.

el zócalo, a public square/town square
el Mercado, the market
la basilica, the church

92

TESOL Standards

Goal 1, Standard 1—To use English to communicate in social settings: Students will use English to participate in social interactions.
Descriptors—Expressing needs, feelings, and ideas.

Soap Carving

Here's how you can learn to carve soap like Naomi.

What you will need:

- Newspapers or a tray or a bowl (something to catch the soap shavings)
- Scissors
- Craft sticks
- Tracing paper (optional)

- A bar (or bars) of pure and natural soap that will need to be aired overnight (see steps 2 and 3 below)
- Pencil or ballpoint pen
- Sheet of paper

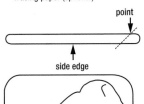

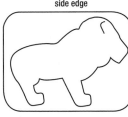

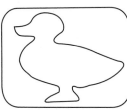

1. Using your scissors, cut off the tip of your craft stick at an angle, creating a point.

2. Unwrap the soap. Using the long edge of a craft stick, scrape the logo from each side of the bar so that you will have a flat surface.

3. Let the soap air out overnight.

4. Draw or trace a design (or create your own) onto a piece of paper such as the ones on the left. Remember, the design should be no larger than your bar of soap. Or you can carve without a pattern and create your own abstract design.

5. Place the piece of paper with the design against the broad, flat side of the soap. Using a ballpoint pen or a pencil, trace the outline of the design, pressing hard so it will leave an impression on your soap.

6. Following the basic rectangular shape of the soap, block out your design. Using the side edge of the angled craft stick, cut away the soap you don't need in thin layers. (Note: Cutting away too much at once will likely cause your soap to crumble apart.)

7. Once the basic angles have been established, start rounding your form. Keep turning your piece, working evenly and from all angles.

ABOUT THE **AUTHOR**

Pam Muñoz Ryan grew up in California's San Joaquin Valley. Her grandparents and many of her aunts and uncles lived nearby. The stories her family told had a big influence on her as she was growing up. Ryan loved reading as a child and became a bilingual teacher before she began writing her own stories for children. Some of her other well-known novels include *Riding Freedom* and *Esperanza Rising,* both of which have won many literary awards. Ryan still lives in southern California with her husband and four teenage children.

BEFORE YOU GO ON

1 Where do Owen and Naomi go on their last days in Oaxaca?

2 What does Santiago give to Owen and Naomi before they leave?

On Your Own
How might creating something in writing, carving, or some other artistic form make an unhappy person feel better?

93

Study Skills: Internet

Students can use the internet to learn more about Pam Muñoz Ryan. Ryan's ethnic background is Spanish, Mexican, Basque, Italian, and Oklahoman, and she has been to Mexico many times. To research *Becoming Naomi León,* she went to Oaxaca. Use search engines to find useful pages and sources of information, like the author's homepage, and her publishers' pages. Ask them to find a bibliography, or list of books she has written. Students can also find out what other people think of the author's books and stories, or look up more about where she came from.

STEP 7: Monitor Progress

Ask students to check what they have understood in the reading.

Before You Go On

Point out that sometimes you need to go far back in a story to find an answer to a question. Suggest that students start at page 92.

ANSWERS

1. Naomi and Owen go to visit Aunt Teresa, to el zócalo (the town square), el Mercado (the market), and la basilica (the church) to see la Soledad.
2. Santiago gives them the carvings which were hanging from the tree.

On Your Own Have students write an answer to the On Your Own question on a separate sheet of paper. Encourage volunteers to share their responses with the class. Then collect student responses to monitor their comprehension, writing skills, and fluency.

Review the Purpose for Reading

Elicit responses to the Set a Purpose for Reading questions at the beginning of this reading. Remind students to relate their responses to the Big Question.

Teach & Apply

STEP 1: Introduce

Speaking Tip

Point out that in a play, you need to look like you do in real life. Facing the other character makes it look realistic. Speaking clearly and loudly helps the audience hear every word you say.

Reader's Theater

Performing by reading aloud is excellent practice for students. It gives them a reason to rehearse their reading several times, to increase fluency, and to improve expression and intonation.

Suggest that students think about how their character feels at this point in the story.

Divide students into pairs to practice and perform. Have students decide who will play which role. Ask them to find a quiet corner in which to rehearse and practice their lines. Then ask volunteers to perform for the class.

STEP 2: Practice

Comprehension

Have students work individually or in small groups to write answers to the questions. Encourage students to answer in complete sentences.

ANSWERS

1. Mrs. Maloney says the Leons will be back from their vacation in time for the interview.
2. Santiago expresses that he would like to be more a part of the children's lives.
3. Naomi wants to stay in Oaxaca because she enjoys it there and she can see her father.
4. It would be hard for Santiago to go to California because his livelihood is selling carvings only sold in Oaxaca.
5. Naomi is expressing how sad and upset she is when she says her pen is too heavy to lift.
6. **Possible response:** I think Naomi will be able to stay with Gram because of Santiago's letter.
7. Answers will vary.
8. Answers will vary.

Teaching Resources

- *Workbook*, p. 44
- CD-ROM/e-book, Reader's Theater, Comprehension, Response to Literature

---

READER'S THEATER

Act out the following scene between Naomi and her father.

Santiago: Let me teach you how to carve. Be careful with the tools.

Naomi: I'll try, but the soap gets slippery in my hands.

Santiago: Start by drawing the design you want on the soap. Choose something simple, like a dog or cat.

Naomi: I'll draw a dog. There . . . that looks good. Now I'm ready to start carving. First, I'll carve the outside pieces. This will be the dog's shape.

Santiago: Wonderful, Naomi! Now, be very careful when you start carving the legs. They're more difficult to carve because they are so thin.

Naomi: Oh, no! Look what I've done. I cut off the running leg!

Santiago: Don't worry. We'll make a different kind of dog, one that has lost something. Look now. Isn't this three-legged dog even more lovely?

Naomi: Yes, it's not the dog I planned, but it is beautiful.

COMPREHENSION — Workbook Page 44

Right There

1. What does Mrs. Maloney tell the mediator about the Leóns?
2. What wishes does Santiago express in his letter to the judge?

Think and Search

3. What are several reasons why Naomi wants to stay in Oaxaca?
4. Why would it be hard for Santiago to go to California?

Author and You

5. Why does Naomi say, "My pen seemed too heavy to lift"?
6. Will Naomi be allowed to stay with Gram? Predict what will happen.

94

Speaking TIP

Face your partner when you are speaking to him or her. Speak clearly and loudly so that your audience can hear you.

🌐 TESOL Standards

Goal 1, Standard 1—To use English to communicate in social settings: Students will use English to participate in social interactions.
Descriptors—Using nonverbal communication in social interactions; Conducting transactions.

Goal 1, Standard 3—To use English to communicate in social settings: Students will use learning strategies to extend their communicative competence.
Descriptors—Selecting different media to help understand language.

Goal 2, Standard 3—To use English to achieve academically in all content areas: Students will use appropriate learning strategies to construct and apply academic knowledge.
Descriptors—Determining and establishing the conditions that help one become an effective learner (e.g., when, where, how to study); Recognizing the need for and seeking assistance appropriately from others (e.g., teachers, peers, specialists, community members); Knowing when to use native language resources (human and material) to promote understanding.

On Your Own

7. With what person in your life do you have a strong bond? Why?

8. Have you ever loved a place so much that you felt that it was "part of you"? Describe the place and your feelings about it.

DISCUSSION

Listening TIP

If you don't understand an answer, ask the person to repeat or explain his or her answer.

Discuss in pairs or small groups.

1. In your opinion, should Naomi and Owen live with Santiago, Gram, or Skyla? Give reasons for your answer.

2. Imagine that you could travel anywhere in the United States or Mexico. Where would you go and why?

Q **How does growing up change us?** What sorts of feelings did Naomi have when she had to say good-bye to her father? Why do you think that she felt the way she did? How do you think that kind of experience affects a person her age?

RESPONSE TO LITERATURE

Workbook
Page 44

Think about what you have learned about Oaxaca from *Becoming Naomi León*. Jot down words and phrases that the author uses to describe the setting. Based on what you have learned, write a short travel brochure in which you tell people why Oaxaca would be a nice place to visit. Describe three features of Oaxaca that would attract tourists. Use descriptive words that will make people want to travel there. You may want to find several photographs or make some drawings for your brochure. Share your completed travel brochure with a classmate.

◄ The streets of Oaxaca City

95

Differentiated Instruction

Beginning	Ask students to name the characters in the illustration on page 92. (Naomi, Santiago, Gram, and Owen)
Early Intermediate	In pairs, give students the opportunity to practice two lines from the Reader's Theater. Encourage students to act rather than read.
Intermediate	In small groups, ask students to summarize the reading and then present their summary to the class.
Greater Challenge	Have students act out the entire Reader's Theater for the class.

STEP 3: Extend

Listening Tip

Point out the Listening Tip in the student book. **SAY:** *There are many reasons why someone might not understand what you have said. Be sure to speak clearly, and use different words than you did before if you are asked to explain your answer.* Remind students to be polite, and ask them to practice this tip when it is necessary in the discussion.

(CRI) Discussion

Congratulate students on successfully completing the reading. **SAY:** *We've learned a lot about the Big Question, "How does growing up change us?" from the reading. Now let's discuss a few questions about the reading.* Model a discussion starter for each question. **SAY:** *For the first question, What do you think should control who takes care of the children? Naomi thinks she will be happy with Santiago. Is that the most important thing? For the second question, think of a place you would love to go, that you've been to. Why would you recommend that other people go there?*

Q **How does growing up change us?** Read the first question to the students. Santiago told Naomi to be brave, but she didn't feel brave saying goodbye. **SAY:** *How do you think Naomi will be brave? How do you think children and adults are expected to be brave?*

STEP 4: Assess

Response to Literature

Read over the instructions for this activity. Bring in some brochures so that students know what they are to create. Point out that brochures are designed to interest the reader in traveling to the place advertised, so they include lots of description and pictures. Students can create pictures based on the author's descriptions, or find pictures of places and things from the story on the Internet.

Teach & Apply

STEP 1: Introduce

Tell students that there are verbs to describe what action we are doing, like *run* and *jump*, and there are verbs to describe what we are thinking, feeling, sensing, or being. Ask them to look at page 96 and tell them you will be reviewing non-action verbs.

STEP 2: Teach

Grammar and Writing

Non-action Verbs Read aloud the information regarding non-action verbs on the pupil page. Create a chart with the five categories: mental states, emotional states, possession, senses, other states. Help students place the verbs in the appropriate category and then search for additional examples in the reading.

STEP 3: Practice

Read over with students the instructions for this practice exercise. Write the first Practice sentence on the board. **SAY:** *This sentence seems to be about how Naomi's father feels about carving—his emotional state. Choose one of the words from the list that seems to fit in this sentence, and then change it so that it matches the subject of the verb—her father. The right word is 'love'—it describes his emotion. This should be changed to 'loves' because the subject, 'her father,' is in the third person singular.* All of the subjects in this exercise are in the third person singular.

Pair English learners with proficient English speakers to work on the rest of the sentences. Have volunteers write their answers on the board.

ANSWERS
1. loves
2. has
3. hears
4. wants/looks like
5. feels

Teaching Resources

- *Workbook*, pp. 45–46
- *CD-ROM/e-book*, Grammar, Writing
- *Transparencies*, Writing Model 27
- *Transparencies*, *Resources*, Graphic Organizer 10
- *Assessment*, Reading 2 Test, pp. 55–58

T96

Grammar and Writing

GRAMMAR, USAGE, AND MECHANICS

Non-action Verbs

Use non-action verbs to describe conditions or situations. Non-action verbs are mostly used only in the simple present, past, or future. Non-action verbs express mental states (*want*, *need*, *know*), emotional states (*like*, *love*, *prefer*), possession (*have*, *own*, *belong*), senses (*taste*, *smell*, *feel*, *see*, *hear*), and other states of being (*seem*, *sound*, *look like*). Notice that all the examples below are in the simple present, past, or future.

> Skyla **wants** to obtain legal custody of Naomi.
> The woman **needs** to talk to all of us by Friday, January third.
> You **like** it here.
> We **have** much for which to be thankful. You **will see**.
> My pen **seemed** too heavy to lift.

Practice Workbook Page 45

Copy the sentences below into your notebook. Complete each sentence with the correct form of a non-action verb from the box. The first one has been done for you.

| feel | have | hear | look like | love | want |

1. Naomi discovers her father *loves* carving, too.
2. Santiago _____ many carved wooden animals hanging in his tree.
3. Naomi _____ the raspy sound of her brother giggling.
4. Santiago _____ to carve a parrot, but in the end it _____ a fish.
5. Naomi _____ sad that she can't be with her father.

96

WRITING A NARRATIVE PARAGRAPH

Write about a Character and Setting

On this page, you will write a narrative about a made-up character in a realistic setting. You'll use a graphic organizer like the one at the right to gather details about the character and setting.

When you write a narrative about a character in a particular setting, you include character and physical traits and sensory details. To describe the character, you tell how the character looks, acts, and thinks. To describe the setting, you tell about the time and place.

Here is a model of a paragraph that describes a character in a realistic place during the present. Notice the words the writer uses to tell you what the character and setting are like and how the character and setting are connected.

Character (Who)
Setting (Where and When)

Talia Marcus

At Camp

I will never forget the day I met Laura at Camp Hillcrest. It was Laura's first day at sleep-away camp, but I had been going there for three years and loved Hillcrest. It's located on a beautiful hill near a huge lake and has great activities. I had just arrived when I noticed her. She's a very tall girl with very short hair, and she was standing all by herself. She seemed shy, so I talked to her and tried to make her feel comfortable. I discovered we both play tennis! For a while, Laura seemed fine. Then, at bedtime, she suddenly felt homesick and wanted to see her parents. She looked distraught! I told her that everyone feels this way at first, and if she gave Hillcrest a try, she would really like it. After that, Laura calmed down and went to sleep. She ended up loving camp, just like I knew she would.

Practice **Workbook Page 46**

Write a narrative paragraph about a made-up character in a realistic setting. Start your paragraph with this sentence: *I will never forget the day I met (character's name) in (real place).* Use a character/setting chart to gather details for your paragraph. Put your details in an order that makes sense. Use non-action verbs to describe the situation and the character's appearance and feelings.

Writing Checklist

IDEAS:
- ☑ I created a clear picture of a character in a particular place.

CONVENTIONS:
- ☑ I checked my grammar, spelling, and punctuation.

97

Accelerate Language Development

Action and Non-action Verbs

Point out that there are a few verbs that can be both action and non-action verbs. Example: *She looks beautiful.* Here *look* is a non-action verb. *I am looking out of the window.* Here *look* is an action verb. The difference between action and non-action usage of these verbs can be made clear with their synonyms. *Look* as a non-action verb is synonymous with *is,* but *looks* as an action verb is synonymous with *see.* Other verbs that can be used as both are: *think, taste, weigh,* and *be.*

STEP 1: Introduce

Tell students a narrative paragraph is often used to introduce the elements of a story. This kind of paragraph can include information about a character or setting in a story.

STEP 2: Teach

Writing a Narrative Paragraph

Create a Character and Setting Read over the instructions with students. Be sure they understand that "made up" characters means that that these people are not real. Read aloud the student sample, and ask students to listen for the details and description that make the character and setting seem real. Point out how the setting is introduced. Explain that students will be creating a paragraph that includes both.

Model Writing Skill Point out the chart on the student page, and draw it on the board. Label the columns *Character* and *Setting.* Ask a volunteer to read aloud the paragraph about Laura at camp, and with students, fill in the setting and character information on the chart. **SAY:** *I know the paragraph's setting—it's at the author's camp, her fourth year there. I will write that under* Setting. *I know how Laura acts and what she likes—she likes tennis and gets homesick. I will write that under* Character.

Now have students create a chart for their own character, listing things about their character, and their setting.

STEP 3: Assess

Many standardized tests have writing sections that use a prompt or sentence starter. Discuss with students that it is important to follow the directions and to stick to the given topic. Explain that this prompt lets the writer know that the paragraph is supposed to describe an unforgettable character in a realistic setting. Brainstorm possible responses.

Writing Checklist Note

Have students evaluate their work using the Writing Checklist.

Ideas Check that students' paragraphs introduce a single character who is well described, and is clearly set in a real place.

Conventions Check that students have used correct punctuation and spelling in their paragraphs.

Teach

STEP 1: Introduce

Objectives

Read the list of objectives in the What You Will Learn section, encouraging students to join in. Tell students that this reading will be about one brother who is jealous of another.

 The Big Question

Ask students the Big Question: *How does growing up change us?* Many children have pets. Pets teach responsibility, and offer companionship. Discuss what pets students have and ask which is the most unusual. Discuss how pets get their names. Ask them what pet they would have if they were allowed.

Build Background

SAY: *There are many stories about brothers and sisters who are jealous of each other. Sometimes siblings are jealous, whether they are children or adults.* One story about sibling jealousy is about Baldur, the Norse god who was killed by his brother Loki. Everyone loved Baldur, and Loki was jealous because he did not feel as loved. Loki, the god of mischief, arranged a trap for Baldur. When Baldur was killed, everyone was sad, and Loki still didn't feel loved. Tell students about this story, and **SAY:** *How is Loki's behavior similar to the behavior of children like Teddy and Bobby?* With help from students, make a list of other examples of jealousy between siblings in stories, and ask them for their own experiences.

STEP 2: Teach

Understanding the Genre:
Novel Excerpt

A novel is a long work of fiction. Novels contain such elements as characters, plot, conflict, and setting. The writer develops these elements. This reading is an excerpt. An *excerpt* is an episode or an event from a novel.

Teaching Resources

• CD-ROM/e-book, Literary Words
• Audio CD 2, track 10
• *Workbook*, p. 47

What You Will Learn

Reading
■ Vocabulary building: *Literary terms, word study*
■ Reading strategy: *Recognize sequence*
■ Text type: *Literature (novel excerpt)*

Grammar, Usage, and Mechanics
Making comparisons

Writing
Write a story from another point of view

 THE BIG QUESTION

How does growing up change us? Why do pets often play an important role in our lives when we're growing up? What kind of a pet would you like to have? Would you choose a common pet such as a dog, cat, or bird? Or would you prefer a less common pet like a pig, rabbit, or snake?

Work with a partner. Talk about what kind of pets you like and what kind you do not like. Then share your ideas with the class. Explain why you prefer a certain kind of pet.

BUILD BACKGROUND

Later, Gator is a realistic and funny novel about two brothers who are very different from each other. The older brother, Teddy, is jealous of his younger brother, Bobby.

Jealousy is a strong feeling that can sometimes make people (and characters) say mean things or act badly. As children grow up, they often have feelings of jealousy. Sometimes a younger child is jealous of an older child because he or she can do more things. Sometimes an older child is jealous of a younger child because he or she gets more attention. In *Later, Gator*, jealousy plays a big part in what happens between Teddy and his brother.

▲ Dogs are popular pets with children and adults.

98

TESOL Standards

Goal 1, Standard 3—To use English to communicate in social settings: Students will use learning strategies to extend their communicative competence.
Descriptors—Selecting different media to help understand language; Using context to construct meaning.

Goal 2, Standard 3—To use English to achieve academically in all content areas: Students will use appropriate learning strategies to construct and apply academic knowledge.
Descriptors—Focusing attention selectively; Applying basic reading comprehension skills such as skimming, scanning, previewing, and reviewing text; Using context to construct meaning.

VOCABULARY

Learn Literary Words

Plot is what happens in a story. Most plots include a problem, the events that lead to solving the problem, and the solution to the problem. Usually, plots move forward in time. They have a beginning, middle, and end.

Point of view is the position from which a story is told. Some stories are told from the point of view of one of the characters. The character tells the events as if they are happening to him or her. This is called *first-person point of view*. The person telling the story uses the pronouns *I, me, my,* and *we*. Other stories are told from the *third-person point of view*. The narrator, or person telling the story, uses the pronouns *she, he,* and *they*. The narrator can be one of the characters in the story, or just someone telling the story from the outside. Read the examples below and notice the pronouns.

Literary Words

plot
point of view
narrator

First-person point of view: I was so excited when my older sister bought me a blue parakeet for my birthday.

Third-person point of view: Gerry was overjoyed when he received a blue parakeet from his sister on his sixth birthday.

Practice Workbook Page 47

Work with a partner. Reread the chapter from *Becoming Naomi León* on pages 88–92. Then answer the questions below in your notebook:

1. What is the plot of the story? Describe the problem, events that lead to a solution, and the solution?

2. Is the story told from the first-person point of view or the third-person point of view? How can you tell?

3. How would the story have been different if it had been told from Santiago's point of view?

A blue parakeet can be a nice pet. ▶

99

Differentiated Instruction

Beginning	Have students name the pets seen in the photos on pages 98, 99, and 100.
Early Intermediate	Have students look at each of the illustrations on pages 102–107. Ask students what they think the story is about.
Intermediate	Have students write example sentences in the first-person and the third-person point of view.
Struggling Readers	Ask students if they have any pets. If not, ask them if they'd like to get one. Ask why or why not.

CD2 T10

 Vocabulary

Learn Literary Words Play the CD. Have students listen and repeat. Read the Literary Words aloud. **SAY:** *These are called literary words because in the discussion of literature they have a unique meaning.* Write down the following key points on the board.

plot: the action that happens in the story

point of view: the position from which the story is told

narrator: the person who tells the story. The narrator can be one of the characters in the story or someone outside the story. Provide examples of plot, point of view, and narrator. **SAY:** *In the reading, the plot is Naomi's trip to Mexico to see her father. If you talk about yourself, you'll use the first person POV, but if you are talking about someone else, you will use the third person POV. In this story, the narrator is Naomi, who is telling about what has happened to her.* Ask students to use the words plot, point of view, and narrator in new sentences. Have students use the corresponding Workbook page for extra practice.

STEP 3: Practice

Read aloud the instructions for this practice exercise. Model how to answer the first question. **SAY:** *I know that the plot is the series of events and action in a story.* Then read aloud the answer given for the first question.

ANSWERS

1. The plot concerns Naomi Leon and her younger brother, who have been living happily with their grandmother for some time. The problem is that the children's mother tries to get custody of them. Gram and the children flee to Mexico to find Naomi's father and ask him to help Gram get custody of the children. The problem appears to be solved when Naomi's father says he has written to the judge, asking that Gram be made the children's guardian. Naomi also learns that she has a lot in common with her father and that he loves her very much.

2. The story is told from the first-person point of view, and uses the words *I* and *me* to refer to Naomi.

3. Possible Answer: If the story had been told from Santiago's point of view, we might have read more about Naomi's mother, and Santiago's plans to be with his kids later on.

STEP 1: Teach

CD2 T11–T12

Vocabulary

Learn Academic Words Play the CD. Have students listen and repeat. The Academic Words box at the top of the page is useful when talking and writing about ideas and new concepts. Read aloud each academic word, discuss its meaning, and model an example. **SAY:** *Look at the Academic Word list. The chart below contains two parts: the definition on the left and a sentence containing the word on the right. Work with a partner to add another sentence using the academic word. Write each word, its definition, and the sentence in your notebook. Example: "The author of the story is Laurence Yep."*

STEP 2: Practice

Write the following question on the board and underline the words as shown: How does a lack of sleep affect you? **SAY:** *When you are asked a question, try to include words from the question in your answer. Look at the question on the board.* Write this sample answer on the board: *A lack of sleep affects me by making me cranky, forgetful, and sleepy during the day.* Be sure to underline the words as shown so students can clearly see the connection.

ANSWERS

Possible responses:
1. A lack of sleep affects me by making me cranky, forgetful, and sleepy during the day.
2. My favorite author is Bill Peet because he creates wacky characters.
3. A new pet would have the effect of creating chaos in our family.
4. From my perspective, a snake is not a real pet because it isn't cuddly.

Teaching Resources

- Audio CD 2, tracks 11–12
- *Workbook*, pp. 48-50
- CD-ROM/e-book, Academic Words, Word Study

Learn Academic Words

Study the red words and their meanings. You will find these words useful when talking and writing about literature. Write each word and its meaning in your notebook. After you read the excerpt from *Later, Gator,* try to use these words to respond to the text.

Academic Words

affect
author
effect
perspective

affect = do something that produces a change in someone or something; influence	Jealousy can **affect** the way people act. Sometimes, it can change how two people feel about each another.
author = someone who writes a book, story, article, or play	Laurence Yep is the **author** of *Later, Gator.* He is the writer of this novel.
effect = a result, or a reaction to something or someone	Owning a pet can have a good **effect** on a person. It gives people a sense of responsibility and companionship.
perspective = a way of thinking about something that is influenced by the type of person you are or what you do	From my **perspective**, dogs are better pets than cats because they are more friendly and loyal. However, my sister has the opposite point of view.

Hint: People often confuse the words *affect* and *effect*. Use the verb *affect* to talk about making changes, and use the noun *effect* to talk about the results of changes. Remember, *effect* is almost always a noun that means "result."

Practice Workbook Page 48

Work with a partner to answer these questions. Try to include the red word in your answer. Write the sentences in your notebook.

1. How does a lack of sleep **affect** you?
2. Who is your favorite **author**? Why?
3. What **effect** would a new pet have on your family?
4 What is your **perspective** on having a snake as a pet?

How would having a pet iguana affect your day-to-day life? ▶

100

TESOL Standards

Goal 1, Standard 3—To use English to communicate in social settings: Students will use learning strategies to extend their communicative competence.
Descriptors—Listening to and imitating how others use English; Exploring alternative ways of saying things.

Goal 2, Standard 1—To use English to achieve academically in all content areas: Students will use English to interact in the classroom.
Descriptors—Participating in full-class, group, and pair discussions; Negotiating and managing interaction to accomplish tasks.

Goal 3, Standard 1—To use English in socially and culturally appropriate ways: Students will use the appropriate language variety, register, and genre according to audience, purpose, and setting.
Descriptors—Recognizing and using Standard English and vernacular dialects appropriately.

Word Study: Animal Verbs and Idioms

Writers often use colorful verbs and idioms to make their writing more lively. Some of the most vivid English verbs and idioms involve animals and animal comparisons. Read the sentences and definitions below. Think about why these words and phrases have these meanings.

Jody always tries **to weasel out of** doing her chores.
[*To weasel out of* means "to avoid."]

It bugs me when you yell in my ear.
[*To bug* means "to annoy someone."]

Why don't you **hold your horses**? We'll be there soon.
[*To hold your horses* means "to be patient."]

I'm completely soaked. It's **raining cats and dogs** outside.
[*To rain cats and dogs* means "to rain very heavily."]

Practice Workbook Page 49

Work with a partner to write a sentence of your own for each of the animal verbs and idioms above.

READING STRATEGY | **RECOGNIZE SEQUENCE**

Recognizing sequence will help you understand what you read. Knowing the sequence, or order, of events in a story helps you to understand the plot. To recognize sequence, follow these steps:

- As you read, look for words that show sequence, such as *first, second, then, next, last,* and *after.*
- Look for dates, days of the week, and times, such as *morning, next Thursday, yesterday, in 2010.*

As you read the excerpt from *Later, Gator,* identify the sequence of events. Ask yourself, "What happens at the beginning, in the middle, and at the end of the story?"

 Workbook Page 50

101

Linguistic Note

False Relatives

Many animal verbs directly derive from the animal noun itself. Point out that the animal noun probably existed first, and over time the nouns were being used as verbs to describe animal-like behavior. For example, a person who *squirrels things away* is someone who provides for later, just like a squirrel hides food for winter. Point out that there are a few verbs that have the same spelling and pronunciation as an animal noun, yet their meaning is very different. *Yak,* means *talk endlessly,* but the animal *yak* is not that talkative. *Batting* in baseball is not related to the animal *bat.* These verbs have a different origin from the seemingly related animal noun. Mention other examples of unrelated verb/noun pairs: *tick, sow, seal,* and *whale.* Then contrast them with a few related verb/noun pairs: *duck, monkey, worm,* and *horse.*

STEP 1: Teach

Word Study:

Animal Verbs and Idioms Read aloud the introductory paragraph and example idioms, and explain to the students that these are examples of descriptive language that have no literal connection to animals. Remind them that prepositions in phrasal verbs cannot be changed.

STEP 2: Practice

Read aloud the instructions for this practice exercise, and review each verb or idiom with your students. Ask them first to volunteer sentences, and write these on the board or overhead. Then ask students to write their own sentences using them.

ANSWERS

Answers will vary.

STEP 3: Teach

Reading Strategy

Recognize Sequence Good writers use sequence to help them organize their writing in a logical order. Sequence, or order of events, is a series of related events or actions that has a particular result. In both fiction and nonfiction writing, the sequence of events is often in chronological order. Model how to follow the order of events as a way of remembering what is read. Write on a chart the bulleted points on the pupil page to help students remember how to recognize sequence when they read.

Assign the corresponding workbook page for extra practice or homework.

Read

Set a purpose for reading How might jealousy change the relationship between two brothers as they grow up? Read to find out how jealousy affects the characters and plot of this story.

STEP 1: Introduce

Reading Summary

This episode tells about two brothers from the point of view of the older brother. His mother tells him to buy a pet for his brother's birthday. He decides to buy a baby alligator.

 The Big Question

Remind students that the Big Question is "How does growing up change us?" **SAY:** *Part of growing up is influenced by jealousy between brothers or sisters in a family, but also of friends and other people. As people grow up, they may become jealous of different people or things.* Ask students for their experiences seeing jealousy outside of sibling rivalry.

STEP 2: Teach

Set a Purpose for Reading

Illustrations can help the reader to predict what will occur in the story. **SAY:** *Look at the picture on the title page of this story. Describe the visible emotions of the characters pictured. Predict which character will get on the nerves of the other. Why do you think that?*

Preteaching Highlighted Words

With students, preview the highlighted selection vocabulary on pages 102–103. Write the words on the board and point out that they are defined at the bottom of each page. **SAY:** *Some words in this reading are related to popular culture, such as* neat-o, Willie Mays, *and the* Three Stooges. *Other words are action verbs, such as* wriggle *and* squirmed. Ask volunteers to find and read the definitions, then model using the words in original sentences. For example, *Writing stories about things you've never done takes a great imagination.* Then ask for volunteers to do the same, and create a word book including a definition, sentence, and image, if appropriate, for each word.

CD2 T13 **Scaffolding: Listen and Read**

Have students read along as you play the audio CD recording of the reading. Pause the recording at the end of each page to ask and answer questions students may have.

Teaching Resources

- *Resources*, Summaries, pp. 135–136
- Audio CD 2, track 13

---

from

Later, Gator

Laurence Yep

In this story, Teddy, the narrator, is jealous of his younger brother, Bobby, because everyone likes him. When their mother asks Teddy to buy Bobby a birthday present, Teddy plans to buy him something that he hopes will scare Bobby.

The alligator was Mother's fault. She told me to buy something special. Mother, as usual, blames me. She says that I've got more imagination than brains.

That's not my little brother's problem. Last Christmas I gave him a pair of socks. Bobby was too dumb to understand the insult. Instead of getting mad, he said to me, "They're neat-o and just what I wanted."

Yeah, sure, I thought to myself.

Bobby had to put on his new socks right away and wriggle his toes at me. "They're very warm and comfortable. Thank you," he said.

Do you see what I mean? Bobby is a walking Hallmark card.

---

blames me, says I did something bad
imagination, ability to form pictures or ideas in the mind
neat-o, great (slang)
wriggle, turn or twist with small, quick movements

102

 TESOL Standards

Goal 1, Standard 1—To use English to communicate in social settings: Students will use English to participate in social interactions.
Descriptors—Sharing and requesting information; Expressing needs, feelings, and ideas.

Goal 2, Standard 1—To use English to achieve academically in all content areas: Students will use English to interact in the classroom.
Descriptors—Asking and answering questions; Requesting information and assistance.

Goal 2, Standard 2—To use English to achieve academically in all content areas: Students will use English to obtain, process, construct, and provide subject matter information in spoken and written form.
Descriptors—Selecting, connecting, and explaining information; Analyzing, synthesizing, and inferring from information.

Mother had understood, though. So this year, on Friday, the week before Bobby's eighth birthday, she took me aside. "Why can't you get along with your little brother? What has he ever done to you?"

"Nothing," I confessed. That was the trouble. What kind of little brother doesn't bug his big brother? Bobby was not normal.

Mother clicked her tongue. "Everybody else likes your brother. He's so sweet."

"Bobby's a regular mint chocolate bar, all right," I said, and thought to myself, And I am a raisin cookie.

"Then why haven't you ever bought him something special?" Mother demanded. She would make a good prosecutor.

"You always said it's the spirit that counts," I grumbled.

Mother frowned. "Only a mean person buys a cheap pair of white cotton socks."

"He liked the baseball."

Mother folded her hands in front of her. "Which you then used and lost."

"The Christmas before I got him comic books," I pointed out.

"Which he couldn't read."

"I read them to him," I said. Mother just looked at me until I admitted, "Sometimes."

"You treat him like he's an enemy. Don't you love your brother?" Mother asked.

"Of course I do," I lied. (But really, how can I love a little angel who makes me feel mean and selfish and bad?)

"Then show your love," Mother said. "Get something Bobby wants."

I tried to weasel out of it. "I can't afford the official Willie Mays baseball glove."

"No, I mean something he wants even more. I've talked it over with your father, and he's agreed that Bobby is now old enough to have a pet," Mother said.

She went to a cabinet and took out a big paper bag. From the bag, she slid out a kidney-shaped plastic tray. A wall of transparent plastic some three inches high ran around the edge of the tray. Part of the bottom rose up into an island in the center. A plastic palm tree grew from the island's middle.

---

get along with, have a friendly relationship with
prosecutor, lawyer who asks questions in court
spirit, thought or attitude
Willie Mays, a famous baseball player
kidney-shaped, having a wide, curved shape
island, land surrounded by water

LITERARY CHECK
Who is the narrator of this selection?

BEFORE YOU GO ON

1 Why does Teddy have trouble loving his younger brother?

2 What does Mother want Teddy to do for Bobby?

🔦 **On Your Own**
What are the advantages of growing up with brothers and sisters? What are the advantages of being an only child?

103

Differentiated Instruction

Beginning	Ask students to point to the younger brother in the illustration on page 102.
Early Intermediate	Have students point to the picture of the younger brother. Ask students if he is the biggest or the smallest boy in the picture.
Intermediate	Ask students how they can tell which is the older brother and which is the younger brother.
Standard English Learners (CRI)	Ask students to think of reasons why siblings don't always get along. Encourage them to share their reasons with the class.

Study Skills: Encyclopedia

In the story, Teddy mentions Willie Mays, Bobby's hero. Willie Mays was a famous baseball player. Students can find information on Willie Mays, his accomplishments, and the game of baseball by using an encyclopedia. Remind them that names listed in an encyclopedia will always be listed last name first (i.e., "Mays, Willie", not "Willie Mays"). Ask students if they know any other sports stars, and write names on the board. Next to these, write names as they would be found in reference books. Remind them also that famous people may have nicknames which are not their real names.

Name	Look up
Willie Mays	Mays, Willie
Hank Aaron	Aaron, Hank
Babe Ruth	Ruth, George

STEP 3: Monitor Progress

Ask students to check what they have understood in the reading. If you are using the Audio CD, pause the recording.

Before You Go On

Remind students that the reading strategy is recognizing sequence. Have students notice the sequence of events as they read. You can verify student comprehension by having students answer these questions before they go on to the next page. When they answer questions, ask where they found the information.

ANSWERS

1. Teddy feels Bobby is an "angel" who makes him feel mean, selfish, and bad.
2. Mother wants Teddy to buy Bobby a special birthday present.

On Your Own Have students write an answer for this question on a separate sheet of paper. Encourage volunteers to share their responses. Collect student responses to check their understanding, writing skills, and fluency.

✔ LITERARY CHECK

Point out the Literary Check box, and read the question aloud. Extend the question into an open-ended discussion about the narrator's point of view, if possible. If students need help with the word *narrator*, refer to page 99.
Answer: The narrator of this story is Teddy.

STEP 4: Teach

Preteaching Highlighted Words

Before reading this spread, review the highlighted words and terms on page 105 with students. Define each one, pointing out the location of the definition in the gloss at the bottom of the student book page. Make sure that students understand each highlighted word. If appropriate, ask students to generate original sentences using the highlighted words. When correcting original sentences, focus on usage of the highlighted word.

Model the
READING STRATEGY

Recognize Sequence

Have students read page 105 again, and look for words that show sequence, or that indicate time or date. **SAY:** *When does Mother first suggest buying Bobby a turtle? What day is it when she talks to Teddy again? What are the words that indicate this?* Have students write out the things that happen on the morning of Bobby's birthday in order from first to last. Ask students why it matters that some things happen before others.

104

🌐 TESOL Standards

Goal 2, Standard 2—To use English to achieve academically in all content areas: Students will use English to obtain, process, construct, and provide subject matter information in spoken and written form.
Descriptors—Comparing and contrasting information; Persuading, arguing, negotiating, evaluating, and justifying.

Goal 2, Standard 3—To use English to achieve academically in all content areas: Students will use appropriate learning strategies to construct and apply academic knowledge.
Descriptors—Actively connecting new information to information previously learned.

"I got the idea when he was watching a nature show on TV. He likes animals," Mother said. "He always wants to go to the zoo or the Academy of Sciences." The academy was in Golden Gate Park and had an aquarium, a hall with stuffed animals, and a reptile section.

It wasn't fair, I told myself. I figured he watched educational shows to please our parents and to make me look bad. I'll take the Three Stooges over a nature show anytime.

"Then I saw an ad in the newspaper," Mother said, "and I bought this. It's a turtle home. You go down to the department store. They've got turtles on sale. You can buy him a pet."

Feeling miserable but caught, I promised.

For the rest of the week, I put it off. There was no fun in giving Bobby something he wanted. Instead, I just hung around the apartment and moped.

On the morning of his birthday, he was up bright and early and jumping around, pretending to catch fly balls over the shoulder like Willie Mays. He had made so much noise that I had got up early, too, even though it was Saturday.

Mother served his favorite breakfast. We each had a scrambled egg with rice and slices of Chinese sausage. The problem was that Mother served it every morning. It was typical of Bobby to play up to Mother that way. I would have asked for scrambled eggs, bacon, and toast.

When Father asked Bobby what he wanted to do on his birthday, Bobby volunteered to help him in the fish shop. Any normal kid would have asked for money for a movie—for him and for his older brother. Boy, he really drove me crazy.

After Father and Bobby left for work, Mother stood over me. "Well, did you buy Bobby's pet?" she asked.

I squirmed on my chair. "I didn't want to get it too soon. If Bobby found it, it would ruin the surprise."

"I thought so." Mother handed me a folded-up piece of paper. "I cut out the ad from the newspaper so you would know where to go. After you wash the dishes, go down and buy Bobby's pet."

"That's Bobby's chore today," I whined.

Three Stooges, popular TV comedy, starring three comedians
miserable, very unhappy
moped, felt sad
volunteered, offered
drove me crazy, made me angry
squirmed, turned and twisted

✔ LITERARY CHECK

Is this narrative told from the first-person point of view or the third-person point of view? How can you tell?

BEFORE YOU GO ON

1 Why does Mother think Bobby likes animals?

2 Why doesn't Teddy want to buy Bobby a turtle?

💡 **On Your Own**
What do you like to do on your birthday?

105

Study Skills: Thesaurus

Teddy uses lots of descriptive words to tell how he is feeling or acting. Help students to expand their vocabulary by finding different ways to say the same thing. **SAY:** *Look for the word* sad *in your thesaurus. Here are some other words that mean* sad *or* sadness *(miserable, mopey, gloomy, unhappy, discouraged, depressed). Each word has a slightly different meaning. Why would Teddy use these words instead of just saying* sad? Have students give examples of other synonyms, and provide sentences using each one.

✔ **LITERARY CHECK**

Point out the Literary Check box, and read the question aloud. If students need help remembering the meaning of *first-person* or *third-person point of view*, refer to pg. 99. Ask them what words let you know which POV it is. Extend the discussion by asking students why this point of view works best for this story. Answer: The story has a first-person point of view. The narrator uses I, me, and my.

STEP 5: Monitor Progress

Ask students to check what they have understood in the reading. If you are using the Audio CD, pause the recording.

Before You Go On

Remind students that the reading strategy is recognizing sequence. Have students notice the sequence of events as they read. You can verify student comprehension by having students answer these questions before they go on to the next page. When they answer questions, ask where they found the information.

ANSWERS

1. Mother thinks that Bobby likes animals because he watches nature shows, and he always wants to go to the zoo or the Academy of Sciences.
2. Teddy doesn't want to buy Bobby a turtle because Bobby would like it, and he doesn't want to make him happy.

On Your Own Have students write an answer to this question on a separate sheet of paper. Encourage volunteers to share their responses. Then collect student responses to check their understanding, writing skills, and fluency.

Read

STEP 6: Teach

Preteaching Highlighted Words

Before reading this spread, review the highlighted words and terms with students. Define each one, pointing out the location of the definition in the gloss at the bottom of the student book page. Make sure that students understand each highlighted word. If appropriate, ask students to generate original sentences using the highlighted words. When correcting original sentences, focus on usage of the highlighted word.

Across the Curriculum:
Science

Alligators and crocodiles are both large lizards from the crocodilian family that spend time in the water and on the land. Like turtles, they are reptiles, and therefore cold-blooded. They look similar and are often confused for each another, but there are a few noticeable differences. Alligators have broad snouts which show only their upper teeth when their mouth is closed. Crocodiles have narrow snouts that show all their teeth even when the mouth is closed! In most species, crocodiles are more aggressive than alligators, although both are dangerous. Both can also grow to be extremely large—the largest species of crocodiles, saltwater crocodiles, can be up to 19 feet long.

✔ LITERARY CHECK

Point out the Literary Check question, and read it aloud to students. Ask students to work in pairs and look back over the reading. Have them discuss what they think has happened in the story, then share their ideas with the rest of the class.

"It's his birthday," Mother said. "I have to buy tonight's dinner. When I come home, I want to find that turtle waiting for me. You can leave it in our bedroom until we give out the presents." She wasn't going to leave me any way to escape. "If you need money, go down to the garbage cans. I saw lots of empty soda bottles."

After Mother left, I heaved a big sigh. Going into the kitchen, I turned on the radio for music and began washing the dishes.

As I was finishing up, I saw the newspaper ad on the table. It was for a department store in the Stonestown mall, where Mother worked. It would take me most of the morning to get out there.

Above the address was a big drawing of a boy and girl gazing happily at a turtle. It was grinning back from a plastic bowl like the one Mother had bought. In big type, the ad announced the turtles were on sale for fifty cents. Then I saw the small print: BABY ALLIGATORS ON SALE. And like an omen, the radio began playing a funny song from the past. "See you later, alligator," the radio sang. "After a while, crocodile."

If there had been a light bulb over my head, it would have suddenly shone as bright as the sun. Carefully I reviewed Mother's words. As far as I could remember, she had said to buy Bobby a pet. I chuckled. Poor Mother. She thought she had trapped me, but she had given me a loophole.

✔ LITERARY CHECK
*What is the **plot** of the story so far?*

---

escape, get away from something
gazing, staring
type, printed letters
omen, sign that something will happen
loophole, way to escape

🌐 TESOL Standards

Goal 1, Standard 1—To use English to communicate in social settings: Students will use English to participate in social interactions.
Descriptors—Expressing needs, feelings, and ideas; Engaging in conversations.

Goal 3, Standard 3—To use English in socially and culturally appropriate ways: Students will use appropriate learning strategies to extend their sociolinguistic and sociocultural competence.
Descriptors—Self-monitoring and self-evaluating language use according to setting and audience.

A plan began to build in my mind. First, though, I called up the department store having the sale. When I got the operator, I asked her, "I'd like to buy my brother something special from your pet department. If he doesn't like it, can I return it?"

"You can return anything within seventy-two hours after the sale." She added, "But the pet has to be alive."

"It won't be here long enough to die," I laughed, and hung up. I imagined what would happen tonight when Bobby opened his present. He would probably run shrieking from the room.

In my mind, I played out many marvelous scenes, ranging from a horrified Bobby to an outraged one. In any case, I would have to return it and get my money back. At the same time Mother would learn her lesson too.

It was the perfect gift. I could keep my promise to Mother because it would be nature stuff as well as something special. I could keep my promise to myself because it would be weird enough.

---

operator, person who answers phone calls
shrieking, screaming
marvelous, good; wonderful
horrified, very upset
outraged, extremely angry

✔ LITERARY CHECK
Why would this narrative have been very different if the story had been told from Bobby's point of view?

ABOUT THE **AUTHOR**

Laurence Yep has written many award-winning books for children and adults, including the Newbery Honor Books *Dragonwings* and *Dragon's Gate*. He was born in 1948, in California. He wrote his first stories for a science-fiction magazine when he was in high school. When he was growing up, Yep really did buy his little brother an alligator as a pet!

BEFORE YOU GO ON

1. What does Teddy think Bobby will do when he opens the present?

2. Does Teddy have a good imagination? Explain.

💡 **On Your Own**
When you were Bobby's age, would you have liked to get an alligator as a birthday present? Why or why not?

107

Study Skills: Internet

Students can use the Internet to learn more about Laurence Yep. Use search engines to find useful information on the author and his books. Laurence Yep has written many books about Chinese-American immigrants. Many of the events in his books are based on his own experiences, like buying his brother an alligator. Ask students to find out more about the subjects of Yep's books and the experiences he writes about. Students can find interviews or quotes from Yep about his books. Make clear the distinction between a quotation from the author and commentary on his work.

STEP 7: Monitor Progress

Ask students to check what they have understood in the reading.

Before You Go On

Remind students that the reading strategy they are practicing is recognizing sequence. Have students notice the sequence of events as they read. Answering questions before going on to the next page in the story is one way to verify student comprehension. **SAY:** *When you answer the first two questions, look for the place on the page that gives you that information.*

ANSWERS

1. Teddy thinks Bobby will be very upset.
2. Yes, Teddy has a good imagination. He schemes how to comply with his promise to his mother, but bug his brother in the process.

On Your Own Have students write an answer to the On Your Own question on a separate sheet of paper. Encourage volunteers to share their responses. Collect student responses to check their comprehension, writing skills, and fluency.

Review the Purpose for Reading

Elicit responses to the Set a Purpose for Reading questions at the beginning of this reading. Remind students to relate their responses to the Big Question.

Teach & Apply

STEP 1: Introduce

Speaking Tip

Remind students that the characters in the story speak and act in believable ways, and that when they are acting, they should also be believable. Using a dull, monotonous voice is boring and hard to understand, and being too exaggerated makes the characters silly.

Reader's Theater

Performing is excellent practice for students. It gives them an authentic reason to rehearse, to increase fluency, and to improve expression and intonation. Divide students into pairs to practice and perform. **SAY:** *This scene is written as a script. When actors prepare to perform, they receive a script that tells them what to say and how to say it. This script has two characters. How is the script different from the original story?*

Have students decide who will play which role. Point out that they should read only the text that follows their character's name. Have them practice delivering their dialogue clearly. Note the use of punctuation, such as exclamation and question marks, as indicating how the dialogue should be read.

STEP 2: Practice

Comprehension

Students can answer these questions independently or in groups. They can respond orally or in writing. Model the first question for the class in a complete sentence. **SAY:** *Teddy bought Bobby cheap white socks.*

ANSWERS

1. Cheap white socks
2. Turtles and baby alligators
3. Teddy's gift has no effect on Bobby because Bobby loves it.
4. Mother tells Teddy what to buy Bobby for his birthday because she doesn't want Bobby to be disappointed.
5. The story is told from Teddy's point of view. I can tell because the author uses words like *I*, *me*, and *my*.
6. Teddy is always trying to find things that will make Bobby unhappy.
7. Answers will vary.
8. Answers will vary.

Teaching Resources

- *Workbook*, p. 51
- CD-ROM/e-book, Reader's Theater, Comprehension, Response to Literature

---

READER'S THEATER

 Speaking TIP
Use realistic voices and facial expressions so that your audience can visualize the characters and their feelings.

Act out this scene between Teddy and his mother.

Teddy: It's not fair, Mom! Why do I have to buy my little brother a birthday present? He gets presents from you and Dad.

Mother: Teddy, stop whining. You should *want* to buy your brother a present. Bobby's your brother. Don't you love him?

Teddy: I do, but we don't get along. You know that, Mom.

Mother: Why can't you get along? He's nice to you.

Teddy: Mom! He's so good that he makes me look bad. Everyone likes him better than they like me.

Mother: You don't have any reason to be jealous of Bobby, dear. Your father and I love you both the same.

Teddy: Okay, Mom. I'll get him a pet at the pet store tomorrow.

Mother: Thank you, Teddy. I'm sure Bobby will be very pleased.

COMPREHENSION

Workbook Page 51

Right There

1. What gift did Teddy buy his little brother Bobby for Christmas?
2. What is on sale at the department store?

Think and Search

3. What effect does Teddy's Christmas gift have on Bobby?
4. Why does Mother tell Teddy what to buy Bobby for his birthday?

Author and You

5. From whose point of view is this story told? How can you tell?
6. How does Teddy's jealousy of Bobby affect his actions?

On Your Own

7. "Sibling rivalry" is a term used to describe the competition between brothers and sisters. What do you think causes sibling rivalry? What are some ways to avoid it?
8. When were you jealous of someone? Describe the experience.

108

🌐 TESOL Standards

Goal 3, Standard 1—To use English in socially and culturally appropriate ways: Students will use the appropriate language variety, register, and genre according to audience, purpose, and setting.
Descriptors—Using the appropriate degree of formality with different audiences and settings; Determining when it is appropriate to use a language other than English; Determining appropriate topics for interaction.

Goal 3, Standard 2—To use English in socially and culturally appropriate ways: Students will use nonverbal communication appropriate to audience, purpose, and setting.
Descriptors—Interpreting and responding appropriately to nonverbal cues and body language; Using acceptable tone, volume, stress, and intonation in various social settings; Recognizing and adjusting behavior in response to nonverbal cues.

DISCUSSION

Discuss in pairs or small groups.

1. Why do you think Teddy called the pet store to make sure that he can return pets? What does this tell you about Teddy?

2. What do you predict will happen when Teddy brings home the alligator? What will Bobby do? What will Teddy's parents do?

3. Do you think that wild animals such as alligators should be sold as pets? Why or why not?

Q **How does growing up change us?** Imagine that you have a younger brother who gets all the attention. What things might you do so that you could get some positive attention?

 Listening TIP

Take notes as you discuss the questions about the story and growing up. This will help you remember what you and your classmates said.

RESPONSE TO LITERATURE

 Workbook Page 51

Teddy is very jealous of his younger brother Bobby. Imagine that twenty years have passed. Teddy and Bobby have grown up. How do they get along now? Are they close friends? Is Teddy still jealous of Bobby? Is Bobby still as popular and nice? Imagine that you are the boys' mother. Write a journal entry in which you describe how the boys get along with each other now. Use the chart below to help you begin.

Then		Now
Teddy was jealous of Bobby.	➡	
Bobby was popular.	➡	
Bobby did not know that Teddy was jealous of him.	➡	

When you are finished writing, share your journal entry with a partner. See whether your partner agrees with your description of the boys' relationship in the future.

109

Differentiated Instruction

Beginning	Ask students which character from the story they liked better, Teddy or Bobby.
Early Intermediate	Ask students to share with the class what they think Bobby's reaction to his birthday present will be.
Intermediate	Have students act out the Reader's Theater for the class. Encourage students to act rather than just read.
Greater Challenge	Have students brainstorm ideas about how the story relates to the Big Question. Have students share their ideas with the class.

STEP 3: Extend

Listening Tip

Remind students that notes should not be in complete sentences. **SAY:** *These notes are to remind you about what was discussed. Because people may talk faster than you can write, write only the most important words and points.*

CRI Discussion

Before discussion, decide if students will work as a class, in teams, or as partners. Consider dividing up the questions so each group has a different topic. Make sure that all participants are heard and that ideas are challenged but not discarded. Explain that the purpose is to allow everyone a chance to be heard. Remind students to use the academic words they have learned and to refer to their notebooks for help.

ANSWERS

Possible responses:

1. Teddy called the pet store because he expected to take the alligator back. This tells us Teddy cares about what happens to the alligator.

2. I predict that Bobby will love the alligator and will thank his brother for it. His parents will be angry and will want Teddy to take it back.

3. I don't think wild animals should be pets because they will not be happy.

Q **How does growing up change us?** Guide students in a discussion about how growing up changes people.

STEP 4: Assess

Response to Literature

Read aloud the instructions for this activity. Brainstorm with students how things might be different for Teddy and Bobby in twenty years. Model by drawing a T-chart like the one below. Write in some answers. Then ask the class to determine how realistic answers are.

Then	Now
Teddy was jealous of Bobby.	Teddy has succeeded on his own and isn't competing with Bobby.
Bobby was popular.	Bobby has many friends, and so does Teddy.
Bobby did not know that Teddy was jealous.	Teddy teases Bobby about how perfect he was.

Grammar and Writing

STEP 1: Introduce

Tell students that we often describe people or things by comparing them to something that is familiar. Ask them to look at page 110 and tell them you will be reviewing how to construct comparisons.

STEP 2: Teach

Grammar and Writing

Making Comparisons This lesson shows students that there are several ways to make comparisons in English. Post the rules on chart paper and have students read each example. Then look for other examples in the reading to add to the list.

STEP 3: Practice

Read aloud the instructions for this practice exercise. Model how to complete the first one by showing students how to try each pair of responses to see which one makes sense and best completes the sentence frame.

ANSWERS

1. not as … as
2. more … than
3. not as … as
4. less … than

Teaching Resources

- *Workbook*, pp. 52–53
- CD-ROM/e-book, Grammar, Writing
- *Transparencies*, Writing Model 28
- *Transparencies*, *Resources*, Graphic Organizer 4
- *Assessment*, Reading 3 Test, pp. 59–62

GRAMMAR, USAGE, AND MECHANICS

Making Comparisons

Making comparisons can help you write clear descriptions and lively narratives. You can use a comparative adjective + *than* to compare two people, places, or things. For most one-syllable adjectives, add -*r* or -*er* to form a comparative. For two-syllable adjectives that end in *y*, change the *y* to *i* and add -*er*. For adjectives that are two syllables or more, use *more . . . than* or *less . . . than*. When you want to point out that two people, places, or things are equal or unequal, use *as . . . as* or *not as . . . as*.

Comparatives with -*er* + *than*:
Bobby is **sweeter than** Teddy.
My dog is **heavier than** your dog.
Comparatives with *more . . . than* and *less . . . than*:
Teddy is **more imaginative than** Bobby.
Teddy is **less helpful than** Bobby.
Comparatives with *as . . . as* and *not as . . . as*:
Tony is **as tall as** his mother.
The moon is **not as bright as** it was a week ago.

Practice
Workbook
Page 52

Work with a partner. Copy the sentences below into your notebook. Decide which choice best completes each sentence. Write the answers in your notebook.

1. Bobby is _____ old _____ Teddy.
   (not as . . . as / as . . . as)
2. Teddy thinks alligators are _____ scary _____ turtles. (as . . . as / more . . . than)
3. Bobby _____ jealous _____ Teddy.
   (more . . .than / not as . . . as)
4. Teddy thinks scrambled eggs with rice is _____ tasty _____ scrambled eggs with bacon. (less . . . than / as . . . as)

110

WRITING A NARRATIVE PARAGRAPH

Write a Story from Another Point of View

You have written two narratives. Now you will write a known story from another character's perspective. You'll use a graphic organizer to contrast different characters' points of view.

Have you ever noticed how a story can change depending on who is telling it? Each character in a story acts and thinks in a unique way. One character may see an event or object from one perspective, but another character may have a completely different point of view.

Here is a model of a familiar story (*Later, Gator*) from the mother's point of view. The writer used a T-chart to contrast the original narrator's and the new narrator's perspectives. Notice how the mother's point of view is different from Teddy's.

Teddy's POV	Mother's POV

Koji Mori

That Teddy!

I can't believe what Teddy has done this time! He's very imaginative, but he's full of mischief and loves to torment his brother. He's jealous of Bobby, my younger son, who is certainly a calmer, easier child than Teddy. Anyway, I suppose I should have known better when I told Teddy to buy Bobby something special for his birthday. I even made a suggestion! I thought a little turtle would be a wonderful gift, since Bobby is just old enough to care for a pet. I should have guessed that Teddy would outsmart me. As it turns out, he saw a newspaper ad for a different kind of reptile. When I came home from work, I found a baby alligator in the turtle bowl! I shrieked, which is what Teddy probably hoped that Bobby would do. Of course, I made Teddy take the alligator back. I have to admit, though, I had to laugh!

Practice *Workbook Page 53*

Write a paragraph telling a familiar story from another character's point of view. Use a T-chart to contrast the perspectives of the original narrator and the new one. Use the pronouns *I, me, my, we,* and *us* to tell the story from the first-person point of view. To compare and contrast characters and events, use comparatives.

Writing Checklist

VOICE:
☑ I used a new voice that reflects the new narrator's point of view.

CONVENTIONS:
☑ I used the pronouns *I, me, my, we,* and *us* to tell the story from a character's point of view.

111

Accelerate Language Development

Figurative Comparisons

Point out that the comparison structures *as . . . as* and *more/less . . . than* produce many idiomatic expressions. Examples are: *as white as a sheet*, *as deaf as a post*, *as mad as a hatter*, *as quiet as a mouse*, *as good as gold*. Taken literally, these expressions make little sense. Explain that these expressions often originate in literature and become part of common language over time. For example, the expression *mad as a hatter* is credited to Lewis Carroll's *Alice in Wonderland*, which did not invent the phrase but helped spread it all over the English-speaking world.

STEP 1: Introduce

Tell students that a narrative paragraph is often used to tell a story. This kind of paragraph uses the point of view of the narrator, and what they think happened.

STEP 2: Teach

Writing a Narrative Paragraph

Another Point of View Begin by reading the writing model aloud. Explain that the student wrote from Mother's POV rather than Teddy's. Review how it differs from the original. Explain that they will rewrite a familiar story from a different point of view.

Model Writing Skill Point out the T-chart on the student book page, and draw it on the board. Label the columns *Teddy's POV* and *Mother's POV*. Then ask a volunteer to read the model paragraph from Mother's POV. **SAY:** *We know how Teddy felt about what happened from the story. He knew Mother wanted him to buy a turtle but decided to get an alligator instead. I'll write that under Teddy's POV. The model paragraph tells us how Mother felt about what happened—she expected to come home to find a turtle, and found an alligator instead! I'll write that under Mother's POV.*

Read aloud the instructions for the practice exercise. Help students brainstorm stories that lend themselves to retelling from a different point of view. Pair students to develop the T-chart organizer on the story they select.

STEP 3: Assess

Writing Checklist Note

Have students evaluate their work, using the Writing Checklist.

Voice Check that students' paragraphs use the voices of different narrators to reflect the character telling the story.

Conventions Check that students have used the appropriate pronouns for the first-person point of view, describing the narrator's thoughts and actions.

Teach

Objectives

Read aloud the list of objectives in the What You Will Learn section, encouraging students to join in. Tell students that these readings will be an article about amazing growth facts and a Russian folktale. Have students work together to restate things they will learn.

The Big Question

Remind students that the Big Question is "How does growing up change us?" Remind them that all living things grow and change as they mature. This article focuses on animals and how they change. Some animals have different names when they are babies. Baby frogs are tadpoles, baby bears are cubs, baby chickens are chicks, and baby horses are foals.

Build Background

Draw a KWL (What I **K**now, What I **W**ant to Know, and What I **L**earned) chart and ask students to brainstorm some interesting animal facts they know. Place these in the K column. Have them fill in the W column with facts about animals they want to know. Discuss how and where students can go to check their facts. When students finish reading the article, come back and add information to the chart.

STEP 2: Teach

Understanding the Genre:
Science Article; Folk Tale

Tell students that a science article is an informational text. Its purpose is to present facts and other information about real people, events, places, and situations. The first reading is a science article about amazing growth facts.

A folk tale is a fictional text without a specific author. It is a story from a particular culture. This Russian folktale has been adapted by Leo Tolstoy.

Teaching Resources

- CD-ROM/e-book, Key Words
- Audio CD 2, tracks 14–15
- *Workbook*, p. 54

What You Will Learn

Reading
- Vocabulary building: *Context, dictionary skills, word study*
- Reading strategy: *Use visuals 2*
- Text type: *Informational text (science article); Literature (folk tale)*

Grammar, Usage, and Mechanics
Simple past: regular and irregular verbs

Writing
Write a personal narrative

THE BIG QUESTION

How does growing up change us? How is growing up different for plants and animals than it is for human beings? Some plants and animals are very small when they are fully grown. Others are very big. Which animals are very small even when they are completely grown? What are the largest animals you can name? What are the tallest plants you can name? Share what you know with the class.

BUILD BACKGROUND

"Amazing Growth Facts" and **"The Old Grandfather and His Little Grandson"** are two very different kinds of texts. The first is a science article about physical growth. It presents interesting facts about how living things grow in size. The second text is a folk tale about another kind of growth. It is a narrative about a young child who teaches his parents a lesson. The child's actions help the parents grow as human beings.

Folk tales are old stories that are passed down over the years. They are often told to children to teach them lessons. Some folk tales warn children to stay away from danger. Others teach children to be kind to others.

▲ Giant Sequoias are the tallest trees in the world.

Giraffes are 1.83 meters (6 ft.) tall when they are born, but they grow to be 5.49 meters (18 ft.) tall. ▶

112

TESOL Standards

Goal 1, Standard 2—To use English to communicate in social settings: Students will interact in, through, and with spoken and written English for personal expression and enjoyment.
Descriptors—Sharing social and cultural traditions and values; Participating in popular culture.

Goal 3, Standard 1—To use English in socially and culturally appropriate ways: Students will use the appropriate language variety, register, and genre according to audience, purpose, and setting.
Descriptors—Responding to and using slang appropriately; Responding to and using idioms appropriately.

VOCABULARY

Learn Key Words

Read these sentences. Use the context to figure out the meaning of the red words. Use a dictionary to check your answers. Then write each word and its meaning in your notebook.

1. At birth, the average baby weighs about 3.5 kilograms (7 or 8 lbs.).

2. We use a conversion chart to change numbers from one system of measurement to another. For example, we can change centimeters to inches, meters to feet, or kilograms to pounds.

3. The building's height is 30 meters (around 100 ft.) from the bottom to the top.

4. The anaconda is the longest snake in the world. It can grow to more than 10.5 meters (close to 35 ft.) in length.

5. A baby has a very fast rate of growth. It can grow almost 18 centimeters (about 7 in.) in one year!

6. We measure weight to figure out how heavy someone or something is.

Practice Workbook Page 54

Work with a partner to answer these questions. Try to include the red word in your answer. Write the sentences in your notebook.

1. How do you figure out the average of a series of ten numbers?

2. When might you need to use a conversion chart?

3. What tools could you use to measure someone's height?

4. How does the length of your hand compare to the length of your feet?

5. Why do you think that babies grow at such a fast rate?

6. What can people do to lower their weight?

Key Words

average
conversion
height
length
rate
weight

▲ Anacondas are also the world's heaviest snakes, sometimes reaching 200 kilograms (440 lb.) in weight.

113

 ## Vocabulary

Learn Key Words Play the CD. Have students listen and repeat. Direct students to the Key Words at the top of the page, and read them aloud. **SAY:** *These words are called key words because they are words that are important in the text we are reading.* On the board or an overhead, write the Key Words below and their definitions.

Average: having qualities that are typical of most people or things
Conversion: the act of changing something from one form, system, or purpose to another
Height: how tall someone or something is
Length: the measurement of something from one end to another
Rate: the number of times something happens over a period of time
Weight: how heavy someone or something is

Have students copy the definitions into their Word Books or notebooks and generate original sentences for them. For extra practice, assign Workbook page 54.

STEP 3: Practice

Read aloud the instructions for this practice exercise. Model the first question and answer.

ANSWERS

1. To average ten numbers, you add them together and divide by ten.
2. You might need to use a conversion chart for money when traveling abroad.
3. You could use a measuring tape to measure someone's height.
4. The length of your hand is about the same as the length of your foot.
5. Babies grow at such a fast rate because they are so tiny to begin with.
6. People can exercise more and eat less to reduce their weight.

Differentiated Instruction

Beginning	Ask students to name each of the animals that appear on page 117.
Early Intermediate	Have students find a picture or illustration on pages 112–117 that demonstrates height.
Intermediate	Have students look at the illustrations on pages 116–117. Have them predict what the reading will be about.
Standard English Learners (CRI)	Have students write example sentences of their own that use the key words on page 113.

Teach

CD2 T16–T17

 Vocabulary

Learn Academic Words Play the CD. Have students listen and repeat. Read aloud each Academic Word and discuss its possible meaning. Then model how to use the chart. **SAY:** *Notice that the chart on this page contains two parts: academic words and their definitions are on the left and sentences containing the words on the right. What other sentence can we create with the word* enormous? (Possible response: The model of the blue whale at the museum is enormous.)

Partners work together to add another sentence for each academic word. They write each word, its definition, and the sentence in their personal word book.

STEP 2: Practice

Read aloud the instructions for this practice exercise. Write the following question on the board and underline the words as shown: "What is a benefit of living in your city or town?" **SAY:** *When you are asked a question, try to include words from the question in your answer. Look at the question on the board.* Write this sample answer on the board: "A benefit of living in our town is that there are plenty of places to play baseball." Be sure to underline the words as shown so students clearly see the connection.

ANSWERS
Possible responses:
1. A benefit of living in our town is that there are plenty of places to play baseball.
2. Cars, trucks, boats, and trains fit in the category of transport vehicles.
3. The most enormous animal I have ever seen is a whale.
4. I feel great when I get 100 percent on my tests because it shows I learned the material.

Teaching Resources

- Audio CD 2, tracks 16–17
- *Workbook*, pp. 55–57
- CD-ROM/e-book, Academic Words, Word Study

Learn Academic Words

Study the red words and their meanings. You will find these words useful when talking and writing about informational texts and literature. Write each word and its meaning in your notebook. After you read "Amazing Growth Facts" and "The Old Grandfather and His Little Grandson," try to use these words to respond to the text.

Academic Words
benefit
category
enormous
percent

benefit = something that gives you an advantage, that helps you, or that has a good effect	Growing fast is a great **benefit** to animals. It helps them live on their own sooner.
category = group of people or things that have related characteristcs	Bears and deer belong to the **category** of warm-blooded animals. Snakes and lizards belong to a different group.
enormous = extremely large in size or amount	The elephant is **enormous**! It is a huge animal.
percent = equal to a particular amount in every hundred	About 75 **percent** of the eggs hatched. The rest of the eggs did not hatch.

Practice **Workbook Page 55**

Work with a partner to answer these questions. Try to include the red word in your answer. Write the sentences in your notebook.

1. What is a benefit of living in your city or town?
2. What category would you use to group cars, trucks, boats, and trains?
3. What are some of the most enormous animals you have seen in pictures or at a nature preserve?
4. Why do students feel good when they get 100 percent on a test?

114

▲ Bears are in the category of warm-blooded animals.

Word Study: Spelling Words with Long Vowel Sound /ō/

Learning to identify sound-spelling patterns will help you read and spell words correctly. The long vowel sound /ō/ can be spelled in many ways. Four common spellings are *o* as in *cold*, *o_e* as in *bone*, *oa* as in *roast*, and *ow* as in *snow*. Look at the chart below. Take turns reading the words aloud with a partner. Notice the sound-spelling patterns for /ō/.

/ō/ spelled *o*	/ō/ spelled *o_e*	/ō/ spelled *oa*	/ō/ spelled *ow*
scold	stone	toast	grown
so	close	loaf	slow
kilo	stove	coast	below

Practice Workbook Page 56

Work with a partner. Copy the chart above into your notebook. Say a word from the chart, and ask your partner to spell it aloud. Then have your partner say the next word. Continue until you can spell all of the words correctly. Now work with your partner to spell these words: *jumbo, soap, tone, bowl, home, gold, show, oak*. Add them to the chart under the correct headings.

READING STRATEGY | **USE VISUALS 2**

Using visuals helps you understand what you are reading. Visuals include photographs, art, diagrams, charts, and maps. Informational texts often have visuals. Sometimes visuals give you information that is not in the text. To use visuals, follow these steps:

- Look at the visual. Ask yourself, "What does it show? How does it help me understand what I am reading?"
- Read the titles, headings, labels, or captions carefully.
- Think about how the visual helps you understand what is in the text. Does the visual give you extra information? In what way?

As you read "Amazing Growth Facts," pay close attention to the visuals. What do they show? How do they help you understand the text better?

 Workbook Page 57

115

STEP 1: Teach

Word Study

Spelling Words with Long Vowel Sound /ō/ English vowel sounds can be spelled in a variety of ways. This does not occur in all other languages. Copy the chart on page 115 onto the board. Review each section, and have students look for other examples to add to the chart.

STEP 2: Practice

Read aloud the instructions for this practice exercise. Model the first two words so that students understand how to place the words on the chart.

ANSWERS

/ō/ spelled *o*	/ō/ spelled *o_e*	/ō/ spelled *oa*	/ō/ spelled *ow*
jumbo	tone	soap	bowl
gold	home	oak	show

STEP 3: Teach

Reading Strategy

Use Visuals 2 Visual supports such as photographs, charts, photos, and diagrams can greatly enhance comprehension. These visual references are especially critical for English Learners when reading dense academic material. Previewing topics by using related illustrations supports comprehension of the text. With students, review the steps of the Reading Strategy. **SAY:** *What kind of visuals do you expect to see in this article?* Then, have the class preview "Amazing Growth Facts" for its visuals. **SAY:** *What images are compared by height on page 116?* (Pictures of giant kelp, bamboo, and an average man are compared.)

Assign the corresponding Reading Strategy workbook page for extra practice or homework.

Accelerate Language Development

Pronunciation

English learners often have difficulty mastering English pronunciation because English is not a perfectly phonetic language. This means one letter can have several different pronunciations, and one sound can have several different spellings. Remind your students of the various spellings of the long /ē/ sound. Point out that just as the different spellings of the long /ē/ sound produce homophones, the different spellings of the long /ō/ sound do as well. Examples for homophones with the long /ō/ sound are: toe/tow, for/four/fore, ode/owed, and doe/dough. Then point out that the same letters can be pronounced differently as well. Demonstrate the difference between the vowel sound in *slow* and *cow*, or *flower* and *lower*.

Read

STEP 1: Introduce

Reading Summary

"Amazing Growth Facts," the first part of this reading, presents unusual facts about plant and animal growth.

The Big Question

Remind students that the Big Question is "How does growing up change us?" **SAY:** *What is the average lifespan of a human being? Is it the same everywhere? What influences how long a person lives? We think of growing up in reference to children, but adults also continue to grow and change. In what ways to adults keep growing up?* Discuss student opinion about what lessons grownups should learn.

STEP 2: Teach

Set a Purpose for Reading

SAY: *Everything changes as it grows. Look for some specific ways that plants and animals change as they grow. How are these changes different from the ways people grow? Look for visuals that compare human growth and characteristics to those of plants and animals.*

Preteaching Highlighted Words

With students, preview the highlighted selection vocabulary on pages 116–117. Write the words on the board and point out that they are defined at the bottom of each page. Model how to use the words in a sentence like *The employees worked hard to increase the number of machines produced.* Ask students to do the same, and create a word book including the definition, a sentence using the word, and possibly an image.

CD2 T18 Scaffolding:
Listen and Read

Have students read along as you play the Audio CD recording of the reading. Pause the recording at the end of each page to ask questions and answer any questions students may have.

Teaching Resources

- *Resources, Summaries,* pp. 137–138
- Audio CD 2, track 18
- *Reader's Companion Workbook,* pp. 39–43

Set a purpose for reading How do different plants and animals grow? As you read the article, think about how all living things change when they grow up.

AMAZING GROWTH FACTS

It is one of the wonders of nature that all living things increase in size. Think about how a tiny acorn can grow into an enormous oak tree. Growth occurs at different rates. Sometimes growth is very fast. Other times it is very slow.

The average newborn baby is 50 centimeters long and weighs 3.4 kilograms. When the baby grows up and becomes an adult, he or she increases on average to 3.4 times that length and 21 times that weight. Girls and boys are about the same height and weight until early adulthood. Then boys usually grow taller and weigh more than girls.

Bamboo can grow 90 centimeters in one day—the height of an average three-year-old child. Pacific giant kelp (a kind of seaweed) can grow as much as 45 centimeters in one day.

An ant can lift more than 100 times its weight. One hundred times the weight of a 64-kilogram person would be the same weight as three cars!

A baby kangaroo is the size and weight of a paper clip (1 gram). An adult kangaroo is 30,000 times heavier (30 kilograms). If a human grew at this rate, a 3.4-kilogram baby would weigh 102,000 kilograms as an adult—that's as much as

increase, become bigger

116

▲ If we were as strong as ants, we could lift three cars!

— Pacific giant kelp: 60 m

— Bamboo: 30 m

— Average man: 1.75 m

🌐 TESOL Standards

Goal 2, Standard 2—To use English to achieve academically in all content areas: Students will use English to obtain, process, construct, and provide subject matter information in spoken and written form.
Descriptors—Comparing and contrasting information; Retelling information; Selecting, connecting, and explaining information; Analyzing, synthesizing, and inferring from information; Understanding and producing technical vocabulary and text features according to content; Formulating and asking questions.

Goal 2, Standard 3—To use English to achieve academically in all content areas: Students will use appropriate learning strategies to construct and apply academic knowledge.
Descriptors—Focusing attention selectively; Using context to construct meaning.

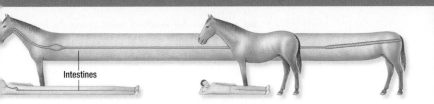

Intestines

a large whale! An average man weighs about 80 kilograms.

The egg of a golden eagle and the egg of a Nile crocodile are both 8 centimeters long. But look how much bigger the crocodile grows!

A 26-centimeter baby crocodile can grow into a 5-meter adult crocodile. If humans grew at the same rate as Nile crocodiles, a 50-centimeter baby would grow into a 9.5-meter adult—more than 5 times as tall as the average person!

Clams are among the longest living and slowest growing of all creatures. A deep-sea clam takes 100 years to grow 8 millimeters. That's as big as your fingernail!

In the average human life of 70 years, a heart pumps enough blood around the body to fill the fuel tanks of 700 jumbo jets. The food that we eat in our lifetime is equal in weight to the weight of six elephants! A horse's intestines are about 27 meters long. A human's intestines are about 7.5 meters long. Luckily, the intestines are curled up inside the body. Otherwise, people and horses would look very strange!

jumbo jets, very large airplanes
intestines, tubes that take food from the stomach out of the body

Conversion Chart	
Metric	**U.S. Customary Units**
1 millimeter =	0.039 inch
1 centimeter =	0.39 inch
1 meter =	3.28 feet
1 gram =	0.035 ounce
1 kilogram =	2.2 pounds

Egg: 8 cm   Chick: 13 cm

Adult golden eagle: 88 cm

Adult Nile crocodile: 5 m

Egg: 8 cm

Baby crocodile: 26 cm

BEFORE YOU GO ON

1 Using the Conversion Chart, change the metric measurements in the text to U.S. Customary Units.

2 Which grows to be the biggest—an eagle, a crocodile, or a human?

On Your Own
What growth fact do you find most interesting? Why?

117

Differentiated Instruction

Beginning	Have students draw a picture of the biggest and smallest animals they know.
Early Intermediate	Ask students what the biggest and smallest animals they know are.
Intermediate	Have students describe the biggest and smallest animals they know. Have other students try to guess what the animal being described is.
Special Needs	Ensure that students are sitting in a quiet area before they begin reading. Provide paper and pencils so that they can note any problematic words as they read.

Study Skills: Conversion Chart

The chart illustrating the text teaches students to convert one type of measurement to another. This is a very small example of a conversion chart. Another use for a conversion chart of measurements is in a cookbook. Different recipes might use metric measurements, cups, tablespoons, pounds, or ounces. A basic cookbook may contain a chart which allows cooks to use recipes by converting the measurements. Find a chart like this in a cookbook, and ask students to convert a basic amount, like a cup of flour, into liters, tablespoons and teaspoons, or a basic weight, like a pound of butter, into grams, kilograms, and ounces.

STEP 3: Monitor Progress

Ask students to check what they have understood in the reading.

Before You Go On

Remind students that the reading strategy they are practicing is using visuals. Remind students that visuals can provide information that is not in the text. **SAY:** *What information is shown by the visuals? What do the captions or titles tell us about the images shown?*

ANSWERS

1. Egg 8 cm. = 3.12 in.
   Adult golden eagle: 88 cm. = 34.32 in.;
   Adult Nile crocodile 5 m. = 16.4 ft.
   Pacific giant kelp: 60 meters = 196.8 ft.
   Bamboo: 30 meters = 98.4 ft.
   Average man: 1.75 meters = 5.74 ft.
2. A crocodile grows to be the biggest.

On Your Own Have students write an answer to the On Your Own question on a separate sheet of paper. Encourage volunteers to share their responses. Collect student responses to monitor their comprehension, writing skills, and fluency.

Review the Purpose for Reading

Elicit responses to the Set a Purpose for Reading questions at the beginning of this reading. Remind students to relate their responses to the Big Question.

Read

STEP 1: Introduce

Reading Summary

The short folktale "The Old Grandfather and His Little Grandson" tells how a grandfather becomes feeble and is treated like a baby until his little grandson imitates his parents' behavior, causing them to realize their wrongdoing.

The Big Question

Remind students that the Big Question is "How does growing up change us?" Point out that sometimes adults need to grow up, too. Ask students what they think being *grown up* really means.

STEP 2: Teach

Read the questions at the top of the page aloud, and discuss the meaning of the saying "Do as I say and not as I do." Ask students if they think that is possible. Ask them what is meant by setting an example. **SAY:** *Misha learned from his parents' example. What do they learn from his actions?*

Preteaching Highlighted Words

With students, preview the highlighted selection vocabulary on page 118. Ask volunteers to find and read the definitions. Model using the words in original sentences. For example, *He felt ashamed when he refused to help his mother with the dishes.* Then ask for students to do the same, and then write the definitions and original sentences in their word books.

CD2 T19 Scaffolding:
Listen and Read

Have students read along as you play the audio CD recording of the reading. Pause the recording at the end of each page to ask questions and answer any questions students may have.

Teaching Resources

- *Resources*, Summaries, pp. 137–138
- Audio CD 2, track 19

LITERATURE

FOLK TALE

Set a purpose for reading How can a young boy help his parents grow up? As you read this folk tale, think about how Misha's actions help his parents grow and change.

The Old Grandfather and His Little Grandson

An adapted folk tale by Leo Tolstoy

The grandfather had become very old. His legs would not carry him. His eyes could not see and his ears could not hear. He had no teeth. Sometimes when he ate, bits of food dropped out of his mouth. His son and his son's wife no longer let him eat with them at the table. He had to eat his meals in the corner near the stove.

One day they gave the grandfather his food in a bowl. He tried to move the bowl closer. It fell to the floor and broke. His daughter-in-law scolded him. She told him that he spoiled everything in the house and broke their dishes. She said that from now on, he would get his food in a wooden dish.

The old man sighed and said nothing.

A few days later, the old man's son and his wife were in their hut, resting. They watched their little boy playing on the floor. He was making something out of small pieces of wood. His father said, "What are you making, Misha?"

The little grandson said, "I'm making a wooden bucket. When you and Mama get old, I'll feed you out of this wooden dish."

The young man and his wife looked at each other. Tears filled their eyes. They were ashamed they had treated the old grandfather so badly. From that day on, they let the old man eat at the table with them, and they took better care of him.

---

scolded, spoke angrily to
spoiled, ruined

ashamed, embarrassed or guilty

118

TESOL Standards

Goal 3, Standard 3—To use English in socially and culturally appropriate ways: Students will use appropriate learning strategies to extend their sociolinguistic and sociocultural competence.
Descriptors—Experimenting with variations of language in social and academic settings; Seeking information about appropriate language use and behavior; Analyzing the social context to determine appropriate language use.

BEFORE YOU GO ON

1. Why do the man and his wife make the grandfather eat his meals in the corner?
2. Why does Misha's bowl make his parents feel ashamed?

🔔 **On Your Own**
How can children benefit from living with their grandparents?

119

Study Skills: Encyclopedia

Students can learn more about the author, Leo Tolstoy, by looking in an encyclopedia. Tolstoy was a famous Russian writer who lived in the nineteenth century. He wrote many books about the relationships between people, like *War and Peace* and *Anna Karenina*. He also wrote many short stories like this one, many of which are also based on Russian folktales. Tolstoy enjoyed these traditional stories from the Russian people. In an encyclopedia, students can learn about his life, his other writings, and the politics of Russia that affected his writing.

STEP 3: Monitor Progress

Ask students to check what they have understood in the reading.

Before You Go On

Remind students that reading the questions before reading the text can help them understand the text. Preview these questions with students before they go on.

ANSWERS

1. They made the grandfather eat in the corner because he was messy and food dropped from his mouth.
2. Misha's parents would not like to eat from the bowl he has made, and they realize the grandfather doesn't like it either.

On Your Own Have students write an answer to the On Your Own question on separate sheets of paper. Encourage volunteers to share their responses with the class. Then collect student responses to monitor their comprehension, writing skills, and fluency.

Review the Purpose for Reading

Elicit responses to the Set a Purpose for Reading questions at the beginning of this reading. Remind students to relate their responses to the Big Question.

STEP 1: Practice

Comprehension

Ask students to complete the questions in the Comprehension section either independently or in groups. They can respond orally or in writing. Model the first question with the class so they can see how to answer in a complete sentence.

ANSWERS

1. 100 years
2. Misha makes a wooden bucket.
3. Bamboo and Pacific giant kelp are both plants that grow very fast.
4. The man and his wife are angry with the grandfather because he spills his food and breaks dishes.
5. "Amazing Growth Facts" is both informative and entertaining in the way it compares other kinds of growth to human growth.
6. Misha teaches his parents that one day they will be old, too. They learn to be more patient with the grandfather.
7. Answers will vary.
8. Answers will vary.

(CRI) In Your Own Words

Remind students that *summarizing* means to focus on the most important main ideas, to use their own words, and to be concise. Read aloud the instructions for this activity, and model the first entry for students.

Speaking Tip

Remind students that visuals help readers to associate main ideas or specific facts with an image. Taking notes also helps readers to reduce a fact to its most important points.

Teaching Resources

- *Workbook*, p. 58
- CD-ROM/e-book, Comprehension, Extension
- *Reader's Companion Workbook*, pp. 44–48

COMPREHENSION Workbook Page 58

Right There

1. According to the article, how long does it take a clam to grow 8 millimeters?
2. In the folk tale, what object does Misha make for his parents?

Think and Search

3. Based on "Amazing Growth Facts," what category would you use to group bamboo and Pacific giant kelp together?
4. In the folk tale, why are the man and his wife angry with the grandfather?

Author and You

5. In what ways is "Amazing Growth Facts" both informative and entertaining?
6. What lesson does Misha teach his parents?

On Your Own

7. What advantages do enormous animals have?
8. What can children learn from their parents? What can parents learn from their children?

▲ How does this artwork help you visualize the size of a slow-growing clam?

IN YOUR OWN WORDS

Summarize each of the readings. Copy the following chart into your notebook. Use it to help you organize your summaries. Then share your summaries with a partner.

🗣 *Speaking* TIP

Use notes and pictures to help you remember important facts.

"Amazing Growth Facts"	"The Old Grandfather and His Little Grandson"
Fact 1:	Beginning:
Fact 2:	Middle:
Fact 3:	End:
Overall summary:	Overall plot summary:

120

🌐 TESOL Standards

Goal 2, Standard 3—To use English to achieve academically in all content areas: Students will use appropriate learning strategies to construct and apply academic knowledge.
Descriptors—Applying self-monitoring and self-corrective strategies to build and expand a knowledge base; Determining and establishing the conditions that help one become an effective learner (e.g., when, where, how to study).

Goal 3, Standard 1—To use English in socially and culturally appropriate ways: Students will use the appropriate language variety, register, and genre according to audience, purpose, and setting.
Descriptors—Responding to and using humor appropriately; Using the appropriate degree of formality with different audiences and settings; Recognizing and using Standard English and vernacular dialects appropriately.

Goal 3, Standard 3—To use English in socially and culturally appropriate ways: Students will use appropriate learning strategies to extend their sociolinguistic and sociocultural competence.
Descriptors—Deciding when use of slang is appropriate.

Discuss in pairs or small groups.

1. Why do you think the two readings were paired? How are they similar? How are they different?

2. What other information would you like to learn about growth? Give at least two examples.

3. Are you more interested in very large animals or very small ones? Why?

Q How does growing up change us? What do you think your life will be like sixty-five years from now? Describe what you think you will be like. Will you want to be with people your own age, with younger people, or both? Why?

READ FOR FLUENCY

Reading with feeling helps make what you read more interesting. Work with a partner. Choose a paragraph from the folk tale. Read the paragraph to yourselves. Ask each other how you felt after reading the paragraph. Did you feel happy or sad?

Take turns reading the paragraph aloud to each other with a tone of voice that represents how you felt when you read it the first time. Give each other feedback.

EXTENSION

Workbook
Page 58

"Amazing Growth Facts" presents interesting information about how certain living things grow. Learn more about the growth of other plants and animals. Use encyclopedias, reference books, and the Internet. Share your findings with your classmates.

Listening TIP

Do not interrupt your classmates when they are speaking. Save your questions until a speaker is finished.

▲ You can track your growth by measuring yourself against a wall every few months.

121

Differentiated Instruction

Beginning	Tell students that answers to the Right There questions can be found in sentences in the reading. Ask students to point to the sentences that contain answers to these questions.
Early Intermediate	Ask students what they think is the most amazing growth fact.
Intermediate	Have students write a few sentences describing their reaction to how the grandfather was treated in the folktale.
Greater Challenge	Have students explain the lesson from the folktale to the rest of the class.

STEP 2: Extend

Listening Tip

Remind students that interruptions are bad for two reasons: first, they are disrespectful, and second, they may be distracting or make a classmate lose her train of thought. Waiting until the end of presentations means you will get all the information before asking questions.

(CRI) Discussion

Model for students how to discuss ideas in a group. Students should state an opinion as well as why they hold that opinion. Remind students how to politely disagree with another person's opinion. Suggest that even when someone else has stated an idea, they can agree and add to that idea to enrich the discussion. "That's what I was going to say" is not enough. Instead, it is better to **SAY:** "I agree because . . ." or "That is a great point because . . ."

ANSWERS

1. **Possible response:** The article was about changes as we age, and the story reminded us that we change as we get old, too. They treat the same topic but are different genres.
2. Answers will vary.
3. Answers will vary.

Q How does growing up change us? SAY: *How did reading this story make you think about what may happen as you age? How is this different from how people usually think about 'growing up'?*

STEP 3: Assess

Read for Fluency

If students report that they are not understanding after several readings, examine the students' understanding of the passage vocabulary. Suggest that students listen to the CD recording.

Extension

Read aloud the instructions for this exercise. Have students brainstorm a way to display the facts they find. For example, they could create a book or bulletin board display.

STEP 1: Introduce

Point out to students that the simple past is often used in narrative writing. Ask them to look through the student book for texts that use the simple past and identify regular and irregular verbs.

STEP 2: Teach

Grammar and Writing

Simple Past: Regular and Irregular Verbs Read aloud the information on the student book page. Discuss the meaning of *regular* and *irregular* verbs as given in the student book. Post the rules for simple past tense on a chart or on the board.

STEP 3: Practice

Model the first sentence so students know what to do. It may help students to conjugate the verb *be* so that they can see which word to use.

Person	Present	Past
I	am	was
you	are	were
we	are	were
he, she, it	is	was
they	are	were

ANSWERS

1. was/were
2. let
3. watched
4. said
5. dropped
6. gave

Teaching Resources

- *Workbook*, pp. 59–60
- CD-ROM/e-book, Grammar, Writing
- *Transparencies*, Writing Model 29
- *Transparencies, Resources*, Graphic Organizer 11
- *Assessment*, Reading 4 Test, pp. 63–66

Grammar and Writing

GRAMMAR, USAGE, AND MECHANICS

Simple Past: Regular and Irregular Verbs

Use the simple past to talk about actions that began and ended in the past. Form the simple past of regular verbs by adding -*d* or -*ed* to the base form of the verb. If the verb ends in *y*, change the *y* to *i* and add -*ed*. Sometimes you must double the consonant and then add -*ed*. Study the examples.

Base Form	Simple Past
watch	They watch**ed** their little boy playing on the floor.
drop	Bits of food drop**ped** out of his mouth.
try	He tr**ied** to move the bowl closer.

Many common verbs are irregular and must be memorized.

Base Form	Simple Past
have	He **had** a grandson.
give	One day they **gave** the grandfather his food in a bowl.
say	The old man sighed and **said** nothing.
be	The old man's son and his wife **were** in their hut.
let	They **let** the old man eat at the table with them.

Practice **Workbook Page 59**

Work with a partner. Copy the sentences below into your notebook. Complete the sentences with the simple past of the verbs in parentheses. Use a dictionary if necessary.

1. When I _____ (be) six, my two front teeth _____ (be) missing.
2. My mother _____ (let) me eat lots of custard and ice cream.
3. My brother or sister _____ (watch) me every day after school until my parents came home from work.
4. They _____ (say) they didn't mind baby-sitting.
5. The school bus _____ (drop) me off about a block from our house.
6. Sometimes my sister _____ (give) me help with my homework.

122

TESOL Standards

Goal 1, Standard 1—To use English to communicate in social settings: Students will use English to participate in social interactions.
Descriptors—Sharing and requesting information; Expressing needs, feelings, and ideas.

Goal 1, Standard 2—To use English to communicate in social settings: Students will interact in, through, and with spoken and written English for personal expression and enjoyment.
Descriptors—Describing, reading about, or participating in a favorite activity; Expressing personal needs, feelings, and ideas.

Goal 3, Standard 1—To use English in socially and culturally appropriate ways: Students will use the appropriate language variety, register, and genre according to audience, purpose, and setting.
Descriptors—Using a variety of writing styles appropriate for different audiences, purposes, and settings; Responding to and using idioms appropriately; Responding to and using humor appropriately; Determining when it is appropriate to use a language other than English; Determining appropriate topics for interaction.

Write a Personal Narrative

You have written three narratives and explored plot, setting, character, and point of view. Now you will write a personal narrative about something that occurred when you were growing up. You'll use a graphic organizer like the one at the right to put the events in your narrative in chronological order.

When you write a personal narrative, you create and develop a situation, including what happened at the beginning, during the middle, and at the end. You use concrete details to describe the setting and people involved. You also try to explain why the experience or situation was memorable.

Here is a model of a personal narrative about a boy's relationship with his grandfather. Notice how the writer has put the events in time order and has explained why the events were worth writing about.

Beginning

↓

Middle

↓

End

Brandon Saiz

My Abuelo

One day I went to my abuelo's house to visit. My abuelo said, "Do you want to help me learn how to use the computer?" He is kind and has helped me with many things, so I was happy that I could help him this time. We sat down in the kitchen, where he had set up the computer on the counter. He said, "Show me how to turn on the Internet." I automatically clicked the browser because that is what I do on my computer at home. I could see Abuelo was pleased because his eyes opened wider as he studied the screen through his reading glasses. Then he asked me if I could find the Spanish newspaper for him on the Internet, which I did. Finally, I showed him how to turn off the computer. He liked that. Abuelo is now able to show other people how to use the Internet.

Practice **Workbook Page 60**

Write a personal narrative about some aspect of growing up. You might want to write about a game you played with an adult or about a lesson you taught or learned. Use a sequence-of-events chart to put your narrative in chronological order. Remember to use regular and irregular verbs in the simple past correctly.

Writing Checklist

VOICE:
☑ I told the narrative from my point of view.

IDEAS:
☑ I used concrete details to describe the events, people, and setting.

123

Link the Readings

Critical Thinking SAY: *What do the readings in this unit have in common? They all talk about change and growing up. However, they do not all have the same purpose, and they each discuss change differently. Fill in the chart with a partner.*

ANSWERS

Title of Reading	Purpose of Reading	How Reading Relates to Theme
"Ancient Kids"	to inform	compares growing up in three ancient civilizations
From *Becoming Naomi León*	to entertain	describes a difficult time in her childhood when she had to grow up
From *Later, Gator*	to entertain	tells about brothers growing up
"Amazing Growth Facts"	to inform	describes some amazing facts about how some living things grow
"The Old Grandfather and His Little Grandson"	to teach a lesson	shows the importance of role models for children and respecting the elderly

 Discussion

Preview the discussion questions and assign groups to work together. Remind students to refer to the charts they created to find information for their discussion. Answers will vary.

Fluency Check

Pair students and have them time each other's reading and record the times. Emphasize that precise timing is important in getting comparable scores. Tell students to draw the fluency check chart, and show them how to write minutes and seconds. (1:15, for example.) Remind them that reading quickly is important, but they also need to understand what they are reading.

Teaching Resources

- *Assessment*, Unit 2 Test, pp. 143–152
- CD-ROM/e-book, Fluency Check, Projects

Link the Readings

Critical Thinking

Look back at the readings in this unit. Think about what they have in common. They all tell about growing up. Yet they do not all have the same purpose. The purpose of one reading might be to inform, while the purpose of another might be to entertain or persuade. In addition, the content of each reading relates to growing up differently. Now copy the chart below into your notebook and complete it.

Title of Reading	Purpose	Big Question Link
"Ancient Kids"		
From *Becoming Naomi León*		
From *Later, Gator*	*to entertain*	*tells about brothers growing up*
"Amazing Growth Facts," "The Old Grandfather and His Little Grandson"		

Discussion

Discuss in pairs or small groups.

- What similarities can you see between *Becoming Naomi León* and "The Old Grandfather and His Little Grandson"?

- **How does growing up change us?** What conclusions can you draw about growing up, based on what you learned in each of the readings?

Fluency Check

Work with a partner. Choose a paragraph from one of the readings. Take turns reading it for one minute. Count the total number of words you read. Practice saying the words you had trouble reading. Take turns reading the paragraph three more times. Did you read more words each time? Copy the chart below into your notebook and record your speeds.

	1st Speed	2nd Speed	3rd Speed	4th Speed
Words Per Minute				

TESOL Standards

Goal 1, Standard 1—To use English to communicate in social settings: Students will use English to participate in social interactions.
Descriptors—Engaging in conversations; Conducting transactions.

Goal 1, Standard 3—To use English to communicate in social settings: Students will use learning strategies to extend their communicative competence.
Descriptors—Seeking support and feedback from others; Using the primary language to ask for clarification; Selecting different media to help understand language.

Goal 2, Standard 2—To use English to achieve academically in all content areas: Students will use English to obtain, process, construct, and provide subject matter information in spoken and written form.
Descriptors—Listening to, speaking, reading, and writing about subject matter information; Gathering information orally and in writing; Selecting, connecting, and explaining information; Analyzing, synthesizing, and inferring from information; Responding to the work of peers and others; Representing information visually and interpreting information presented visually; Understanding and producing technical vocabulary and text features according to content area; Demonstrating knowledge through application in a variety of contexts.

Projects

1 What do you think happens at the end of *Becoming Naomi León*? Write a paragraph that predicts what will happen. Then read the book to see if your prediction is correct.

2 Make a thank-you card that Bobby might send to Teddy to thank him for the alligator. Include a drawing of the alligator, as well as a note about how Bobby feels about the gift.

3 Make a soap carving. Follow the directions in "Soap Carving" on page 93. You may want to make an animal, as Naomi does. Or you can make something else. Write a title for the figure on an index card to put with it. Have your classmates place their carved figures next to yours to make a class art display.

4 Share a folk tale with your class. You can retell "The Old Grandfather and His Little Grandson" in your own words. Or you can choose another folk tale to share.

Further Reading

To find out more about the theme of this unit, choose from these reading suggestions.

Rip Van Winkle and the Legend of Sleepy Hollow,
Washington Irving
This Penguin Reader® includes adaptations of Irving's two beloved classics.

The Barefoot Book of Heroic Children, Rebecca Hazel
This book presents inspiring stories of some of the most amazing young people in history.

Just Juice, Karen Hesse
A family in Appalachia faces many challenges and, together, overcomes them.

125

 ## Home-School Connection

These projects provide students with several ways to practice and apply what they have learned in the unit. The projects can be completed alone, with partners, or in small groups. They can be completed in the classroom or at home.

Further Reading

Each book listed on this page pertains to the Big Question. Encourage students to peruse them in their free time or read them for extra-credit book reports. The first book on the list is easily accessible, the second is accessible, and the third is challenging.

Websites

Log onto www.LongmanKeystone.com for links to other interesting websites about growing up.

Differentiated Instruction

Beginning	Ask students which reading selection they liked best.
Early Intermediate	Have students explain why they enjoyed a particular reading.
Intermediate	Have students briefly explain the connection between one of the readings and the Big Question.
Struggling Readers	Ask students to identify the author of the folk tale from this unit.

Listening & Speaking Workshop

STEP 1: Introduce

(CRI) Remind students that this workshop will be similar to Reader's Theater, but that they will need to write what they will say. Explain that a skit is informal theater, often demonstrating something, where each person has a part.

Think About It Help students brainstorm topic ideas that would make a good skit about ancient times. As they brainstorm, students should write down what kinds of characters would be in each skit. Encourage students to choose the skit that has good parts for all students and will be fun to perform.

STEP 2: Teach

Gather and Organize Information Write the organizational steps that appear on this page on the board—Research, Order Your Notes, Prepare a Script, and Use Visuals. Students will need to choose a culture to act out a skit from. Ask a pair of students to read aloud the model script that is given. The word *visuals* is used to describe the costumes, props, or scenery indicators students will need for their skits.

Teaching Resources

- CD-ROM/e-book, Gather and Organize Information

Put It All Together

LISTENING & SPEAKING WORKSHOP

Skit

You will write and perform a skit about growing up in ancient times.

1 THINK ABOUT IT Work in small groups. Choose one of the ancient cultures you read about in "Ancient Kids": Greek, Roman, or Maya. Talk about growing up in that time and place. Focus on topics such as school, families, ceremonies, gifts, toys, and foods. Also, discuss how girls and boys were treated and how brothers and sisters might have felt about each other. Do you think that ancient kids felt jealous, the way Teddy did in *Later, Gator*? Think of a situation in your ancient culture that you could present as a skit, or short play. Write down your ideas.

2 GATHER AND ORGANIZE INFORMATION Work with your group to plan your skit. Include a character for each group member.

Research Go to the library or use the Internet to gather more information about your ancient culture. Take notes on what you find. Discuss which information you can use to create a clear picture of your ancient culture.

Order Your Notes Write these headings in your notebook: *Characters, Setting, Plot*. Make notes under each heading. For example, under *Plot*, list the main events you will include in your skit.

Prepare a Script Use your notes to write a script for your skit. The dialogue should look like this:

> **Jason:** I don't want to go to school today. I want to stay home and play with my new yo-yo.
> **Jacinda:** You should be grateful that you can go to school! Girls like me have to stay home all the time.
> **Jason:** That sounds like fun.
> **Jacinda:** Well, you're wrong! I hardly ever have time to play. Mother keeps me busy doing chores all day.

Include important details about the setting, props, and action:

> *Jason stops playing with his yo-yo and frowns. Then he starts to get ready for school.*

Use Visuals Make or find the costumes and props you need for your skit.

126

TESOL Standards

Goal 3, Standard 2—To use English in socially and culturally appropriate ways: Students will use nonverbal communication appropriate to audience, purpose, and setting.
Descriptors—Interpreting and responding appropriately to nonverbal cues and body language; Demonstrating knowledge of acceptable nonverbal classroom behaviors; Using acceptable tone, volume, stress, and intonation, in various social settings; Recognizing and adjusting behavior in response to nonverbal cues.

Goal 3, Standard 3—To use English in socially and culturally appropriate ways: Students will use appropriate learning strategies to extend their sociolinguistic and sociocultural competence.
Descriptors—Experimenting with variations of language in social and academic settings; Seeking information about appropriate language use and behavior; Analyzing the social context to determine appropriate language use; Rehearsing variations of language use in different social and academic settings.

3 PRACTICE AND PRESENT As a group, practice your skit until you can perform it without looking at the script. If possible, ask a friend or family member to serve as *prompter* while you practice. (A prompter watches the skit and follows along in the script. If someone forgets what to say or do, the prompter quietly reminds him or her.) Practice using your props and wearing your costumes.

Perform Your Skit Speak loudly enough so that everyone in the class can hear you. Say each word carefully so that it is clear. Be sure to face the audience as you speak, even if your body is pointing in another direction. Pay attention to the other actors, and be ready when it's your turn to speak or move!

4 EVALUATE THE PRESENTATION
A good way to improve your speaking and listening skills is to evaluate your own performance and the performances of your classmates. When you evaluate yourself, you think about what you did well and what you can do better. Use this checklist to help you judge your group's skit and the skits of your classmates.

- ☑ Could you understand the plot?
- ☑ Did the skit show what it was like to grow up in an ancient time?
- ☑ Were the costumes and props helpful and appropriate?
- ☑ Could you hear and understand the actors' words?
- ☑ What suggestions do you have for improving the skit?

> ### 🔊 Speaking TIPS
> Speak naturally and with feeling.
> Use gestures and facial expressions to help convey your character's actions and emotions to the audience.

> ### 🔊 Listening TIPS
> Listen carefully to the other actors so that you know when to say your lines. Learn your *cues*—words or actions that signal when it is your turn to speak.
>
> When you watch a skit, look for actions and gestures to help you understand what people are saying.

127

Practice and Present Read over with students the information about preparing for their performance. As students prepare their delivery, remind them that the more they rehearse, the more comfortable they are likely to be during the performance. Becoming familiar with their props and costumes will also make the skit go more smoothly. In addition, remind students to review the Speaking and Listening Tips at the right side of the page.

Speaking Tips

Remind students that when they are acting out a part, they should try to act the same way they would in real life. Point out that breathing naturally and not putting their hands in their pockets will make their acting seem more realistic.

Listening Tips

Remind students that as they are performing, they should always let other actors finish their lines before starting their own lines, and they should watch other actors' faces. When watching a skit, point out that we can often tell what is going on just by watching how people are moving.

Evaluate the Presentation Suggest that students use the checklist on this page to evaluate the skits. On a sheet of paper, have students number 1 to 5 for each skit. After they listen to a speaker, they read the five questions on the checklist and write *Yes* or *No* next to the first four. For the fifth question, they offer specific examples taken directly from the presentation. Remind students that feedback should be given in a kind, helpful way.

Differentiated Instruction	
Beginning	Before students start writing, have them recall details about growing up in ancient times from the reading to include in their skit.
Early Intermediate	Brainstorm with students. Try to come up with situations that they would encounter as they grow up. Could these situations be applied to the ancient world?
Intermediate	Before students start writing, have them organize the characters, plot, and setting in the chart in their notebook.
Standard English Learners (CRI)	Before students perform their skits, have them read the speaking tips on page 127. Tell them that following these tips will greatly enhance their skit.

Writing Workshop

STEP 1: Introduce

In this workshop, students review the steps of the writing process. They will apply each of the steps from prewriting to publication while applying the characteristics of fictional narrative paragraphs they have learned.

STEP 2: Teach

Prewrite Review the steps of the writing process with students: prewrite, draft, revise, edit and proofread, and publish. Point out that these steps will help make the job of writing their fictional narrative easier and more orderly. Write the words *fictional narrative* on the board. **SAY:** *A fictional narrative is a make-believe story. The plot, characters, and action are made up to entertain the reader.*

Draft Explain that a draft is a work in progress, and that it does not have to be perfect. Students can make further changes later on. Review the parts of a fictional narrative and the draft of Wendy's narrative. Ask students to identify the characters, setting, conflict, and resolution to the conflict.

Teaching Resources

- *Transparencies*, Writing Model 30, Proofreader's Marks 51
- CD-ROM/e-book, Writing Workshop
- *Workbook*, pp. 61–62

WRITING WORKSHOP
Fictional Narrative

You've learned how to write a variety of narrative paragraphs. Now, you'll use your skills to write a longer fictional narrative. A fictional narrative is a make-believe story. Two important features of a fictional narrative include the setting, or the time and place of events, and the characters. The characters can be people or animals. Another important feature of a fictional narrative is the plot. The plot is the series of events in a story. These events usually take place in chronological order and build to a climax, or high point. Most plots focus on a problem or conflict that is resolved by the story's end. The point of view, or the perspective from which a story is told, helps shape readers' understanding of what happens. Dialogue also helps show what the characters think and feel.

Your assignment for this workshop is to write a fictional narrative about jealousy between two friends or family members.

1 **PREWRITE** Brainstorm some ideas for your story in your notebook. What sort of characters would be jealous of each other? Why would the jealousy occur? What effect would it have on the characters' relationship? What would be the story's climax, or high point? How would the story end?

Develop and Organize Ideas Use one or more graphic organizers to develop your story. For example, you might use a T-chart to list the traits of your two characters or a sensory details web to develop a setting. A student named Wendy decided to write about a brother who is jealous of his sister. She used this story chart to organize her ideas:

CHARACTERS Who?	SETTING Where?	PROBLEM What is the conflict?	SOLUTION What is the resolution?
Max Joni their parents	their home	Joni gets all the family's attention. Max is jealous.	Max tells about volunteering. Parents are proud of him.

2 **DRAFT** Use your graphic organizer and the model on page 131 to help you write a first draft. Remember to tell events in chronological order. Include dialogue to help show what your characters are thinking and feeling.

128

TESOL Standards

Goal 2, Standard 2—To use English to achieve academically in all content areas: Students will use English to obtain, process, construct, and provide subject matter information in spoken and written form.
Descriptors—Listening to, speaking, reading, and writing about subject matter information; Gathering information orally and in writing; Understanding and producing technical vocabulary and text features according to content area; Demonstrating knowledge through application in a variety of contexts.

3 REVISE Read over your draft. As you do so, ask yourself the questions in the writing checklist. Use the questions to help you revise your fictional narrative.

SIX TRAITS OF WRITING CHECKLIST

- ☑ **IDEAS:** Is my plot focused on jealousy between two characters?
- ☑ **ORGANIZATION:** Does my story have a beginning, middle, and end?
- ☑ **VOICE:** Does my story have a clear point of view?
- ☑ **WORD CHOICE:** Do I include realistic dialogue?
- ☑ **SENTENCE FLUENCY:** Do my sentences vary in length and type?
- ☑ **CONVENTIONS:** Does my writing follow the rules of grammar, usage, and mechanics?

Here are the changes Wendy plans to make when she revises her first draft:

Max Learns a Lesson

For a long time,
I thought my sister was better than I was at everything. I ~~worked~~ struggled
~~so hard for a B average.~~ Yet Joni ~~got an A in~~ just breezed through with every class My parents

weren't upset with my grades; they just paid a lot more attention

to Joni. My sister also is a ~~good~~ terrific athlete.

Last month,
I helped rebuild homes damaged by a flood in a nearby community.
was excited about   On the other hand,
I ~~liked~~ making a difference in other people's lives. ~~Every afternoon,~~

the only thing Joni and my parents talked about was Joni!
as we were having dinner
One night, I got sick and tired of the world revolving around her.
                                        "I demanded. "
~~Doesn't anybody ever want to hear about me?~~ I'm working with a

family whose house was really messed up by the flood."

129

Differentiated Instruction

Beginning	Ask students to point out an example of dialogue from Wendy's first draft.
Early Intermediate	Have students give reasons why dialogue might be important in writing. How does it enhance writing?
Intermediate	Put students in pairs and have them compare their story charts. What do they have in common? In what ways are they different?
Special Needs	Explain to students that they may use the spell-checking tool on a computer to revise their work.

Revise Point out that the revising step focuses on improving the content and wording of a draft. Have students look over Wendy's first draft and notice the kinds of changes she made. Ask students to look at their own drafts and make changes. They should use the Six Traits of Writing Checklist. SAY: *Revising a draft means looking at it again and making changes in content or wording. It can be very difficult to make changes to your own writing since you know what you meant when you wrote it. That is why getting feedback from other readers is helpful. Ask a partner to read your draft and read his or hers. Remember to give specific feedback about what you liked. If your reviewer does not understand something, others may misunderstand, too. Decide which suggestions you will include in your writing, and make changes to your draft.*

STEP 3: Assess

Writing Checklist Note

Ideas: SAY: *Check that your plot is focused on the jealousy between characters and how this is resolved.*

Organization: SAY: *Check that your essay is in sequence. Is it clear what happens first, next, and at the end?*

Voice: SAY: *Check that your point of view is consistent, and your narrator does not change.*

Word Choice: SAY: *Check that your dialogue sounds believable and natural and matches the character's traits.*

Sentence Fluency: SAY: *Check that your essay contains a variety of simple and complex sentences.*

Conventions: SAY: *Check that you use complete sentences.*

Edit and Proofread Review with students the preliminary draft of the student essay and the final revised essay. List the differences between these versions. What changed from draft to draft?

Grouping for Collaboration—pair English Learners with English proficient students. Review with students the edits on the student's final draft. Discuss why you think each edit was made. Keep dictionaries nearby for checking spelling.

My parents looked at me. "Of course we want to hear about you," my father said. "You don't always seem to want to tell us anything. Usually, when we ask, you just shrug." I had to admit to myself that was true.

"I knew the school asked you to volunteer," my mother said slowly. "But I wasn't sure exactly what you were doing." So I told them about working hard to repair soggy floors and repaint water-stained walls.

Just then, joni spoke up. I figured she was about to say something even more wonderful about herself, but instead She said, "Max, did you tell Mom and Dad you made the debate team." I was stunned she cared! Since then, I try to share more about my interests and activities. My parents congratulated me on volunteering and making the team. I'm no longer jealous of Joni because my parents seemed just as proud of me. They know that we are each special in our own way.

4 EDIT AND PROOFREAD Workbook Page 61

Copy your revised story onto a clean sheet of paper. Read it again. Correct any errors in grammar, word usage, mechanics, and spelling. Here are the additional changes Wendy plans to make when she prepares her final draft.

130

 TESOL Standards

Goal 3, Standard 1—To use English in socially and culturally appropriate ways: Students will use the appropriate language variety, register, and genre according to audience, purpose, and setting.
Descriptors—Using the appropriate degree of formality with different audiences and settings; Recognizing and using Standard English and vernacular dialects appropriately; Using a variety of writing styles appropriate for different audiences, purposes, and settings; Determining appropriate topics for interaction.

Wendy Willner

Max Learns a Lesson

For a long time, I thought my sister was better than I was at everything. I struggled for a B average. Yet Joni just breezed through with an A in every class My parents weren't upset with my grades; they just paid a lot more attention to Joni. My sister also is a terrific athlete.

Last month, I helped rebuild homes damaged by a flood in a nearby community. I was excited about making a difference in other people's lives. On the other hand, every afternoon, the only thing Joni and my parents talked about was Joni!

One night as we were having dinner, I got sick and tired of the world revolving around her. Doesn't anybody ever want to hear about me?" I demanded. "I'm working with a family whose house was really messed up by the flood."

My parents looked surprised. "Of course we want to hear about you," my father said. "You don't always seem to want to tell us anything. Usually, when we ask, you just shrug." I had to admit to myself that was true.

"I knew the school asked you to volunteer," my mother said slowly. "But I wasn't sure exactly what you were doing." So I told them about working hard to repair soggy floors and repaint water-stained walls.

Just then, joni spoke up. I figured she was about to say something even more wonderful about herself, but instead she said, "Max, did you tell Mom and Dad you made the debate team." I was stunned she cared!

My parents congratulated me on volunteering and making the team. Since then, I try to share more about my interests and activities. I'm no longer jealous of Joni because my parents seem just as proud of me. They know that we are each special in our own way.

5 PUBLISH Prepare your final draft. Share your fictional narrative with your teacher and classmates.

Workbook Page 62

131

STEP 1: Introduce

Remind students that the Big Question is *How does growing up change us?* **SAY:** *You have learned about growth and read about growing up in different historical periods. Throughout American history, artists have captured childhood in photographs, paintings, and other media that show childhood then and now.* Go to the Smithsonian National Museum of African Art online exhibition "Exploring the World at Play" (www.LongmanKeystone.com) to learn more about how children around the world play. Have students study the children in the five photographs.

STEP 2: Teach

Visual Literacy

Albert Bisbee Help students analyze photographs more effectively by showing them a technique that involves covering portions of the image so the viewer can focus in on just one section at a time. Create an enlarged photocopy of Bisbee's *Child on a Rocking Horse* and cover the bottom half of the image with a sheet of paper. The students will be able to see only the little girl's upper torso and the head of the horse. **ASK:** *What do you think of the girl's hairstyle? What about the expression on her face? How accurate are the reins on the horse in comparison with those used in real life?* Now cover the top half of the photograph and show the class the bottom half. Point out the girl's shoes, her small riding crop, and the fine woodworking on the horse's legs. Do students have a better feel for the overall story that the portrait tells, now that they have looked at the two sections in more detail? To extend this lesson, go to the Smithsonian American Art Museum online exhibition "Helios: Photography Online" (www.LongmanKeystone.com). Ask students to choose a photograph and print a black and white copy. Have them divide the photograph into quarters and use pieces of paper to cover all but one quarter. Have them examine the details of their photograph one quarter at time and record their observations. Then have them study the picture as a whole and write their final comments on the photograph. Ask for volunteers to discuss their photographs in class.

Explain that when Bisbee took his photograph *Child on a Rocking Horse*, he captured a girl perched on one of the most popular (and expensive) toys of the mid-nineteenth century.

Teaching Resources

- *Workbook*, pp. 63–64
- CD-ROM/e-book, Smithsonian

Capturing Childhood

*A*rtists have used many methods to try to capture how people grow up. Many use photographs and paintings. Sometimes families hand these images down over the years, from generation to generation. The clothes and the favorite toys in the images may change over time. Usually, though, there's something familiar in the parade of family faces.

Albert Bisbee, *Child on a Rocking Horse* (about 1855)

This little girl with curly hair stares out at you. She looks a bit uncertain about sitting on the rocking horse. Albert Bisbee, who took a lot of family portraits, once said that he liked to photograph children as soon as they sat on the horse. If he missed his early chance, he felt it got more difficult with each passing minute because the child would get restless.

It took a lot more time to create a photograph in 1855 than it does today. The child had to sit very still. This was because Bisbee used an early photographic process called a daguerreotype. The image was printed directly on a sheet of silver-plated copper. If someone moved even a little bit, the photograph would be blurry.

Photographs were expensive over 150 years ago. Many families had only one or two pictures taken of their children as they grew up. Most of them wanted their child's photograph to be taken on a toy horse. The rocking horse was a very popular toy in nineteenth-century America. The little girl's face in this photograph shows how serious it was to have your picture taken. She wears a checkered dress trimmed with lace. She also wears fancy shoes. She is all dressed up for this important event.

▲ Albert Bisbee, *Child on a Rocking Horse*, about 1855, daguerreotype, 4¼ x 4½ in., Smithsonian American Art Museum

132

William Holbrook Beard, *The Lost Balloon* (1882)

The balloon off in the distance in William Holbrook Beard's painting *The Lost Balloon* is not a toy. It is a hot-air balloon floating beneath the clouds. A group of nine children and a dog are on the edge of a great ledge, watching the balloon as it moves through the sunlight.

An enormous rock face, which rises to their right, is partly hidden by stormy clouds. The children stand very close to the rim of a sharp drop-off in the landscape. Oddly, there are no adults with them. Perhaps Beard was trying to capture the quickly changing nature of childhood. In the painting, he seems to be saying that childhood is like the lovely balloon hanging on the edge of a storm. The children certainly seem very small against the wilderness.

Both of these artists captured an instant in childhood that's temporary, but somehow timeless. Each of us must move on from being ten or twelve or fourteen and face the next stage in life.

◀ William Holbrook Beard, *The Lost Balloon*, 1882, oil, 47¾ x 33¾ in., Smithsonian American Art Museum

Apply What You Learned

1 In what way does each of these artworks capture a moment in childhood?

2 Which medium do you feel is better at capturing the feelings of childhood—photography or painting? Explain.

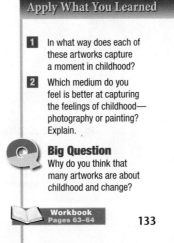

Big Question
Why do you think that many artworks are about childhood and change?

Workbook
Pages 63–64

133

Despite the many hi-tech toys available today, many old fashioned items like the rocking horse continue to be popular. Download the *Smithsonian* magazine article "Happy Trails" (www.LongmanKeystone.com) about a company that produces handcrafted rocking horses. Have students work in groups to research the history of a toy or game that does not involve electronics, such as dolls, dominoes, and jacks. Have students discuss why they think the toys and games they've researched have survived through the ages.

William Holbrook Beard Explain that in *The Lost Balloon*, Beard depicts a group of children walking through the outdoors where they catch sight of a balloon in the distance. Many children today have very little unstructured playtime outside, but this sort of experience offers its own special rewards. **ASK:** *What do you do in your free time, either alone or in a group? What percentage of your day is completely unstructured?* Create a circle chart that represents 24 hours in a day. Tally up the average number of hours (or minutes) of free time that students have each day. Make a second circle chart that shows the average number of hours (or minutes) that students play freely outdoors with their friends each day. **ASK:** *What are the pros and cons of structured and unstructured free time? What do you learn in unstructured, unsupervised settings that you can't learn in school or at home?*

STEP 3: Apply

Apply What You Learned

Have volunteers read the questions aloud, and be sure students understand the meaning of difficult words and concepts. Encourage students to carefully study the artworks, and if necessary, reread the text to help them.

ANSWERS

1. By taking the photo of the *Child on a Rocking Horse*, the photographer captures one moment from the little girl's childhood. When that moment is over, the girl changes forever. The painter of *The Lost Balloon* also captures a moment in childhood with nine children near the edge of a cliff with a storm coming. The children will have to leave and move on toward adulthood.

2. **Possible response:** Photography is a better medium for capturing childhood because it seems more realistic. A painter might work in a style that intentionally changes the way things really look.

Q Possible response: Artists may choose to show scenes of childhood because it is a subject that most people can relate to.

Differentiated Instruction

Beginning	Have students draw a picture that captures one of their favorite childhood memories.
Early Intermediate	Ask students which of the two artworks on this spread they prefer. Encourage them to explain reasons for their preference.
Intermediate	Have students describe a favorite childhood memory for the class.
Struggling Readers	Ask students to identify the artist's name on page 133.

UNIT 3

 How does helping others help us all?

134

THE BIG QUESTION

STEP 1: Introduce

Unit Content

Tell students that in this unit they will read four different selections about how helping others helps us all. These readings include a novel excerpt, a diary excerpt, and two informational articles. As they read, students will learn new vocabulary, grammar, and reading skills, such as making inferences, identifying problems and solutions, distinguishing fact from opinion, and more. At the end, students will write a speech focusing on the theme of helping others.

The Big Question

Introduce the Big Question "How does helping others help us all?" Encourage students to give some potential answers to the question. Express interest in students' answers and probe their thinking. Emphasize that there is no right or wrong answer to the question. To facilitate class discussion, ask the following questions.

- Have you ever helped anyone? What did you do? (Helping can be as small as opening a door for another person.)
- How did that person feel when you helped him or her?
- How did helping someone else make you feel?

STEP 2: Teach

Visual Literacy

With students, preview the selections in the unit for photos, illustrations, and maps that relate to how people and animals help one another. Some questions to ask about the illustrations are:

- On page 140, how are the mother and daughter helping the boy?
- On pages 154–156, who are the famous people who have helped people in the past?
- On page 168, what kind of help is being given to this woman?
- On page 181, what does the map show you? From the photos in this article, which animals are helping each other?

Teaching Resources

- *Resources*, Unit 3 Lesson Plans, pp. 27–38
- *Transparencies*, Unit 3 Daily Language Practice
- CD-ROM/e-book, Big Question
- Video, Segment 3
- *Resources*, Letters Home, pp. 113–114

TESOL Standards

Goal 2, Standard 1—To use English to achieve academically in all content areas: Students will use English to interact in the classroom.
Descriptors—Asking and answering questions.

Goal 2, Standard 2—To use English to achieve academically in all content areas: Students will use English to obtain, process, construct, and provide subject matter information in spoken and written form.
Descriptors—Hypothesizing and predicting; Formulating and asking questions.

Goal 2, Standard 3—To use English to achieve academically in all content areas: Students will use appropriate learning strategies to construct and apply academic knowledge.
Descriptors—Actively connecting new information to information previously learned.

This unit is about living creatures helping one another. You'll read about an Apache boy who receives help from a farm family and biographies about people who devoted their lives to helping others. You'll read a girl's diary entries that ask for peace in her war-torn country, and you'll read about a baby hippo that receives help from an unlikely fellow creature. As you read, you'll practice the academic and literary language you need to use in school.

READING 1: Novel Excerpt
■ From *Run Away Home* by Patricia C. McKissack

READING 2: Social Studies Article
■ "Extraordinary People: Serving Others"

READING 3: Diary Excerpt
■ From *Zlata's Diary* by Zlata Filipović

READING 4: Science Article
■ "Friendship and Cooperation in the Animal Kingdom"

Listening and Speaking

At the end of this unit, you'll present a **TV talk show** about a person you admire.

Writing

In this unit, you will practice **persuasive writing**. This type of writing tries to get the reader to do something or agree with a viewpoint. After each reading, you will learn a skill to help you write a persuasive paragraph. At the end of the unit, you will write a persuasive speech.

QuickWrite
In your notebook, write several persuasive sentences about why it is important for friends to help one another.

Visit *LongmanKeystone.com*

135

QuickWrite

Draw an idea web on the board and write *Why do friends help one another?* in the center circle. Ask students for ideas and write them in the outer circles of the web. Some examples are *It makes them feel good about themselves; Helping shows how much they care; Friends are important.* Then write the following sentence frame on the board for students to copy: *It is important for friends to help one another because _____.* Use this sentence frame to generate a few persuasive sentences for students to use as models.

STEP 4: Extend

Have students read aloud the titles of the selections, and ask them how they think each reading will relate to the Big Question. **SAY:**

● What do you think *Run Away Home* may have to do with helping others?

● What kind of people do you think "Extraordinary People: Serving Others" will be about?

● Zlata's Diary is about her life during the Bosnian War. What kind of help might Zlata need?

● What do you think "Friendship and Cooperation in the Animal Kingdom" will be about? Can you think of any animals that help one another?

Tell students they will find out how each reading relates to the Big Question as they work through the unit.

Teach

STEP 1: Introduce

Objectives

Read aloud the list in the What You Will Learn section, encouraging students to join in. Tell students that *Run Away Home* is about a family who helps a stranger. Have students work in pairs to restate the list of things they will learn.

 The Big Question

Remind students that the Big Question is "How does helping others help us all?" Have students read the first paragraph on page 136. Offer an example answer from your own experience and ask students to share their own experiences or points of view.

Build Background

By the late 1800s, many Native Americans were forcibly relocated to reservations. These areas were on land that was unwanted; those in power wanted the land previously occupied by Native Americans for farming and mining. They also wanted to assimilate Native Americans into American life. Laws were passed that made Native American religious practices such as the Ghost Dance illegal. Native American children were sent to schools like the Carlisle School. Ask students to do research on the Internet to find out more about this time in American history.

STEP 2: Teach

Understanding the Genre:
Novel Excerpt

Point out that a novel is a long work of fiction. Novels contain elements such as characters, plot, setting, and conflict. They are usually not about real people and events but may refer to them.

The excerpt from *Run Away Home* is an example of historical fiction. Point out that historical fiction is set in a specific time and place in history.

Teaching Resources

- CD-ROM/e-book, Literary Words
- Audio CD 3, track 1
- *Workbook*, p. 65

What You Will Learn

Reading
- Vocabulary building: *Literary terms, word study*
- Reading strategy: *Make inferences*
- Text type: *Literature (novel excerpt)*

Grammar, Usage, and Mechanics
Simple and compound sentences

Writing
Write a book review

 THE BIG QUESTION

How does helping others help us all? Everyone needs help sometimes. Sometimes we need help because of a big problem or a small problem. Think about a time when you needed help. What was the situation? How did that person help you? Think about a time when you helped someone else. What happened? How did you feel? Discuss with a partner.

BUILD BACKGROUND

Run Away Home takes place on a farm in Alabama in 1888. Novels that take place in a real time and place in the past are called historical fiction. In *Run Away Home*, the main characters are an African-American farm family and an Apache boy. The main characters and plot are imaginary, but certain people and events mentioned in the novel are real.

In 1888, many Apaches were forced to move onto reservations in Alabama. A reservation is land set aside for Native Americans by the U.S. government. Living conditions on the reservations were poor, and many Native Americans became sick.

Some Native American children were sent from reservations to schools far away. At school, they had to stop speaking their native languages and speak only English. They had to eat, dress, and act like whites. The Apache boy in *Run Away Home* doesn't want to be sent to the Carlisle Indian School. This was a real school for Native Americans in Carlisle, Pennsylvania, near Harrisburg.

▲ An 1880 class photo from the Carlisle Indian School

136

TESOL Standards

Goal 1, Standard 3—To use English to communicate in social settings: Students will use learning strategies to extend their communicative competence.
Descriptors—Listening to and imitating how others use English; Exploring alternative ways of saying things; Focusing attention selectively.

Goal 2, Standard 1—To use English to achieve academically in all content areas: Students will use English to interact in the classroom.
Descriptors—Requesting and providing clarification; Participating in full-class, group, and pair discussions; Negotiating and managing interaction to accomplish tasks.

Goal 2, Standard 2—To use English to achieve academically in all content areas: Students will use English to obtain, process, construct, and provide subject matter information in spoken and written form.
Descriptors—Selecting, connecting, and explaining information; Understanding and producing technical vocabulary and text features according to content area.

Learn Literary Words

To make stories realistic, writers sometimes use dialect when they write dialogue. Dialect is the way people speak in a specific region. For example, in the southern part of the United States, people use different expressions and may say words differently from the way people do in other parts of the country. Read the examples of dialect. How are these examples of dialect different from the English you are asked to use in school?

> I **might can't** save him. (I may not be able to save him.)
> He's **fixin'** to leave. (He's getting ready to leave.)

Usually, writers create a mood, or feeling, in a narrative. For example, they might create a funny, sad, hopeful, or tense mood. One mood that many writers create is a feeling of suspense, or uncertainty about what will happen. Suspense keeps readers interested and makes them want to read on to find out what will happen. Read the example below. What mood does the writer create?

> It was a dark moonless night outside the cabin. My father and I were alone for the weekend and were about to go to bed. Suddenly, we heard the sound of heavy footsteps coming closer. We stayed very still and listened. The footsteps sounded like a steady heartbeat getting louder and louder. I shivered.

Practice

Workbook Page 65

Work with a partner. Take turns reading the examples of dialect from *Run Away Home*. Discuss how the dialect might be different from the English you hear at school.

> "What are you thinkin' 'bout, Georgianne? How could you bring trouble to our front door like this? Mr. Wratten was just here lookin' for this boy, and here we got him in our house, takin' care of him."
>
> "Aine it enough 'round here to do, besides taking on a sick boy, somebody we don't even-now know. What business is it of ours?"

Now read these sentences aloud in the English you hear at school. There might be many ways to say the same sentence.

Literary Words
- dialect
- mood
- suspense

137

CD3 T1

 Vocabulary

Learn Literary Words Play the CD. Have students listen and repeat. If you are not using the CD, read the Literary Words aloud. Ask students what comes to mind when they hear each word. Write down students' responses. **SAY:** *These words are called literary words because in a discussion of literature, they have a unique meaning.* Ask students to read the paragraphs and examples that illustrate *dialect*, *mood*, and *suspense*.

Write the following definitions for *dialect*, *mood*, and *suspense* on the board or an overhead transparency to reinforce learning.

- **dialect:** the way people speak in a specific region
- **mood:** the atmosphere or feeling of the literary work
- **suspense:** a feeling of excitement or anxiety that comes from not knowing what will happen next

Provide examples of dialect, mood, and suspense. For example, explain that people in different parts of the United States have their own dialects. They sometimes use special words and ways of pronouncing words that are not used elsewhere. Ask students to use the Literary Words in new sentences. Then refer students to the corresponding Workbook page for further practice.

STEP 3: Practice

Read aloud the passage on page 137, and play the CD. **SAY:** *Do you notice any difference between the way the people in the story talk and the way you talk? What literary word that we've just learned is this an example of?*

Differentiated Instruction

Beginning	Ask students if they have ever helped someone else.
Early Intermediate	Have students say what they have done to help someone else.
Intermediate	Have students describe how they helped someone else and how it made both them and the person feel.
Greater Challenge	Have students research ways they can help others within their community.

Teach

STEP 1: Teach

CD3 T2–T3

 Vocabulary

Learn Academic Words Play the CD. Have students listen and repeat. If you are not using the CD, read the Academic Words aloud.
SAY: *Look at the Academic Words chart. The definition for each word is on the left side. On the right side, each word is used in a sentence. Work with a partner to write an additional sentence for each Academic Word. Write each word, its definition, and the sentence in your notebook.*

STEP 2: Practice

Model how to answer the questions on page 138 by doing the first one with the whole group. **SAY:** *The first question reads, "What is appropriate to say to someone after he or she has helped you?" I know that the word* appropriate *is defined as "something that is suitable for a particular time, situation, or purpose." I think "Thank you" is something suitable, or appropriate, to say after someone has helped me.*

ANSWERS
Possible responses:
1. It is appropriate to say, "Thank you" to someone who has helped me.
2. To communicate that I need help, I might say, "Excuse me" or "Could you assist me?" In an emergency, I might wave my arms or shout.
3. The period in history I like to read about is ancient Rome. This is because I'm interested in Julius Caesar.
4. Travelers need precise directions so they won't get lost.

Teaching Resources
- Audio CD 3, tracks 2–3
- *Workbook*, pp. 66–68
- CD-ROM/e-book, Academic Words, Word Study

Learn Academic Words

Study the **red** words and their meanings. You will find these words useful when talking and writing about literature. Write each word and its meaning in your notebook. After you read the excerpt from *Run Away Home*, try to use these words to respond to the text.

appropriate = suitable for a particular time, situation, or purpose	➡	It is **appropriate** to say "thank you" when someone helps you.
communicate = express your thoughts and feelings so that others understand them	➡	Some people **communicate** their ideas by writing fiction.
period = a particular length of time in history or in a person's life	➡	Some novels take place during a specific **period** in history. For example, historical fiction might be set in the nineteenth century.
precise = exact and correct in every detail	➡	Directions must be **precise** so that students know exactly what to do.

Practice **Workbook Page 66**

Work with a partner to answer these questions. Try to include the **red** word in your answer. Write the sentences in your notebook.

1. What is **appropriate** to say to someone after he or she has helped you?
2. What might you do to **communicate** that you need help?
3. Which **period** in history do you like to read about? Why?
4. Why is it important for travelers to get **precise** directions?

Apache "burden baskets" were used to carry loads during the 1800s—a period of great change for the Apache people. ▶

138

TESOL Standards

Goal 1, Standard 3—To use English to communicate in social settings: Students will use learning strategies to extend their communicative competence.
Descriptors—Self-monitoring and self-evaluating language development; Learning and using language "chunks; Practicing new language.

Goal 2, Standard 3—To use English to achieve academically in all content areas: Students will use appropriate learning strategies to construct and apply academic knowledge.
Descriptors—Focusing attention selectively; Applying basic reading comprehension skills such as skimming, scanning, previewing, and reviewing text; Planning how and when to use cognitive strategies and applying them appropriately to a learning task.

Goal 3, Standard 3—To use English in socially and culturally appropriate ways: Students will use appropriate learning strategies to extend their sociolinguistic and sociocultural competence.
Descriptors—Analyzing the social context to determine appropriate language use.

Word Study: Uses of the Apostrophe

A contraction is a word that is made up of two words that have been shortened into one. An apostrophe is a mark of punctuation that shows where letters have been left out in contractions. Read the examples below.

Two Words	Contraction
is not	isn't
do not	don't

An apostrophe is also used in dialect to show that letters are missing. Read the examples below. What letters does the apostrophe replace in each example of dialect?

Word	Dialect
thinking	thinkin'
children	chil'en or chill'un

▲ The sun is shining. There isn't a cloud in the sky.

Practice
Workbook Page 67

Write these contractions and examples of dialect in your notebook: *I'll, he'd, shouldn't, 'cause, 'round, 'til*. Work with a partner to identify the letter or letters each apostrophe replaces. Then rewrite the words by replacing apostrophes with the letters that are missing.

READING STRATEGY | MAKE INFERENCES

Making inferences helps you figure out information that authors do not state directly. When you make inferences, you are figuring out what the author means. To make inferences, follow the steps in this example:

- Read the sentence: *By then, the boy was shaking with chills.*
- Think about your own experiences. Ask yourself: "What are chills? How do I feel when I shake with chills?"
- Use the information in the text and your own experiences to make an inference. You can infer (or make the inference) that the boy is probably shaking with chills because he is sick.

As you read the excerpt from *Run Away Home*, make inferences. Think about what the author means but does not say directly.

Workbook Page 68

139

STEP 1: Teach

Word Study

Uses of the Apostrophe Review the fact that apostrophes are used in contractions and in dialect, where letters have been left out. Read the words in the chart aloud, emphasizing the change in pronunciation. Explain the difference between grammatically correct contractions and contractions that are used in dialect, which are not Standard English.

STEP 2: Practice

To help students with this activity, **SAY:** *Let's identify the missing letters in I'll. Will is the second word in the contraction I'll. Write I'll and I will in your notebooks. Then work with a partner to do the same for the other words.*

ANSWERS
I'll, I will; he'd, he would; shouldn't, should not; 'cause, because; 'round, around; 'til, until

STEP 3: Teach

Reading Strategy

Make Inferences To emphasize the step-by-step nature of using the reading skill, **SAY:** *I had to wear my coat, hat, and winter boots today. Using what you know about situations in which people wear those things, you can infer that it is cold outside.*

Assign the reading strategy Workbook page for extra practice.

Linguistic Note

The Genitive Apostrophe

Remind students that the apostrophe is not only used to indicate omission of a letter in contraction, but also to indicate possession. Most singular nouns add *'s*, as in *The dog's fur is black.* Plural nouns ending in *s* only add the apostrophe, as in *The two dogs' puppies looked alike.* Be aware that many people, and not only English learners, wrongly use *it's* for the possessive of *it,* but *it's* can only be a contraction of *it is* or *it has.* Point out that the possessive pronouns and adjectives *yours, his, hers, ours, its, theirs,* do <u>not</u> use an apostrophe.

T139

STEP 1: Introduce

Reading Summary

This reading is about a family who helps an Apache boy in Alabama in 1888. He escapes from a train that is taking him to a school where Native American children are sent to learn American ways and culture.

 The Big Question

Read aloud the Big Question. Ask students how helping an Apache boy might possibly benefit the family who takes him in. List students' ideas on the board and refer to them again after students have read the excerpt.

STEP 2: Teach

Set a Purpose for Reading

Tell students that when they read *Run Away Home*, they should try to use their own knowledge and experience to make inferences about who Sky is and the reasons why the Crossman family helps him.

Preteaching Highlighted Words

With students, preview the highlighted selection vocabulary on pages 140–141. **SAY:** *Many of the words in this reading are idioms, such as* larger than life, out of the woods, *and* bone tired.

Ask volunteers to read the definitions aloud. Model how to use the words in original sentences—for example, *People with a contagious disease can infect others.* Then ask volunteers to do the same for each word.

 CD3 T4 Scaffolding:
Listen and Read

Have students read the text as they listen to the CD recording. Pause at the end of each page so you can ask and answer questions. Model the reading strategy in your questions.

Teaching Resources

• *Resources*, Summaries, pp. 139–140
• Audio CD 3, track 4

Set a purpose for reading Does it take courage to help someone who is very ill? Read to find out what happens to the sick boy that Sarah and her mother find in their barn. Who is he, and why does he need their help?

from

Run Away Home

Patricia C. McKissack

It is 1888 in Alabama when eleven-year-old Sarah Crossman sees an Apache boy escape from a train taking him to a reservation. Later Sarah and her mother find the boy dying of swamp fever in their barn.

When we pulled the shirt over Sky's head, Mama sucked in her breath and clicked her teeth. I covered my mouth to keep from screaming. He was covered with what looked like hundreds and hundreds of mosquito bites. He had scratched them and they had formed sores.

"Swamp fever," Mama whispered. By then, the boy was shaking with chills. We covered him with quilts, and wrapped his hands with strips of cloth so he couldn't scratch and infect himself more.

---

infect, spread disease throughout

140

 TESOL Standards

Goal 1, Standard 3—To use English to communicate in social settings: Students will use learning strategies to extend their communicative competence.
Descriptors—Using the primary language to ask for clarification; Using context to construct meaning.

Goal 2, Standard 1—To use English to achieve academically in all content areas: Students will use English to interact in the classroom.
Descriptors—Asking and answering questions.

Goal 2, Standard 2—To use English to achieve academically in all content areas: Students will use English to obtain, process, construct, and provide subject matter information in spoken and written form.
Descriptors—Analyzing, synthesizing, and inferring from information; Hypothesizing and predicting; Formulating and asking questions.

"Boil water for sassafras tea," Mama snapped an order. "We've got to drive the impurities out of his body."

Mama began humming, the way she did when she was deep thinking, worried, or unsure. "I need quinine," she said. "Run get yo' daddy."

Turning around, I ran right into Mr. Wratten, who looked larger than life, framing the doorway. "I have some quinine in my saddlebag," he said. Right away, I guessed Mr. Wratten had not gone back to Mount Vernon, but had hung around, suspecting maybe that Sky was hiding out at our place, or we were hiding him. He'd probably seen us carry Sky into the house and come to get him. Seeing how sick Sky was, Mr. Wratten's face softened with concern. "Looks bad," he said. "If I try to take him back to Mount Vernon, he'll never make it."

"Leave him here, then." I said, knowing I was speaking out of place, getting deeper and deeper into trouble with Mama. But I couldn't help myself. I went right on talking. "Mama knows Indian ways; she can help him."

Mr. Wratten looked to Mama for her consent. Sky coughed and moaned. She mopped his forehead with a cool cloth. "I might can't save him," she said. "But I can try."

Mr. Wratten studied on the idea, shifting his weight from foot to foot. "So many Apaches died in Florida," he said, looking beyond Mama to some place in his past. "They're a mountain people, used to dry, cool weather." He mumbled something about the damp climate that seemed to sap the life right out of the Apaches. He was talking more to himself than us.

"Can the boy speak English?" Mama asked. "That might make things a whole lot easier later on."

"Sky speaks Apache and Spanish," he answered. "But he can manage English better than most. He learned it mostly by listening and from a few nuns who used to come several times a week to teach those who were interested. Sky is interested in everything."

---

impurities, poisons, or unclean substances that cause sickness
quinine, a drug used for treating fevers
larger than life, important and exciting
suspecting, thinking that
consent, permission
sap, drain

✔ **LITERARY CHECK**

*What is the **mood** of the story at this point? Do you feel any **suspense**? Why?*

BEFORE YOU GO ON

1 Why does Mama ask Sarah to boil sassafras tea for Sky?

2 Why did many Apaches die in Florida?

💡 **On Your Own**
Have you or someone close to you ever nursed someone who was very sick? What was it like?

141

Study Skills: Internet

Students can use the Internet to research the Carlisle School or the state of Pennsylvania. Suggest that they look for URLs that end in .edu or .org. Explain that these websites are not commercially-owned, unlike those that end in .com.

✔ LITERARY CHECK

Point out the Literary Check box. If students need help with the word *mood*, refer to page 137. Answer: Possible response: The mood of the story is anxious and suspenseful. I feel suspense because I don't know what will happen to Sky.

STEP 3: Monitor Progress

Ask students to check what they have understood in the reading. If you are using the Audio CD, pause the recording.

Before You Go On

Have students read and answer the questions. Explain that answering these questions will help students monitor their progress.

ANSWERS

1. Mama asks Sarah to boil sassafras tea because she believes it will help cure him.
2. Many Apaches died in Florida because they were used to dry, cool weather, unlike Florida.

On Your Own Have students write an answer to the On Your Own question. Encourage volunteers to share their responses with the class. Then collect student responses to monitor their comprehension, writing skills, and fluency.

Differentiated Instruction	
Beginning	Have students point to the name of the girl who found Sky.
Early Intermediate	Have students fill in the blank. The name of the girl who found Sky is _____.
Intermediate	Describe Georgianne's explanation to her husband upon seeing Sky.
Standard English Learners (CRI)	Point out phrases from the story that are not Standard English. Have students rewrite the phrases in Standard English, e.g. ". . . talkin' 'bout how you s'posed to love yo' neighbor as yo'self."

Read

Preteaching Highlighted Words

Preview the vocabulary by writing on the board the highlighted words on pages 142–143. Make sure students understand each highlighted word. Ask students to create original sentences using the highlighted words.

Across the Curriculum:
Social Studies

The Carlisle School in Pennsylvania was an actual school. It was run as a military school; its young students had to wear uniforms and shoes instead of moccasins. Students were required to speak only English and to cut their hair (in some Native American cultures this was only done at times of mourning). Native American students had to participate in military drills and were subject to a military court system that imposed punishments. During the summer, the children were sent to live with non-Native American families instead of being able to go home.

Model the
READING STRATEGY

Make Inferences
Return to the Reading Strategy exercise on page 139. **SAY:** *Why do you think Sky would run if he knew Mr. Wratten had seen him? You can infer that Sky is a fugitive, someone who has broken the law* (by not going to the school) *and is hiding. He may think that Mr. Wratten will turn him over to the authorities.*

✔ LITERARY CHECK

Ask students the Literary Check question, and extend the discussion if students seem engaged. If students need help remembering the meaning of *dialect*, have them look back at page 137. Answer: Possible response: The dialect on this page tells us that Mama and Papa come from the South and don't speak standard English.

Mr. Wratten sighed deeply. "Sky will be better off here for the time being," he said. "I guess I'll just say I couldn't find him."

I felt relieved. "If he doesn't make it," he added, "wire me that *the quilt is torn.* If he makes it, wire me that *the quilt is ready,* and I'll come get him. Don't let Sky know I've been here or he'll run again." Mama agreed.

Following Mr. Wratten out to his horse to get the quinine, I asked, "Why did Sky run?"

"Sky is the first Apache who has run away. I don't think he wants to go to Carlisle School for Indians up in Pennsylvania. And I can't say as I blame him. Most Apaches who go there come back home in a coffin. As many of them die of homesickness as they do from diseases."

I had many more questions, but it was not the time to ask. Mr. Wratten was gone by the time Papa came in from the fields for noontime meal.

When Papa didn't smell anything cooking and saw who we had made the sickroom for, he commenced to fussing. "What are you thinkin' 'bout, Georgianne? How could you bring trouble to our front door like this? Mr. Wratten was just here lookin' for this boy, and here we got him in our house, takin' care of him."

"He's sick and needs our help," Mama said. "And besides," she added, "Mr. Wratten knows he's here and asked me to care for him 'til he gets better."

"Aine it enough 'round here to do, besides taking on a sick boy, somebody we don't even-now know. What business is it of ours?"

Mama had started a pot to boil some rice. But she stopped and raised the wooden spoon as if she planned to use it as a weapon. "Lee Andy, you the one always talkin' 'bout how you s'posed to love yo' neighbor as yo'self. What meaning is in them words?" Mama asked.

Right away, Papa fled to the barn. Within the half hour he came back, Bible story in hand.

"I'm reminded here of the parable of the Good Samaritan who took care of a stranger he found 'side the road. It is right that we should take care of this poor soul who is in need. I've made up my mind, now. So, don't try to talk me out of it."

"Yes, you're right, Lee Andy," Mama said.

I turned away so Papa wouldn't see me smiling as I spooned hot tea into Sky's mouth.

---

for the time being, for now
homesickness, feelings of sadness when away from home
diseases, illnesses
commenced to, began
business, personal responsibility or task

142

✔ LITERARY CHECK
How do the examples of dialect on this page help to communicate what Mama and Papa are like?

TESOL Standards

Goal 1, Standard 2—To use English to communicate in social settings: Students will interact in, through, and with spoken and written English for personal expression and enjoyment.
Descriptors—Sharing social and cultural traditions and values.

Goal 2, Standard 3—To use English to achieve academically in all content areas: Students will use appropriate learning strategies to construct and apply academic knowledge.
Descriptors—Using context to construct meaning; Applying self-monitoring and self-corrective strategies to build and expand a knowledge base.

Goal 3, Standard 3—To use English in socially and culturally appropriate ways: Students will use appropriate learning strategies to extend their sociolinguistic and sociocultural competence.
Descriptors—Experimenting with variations of language in social and academic settings.

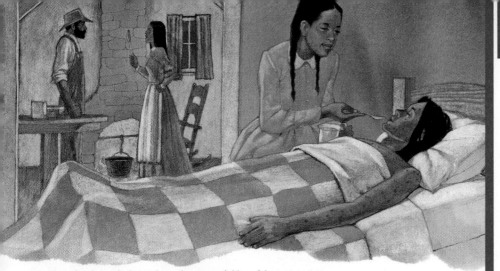

Getting Sky through the night took a powerful lot of doctoring. I sat by his bedside, hoping some and praying some, always helping Mama by fetching and carrying whatever was needed. Sky tossed and turned, and yelled out in his feverish sleep, calling Geronimo's name, and mumbling words in Apache. "Fight," I whispered to him. "Fight to stay alive. Don't give up."

Mama burned herbs and called upon her grandmother for guidance. And then she rattled her bag of bones over his body and sang a song her father had taught her. . . .

All through the night I rubbed Sky's arms and legs with a soothing paste Mama'd made from dried roots. . . .

Sky's fever broke early the next morning, shortly before the southbound rumbled through Quincy. But he wasn't out of the woods yet—far from it. On the third day, his breathing settled into a steady rhythm as his body stayed cool. "He'll make it," said Mama, giving her head a quick nod, the way she did when she felt triumphant. Strengthened by her success, Mama stopped humming and sang a happy tune while preparing breakfast.

But I was bone tired because I hadn't slept more than a few hours in days. Now that it looked like Sky would live, I yawned and stretched and dragged into the kitchen. "Put a little life in your step," Mama said in a lively way. "You're too young to know what tired is."

Geronimo, a famous Apache chief who fought to protect his people's lands
guidance, help and advice
out of the woods, out of trouble
triumphant, victorious
bone tired, extremely tired

BEFORE YOU GO ON

1 What does Mama say to convince Papa to help Sky?

2 Why is Sarah bone tired?

On Your Own
What does it mean "to love yo' neighbor as yo'self"? Is this a good saying? Why?

143

Study Skills: Dictionary

To better understand what they are reading, students should use a dictionary to find the definitions of unfamiliar words. As they read, have students look up unfamiliar words and write them and their definitions in their notebooks. Students should keep their notebooks at hand for easy reference while reading and during classroom discussion.

STEP 5: Monitor Progress

Ask students to check what they have understood in the reading. If you are using the Audio CD, pause the recording.

Before You Go On

Have students read and answer the questions. Explain that answering these questions will help students monitor their progress.

ANSWERS
1. Mama reminds Papa that he always says to love one's neighbor as oneself.
2. Sarah is bone tired because she has hardly slept in days. She has been taking care of Sky.

On Your Own Have students write an answer to the On Your Own question on a separate sheet of paper. Encourage volunteers to share their responses with the class. Then, collect student responses to monitor their comprehension, writing skills, and fluency.

Read

Preteaching Highlighted Words

Preview the vocabulary by writing the highlighted words from pages 144–145 on the board. Make sure students understand each highlighted word. Ask students to create original sentences using the highlighted words. When you correct their sentences, focus on their usage of the highlighted word instead of other kinds of errors.

Across the Curriculum:
Science

Swamp fever is a term that refers to a number of diseases people can get from being in a damp, swampy environment. These include leptospirosis, which is a bacterial infection, and malaria, which is caused by parasites commonly carried by mosquitoes.

Model the
READING STRATEGY

Make Inferences

To further model the strategy, **SAY:** *Why do you think Sky was unfriendly to the Crossman family when he first saw them? You can infer that Sky is afraid to be with people who are not Native Americans, such as those who are trying to send him to the Carlisle School. Also, the culture of the Crossman family (for example, their food) is clearly unfamiliar to him.*

Yes I do, I wanted to say, but dared not be that sassy. I was forever getting my legs switched for talking back, talking out of turn, or just plain talking too much. When I'm all grown up, I thought, I'm going to say what's on my mind. But that was a ways off. As far as I knew I was still on the wrong side of Mama, even though she hadn't mentioned anything to Papa about my part in Sky's escape. I decided it was best not to rile her. So I kept my mouth shut and took joy in knowing we would not have to wire Mr. Wratten that *the quilt is torn.*

Buster met me at the door, yelping all kinds of questions. I explained everything to him, putting in all the details about how we'd saved Sky's life. He listened, head cocked to one side as if he understood everything I was saying. "Buster, I'm so glad I've got you to talk to," I said. "You're a good dog, no matter what Papa thinks."

The smells of Mama's kitchen must have awakened Sky. He was sitting bolt straight in the bed, looking wild-eyed and frightened when I brought a plate of food to him. He asked something in Apache. When I shook my head to show I didn't understand, he switched to English. "Where is this place?" he asked, trying to get up, but he was too weak.

Putting my hand on his shoulder, I smiled, saying, "Here, lie back down, before you . . . "

Sky pulled away and his first words to me were, "I don't know you!" He snapped at me in very clear English, "I don't know you." This time, I snatched my hands away like I'd touched a sleeping alligator by accident. He tried to sit up, but once more he flopped back down on his pallet.

"I was just trying to help," I said, feeling put out. The past few days, I'd imagined a lot of things about Sky, but I never expected him to be an Un-person. In my way of thinking, an Un-person was one who was unkind, ungrateful, unpleasant, unfair, unanything.

The patient wasn't any nicer to Mama. When she tried to get him to eat, he shoved it away. "No pig meat," he said, looking down in disgust.

---

rile, anger or upset
put out, hurt or unfairly treated
patient, person getting medical care

144

🌐 TESOL Standards

Goal 1, Standard 3—To use English to communicate in social settings: Students will use learning strategies to extend their communicative competence.
Descriptors—Testing hypotheses about language.

Goal 2, Standard 1—To use English to achieve academically in all content areas: Students will use English to interact in the classroom.
Descriptors—Explaining actions.

Goal 2, Standard 2—To use English to achieve academically in all content areas: Students will use English to obtain, process, construct, and provide subject matter information in spoken and written form.
Descriptors—Retelling information.

Maybe the fever had addled his brain, I thought.

"Eat a few grits, then," Mama insisted. "You need to build up your strength again. You're still sick."

"I am not sick!" he scoffed. Sky would have nothing to do with us. He pulled the sheet up to his chin, and refused everything we offered him. By then I was close to tossing the food on his head. Just then Papa came in.

Papa introduced everybody by name, including himself. "This is my family." Sky shook his head, never taking his eyes off Mama, who stood at the foot of the bed. "Son, you're 'mongst the living this morning, 'cause of the Good Lord working through my wife and daughter." Sky seemed to be hanging on every word Papa said. "Now, let's get this understanding," Papa went on. "As long as you're in this house, you'll treat them with respect or I'm gon' know why. Clear?"

It took me back when Sky's whole attitude changed in a hurry—I mean, right now. He commenced to eating, shoving down three helpings of grits, eggs, and biscuits—but he still wouldn't touch the pork.

He was still an Un-person, I decided—ungrateful! But I remembered one of Papa's favorite sayings. "Tote the load of another person 'fore you pass judgment." So I put myself in Sky's shoes. He had awakened in a strange man's house and bed with that man's family attending to him in a very personal way. Maybe he wasn't being rude, but waiting until he had been welcomed by the head of the household—Papa. Somehow Sky had gotten a welcome in Papa's words—the permission he needed to feel comfortable with us. I may have been all wrong, but my reason made good sense to me.

addled his brain, confused him
grits, crushed dried corn that is cooked and eaten for breakfast
hanging on every word, listening closely to every word
tote, carry
put myself in Sky's shoes, put myself in his place
attending to, taking care of
personal, private

✔ **LITERARY CHECK**

*Why do you think the author has Papa speak in **dialect**? How does his way of speaking reveal his character?*

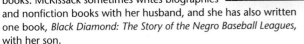

ABOUT THE AUTHOR

Patricia C. McKissack based *Run Away Home* in part on a family story her great-uncle told about her great-great-great-great-grandfather, who was a Native American. She has written numerous award-winning novels and nonfiction books. McKissack sometimes writes biographies and nonfiction books with her husband, and she has also written one book, *Black Diamond: The Story of the Negro Baseball Leagues*, with her son.

BEFORE YOU GO ON

1. Why does Sarah snatch her hands away as if she had touched an alligator?

2. What does Sarah mean when she calls Sky an Un-person?

On Your Own
What do you think of the Crossmans? What kind of people are they?

145

Study Skills: Encylopedia

An encyclopedia is an easy-to-use reference for students seeking background information or an overview of a topic. For example, students can use an encyclopedia to look up the history and culture of the Apache people. The references in an encyclopedia can direct students to primary and secondary sources for more in-depth exploration. Have students fill in a word web with information that they learn.

✔ **LITERARY CHECK**

Ask students the Literary Check question. If students need help with the word *dialect*, refer to page 137. Answer: Possible Answer: Pa's dialect shows where he grew up. His way of speaking reveals that he is used to being an authority.

STEP 7: Monitor Progress

Ask students to check what they have understood in the reading.

Before You Go On

Have students read and answer the questions.

ANSWERS

1. Sarah snatched her hands away because her feelings were hurt.
2. When she calls Sky an un-person, she means that he has an unpleasant characteristic—in this case, unkind.

On Your Own Have students write an answer to the On Your Own question. Encourage volunteers to share their responses with the class. Then collect student responses to monitor their comprehension, writing skills, and fluency.

Review the Purpose for Reading

Elicit responses to the Set a Purpose for Reading questions at the beginning of this reading. Remind students to relate their responses to the Big Question.

STEP 1: Introduce

Speaking Tip

Suggest to students that Sarah's voice would probably sound less self-confident than her mother's.

Reader's Theater

Reader's Theater gives students a reason to rehearse their reading several times, increase their fluency, and improve expression and intonation. Invite pairs of students to practice and perform. Have partners decide who will play which roles. Suggest that they think about how their character feels at this point in the story.

Students should find a quiet corner in which to rehearse. When they are ready, ask volunteers to perform before the class.

STEP 2: Practice

Comprehension

Ask students to read and answer the questions.

ANSWERS

1. Sky has swamp fever.
2. If Sky lives, the message she is to send is that the quilt is ready.
3. 1888
4. To help Sky get well, Mama covers him, wraps his hands so that he can't scratch himself, feeds him, and gives him quinine and sassafras tea.
5. **Possible response:** Sky only listens to Papa because Papa is the head of the household.
6. The writer creates suspense because the reader doesn't know if Sky will live or die. I knew that Sky would get better when his fever broke.
7. **Possible response:** It helps to put yourself in someone else's shoes because then you can try to understand their point of view.
8. **Possible response:** I felt homesick when my family went on vacation and when we went to visit relatives.

Teaching Resources

- *Workbook*, p. 69
- CD-ROM/e-book, Reader's Theater, Comprehension, Response to Literature

---

READING 1 | # Review and Practice

READER'S THEATER

Act out this scene between Sarah and her mother.

Sarah: Mama, how sick is Sky? All those sores look pretty bad.

Mama: He is very sick, Sarah. He has a bad disease. Sky might die.

Sarah: Oh, no! Can you cure him, Mama? How can you help him?

Mama: I am going to give him a medicine called quinine. It will help lower his fever. If we can get his fever down, he will probably recover. I will wash him with cool water, too.

Sarah: What can I do to help you? Should I get some water?

Mama: Get your father. I need his help, too. Then boil some water for sassafras tea. Sky will need to drink a lot of this tea in order to get the poisons out of his body.

Sarah: Okay, Mama. I really hope that Sky gets better.

Mama: Hurry up now, and get your Papa.

COMPREHENSION Workbook Page 69

Right There

1. What illness does Sky have?
2. What message is Mama to send if Sky lives?

Think and Search

3. During what time period does this novel take place?
4. What are some things that Mama does to help Sky get well?

Author and You

5. Why do you think that Sky only listens to Papa?
6. How does the writer create suspense? At what point in the selection did you know that Sky would get better?

On Your Own

7. Does it help to try to put yourself in someone else's shoes? Why?
8. When have you or someone close to you felt homesick?

146

▲ This advertisement shows how quinine was once used to treat fevers.

🔊 *Speaking* TIP

Try to use your voice to communicate your character's traits. For example, Mama would speak in a strong, grown-up way, but Sarah would sound less sure of herself.

🌐 TESOL Standards

Goal 1, Standard 1—To use English to communicate in social settings: Students will use English to participate in social interactions.
Descriptors—Sharing and requesting information; Engaging in conversations.

Goal 1, Standard 2—To use English to communicate in social settings: Students will interact in, through, and with spoken and written English for personal expression and enjoyment.
Descriptors—Participating in popular culture.

DISCUSSION

Discuss in pairs or small groups.

1. How does Mama get Papa to do what she wants? Explain.

2. Papa says, "Tote the load of another person 'fore you pass judgment." What does he mean by this?

3. How do you think Sky knew that he would not like the Carlisle Indian School? What inferences can you make about Sky's character and feelings?

Q **How does helping others help us all?** How do the Crossmans feel when Sky gets better? Do they feel better about themselves for helping him? Why?

 Listening TIP

Ask questions if you want more information. If you don't understand what someone is saying, ask the person to repeat or explain his or her answer.

RESPONSE TO LITERATURE

 Workbook Page 69

Imagine that you are in Sky's shoes. Why did you run away? How do you feel about having Mama and Sarah take care of you? Write a journal entry in which you communicate your experiences and feelings. Describe the following:

- Why I ran away
- What happened to me
- How I feel about being sick
- How I feel about being cared for by a girl and her mother

When you are done writing, share your journal entry with a partner. Discuss which details in the selection helped you write your journal entry.

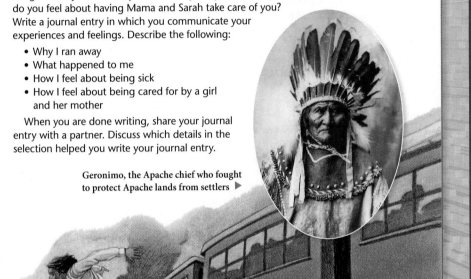

Geronimo, the Apache chief who fought to protect Apache lands from settlers ▶

147

STEP 3: Extend

Congratulate students on successfully completing the reading. **SAY:** *We've learned a lot about helping people from the reading. Now, let's discuss a few questions about the reading.*

Listening Tip

Tell students that they should say, "Excuse me," "Please," and "Thank you" when asking for more information. Explain that it is always acceptable to ask someone to repeat what they said and to ask for clarification.

(CRI) Discussion

Draw students into a conversation about the questions. **SAY:** *The Golden Rule says to do unto others as you would have them do unto you. Do you think that rule is important today?*

Model the first question. **SAY:** *Mama gets Papa to help Sky by citing the Golden Rule.* Be sure to model listening skills by listening carefully and patiently to students.

Q **How does helping others help us all?** Ask students how helping Sky also helped the Crossmans.

STEP 4: Assess

Response to Literature

To help students see the story from Sky's point of view, have them copy a word web and write Sky in the center oval. In the lines coming from the circle, they should write what they know or have inferred about Sky.

Differentiated Instruction

Beginning	Tell students that answers to the Right There questions can be found in sentences in the reading. Ask students to point to the sentences that contain answers to these questions.
Early Intermediate	Ask students why they think Sarah wanted to help Sky.
Intermediate	Ask students if they think Sarah did the right thing. Should she have left Sky or helped him. Why?
Struggling Readers	Have students point out the illustration from the story where Sarah is helping Sky by spooning hot tea into his mouth.

Teach & Apply

STEP 1: Introduce

Tell students that it is important to use both simple and compound sentences in writing. Ask them to look at page 148 and tell them you will be reviewing examples of both simple and compound sentences.

STEP 2: Teach

Grammar and Writing

Simple and Compound Sentences Read aloud the information in this section. Write on the board the examples on page 148. Have students come up and underline the subject, verb, and conjunction (if there is one) in each sentence. **SAY:** *Let's read aloud the first sentence. What are the subject and verb in this sentence? Now let's read the next sentence. What are the subject and verb in the sentence? What is the conjunction?* Continue in the same manner with the remaining sentences.

Have students break the compound sentence into two sentences. They should write the sentences in a two-column chart as follows.

He had scratched them.	They had formed sores.
I had more questions.	It was not the time to ask.

STEP 3: Practice

Review with students how to write simple and compound sentences. Ask them to write two original simple sentences and two original compound sentences for more practice.

ANSWERS
1. Sky could die, or he could get better.
2. Mama stopped humming nervously, and she started whistling a happy tune.
3. I may be wrong about Sky, but my reason made sense to me.

Teaching Resources

- *Workbook*, pp. 70–71
- CD-ROM/e-book, Grammar, Writing
- *Transparencies*, Writing Model 31
- *Transparencies*, *Resources*, Graphic Organizer 13
- *Assessment*, Reading 1 Test, pp. 67–70

Grammar and Writing

GRAMMAR, USAGE, AND MECHANICS

Simple and Compound Sentences

Remember that a sentence is a group of words that expresses a complete thought. A simple sentence has a subject and a verb. Read the example of a simple sentence from *Run Away Home*.

subject	verb
Mr. Wratten sighed.	

Good writers include sentences of varying lengths in their writing. When you want to combine two simple sentences, use a coordinating conjunction, such as *and*, *but*, or *or*. This will make your writing flow better. Two simple sentences joined by a coordinating conjunction form a compound sentence. When joining two simple sentences, you usually place a comma before the coordinating conjunction. Read these examples.

> He had scratched them, **and** they had formed sores.
> I had more questions, **but** it was not the time to ask.

Practice Workbook Page 70

Work with a partner. Copy the pairs of simple sentences below into your notebook. Then combine each pair into a compound sentence, using a coordinating conjunction, such as *and*, *but*, or *or*. Write the compound sentences.

1. Sky could die.
   He could get better.
2. Mama stopped humming nervously.
   She started whistling a happy tune.
3. I may be wrong about Sky.
   My reason made sense to me.

148

TESOL Standards

Goal 2, Standard 1—To use English to achieve academically in all content areas: Students will use English to interact in the classroom.
Descriptors—Following oral and written directions, implicit and explicit; Elaborating and extending other people's ideas and words.

Goal 2, Standard 2—To use English to achieve academically in all content areas: Students will use English to obtain, process, construct, and provide subject matter information in spoken and written form.
Descriptors—Listening to, speaking, reading, and writing about subject matter information; Gathering information orally and in writing; Responding to the work of peers and others.

Goal 3, Standard 1—To use English in socially and culturally appropriate ways: Students will use the appropriate language variety, register, and genre according to audience, purpose, and setting.
Descriptors—Using a variety of writing styles appropriate for different audiences, purposes, and settings.

WRITING a PERSUASIVE PARAGRAPH

Write a Book Review

On this page, you'll use a graphic organizer like the one at the right to help you write a book review. When you write a review, you state your opinion of the book and tell whether it is worth reading or not. In either case, you give reasons for your point of view and support them with convincing examples. Providing one or more reasons and presenting them simply and logically makes the review persuasive. Begin by stating your opinion. Then give reasons and provide examples from the book. End your review with a persuasive conclusion. For example, you might recommend the book to others.

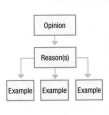

   Here is a model book review of *Run Away Home*. Notice how the writer gives her opinion and a recommendation, and supports her opinion and recommendation with reasons and examples.

> *Danielle Christian*
>
> ### Run Away Home
>
> *Run Away Home* is the most exciting book I've read in a long time, and I think that many students would feel the same way. It is the story of a runaway Apache boy who is helped by an African-American farm family in Alabama in 1888. One reason why I liked the book is that it is full of suspense. When the Crossmans find Sky dying of swamp fever, I was in suspense until I knew whether Sky would live or die. I had to keep reading until I found out. I also liked the book because I identify with the main characters. I liked all of the characters, but I identify most with Sarah. She is brave, kind, and rebellious. I would choose someone like Sarah for my friend. In addition, I enjoyed the book because it was about people who care for others. Each of the Crossmans helped to protect Sky. I recommend *Run Away Home* to anyone who likes suspense, real-life characters, or stories about helping others.

Practice  **Workbook Page 71**

Review a book or story that you like very much. Use an opinion and reasons chart to list your ideas. Include both simple and compound sentences in your review.

Writing Checklist

IDEAS:
- ☑ I included my opinion, reasons that support it, and a recommendation.

SENTENCE FLUENCY:
- ☑ I used both simple and compound sentences.

149

STEP 1: Introduce

Objectives

Read the list in the What You Will Learn section, encouraging students to join in. Tell students that "Extraordinary People: Serving Others" is about heroic people who have significantly helped others. Have students work in pairs to restate the list of things they will learn.

The Big Question

Remind students that the Big Question is "How does helping others help us all?" Have them read the first paragraph on page 150 of the student book. Answer one of the questions from your own personal experience. Ask students to share their own experiences or points of view.
SAY: *"Extraordinary People: Serving Others" tells about Helen Keller, who became blind and deaf as a child, and Franklin Delano Roosevelt, a U.S. president who lost the ability to walk. Both wanted to help others despite their own struggles.*

Build Background

Read aloud the Build Background section from page 150 of the student book. Show students a world map, and point out the countries/states where the extraordinary people in the reading came from. Help students see that remarkable people help others all over the world and not in just one country or place.

STEP 2: Teach

Understanding the Genre:
Informational Text

Tell students that an informational text is a work of nonfiction. Its purpose is to present facts and other information about real people, events, places, and situations. This informational text is a social studies article. It is about heroes who overcame their own challenges and helped others.

Teaching Resources

- CD-ROM/e-book, Key Words
- Audio CD 3, tracks 5–6
- *Workbook*, p. 72

What You Will Learn

Reading
- Vocabulary building: *Context, dictionary skills, word study*
- Reading strategy: *Identify problems and solutions*
- Text type: *Informational text (social studies)*

Grammar, Usage, and Mechanics
Prepositions of time: *in, on,* and *at*

Writing
Use a question-and-answer format

THE BIG QUESTION

How does helping others help us all? Heroes are people whom we admire and respect because they've helped others. Sometimes people do heroic things because of their work. Firefighters, teachers, doctors, men and women who serve in the military—they can all be heroes. Who are your heroes? How are, or were, they heroic? How do, or did, they help others?

BUILD BACKGROUND

"Extraordinary People: Serving Others" is a series of short biographies of heroic figures from around the world. Many readers will be inspired by the stories of these remarkable people and how they helped change the world. All of these heroic figures are greatly admired for their bravery, strength, and willingness to help others.

Two of the people you will read about also had to face their own physical challenges. Helen Keller became blind and deaf as a young child. Franklin Delano Roosevelt lost the ability to walk when he was thirty-nine years old. Both of these extraordinary people worked hard to conquer their physical challenges. Heroes always face challenges, but they don't give up.

▲ President Roosevelt had to wear leg braces to help him walk.

◄ Anne Sullivan (right) helped Helen Keller (left) learn how to communicate.

150

TESOL Standards

Goal 2, Standard 2—To use English to achieve academically in all content areas: Students will use English to obtain, process, construct, and provide subject matter information in spoken and written form.
Descriptors—Demonstrating knowledge through application in a variety of contexts.

Goal 3, Standard 1—To use English in socially and culturally appropriate ways: Students will use the appropriate language variety, register, and genre according to audience, purpose, and setting.
Descriptors—Using a variety of writing styles appropriate for different audiences, purposes, and settings.

Goal 3, Standard 3—To use English in socially and culturally appropriate ways: Students will use appropriate learning strategies to extend their sociolinguistic and sociocultural competence.
Descriptors—Observing and modeling how others speak and behave in a particular situation or setting; Rehearsing variations of language use in different social and academic settings.

Learn Key Words

Read these sentences. Use the context to figure out the meaning of the red words. Use a dictionary to check your answers. Then write each word and its meaning in your notebook.

Key Words

- assassinated
- extraordinary
- founders
- resistance
- superintendent
- tolerance

1. Sometimes leaders are assassinated. Kings, presidents, and other important people have been killed by surprise attack.

2. The doctor had extraordinary abilities. She saved the lives of three children whose injuries were thought to be beyond hope.

3. The founders of this school wanted to establish a place of learning for students with special needs.

4. The people showed resistance to the law by voting against it.

5. The superintendent of our group makes all the rules and is in charge.

6. You show tolerance by respecting other people's ideas.

Practice | Workbook Page 72

Write the sentences in your notebook. Choose a red word from the box above to complete each sentence. Then take turns reading the sentences aloud with a partner.

1. At first there was much _____ to the new idea, but everyone finally came to accept it.

2. _____ helps people live peacefully because it encourages people to respect one another's ideas.

3. In the 1960s, three important U.S. leaders—John F. Kennedy, Martin Luther King Jr., and Robert F. Kennedy—were all _____ by gunmen.

4. The doctor was one of the three _____ of the hospital in 1938.

5. Tiger Woods is an _____ golfer. He has amazing abilities.

6. The _____ hired all the nurses and was in charge of running the hospital.

▲ Senator Robert F. Kennedy attends the funeral of assassinated civil rights leader Dr. Martin Luther King Jr.

151

CD3 T5–T6

Vocabulary

Learn Key Words Play the CD. Have students listen and repeat. If you are not using the CD, read the Key Words aloud. **SAY:** *These words are called key words because they are important to the subject matter of the text we are reading.* On the board or an overhead transparency, write the Key Words below and their definitions.

- **assassinated:** murdered (an important person)
- **extraordinary:** very unusual and special
- **founders:** people who start a business, school, and so on
- **resistance:** refusal to accept new ideas or change
- **superintendent:** someone who runs the schools in a district or runs any large group
- **tolerance:** a willingness to let people do, say, and believe what they want

Have students copy the definitions into their notebooks and generate original sentences for each word. For extra practice, assign the corresponding Workbook page.

STEP 3: Practice

Have students work with partners to complete the activity. **SAY:** *Take turns reading the sentences aloud. As you read each sentence, think about the Key Word that makes the most sense in that sentence. Then write that word in your notebook.*

ANSWERS
1. resistance
2. Tolerance
3. assassinated
4. founders
5. extraordinary
6. superintendent

Differentiated Instruction	
Beginning	Have students name a person they consider to be extraordinary.
Early Intermediate	Have students research one of the people from the reading. Have them tell the class three facts about that person.
Intermediate	Have students write their own example sentences for two of the Key Words.
Standard English Learners (CRI)	Have students name a person they consider to be extraordinary. Ask the student to explain why they think that person is special.

STEP 1: Teach

CD3 T7–T8

Vocabulary

Learn Academic Words Play the CD. Have students listen and repeat. If you are not using the CD, read the Academic Words aloud. **SAY:** *Look at the Academic Word list. The chart below it contains two parts: the definition on the left and a sentence containing the word on the right. Work with a partner to add another sentence using the Academic Word. Write each word, its definition, and the sentence in your notebook. Example: My older sister altered her appearance by cutting her hair.*

STEP 2: Practice

Have students work with partners to complete the practice activity. **SAY:** *Take turns reading the sentence starters aloud with your partner. As you read each sentence starter, think about how to use the Academic Word to complete that sentence. Once you decide what completes the sentence best, write the sentence in your notebook.*

ANSWERS

1. By the time I am grown up, I would like to achieve my goal of graduating from college.
2. When it rains, I alter my plans by riding the bus to school.
3. I think my teachers have an impact on my life because they show me how to be my best.
4. First-grade teachers play an important role in a child's life because they affect how a child feels about himself or herself.

Teaching Resources

- Audio CD 3, tracks 7–8
- *Workbook*, pp. 73–75
- CD-ROM/e-book, Academic Words, Word Study

T152

Learn Academic Words

Study the red words and their meanings. You will find these words useful when talking and writing about informational texts. Write each word and its meaning in your notebook. After you read "Extraordinary People: Serving Others," try to use these words to respond to the text.

Academic Words
achieve
alter
impact
role

achieve = succeed in doing or getting something as a result of your actions	➡	Some people **achieve** success by getting important things done.
alter = change in some way	➡	Many people want to **alter** the health-care system in the United States.
impact = the effect that something or someone has on someone or something	➡	Doctors have a big **impact** on the health and well-being of their patients.
role = the position, job, or function someone or something has in a particular situation or activity	➡	Nurses play an important **role** in a hospital. They help doctors, and they help sick people get well.

Practice Workbook Page 73

Work with a partner to complete these statements. Try to include the red word in your answer. Write the sentences in your notebook.

1. By the time I am a grown-up, I would like to **achieve** . . .
2. When it rains, I **alter** my plans by . . .
3. I think my close friends have an **impact** on my life because . . .
4. First-grade teachers play an important **role** in a child's life because . . .

▲ This nurse plays an important role in caring for senior citizens.

152

 ## TESOL Standards

Goal 1, Standard 3—To use English to communicate in social settings: Students will use learning strategies to extend their communicative competence.
Descriptors—Comparing nonverbal and verbal cues.

Goal 2, Standard 2—To use English to achieve academically in all content areas: Students will use English to obtain, process, construct, and provide subject matter information in spoken and written form.
Descriptors—Representing information visually and interpreting information presented visually.

Goal 2, Standard 3—To use English to achieve academically in all content areas: Students will use appropriate learning strategies to construct and apply academic knowledge.
Descriptors—Imitating the behaviors of native English speakers to complete tasks successfully.

Word Study: Spelling Words with Silent *gh*

In English, the letters *gh* are often, but not always, silent. Study the words in the chart. You will read some of these words in "Extraordinary People: Serving Others." Notice that in these words, the letters *gh* are silent.

brought	daughter	fought	night	rights	sight

Practice **Workbook Page 74**

Say a word from the chart, and ask your partner to spell it aloud. Then have your partner say the next word. Continue until you can spell all of the words correctly. Now think of three more words that contain the silent letters *gh*. Say the words one by one. Ask your partner to spell each word.

READING STRATEGY | IDENTIFY PROBLEMS AND SOLUTIONS

Identifying problems and solutions helps you understand a text better. Many texts include a problem that a person, group, or character has to solve (or find a solution to). To identify problems and solutions, ask yourself:

- What problem or problems does the person or group have?
- How does the person or group solve or try to solve the problem?

In "Extraordinary People: Serving Others," heroes face problems and find solutions. As you read the biographies, think about each problem and its possible solutions. Read to find out how the problem was solved.

Workbook Page 75

153

Read

STEP 1: Introduce

Reading Summary

This is an informational text about people who have made extraordinary achievements. Included are people from the 19th, 20th, and 21st centuries who went above and beyond what was expected in order help others.

 The Big Question

Remind students that the Big Question is, "How does helping others help us all?" By helping a few, people can sometimes improve the lives of many. Ask students how their own lives have been improved by helping others.

STEP 2: Teach

Set a Purpose for Reading

Point out that people are often motivated by a desire to make the world a better place. **SAY:** *Look for the reasons and motivations behind these peoples' actions as you read.*

Preteaching Highlighted Words

With students, preview the highlighted vocabulary on student book pages 154–155. Write the words on the board, and point out that they are defined at the bottom of each page. Ask volunteers to find and read the definitions. Model using the words in original sentences— for example, *They all felt inspired by the missionary's speech.* Then ask for volunteers to do the same and create a word book including the definition, a sentence using the word, and an image.

CD3 T9 **Scaffolding:**
Listen and Read

Have students read the text as you play the audio CD. Pause the recording at the end of each page to answer questions students may have.

Teaching Resources

- *Resources*, Summaries, pp. 141–142
- Audio CD 3, track 9
- *Reader's Companion Workbook*, pp. 49–55

Set a purpose for reading What motivates certain people to spend their lives helping others? Read these biographies of extraordinary people to find out.

Extraordinary People: Serving Others

In different places and at different times, people have achieved extraordinary things. In the short biographies that follow, you will read about people from different times in history who helped others in many ways. You will also read about a group of people who continue to do extraordinary things in troubled parts of the world today.

Benito Juárez

Benito Juárez (1806–1872) is a national hero in Mexico. He was the son of poor Zapotec Indian farmers in the state of Oaxaca, Mexico. At age thirteen he couldn't read, write, or speak Spanish. He trained to become a priest, but later he decided to become a lawyer. As a young man, he became interested in social justice, especially the rights of native peoples. He was very popular among the native Indian population. In 1847, he was elected governor of Oaxaca.

In 1861, Juárez became the first Zapotec Indian president of Mexico. He improved education. For the first time, it was possible for every child to go to school. He stopped the French from colonizing Mexico. His many reforms made Mexico a fairer, more modern society.

▲ Benito Juárez fought for the rights of all people in Mexico.

---

social justice, fairness for all people
colonizing, controlling a country and sending your own people to live there
reforms, changes that improve a system

154

 ## TESOL Standards

Goal 1, Standard 2—To use English to communicate in social settings: Students will interact in, through, and with spoken and written English for personal expression and enjoyment.
Descriptors—Expressing personal needs, feelings, and ideas

Goal 2, Standard 3—To use English to achieve academically in all content areas: Students will use appropriate learning strategies to construct and apply academic knowledge.
Descriptors—Taking notes to record important information and aid one's own learning; Actively connecting new information to information previously learned.

Florence Nightingale

Florence Nightingale (1820–1910) came from a wealthy English family. Against her parents' wishes, she became a nurse.

In 1853, she became superintendent of a hospital for women in London. In 1854, Britain, France, and Turkey fought against Russia in the Crimean War. Nightingale volunteered to go to Turkey to help. She took thirty-eight nurses with her. They helped many wounded soldiers recover. Nightingale often visited the soldiers at night, carrying a lamp. Soldiers called her "the lady with the lamp."

When Nightingale returned to England, she started a school for nurses. The school still exists today.

Mohandas Gandhi

Mohandas Gandhi (1869–1948) was born in the coastal city of Porbandar, in the western part of India. At that time, India was a British colony. Gandhi went to England in 1888 and studied law. He returned to India and worked as a lawyer in Bombay (Mumbai).

In 1893, Gandhi traveled to South Africa. The government of South Africa had a system of racial separation, called apartheid. A group of white South Africans attacked Gandhi and beat him. After this experience, he encouraged people to practice passive resistance against the South African authorities and apartheid.

After he returned to India in 1915, Gandhi became a leader in India's struggle for independence. He became the international symbol of nonviolent protest. He believed in religious tolerance. In 1947, Britain finally ended its 190-year rule in India. Then, in 1948, Gandhi was assassinated by someone who didn't agree with his beliefs.

Gandhi inspired nonviolent movements elsewhere. In the United States, Dr. Martin Luther King Jr. used passive resistance when he became leader of the civil rights movement in the 1950s and 1960s.

---

wealthy, very rich
apartheid, a system in which different races in a country are separated
inspired, caused; influenced people to express interest in

▲ Florence Nightingale worked for many long hours to help the sick and dying men.

▲ Gandhi was imprisoned many times for his beliefs.

BEFORE YOU GO ON

1 What role did Florence Nightingale play during the Crimean War?

2 What system was Mohandas Gandhi trying to change through passive resistance?

On Your Own
Why do you think Benito Juárez wanted to stop the French from colonizing Mexico?

155

STEP 4: Teach

Preteaching Highlighted Words

Before reading this spread, point out the highlighted words and terms to students. Define each one, pointing out the location of the definition in the gloss at the bottom of the student book page. Make sure that students understand each highlighted word. If appropriate, ask students to generate original sentences using the highlighted words. When correcting original sentences, focus on usage rather than other kinds of errors.

Across the Curriculum:
Science

Sound travels in waves, which reach our ears as vibrations. These vibrations enter the ear canal and hit the eardrum, which transmits sounds from the air to the middle ear, and the nerve centers of the inner ear. If the eardrum or nerve centers are damaged, deafness can result. However, these are not the only ways we have of sensing vibrations or telling what people are saying. Helen Keller learned to "hear" speech by touching a person's throat, to feel the vibrations created, and by touching their lips, to feel the shapes created by speech. Keller was also sight-impaired, but many hearing-impaired people can tell what is being said just by watching the way a person's lips move as he or she speaks.

Franklin Delano Roosevelt

Franklin Delano Roosevelt (1882–1945) was elected as the thirty-second president of the United States in 1932. During the 1930s, the country was experiencing deep economic troubles. This period in American history is called the Great Depression. Banks shut down, workers lost their jobs, and farms failed. Roosevelt declared that Americans had "nothing to fear but fear itself." He put into place a series of new government programs that brought hope to the American people. Many people returned to work.

Roosevelt soon faced another challenge. The Second World War in Europe and the Pacific began in 1939. Great Britain, France, Russia, and other countries (the Allies) fought against Germany and Japan. In 1941, the Japanese bombed Pearl Harbor in Hawaii. Roosevelt asked for and received a declaration of war on Japan, and the United States entered the war. The United States and the Allies fought many brave battles and eventually won the war in 1945.

Roosevelt faced personal challenges as well. He came down with polio at the age of thirty-nine, and lost the use of his legs. However, Roosevelt did not allow his physical condition to prevent him from contributing to society. Roosevelt is now considered by many historians to be one of the greatest U.S. presidents.

▲ President Roosevelt overcame polio to lead the United States through two of its most difficult times: the Great Depression and World War II.

Helen Keller

Helen Keller (1880–1968) was nineteen months old when she became sick with a fever. The sickness left her without sight or hearing. Because she was so young when this happened, it was hard for her to learn to communicate. Because she could not see, she was unable to use sign language—the language of hearing-impaired people. She also couldn't "read lips," as many hearing-impaired people do. Although these challenges made young Helen very frustrated, she was also extremely intelligent. With the help of a skilled teacher, named Anne Sullivan, she learned that everything had a name and that these names were words. Because of the help of others and her own determination, she was eventually able to learn different ways to communicate. For instance, she learned to "hear" and understand speech by touching a speaker's lips and throat.

▲ Helen Keller was the first sight- and hearing-impaired person to graduate from college.

economic, relating to business, industry, and managing money
polio, an infectious disease of the nerves in the spine that can cause paralysis
impaired, damaged, or less strong, or less good
frustrated, upset because you can't do something

156

TESOL Standards

Goal 1, Standard 1—To use English to communicate in social settings: Students will use English to participate in social interactions.
Descriptors—Expressing needs, feelings, and ideas.

Goal 1, Standard 3—To use English to communicate in social settings: Students will use learning strategies to extend their communicative competence.
Descriptors—Using the primary language to ask for clarification; Using context to construct meaning.

Goal 2, Standard 1—To use English to achieve academically in all content areas: Students will use English to interact in the classroom.
Descriptors—Requesting information and assistance.

Keller gave lectures (with her teacher's help) and wrote a number of books. Her public talks and her writings inspired countless people with hearing, sight, and other physical problems. She inspired others to not give up in the face of adversity. Keller also toured the world. She raised funds for programs to help people with impaired hearing and sight. To this day, Helen Keller remains a figure of inspiration.

Doctors Without Borders

Doctors Without Borders is an international organization whose members believe that every person in every country has the right to medical care. It helps victims of war, disease, and natural disasters. A small group of French doctors started Doctors Without Borders (Médecins Sans Frontières) in 1971. Each year, thousands of volunteer doctors, nurses, and administrators from countries all over the world provide medical aid to people in more than seventy countries. They provide health care, perform surgery, organize nutrition and sanitation programs, train local medical staff, and provide mental health care.

Doctors Without Borders works with the United Nations, governments, and the media to tell the world about their patients' suffering and concerns. For example, Doctors Without Borders volunteers told the media about the atrocities they saw in Chechnya, Angola, and Kosovo.

Doctors Without Borders won the Nobel Peace Prize in 1999. Accepting the award, one of the organization's founders, Bernard Kouchner, said, "I'm deeply moved, and I'm thinking of all the people who died without aid, of all those who died waiting for someone to knock on their door."

---

adversity, difficulties or problems
borders, official lines that separate two countries
administrators, people who manage businesses or organizations
nutrition, food for good health and growth
sanitation, hygiene; cleanliness
atrocities, extremely violent actions

▲ A doctor helps a child in Angola, where many children die of starvation or disease.

BEFORE YOU GO ON

1. How did Franklin Delano Roosevelt help pull the United States out of the Depression?

2. Why did Helen Keller have trouble communicating?

On Your Own
Would you like to work for Doctors Without Borders? Why or why not?

157

Study Skills: Atlas

An atlas provides not only world maps, but detailed maps of different regions in the world. Students can use an atlas to find the places mentioned in this reading. *Doctors Without Borders* has worked in Angola, Chechnya, and Kosovo. Students can find out where each place is located by using the index. Regional maps of Europe and Africa will give students more information about an area than a full world map would. Students can also look up India, South Africa, Oaxaca (Mexico), and Turkey.

STEP 5: Monitor Progress

Ask students to check what they have understood in the reading.

Before You Go On

Tell students that when they answer each question, they should look for the place on the spread that substantiates that information.

ANSWERS

1. Franklin Delano Roosevelt pulled the United States out of the Depression by putting a series of government plans into place that gave people work.
2. Helen Keller had trouble communicating because she was both sight- and hearing-impaired.

On Your Own Have students write an answer to the On Your Own question on a separate sheet of paper. Encourage volunteers to share their responses with the class. Then collect student responses to monitor their comprehension, writing skills, and fluency.

Review the Purpose for Reading

Elicit responses to the Set a Purpose for Reading question at the beginning of this reading. Remind students to relate their responses to the Big Question.

Teach & Apply

STEP 1: Practice

Comprehension

These questions help students review and extend what they have read. Have students work in pairs or small groups. They can respond orally or in writing. Answer the first question with the class.

ANSWERS

1. In 1861, Benito Juarez was elected president of Mexico.
2. World War II
3. Helen Keller's childhood was difficult because she became sight- and hearing-impaired. She could not communicate with other people.
4. Martin Luther King Jr.
5. Possible response: I think the author wrote about Florence Nightingale because she healed and brought hope to soldiers voluntarily.
6. Answers will vary.
7. Answers will vary.
8. Answers will vary.

STEP 2: Extend

Speaking Tips

Point out the Speaking Tips on the right side of the page. Remind students that when they are speaking, they need to connect with their audience. **SAY:** *Making eye contact helps keep people interested and also makes it easier for people to hear you.*

In Your Own Words

Read aloud the instructions for this activity. **SAY:** *Reading the text has probably given you a good sense of these remarkable individuals and their achievements. Using the chart on page 158 as your guide, summarize each person's life and history, and then share your summaries with a classmate.*

Teaching Resources

- *Workbook*, p. 76
- CD-ROM/e-book, Comprehension, Extension
- *Reader's Companion Workbook*, pp. 56–60

COMPREHENSION Workbook Page 76

Right There

1. What happened to Benito Juárez in 1861?
2. Franklin Delano Roosevelt was president during which war?

Think and Search

3. Why was Helen Keller's childhood so difficult?
4. What North American leader believed in passive resistance?

Author and You

5. Why do you think the author chose to write about Florence Nightingale?
6. Who do you think had the most lasting impact on others? Why?

On Your Own

7. Why is it important for all children to get an education?
8. Describe someone you think is extraordinary. Why is that person special?

IN YOUR OWN WORDS

Imagine that you are telling a small group of friends about "Extraordinary People: Serving Others." Tell your friends about each person or organization in the text. Use the chart to help you summarize the history of each person or organization. Then share your summaries with a classmate. See how they compare.

> **Speaking TIPS**
>
> Make eye contact with your classmates.
>
> Talk to your audience, not your chart.

Famous People	Summary
Benito Juárez	
Florence Nightingale	
Mohandas Gandhi	
Franklin Delano Roosevelt	
Helen Keller	
Doctors Without Borders	

158

TESOL Standards

Goal 1, Standard 1—To use English to communicate in social settings: Students will use English to participate in social interactions.
Descriptors—Using nonverbal communication in social interactions; Conducting transactions.

Goal 1, Standard 3—To use English to communicate in social settings: Students will use learning strategies to extend their communicative competence.
Descriptors—Selecting different media to help understand language.

Goal 2, Standard 3—To use English to achieve academically in all content areas: Students will use appropriate learning strategies to construct and apply academic knowledge.
Descriptors—Determining and establishing the conditions that help one become an effective learner (e.g., when, where, how to study); Recognizing the need for and seeking assistance appropriately from others (e.g., teachers, peers, specialists, community members); Knowing when to use native language resources (human and material) to promote understanding.

DISCUSSION

Discuss in pairs or small groups.

1. In what ways did Helen Keller's teacher, Anne Sullivan, help her?
2. How are Benito Juárez and Mohandas Gandhi similar? How are they different?
3. What kind of qualities do you think members of Doctors Without Borders have in common?

Q How does helping others help us all? In what ways did Mohandas Gandhi, Helen Keller, and Doctors Without Borders make the world better for all of us?

Listening TIP

When listening to your classmates, listen for examples they use to illustrate their ideas. Think about how these ideas are similar to or different from your own.

READ FOR FLUENCY

When we read aloud to communicate meaning, we group words into phrases, pause or slow down to make important points, and emphasize important words. Pause for a short time when you reach a comma and for a longer time when you reach a period. Pay attention to rising and falling intonation at the end of sentences.

Work with a partner. Choose a paragraph from the reading. Discuss which words seem important for communicating meaning. Practice pronouncing difficult words. Take turns reading the paragraph aloud and give each other feedback.

▲ Helen Keller had to rely on her sense of touch and smell.

EXTENSION Workbook Page 76

Learn more about the people and organization described in "Extraordinary People: Helping Others." Choose any two subjects described in the text. Use encyclopedias, reference books, and reliable websites to do research. Then share your findings with a classmate.

A Belgian doctor treats a woman in Zaire. ▶

159

Listening Tip

Point out the Listening Tip and read it aloud. Remind students that if someone has already said what they were thinking, they should expand on that thought instead of repeating it.

(CRI) Discussion

Decide whether students will work in small groups or as partners. Consider dividing up the questions so each group has a different topic. Try to ensure that all participants are heard and that ideas are challenged but not discarded.

ANSWERS
Possible responses:
1. Anne helped Helen to understand that words were names for things.
2. Both men were leaders who worked towards justice and against colonization. Juárez was a president of Mexico. Ghandi was never the president of India, but he was one of its greatest leaders.
3. Members of Doctors Without Borders are likely to be brave, compassionate, and honest.

Q How does helping others help us all?
Ask students to consider the impact that these people have made. Answers will vary.

STEP 3: Assess

Read for Fluency

Suggest that students use a stopwatch or read the second hand on a clock. Emphasize that precise timing is needed to get comparable scores. If students report that they are still not understanding better after several readings, examine their comprehension of the passage vocabulary. Suggest that students listen to the CD recording.

Extension

Suggest that students compare and contrast the subjects they choose. This may lend focus to their research.

Differentiated Instruction

Beginning	Ask students where Benito Juarez is from. Mohandas Gandhi? Florence Nightingale? (Mexico, India, England)
Early Intermediate	Ask students to explain why the painting of Florence Nightingale shows her carrying a lamp.
Intermediate	Have students write one sentence for each person in the reading, telling why that person is extraordinary.
Struggling Readers	Have students write down 5 words in the reading that they found difficult and look up the definitions to the words in a dictionary.

STEP 1: Introduce

Review the use of prepositions of time with students. Explain that *in*, *on*, and *at* are each used with different words and phrases.

STEP 2: Teach

Grammar and Writing

Prepositions of Time Biographies like those in the reading refer to specific times, which require using prepositions. Write the sample sentences on page 160 on the board. Read aloud the sentences with the class. **SAY:** *There are three main prepositions we use to show time: in, on,* and *at. In is used for periods of time like months or years, on is used for exact days or dates, and at is used for times of day.* Have students write the examples in their Word Books for reference.

STEP 3: Practice

Read aloud the instructions. Model answering the first question. **SAY:** *1861 is a year, but there is no specific date or time given, so the answer is* In. Ask students to complete the remaining questions. You may wish to pair English learners with proficient English speakers.

ANSWERS

1. In
2. on
3. in
4. On
5. at
6. at

Teaching Resources

- *Workbook*, pp. 77–78
- *CD-ROM/e-book*, Grammar, Writing
- *Transparencies*, Writing Model 32
- *Transparencies, Resources*, Graphic Organizer 13
- *Assessment*, Reading 2 Test, pp. 71–74

Grammar and Writing

GRAMMAR, USAGE, AND MECHANICS

Prepositions of Time: *in, on,* and *at*

Biographies refer to specific moments in time. The prepositions *in, on,* and *at* can be used to show a point in time. Use *in* for months, years, centuries, and seasons. Use *on* for days and exact dates, and use *at* for times of day. Read these examples.

> **In** 1893, Mohandas Gandhi traveled to South Africa.
> **On** Friday, Helen Keller started to study with her teacher.
> During the day and **at** night, Florence Nightingale took care of her patients.

Study the chart below. It shows how prepositions of time are used.

in	on	at
October 2009	October 7	twelve o'clock
a month	Friday	noon
the summer	Friday morning	midnight
the morning	a winter day	dawn
	my birthday	sunset

Note: The preposition *in* is used with *in the morning, in the afternoon,* and *in the evening,* but the preposition *at* is used with *at night.*

The sky at night ▼

Practice
Workbook Page 77

Work with a partner. Write the sentences in your notebook. Use the correct preposition for each sentence.

1. _____ 1861, Benito Juárez became president.
2. Congress declared war _____ December 8, 1941.
3. Florence Nightingale visited the patients _____ the morning.
4. _____ December 17, the doctors accepted the award.
5. Gandhi met with the government of South Africa _____ five o'clock.
6. The doctor received a call for help _____ night.

160

TESOL Standards

Goal 2, Standard 1—To use English to achieve academically in all content areas: Students will use English to interact in the classroom.
Descriptors—Following oral and written directions, implicit and explicit.

Goal 2, Standard 2—To use English to achieve academically in all content areas: Students will use English to obtain, process, construct, and provide subject matter information in spoken and written form.
Descriptors—Gathering information orally and in writing; Representing information visually and interpreting information presented visually; Demonstrating knowledge through application in a variety of contexts.

Goal 2, Standard 3—To use English to achieve academically in all content areas: Students will use appropriate learning strategies to construct and apply academic knowledge.
Descriptors—Evaluating one's own success in a completed learning task.

WRITING A PERSUASIVE PARAGRAPH

Use a Question-and-Answer Format

On this page, you'll write a persuasive paragraph that asks and answers a specific question. Your paragraph will justify, or give reasons why, someone is extraordinary and admirable. You'll use a graphic organizer like the one at the right to structure your paragraph.

Asking and answering a question is one way to focus and organize a paragraph. First, you pose a question. Then you not only give an answer, but you explain your answer by giving facts, details, and examples to support it. The support you give should convince readers to agree with your point of view.

Here is a model of a paragraph that uses a question-and-answer format. Notice how the writer asks a question first, then follows with a persuasive answer that is supported by facts, details, and examples.

```
                    Question
                       │
                       ▼
                    Answer
              ┌────────┼────────┐
              ▼        ▼        ▼
           Reason   Reason   Reason
```

Tamar Honig

Mohandas Gandhi

What extraordinary things did Gandhi do that set him apart from other people of his time? He developed peaceful, nonviolent methods of protest in the face of violence and injustice, and he was an inspiration to millions of people around the world. While in South Africa, he encouraged people to practice passive resistance against apartheid. In India, he played a major role in the country's struggle for independence by organizing nonviolent demonstrations. Lastly, Gandhi inspired others, including leaders of the U.S. civil rights movement to use nonviolent methods of protest. Tragically, this peaceful man was assassinated on January 30, 1948.

Practice  **Workbook** Page 78

Choose someone who you think is truly extraordinary. Then write a persuasive paragraph that answers the question, What extraordinary things did this person do? Use a question-and-answer chart like the one above to organize your ideas. Include at least three reasons for your opinion. Justify each reason with facts, details, or examples. Use prepositions of time if this will make your explanation clearer.

 Writing Checklist

ORGANIZATION:
☑ I posed a question and justified my answer with facts, details, and examples.

CONVENTIONS:
☑ I used prepositions of time correctly.

161

STEP 1: Introduce

Tell students that presenting an argument is one type of persuasive writing. In this kind of writing, it is important to include supporting information to make your point of view convincing.

STEP 2: Teach

Writing a Persuasive Paragraph

Use a Question-and-Answer Format
Review the structure of a persuasive paragraph. Point out that the argument is first presented and then supported by reasons and examples. Tell students that the graphic organizer will help them plan their paragraph in question-and-answer format.

Model Writing Skill Read aloud the model paragraph. **SAY:** *When writing a paragraph in question-and-answer format, you must support your answer with reasons that include facts, details, and examples. The reasons that support your answer will help to persuade your reader that your argument is sound.*

STEP 3: Assess

Have students evaluate their work using the Writing Checklist.

Writing Checklist Note

Organization: Check that students' paragraphs include good questions and examples that support their answers.

Conventions: Check that students' paragraphs correctly use *in*, *on*, and *at*.

Accelerate Language Development

Use of Prepositions

Prepositions are one of the most difficult aspects of a language for non-native speakers. Where English uses a preposition, other languages may not use prepositions at all, or use different ones altogether. For example, the English *in the afternoon* becomes the German *am Nachmittag*, while the English *at night* becomes the German *in der Nacht*. The matter is confused further as the prepositions *in*, *on*, and *at* can also be used for place as well. Prepositions have no real meaning on their own, but only describe the relationship of words to each other. If you will, prepositions place the other words in relation to time and place.

Teach

STEP 1: Introduce

Objectives

Read the list of objectives in the What You Will Learn section, and encourage students to join in. Tell them that this reading will be about a Bosnian girl who lives in a war zone. Have students work in pairs to restate the list of things they will learn.

The Big Question

Remind students that the Big Question is "How does helping others help us all?" **SAY:** *Can you imagine living in a war zone? People use diaries to express their feelings about what is happening to them. How do you think reading Zlata's Diary will help you understand what Zlata experienced? Keep that question in mind as you read.*

Build Background

Read aloud the Build Background section. Help students understand the time in which *Zlata's Diary* was written. It was during the 1990s, following the breakup of the former Yugoslav Republic. The conflicts between ethnic groups in the former Yugoslavia had been suppressed during the time of the Soviet Union. Once the Soviet Union fell apart, other countries, like the Yugoslav Republic, soon followed, leading to war. Have students look at the map on page 162 and a world map to understand the geographic context.

STEP 2: Teach

Understanding the Genre: Diary Entry

Tell students that a diary is a personal record kept by an individual on a regular basis, sometimes daily. Diary keepers write about their experiences and thoughts. They often write using the format of a letter to the diary or to a person.

Teaching Resources

- CD-ROM/e-book, Literary Words
- Audio CD 3, track 10
- *Workbook*, p. 79

What You Will Learn

Reading
- Vocabulary building: *Literary terms, word study, dictionary skills*
- Reading strategy: *Distinguish fact from opinion*
- Text type: *Literature (diary excerpt)*

Grammar, Usage, and Mechanics
Placement of adjectives

Writing
Write a diary entry

THE BIG QUESTION

How does helping others help us all? Have you ever kept or wanted to keep a diary? People who keep a diary write about their experiences, observations, and feelings. How could keeping a diary help someone get through a difficult time? What can others learn from that diary if they read it? Discuss with a partner.

BUILD BACKGROUND

Zlata Filipović, an eleven-year-old Bosnian girl, wrote **Zlata's Diary** in 1992, during the Bosnian War. Zlata lived in Sarajevo, the capital of Bosnia and Herzegovina, where some of the worst fighting occurred. She used her diary to write about her daily experiences during the war.

Look at the map. It shows the borders of the former Yugoslavia in 1991, just before the Bosnian War. It also shows the six republics that once had been part of the Yugoslav Federation: Bosnia and Herzegovina, Croatia, Macedonia, Montenegro, Slovenia, and Serbia. During the 1980s and 1990s, long-standing national and ethnic conflicts caused war among citizens of Yugoslavia. Before the war, Bosnia and Herzegovina had been a republic within Yugoslavia. As a result of the war, Bosnia and Herzegovina and other republics within Yugoslavia broke away and declared their independence. During this time, much blood was shed.

▲ The six republics of the former Yugoslav Federation

162

TESOL Standards

Goal 1, Standard 3—To use English to communicate in social settings: Students will use learning strategies to extend their communicative competence.
Descriptors—Selecting different media to help understand language; Using context to construct meaning.

Goal 2, Standard 3—To use English to achieve academically in all content areas: Students will use appropriate learning strategies to construct and apply academic knowledge.
Descriptors—Focusing attention selectively; Applying basic reading comprehension skills such as skimming, scanning, previewing, and reviewing text; Using context to construct meaning.

VOCABULARY

Learn Literary Words

People often use words in ways that do not match the literal, or basic, dictionary definitions of the words. For example, when we say that someone is *driving us crazy*, we do not mean this literally. We are trying to express a feeling of frustration.

A group of words that is used in a different way from the usual meanings of the words is called a figure of speech. Here are some examples.

> The girl **jumped out of her skin** when she heard a blast.
> The man's **head was spinning** after hearing all the bad news.

The girl can't really jump out of her skin. This figure of speech means that the girl was very frightened. Likewise, the man's head does not go around and around. This is another way of saying that the man was confused and upset.

A figure of speech that uses exaggeration, or overstatement, is called hyperbole. Many everyday expressions are examples of hyperbole. For example, when we are hungry, we say: *I could eat a horse.*

Writers use hyperbole to create an effect, emphasize something, or express a feeling. Here are two examples of hyperbole. What do these figures of speech mean to you?

> Her laughter was **like a meteor shower** brightening up the dark room.
> It would **take a thousand years** to figure out what happened.

Practice Workbook Page 79

Take turns reading these everyday figures of speech with a partner. Rephrase each one in your own words.

1. I've told you **a million times** to be more careful.
2. Her love for her parents was **deeper than the ocean**.
3. During the war, she and her friends didn't know what would happen. They were all **in the same boat**.

In your notebook, list several other everyday examples of hyperbole. Then try to create two exaggerated statements of your own.

163

CD3 T10

Vocabulary

Learn Literary Words Play the CD. Have students listen and repeat. If you are not using the CD, read the Literary Words aloud. Ask students what comes to mind when they hear each word. Write down student responses.

Write these definitions for *figures of speech* and *hyperbole* on the board or a transparency to reinforce learning.

- **figure of speech:** a group of words different from their literal meaning
- **hyperbole:** figure of speech that uses exaggeration

Provide examples of figures of speech and hyperboles. **SAY:** *"It's raining cats and dogs" is a figure of speech. It means that it is raining very hard, but does not mean that pets are falling from the sky. "Her hands were as cold as ice" is a hyperbole. It overstates the coldness of the woman's hands.*

For extra practice, have students use the corresponding Workbook page.

STEP 3: Practice

Pair English learners with proficient English speakers to aid pronunciation. Ask volunteers to write their answers on the board.

ANSWERS
Possible responses:
1. many times
2. very intense
3. having the same experience

Differentiated Instruction

Beginning	Ask students how old Zlata is and where she lives. (11, Sarajevo, Bosnia and Herzegovina)
Early Intermediate	Have students describe Zlata and where she lives.
Intermediate	Ask students to write a sentence that is an example of hyperbole and share it with the class.
Standard English Learners (CRI)	Have students discuss why someone might want to keep a diary.

Teach

 Vocabulary

Learn Academic Words Play the CD. Have students listen and repeat. If you are not using the CD, read the Academic Words aloud. **SAY:** *Work with a partner to write an additional sentence for each Academic Word.* (Example: I learned a new method for taking notes.) *Write each word, its definition, and the sentence in your notebook.*

STEP 2: Practice

Write the following question on the board and underline the word as shown: *In your opinion, what does a perfect graduation party consist of?* **SAY:** *When you are asked a question, try to include words from the question in your answer.* Write this example on the board: *In my opinion, a perfect graduation party consists of family, friends, and good food.*

ANSWERS
Possible responses:
1. In my opinion, a perfect graduation party would consist of family, friends, and good food.
2. Countries can establish peace after a war by helping people realize that peace benefits both sides. Weapons can never make friends.
3. My method for getting to school in the morning is to walk down Maple Street. My way of getting to school on time is to leave my house early enough so I don't have to run all the way there.
4. I deal with stress by listening to soft music. To relax, I go for a walk.

Teaching Resources
- Audio CD 3, tracks 11–12
- *Workbook*, pp. 80–82
- CD-ROM/e-book, Academic Words, Word Study

Learn Academic Words

Study the red words and their meanings. You will find these words useful when talking and writing about literature. Write each word and its meaning in your notebook. After you read this excerpt from *Zlata's Diary,* try to use these words to respond to the text.

Academic Words
consist
establish
method
stress

consist = are made up of or contain particular things or people	➡	Diaries **consist** of a writer's feelings and observations. They are made up of daily entries.
establish = create; organize	➡	Concerned people in our community want to **establish** a neighborhood cleanup project.
method = a planned way of doing something	➡	The girl had her own **method** of keeping her house safe during bombings. Many of the neighbors liked her way of doing this.
stress = continuous feelings of worry caused by difficulties in your life	➡	People in wars are under a lot of **stress**. They feel great anxiety and worry.

Practice

Work with a partner to answer these questions. Try to include the red word in your answer. Write the sentences in your notebook.

1. In your opinion, what does a perfect graduation party **consist** of? What things or people would it include?
2. How can countries **establish** peace after a war? What can be done to make people put down their weapons and live peacefully together?
3. What is your **method** of getting to school in the morning? What is your way of getting there on time?
4. How do you deal with **stress**? What do you do to relax?

▲ It is important to take breaks from your work if you are under a lot of stress.

164

🌐 TESOL Standards

Goal 1, Standard 3—To use English to communicate in social settings: Students will use learning strategies to extend their communicative competence.
Descriptors—Listening to and imitating how others use English; Exploring alternative ways of saying things.

Goal 2, Standard 1—To use English to achieve academically in all content areas: Students will use English to interact in the classroom.
Descriptors—Participating in full-class, group, and pair discussions; Negotiating and managing interaction to accomplish tasks.

Goal 3, Standard 1—To use English in socially and culturally appropriate ways: Students will use the appropriate language variety, register, and genre according to audience, purpose, and setting.
Descriptors—Recognizing and using Standard English and vernacular dialects appropriately.

Word Study: Synonyms and Antonyms

Use context clues to figure out the meanings of unfamiliar words. Look for definitions, synonyms, and antonyms. Synonyms are words with the same or nearly the same meanings. Antonyms are words with the opposite or nearly the opposite meanings. Read the examples. Clues to the meanings of the boldfaced words are underlined.

> The war made people go **berserk**, or act <u>crazy</u>. (synonym clue)
> I was filled with <u>sadness</u>. He felt a similar **sorrow**. (synonym clue)
> This war is <u>madness</u>. We have lost our **sanity**. (antonym clue)

Practice

Copy the sentences into your notebook. Work with a partner to figure out the meanings of the boldfaced words. Circle words or phrases that are clues to meaning. Then write your own definition of each boldfaced term. Check your definitions in a dictionary.

1. We saw the worst **massacre**, or killing of many helpless people.
2. During the war, we never lost hope. We never gave in to **despair**.
3. People who were welcomed before are now being **expelled**.
4. The warring groups need to talk and come to an agreement. When will they begin to **negotiate** a settlement?

▲ *Tragedy* is the antonym of *comedy*.

READING STRATEGY	DISTINGUISH FACT FROM OPINION

Distinguishing a fact from an opinion will help you evaluate what you read. A fact is something that can be proven through evidence. An opinion is what someone believes or thinks. Opinions express a point of view, but aren't necessarily wrong. They just can't be proven. To distinguish facts from opinions, follow these steps:

- Read the text. Then ask yourself: "Can I check this information in a reliable source?" If you can, it's probably a fact.
- Look for words that signal opinions, such as *I think* and *to me*.
- Ask yourself: "Is this what someone thinks or believes? Can it be proven?" If it cannot be proven, it's probably an opinion.

As you read *Zlata's Diary*, distinguish between the facts and opinions.

Workbook Page 82

165

Linguistic Note

Subtle Differences among Synonym and Antonym Pairs

Writers express different meanings and evoke different feelings when choosing a particular synonym. Point out that the words in a synonym pair may be more or less formal (*dead/deceased*), more or less taboo (*handicapped/physically challenged*), or more or less ambiguous (*love/romance*). Words in a synonym pair may be specific to different geographic regions, social backgrounds or age groups. A common example is the word *bad* as a synonym for *cool*. Similarly, using a certain antonym may highlight a specific aspect of a word's meaning. For example, *disappear* is an antonym for both *leave* and *vanish*.

Read

Reading Summary

This reading is an excerpt from *Zlata's Diary*. Zlata wrote it during the Bosnian War, when she was eleven. It describes the difficulties, terror, sadness, and despair of living in a war-torn place.

 **The Big Question**

Remind students that the Big Question is "How does helping others help us all?" **SAY:** *How does Zlata show us what war time is like?*

STEP 2: Teach

Set a Purpose for Reading

SAY: *Zlata deals with many strong emotions brought on by the difficulties of war. How does she use her diary to deal with her emotions? How does reading the diary help you and others?*

Preteaching Highlighted Words

With students, preview the highlighted vocabulary on pages 166–167. Write the words on the board and point out that they are defined at the bottom of each page. **SAY:** *Some words in this reading are idioms, such as* beside ourselves, tearing our hair out, *and* knot in my tummy. Ask volunteers to find and read the definitions. Model how to use the words in original sentences—for example, *When they said that I was the next speaker, I got a knot in my tummy.* Then ask volunteers to do the same and write them in their notebook.

CD3 T13 **Scaffolding: Listen and Read**

Have students read the text as you play the Audio CD. Pause the recording at the end of each page to answer students' questions.

Teaching Resources

- *Resources,* Summaries, pp. 143–144
- Audio CD 3, track 13

Set a purpose for reading How does Zlata use her diary to help herself and others? Read this important account of the Bosnian War to find out.

from ZLATA'S DIARY
Zlata Filipović

When Zlata Filipović wrote her diary, which she calls "Mimmy," she was eleven years old and living in Sarajevo. The people of Sarajevo, including Zlata's family and friends, were caught in the middle of a war.

▲ Zlata Filipović

Saturday, May 23, 1992

Dear Mimmy,

I'm not writing to you about me anymore. I'm writing to you about war, death, injuries, shells, sadness and sorrow. Almost all my friends have left. Even if they were here, who knows whether we'd be able to see one another. The phones aren't working, we couldn't even talk to one another. Vanja and Andrej have gone to join Srdjan in Dubrovnik. The war has stopped there. They're lucky. I was so unhappy because of that war in Dubrovnik. I never dreamed it would move to Sarajevo. . . .

I now spend all my time with Bojana and Maja. They're my best friends now. Bojana is a year-and-a-half older than me, she's finished seventh grade and we have a lot in common. Maja is in her last year of school. She's much older than I am, but she's wonderful. I'm lucky to have them, otherwise I'd be all alone among the grown-ups.

---

shells, bombs
grown-ups, adults

166

 ## TESOL Standards

Goal 1, Standard 1—To use English to communicate in social settings: Students will use English to participate in social interactions.
Descriptors—Sharing and requesting information; Expressing needs, feelings, and ideas.

Goal 2, Standard 1—To use English to achieve academically in all content areas: Students will use English to interact in the classroom.
Descriptors—Asking and answering questions; Requesting information and assistance.

Goal 2, Standard 2—To use English to achieve academically in all content areas: Students will use English to obtain, process, construct, and provide subject matter information in spoken and written form.
Descriptors—Selecting, connecting, and explaining information; Analyzing, synthesizing, and inferring from information.

On the news they reported the death of Silva Rizvanbegović, a doctor at the Emergency Clinic, who's Mommy's friend. She was in an ambulance. They were driving a wounded man to get him help. Lots of people Mommy and Daddy know have been killed. Oh, God, what is happening here???

Love, Zlata

Tuesday, May 26, 1992

Dear Mimmy,

I keep thinking about Mirna; May 13 was her birthday. I would love to see her so much. I keep asking Mommy and Daddy to take me to her. She left Mojmilo with her mother and father to go to her grandparents' place. Their apartment was shelled and they had to leave it.

There's no shooting, the past few days have been quiet. I asked Daddy to take me to Mirna's because I made her a little birthday present. I miss her. I wish I could see her.

I was such a nag that Daddy decided to take me to her. We went there, but the downstairs door was locked. We couldn't call out to them and I came home feeling disappointed. The present is waiting for her, so am I. I suppose we'll see each other.

Love, Zlata

Emergency Clinic, place to go for emergency medical attention

nag, person who asks for something again and again

United Nations peacekeepers arrive. ▶

BEFORE YOU GO ON

1 What fact do you learn about Silva Rizvanbegović?

2 Why is Zlata disappointed when she goes to visit Mirna?

On Your Own
How do you think you would feel if you were living in Sarajevo in 1992?

167

Study Skills: Thesaurus

Zlata uses some descriptive words again and again for emphasis, like *horrible*. Zlata also emphasizes significant things by using synonyms. A thesaurus is a good place to find specific descriptive words. Have students choose descriptive words from *Zlata's Diary* and look them up in a thesaurus. Remind students that a thesaurus lists words alphabetically, like a dictionary.

STEP 3: Monitor Progress

Ask students to check what they have understood in the reading. If you are using the Audio CD, pause the recording.

Before You Go On

Remind students that distinguishing fact from opinion helps them understand what is happening in the text. Preview these questions with students before they read the page so they know what to look for.

ANSWERS

1. We learn that Silva was killed.
2. Zlata is disappointed when she goes to visit Mirna because the door is locked and she can't give her the birthday present.

On Your Own Have students write an answer to the On Your Own question on a separate sheet of paper. Encourage volunteers to share their responses with the class. Then collect student responses to monitor their comprehension, writing skills, and fluency.

Differentiated Instruction	
Beginning	Have students point to the composers Zlata studies.
Early Intermediate	Ask students how long Zlata has been playing music. (5 years)
Intermediate	Have students describe Zlata's piano lesson on December 28, 1992.
Struggling Readers	Have students point to the diary entry that talks about Zlata's piano lesson.

Preteaching Highlighted Words

Before reading this spread, review the highlighted words and terms with students. Define each one, pointing out the location of the definition in the gloss at the bottom of the student book page. Make sure that students understand each highlighted word. If appropriate, ask students to generate original sentences with each word.

Model the
READING STRATEGY

Distinguish Fact from Opinion

Have students go back to page 165 and review the questions for distinguishing fact from opinion. Use these questions to guide a class discussion about Zlata's reports of what's happening in Sarajevo. **SAY:** *Which sentences from Zlata's story are facts? Which information is her opinion? How and where would you check the facts that Zlata has provided? Why is her opinion useful to readers?*

✔ LITERARY CHECK

Point out the Literary Check box, and read the question aloud. If students need help remembering the meaning of *figures of speech,* go back to page 163. Encourage students to think of other figures of speech that Zlata might use. **Answer:** Zlata uses the following figures of speech to express her feelings: *beside ourselves, lump in my throat, knot in my tummy, madhouse,* and *tearing our hair out.*

Wednesday, May 27, 1992

Dear Mimmy,

SLAUGHTER! MASSACRE! HORROR! CRIME! BLOOD! SCREAMS! TEARS! DESPAIR!

That's what Vaso Miskin Street looks like today. Two shells exploded in the street and one in the market. Mommy was nearby at the time. She ran to Grandma and Granddad's. Daddy and I were beside ourselves because she hadn't come home. I saw some of it on TV but still can't believe what I actually saw. It's unbelievable. I've got a lump in my throat and a knot in my tummy. HORRIBLE! They're taking the wounded to the hospital. It's a madhouse. We kept going to the window hoping to see Mommy, but she wasn't back. They released a list of the dead and wounded. Daddy and I were tearing our hair out. We didn't know what had happened to her. Was she alive? At 4:00 Daddy decided to go and check the hospital. He got dressed, and I got ready to go to the Bobars', so as not to stay home alone. I looked out the window one more time and . . . I SAW MOMMY RUNNING ACROSS THE BRIDGE. As she came into the house she started shaking and crying. Through her tears she told us how she had seen dismembered bodies. All the neighbors came because they had been afraid for her. Thank God, Mommy is with us. Thank God.

A HORRIBLE DAY. UNFORGETTABLE. HORRIBLE! HORRIBLE!

Your Zlata

✔ LITERARY CHECK

*What **figures of speech** does Zlata use to express her feelings of fear and horror?*

▲ An injured woman is taken to the hospital.

---

beside ourselves, very worried
I've got a lump in my throat, I feel like crying
knot in my tummy, bad feeling about something
madhouse, place where everyone seems crazy
tearing our hair out, feeling very worried
dismembered bodies, bodies with missing arms or legs

168

TESOL Standards

Goal 2, Standard 2—To use English to achieve academically in all content areas: Students will use English to obtain, process, construct, and provide subject matter information in spoken and written form.
Descriptors—Comparing and contrasting information; Persuading, arguing, negotiating, evaluating, and justifying.

Goal 2, Standard 3—To use English to achieve academically in all content areas: Students will use appropriate learning strategies to construct and apply academic knowledge.
Descriptors—Actively connecting new information to information previously learned.

Thursday, October 1, 1992

Dear Mimmy,

Spring has been and gone, summer has been and gone, and now it's autumn. October has started. And the war is still on. The days are getting shorter and colder. Soon we'll move the stove upstairs to the apartment. But how will we keep warm? God, is anyone thinking of us here in Sarajevo? Are we going to start winter without electricity, water or gas, and with a war going on?

The "kids" are negotiating. Will they finally negotiate something? Are they thinking about us when they negotiate, or are they just trying to outwit each other, and leave us to our fate?

Daddy has been checking the attic and cellar for wood. It looks to me as though part of the furniture is going to wind up in the stove if this keeps up until winter. It seems that nobody is thinking of us, that this madness is going to go on and on. We have no choice, we have to rely on ourselves, to take care of ourselves and find a way to fight off the oncoming winter.

Mommy came home from work in a state of shock today. Two of her colleagues came from Grbavica. It really is true that people are being expelled from there. There's no sign of Mommy's and Nedo's relatives or of Lalo. Nedo is going berserk.

Your Zlata

---

the "kids," Zlata's slang for the politicians
outwit, be more clever than; trick
wind up, end up; finally be
colleagues, fellow workers

▲ Cooking is quite an achievement without electricity.

BEFORE YOU GO ON

1. How do Zlata and her father feel after the massacre on Vaso Miskin Street? Why?

2. What is the "madness" that Zlata refers to?

☀ **On Your Own**
What would you do if you were in Zlata's family?

169

Study Skills: Almanac

Zlata writes about the changing seasons and the onset of winter in Sarajevo. An almanac is a book, published annually, which gives information about the times of sunrise and sunset, average temperature and precipitation amounts, and long-term weather forecasts for a region. Zlata says that the days are growing shorter and colder. Using an almanac, students can find out how cold it gets in the Bosnian winter. The almanac may also give information about how this year will differ from past years, and what the records are. Almanacs may also contain information and statistics about countries, places, people, and events.

STEP 5: Monitor Progress

Ask students to check what they have understood in the reading. If you are using the Audio CD, pause the recording.

Before You Go On

Remind students that when they answer each question, they should look for the place on the spread that gives that information.

ANSWERS

1. Zlata and her father are panicked after the massacre on Vaso Miskin Street. They are worried about Mommy.
2. The "madness" that Zlata refers to is the chaos and difficulties of the war.

On Your Own Have students write an answer to the question on a separate sheet of paper. Encourage volunteers to share their responses with the class. Then collect student responses to monitor their comprehension, writing skills, and fluency.

STEP 6: Teach

Preteaching Highlighted Words

Review the highlighted words and terms with students. Define each one, pointing out the location of the definition in the gloss at the bottom of the page. Make sure that students understand each highlighted word. If appropriate, ask students to generate original sentences with each word.

Across the Curriculum:
Social Studies

The composers that Zlata studies are Karl Czerny, Johann Sebastian Bach, Wolfgang Amadeus Mozart, and Frederic Chopin. All of these men were European composers. Mozart and Czerny were Austrian, Bach was German, and Chopin was Polish, but lived in France. They all lived between 1685 and 1857, during a period of great musical development in Europe. Many of the greatest classical composers of all time lived during this period, and they were often influenced by one another. Bach was the earliest of these four, and his compositions are thought to have had a great impact on all classical music that followed him.

✔ LITERARY CHECK

Tell students to read the question in the box before reading the text on the page. This way, they'll know what to look for as they read. This strategy can be used by good readers and successful test takers. Remind students that they learned the term *figure of speech* on page 163 and that they can review its meaning on that page. **Answer:** The figure of speech "I'll give it my all" means I'll do my best.

Monday, December 28, 1992

Dear Mimmy,

I've been walking my feet off these past few days.

I'm at home today. I had my first piano lesson. My teacher and I kissed and hugged, we hadn't seen each other since March. Then we moved on to Czerny, Bach, Mozart, and Chopin, to the étude, the invention, the sonata and the "piece." It's not going to be easy. But I'm not going to school now and I'll give it my all. It makes me happy. Mimmy, I'm now in my fifth year of music.

You know, Mimmy, we've had no water or electricity for ages. When I go out and when there's no shooting it's as if the war were over, but this business with the electricity and water, this darkness, this winter, the shortage of wood and food, brings me back to earth and then I realize that the war is still on. Why? Why on earth don't those "kids" come to some agreement? They really are playing games. And it's us they're playing with.

As I sit writing to you, my dear Mimmy, I look over at Mommy and Daddy. They are reading. They lift their eyes from the page and think about something. What are they thinking about? About the book they are reading or are they trying to put together the scattered pieces of this war puzzle? I think it must be the latter. Somehow they look even sadder to me in the light of the oil lamp (we have no more wax candles, so we make our own oil lamps). I look at Daddy. He really has lost a lot of weight. The scales say 25 kilos, but looking at him I think it must be more. I think

▲ Zlata expresses her concern about her family in her diary.

✔ LITERARY CHECK

What does the figure of speech "I'll give it my all" mean?

---

walking my feet off, walking a lot
Czerny, Bach, Mozart, and Chopin, composers who wrote piano music
for ages, for a long time
shortage, lack
back to earth, back to reality
scattered, spread out
latter, the second of two things or people

170

🌐 TESOL Standards

Goal 1, Standard 1—To use English to communicate in social settings: Students will use English to participate in social interactions.
Descriptors—Expressing needs, feelings, and ideas; Engaging in conversations.

Goal 3, Standard 3—To use English in socially and culturally appropriate ways: Students will use appropriate learning strategies to extend their sociolinguistic and sociocultural competence.
Descriptors—Self-monitoring and self-evaluating language use according to setting and audience.

▲ Sarejevo

even his glasses are too big for him. Mommy has lost weight too. She's shrunk somehow, the war has given her wrinkles. God, what is this war doing to my parents? They don't look like my old Mommy and Daddy anymore. Will this ever stop? Will our suffering stop so that my parents can be what they used to be—cheerful, smiling, nice-looking?

This stupid war is destroying my childhood, it's destroying my parents' lives. WHY? STOP THE WAR! PEACE! I NEED PEACE!

I'm going to play a game of cards with them!

Love from your Zlata

---

wrinkles, lines on the face or skin that people get as they age

✔ LITERARY CHECK

Why do you think that Zlata uses hyperbole to describe how her parents look?

ABOUT THE **AUTHOR**

Zlata Filipović escaped to Paris in December 1993, where she began to study at the International School. Her diary has been translated into more than twenty languages. With the money from her book, Zlata helped to start a charity for victims of the Bosnian War. Zlata was awarded the Special Child of Courage Award. She is also co-editor of *Stolen Voices: Young People's Diaries from World War I to Iraq.*

BEFORE YOU GO ON

1 What has Zlata begun studying again?

2 Why is Zlata worried about her parents?

💡**On Your Own**
How can a diary like Zlata's help people today?

171

✔ LITERARY CHECK

Tell students to read the question in the box before reading the text on the page. This way, they know what to look for as they read. Remind students that the meaning of *hyperbole* is on page 163. Answer: Zlata's uses hyperbole to describe her father's glasses and her mother's skin to convey how much her parents have changed as a result of the war.

Study Skills: Internet

Zlata Filipovic experienced many awful things during the Bosnian War, including the death of a close friend. She now lives in Ireland, and is still working and writing to achieve peace. Students can research Zlata using the Internet. A search engine can help them find more information about Zlata's life since the war, her family and her charity.

STEP 7: Monitor Progress

Ask students to check what they have understood in the reading.

Before You Go On

Tell students to read and answer these questions.

ANSWERS
1. Zlata is studying the piano again.
2. Zlata is worrying about her parents because they are both losing weight.

On Your Own Have students write an answer to the question on a separate sheet of paper. Encourage volunteers to share their responses with the class. Then collect student responses to monitor their comprehension, writing skills, and fluency.

Review the Purpose for Reading

Elicit responses to the Set a Purpose for Reading question at the beginning of this reading. Remind students to relate their responses to the Big Question.

Teach & Apply

STEP 1: Introduce

Speaking Tip

Point out the Speaking Tip and discuss ways that people show emotion with their voices. Remind students excitement is often indicated by higher vocal pitches.

Reader's Theater

Reader's Theater gives students an opportunity to rehearse their reading, increase fluency, and improve expression and intonation.

Suggest that students think about how their character feels at this point in the story. Have them note vocabulary clues to their character's feelings and how the dialogue should be read.

Have pairs of students practice and perform. They should decide who will play which role. Ask them to find a quiet area and practice delivering their dialogue clearly.

STEP 2: Practice

Comprehension

Have students work in small groups to read questions and write responses.

ANSWERS

1. She writes about the war now.
2. Two shells hit and exploded there.
3. Since the war began, Zlata's parents have lost weight and aged.
4. Zlata writes in her diary to cope with the stress of war.
5. **Possible response:** Zlata writes that there is no electricity or heating fuel, and that many people have left Sarajevo.
6. Zlata thinks the "kids" are playing games and not really trying to agree.
7. Answers will vary.
8. Answers will vary.

Teaching Resources

- *Workbook*, p. 83
- CD-ROM/e-book, Reader's Theater, Comprehension, Response to Literature

---

READER'S THEATER

 Speaking TIP

Use your voice to express the emotions Zlata and her mother are feeling.

Act out this scene between Zlata and her mother.

Zlata: MOMMY! I am so glad to see you! When the shells exploded in the market and you did not come home, I was so so worried. Are you okay?

Mother: Yes, Zlata, dear. I'm all right. When I heard the explosion, I ran to Grandma and Granddad's home. I am safe and not harmed, but I saw the most terrible things.

Zlata: What happened? What did you see?

Mother: I saw people lying wounded on the ground. Some had lost limbs. It was the most horrible thing I have ever seen. I couldn't stop crying and shaking!

Zlata: Mommy, how awful. Why is this happening in Sarajevo?

Mother: I don't know, but this war must stop. We need peace in our country. We have been torn apart by fighting for too long.

▲ The historic Stari Most bridge in Bosnia was nearly destroyed during the war in 1993.

COMPREHENSION

Workbook Page 83

Right There

1. Zlata says that she does not write about herself anymore. What does she write about now?
2. What happened on Vaso Miskin Street?

Think and Search

3. How have Zlata's parents changed since the war began?
4. What is Zlata's method for coping with the stress of war?

Author and You

5. How does Zlata think life in Sarajevo has changed since the war started?
6. What does Zlata think about the "kids'" ability to establish peace?

▲ After being rebuilt to look as it did originally, the bridge was reopened in July 2004.

172

 TESOL Standards

Goal 3, Standard 1—To use English in socially and culturally appropriate ways: Students will use the appropriate language variety, register, and genre according to audience, purpose, and setting.
Descriptors—Using the appropriate degree of formality with different audiences and settings; Determining when it is appropriate to use a language other than English; Determining appropriate topics for interaction.

Goal 3, Standard 2—To use English in socially and culturally appropriate ways: Students will use nonverbal communication appropriate to audience, purpose, and setting.
Descriptors—Interpreting and responding appropriately to nonverbal cues and body language; Using acceptable tone, volume, stress, and intonation, in various social settings; Recognizing and adjusting behavior in response to nonverbal cues.

On Your Own

7. Do you think that a diary could influence people to be more tolerant and less likely to go to war? Explain.

8. If you kept a diary, would you want it to be published and read by others? Or would you want it to be only for yourself? Explain.

DISCUSSION

Discuss in pairs or small groups.

1. What do you predict will happen to Zlata and her family when the war finally ends?

2. How is Zlata's diary a clear account of the Bosnian War? How is it not? Discuss some of the facts Zlata presents about the war. Then discuss some of her opinions.

3. Do you think people who live in a country that is at war feel helpless? Why or why not?

Q How does helping others help us all? What are some other difficult experiences that a person might go through? What can a person do to help him or herself and others get through these events?

Listening TIP

When you listen to your classmates debate an issue, take notes. This will help you evaluate other people's points of view.

◄ Zlata writes at her desk, as the sound of guns echoes from the hills. ▶

RESPONSE TO LITERATURE

Workbook
Page 83

Reread the excerpt from *Zlata's Diary*. In your notebook, write the dates of the five days she writes about. Then write something important that happened to Zlata on each of these days. Compare what you write in pairs or small groups.

173

STEP 3: Extend

Listening Tip

Point out the Listening Tip. **SAY:** *Taking notes will help you keep track of what points have been made, who said what, and what arguments were made. Remembering who made an argument may help you remember what they said.*

(CRI) Discussion

Before students begin their discussion, decide if they will work as a class, in groups, or as partners. Consider dividing up the questions so each group has a different topic. Try to ensure that all participants are heard and that ideas are challenged but not discarded.

Q How does helping others help us all?
SAY: *Zlata, her parents, and her neighbors all have different ways of dealing with the war, and of helping one another. Why is it important for everyone to be able to cope during difficult times?*

STEP 4: Assess

Response to Literature

Help students reread the excerpts from *Zlata's Diary* and then, in their notebook, write the dates of the five days she writes about. **SAY:** *In your notebook, write about something significant that happened to Zlata on each of the five days she writes about.* Have students share their entries with the class.

Differentiated Instruction

Beginning	Ask students if they think Zlata and other children who are surrounded by war share similar feelings.
Early Intermediate	Have students name two traits that children who grow up during wars might have in common.
Intermediate	Have students name the traits that Zlata and other children of war have in common and explain why they share those traits.
Standard English Learners (CRI)	Have students read the speaking tip on page 172. Ask students to think of ways you can use your voice to express emotions. Ask them to give examples.

Teach & Apply

STEP 1: Introduce

Tell students that adjectives describe nouns and pronouns. In English, adjectives either go before the noun they describe or after a linking verb like *be, feel,* and *seem.*

STEP 2: Teach

Grammar and Writing

Placement of Adjectives Read aloud the information about adjectives. Write the list of linking verbs on the board. Then read aloud the samples in the text box on page 174, so that students will hear how to place adjectives in a sentence. **SAY:** *Follow along in your book on page 174 as I read the sentences in the text box. Notice that on the left side of the box, the noun being described is underlined, and on the right side, the linking verb is underlined. Write the linking verbs on page 174 in your notebooks for future reference.*

STEP 3: Practice

Write the first sentence on the board. **SAY:** *In this sentence, the noun being described is* birthday. *Choose the adjective from the list that makes the most sense to complete the sentence. Say the sentence aloud to make sure it sounds right.* Have students work with a partner to complete the activity.

ANSWERS
1. eleventh
2. eager
3. humorous
4. violent
5. troubled

Teaching Resources

- *Workbook,* pp. 84–85
- CD-ROM/e-book, Grammar, Writing
- *Transparencies,* Writing Model 33
- *Transparencies, Resources,* Graphic Organizer 4
- *Assessment,* Reading 3 Test, pp. 75–78

GRAMMAR, USAGE, AND MECHANICS
Placement of Adjectives

Zlata uses many adjectives to describe her feelings and observations about the war around her. Using well-chosen adjectives helps to make writing precise. It also helps writers persuade readers to agree with their point of view.

An adjective describes a noun. It can appear before the noun it describes or after a linking verb. Linking verbs describe states of being. They include such verbs as *get, become, seem, appear, feel, taste, sound, smell,* and *look,* and forms of *be.* Study the examples below.

Adjective + Noun	Linking Verb + Adjective
They were driving a **wounded man** to get him help.	I **am lucky** to have them.
I'm now in my **fifth year** of music.	I **felt disappointed**.
This **stupid war** is destroying my childhood.	The days **are shorter** and **colder**.
	My parents **were cheerful**, smiling, **nice-looking**.

Practice

Write these sentences in your notebook. Choose one adjective from the box below to complete each sentence.

eager	eleventh	humorous	troubled	violent

1. On my _____ birthday, my parents gave me a diary.
2. I was _____ to begin recording my thoughts and feelings.
3. I wrote _____ entries about funny events in my life.
4. Then a _____ tornado struck our house, and our lives changed.
5. I was _____ by the changes that occurred, so I wrote about them.

▲ A teenager writes in his diary.

174

 TESOL Standards

Goal 1, Standard 2—To use English to communicate in social settings: Students will interact in, through, and with spoken and written English for personal expression and enjoyment.
Descriptors—Describing, reading about, or participating in a favorite activity.

Goal 3, Standard 1—To use English in socially and culturally appropriate ways: Students will use the appropriate language variety, register, and genre according to audience, purpose, and setting.
Descriptors—Responding to and using slang appropriately; Responding to and using idioms appropriately.

Goal 3, Standard 3—To use English in socially and culturally appropriate ways: Students will use appropriate learning strategies to extend their sociolinguistic and sociocultural competence.
Descriptors—Experimenting with variations of language in social and academic settings.

WRITING a PERSUASIVE PARAGRAPH

Write a Diary Entry

On this page, you'll write a persuasive paragraph in the form of a diary entry. You'll present *both* sides of an issue before stating your opinion. You'll use a graphic organizer like the one at the right to organize your argument, or position.

ISSUE	
For	Against
Facts Opinions	Facts Opinions

Many people who keep diaries describe the world around them. They also examine their feelings and ideas about issues and express their opinions. Look back at Zlata's entries. Notice the format she uses. She dates each entry and addresses it to "Mimmy."

Here is a model of a diary entry. Notice how the writer, Talia Marcus, presents both sides of an issue that she feels strongly about. Then she states an opinion. Notice the adjectives she uses to persuade.

August 20, 2009

Dear Diary,

It is clear after reading Zlata's Diary and "Extraordinary People" that violence and war have a negative effect on people's lives. Zlata wrote her diary during the war in Sarajevo. She could rarely leave her house because of the violence. Her family was scared and didn't have electricity, water, or gas. In war, innocent people, like Zlata and her family, suffer. Gandhi understood the senselessness of violence and showed how passive resistance was a better way to solve problems. In my opinion, it is much smarter to follow Gandhi's example. The people who fought in Sarajevo couldn't come to an agreement and resorted to violence. They thought the only way to respond to violence was with more violence. However, violence hurts everybody. Peaceful protest sends a powerful message and is less likely to harm others.

Practice

Workbook Page 85

Write a diary entry about an important issue. Use a T-chart to list facts and opinions about both sides of the issue. Then write a diary entry that examines both sides and comes to a conclusion. Use figurative expressions and adjectives to help bring your feelings across. Place your adjectives before nouns and after linking verbs.

Writing Checklist

VOICE:
☑ I used strong words and phrases that expressed my argument clearly.

WORD CHOICE:
☑ I used adjectives to persuade.

175

STEP 1: Introduce

Tell students that a diary is subjective. It expresses the opinions, thoughts, and feelings of the writer. Entries that are emotionally charged can be very persuasive.

STEP 2: Teach

Writing a Persuasive Paragraph

Write a Diary Entry Read over the instruction with students. Be sure they understand the format of a diary entry, including a date. **SAY:** *Look for the issue and supporting facts and examples in the model. You will write a diary entry about an important world issue.*

Model Writing Skill Point out the model of a diary entry. Ask a volunteer to read it aloud to the class. **SAY:** *It is important to support your opinion with facts and examples. This paragraph offers support FOR the argument. What examples or reasons could be given AGAINST the main idea?* With students, brainstorm some possible examples, like one country coming to the aid of another, (i.e. Britain entering WWII after the German invasion of Poland.)

STEP 3: Assess

Have students evaluate their work using the Writing Checklist.

Writing Checklist Note

Voice Check that students' paragraphs make their opinion clear and use powerful and persuasive language.

Word choice Check that students use a variety of well-chosen adjectives.

Accelerate Language Development

Adjective or Adverb?

Students may confuse an adjective used with a linking verb and an adverb describing a verb. Example: *My mother turned red with anger.* In this sentence *red* is an adjective describing the mother, used after the linking verb *turn.* *My mother turned quickly to see what had happened.* Here *quickly* is an adverb, describing the verb *turn.* Some linking verbs can be used as regular verbs, which complicates the matter. Example: *Sandra looked quickly into the mirror to check whether her hair looked beautiful.* In this sentence, *quickly* is an adverb, describing the verb *look,* whereas *beautiful* is an adjective describing the noun *hair.*

STEP 1: Introduce

Objectives

Read the list of objectives in the What You Will Learn section, encouraging students to join in. Tell students that this reading will be about animals that help each other. Have pairs of students work together to restate the list of things they will learn.

 The Big Question

Remind students that the Big Question is "How does helping others help us all?" **SAY:** *Do you know of any animals who have animal friends? If so, are they of the same species or of different species? Do they help each other? How?*

Build Background

Read aloud the Build Background section from the student text. Explain to students the meaning of *symbiosis.* **SAY:** *When two living things have a relationship where the actions of one are necessary to the other, we say they have a symbiotic relationship. In a mutually symbiotic relationship, both animals benefit from the other. Sometimes, the relationship is just friendship—animals who enjoy the company of other animals.*

STEP 2: Teach

Understanding the Genre:
Informational Text

An informational text is a piece of nonfiction. Its purpose is to present facts and other information about real people, events, places, and situations. This informational text is about the way some animals befriend each other or cooperate with each other.

Teaching Resources

- CD-ROM/e-book, Key Words
- Audio CD 3, tracks 14–15
- *Workbook*, p. 86

What You Will Learn

Reading
- Vocabulary building: *Context, dictionary skills, word study*
- Reading strategy: *Identify main idea and details*
- Text type: *Informational text (science)*

Grammar, Usage, and Mechanics
Prepositions of location

Writing
Write a critical evaluation

 THE BIG QUESTION

How does helping others help us all? What do you know about animal friendships? Which animals help each other? Are they usually in the same family group, such as monkeys and gorillas? Are they in packs or herds, such as wolves or horses?

Work with a partner to see what you know about animal friendship and cooperation. In your notebook, make a T-chart with two headings: *Kind of Animal* and *How They Act Together.* Complete the chart with the facts you know. Then share what you know with the class.

BUILD BACKGROUND

"Friendship and Cooperation in the Animal Kingdom" is a science article. It describes how certain animals rely on one another, often in unusual ways.

Symbiosis means "living together." When two living things help each other, we say that they have a *symbiotic relationship.* One example of a symbiotic relationship is that between the tickbird and the rhinoceros. The tickbird picks insects called ticks off the rhino. Both animals are helped by this relationship. The tickbird gets food and protection (other animals don't attack the tickbird because it is sitting on the rhino!), and the rhino is not bothered by ticks.

Animals can be friends, too. Like people, animals can enjoy one another's company. Perhaps you have a cat and a dog. They may fight a lot—or they may be best friends.

▲ The rhino and the tickbird have a symbiotic relationship.

176

 TESOL Standards

Goal 1, Standard 2—To use English to communicate in social settings: Students will interact in, through, and with spoken and written English for personal expression and enjoyment.
Descriptors—Sharing social and cultural traditions and values; Participating in popular culture.

Goal 3, Standard 1—To use English in socially and culturally appropriate ways: Students will use the appropriate language variety, register, and genre according to audience, purpose, and setting.
Descriptors—Responding to and using slang appropriately; Responding to and using idioms appropriately.

VOCABULARY

Learn Key Words

Read these sentences. Use the context to figure out the meaning of the red words. Use a dictionary to check your answers. Then write each word and its meaning in your notebook.

1. Lions have an **arrangement**. The females hunt in a group. The males eat first.

2. Some animals, such as buffalo, **cooperate** with one another. They work together to help the whole herd.

3. A strong wind can do a lot of **damage** to trees. It can tear off branches and blow the trees down.

4. The blue whale is a **gigantic** mammal—the biggest in the world.

5. An **intruder** broke into the herd of zebras. The unwelcome creature was a hungry lion.

6. After the earthquake, a **tsunami** crashed into the shore. This series of huge waves destroyed many houses and trees.

Key Words

arrangement
cooperate
damage
gigantic
intruder
tsunami

▲ Blue whales are gigantic compared to humans.

Practice **Workbook Page 86**

Write the sentences in your notebook. Choose a red word from the box above to complete each sentence. Then take turns reading the sentences aloud with a partner.

1. A hippo is a _____ animal. Even a baby hippo weighs 272 kilograms (or 600 lb.).

2. A _____ looks like a huge wall of water. It is often caused by an earthquake.

3. Sometimes my three cats _____. They work together to chase mice.

4. I made an _____ with my best friend to take care of my pets while I'm away.

5. The storm caused a lot of _____. The town was destroyed.

6. The _____ broke into the nature preserve at night. He knew he wasn't supposed to be there, but he loved watching the seals.

177

Vocabulary

Learn Key Words Play the CD. Have students listen and repeat. If you are not using the CD, read the Key Words aloud. **SAY:** *These words are important to the content of the text we are reading.* On the board or an overhead transparency, write the Key Words below and their definitions.

- **arrangement:** something that has been agreed on
- **cooperate:** to work together to get something done
- **damage:** do harm to something
- **gigantic:** extremely large
- **intruder:** someone who comes without welcome
- **tsunami:** a very large ocean wave caused by an underwater earthquake

Have students copy the definitions into their Word Books or notebooks and generate original sentences for them. For extra practice, assign the corresponding Workbook page.

STEP 3: Practice

Have students work with partners. Suggest that students read aloud the practice items to help them identify which word fits best. Pair English learners with proficient English speakers to aid pronunciation. Ask volunteers to write their answers on the board.

ANSWERS

1. gigantic
2. tsunami
3. cooperate
4. arrangement
5. damage
6. intruder

Differentiated Instruction	
Beginning	Have students point to the phrase that means "living together."
Early Intermediate	Have students fill in the blank. A word that means "living together" is _____.
Intermediate	Ask students to write two sentences of their own that include the keyword *cooperate* and the academic word phrase *rely on.*
Standard English Learners (CRI)	Have students find another symbiotic relationship in nature. Have students name the two animals and explain how each one benefits from the relationship.

Teach

CD3 T16–T17

 Vocabulary

Learn Academic Words Play the CD. Have students listen and repeat. If you are not using the CD, read the Academic Words aloud. **SAY:** *What other sentence can we create with the word* comment? (Possible response: Everyone had a comment about her new haircut.) Students should work together as partners to add another sentence for each Academic Word. They should write each word, its definition, and the sentence in their personal Word Book.

STEP 2: Practice

Model answering the first question. Write the sentence on the board, and **SAY:** *This is a fill in the blank question. I need to look at the list of words at the top of the page to see which one best fits in the blank. At first I thought the answer was* idea, *but that word isn't on the list. The word* concept *means something similar and fits with this sentence.* Have students work with partners to complete the practice activity. **SAY:** *Take turns reading the sentences aloud with your partner. As you read each sentence, think about the word that makes the most sense in that sentence. Once you know which word best completes it, write the sentence in your Word Book.*

ANSWERS

1. concept
2. rely on
3. attitude
4. comment

Teaching Resources

- Audio CD 3, tracks 16–17
- *Workbook*, pp. 87–89
- CD-ROM/e-book, Academic Words, Word Study

Learn Academic Words

Study the **red** words and their meanings. You will find these words useful when talking and writing about informational texts. Write each word and its meaning in your notebook. After you read "Friendship and Cooperation in the Animal Kingdom," try to use these words to respond to the text.

Academic Words

attitude
comment
concept
rely on

attitude = the opinions and feelings that you usually have about someone or something	⟹	After she fell off her horse, she developed a negative **attitude** about horses.
comment = a stated opinion made about someone or something	⟹	The speaker made a short **comment** about the hippo. Then he went on to speak about birds.
concept = an idea of how something is or how something should be done	⟹	We learned the **concept** of animal cooperation. It was fun to know that they helped each other.
rely on = trust or depend on someone or something	⟹	Some animals **rely on** one another for safety.

Practice Workbook Page 87

Write the sentences in your notebook. Choose a **red** word from the box above to complete each sentence. Then take turns reading the sentences aloud with a partner.

1. The boy began to understand the _____ of two animals working together. He listened as the scientist talked about how it happens.
2. The cub will _____ his mother for care. The cub needs her to help find food.
3. The girl's _____ toward crocodiles changed when she saw the movie about them.
4. The vet made an important _____ about pets and their need for attention. The pet owner listened to his opinion.

▲ Crocodiles in Long Xuyen, Vietnam

178

TESOL Standards

Goal 1, Standard 3—To use English to communicate in social settings: Students will use learning strategies to extend their communicative competence.
Descriptors—Testing hypotheses about language.

Goal 2, Standard 2—To use English to achieve academically in all content areas: Students will use English to obtain, process, construct, and provide subject matter information in spoken and written form.
Descriptors—Hypothesizing and predicting; Formulating and asking questions.

Goal 2, Standard 3—To use English to achieve academically in all content areas: Students will use appropriate learning strategies to construct and apply academic knowledge.
Descriptors—Applying basic reading comprehension skills such as skimming, scanning, previewing, and reviewing text.

Word Study: Greek and Latin Roots

English has borrowed many words from other languages. Many English words come from ancient Greek or Latin word parts, called roots. For example, the word *disaster* contains a Greek root (*aster*), meaning "star." In ancient times, people who suffered disasters were thought to be living under a "bad star." Study the chart below. Notice the relationships between the roots, their meanings, and the English words that contain them.

Root	Meaning	Origin	English Words
anima	breath, life, spirit	Latin	animal, animation
aster/astro	star	Greek	aster, astrology
bios	life	Greek	biology, symbiosis

▲ The aster is a star-shaped flower.

Practice — Workbook Page 88

Work with a partner. Use a large dictionary to look up each of the English words in the chart above. Discuss how the meaning of each Greek or Latin root is related to the meaning of each English word.

READING STRATEGY — IDENTIFY MAIN IDEA AND DETAILS

Identifying the main idea and details in a reading helps you see the key points the author is making. The main idea is the most important idea about a topic. Details are small pieces of information that support the main idea. To identify the main idea and details, follow these steps.

- Look at the title. Ask yourself: "What is the topic of this text?"
- As you read each paragraph, identify the author's main idea about the topic. Sometimes the author will state the main idea in a sentence. Other times you will have to put the main idea into your own words.
- As you read, look for examples, facts, dates, and sentences that tell more about the main idea. These are the supporting details.

As you read "Friendship and Cooperation in the Animal Kingdom," identify the main idea of each paragraph and of the whole article. Then find details that support the author's main idea about the topic.

Workbook Page 89

179

Linguistic Note

Numerals

Most European languages have Latin or Greek roots. Point out that entire word groups in English, such as numerals, show clusters of Latin and Greek roots. Write the words *semester* and *trimester* on the board, and circle the Greek root *sem* meaning *half*, and the Latin root *tri* meaning *three*. Write other words with numeral roots on the board: *uni-versal, du-plicate, tri-pod, quar-ter, Penta-gon, sex-tet, sept-ennial, oct-ave, deci-mal, centi-meter*. Mention that the English names of the months go back to the ancient Roman calendar, which divides the year into 10 months: September was the seventh, October the eighth, November the ninth, and December the tenth month of the year.

STEP 1: Teach

Word Study

Greek and Latin Roots Copy the table on page 179 onto the board. Read the words aloud with students, then ask them to work in small groups to practice pronouncing the words in the table. **SAY:** *A root is the basic part of the word. The basic part, or root, of many English words comes from Greek or Latin. Do you know of any others?*

STEP 2: Practice

Keep the chart from page 179 on the board for reference. **SAY:** *Working with a partner, you will look up the definition of a word and discuss how the meaning of the root is related to the meaning of the word.* Provide dictionaries with word roots and pair English learners with proficient English speakers.

ANSWERS

1. **animal:** a living creature, such as a dog or cat, that is not a plant or fungus
   animation: a film, computer game, or image that has pictures, clay models, or computer graphics that move
2. **aster:** a star-shaped flower
   astrology: the study of the positions and movements of the stars and how they might influence people and events
3. **biology:** the scientific study of living things
4. **symbiosis:** the relationship between different living things that depend on each other

STEP 3: Teach

Reading Strategy

Identify Main Idea and Details With students, read the strategy information and review the steps shown. **SAY:** *Very often the main idea will be stated or suggested in the first part of a paragraph. Specific details, including examples and facts given should support the main idea.*

Read

STEP 1: Introduce

Reading Summary

This nonfiction reading is about symbiotic relationships between two pairs of animals.

 The Big Question

Remind students that the Big Question is, "How does helping others help us all?" **SAY:** *All living things are part of an ecosystem, and each species affects many other species or the environment in some way. Imagine how symbiosis between two animals could affect the rest of the ecosystem.*

STEP 2: Teach

Set a Purpose for Reading

Remind students that they should be looking for the main idea and supporting details of the article. **SAY:** *We know from the title what the article is about. However, we need to know more about how animals cooperate. Look for details that support the main idea as you read.*

Preteaching Highlighted Words

With students, preview the highlighted selection vocabulary on student book pages 180–181. Write the words on the board, and point out that they are defined at the bottom of each page. **SAY:** *Some of the vocabulary words in this reading are about the natural world, such as* coral reef *and* tickle. Ask volunteers to find and read the definitions. Model using the words in original sentences—for example, *My dog likes it when I tickle his belly.* Then ask for volunteers to do the same.

CD3 T18 Scaffolding:
Listen and Read

Have students read along as you play the audio CD recording of the reading. Pause the recording at the end of each page to answer questions students may have.

Teaching Resources

- *Resources*, Summaries, pp. 145–146
- Audio CD 3, track 18
- *Reader's Companion Workbook*, pp. 61–67

READING 4 INFORMATIONAL TEXT

SCIENCE

Set a purpose for reading Can animals really cooperate and form friendships? As you read, think about the friendships animals develop. Why do you think animals help each other?

Friendship and Cooperation in the Animal Kingdom

You know that people help other people, but do animals help other animals? It's a "dog-eat-dog" world out there, isn't it? Not always! It's true that animals often fight. However, at other times, they help each other out.

Life in the wild can be very difficult for animals. It is not easy for them to find food and water and stay safe. Animals struggle every day to survive.

That's why animals of the same species, or group, such as lions or blue jays, sometimes cooperate. By helping one another, they help their group survive.

Some animals become partners with other kinds of animals. The two types of animals depend on each other for survival.

This is called symbiosis, and animals who depend on each other are said to be in a symbiotic relationship. Sometimes the two animals would die without each other. Other times, they might be able to live, but they would not be as healthy.

One example of symbiosis is the relationship between the plover and the crocodile. The plover is a small wading bird. It helps pick clean the Nile crocodile's body and even its teeth. The crocodile will open its jaws and let the bird enter its mouth safely. Amazingly, the crocodile will not snap its jaws shut. Instead, it patiently allows the plover to eat the small, harmful animals on the crocodile's teeth. The crocodile gets its teeth cleaned, and the plover gets an easy meal!

"dog-eat-dog," very competitive

◀ A Nile crocodile keeps its jaws open while a plover is in its mouth.

180

🌐 TESOL Standards

Goal 2, Standard 2—To use English to achieve academically in all content areas: Students will use English to obtain, process, construct, and provide subject matter information in spoken and written form.
Descriptors—Comparing and contrasting information; Retelling information; Selecting, connecting, and explaining information; Analyzing, synthesizing, and inferring from information; Understanding and producing technical vocabulary and text features according to content; Formulating and asking questions.

Goal 2, Standard 3—To use English to achieve academically in all content areas: Students will use appropriate learning strategies to construct and apply academic knowledge.
Descriptors—Focusing attention selectively; Using context to construct meaning.

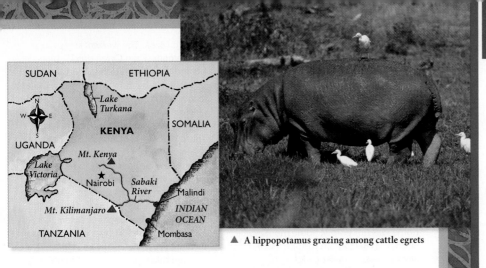

▲ A hippopotamus grazing among cattle egrets

Symbiosis is a working relationship. Many animal species have worked out this arrangement with other animal species. Sometimes, however, animals simply become friends with other animals. There may not be an obvious reason. Perhaps they just like the companionship.

Animals can find friends in the strangest places. For an example, take Owen, a baby hippopotamus. It is hard to believe, but Owen actually became best friends with a 318-kilogram (700-lb.) tortoise named Mzee (mm-ZAY).

Owen, the hippo, lived in the country of Kenya on the east coast of Africa. He was just one year old, and he already weighed 272 kilograms (600 lb.). He lived happily with his mother in a group of about twenty hippos. They grazed on the grass along the Sabaki River near the small village of Malindi.

On December 26, 2004, a disaster struck. There was a huge earthquake under the ocean floor near Indonesia. This caused a gigantic tsunami. The tsunami wiped out towns and villages throughout

Asia. Around 230,000 people died. By the time the tsunami reached the east coast of Africa, the waves had lost a great deal of power. However, they still caused flooding and widespread damage. Owen had been swimming in the river with his mother when the tsunami hit. The enormous waves separated Owen from his mother and swept him out to sea.

The next day, the people of Malindi saw the struggling baby hippo, without its mother, stranded on a coral reef. It was Owen. He was tired and frightened. Owen could not reach the shore on his own. It took hours for the villagers to rescue Owen from the coral reef.

BEFORE YOU GO ON

1 What is the main idea of the second paragraph on page 180?

2 How do plovers help Nile crocodiles?

On Your Own
What do you think the villagers will do to help Owen?

coral reef, line of hard material formed by the skeletons of small ocean creatures that live in warm water

181

Study Skills: Chart

Conversion from metric measurements to American Standard measurements is common in scientific articles. The scientific community uses metric measurements, but everyday use in the U.S. is done in Standard. A conversion chart can often be found in a science or math textbook or an almanac. Ask students to use a chart to check the conversions in the article. Then practice converting other measurements.

STEP 3: Monitor Progress

Ask students to check what they have understood in the reading. If you are using the Audio CD, pause the recording.

Before You Go On

When they answer each question, students should look for the spread or the page that gives that information.

ANSWERS

1. The main idea is that life in the wild can be difficult and dangerous.
2. Plovers help Nile crocodiles by cleaning their teeth.

On Your Own Have students write an answer to the On Your Own question on a separate sheet of paper. Encourage volunteers to share their responses with the class. Then collect student responses to monitor their comprehension, writing skills, and fluency.

Differentiated Instruction

Beginning	Have students point to the expression on page 180 that means "very competitive."
Early Intermediate	Have students fill in the blank. An expression that means "very competitive" is _____.
Intermediate	Ask students what the expression "dog-eat-dog" means.
Special Needs	Break the task into small steps and give clear step-by-step instructions, e.g. first read the title, next read the first line of the first paragraph. Be sure that students understand your expectations.

Read

Preteaching Highlighted Words

Before reading this spread, point out the highlighted words and terms to students. Define each one, pointing out the location of the definition in the gloss at the bottom of the student book page. Make sure that students understand each highlighted word. If appropriate, ask students to generate original sentences using the highlighted words. When correcting original sentences, focus on usage rather than on other kinds of errors.

Model the
READING STRATEGY

Identify Main Idea and Details

Remind students that the main idea of the article is that animals form friendships and cooperate with each other. However, each paragraph in the article also has its own main idea. **SAY:** *Look at the first paragraph on page 182. The main idea of this paragraph is that Owen cannot be released into the wild. Three reasons supporting this main idea are given in the paragraph.* Ask students to identify these reasons. (Owen cannot take care of himself, other hippos would reject him and would probably attack him) Then choose one or more other paragraphs to break down in a similar way.

But what should they do with a 272-kilogram (600-lb.) baby hippo? The people could not return him to the wild. Owen had not yet learned to take care of himself. Another hippo group would not accept him. Other hippos would think Owen was an intruder and probably attack him.

Luckily for Owen, there was an animal shelter nearby named Haller Park. The workers prepared a perfect home for Owen. It had a pond, a mud hole, tall trees, and lots of grass. This seemed perfect for a hippo, but Owen's new home was not empty. Some monkeys and the 318-kilogram tortoise Mzee already lived in Haller Park.

It took hours for the people of Malindi to load Owen into a pickup truck. Owen was very angry, and he was also very frightened. He had lost his mother and his friends. He did not know where he was or where he was going.

When Owen arrived at Haller Park, he quickly left the pickup truck and ran right to Mzee. The workers looked in amazement when Owen quickly hid behind the giant tortoise. This is exactly the way a baby hippo would hide behind its mother if it felt the need for protection.

Mzee was shocked and surprised. He had originally come from Aldabra Island. This is part of the country of Seychelles in the Indian Ocean. Sailors had probably taken Mzee from his home to be used for food. He must have escaped from the ship, maybe during a shipwreck, and come ashore somewhere on the eastern coast of Africa. That was a long time before, because Mzee was about 130 years old. (Some giant tortoises live to be 200 years old!)

Mzee must have seen a lot in his long life. Like most giant tortoises, he was not very friendly. He preferred to be left alone. So, at first, Mzee tried to crawl away from Owen. However, as you know, tortoises cannot move very quickly. Owen just watched where Mzee went and then followed him around. For some reason, Mzee began to like his new companion.

◄ Owen following Mzee

182

TESOL Standards

Goal 3, Standard 3—To use English in socially and culturally appropriate ways: Students will use appropriate learning strategies to extend their sociolinguistic and sociocultural competence.
Descriptors—Experimenting with variations of language in social and academic settings; Seeking information about appropriate language use and behavior; Analyzing the social context to determine appropriate language use.

▲ Owen and Mzee nuzzling

Over the next few days, the two giant animals became good friends. Then they became great friends. In fact, Owen and Mzee soon refused to be separated. They would spend all their time together, eating, swimming, sleeping, and playing. Mzee would stretch out his neck and Owen would tickle it. At night, the two huge animals would cuddle up next to each other. Mzee and Owen even developed their own way of "talking" with each other.

It is a bit of a mystery why Owen and Mzee became such good friends. After all, Owen is a mammal and Mzee is a reptile. Perhaps Mzee's coloring and round shape reminded Owen of his mother. Maybe

Owen looked like another tortoise to Mzee. For whatever reason, they surprised scientists with the strength of their friendship.

Mzee's name means "wise man" in Swahili (one of the main languages of Kenya). It turned out that Mzee's name was well chosen. When Owen the hippo needed a friend, Mzee was there for him. Owen suffered a tremendous loss, but he never gave up. He kept trying and now has a happy life.

---

tickle, touch a person or animal lightly, often in order to make him or her laugh

BEFORE YOU GO ON

1. Why is Owen upset when the people of Malindi put him into the truck?

2. What does Mzee's name mean in Swahili?

On Your Own
What do you think about the friendship between Owen and Mzee?

183

Study Skills: Map

Study Skills: Map

This article includes a map on page 181. Students can use this map to identify where the story took place. Ask students to find places and geographical features on the map which are mentioned in the article. Using a larger map offers context for the places shown. Students can see that Kenya is bordered by Somalia, Ethiopia, Sudan, Uganda, and Tanzania. A larger map shows that all of these countries are located on the east coast of Africa. Ask students to also find Seychelles, where Mzee came from, and Indonesia, where the tsunami struck first.

STEP 5: Monitor Progress

Ask students to check what they have understood in the reading.

Before You Go On

When they answer each question, students should look for the source of the information on that page.

ANSWERS

1. Owen is upset when he is put into the truck because he is alone and he doesn't know what's happening.
2. Wise man

On Your Own Have students write an answer to the On Your Own question on a separate sheet of paper. Encourage volunteers to share their responses with the class. Then collect student responses to monitor their comprehension, writing skills, and fluency.

Review the Purpose for Reading

Elicit responses to the Set a Purpose for Reading questions at the beginning of this reading. Remind students to relate their responses to the Big Question.

Teach & Apply

STEP 1: Practice

Comprehension

Ask students to complete the questions either independently or in groups. Model the first question with the class, so they can see how to answer in a complete sentence.

ANSWERS

1. Owen can't be returned to the wild because he can't take care of himself and other hippos will reject him.
2. Kenya
3. At first Mzee prefers to be left alone. Soon Owen and Mzee spend all their time together.
4. Symbiosis and friendship are both working relationships, but friendship is based on companionship instead of a specific benefit received.
5. **Possible response:** The writer infers that they are friends because they play together and won't be separated.
6. **Possible response:** The main idea is that animals can have friendly and cooperative relationships.
7. Answers will vary.
8. Answers will vary.

Speaking Tip

Have students read the Speaking Tip. **SAY:** *Sometimes it only takes one word to remind us of what we intended to say. Notes that are too thorough can be confusing.*

In Your Own Words

Ask students to summarize the reading, using the chart on page 184 as a guide. Have students work in groups to fill in the chart outline and then write a summary from that information.

Teaching Resources

- *Workbook*, p. 90
- CD-ROM/e-book, Comprehension, Extension
- *Reader's Companion Workbook*, pp. 68–72

COMPREHENSION Workbook Page 90

Right There

1. Why can't Owen be returned to the wild?
2. Where was Owen born?

Think and Search

3. How does Mzee's attitude toward Owen change?
4. How is symbiosis similar to friendship? How is it different?

Author and You

5. What helps the writer infer that Mzee and Owen have become great friends?
6. What main idea, or overall concept, does "Friendship and Cooperation in the Animal Kingdom" present?

On Your Own

7. Why do you think the author says, "It's a 'dog-eat-dog' world out there"? What do you think the author means?
8. What examples can you think of in which animals help people survive?

▲ Some dogs and cats get along well together.

IN YOUR OWN WORDS

Imagine that you are telling a classmate about "Friendship and Cooperation in the Animal Kingdom." Use a chart like the one below to help you organize your ideas. Then share your summary with a classmate.

Main Idea about Symbiosis	Main Idea about Friendship
Definition of *symbiosis*:	Definition of *friendship*:
Examples:	Examples:

 Speaking TIP

Write your main ideas on note cards. Put just a few words in big letters on each card. Use the cards to help you remember your main ideas.

184

TESOL Standards

Goal 2, Standard 3—To use English to achieve academically in all content areas: Students will use appropriate learning strategies to construct and apply academic knowledge.
Descriptors—Applying self-monitoring and self-corrective strategies to build and expand a knowledge base; Determining and establishing the conditions that help one become an effective learner (e.g., when, where, how to study).

Goal 3, Standard 1—To use English in socially and culturally appropriate ways: Students will use the appropriate language variety, register, and genre according to audience, purpose, and setting.
Descriptors—Responding to and using humor appropriately; Using the appropriate degree of formality with different audiences and settings; Recognizing and using Standard English and vernacular dialects appropriately.

Goal 3, Standard 3—To use English in socially and culturally appropriate ways: Students will use appropriate learning strategies to extend their sociolinguistic and sociocultural competence.
Descriptors—Deciding when use of slang is appropriate.

Discuss in pairs or small groups.

1. Which do you think is more common in the animal kingdom— symbiosis or friendship? Why?

2. Owen and Mzee live in Haller Park, an animal shelter. Do you think animals should live in shelters and nature preserves? Or should they be allowed to live in the wild? Explain.

Q How does helping others help us all? You have thought about how animals can help people. Now describe some specific examples in which people can help animals.

 Listening TIP

Respect each speaker. Listen politely, even if you disagree with the speaker's ideas.

READ FOR FLUENCY

Reading with feeling helps make what you read more interesting. Work with a partner. Choose a paragraph from the reading. Read the paragraph. Ask each other how you felt after reading the paragraph. Did you feel happy or sad?

Take turns reading the paragraph aloud to each other with a tone of voice that represents how you felt when you read it the first time. Give each other feedback.

EXTENSION **Workbook Page 90**

In "Friendship and Cooperation in the Animal Kingdom," you learned about different kinds of animals. Learn more about one of the animals described in the article. Use encyclopedias, reference books, and reliable websites. Copy the chart below into your notebook. Use it to organize the information you find. Add more columns if necessary. Share your findings with the class.

Animal	Habitat (where the animal lives)	Size	Life Span	Foods

185

Listening Tip

Point out the Listening Tip. Remind students that if they are respectful in discussion, others are more likely to be respectful as well.

(CRI) Discussion

Congratulate students on successfully completing the reading. **SAY:** *We've learned a lot about animals helping others from the reading. Now let's discuss a few questions about the reading.* Model a discussion starter for the questions. **SAY:** *Review the difference between symbiosis and friendship. Do you think friendship happens in the wild as often as in a zoo or park? How do wildlife parks benefit people and animals?*

Q How does helping others help us all?
Possible response: People can learn how to protect and preserve endangered species.

Read for Fluency

Help students to recognize that when we read aloud, we use tone to place emphasis. **SAY:** *When reading aloud, pay attention to your tone and that of your partner. Does your partner drop his or her voice at the end of a sentence?*

Extension

Have students select one of the animal species from the article to learn more about. They should copy the chart on page 185 in their notebooks, fill in the chart with details, and share their findings with the class.

Differentiated Instruction	
Beginning	Ask students if they think Owen and Mzee were good friends.
Early Intermediate	Ask students to name the park where Owen was brought after being rescued. (Haller Park)
Intermediate	Ask students why they think the relationship between Owen and Mzee worked.
Greater Challenge	Have students explain the similarities and differences between Giant Tortoises and Hippos.

Teach & Apply

STEP 1: Introduce

Remind students that prepositions are words that can show position, location, or time. Changing a preposition can change the meaning of a sentence entirely.

STEP 2: Teach

Grammar and Writing

Prepositions of Location Using the correct preposition makes writing more specific. Write the prepositions of location on the board. Read the words aloud. Then read aloud the examples in the text box. **SAY:** *Prepositions of location indicate where an object or person is in relation to something else, such as below the tree. What is being described in relation to the position of other things in the example sentences?*

STEP 3: Practice

Have students work with a partner to complete the practice activity. Write one model sentence, using one of the prepositions of location. Ask volunteers to share them with the class. Pair English learners with proficient English speakers.

ANSWERS
Possible responses:
1. The ball is under the table.
2. The book is behind the chair.
3. Jorge is sitting beside Jamie.
4. I sat between my two brothers.
5. The fish is in the water.

Teaching Resources

- *Workbook*, pp. 91–92
- CD-ROM/e-book, Grammar, Writing
- *Transparencies*, Writing Model 34
- *Assessment*, Reading 4 Test, pp. 79–82

Grammar and Writing

GRAMMAR, USAGE, AND MECHANICS

Prepositions of Location

Remember that a preposition is a word that shows location or time. Using the correct preposition in your persuasive writing helps you be specific when giving information.

Here are some common prepositions of location: *above, across, behind, below, beside, between, in, near, on, outside,* and *under.* Read the example sentences below. Notice the prepositions.

> There was a huge earthquake **under** the ocean floor **near** Indonesia.
> Owen quickly hid **behind** the giant tortoise.
> The hippo cuddled up **beside** the tortoise.
> The plover picked clean the area **between** the crocodile's teeth.
> Owen, the hippo, lived **in** the country of Kenya **on** the east coast of Africa.

Practice Workbook Page 91

Choose five prepositions from the example sentences above. Write a sentence in your notebook using each preposition. Compare your sentences with a partner's.

▲ Koko the gorilla holds a visiting kitty in her arms.

186

 TESOL Standards

Goal 1, Standard 1—To use English to communicate in social settings: Students will use English to participate in social interactions.
Descriptors—Sharing and requesting information; Expressing needs, feelings, and ideas.

Goal 1, Standard 2—To use English to communicate in social settings: Students will interact in, through, and with spoken and written English for personal expression and enjoyment.
Descriptors—Describing, reading about, or participating in a favorite activity; Expressing personal needs, feelings, and ideas.

Goal 3, Standard 1—To use English in socially and culturally appropriate ways: Students will use the appropriate language variety, register, and genre according to audience, purpose, and setting.
Descriptors—Using a variety of writing styles appropriate for different audiences, purposes, and settings; Responding to and using idioms appropriately; Responding to and using humor appropriately; Determining when it is appropriate to use a language other than English; Determining appropriate topics for interaction.

Write a Critical Evaluation

On this page, you'll write a critical evaluation of a person or issue, using an outline. When you evaluate a topic critically, you examine it against a set of standards. You then make a judgment about whether the person or thing meets those standards. Imagine that you are writing a critical evaluation of someone who is running for class president. You might use the outline below.

I. Class presidents must have certain traits.
  A. leadership ability (standard)
  B. good communication skills (standard)

II. Joe is a good candidate in my judgment.
  A. examples of his leadership ability
  B. examples that prove he can communicate well

Here is a model of a critical evaluation. Notice how the writer presents the topic and a set of standards to judge it against.

> I. Main idea
> (introduce standards)
>
> A.
>
> B.
>
> II. Main idea
> (judge topic)
>
> A.
>
> B.

Tyler Welsh

The Perfect Student

Good students need to have certain traits. They must be smart. They also must be dedicated, proud, confident, and willing to share what they know. Many students possess one or two of these traits, but very few possess them all. Michaela, a classmate who sits next to me, is an exception. She is very smart. She reads everything, from science to historical fiction. She studies hard and does well in school. Michaela takes pride in her work. She has a relaxed and friendly attitude in class. When she gives an oral report, she speaks clearly and with confidence. In addition, she is very willing to help others. This year, she helped me when I was having trouble in one of my classes. To me, Michaela is the perfect example of a good student.

Practice  Workbook Page 92

Write a critical evaluation of a person or issue. Use an outline to organize your ideas. First, present your standards for judging the topic. Then make a judgment supported by examples. Use prepositions of location to help clarify your ideas.

 Writing Checklist

ORGANIZATION:
☑ I introduced the topic and explained my critical standards.

CONVENTIONS:
☑ I checked my writing for errors in grammar and spelling.

187

Tell students that a persuasive paragraph can evaluate a person or an idea.

Writing a Persuasive Paragraph

Write a Critical Evaluation Evaluating a subject critically requires determining standards, and then evaluating the subject against those standards. With students, brainstorm a list of potential topics which might be evaluated against certain standards.

Model Writing Skill Point out the outline in the student book, and copy it onto the board. Review it with the students. Then read the student model aloud. Hearing the paragraph helps students recognize the elements from the organizer. **SAY:** *The model paragraph states that good students should have the traits of intelligence, dedication, confidence, and a willingness to share knowledge.*

Have students evaluate their work using the Writing Checklist.

Writing Checklist Note

Organization: Check that students' paragraphs make their standards clear and evaluate the topic against them.

Conventions: Check that students' paragraphs do not contain misspelled words or misplaced punctuation.

Accelerate Language Development

Dangling Prepositions

Tell students to avoid ending a sentence with a preposition. This is called a dangling preposition. Often it is easy to move the dangling preposition, but sometimes it isn't and may result in a clumsy sentence. *Tell me from where you are,* is grammatically correct, but sounds rather stilted and is not at all as idiomatic as its counterpart, *tell me where you are from.* Point out that, if avoiding a dangling preposition makes for stilted language, students should try to use a synonym without a preposition. Example: *Tell me where you are from* can be replaced by *Tell me where you were born.*

Unit Wrap-Up

Link the Readings

Critical Thinking Have students copy the chart. **SAY:** *All these readings tell about helping others. However, they do not all have the same purpose. The nonfiction pieces are informational, while the story is designed to entertain as well as provoke thought.* Point out the completed parts of the chart, and ask students to complete it.

ANSWERS

Title of Reading	Purpose	Big Question Link
From *Run Away Home*	to entertain	shows how strangers are willing to help one another.
"Extraordinary People: Serving Others"	to inform	shows people who helped the world by their actions.
From *Zlata's Diary*	to persuade	shows how people are affected by war.
"Friendship and Cooperation in the Animal Kingdom"	to teach	discusses how animals help each other.

 Discussion

With students, preview the discussion questions, and assign pairs or groups to work together. Point out that in the first question, *Run Away Home* is fictional, while the article is about real events.

Q How does helping others help us all? **SAY:** *How do the readings affect the way you would answer the Big Question? Which reading most inspired you to help others? Do you think helping others also helps you? Explain.*

Fluency Check

Arrange students in small groups and have them time and record each other's reading. Tell students to fill in the fluency check chart. If students report they are not improving after several readings, examine their comprehension. Select a paragraph to read aloud to the class.

Teaching Resources

- *Assessment*, Unit 3 Test, pp. 153–162
- CD-ROM/e-book, Fluency Check, Projects

T188

Link the Readings

Critical Thinking

Look back at the readings in this unit. Think about what they have in common. They all tell about helping others. Yet they do not all have the same purpose. The purpose of one reading might be to inform, while the purpose of another might be to entertain or persuade. In addition, the content of each reading relates to helping others differently. Now copy the chart below into your notebook and complete it.

Title of Reading	Purpose	Big Question Link
From *Run Away Home*		
"Extraordinary People: Serving Others"		
From *Zlata's Diary*	*to persuade*	
"Friendship and Cooperation in the Animal Kingdom"		*discusses how animals help each other*

Discussion

Discuss in pairs or small groups.

- How does the purpose of *Run Away Home* differ from the purpose of "Friendship and Cooperation in the Animal Kingdom"?

Q How does helping others help us all? Compare and contrast the readings in this unit. In your opinion, which reading best expresses the importance of helping others? Why? Based on the readings, do you think it's more important to help others or to help yourself? Explain.

Fluency Check

Work with a partner. Choose a paragraph from one of the readings. Take turns reading it for one minute. Count the total number of words you read. Practice saying the words you had trouble reading. Take turns reading the paragraph three more times. Did you read more words each time? Copy the chart below into your notebook and record your speeds.

	1st Speed	2nd Speed	3rd Speed	4th Speed
Words Per Minute				

188

 TESOL Standards

Goal 1, Standard 1—To use English to communicate in social settings: Students will use English to participate in social interactions.
Descriptors—Engaging in conversations; Conducting transactions.

Goal 1, Standard 3—To use English to communicate in social settings: Students will use learning strategies to extend their communicative competence.
Descriptors—Seeking support and feedback from others; Using the primary language to ask for clarification; Selecting different media to help understand language.

Goal 2, Standard 2—To use English to achieve academically in all content areas: Students will use English to obtain, process, construct, and provide subject matter information in spoken and written form.
Descriptors—Listening to, speaking, reading, and writing about subject matter information; Gathering information orally and in writing; Selecting, connecting, and explaining information; Analyzing, synthesizing, and inferring from information; Responding to the work of peers and others; Representing information visually and interpreting information presented visually; Understanding and producing technical vocabulary and text features according to content area; Demonstrating knowledge through application in a variety of contexts.

Projects

Work in pairs or small groups. Choose one of these projects.

1 Work in small groups to think of some ways in which people help others. You might research a recycling project or volunteers who take food to homebound people.

2 What do you think happens at the end of *Run Away Home*? Write a summary of what you think will happen at the end. Then read the entire book to see if your prediction is correct.

3 Think about a time when you helped a friend. Write a diary entry about what you did and how you felt about the experience.

4 Look for a documentary about Kenya's wildlife in your library. View it with your class.

5 Prepare an oral report about Sarajevo today. The war has ended, but has the country been rebuilt? Look for visuals to use in your presentation. Be sure to use reliable sources for your report.

Further Reading

To find out more about the theme of this unit, choose from these reading suggestions.

Gandhi, Jane Rollason
This Penguin Reader® biography describes the life of Mohandas Gandhi, whose message of peaceful resistance changed the world.

Anne Frank: The Diary of a Young Girl, Anne Frank
To escape Nazi persecution in Holland, Anne Frank and her family hid for two years in a secret warehouse annex. There, Anne wrote her extraordinary diary.

Free At Last, The Story of Martin Luther King Jr., Angela Bull
Civil rights leader Martin Luther King Jr. dreamed of an America where people would be judged by "the content of their character, not the color of their skin."

189

 Home-School Connection

These projects provide students with several ways to practice and apply what they have learned in the unit. The projects can be completed alone, with partners, or in small groups. They can be completed in the classroom or at home.

Further Reading

Each book listed on this page pertains to the Big Question of this unit. Encourage students to peruse them in their free time and, if applicable, to read them for extra credit. The first book on the list is easily accessible, the second is accessible, and the third is challenging.

Websites

Log onto www.LongmanKeystone.com for links to other interesting websites about helping people.

Differentiated Instruction

Beginning	Ask students to tell you which reading they enjoyed the most.
Early Intermediate	Have students explain why they enjoyed a particular reading.
Intermediate	Have students explain how one of the readings helps them understand the Big Question better.
Standard English Learners (CRI)	Ask students to write a paragraph about how helping others helps us all.

Listening & Speaking Workshop

STEP 1: Introduce

(CRI) Begin this workshop by discussing the formats of some TV talk shows. Ask students for examples of common questions and topics that people discuss on these shows. Point out that talk shows should appeal to a wide audience.

Think About It Read over the instructions with students. Then have students brainstorm to list other public servants and humanitarians they know of. Suggest that students list people about whom there will be a lot of information, which will make it easier to prepare and deliver the presentation.

STEP 2: Teach

Gather and Organize Information Encourage students to distribute the tasks among the group members fairly. Then write the organizational steps on the board: Research, Order Your Notes, and Use Visuals. Have students list any questions they have about their talk show below the correct organizational step. Explain that visuals are things you can see, including props, photos, posters, drawings, and video clips that can enhance discussion.

Teaching Resources

- CD-ROM/e-book, Gather and Organize Information

Put It All Together

LISTENING & SPEAKING WORKSHOP
TV Talk Show

With a group, you will present a TV talk show about a person you admire for his or her efforts to help others. One person will be the talk show host, and another will be the special guest. The remaining group members will play other guests who give their perspectives on the person's life or work.

1 THINK ABOUT IT In a group, discuss the selection "Extraordinary People: Serving Others." Then talk about what it would be like to host one of those amazing people on your own TV talk show. Discuss how you would introduce the person and what questions you would ask him or her.

Work together to develop a list of other people, living or dead, who have done a lot to help others. For example:

- Eleanor Roosevelt
- Bono
- Jonas Salk

Jonas Salk, developer of the polio vaccine ▶

2 GATHER AND ORGANIZE INFORMATION With your group, choose a person from your list. Write down what you already know and what you want to find out about the person. Decide who will play the talk show host and the special guest. Then decide what parts the other group members will play (for example, a coworker or someone the person helped).

Research Go to the library or use the Internet to gather information about your person's efforts to help others. Look for facts, details, and examples that show why the person is great and why the audience should admire him or her. Take notes on what you find.

Order Your Notes Use your notes to make an outline for your TV show. Choose which information the host will include in the introduction and what questions he or she will ask each guest. Decide the order in which the guests will appear, and create a list of main points for each one to discuss.

Use Visuals Think about how you should dress for the show. Wear a simple costume, or bring an appropriate prop to help express your role. You may also wish to display a photo of the person your show is about.

190

TESOL Standards

Goal 3, Standard 2—To use English in socially and culturally appropriate ways: Students will use nonverbal communication appropriate to audience, purpose, and setting.
Descriptors—Interpreting and responding appropriately to nonverbal cues and body language; Demonstrating knowledge of acceptable nonverbal classroom behaviors; Using acceptable tone, volume, stress, and intonation, in various social settings; Recognizing and adjusting behavior in response to nonverbal cues.

Goal 3, Standard 3—To use English in socially and culturally appropriate ways: Students will use appropriate learning strategies to extend their sociolinguistic and sociocultural competence.
Descriptors—Experimenting with variations of language in social and academic settings; Seeking information about appropriate language use and behavior; Analyzing the social context to determine appropriate language use; Rehearsing variations of language use in different social and academic settings.

3 **PRACTICE AND PRESENT** As a group, practice your TV talk show. Keep your outline handy for reference, but try to speak naturally, without reading. Place your chairs at an angle so that the host and guests can see each other and the audience. Be careful not to turn your face away from the audience when you speak. Keep practicing until you can present your show confidently, with smooth transitions between speakers.

Deliver Your TV Talk Show TV talk shows are informal and relaxed. Try to create that atmosphere during your presentation. Saying things you didn't rehearse ("ad-libbing") can help. Speak loudly enough so that everyone in the class can hear you. Use natural hand and body movements, too. For example, lean forward and reach out when you are making an important point.

4 **EVALUATE THE PRESENTATION**
You can improve your skills as a speaker and a listener by evaluating each presentation you give and hear. Use this checklist to help you judge your group's TV talk show and the talk shows of other groups.

- ☑ Did the group clearly show how this person has helped others and why he or she is admirable?
- ☑ Did the host give a persuasive introduction?
- ☑ Did the guests provide interesting examples and opinions?
- ☑ Did you understand each speaker's relationship to the special guest?
- ☑ Could you hear and understand the speakers easily?
- ☑ What suggestions do you have for improving the talk show?

🗣️ *Speaking* TIPS

Ask a friend or classmate to listen and give feedback as your group practices. Or tape-record your rehearsal, if possible. Listen to the tape together, and find the places where you can improve your presentation.

Use specific details to present your facts. Use persuasive words to give your opinions.

👂 *Listening* TIPS

As you listen, think about what you already know about this person. Has the presentation changed your feelings about him or her?

When you participate in a talk show, listen carefully. If you don't understand a question or answer, ask the host or guest to repeat or explain it.

191

Practice and Present With students, read the information about preparing for their TV talk show. Remind them that the interactive nature of talk shows allows for including discussion that is not rehearsed.

Speaking Tips

Point out the Speaking Tips and read them. Remind students that watching or listening to a recording of themselves offers them a chance to see themselves as other people see them. **SAY:** *It may seem strange to watch, but it can be useful.*

Listening Tips

Point out the Listening Tips and read them. Remind students that the informal nature of the talk show may mean that things may not happen exactly as they rehearsed. They should expect classmates to ad lib from time to time.

Evaluate the Presentation Suggest that students use the checklist on this page to evaluate the group presentations for the purpose of giving feedback. Have students rate each presentation from 1 to 6. After they watch each performance, they should read the questions on the checklist, and answer *Yes* or *No* for all but the last question. Giving specific examples directly from the presentation is most helpful to the performers.

Differentiated Instruction

Beginning	With students, brainstorm a list of possible people to interview on the TV talk show. List the names on the board.
Early Intermediate	Work with students to develop a list of possible interview questions to ask the person being featured in the TV talk show.
Intermediate	Ask students if they could interview any one person, who it would be. Have students give reasons why they chose their person.
Struggling Readers	Have students give an example of when you might see or hear an interview.

Writing Workshop

In this workshop, students will write a speech, using elements of persuasive writing from previous assignments. They will follow the steps in the writing process, from prewriting to publication.

STEP 2: Teach

Prewrite Review the steps in the writing process with students: prewrite, draft, revise, edit and proofread, and publish. Point out that using these steps will help them write a better and more persuasive speech. Remind students to begin by presenting both sides, but to make their opinion clear and support it with persuasive examples and reasons.

SAY: *The point of persuasive writing is to persuade the reader to agree with you. Think about how to state your opinion in a way that is memorable. Using well-chosen adjectives and inspiring examples will make your speech more interesting for your audience.*

Have students read the instructions on this page and brainstorm possible topics. Then model filling in a graphic organizer like the one shown. **SAY:** *The supporting examples go below the main idea.* Once students have selected a topic, have them list ideas for their speech in a graphic organizer.

Draft Explain that a draft is a work in progress; it does not have to be perfect. Students can make changes later on. Have students use their graphic organizers to help create a draft.

Teaching Resources

- *Transparencies, Resources,* Graphic Organizer 16
- *Transparencies,* Writing Model 35, Proofreader's Marks 51
- CD-ROM/e-book, Writing Workshop
- *Workbook,* pp. 93–94

WRITING WORKSHOP
Persuasive Speech

You have written four persuasive paragraphs. Now you will use your skills to write a persuasive speech. In a persuasive speech, you try to convince listeners to agree with your opinion on an issue. A good persuasive speech begins with a paragraph that introduces the issue. This paragraph presents both sides of the argument and then gives the writer's own opinion. Body paragraphs support the writer's position with carefully organized reasons, facts, and examples. Most persuasive speeches conclude with a paragraph that restates the writer's opinion in a new and memorable way. Speechwriters often use strong and persuasive words to appeal to listeners' emotions.

You will write a five-paragraph speech that tries to persuade listeners to agree with your opinion on an issue you care about.

1 PREWRITE Brainstorm possible topics for your speech. You might focus on the theme of helping others. For example, is there something you believe your school should do to help the community? Is there a leader who in your opinion deserves extra praise for helping humanity? Do you want your friends to volunteer for a specific cause? Choose a topic. Then think about how you can persuade listeners to agree with your opinion on the issue.

List and Organize Ideas and Details Use a graphic organizer to gather your ideas and information. A student named Tyler decided to write a persuasive speech about a man he admired—former president Franklin D. Roosevelt. Here is the opinion-and-reason chart Tyler prepared.

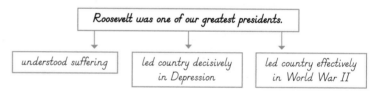

> Roosevelt was one of our greatest presidents.

| understood suffering | led country decisively in Depression | led country effectively in World War II |

2 DRAFT Use the model on page 195 and your graphic organizer to help you write your first draft. Remember to state your opinion clearly in your first paragraph and to restate your opinion in your conclusion.

192

TESOL Standards

Goal 2, Standard 2—To use English to achieve academically in all content areas: Students will use English to obtain, process, construct, and provide subject matter information in spoken and written form.
Descriptors—Listening to, speaking, reading, and writing about subject matter information; Gathering information orally and in writing; Understanding and producing technical vocabulary and text features according to content area; Demonstrating knowledge through application in a variety of contexts.

3 **REVISE** Read over your draft. As you do so, ask yourself the questions in the writing checklist. Use the questions to help you revise your speech.

SIX TRAITS OF WRITING CHECKLIST

- ☑ **IDEAS:** Do I present both sides of the issue?
- ☑ **ORGANIZATION:** Do I support my opinion with persuasive reasons, facts, and examples?
- ☑ **VOICE:** Does my writing show my feelings about the issue?
- ☑ **WORD CHOICE:** Do I use vivid words that will appeal to listeners?
- ☑ **SENTENCE FLUENCY:** Do my sentences flow well when read aloud?
- ☑ **CONVENTIONS:** Does my writing follow the rules of grammar, usage, and mechanics?

Here are the changes Tyler plans to make when he revises his first draft:

A Great President

Franklin Delano Roosevelt, the 32nd President of the United States,

is known for overcoming hardships. He became president at a time

of world and national crisis ~~on~~ in 1933. Some people believe Roosevelt

created even more problems by increasing the government's powers. but

I believe he used the government's powers in exciting new ways to help people.

In my opinion, Roosevelt was one of the greatest presidents in U.S. history.

Roosevelt himself understood human suffering, in part because he

had experienced tragedy. He was born on January 30 1882, in Hyde

Park, New York. ~~On~~ In 1921, at age 39, he was diagnosed with polio. The

disease left him partially paralyzed. He felt despair at first. but Then he

fought with all his strength to regain use of his legs. Although he

193

Revise Point out that the revising step focuses on improving the content and wording of a draft. Have students look over Tyler's first draft and notice the kinds of changes he made. (He reordered sentences, corrected prepositions, and added linking words.) Ask students to look at their own drafts and make changes in organization, content, or wording. Be sure they ask themselves the questions in the Six Traits of Writing Checklist.

STEP 3: Assess

Writing Checklist Notes

Read aloud the Writing Checklist and go over the entries with students.

Ideas *Check that your speech introduces both sides of the issue.*

Organization *Check that your speech includes persuasive reasons, facts and examples.*

Voice *Check that your writing makes your opinion on the topic clear.*

Word Choice *Check that you have chosen descriptive, powerful, and persuasive words to make your point.*

Sentence Fluency *Check that your sentences are not overly complex or clunky.*

Conventions *Check that you follow rules of grammar, usage, and mechanics.*

Differentiated Instruction

Beginning	Ask students if they can come up with an example of persuasion, e.g. convincing a parent to let them stay up late.
Early Intermediate	After reading Tyler's persuasive speech, ask students who they think the audience is. Who is he trying to persuade?
Intermediate	After reading Tyler's persuasive speech, ask students if they were persuaded to think that FDR was one of the greatest presidents. If so, have them give examples and reasons why.
Special Needs	Refer students to the *How To Use Technology in Writing* section of the handbook at the back of their books for hints and tips on saving drafts.

Edit and Proofread Review with students the preliminary drafts of the model speech and the final revised version. Identify the differences between these versions. Ask how the changes improved the writing. Tell students to keep these changes in mind as they work on their own essay. Pair English learners with English proficient students. Keep dictionaries handy for students to use as they work.

never was able to walk again without assistance he went on to a brilliant political career.

Elected president during the Great Depression, Roosevelt was a (leader) decisive and passionate, who wanted to get the country back on
                                                                    also
its feet. His administration ^ worked to create jobs for the unemployed to assist struggling farmers, to feed the hungry, and to provide for the elderly. (During his presidency, laws were passed to regulate the stock market.) Roosevelt cared about everyone!

Roosevelt was equally effective during wartime. In World War II, he showed tremendous leadership in preparing the way for an Allied victory. In addition, he thought about the future of peace. He supported the idea of a global peacekeeping organization. Today, that organization is called the United Nations.

At age 63, Roosevelt died suddenly during his fourth term in
                                   across
office. His death caused sorrow to the country. Roosevelt was a great president. He inspired hope, introduced important social programs, and led the nation brilliantly during wartime. Without his decisiveness and passion, the United states would not be the country it is today.

4 EDIT AND PROOFREAD Workbook Page 93

Copy your revised speech onto a clean sheet of paper. Read it again. Correct any errors in grammar, word usage, mechanics, and spelling. Here are the additional changes Tyler plans to make when he prepares his final draft.

194

🌐 TESOL Standards

Goal 3, Standard 1—To use English in socially and culturally appropriate ways: Students will use the appropriate language variety, register, and genre according to audience, purpose, and setting.
Descriptors—Using the appropriate degree of formality with different audiences and settings; Recognizing and using Standard English and vernacular dialects appropriately; Using a variety of writing styles appropriate for different audiences, purposes, and settings; Determining appropriate topics for interaction.

Tyler Welsh

A Great President

Franklin Delano Roosevelt, the 32nd President of the United States, is known for overcoming hardships. He became president at a time of world and national crisis in 1933. Some people believe Roosevelt created even more problems by increasing the government's powers, but I believe he used the government's powers in exciting new ways to help people. In my opinion, Roosevelt was one of the greatest presidents in U.S. history.

Roosevelt himself understood human suffering, in part because he had experienced tragedy. He was born on January 30, 1882, in Hyde Park, New York. In 1921, at age 39, he was diagnosed with polio. The disease left him partially paralyzed. He felt despair at first, but then he fought with all his strength to regain use of his legs. Although he never was able to walk again without assistance, he went on to a brilliant political career.

Elected president during the Great Depression, Roosevelt was a decisive and passionate leader who wanted to get the country back on its feet. During his presidency, laws were passed to regulate the stock market. His administration also worked to create jobs for the unemployed, to assist struggling farmers, to feed the hungry, and to provide for the elderly. Roosevelt cared about everyone!

Roosevelt was equally effective during wartime. In World War II, he showed tremendous leadership in preparing the way for an Allied victory. In addition, he thought about the future of peace, and he supported the idea of a global peacekeeping organization. Today, that organization is called the United Nations.

At age 63, Roosevelt died suddenly during his fourth term in office. His death caused sorrow across the country. Roosevelt was a great president, He inspired hope, introduced important social programs, and led the nation brilliantly during wartime. Without his decisiveness and passion, the United states would not be the country it is today.

5 PUBLISH Prepare your final draft. Share your speech with your teacher and classmates.

Workbook
Page 94

195

Career Connection

Helping Careers Many careers and career fields focus on helping people. Doctors and nurses are two obvious examples, but there are many other humanitarian professions. Lawyers can work for justice when someone has been wronged or falsely accused. Social workers help troubled families and protect children in bad situations. Teachers and professors work to educate and share knowledge, making it possible for others to improve their own lives and be aware of the struggles of others. Inventors make new creations, some of which may change the everyday lives of millions. Finally, there are many careers that involve working directly for charitable causes, providing food, water, housing, education, and support for people in need everywhere.

Accelerate Language Development

The Elements of a Paragraph

Remind students to include the elements of a paragraph in their essays as they write. Ask them to check each paragraph to make sure it contains:

- a topic sentence that introduces the main idea;
- details, such as facts and examples, in the body;
- a concluding sentence that restates the topic sentence and summarizes the main idea.

Also, remind students to follow the rules of grammar, usage, and mechanics.

Remind students that the Big Question is *How does helping others help us all?* **SAY:** *You have read about how both people and animals help one another and that many small acts of kindness enrich the larger community. The artworks shown celebrate how people help one another through respecting others and therefore improving the lives of those in the whole community.*

STEP 2: Teach

Visual Literacy

Jesse Treviño Explain that Treviño celebrates close family and cultural ties in his painting. Many families and communities celebrate these ties by gathering together at parties and picnics. Go to the Smithsonian Global Sound website feature "Recording Details" (www.LongmanKeystone.com) to listen to samples from "Music of New Mexico: Hispanic Traditions." Play excerpts from soundtracks such as "Pecos Polka" by Gregorio Ruiz and Henry Ortiz, or "Mañanitas Tapatias" by Coro Cristo Rey. Also go to the Smithsonian Global Sound web site (www.LongmanKeystone.com) and choose songs from a variety of African nations and African-American folksinger Ella Jenkins ("No More Pie" and "I'm Gonna Sing"). Use the soundtracks to initiate a discussion on the ways groups use music to build community. **ASK:** *What sort of cultural music might you play at family gatherings like the one Treviño captures in his painting? How does music add to the mood of the gathering?* Have students share their selections with the class.

Jacob Lawrence Explain that Lawrence was commissioned to create a painting based on a quotation by the ancient Roman author Marcus Aurelius Antoninus. Read the full quotation to the class: *Men exist for the sake of one another. Teach them then, or bear with them.* Explain that the author was encouraging people to help one another. He was saying that people need to work toward understanding and acceptance of one another.

Teaching Resources

- *Workbook*, pp. 95–96
- CD-ROM/e-book, Smithsonian

Learn about *Art* with the
Smithsonian American Art Museum

Respect

Sometimes the best way to help someone else is to listen. When you are silent and just listen, you show that you care and respect the person you are listening to. Caring about someone and respecting that person are all important pieces of a larger feeling we call love. Many American artists try to show this emotion in their work.

Jesse Treviño, *Mis Hermanos* (1976)

In this painting, Mexican-born Jesse Treviño uses a large canvas to capture the daily life of Mexican Americans in San Antonio, Texas, the city where he lives. The title of the painting, *Mis Hermanos,* is Spanish for "My Brothers." But the title refers to both members of the Mexican-American community, as well as Treviño's actual family. The sunlight shines across the shirts of his six brothers and the artist himself (center, in striped shirt). The sunlight brings the men together like a strong emotion. Treviño shows the men standing or sitting in different positions against a fence. He captures the crinkles in their shirts and the liquid in the glasses that several of them hold in their hands. Treviño uses a painting style that creates an image almost as realistic as a photograph.

Treviño showed great promise as an artist when he was a young man. Then he lost his right arm when he served as a soldier in the Vietnam War. When he returned to the

▲ Jesse Treviño, *Mis Hermanos*, 1976, acrylic, 48 × 70 in., Smithsonian American Art Museum

196

TESOL Standards

Goal 2, Standard 2—To use English to achieve academically in all content areas: Students will use English to obtain, process, construct, and provide subject matter information in spoken and written form.
Descriptors—Analyzing, synthesizing, and inferring from information; Hypothesizing and predicting; Formulating and asking questions.

Goal 2, Standard 2—To use English to achieve academically in all content areas: Students will use English to obtain, process, construct, and provide subject matter information in spoken and written form.
Descriptors—Representing information visually and interpreting information presented visually.

Goal 2, Standard 3—To use English to achieve academically in all content areas: Students will use appropriate learning strategies to construct and apply academic knowledge.
Descriptors—Focusing attention selectively; Applying basic reading comprehension skills such as skimming, scanning, previewing, and reviewing text; Planning how and when to use cognitive strategies and applying them appropriately to a learning task.

United States, he had to teach himself to paint all over again with his left hand. His family and friends helped him as he recovered from his war injury. In *Mis Hermanos*, Treviño captures the respect and support the brothers give each other. Notice the hand of the brother in the back row resting on Treviño's shoulder. Each of the men touches another in some fashion, which adds to the warmth of the portrait.

Jacob Lawrence, *"Men exist for the sake of one another . . ."* (1958)

In *"Men exist for the sake of one another . . . ,"* an adult sits among four children. The man, though very large, bends gently toward the children. He holds a small tree that still has its roots. This means that the tree can be replanted. The older children, two girls, look sad and in need of comfort. The blue background mirrors their unhappy mood. But the child in the center smiles up at the man. The man's long fingers seem to touch her face, and her hand touches his leg. The warmth they show each other also envelops the smallest child, who looks up at the adult with a happy expression. Flowers bloom at their feet.

Jacob Lawrence had a difficult childhood. His father left when Lawrence was young, and his mother moved many times to find work. Lawrence lived in foster care—where another family takes you in until your own family can support you again. Fortunately, like the girls in this painting, Lawrence got support from adults in his community who cared for him.

Lawrence and other artists were hired by a company to create paintings that matched quotations from famous works in Western literature. Lawrence based his painting on a quotation from the Roman emperor Marcus Aurelius Antoninus. The emperor's statement (the title of Lawrence's painting) tells people that they should respect one another.

Respecting others strengthens our sense of community and the quality of our own lives. Both of these artists' works celebrate this give and take.

▲ Jacob Lawrence, *"Men exist for the sake of one another . . . ,"* 1958, oil, 20¾ x 16¾ in., Smithsonian American Art Museum

Apply What You Learned

1 In what ways are these two paintings similar? How are they different?

2 Why do you think that Jacob Lawrence showed a tree that could be replanted in his painting? What do you think this tree stands for?

Q Big Question
In what ways are helping people and having respect for them related?

Workbook
Pages 95–96

197

Go to the Smithsonian American Art Museum website feature "1001 Days & Nights of American Art" (www.LongmanKeystone.com) for information about John Bartlett, whose famous book, *Bartlett's Familiar Quotations*, is still regularly used in libraries and classrooms around the world. Have students choose a quotation that relates to helping others. Then have them create a work of art that captures the meaning of the quotation. Suggest that they include the quotation in their artwork.

Invite someone from a helping profession or organization (such as a doctor, nurse, social worker, foster care worker, Red Cross volunteer, etc.) to speak to the class about his or her work, explaining how it helps individuals as well as the wider community. Encourage students to ask questions afterwards.

Ask for volunteers who have resettled in an unfamiliar place with new customs, food, and language to write a letter to a family member or friend in their native country describing their feelings about the new situation. **ASK:** *What do you think you might need help with? What sort of help could this person offer from a distance? What do you have to figure out for yourself?* Have volunteers share their letters with the class.

STEP 3: Apply

Apply What You Learned

Have volunteers read the questions aloud, and be sure students understand the meaning of difficult words and concepts. Encourage students to carefully study the artworks, and if necessary, reread the text to help them.

ANSWERS

1. These paintings are similar in that they both portray groups of people who are loving and caring of each other. They are different in that the subject of *Mis Hermanos* is the respect and support of men who are like brothers to each other, while the subject of "Men exist for the sake of one another … ." is the support that an adult gives to children.

2. Possible response: Lawrence showed a tree that could be transplanted because as a child Lawrence himself felt transplanted and nourished in foster homes. He also got support from other adults in his community. The tree may stand for possibilities of a new life.

Q Possible response: If you have respect for someone, you are more likely to want to help the person.

<table>
<tr><td colspan="2">Differentiated Instruction</td></tr>
<tr><td>Beginning</td><td>Ask students which of the paintings on pages 196–197 they prefer. Why?</td></tr>
<tr><td>Early Intermediate</td><td>Ask students to brainstorm adjectives that they think best describes either of the paintings on this spread.</td></tr>
<tr><td>Intermediate</td><td>Ask students to describe either of the paintings on this spread in their own words.</td></tr>
<tr><td>Standard English Learners (CRI)</td><td>Have students think about well-known paintings from their home culture. How are they similar to or different from those on this spread?</td></tr>
</table>

 What do we learn through winning and losing?

198

STEP 1: Introduce

Unit Content

Tell students that they will read selections from a variety of genres about winning and losing, including: three nonfiction articles, three poems, a fable, and a myth. Students will practice reading and comprehension skills, such as analyzing causes and effects, asking questions to get information, and understanding the author's purpose. They will study words, apply strategies to learn new vocabulary, learn writing skills, and write an expository essay.

The Big Question

Introduce the Big Question, "What do we learn through winning and losing?" Encourage students to give some potential answers to the question. Express interest in students' answers, and probe their thinking. Ask the following questions.

- Have you ever won something? How did it make you feel?
- Have you ever lost a game, a sports match, or a competition? How did you feel?
- What can you learn from winning?
- What can you learn from losing?

STEP 2: Teach

Visual Literacy

Point out that photos and illustrations help readers understand what they are reading. Preview the selections in the unit to find these visuals. Some questions to ask about the illustrations include these:

On page 206, the soccer players have just finished an important match. Do you think they have won or lost? Why?

On page 219, what kind of competition does the illustration show? How do you think the players are feeling? Why?

On page 234, what kind of problem do you see? What do you think will happen?

On pages 244–247, what kind of animals are "going, going, gone"?

Teaching Resources

- *Resources*, Unit 4 Lesson Plans, pp. 39–50
- *Transparencies*, Unit 4 Daily Language Practice
- CD-ROM/e-book, Big Question
- Video, Segment 4
- *Resources*, Letters Home, pp. 115–116

TESOL Standards

Goal 2, Standard 1—To use English to achieve academically in all content areas: Students will use English to interact in the classroom.
Descriptors—Asking and answering questions.

Goal 2, Standard 2—To use English to achieve academically in all content areas: Students will use English to obtain, process, construct, and provide subject matter information in spoken and written form.
Descriptors—Hypothesizing and predicting; Formulating and asking questions.

Goal 2, Standard 3—To use English to achieve academically in all content areas: Students will use appropriate learning strategies to construct and apply academic knowledge.
Descriptors—Actively connecting new information to information previously learned.

This unit is about winning and losing. You'll read about winning a soccer game and winning a race. You'll read about different kinds of loss. You'll learn about sportsmanship and how "it's not whether you win or lose, it's how you play the game." As you read, you'll practice the academic and literary language you need to use in school.

Listening and Speaking

At the end of this unit, you'll present a **TV sports report** as if you were a newscaster.

Writing

In this unit you will practice **expository writing**, or writing that explains a topic. You'll write an expository paragraph after each reading and an expository essay at the end of the unit.

QuickWrite

Write several sentences about a time when you lost a contest, game, or object.

Visit *LongmanKeystone.com*

199

STEP 3: Practice

QuickWrite

To stimulate ideas for the QuickWrite, talk about the difference between losing a contest or game and losing an object. Draw a two-column chart on the board, and label one column *Losing a Game or Contest* and the other column *Losing an Object.* Ask students for words and phrases that describe each and record them on the chart. Students can use the ideas for their sentences. (Column 1 might include: *wasn't prepared, didn't try my best, didn't want to compete in the first place, felt bad about myself.* Column 2 might include: *wasn't my fault, wasn't careful, felt awful, learned a lesson.*)

STEP 4: Extend

Have students read aloud the titles of the selections and decide how each reading might relate to the Big Question. **SAY:** *What do you think the article "Soccer: The World Sport" will tell you about winning and losing? "Casey at the Bat" is a poem. What sport will this probably be about? What might happen to Casey? "The Hare and the Tortoise" and "Orpheus and Eurydice" are a fable and a myth. Who might the winners and losers in these readings be? What does the title "Going, Going, Gone?" tell you about losing?*

Teach

Objectives

Read the list in the What You Will Learn section, encouraging students to join in. Tell students that "Soccer: The World Sport" will be about the experience of playing the world's most popular sport. Have pairs of students work together to restate the list of things they will learn.

The Big Question

Remind students that the Big Question is "What do we learn through winning and losing?" Answer the question from your own experience, for example, **SAY:** *I was on the basketball team in high school. I wasn't such a good player, but the rest of the team members were. We won the school tournament, and I felt two ways. I didn't feel I deserved to win, but I felt very happy that we did.*

Ask students to share their own experiences about winning or losing. To prepare them for the reading selection, **SAY:** *Soccer is played all over the world. Many teams win and others lose. How would you feel if you were on the winning team? How would you feel if you were on the losing team?*

Build Background

With students, review the fact that soccer is a game in which two teams, of eleven people each, compete. Players can use any parts of their bodies, except their hands and arms, to get the ball into the opposing team's goal. The team that scores the most goals wins.

STEP 2: Teach

Understanding the Genre:
Informational Text

An informational text is a work of nonfiction. Its purpose is to present facts and other information about real people, events, places, and situations. This article is about soccer and how it helped some refugees in the United States connect their old lives with their new one.

Teaching Resources

- CD-ROM/e-book, Key Words
- Audio CD 4, tracks 1–2
- *Workbook*, p. 97

READING 1: Prepare to Read

What You Will Learn

Reading
- Vocabulary building: *Context, dictionary skills, word study*
- Reading strategy: *Ask questions*
- Text type: *Informational text (social studies)*

Grammar, Usage, and Mechanics
Present perfect

Writing
Write a newspaper article

THE BIG QUESTION

What do we learn through winning and losing? Why do people admire someone who wins a game, a sports match, an election, or some other type of contest? Winners use their skills to do something better than anyone else. Of course, no one wins all the time. Winning and losing are both part of competing. Giving it your all and achieving your personal best are just as important.

Work with a partner. Look at the events listed below. How do you win each activity? Look up any information you need to know to complete the chart. When you are finished, share your ideas with the class.

▲ Marathon runners

Activity	How to Win
Spelling bee	Spell each word correctly.
Game of chess	
Soccer game	
Marathon race	

BUILD BACKGROUND

"Soccer: The World Sport" is a nonfiction article that gives facts about the world's most popular sport. According to one survey, over 240 million people play soccer regularly. Two people from different parts of the world, who speak different languages, might have nothing in common except for soccer. Soccer is a common interest that almost the whole world shares.

The article explains how soccer is played and traces the history of the game. Soccer has been around longer than any other sport. Historians have found evidence that the game was played in China, Japan, Greece, and Italy as long as 2,000 years ago. Today, soccer is more popular than ever and is still being spread to countries throughout the world.

200

TESOL Standards

Goal 1, Standard 3—To use English to communicate in social settings: Students will use learning strategies to extend their communicative competence.
Descriptors—Listening to and imitating how others use English; Exploring alternative ways of saying things; Focusing attention selectively.

Goal 2, Standard 1—To use English to achieve academically in all content areas: Students will use English to interact in the classroom.
Descriptors—Requesting and providing clarification; Participating in full-class, group, and pair discussions; Negotiating and managing interaction to accomplish tasks.

Goal 2, Standard 2—To use English to achieve academically in all content areas: Students will use English to obtain, process, construct, and provide subject matter information in spoken and written form.
Descriptors—Selecting, connecting, and explaining information; Understanding and producing technical vocabulary and text features according to content area.

VOCABULARY

Learn Key Words

Read these sentences. Use the context to figure out the meaning of the red words. Use a dictionary to check your answers. Then write each word and its meaning in your notebook.

Key Words

- athletes
- boundaries
- professional
- responsibilities
- sacrifice
- uniforms

1. Each team has many fine **athletes**. These players are good at sports.
2. The coach marked the field's **boundaries** with chalk. The players can't kick the ball outside of these lines.
3. **Professional** players get paid for being on a team. It is their job.
4. The players have many **responsibilities**. There are many things that they must do.
5. Players **sacrifice** things in order to have time to practice. They give up TV, or school clubs, or time with friends.
6. You can tell the teams apart by the color of their **uniforms**. Each team wears a different outfit.

Practice

Workbook Page 97

Write the sentences in your notebook. Choose a red word from the box above to complete each sentence. Then take turns reading the sentences aloud with a partner.

1. There are many _____ baseball players. They are paid to play ball.
2. The team's new _____ are blue and white. They have the players' names and numbers on the back.
3. The sports team has five new _____ who all play soccer well.
4. Players often must _____ sleeping late on weekend mornings.
5. Luisa has many _____ as the team captain. There are many things she must do.
6. The _____ of the playing field are clearly marked.

▲ Professional soccer player Mia Hamm goes for the ball at the Olympics, 2004.

201

CD4 T1–T2

 Vocabulary

Learn Key Words Play the CD. Have students listen and repeat. If you are not using the CD, read the Key Words aloud. **SAY:** *These words are important to the content of the text we are reading.* Write the key words below and their definitions.

- **athletes:** people who are good at sports
- **boundaries:** the lines that mark the edges of something, such as a playing field
- **professional:** someone who gets paid to do something
- **responsibilities:** things a person has to do
- **sacrifice:** to give something up
- **uniforms:** outfits worn by members of a group, such as a sports team

Have students copy the definitions into their notebooks and generate original sentences for them. For extra practice, assign corresponding Workbook pages.

STEP 3: Practice

Have students work with a partner to complete the activity. Model answering the first question. **SAY:** *I'll read the entire sentence and say "blank" for the missing word. Then I'll look over the list of Key Words and their definitions to see which one makes the most sense in the sentence. I know that a professional is someone who gets paid to do something. That must be the word.*

ANSWERS

1. professional
2. uniforms
3. athletes
4. sacrifice
5. responsibilities
6. boundaries

Differentiated Instruction

Beginning	Ask students if they have ever won something. Ask them what they won and how they won it.
Early Intermediate	Have students name two things about winning that makes them feel good.
Intermediate	Have students describe how they feel when they win. Ask them to describe how they feel when they lose.
Standard English Learners **CRI**	Ask students to name a sport that is popular. Ask them to name a team they know and like and talk about their favorite athletes.

STEP 1: Teach

CD4 T3–T4

 Vocabulary

Learn Academic Words Play the CD. Have students listen and repeat. If you are not using the CD, read the Academic Words aloud. Then model how to use the chart. **SAY:** *Look at the chart below the Academic Words list. What other sentence can we create with the word element? (Possible response: One element in writing a good story is an exciting plot.)*

Have students work together in pairs to add another sentence for each academic word. They write each word, its definition, and the sentence in their personal Word Book.

STEP 2: Practice

Model how to answer the questions on page 202 by completing the first one with the whole group. **SAY:** *The first question says, "What is the most important element that makes a team successful?" I know that the word element means a part of something, such as a plan or system. The elements of a successful team are such things as cooperation and teamwork. My answer is teamwork.*

ANSWERS

Possible responses:
1. The most important element that makes a team successful is teamwork.
2. When I watch a baseball game, I focus on the pitcher.
3. Playing sports is a positive experience because it is enjoyable, and you get better with practice.
4. Tennis players require a racket, tennis balls, and a tennis court.

Teaching Resources

- Audio CD 4, tracks 3–4
- *Workbook*, pp. 98–100
- CD-ROM/e-book, Academic Words, Word Study

Learn Academic Words

Study the red words and their meanings. You will find these words useful when talking and writing about informational texts. Write each word and its meaning in your notebook. After you read "Soccer: The World Sport," try to use these words to respond to the text.

Academic Words
element
focus
positive
require

element = one part of a plan, system, piece of writing, and so on	Teamwork is an important **element** in baseball, soccer, and football.
focus = give all your attention to a particular person or thing	Baseball players must **focus** on the ball at all times.
positive = good or useful	Team sports can have a **positive** effect. Players learn to help one another.
require = need something	The team will **require** new uniforms. Their old ones are torn.

Practice **Workbook Page 98**

Work with a partner to answer these questions. Try to include the red word in your answer. Write the sentences in your notebook.

1. What is the most important **element** that makes a team successful?
2. What do you **focus** on when you watch a baseball game?
3. Why is playing sports a **positive** experience?
4. What items do tennis players **require**?

Soccer players must focus on the ball. ▶

202

Word Study: Multiple-Meaning Words

Many English words have more than one meaning. You must figure out which meaning fits the particular context. First, look at the context in which you found the word. Are there any clues to meaning in the words and sentences surrounding the word? See which meaning makes most sense in the sentence. Also, identify the word's part of speech. It may be an important clue to the correct meaning. If you still need help, look up the word in a dictionary. Read all the meanings for the word. Select the one that makes most sense in the sentence.

Sentence	Part of Speech	Word and Meaning
In the northeast, each **season** has different weather.	Noun	**season**: one of the four main periods in the year: winter, spring, summer, or fall
We **season** the sauce to make it spicy.	Verb	**season**: add salt, pepper, and other spices to food in order to make it taste better

Practice

Work with a partner to explore the different meanings of these words: *boom, field, goal, matches,* and *meet.* Start by looking up each word in a dictionary. Then use each word in two sentences to show two of the word's meanings. Write the sentences in your notebook.

READING STRATEGY | ASK QUESTIONS

Asking questions makes you a better reader because you get more information from the text. The five questions you should ask are: *Who? Where? When? What? Why?* These questions are sometimes called the 5Ws. They focus on people, places, time, events, and reasons. To ask questions, follow these steps:

- Read a paragraph. Stop and ask yourself one of the five questions.
- Now try to answer the question from what you've learned in the text.
- Read on and see if your answer is correct. Then ask more questions.

As you read "Soccer: The World Sport," ask yourself all of the five questions. Make a note of the answers.

 Workbook Page 100

203

Linguistic Note

The History of Multiple Meaning Words

Point out that multiple meaning words often have very different origins. For example, the word *race* referring to a group of people comes from 16th century French, which comes from Italian *razza; race* referring to a competition comes from Old English *ræsan,* meaning *rush, hasten,* and is related to the 13th century Old Norse *ras,* meaning *running.* The word *pound* demonstrates that language still changes today: *Pound* referring to the currency comes from Old English *pund,* which was the value of a pound weight of silver; *pound* referring to a lost dogs home comes from the 14th century prefix *pund-,* meaning *enclosure; to pound* someone or something with a striking blow comes from Old English *punian,* related to Dutch *puin,* meaning *break down into rubble; to pound the streets,* meaning *to walk with heavy footsteps,* or *to pound at a keyboard,* is a 20th century colloquial use of the word.

STEP 1: Teach

Word Study

Multiple-Meaning Words When words have more than one meaning, you have to look at the context words for clues as to the correct meaning. Read aloud the two meanings of the word *season* on the chart. **SAY:** *Which part of speech is season in the first sentence? (noun) What does season mean in this sentence? (one of the four periods in a year) Which part of speech is season in the second sentence? (verb) What does season mean here? (to add spices)*

STEP 2: Practice

Have students work with a partner to find the different meanings of the words. Have them write these words and their definitions in their Word Book.

ANSWERS
Possible responses:
- **boom:** The thunder made a large boom. We studied the stock market boom.
- **field:** "I will field that question," she said. The soccer field was covered with grass.
- **goal:** Our team scored the first goal of the game. Her goal is to become a doctor.
- **matches:** Lighting matches can be dangerous. We saw two tennis matches today.
- **meet:** I'd like to meet the guest lecturer. There is a swim meet at the pool today.

STEP 3: Teach

Reading Strategy

Ask Questions Model using this reading strategy. On the board, write the statement, "When she finished singing, people applauded wildly." **SAY:** *Asking the 5Ws as you read can help you clarify the facts and keep you focused. For example, Who? (a singer) What? (wild applause) Why? (the audience loved her singing)* You may wish to assign the Workbook page for extra practice.

Read

Reading Summary

This social studies article is about soccer, its world-wide popularity, and refugees to the United States.

The Big Question

Remind students of the Big Question "What do we learn through winning and losing?" Suggest that students discuss this idea: the lessons we learn from losing can eventually lead to our winning.

STEP 2: Teach

Set a Purpose for Reading

Tell students to copy the purpose for reading into their notebooks and to keep it in mind as they read. Explain that they will have to present details that support their answer to the question and to explain how the reading relates to the Big Question.

Preteaching Highlighted Words

In pairs, have students read aloud the highlighted words and their definitions. Answer any questions students have about the use of a word or its meaning before reading the spread.

CD4 T5
Scaffolding:
Listen and Read

Have students listen to the Audio CD as they read the selection to themselves. Then have student pairs alternate reading aloud paragraphs from the selection.

Teaching Resources

- *Resources*, Summaries, pp. 147–148
- Audio CD 4, track 5
- *Reader's Companion Workbook*, pp. 73–81

READING
1
INFORMATIONAL TEXT
SOCIAL STUDIES

Set a purpose for reading Why do soccer players work so hard to win the game, and why do crowds love this sport so much? Read this article to find out.

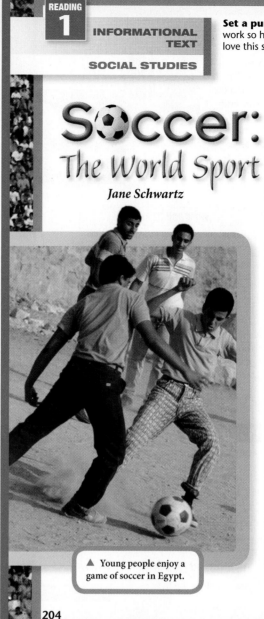

Soccer: The World Sport

Jane Schwartz

▲ Young people enjoy a game of soccer in Egypt.

Americans call the game *soccer*. The British, and almost everyone else in the world, call it *football*. Under either name, soccer has become the most popular sport in the world. It is played almost everywhere. More than 200 countries have national professional teams. Every four years, more people watch the final game of the World Cup tournament on TV than any other sporting event. In 2006, the TV audience was 1.3 billion viewers. Compare that to the Superbowl—the most-watched sports program in the United States. American football, however, is not a major sport in any other country—only 95 million people watched it.

The Simplest Sport

Soccer is often called "the simplest sport." That's probably one reason for its wide appeal. It requires very little equipment. You don't use bats, racquets, clubs, paddles, or sticks. You don't wear gloves, mitts, helmets, or goggles. You don't need skis, sleds, anything that floats, or anything with an engine in it. All you need is a round ball and some space. Even the youngest kids in the poorest parts of the world can usually put together those two things.

---

tournament, sports competition
equipment, things needed for a particular activity
goggles, special glasses that protect the eyes

204

TESOL Standards

Goal 1, Standard 3—To use English to communicate in social settings: Students will use learning strategies to extend their communicative competence.
Descriptors—Using the primary language to ask for clarification; Using context to construct meaning.

Goal 2, Standard 1—To use English to achieve academically in all content areas: Students will use English to interact in the classroom.
Descriptors—Asking and answering questions.

Goal 2, Standard 2—To use English to achieve academically in all content areas: Students will use English to obtain, process, construct, and provide subject matter information in spoken and written form.
Descriptors—Analyzing, synthesizing, and inferring from information; Hypothesizing and predicting; Formulating and asking questions.

The rules of the game are also simple. Two teams of eleven players each try to get the ball into the other team's goal. You can kick the ball or use your head to move it. No one except the goalkeeper (or "goalie") is allowed to touch the ball with hands or arms. This is what makes soccer unique among sports. Think about it. Even in everyday life, what actions do you perform *without* using your hands? The answer is: none or almost none. It's certainly true in sports. You are always using your hands in sports. You *hit*, *shoot*, *pass*, and *carry*. You *serve*, *dunk*, *rebound*, and *throw*. Even in the simple childhood game of "tag," you have to *tag* the other players to get them out!

There is an old saying: "Necessity is the mother of invention." This means that if people need something, they will find a way to invent it. The rules of soccer took away the use of the players' hands. This

▲ A goalkeeper stops the ball from entering the goal.

forced soccer players to "invent" new ways to use their feet. Soccer players don't just *pass* the ball with their feet. They *protect* it, *block* it, and *steal* it from their opponents. Their footwork is so fast and so skillful that sometimes it's hard to follow without replaying the action in slow motion. In addition, players often *dazzle* audiences with leaping kicks that are as awesome as the flying dunks of professional basketball players.

---

goal, area in which you try to put the ball to win a point
goalkeeper, player on a team who tries to stop the ball before it goes into the goal
dunk, jump up and slam the ball from above into the basket in a game of basketball
rebound, catch a basketball after a player has tried but failed to get a point
necessity, being in need

---

dazzle, amaze with an inspiring display

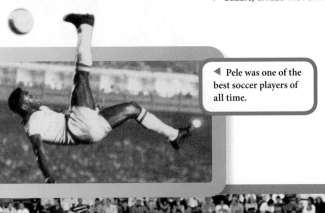

◀ Pele was one of the best soccer players of all time.

BEFORE YOU GO ON

1 What two things do you need to play soccer?

2 What is unique about soccer as a sport?

💡 **On Your Own**
When have you invented something out of necessity?

205

Study Skills: Reference Books

Give students the following directions for using a reference book.

- Look in the library for reference books on a subject, such as sports.
- Use the table of contents and/or the index of books about sports to see whether they include information about soccer.
- Indexes often have subtopic listings under a topic listing. For example, under the topic *soccer*, you might find these subtopics listed: *famous players*, *history of*, or *rules of*.

STEP 3: Monitor Progress

Continue reading and listening to the text with your students. Pause the recording at the end of the page, and invite volunteers to ask the 5Ws.

Before You Go On

Point out the Before You Go On box, and have students read and answer the questions.

ANSWERS

1. You need a round ball and some space to play soccer.
2. Soccer is unique in that it is a sport that you can't play with your hands.

On Your Own Have students write an answer to the On Your Own question on a separate sheet of paper. Collect student responses to monitor their comprehension, writing skills, and fluency.

Differentiated Instruction

Beginning	Provide students with additional visuals of soccer games. Students can look at photographs from newspapers and magazines to answer the Before You Go On questions.
Early Intermediate	Ask students what soccer is called outside of the United States, in other countries.
Intermediate	Ask students to explain to the class why soccer is called the "simplest sport."
Greater Challenge	After completing this reading, have students prepare a short presentation about the Fugees soccer team.

Read

Preteaching Highlighted Words

In pairs, have students read aloud the highlighted words and their definitions. Answer any questions students have about the use of a word or its meaning before reading the spread.

Across the Curriculum:
Social Studies

Brandi Chastain, the athlete who scored the winning goal in the Women's World Cup of 1999, went on to the Olympics after her soccer team's win. She won two gold medals and one silver medal in soccer.

Model the
READING STRATEGY

Ask Questions

Reread the text in the Reading Strategy box on page 203. **SAY:** *Now that we have read a bit of the article, what information can we recall using the 5Ws? Who plays soccer? When did people start playing soccer? Where can soccer be played? What are some of the rules for playing soccer? Why do you think soccer is so popular?*

A Little History

No one knows exactly where or when soccer began. Written records from 2,000 years ago in China describe games in which a ball was kicked into a goal. Other records have been found in Japan, Greece, and Italy.

The modern game of soccer was developed from the eighth to the nineteenth century in England. In 1863, a formal set of rules was adopted. Other countries accepted these rules, and soon international matches were held. At this time, Great Britain ruled colonies all over the world, and British traders, soldiers, and sailors introduced the game to many parts of Asia, Africa, and the Americas.

The *Fédération Internationale de Football Association* (FIFA) was formed in 1904. It is still the governing body of the sport. By 1930, there were professional football leagues in many countries. The first World Cup tournament was held in Uruguay in 1930. It has been held every four years since then.

A Big Boom

Today, about 18 million people play soccer in the United States. It is the fastest growing team sport in the country. Major League Soccer (MLS) was started in 1996, after other professional soccer leagues had failed. The goal of MLS is to make soccer into a mainstream sport like football, baseball, and basketball.

---

traders, people who buy and sell goods
mainstream, popular; accepted

One big boost was the 1999 Women's World Cup played at the Rose Bowl in Palo Alto, California. The U.S. Women's National Team beat China in front of a crowd of 90,185, the largest number of people at a women's sports event ever. The teams were scoreless in regulation time, scoreless in overtime, and the U.S. finally won 5-4 in penalty kicks. Brandi Chastain scored the winning point, and her picture was on the cover of many sports magazines and newspapers. People who had never followed soccer watched this game on television, and the sport began to attract many new fans.

---

regulation time, the normal period of time in which a soccer game is played; 90 minutes
overtime, the period of time added to the end of a sports game to give one of the two teams a chance to win
penalty kicks, chances to kick the ball into the goal that are given because the other team has not obeyed a rule

The U.S. Women's National Team celebrates its World Cup win over China. ▶

206

Something Bigger Than Winning

Most athletes play sports because they want to win. Why else would the players put in hours of practice and travel? Why would they sacrifice their social life and money and sleep to help their team get better and better?

But, if winning is the only goal, most teams will feel like losers, because there can be only one winner at the end of each season.

Is there something about soccer—as it's played in the United States at this time in history—that goes beyond winning and losing? The answer doesn't come from the game, but from the people who play it. The wave of immigrants to the United States in the last ten to fifteen years has been a big part of the soccer boom. These newcomers have arrived from Central and South America, Africa, and parts of Asia. Many have come from countries torn apart by war, poverty, and natural disasters. Soccer is important to people already in the United States, but it has an even deeper meaning to many recent refugees. For them, soccer can sometimes be a lifeline.

One example of this is a team in Clarkston, Georgia, a small town outside of Atlanta. In 2004, a soccer team was organized. It is made up entirely of refugees. In fact, the team calls itself the

▲ The Fugees soccer team

Fugees (as in re**fugees**). The players are all in this country legally, brought by a resettlement agency because of housing and low-paying jobs nearby.

The reporter Warren St. John wrote about the Fugees in the *New York Times*. The boys, all between eight and thirteen, have come from Sudan, Somalia, Bosnia, Iraq, and Afghanistan. Some lived for years in refugee camps. Some have been separated from their families. Some watched their loved ones taken away to prison. One boy saw his father murdered in their home. They have been through a lot in their young lives.

---

refugees, people who have left their country, especially because of a war
lifeline, something that someone depends on completely

resettlement agency, organization that helps refugees adjust to life in the United States

BEFORE YOU GO ON

1. Where was the first World Cup tournament held?
2. Who are the Fugees?

On Your Own
Why do you think that soccer has an even deeper meaning to many recent refugees?

207

Study Skills: Internet

Students can use the Internet for research on the Fugees. Point out that using the Internet involves evaluating the quality of information as well as locating it.

- Use a search engine to do a key word search on *soccer Fugees.*
- In the resulting display of links, look for URLs from reliable sources like newspapers, magazines, and television channels.
- Do key word searches on other interesting facts or names mentioned in the reading.

STEP 5: Monitor Progress

Ask students to check what they have understood in the reading. If you are using the Audio CD, pause the recording.

Before You Go On

Remind students that these questions will help them monitor their progress. Put students in pairs to answer the questions. Encourage them to share their answers with the class.

ANSWERS

1. The first World Cup tournament was held in Uruguay in 1930.
2. The Fugees are a U.S. soccer team made of up children from war-torn or poverty-stricken countries.

On Your Own Have students write an answer to the On Your Own question on a separate sheet of paper. Collect student responses to monitor their comprehension, writing skills, and writing fluency.

Read

Preteaching Highlighted Words

In pairs, have students read aloud the highlighted words and their definitions. Answer any questions students have about the use of a word or its meaning before reading the spread.

Across the Curriculum:
Science

In the game of soccer, the goalkeeper has perhaps the most harrowing job. She or he must wait in one place and try to deflect the ball when it comes. How do goalkeepers know which way to dive to keep a ball from entering the net? Researchers in Britain have found that two clues are the direction that the kicker's hips are facing when he or she approaches the ball and the position of the kicker's nonkicking foot.

Model the
READING STRATEGY

Ask Questions
SAY: *Let's use the reading strategy to help clarify our understanding of the story. Remember the 5Ws. For example, Where do the Fugees play? They play in Clarkston, Georgia.*

▲ The Fugees, led by Coach Luma Mufleh, stretch before a game.

One day a young coach named Luma Mufleh put up a sign announcing tryouts for a soccer team. The team was to be for refugees only, and she was going to be the coach. Those who made the team had to sign a contract accepting certain responsibilities on and off the field. They were going to have to work really hard, but they would have the chance to do something they loved. Before they played their first game, the boys had already "won" several important things: respect, a group they could belong to, and the chance to do really well at something.

The season wasn't perfect. The Fugees did not win every game. The tragedies they had experienced in the past did not suddenly disappear. But other teams admired the way the Fugees played. Parents from the wealthier teams helped the Fugees buy balls, uniforms, and cleated shoes. The boys on the team learned to work together. They had come from different countries, but they all shared a love of soccer. They got to know one another through the sport, and the sport is helping them all to bridge the gap from their old world to their new one.

Throughout U.S. cities and towns soccer is working its magic. It may be "the simplest game," but soccer can have a powerful effect on people's lives. No other sport crosses over so many cultural, racial, and ethnic boundaries as soccer.

---

tryouts, times when people who want to be on a sports team are tested so that the best can be chosen
tragedies, events that cause a lot of sadness

wealthier, richer, having more money
cleated shoes, sneakers that have short pieces of rubber, plastic, or metal attached to the bottom of them, in order to prevent someone from slipping
bridge the gap, reduce or get rid of the difference between two things

208

TESOL Standards

Goal 1, Standard 3—To use English to communicate in social settings: Students will use learning strategies to extend their communicative competence.
Descriptors—Testing hypotheses about language.

Goal 2, Standard 1—To use English to achieve academically in all content areas: Students will use English to interact in the classroom.
Descriptors—Explaining actions.

Goal 2, Standard 2—To use English to achieve academically in all content areas: Students will use English to obtain, process, construct, and provide subject matter information in spoken and written form.
Descriptors—Retelling information.

A Different Ending Every Time

It's true that all sports are different, but they all have one thing in common: Every game is like a story written right there on the spot. It's never the same story, and no one knows the ending ahead of time.

You might lose today, but there will be another game tomorrow. Soccer has attracted millions of fans and created millions of players. Most will never make it to the professional leagues, but they'll probably make some friends, have fun, and experience the satisfaction of working hard to meet a goal. That's not bad for a simple game!

▲ The Fugees play as a team.

---

on the spot, immediately, without careful planning
satisfaction, feeling of happiness or pleasure because of an achievement

ABOUT THE **AUTHOR**

Jane Schwartz writes on many subjects and in many different genres. She is best known for *Ruffian: Burning from the Start*, a nonfiction book about a famous racehorse who suffered a fatal injury. She has also written *Caught*, a novel about a young girl growing up in Brooklyn during the 1950s, and *Grammar Power*, a humorous grammar book. In addition, she writes articles for the *New York Times* and *Sports Illustrated*, and she writes poetry. When she is not busy writing, Schwartz loves to travel.

BEFORE YOU GO ON

1. What three things did the Fugees "win" before their first game?
2. According to the author, what boundaries does soccer cross over?

On Your Own
What does the author compare games to? Do you agree with her? Why?

209

Study Skills: Dictionary

Looking up unfamiliar words is invaluable for students seeking to understand a text. Suggest that students do the following:

- Write down the unfamiliar words in their notebook or their Word Book.
- Look up the definition, pronunciation, and part of speech in a dictionary. Write this information next to the words.
- Keep the list handy for easy reference when reading and during classroom discussion.

STEP 7: Monitor Progress

Ask students to check what they have understood in the reading.

Before You Go On

Remind students that these questions will help them monitor their progress. Put students in pairs to answer the questions. Encourage them to share their answers with the class.

ANSWERS

1. Before their first game, the Fugees won respect, a group to belong to, and a chance to do really well at something.
2. Soccer crosses over cultural, racial, and ethnic boundaries.

On Your Own Have students write an answer to the On Your Own question on a separate sheet of paper. Encourage volunteers to share their responses with the class. Then collect student responses to monitor their comprehension, writing skills, and fluency.

Review the Purpose for Reading

Elicit responses to the Set a Purpose for Reading questions at the beginning of this reading. Remind students to relate their responses to the Big Question.

Teach & Apply

Comprehension

Have students work in pairs or small groups to write their responses.

ANSWERS
1. football
2. The modern game of soccer was developed in England in the 1800s.
3. Soccer is called the "simplest sport" because players only need a round ball and some space to play it.
4. The Women's World Cup of 1999 was exciting because a huge audience watched it, and it went into overtime and was won on a penalty kick.
5. While players in basketball, baseball, and tennis can use their hands, players in soccer can't.
6. The author seems to admire the Fugees because she talks about the hardships they overcame to play soccer.
7. **Possible response:** Baseball is my favorite sport. I like to root for my home team.
8. **Possible response:** In my opinion, there are three traits that make someone a winner: courage, determination, and a good team spirit.

Speaking Tip

Before students tell their partner about the article, ask them to practice reading their summaries aloud a few times. Tell students that the more they practice, the easier it will be for them to remember their ideas without looking so often at their notes.

 In Your Own Words

Read the directions aloud and explain that items in the first column refer to subheadings in the article. Remind students that summaries include only the most important ideas; details can be left out. Suggest that students revise their summaries after they compare their work with a partner.

Teaching Resources

- *Workbook*, p. 101
- CD-ROM/e-book, Comprehension, Extension
- *Reader's Companion Workbook*, pp. 82–86

COMPREHENSION Workbook Page 101

Right There
1. What do British people and almost everyone else call soccer?
2. When and where was the modern game of soccer developed?

Think and Search
3. Why is soccer called "the simplest sport"?
4. What elements made the Women's World Cup in 1999 so exciting?

Author and You
5. How is soccer different from baseball, or basketball, or tennis?
6. What is the author's attitude toward the Fugees? How can you tell?

On Your Own
7. What is your favorite sport? Why do you like to play or watch it?
8. In your opinion, what makes someone a winner? List three traits.

IN YOUR OWN WORDS

Writers of informational texts often use clues to help readers follow the main idea. Section headings, or subheadings, are helpful clues. Imagine that you are telling a partner about "Soccer: The World Sport." Use the subheadings to help you identify the main idea of each section. Complete the chart below to help you organize your ideas. Then share your summary with a classmate. See how they compare.

 Speaking TIP

Use notes and pictures to help you remember and explain the main ideas clearly.

Part of the Text	Summary of Main Ideas
Introduction (no subheading)	Soccer/Football is the most popular sport in the world.
The Simplest Sport	
A Little History	
A Big Boom	
Something Bigger Than Winning	
A Different Ending Every Time	

210

TESOL Standards

Goal 1, Standard 1—To use English to communicate in social settings: Students will use English to participate in social interactions.
Descriptors—Sharing and requesting information; Engaging in conversations.

Goal 1, Standard 2—To use English to communicate in social settings: Students will interact in, through, and with spoken and written English for personal expression and enjoyment.
Descriptors—Participating in popular culture.

DISCUSSION

Discuss in pairs or small groups.

1. What is the history of soccer?
2. What caused soccer to become the fastest-growing sport in the United States?
3. What does the expression "It's not whether you win or lose, it's how you play the game" mean to you?

Q **What do we learn through winning and losing?** Why do you think so many people all over the world enjoy watching sports? Do you think that we learn a lesson when we watch a game like soccer? If so, what is it that we learn?

Listening TIP

If you can't hear a classmate who is speaking, you may say, "Excuse me, could you speak louder, please?"

READ FOR FLUENCY

Reading with feeling helps make what you read more interesting. Work with a partner. Choose a paragraph from the reading. Read the paragraph. Ask each other how you felt after reading the paragraph. Did you feel happy or sad?

Take turns reading the paragraph aloud to each other with a tone of voice that represents how you felt when you read it the first time. Give each other feedback.

▲ Brazilian fans celebrate after a win during the 2002 World Cup.

EXTENSION

Workbook Page 101

"Soccer: The World Sport" provides a lot of information about soccer. Learn more about a member of the Fugees or about a famous soccer star. Choose a player. Use magazine stories, newspaper articles, and reliable web pages to find information. Copy and complete the following chart to organize your ideas. Share your findings with the class.

Player	Team	Country of Birth	Important Games	Outstanding Skills

211

Differentiated Instruction

Beginning	As students complete the Extension chart, help them use an internet search engine to find the information.
Early Intermediate	Ask students whether they prefer soccer or football. Ask them to give reasons for their choice.
Intermediate	Ask students to describe the rules of their favorite sport. Remind them that they can organize their descriptions with sequence words, such as *first*, *then*, and *next*.
Struggling Readers	Encourage students to find a magazine article about their favorite sport. Have them read the article and summarize it for the class.

STEP 2: Extend

Listening Tip

By politely asking someone to speak up, you are showing you value what they are saying.

(CRI) Discussion

Before students begin their discussion, decide whether they will work as a class, in small groups, or in pairs. Consider dividing up the questions so each group has a different topic. Set up class norms to make sure that all participants are heard and that ideas are challenged but not discarded. Explain that the purpose is to allow everyone a chance to be heard. Remind students of the new vocabulary they have learned.

ANSWERS

1. While first origins are unknown, ancient records point back to China, Japan, Greece, and Italy. The modern game developed in England with modern rules coming in 1863.
2. The U.S. Women's National Team winning the 1999 World Cup caused a surge in soccer's popularity in the U.S.
3. Possible answer: To me it means that the benefits of sports are what you get from playing rather than wins/losses.

Q **What do we learn through winning and losing? SAY:** *In what ways do winning and losing go beyond the final score of a game?*

STEP 3: Assess

Read for Fluency

Explain to students how tone affects the way readers understand a passage. Have pairs of students practice reading a sample paragraph.

Extension

Have students research a person whose career is related to soccer or the Fugees. Invite them to share their findings with the class.

STEP 1: Introduce

Remind students that verb tenses indicate when an action takes place.

STEP 2: Teach

Grammar and Writing

Present Perfect The present perfect is formed with the verb *have* plus the past participle. Write and discuss the examples below. Point out that one sentence uses an irregular verb, *be*, and the other uses a regular verb, *play*.

- The Fugees have been a team for four years.
- The Fugees have played soccer together since 2003.

STEP 3: Practice

Have students write the correct verb in each sentence and then ask volunteers to write their answers on the board.

ANSWERS

1. Soccer has become an extremely popular sport.
2. Several attempts to form soccer leagues have failed.
3. Soccer has attracted millions of players over time.
4. The United States has won the Women's World Cup.
5. Soccer has been popular in Europe for a long time.
6. Fans in the United States have begun to enjoy soccer.

Teaching Resources

- *Workbook*, pp. 102–103
- CD-ROM/e-book, Grammar, Writing
- *Transparencies*, Writing Model 36
- *Transparencies*, *Resources*, Graphic Organizer 8
- *Assessment*, Reading 1 Test, pp. 83–86

Grammar and Writing

GRAMMAR, USAGE, AND MECHANICS

Present Perfect

Use the present perfect to talk about actions that happened in the past but not at a specific time. Form the present perfect with *has* or *have* and the past participle. For regular verbs, the past participle ends in *-d* or *-ed*. Irregular verbs have irregular past participles.

have/has + past participle of regular verb		have work**ed**, has work**ed**
have/has + past participle of irregular verb		have **been**, has **been**

You can also use the present perfect for actions that started in the past and continue into the present (with *for* or *since*). Use it with *ever* when asking whether someone has done something "at any time in the past" or "in his or her entire life."

> FIFA **has governed** soccer <u>since</u> 1904.
> The team **has waited** <u>for</u> a long time to win the game.
> **Has** the team <u>ever</u> **won** a city championship?

Practice

Workbook Page 102

Work with a partner. Copy the sentences into your notebook. Complete the sentences using the present perfect form of the verb in parentheses. Then take turns reading the sentences aloud with a partner.

1. Soccer _____ (become) an extremely popular sport.
2. Several attempts to form soccer leagues _____ (fail).
3. Soccer _____ (attract) millions of players over time.
4. The United States _____ (win) the Women's World Cup.
5. Soccer _____ (be) popular in Europe for a long time.
6. Fans in the United States _____ (begin) to enjoy soccer.

212

TESOL Standards

Goal 2, Standard 1—To use English to achieve academically in all content areas: Students will use English to interact in the classroom.
Descriptors—Following oral and written directions, implicit and explicit; Elaborating and extending other people's ideas and words.

Goal 2, Standard 2—To use English to achieve academically in all content areas: Students will use English to obtain, process, construct, and provide subject matter information in spoken and written form.
Descriptors—Listening to, speaking, reading, and writing about subject matter information; Gathering information orally and in writing; Responding to the work of peers and others.

Goal 3, Standard 1—To use English in socially and culturally appropriate ways: Students will use the appropriate language variety, register, and genre according to audience, purpose, and setting.
Descriptors—Using a variety of writing styles appropriate for different audiences, purposes, and settings.

WRITING an EXPOSITORY PARAGRAPH

Write a Newspaper Article

Newspaper articles are a common type of expository writing. On this page, you'll use a graphic organizer like the one at the right to help you write a short newspaper article about a sports event or competition.

When you write an expository paragraph, you explain something about a person, place, event, or thing. You state the main idea about your topic in a topic sentence. You explain the main idea by giving clear supporting details. The supporting details should answer the 5Ws: *Who? Where? When? What? Why?*

Here is a model of a newspaper article. Notice that the writer presents the main idea and gives supporting details.

| Who? |
| Where? |
| When? |
| What? |
| Why? |

Anna Espínola

2006 World Cup

Over the past seventy years, the FIFA World Cup tournament has brought countries together, helping them forget their differences as they play soccer and compete to be the world champions. The 2006 Men's World Cup was held in Germany, from June 9 to July 9. Out of 198 countries, 32 countries qualified to compete in the Cup. To reach the final championship game, teams must first advance past the first round, the quarterfinals, and the semifinals. In 2006, the two finalists were France and Italy. It was a breathtaking game that remained a 0–0 tie after an hour and a half of play. When overtime ended, the teams were still tied. The teams then began a shootout of penalty kicks, the last possible way to determine the winner. In the end, Italy beat France 5–3 and the World Cup was theirs!

Practice

Workbook Page 103

Write a newspaper article about a sports event or some other competition or game that you found exciting. Copy a 5Ws chart like the one above into your notebook. Complete the chart, and use your answers to write a newspaper article. Be sure to use the present perfect and the simple past correctly when you explain events that happened in the past.

Writing Checklist

WORD CHOICE:
☑ I included specific details about each of the 5Ws.

CONVENTIONS:
☑ I used grammar and punctuation correctly.

213

STEP 1: Introduce

Tell students that expository passages, such as newspaper articles, are often used to report factual information.

STEP 2: Teach

Writing an Expository Paragraph

Write a Newspaper Article Tell students that newspaper articles are written for an audience that presumably is just being introduced to the topic under discussion, so the writer needs to include all the basic details. Explain that this is one reason the 5W chart is important: it helps the writer make sure he or she hasn't left anything out.

Model Writing Skill Have a volunteer read the first sentence of the model paragraph aloud. Then have students identify the details contained in that sentence. Write down their answers on the board, paraphrasing as necessary. Continue with the rest of the paragraph, with a different volunteer reading each sentence.

STEP 3: Assess

Have students evaluate their work, using the Writing Checklist.

Writing Checklist Note

Word Choice: Check that students address each of the 5Ws.

Conventions: Check students' grammar, focusing on their use of the present perfect and the simple past.

Accelerate Language Development

Usage of Present Perfect

Students may have difficulty deciding when to use the present perfect rather than the simple past. While many languages have at least one past tense, and most have several of them, other languages are not as strict about when to use them. Point out that English uses the simple past only for events that are over, and the present perfect for events that began in the past and may still continue. This distinction is not important in some languages such as German, for example, where the simple past and the present perfect can be used synonymously. Chinese does not have a past tense *per se*, but uses temporal adverbs instead. Japanese forms the past tense by adding endings to adjectives rather than verbs. Language learners from these backgrounds may need more practice to master the usage present perfect.

Teach

Objectives

Read the list of objectives in the What You Will Learn section. Tell students that this reading consists of a famous poem about baseball and two poems about the natural world. Have pairs of students restate the list of things they will learn.

The Big Question

Remind students that the Big Question is "What do we learn through winning and losing?" Initiate a discussion about loss and the role of literature in helping people deal with loss. Ask students whether they think we can learn from poetry or song lyrics. Point out the difference between the two different meanings of loss, and allow that to guide the discussion.

Build Background

Point out that the poem "Buffalo Dusk" is about the near extinction of the American bison, or buffalo. **SAY:** *Hundreds of thousands of buffalo lived on the American plains for thousands of years. Now there are only a few thousand left. During the 1800s, hunters nearly caused their extinction.* Discuss how this situation relates to the idea of loss.

STEP 2: Teach

Understanding the Genre: Poetry

A poem is a piece of writing that expresses ideas, experiences, and emotions. The lines of a poem are often short and sometimes end with the same sound.

Groups of these lines are called stanzas or verses. Often words in poems have a strong rhythm, or beat, and a regular pattern, like a song. Poets often choose words for the way they sound.

Teaching Resources

- CD-ROM/e-book, Literary Words
- Audio CD 4, track 6
- *Workbook*, p. 104

What You Will Learn

Reading
- Vocabulary building: *Literary terms, word study*
- Reading strategy: *Read for enjoyment*
- Text type: *Literature (poetry)*

Grammar, Usage, and Mechanics
Simple past: more irregular verbs

Writing
Write a response to literature

THE BIG QUESTION

What do we learn through winning and losing?
How do you feel when you lose a game? How is it different from the way you feel when you lose a person, animal, or thing? How could a poem or song help you remember someone or something you have lost?

What are some of your favorite poems and songs? Why are the words to these poems and songs so easy to remember? Are any of them about some kind of loss? Work with a partner. Take turns reciting a stanza, or group of lines, from a poem or song that you like.

BUILD BACKGROUND

In this section, you will read three poems: **"Casey at the Bat," "Swift Things Are Beautiful,"** and **"Buffalo Dusk."** Some poems tell a story. For example, "Casey at the Bat" is a narrative poem about a mighty baseball player named Casey. It is his turn to hit the ball. Will Casey hit the ball far, so his team wins the game? Or will he strike out? Some poems focus on an idea or an image,

but do not tell a story. "Swift Things Are Beautiful" describes things that are fast and things that are slow. "Buffalo Dusk" focuses on the disappearance of huge herds of buffaloes from the United States in the late 1880s.

▲ Once, a million buffaloes lived on the Great Plains of the United States. By the 1800s, only about a thousand were left.

214

🌐 TESOL Standards

Goal 2, Standard 2—To use English to achieve academically in all content areas: Students will use English to obtain, process, construct, and provide subject matter information in spoken and written form.
Descriptors—Demonstrating knowledge through application in a variety of contexts.

Goal 3, Standard 1—To use English in socially and culturally appropriate ways: Students will use the appropriate language variety, register, and genre according to audience, purpose, and setting.
Descriptors—Using a variety of writing styles appropriate for different audiences, purposes, and settings.

Goal 3, Standard 3—To use English in socially and culturally appropriate ways: Students will use appropriate learning strategies to extend their sociolinguistic and sociocultural competence.
Descriptors—Observing and modeling how others speak and behave in a particular situation or setting; Rehearsing variations of language use in different social and academic settings.

Learn Literary Words

Rhythm is the regular repeated pattern of sounds. The rhythm in a poem is like the beat in a piece of music. Read aloud the nursery rhyme below. What words did you stress? How many beats did you hear in each line?

Literary Words

rhythm
repetition
rhyme scheme

> Hickory Dickory Dock.
> The mouse ran up the clock.
> The clock struck one,
> The mouse ran down!
> Hickory Dickory Dock.

As you can see and hear in the nursery rhyme, repetition is another tool used in poems. Repetition involves repeating the same sound, words, or lines in a poem. Words that rhyme have the same ending sound but different beginning sounds. Many poems contain end-rhymes, or rhyming words at the ends of lines.

The rhyme scheme in a poem is the regular pattern of words that end with the same sound. To find the rhyme scheme, look at the end of every line in a poem. Then use the letters *a, b, c* to label the rhyme scheme. Read these lines from the first stanza of "Casey at the Bat." Notice how the rhyme scheme works and is labeled.

▲ This painting is called *Hickory Dickory Dock.*

The outlook wasn't brilliant for the Mudville nine that <u>day</u>;	a
The score stood four to two, with but one inning more to <u>play</u>,	a
And then when Cooney died at first, and Barrows did the <u>same</u>,	b
A sickly silence fell upon the patrons of the <u>game</u>.	b

Practice

Workbook Page 104

Work with a partner to create a rhyming poem in two stanzas. First, think of four pairs of rhyming words, such as *knee/free, light/night, won/fun, toe/slow.* Write the words in your notebook. Then take turns writing a line that ends with one of the rhyming words. Don't worry if the poem is a bit silly. Just play with the rhythm and rhymes. When you have completed your eight-line poem, share it with the class.

215

Vocabulary

Learn Literary Words Play the CD. Have students listen and repeat. If you are not using the CD, read the Literary Words aloud. **SAY:** *These are called literary words because in the discussion of literature they have a unique meaning. Read aloud the lines from "Hickory Dickory Dock."* Listen for the rhythm and rhyme of each line. Students should stress the final word of each line. There are three beats in the first, second, and fifth lines, and two beats in the third and fourth. Write down the following points on the board or on an overhead transparency:

- **rhythm:** a regular repeated pattern of sounds
- **repetition:** repeating the same sounds, words, or lines in a poem
- **rhyme scheme:** regular pattern of words that end with the same sound

STEP 3: Practice

Have students work with partners. Tell them to create a rhyming poem in two stanzas. Explain that a stanza is a group of lines in a repeated pattern forming part of a poem. Suggest that students begin by thinking of four pairs of rhyming words like those on page 215. Ask volunteers to write their poems on the board.

Differentiated Instruction

Beginning	Have students say two words that rhyme.
Early Intermediate	Direct students' attention to the lines from "Hickory Dickory Dock," above. Ask them to find the words that have repeated *-ck* sound. (Hickory, Dickory, Dock, clock, struck)
Intermediate	Have students write a few simple sentences that rhyme.
Standard English Learners (CRI)	Have students write a simple poem about winning and losing. Have them share their poem with the class.

Teach

STEP 1: Teach

CD4 T7–T8

 Vocabulary

Learn Academic Words Play the CD. Have students listen and repeat. If you are not using the CD, read the Academic Words aloud. **SAY:** *Look at the Academic Words chart. Note that it contains two parts: the definitions on the left and sentences containing the words on the right. Work with a partner to add another sentence using each word. Write the words, definitions, and sentences in your personal Word Book.*

STEP 2: Practice

Have students work with partners to complete the practice activity. **SAY:** *Take turns reading aloud the sentences. As you read each, think about how to use the Academic Word to complete that sentence. Write that sentence in your Word Book.*

ANSWERS

1. respond
2. sphere
3. structure
4. final
5. device
6. brief

Teaching Resources

- Audio CD 4, tracks 7–8
- *Workbook*, pp. 105–107
- CD-ROM/e-book, Academic Words, Word Study

Learn Academic Words

Study the red words and their meanings. You will find these words useful when talking and writing about literature. Write each word and its meaning in your notebook. After you read "Casey at the Bat," "Swift Things Are Beautiful," and "Buffalo Dusk," try to use these words to respond to the text.

Academic Words
brief
device
final
respond
sphere
structure

brief = continuing for a short time	➡	Some poems are **brief**, while others are long.
device = a way of achieving a particular purpose	➡	The use of rhyme is a poetic **device** that helps to create rhythm.
final = last in a series of actions, events, or parts of something	➡	The fans watched the **final** minutes of the game. They hoped for a last-minute goal.
respond = react to something that has been said or done	➡	When a team wins a game, fans **respond** with cheers. They jump up and yell.
sphere = something in the shape of a ball	➡	The planet Earth is a **sphere**. It has the same shape as a baseball.
structure = the way in which the parts of something connect with each other to form a whole	➡	"Casey at the Bat" has a definite **structure**. It is divided into thirteen four-line stanzas.

Practice Workbook Page 105

Write the sentences in your notebook. Choose a red word from the box above to complete each sentence. Then take turns reading the sentences aloud with a partner.

1. I didn't know how to _____ when the coach asked me to say yes or no.
2. A _____ is a good shape for a soccer ball because it is easy to kick.
3. All types of writing need some sort of _____ to tie the words together.
4. In the _____ inning of the game, the player hit a home run.
5. Creating suspense is a _____ that many writers use.
6. The chess game was very _____. It lasted for only ten minutes.

216

▲ A baseball is a sphere, but a football is not.

🌐 TESOL Standards

Goal 1, Standard 3—To use English to communicate in social settings: Students will use learning strategies to extend their communicative competence.
Descriptors—Comparing nonverbal and verbal cues.

Goal 2, Standard 2—To use English to achieve academically in all content areas: Students will use English to obtain, process, construct, and provide subject matter information in spoken and written form.
Descriptors—Representing information visually and interpreting information presented visually.

Goal 2, Standard 3—To use English to achieve academically in all content areas: Students will use appropriate learning strategies to construct and apply academic knowledge.
Descriptors—Imitating the behaviors of native English speakers to complete tasks successfully.

Word Study: Spelling Long Vowel Sound /ī/

In English, the long vowel sound /ī/ can be spelled in different ways. When you read "Casey at the Bat," you will read the words below.

vi-o-lence	qui-et	nine	pride	style	bright	died

Say each word with a partner. Notice the /ī/ sound and its spellings. Some of the words above contain one syllable; others contain two or three syllables. Notice that when the letter *i* comes at the end of a syllable as in the word *qui-et*, the *i* often stands for /ī/. Study the chart below for more examples.

i	i_e	y	igh	ie
mind	strike	try	fight	tie
tiny	five	shy	mighty	cried

Practice

Work with a partner. Copy the chart above into your notebook. Say a word from the chart, and ask your partner to spell it aloud. Then have your partner say the next word. Continue until you can spell all of the words correctly. Then work with your partner to spell the following words: *lightning, smile, kind, pie, fry*. Add them to the chart under the correct headings.

▲ A young man enjoys some quiet time with a good book.

READING STRATEGY   READ FOR ENJOYMENT

Sometimes you read for information. Other times you read for enjoyment. When you read for the fun of it, ask yourself these questions:

- What is enjoyable about the characters, setting, and illustrations?
- Which words help me create images in my mind?
- Which parts of the text do I like best? What makes these parts so enjoyable to read?

As you read "Casey at the Bat," "Swift Things Are Beautiful," and "Buffalo Dusk," ask yourself: "How do the poets make their poems fun, interesting, or exciting to read?"

217

Read

LITERATURE

POETRY

Set a purpose for reading What will happen when Casey comes up to bat? Is it better to be fast or slow? What happened to the buffaloes? Read the poems to find out what each one has to say about winning, beauty, power, and loss.

STEP 1: Introduce

Reading Summary

This reading includes three poems. The first is "Casey at the Bat," a poem known to many American school children for the past 100 years. The second poem is about fast and slow things, and the third is about disappearing buffalo.

The Big Question

As students read the poems, invite them to relate the Big Question to specific characters. Ask them what they think Casey learns about winning and losing. Have them consider what the Mudville spectators might learn and whether they might all learn the same thing. When they read the final poem, ask them what they can learn from it.

STEP 2: Teach

Set a Purpose for Reading

Remind students that sometimes we read just for our own enjoyment. Many people enjoy reading poetry or hearing it read aloud. The sounds of the words in a poem create appealing effects such as rhythm and rhyme. Compare a poem to a song, which also has rhythm and rhyme. As students read, ask them to listen for interesting effects created by the sounds of the words.

Preteaching Highlighted Words

In pairs, have students read aloud the highlighted words and their definitions. Answer any questions students have about the use of a word or its meaning before reading the spread.

CD4 T9–T11 Scaffolding:
Listen and Read

Have students read the text as you play the Audio CD. Pause the recording at the end of each page to answer questions students may have.

Teaching Resources

• *Resources*, Summaries, pp. 149–150
• Audio CD 4, tracks 9–11

CASEY AT THE BAT

A Ballad of the Republic, Sung in the Year 1888

The outlook wasn't brilliant for the Mudville nine that day;
The score stood four to two, with but one inning more to play,
And then when Cooney died at first, and Barrows did the same,
A sickly silence fell upon the patrons of the game.

A straggling few got up to go in deep despair. The rest
Clung to that hope which springs eternal in the human breast;
They thought, "If only Casey could but get a whack at that —
We'd put up even money now, with Casey at the bat."

But Flynn preceded Casey, as did also Jimmy Blake,
And the former was a lulu and the latter was a cake;
So upon that stricken multitude grim melancholy sat;
For there seemed but little chance of Casey's getting to the bat.

---

died, was "out"
patrons, spectators; fans
springs eternal, flows always
preceded, went before
lulu, person who is extremely stupid, bad, or
    embarrassing
cake, person who is easy to get out
melancholy, feeling of sadness

218

TESOL Standards

Goal 1, Standard 2—To use English to communicate in social settings: Students will interact in, through, and with spoken and written English for personal expression and enjoyment.
Descriptors—Expressing personal needs, feelings, and ideas.

Goal 2, Standard 3—To use English to achieve academically in all content areas: Students will use appropriate learning strategies to construct and apply academic knowledge.
Descriptors—Taking notes to record important information and aid one's own learning; Actively connecting new information to information previously learned.

But Flynn let drive a single, to the wonderment of all,
And Blake, the much despised, tore the cover off the ball;
And when the dust had lifted, and men saw what had occurred,
There was Jimmy safe at second and Flynn a-hugging third.

Then from 5,000 throats and more there rose a lusty yell;
It rumbled through the valley, it rattled in the dell;
It knocked upon the mountain and recoiled upon the flat,
For Casey, mighty Casey, was advancing to the bat.

dell, small valley with grass and trees

✔ LITERARY CHECK

*Is the **rhythm** of this poem regular or not? How many beats do you hear in each line?*

BEFORE YOU GO ON

1. What do Cooney and Barrows do when they come to bat?
2. Who are the two players who come to bat before Casey?

💡 **On Your Own**
Have you ever watched an exciting baseball game? What was it like?

219

✔ LITERARY CHECK

If students need help remembering the meaning of *rhythm*, have them go back to page 215. Students can determine the number of beats in each line of this poem by tapping out beats with their hands on the desk. Answer: The rhythm of this poem is regular. Each line has seven beats.

STEP 3: Monitor Progress

With students, continue reading and listening to the Audio CD. Pause the recording at the end of the page to monitor students' comprehension.

Before You Go On

Remind students that these questions will help them monitor their progress. Put students in pairs to answer the questions. Encourage them to share their answers with the class.

ANSWERS

1. Cooney and Barrows make outs at first base.
2. Flynn and Jimmy Blake are the two players who came to bat before Casey.

On Your Own Have students write an answer to the On Your Own question on a separate sheet of paper. Invite volunteers to read them aloud to the class.

Differentiated Instruction

Beginning	Ask students who the 5,000 fans in the crowd cheered for.
Early Intermediate	Ask students what Casey did when the second pitch was thrown.
Intermediate	Have students describe why Casey did not swing at the first two pitches thrown to him.
Special Needs	Have students slide their finger along each line of text in order to track text visually, and to see more than one word at a time, without being distracted by the next line.

STEP 4: Teach

Preteaching Highlighted Words

In pairs, have students read aloud the highlighted words and their definitions. Answer any questions students have about the use of a word or its meaning before reading the spread.

Across the Curriculum: Math

Although a baseball field is called a "diamond," it is mathematically a square. Each of the four sides is the same length, and each of the angles is 90°. The distance between each base is 90 feet.

Model the READING STRATEGY

Read for Enjoyment

Say: *This poem has been popular with American readers for the last century. What do you think makes it so popular? Do you think it's the subject matter? What about the fact that it tells a story? Is it the suspense, the humor, or the catchiness of the poem's rhythm and rhyme?* Have students discuss their ideas in pairs or small groups.

✔ LITERARY CHECK

Read the question in the Literary Check box aloud and have students refer back to the definition of *rhyme scheme* on page 215. Then reread the first stanza on page 220, and ask a volunteer to list the last word of each line on the board. (*place, face, hat, bat*). To determine the rhyme scheme, ask students which of these words rhyme. The first pair gets an *a*; the second a *b*. **Answer:** The rhyme scheme of this stanza is a, a, b, b.

There was ease in Casey's manner as he stepped into his place;
There was pride in Casey's bearing and a smile on Casey's face.
And when, responding to the cheers, he lightly doffed his hat,
No stranger in the crowd could doubt 'twas Casey at the bat.

Ten thousand eyes were on him as he rubbed his hands with dirt.
Five thousand tongues applauded when he wiped them on his shirt.
Then while the writhing pitcher ground the ball into his hip,
Defiance flashed in Casey's eye, a sneer curled Casey's lip.

And now the leather-covered sphere came hurtling through the air,
And Casey stood a-watching it in haughty grandeur there.
Close by the sturdy batsman the ball unheeded sped—
"That ain't my style," said Casey. "Strike one!" the umpire said.

From the benches, black with people, there went up a muffled roar,
Like the beating of the storm-waves on a stern and distant shore;
"Kill him! Kill the umpire!" shouted someone on the stand;
And it's likely they'd have killed him had not Casey raised his hand.

With a smile of Christian charity great Casey's visage shone;
He stilled the rising tumult; he bade the game go on;
He signaled to the pitcher, and once more the spheroid flew;
But Casey still ignored it, and the umpire said "Strike two!"

"Fraud!" cried the maddened thousands, and echo answered "Fraud!"
But one scornful look from Casey and the audience was awed.
They saw his face grow stern and cold, they saw his muscles strain,
And they knew that Casey wouldn't let that ball go by again.

---

bearing, way of moving, standing, or behaving
doffed, took off or tipped
writhing, angry; violently twisting
defiance, bold refusal to obey or give in
visage, face
tumult, noisy and excited situation, often caused by a large crowd

✔ LITERARY CHECK
What is the rhyme scheme of the first stanza on this page?

220

TESOL Standards

Goal 1, Standard 1—To use English to communicate in social settings: Students will use English to participate in social interactions.
Descriptors—Expressing needs, feelings, and ideas.

Goal 2, Standard 1—To use English to achieve academically in all content areas: Students will use English to interact in the classroom.
Descriptors—Requesting information and assistance.

The sneer has fled from Casey's lip, the teeth are clenched in hate;
He pounds with cruel violence his bat upon the plate.
And now the pitcher holds the ball, and now he lets it go,
And now the air is shattered by the force of Casey's blow.

Oh, somewhere in this favored land the sun is shining bright,
The band is playing somewhere, and somewhere hearts are light,
And somewhere men are laughing, and little children shout;
But there is no joy in Mudville—mighty Casey has struck out.

—*Ernest Lawrence Thayer*

---

clenched, held together tightly

ABOUT THE POET

Ernest Lawrence Thayer was an American poet who wrote during the 1880s and 1890s. Thayer began his writing career at Harvard, as editor of the school newspaper. He spent most of his career writing humorous pieces for the *San Francisco Examiner*, a paper owned by a fellow Harvard classmate, William Randolph Hearst. "Casey at the Bat" was originally written for the newspaper. However, it didn't become popular until months after it was written, when it was recited on Broadway in front of players from professional baseball teams.

BEFORE YOU GO ON

1. What does Casey do right after he comes to bat?

2. What does the crowd yell at the umpire?

On Your Own
How do you feel about Casey? Is he mighty or not?

221

Study Skills: Internet

For a long time, people weren't sure who wrote "Casey at the Bat." Students can use the Internet for research on the interesting story of Ernest Lawrence Thayer and the writing of "Casey at the Bat."

- Use a search engine to do a key word search on "Ernest Lawrence Thayer" and "Casey at the Bat."

- In the resulting display of links, look for URLs from reliable sources like universities, newspapers, magazines, and television channels.

- Ask students to analyze these sources of information and try to identify any misleading information.

STEP 5: Monitor Progress

Ask students to check what they have understood in the reading. If you are using the Audio CD, pause the recording.

Before You Go On

Remind students that these questions will help them monitor their progress. Put students in pairs to answer the questions. Encourage them to share their answers with the class.

ANSWERS

1. Right after Casey comes to the bat, he takes off his hat.
2. The crowd yells "Fraud!" at the umpire.

On Your Own Have students work in pairs to write an answer to the On Your Own question. Invite volunteers to read their answer aloud.

STEP 6: Teach

Preteaching Highlighted Words

In pairs, have students read aloud the highlighted words and their definitions. Answer any questions students have about the use of a word or its meaning before reading the spread.

Across the Curriculum:
Physics

The "things" that exemplify the ideas of swiftness and slowness in the poem have been chosen to create an emotional impact. Swiftness and slowness are defined in poetic terms—both to be enjoyed for their own particular type of beauty. In physics, however, swiftness, or speed, is defined by a formula that can be measured. Speed equals the change in distance divided by the change in time.

Model the
READING STRATEGY

Read for Enjoyment

Say: *The reading strategy is Read for Enjoyment. When some detail or idea in a poem or story strikes us as true or interesting, it is often because the idea relates to something we know or have experienced. It's almost as though the author has expressed our thoughts in his or her well chosen words. What things in Elizabeth Coatsworth's poem have you seen before? Does the poem remind you of anything in your own life? Do you think swift and slow things are beautiful? What would you add to the list of beautiful swift and slow things?*

Swift Things Are Beautiful

Swift things are beautiful:
Swallows and deer,
And lightning that falls
Bright-veined and clear,
Rivers and meteors,
Wind in the wheat,
The strong-withered horse,
The runner's sure feet.

And slow things are beautiful:
The closing of day,
The pause of the wave
That curves downward to spray,
The ember that crumbles,
The opening flower,
And the ox that moves on
In the quiet of power.
　　　　　　　　—Elizabeth Coatsworth

swift, very fast
meteors, pieces of rock or metal that make a bright line in the night sky when they fall through Earth's atmosphere
withered, referring to the withers, or ridge between a horse's shoulders, the highest part of a horse's back
sure, steady; able to walk or run without sliding or falling
ember, piece of wood or coal that stays red and very hot after a fire stops burning
ox, large bull or cow

ABOUT THE POET

Elizabeth Coatsworth was born in Buffalo, New York, in 1893. As a young child, she lived for a time in Europe and Egypt. She began writing when she was twenty years old and continued until she was in her eighties. Coatsworth wrote over ninety books for children and adults, including poetry, novels, and nonfiction. Her 1930 book *The Cat Who Went to Heaven* won the Newbery Medal.

222

🌐 TESOL Standards

Goal 1, Standard 3—To use English to communicate in social settings: Students will use learning strategies to extend their communicative competence.
Descriptors—Using the primary language to ask for clarification; Using context to construct meaning.

Buffalo Dusk

The buffaloes are gone.
And those who saw the buffaloes are gone.
Those who saw the buffaloes by thousands and how they
    pawed the prairie sod into dust with their great hoofs,
    their great heads down pawing on in a great pageant
    of dusk,
Those who saw the buffaloes are gone.
And the buffaloes are gone.

—*Carl Sandburg*

---

prairie sod, grass that covers a large, wide-open space
pageant, public show or display
dusk, time just before it gets dark

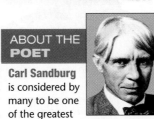

ABOUT THE POET

Carl Sandburg is considered by many to be one of the greatest American writers. Although he is best known for his poetry, Sandburg also wrote nonfiction and folklore. Sandburg won the Pulitzer Prize twice: first in 1926 for a biography titled *Abraham Lincoln: The Prairie Years* and later in 1951 for *The Complete Poems of Carl Sandburg*.

BEFORE YOU GO ON

1. What slow animal is described in the poem on page 222?

2. What do the buffaloes do at dusk in the poem on page 223?

☀ **On Your Own**
Which of the animals in these two poems have you seen up close? Where did you see them?

223

Study Skills: Maps

Point out to students that maps can organize any information that has geographical relevance. For instance, if students were curious about where the buffalo used to live, they could search in the library or online for a map that shows the historical range of the North American Bison.

STEP 7: Monitor Progress

Ask students to check what they have understood in the reading.

Before You Go On

Remind students that these questions will help them monitor their progress. Put students in pairs to answer the questions. Encourage them to share their answers with the class.

ANSWERS

1. An ox is the slow animal described on page 222.
2. In the poem on page 223, buffaloes paw the prairie sod at dusk.

On Your Own Have students write an answer to the On Your Own question on a separate sheet of paper. Encourage volunteers to share their responses with the class. Then collect student responses to monitor their comprehension, writing skills, and fluency.

✔ **LITERARY CHECK**

Ask partners to reread "Buffalo Dusk" together to find the repeated word *gone* and to decide how it makes them feel. If students need to review the meaning of *repetition*, refer them back to page 215. Answer: Possible response: The repetition of the word *gone* makes me feel very sad.

Review the Purpose for Reading

Elicit responses to the Set a Purpose for Reading questions at the beginning of this reading. Remind students to relate their responses to the Big Question.

Teach & Apply

STEP 1: Introduce

Speaking Tip

Remind students that the more relaxed and comfortable they are, the more expressive and confident their reading will be.

Dramatic Reading

Memorizing a poem gives students the opportunity to understand the emotional impact of the poem's cadence, rhythm, and content much better than simply reading it or listening to it. Encourage students to memorize the portion of poem that they feel most strongly about and to try to allow that emotion to enhance their reading.

STEP 2: Practice

Comprehension

Have students answer the questions individually or in pairs.

ANSWERS

1. In "Casey at the Bat," the score is 4 to 2 when Casey comes to bat.
2. Swallows, deer, lightning, rivers, meteors, wind, a horse, and a runner are swift things that are mentioned in "Swift Things Are Beautiful."
3. In "Casey at the Bat," Flynn hits a single. Jimmy Blake hits a double.
4. "Casey at the Bat" is humorous; "Swift Things" is serious and thoughtful; "Buffalo Dusk" is sad.
5. **Possible response:** Carl Sandburg chose to write about buffaloes because they are almost extinct.
6. **Possible response:** Thayer calls Casey "mighty" because he thinks Casey is a strong athlete.
7. Answers will vary.
8. Answers will vary.

Teaching Resources

- *Workbook*, p. 108
- CD-ROM/e-book, Comprehension, Response to Literature

READING 2 — Review and Practice

DRAMATIC READING

Work in small groups to reread, discuss, and interpret "Casey at the Bat," "Swift Things Are Beautiful," and "Buffalo Dusk." Describe what you visualize as you read each poem line by line. How do the authors use rhyme and rhythm? What images do the poems create in your mind? Then with the rest of the class, read the poems aloud.

One of the best ways to understand a poem is to memorize it, or learn it by heart. Start by saying two lines of the poem you like best. Then memorize the next two lines. Keep going as far into the poem as you can. The part you memorize will be yours forever.

> **Speaking TIP**
>
> Have fun. The more you enjoy reading the poems aloud, the more your classmates will enjoy the poems, too.

COMPREHENSION Workbook Page 108

Right There

1. In "Casey at the Bat," what is the score in the baseball game when Casey comes to bat?
2. What swift things are mentioned in "Swift Things Are Beautiful"?

Think and Search

3. In "Casey at the Bat," what happens when Flynn comes to bat? What happens when Jimmy Blake comes to bat?
4. In what ways are the moods of each of the three poems different? Which one contains humor and suspense? Which one expresses a serious and thoughtful mood? Which one expresses sadness?

Author and You

5. Why do you think that Carl Sandburg chose to write about buffaloes in "Buffalo Dusk"?
6. Why do you think that Ernest Lawrence Thayer chose to write about a baseball player who strikes out? Why does he call Casey "mighty"?

On Your Own

7. Which fast-moving things do you think are beautiful? Explain.
8. What animal would you like to write a poem about? What three things about that animal would you include in your poem?

224

TESOL Standards

Goal 1, Standard 1—To use English to communicate in social settings: Students will use English to participate in social interactions.
Descriptors—Using nonverbal communication in social interactions; Conducting transactions.

Goal 1, Standard 3—To use English to communicate in social settings: Students will use learning strategies to extend their communicative competence.
Descriptors—Selecting different media to help understand language.

Goal 2, Standard 3—To use English to achieve academically in all content areas: Students will use appropriate learning strategies to construct and apply academic knowledge.
Descriptors—Determining and establishing the conditions that help one become an effective learner (e.g., when, where, how to study); Recognizing the need for and seeking assistance appropriately from others (e.g., teachers, peers, specialists, community members); Knowing when to use native language resources (human and material) to promote understanding.

Discuss in pairs or small groups.

1. "Casey at the Bat" was written in 1888. Why do you think "Casey at the Bat" is still a popular poem?

2. If you were writing a poem about slow things that are beautiful, what five things would you include in your poem?

Q What do we learn through winning and losing? What did you learn about winning and losing from each of the three poems? Which poem taught you the most? Why?

 Listening TIP

Evaluate what your classmates say and how they say it. Often a speaker's manner and body language can be more or less persuasive than the content of what the person is saying.

RESPONSE TO LITERATURE

Workbook Page 108

"Swift Things Are Beautiful" describes both swift and slow things. Write a short poem of your own in which you describe two things that are swift and two things that are slow. Use a graphic organizer like the one below to list your ideas. Share your poem with a partner.

Swift Things	Why They Are Beautiful	Slow Things	Why They Are Beautiful

◄ Cheetahs are very swift.

225

Differentiated Instruction

Beginning	Have students name a swift animal that they know of, besides the cheetah on page 225.
Early Intermediate	Ask students what swift animals the poet talks about in "Swift Things Are Beautiful."
Intermediate	Have students describe a swift animal.
Struggling Readers	Have students write their own comprehension questions for "Swift Things Are Beautiful." Then have them work in pairs to answer the questions.

STEP 3: Extend

Listening Tip

Point out to students that speakers who are sure of themselves and their topic will look and sound persuasive and confident. Discuss what a confident speaker looks like (good posture, clear voice, fluent phrasing). Explain that paying close attention to a speaker's voice and body language can give listeners clues as to the speaker's comfort with his or her topic.

CRI Discussion

Before students begin their discussion, decide whether they will work as a class, in small groups, or in pairs. Consider dividing up the questions so each group has a different topic. Set up class norms to make sure that all participants are heard and that ideas are challenged but not discarded. Explain that the purpose is to allow everyone a chance to be heard. Remind students of the new vocabulary they have learned

Q What do we learn through winning and losing? Guide students to an understanding of how the Big Question relates to each poem. For "Casey at the Bat," students might discuss how expectations of success can be disappointed. For "Swift Things Are Beautiful," students might discuss how two opposites can both have merit. For "Buffalo Dawn," students might discuss what the loss of the buffalo can teach us about wildlife management for the future.

STEP 4: Assess

Response to Literature

Brainstorm with students to list swift and slow things. Write students' ideas on the board to create a master list for them to use as they write their poems. Suggest that students scan the master list for rhymes among the names of swift and slow things.

STEP 1: Introduce

Many commonly used verbs have irregular forms in the simple past which need to be memorized.

STEP 2: Teach

Grammar and Writing

Simple Past: More Irregular Verbs The simple past for regular verbs is formed by adding *-ed* to the base. Many verbs are irregular. **SAY:** *Many English verbs are irregular in the simple past. Although some of these verbs follow a pattern, which helps when memorizing them, others do not. Let's read the verbs in the table on page 226 together.* Ask volunteers to create original sentences with selected words.

STEP 3: Practice

Have students work with partners to complete the sentences in the activity. Suggest that partners take turns reading the sentences aloud.

ANSWERS

1. threw
2. thought
3. shook
4. knew
5. sang
6. wrote

Teaching Resources

- *Workbook*, pp. 109–110
- CD-ROM/e-book, Grammar, Writing
- *Transparencies*, Writing Model 37
- *Transparencies, Resources*, Graphic Organizer 1
- *Assessment*, Reading 2 Test, pp. 87–90

GRAMMAR, USAGE, AND MECHANICS

Simple Past: More Irregular Verbs

Remember to use the simple past to talk about completed actions or conditions that happened at a specific time in the past. Many common verbs in English are irregular. They do not follow regular rules. Some are formed in surprising ways.

The only way to learn the simple past of irregular verbs is to memorize them. However, there are "groupings" that can be helpful in memorizing irregular verbs. Study the examples in the chart below. Some are from "Casey at the Bat."

Base Form	Simple Past		Base Form	Simple Past
know throw	knew threw		sleep keep	slept kept
come become overcome	came became overcame		ring sing begin	rang sang began
bring think	brought thought		shake take	shook took
stand understand	stood understood		wake break	woke broke
let put hit	let put hit		rise ride write	rose rode wrote

Practice **Workbook Page 109**

Work with a partner. Copy these sentences into your notebook. Then fill in the blanks with the simple past of the verb in parentheses.

1. The pitcher _____ the ball to Casey. (throw)
2. Flynn _____ he could hit the ball. (think)
3. Jimmy's hand _____ when he held the bat. (shake)
4. Everyone _____ that Casey wanted to hit the ball. (know)
5. No one in Mudville _____ that night. (sing)
6. A reporter _____ an article about the big game. (write)

226

 TESOL Standards

Goal 2, Standard 1—To use English to achieve academically in all content areas: Students will use English to interact in the classroom.
Descriptors—Following oral and written directions, implicit and explicit.

Goal 2, Standard 2—To use English to achieve academically in all content areas: Students will use English to obtain, process, construct, and provide subject matter information in spoken and written form.
Descriptors—Gathering information orally and in writing; Representing information visually and interpreting information presented visually; Demonstrating knowledge through application in a variety of contexts.

Goal 2, Standard 3—To use English to achieve academically in all content areas: Students will use appropriate learning strategies to construct and apply academic knowledge.
Descriptors—Evaluating one's own success in a completed learning task.

WRITING AN EXPOSITORY PARAGRAPH

Write a Response to Literature

On this page, you'll write an expository paragraph that explains your response to one of the poems you just read. You'll use a graphic organizer like the one at the right to gather examples and details.

In a response, you give your ideas and opinions about the meaning of a story, poem, or other type of literature. You use examples and other details from the text to support your response. In addition, you show your understanding of the text and give your thoughts and feelings about it.

Here is a model of a response to a poem. Notice how the writer explains his interpretation of and reaction to the poem.

> Andrew C. Dubin
>
> "Buffalo Dusk"
>
> "Buffalo Dusk," by Carl Sandburg, is a peaceful, yet very upsetting poem. It is peaceful because Sandburg talks about buffaloes and how they once lived and roamed free on the prairies. He also mentions "those who saw the buffaloes." These are the Native Americans, who also lived freely. The poem is upsetting because Sandburg tells how both the buffaloes and the Native Americans are gone. Reading this makes me angry and upset. The buffaloes were hunted so much, they nearly died out. Without the buffaloes, the Native Americans had no source of food or clothing and began to disappear as well. Some Native Americans and buffaloes did survive, but far fewer of either are alive today compared to 200 years ago. For this reason, the poem is very powerful and also very sad.

Practice Workbook Page 110

Write a response to "Casey at the Bat" that explains what the poem is about and describes the impact it had on you and why. Include your ideas, opinions, and feelings. Provide reasons and examples to support your opinions. Use a word web to gather examples and details from the poem. Be sure to form the simple past of irregular verbs correctly.

Writing Checklist

IDEAS:
- ☑ I explained my reaction to the poem by providing good examples from the text.

VOICE:
- ☑ My response clearly states my point of view.

227

Accelerate Language Development

Were versus *We're* and *Where*

Some forms of the simple past of *be* may create difficulties for English learners. *Were* is often confused with *we're* and *where*. Help your students distinguish the three words by pointing to the slight difference in pronunciation between the shortened first person plural simple present form *we're* and the simple past form *were*. Mention that *we were* cannot be shortened to *we're*. Explain that *where* is not a verb form, but a question pronoun. Write sentences on the board, at least one with a blank for *we're*, one with a blank for *were*, and one with a blank for *where*. Ask for volunteers to fill in the blanks.

Teach

STEP 1: Introduce

Objectives

Read aloud the list of objectives in the What You Will Learn section. Tell students that they will be reading a fable called "The Hare and the Tortoise," an ancient story about winning and losing. Have students work in pairs to restate the list of things they will learn.

The Big Question

Remind students that the Big Question is "What do we learn through winning and losing?" Point out that "The Grasshopper and the Ant" is an example of a fable. Read the story aloud. **SAY:** *Who is the winner in the story? Who is the loser? What is the moral, or message, of the story?* (It is best to prepare for the future in the present.) Ask students if they know of any similar stories from their own cultures.

Build Background

"The Hare and the Tortoise" was written in the sixth century B.C.E. Have students look at the road signs on page 228. Ask what kind of lesson they think a hare and a tortoise can teach us?

STEP 2: Teach

Understanding the Genre:
Fable and Myth

A fable is a brief story, often with animal characters, that teaches a moral. The moral is usually stated at the end of the fable. Many cultures have created myths to explain natural events or the actions of gods and heroes. The myths were passed as part of a culture's spoken tradition.

Teaching Resources

- CD-ROM/e-book, Literary Words
- Audio CD 4, track 12
- *Workbook*, p. 111

READING 3 — Prepare to Read

What You Will Learn

Reading
- Vocabulary building: *Literary terms, word study*
- Reading strategy: *Identify author's purpose*
- Text type: *Literature (fable and myth)*

Grammar, Usage, and Mechanics
Adverbs with *-ly*

Writing
Write to compare and contrast

THE BIG QUESTION

What do we learn through winning and losing? What can ancient stories teach us about winning and losing? Every culture has stories that teach a lesson. Many of these stories have animal characters that talk, think, and act as if they were human. You may know the story "The Grasshopper and the Ant." Who is the winner in this story?

> All summer long, Grasshopper relaxed, chirping and singing all day. Ant went by carrying an ear of corn to her nest. "Why work so hard?" Grasshopper said to Ant. "It's summer. Come and relax with me." "I can't," Ant replied. "I'm preparing my nest for winter." Grasshopper laughed and began singing again. "Why worry about winter? We have plenty to eat." When winter came, Grasshopper had nothing to eat and was dying of hunger. He watched the ants eating the food they had gathered in summer. Then Grasshopper realized: It is best to prepare for the future in the present.

Work with a partner. Discuss stories you know that teach a lesson or have animal characters that act like human beings. Compare and contrast them.

BUILD BACKGROUND

Almost every culture in the world has fables and myths. These stories are traditionally passed down from one generation to the next. They are wonderful to listen to or read. They often contain wise messages and advice.

"The Hare and the Tortoise" is a fable from ancient Greece about a race between two animals. The main characters are very different from each other. Their character traits lead one to victory and the other to defeat.

"Orpheus and Eurydice" is a myth that is also from ancient Greece. Like many myths, it tells a story and explains how something in nature came into existence.

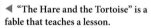

228

◄ "The Hare and the Tortoise" is a fable that teaches a lesson.

TESOL Standards

Goal 1, Standard 3—To use English to communicate in social settings: Students will use learning strategies to extend their communicative competence.
Descriptors—Selecting different media to help understand language; Using context to construct meaning.

Goal 2, Standard 3—To use English to achieve academically in all content areas: Students will use appropriate learning strategies to construct and apply academic knowledge.
Descriptors—Focusing attention selectively; Applying basic reading comprehension skills such as skimming, scanning, previewing, and reviewing text; Using context to construct meaning.

Learn Literary Words

A **fable** is a short story that teaches a lesson called a **moral**. The moral is sometimes stated at the end of the fable in a short sentence. At other times, the moral is implied. You, the reader, must figure it out yourself. You may have heard the word *proverb*. The morals at the ends of fables are like proverbs, or short statements of advice. Here are the titles of two other fables and the morals they teach.

Fable	Moral
"The Lion and the Mouse"	A little friend can be a big help.
"The Wolf in Sheep's Clothing"	Don't be fooled by outward appearances.

As you learned earlier, animal characters in a fable talk and act like human beings. When writers create animal characters that have human traits, this is called **personification**. Most fables, such as the one you are about to read, contain examples of personification.

A **myth** is a story from long ago that has been passed on by word of mouth. Myths often try to explain cultural beliefs and why certain things occur in the natural world, such as thunder and lightning. Many myths also tell stories about the actions of gods and heroes.

Place	Myth	What It Explains
Greece	"Poseidon, the God of the Sea"	earthquakes, shipwrecks, storms
Hawaii	"Pele, Goddess of Fire"	fire and volcanoes

Literary Words

- fable
- moral
- personification
- myth

▲ The little mouse was a big help to the trapped lion.

Practice
Workbook Page 111

Work with a partner to discuss these morals and proverbs. Explain what each one means to you. Write your explanations in your notebook.

1. Absence makes the heart grow fonder.
2. Look before you leap.
3. Evil wishes, like chickens, come home to roost.
4. Little by little does the trick.

229

Vocabulary

Learn Literary Words Play the CD. Have students listen and repeat. If you are not using the CD, read the Literary Words aloud. Ask students what comes to mind when they hear each word. Write down student responses on the board. Then write the following key elements for *fable, moral, personification,* and *myth*.

- **fable:** a short story that teaches a lesson
- **moral:** a lesson taught in a fable
- **personification:** giving human traits to animals or things
- **myth:** a story from long ago that has been passed on by word of mouth

Provide examples of a fable, a moral, personification, and myth, and ask students to contribute any examples they know.

STEP 3: Practice

Have students work with partners. Tell them to take turns reading and paraphrasing the morals and proverbs in the activity.

ANSWERS
Possible responses:
1. Not having someone or something makes you appreciate it more.
2. Think carefully before making a decision.
3. Wishing bad things for others will lead to bad things happening to you.
4. If you do things in small steps you can eventually finish a task.

Differentiated Instruction

Beginning	Ask students what the purpose of a fable is, and what the purpose of a myth is.
Early Intermediate	Have students find examples of personification in "The Grasshopper and the Ant" on page 228.
Intermediate	Have students write two example sentences that demonstrate the literary element, personification.
Standard English Learners (CRI)	Ask students to share a myth or fable that they know with the class.

Teach

STEP 1: Teach

CD4 T13–T14

 Vocabulary

Learn Academic Words Play the CD. Have students listen and repeat. If you are not using the CD, read the Academic Words aloud.
SAY: *Look at the Academic Words chart. The definitions are on the left. On the right, each word is used in a sentence. Write each word, its definition, and the sentence in your Word Books. Then work with a partner to write a new sentence using each Academic Word.*

STEP 2: Practice

Write the following question on the board and underline the words as shown: *What would you say if you <u>were asked to define what a fable is</u>?* **SAY:** *When you are asked a question, try to include words from the question in your answer. Look at the question on the board.*
Write this example on the board: *If I <u>were asked to define a fable</u>, I would say it's a short story with a moral lesson.* Be sure to underline the words as shown so students clearly see the connection.

ANSWERS

Possible responses:
1. If I were asked to define a fable, I would say it is a short story with a moral lesson.
2. I would ask my English teacher to instruct me on how to write a short story.
3. If I were running in a race, my objective would be to do my best.
4. I like a humorous writing style.

Teaching Resources

- Audio CD 4, tracks 13–14
- *Workbook*, pp. 112–114
- CD-ROM/e-book, Academic Words, Word Study

T230

Learn Academic Words

Study the red words and their meanings. You will find these words useful when talking and writing about literature. Write each word and its meaning in your notebook. After you read "The Hare and the Tortoise" and "Orpheus and Eurydice," try to use these words to respond to the text.

Academic Words

define
instruct
objective
style

define = show or describe what something is or means	One way to **define** a word is to use a synonym, another word that has the same meaning.
instruct = teach someone or show him or her how to do something	The teacher planned to **instruct** the class on how to write a fable. His outline helped him teach the lesson.
objective = something that you are working hard to achieve	The author's **objective** was to entertain. She wanted readers to enjoy the story.
style = a way of doing, making, or painting something that is typical of a particular period	The artist who drew pictures for the fable had a good **style**. He drew funny, colorful characters.

Practice **Workbook Page 112**

Work with a partner to answer the questions. Try to include the red word in your answer. Write the sentences in your notebook.

1. What would you say if you were asked to **define** what a fable is?
2. Who would you ask to **instruct** you in how to write a short story?
3. What would be your **objective** if you were running in a race?
4. What kind of writing **style** do you like best?

This woman is dressed in the style of the Hawaiian ◀ goddess Pele.

230

 TESOL Standards

Goal 1, Standard 3—To use English to communicate in social settings: Students will use learning strategies to extend their communicative competence.
Descriptors—Listening to and imitating how others use English; Exploring alternative ways of saying things.

Goal 2, Standard 1—To use English to achieve academically in all content areas: Students will use English to interact in the classroom.
Descriptors—Participating in full-class, group, and pair discussions; Negotiating and managing interaction to accomplish tasks.

Goal 3, Standard 1—To use English in socially and culturally appropriate ways: Students will use the appropriate language variety, register, and genre according to audience, purpose, and setting.
Descriptors—Recognizing and using Standard English and vernacular dialects appropriately.

Word Study: Spellings for *r*-Controlled Vowels

When a vowel is followed by an *r*, the vowel stands for a special sound, called an *r*-controlled vowel. The letters *er, ir,* and *ur* all stand for the same *r*-controlled vowel sound. It is the /ər/ sound you hear in *her, bird,* and *hurt.* The letters *ar* stand for the *r*-controlled vowel sound you hear in *car.* The letters *or* stand for the *r*-controlled vowel sound you hear in *for.*

▲ This bird is perching on a fern.

/är/ as in car	/ər/ as in her	/ər/ as in bird	/ôr/ as in for	/ər/ as in hurt
start	fern	third	horse	turn
dark	certain	first	tortoise	burst

Practice Workbook Page 113

Work with a partner. Copy the chart above into your notebook. Sort the words from the box below by their sound-spelling and add them to the chart. Then add other words with *r*-controlled vowels.

artist	corner	curve	nerve	short
circle	curled	large	person	thirst

READING STRATEGY   IDENTIFY AUTHOR'S PURPOSE

Identifying an author's purpose (or reason for writing) can make you a better reader because you understand *why* the author wrote the text. Authors can choose to write to inform, to entertain, or to persuade. Sometimes an author has more than one purpose for writing. To identify an author's purpose, ask yourself these questions:

- Is this entertaining? Am I enjoying reading it?
- Am I learning new information? Is something being explained?
- Is the author trying to persuade me about something?

As you read "The Hare and the Tortoise" and "Orpheus and Eurydice," identify the author's purpose.

 Workbook Page 114

231

Read

Reading Summary

The fable "The Hare and the Tortoise" explores the question, *What is more important when running a race, speed or endurance?* The myth "Orpheus and Eurydice" is about a husband who descends to the Underworld to try to find his wife.

 **The Big Question**

Remind students that the Big Question is "What do we learn through winning and losing?" Tell them to think about this question as they read the fable. **SAY:** *The text you are going to read is about speed versus slow and steady. Which is better? Why?*

STEP 2: Teach

Set a Purpose for Reading

Tell students to copy the purpose for reading into their notebooks and to keep it in mind as they read. Explain that they will have to present details that support their answer(s) to the question(s) and to explain how the reading relates to the Big Question.

Preteaching Highlighted Words

In pairs, have students read aloud the highlighted words and their definitions. Answer any questions students have about the use of a word or its meaning before reading the spread.

CD4 T15–T16 **Scaffolding: Listen and Read**

Have students listen to the Audio CD as they read the selection to themselves. Then have student pairs alternate reading paragraphs from the selection aloud.

Teaching Resources

- *Resources, Summaries,* pp. 151–152
- Audio CD 4, tracks 15–16

READING 3

LITERATURE

FABLE AND MYTH

Set a purpose for reading Is speed the most important thing in a race? How does the night sky remind us of Orpheus and his loss? Read the classic fable and myth to answer these questions.

The Hare and the Tortoise

Aesop

232

TESOL Standards

Goal 1, Standard 1—To use English to communicate in social settings: Students will use English to participate in social interactions.
Descriptors—Sharing and requesting information; Expressing needs, feelings, and ideas.

Goal 2, Standard 1—To use English to achieve academically in all content areas: Students will use English to interact in the classroom.
Descriptors—Asking and answering questions; Requesting information and assistance.

Goal 2, Standard 2—To use English to achieve academically in all content areas: Students will use English to obtain, process, construct, and provide subject matter information in spoken and written form.
Descriptors—Selecting, connecting, and explaining information; Analyzing, synthesizing, and inferring from information.

On a hot, sunny day, Hare saw Tortoise plodding along on the road. Hare teased Tortoise because she was walking so slowly.

Tortoise laughed. "You can tease me if you like, but I bet I can get to the end of the field before you can. Do you want to race?"

Hare agreed, thinking that he could easily win. He ran off. Tortoise plodded steadily after him.

Before long, Hare began to feel hot and tired. "I'll take a short nap," he thought. "If Tortoise passes me, I can catch up to her." Hare lay down and fell asleep.

Tortoise plodded on steadily, one foot after another.

The day was hot. Hare slept and slept in the heat. He slept for a longer time than he wanted. And Tortoise plodded on, slowly and steadily.

Finally, Hare woke up. He had slept longer than he wanted, but he still felt confident that he could reach the finish line before Tortoise.

He looked around. Tortoise was nowhere in sight. "Ha! Tortoise isn't even here yet!" he thought.

Hare started to run again. He leaped easily over roots and rocks. As he ran around the last corner and stopped to rest, he was amazed to see Tortoise, still plodding steadily on, one foot after another, nearer and nearer the finish line.

Now Hare ran as fast as he could. He almost flew! But it was too late. He threw himself over the finish line, but Tortoise was there first.

"So what do you say?" asked Tortoise. But Hare was too tired to answer.

MORAL: Slow and steady wins the race.

---

plodding, walking slowly
teased, made jokes and laughed at in order to embarrass
steadily, moving in a continuous, gradual way
nap, short sleep
catch up to, come from behind and reach by going fast
confident, sure
finish line, line at which a race ends

ABOUT THE **AUTHOR**

Aesop was a slave in ancient Greece. He was a great storyteller. In many of his fables, Aesop uses personification to teach people lessons. Some historians believe that Aesop gained his freedom because of his stories. His fables are still popular today.

✔ **LITERARY CHECK**
*How might the **moral** of this fable apply to other areas of life besides a race?*

BEFORE YOU GO ON

1. What kind of character is Hare? Describe Hare's traits.

2. What is Tortoise like? How is she different from Hare?

💡**On Your Own**
Who did you want to win the race? Why?

233

Study Skills: Thesaurus

Tell students that using a thesaurus is a great way to improve their vocabulary and to enhance their writing. Pair students and have them find synonyms for *plodding*.

✔ **LITERARY CHECK**

SAY: *Do you think you can apply the moral of this fable to your school work? What about other goals you have?* **Answer:** The moral can apply to areas in our lives in which we are tempted to hurry rather than taking our time and doing a good job.

STEP 3: Monitor Progress

Continue reading and listening to the text, pausing at the end of the page. Invite students to ask questions.

Before You Go On

Remind students that these questions will help them monitor their progress. Put students in pairs to answer the questions. Encourage them to share their answers with the class.

ANSWERS

1. Hare is overconfident, and he isn't nice when he teases Tortoise.
2. Tortoise is slow, steady, and sure of herself.

On Your Own Have students write an answer to the On Your Own question on a separate sheet of paper. Encourage volunteers to share their responses with the class. Then collect student responses to monitor their comprehension, writing skills, and fluency.

Differentiated Instruction

Beginning	Ask students to read the *About the Author* box and to tell you two facts about Aesop.
Early Intermediate	Ask students to look at the photo of a lyre on page 235. Ask them if they can name a similar instrument used today. (harp)
Intermediate	Ask students to determine what kind of friend Tortoise or Hare would be based on their words and actions in the text. Invite students to complete the following sentences and to elaborate on their ideas. *I think Tortoise/Hare would be a good/bad friend because _____.*
Struggling Readers	Read "The Hare and the Tortoise" aloud. Ask students to listen for words that describe the two characters. Then, in pairs, have students describe each of the characters.

STEP 4: Teach

Preteaching Highlighted Words

In pairs, have students read aloud the highlighted words and their definitions. Answer any questions students have about the use of a word or its meaning before reading the spread.

Across the Curriculum:
Social Studies

Many modern words and names come from Greek mythology. Because of Orpheus's musical skill, many cities including Los Angeles, Minneapolis, and Memphis have Orpheum Theatres named for him.

Model the
READING STRATEGY

Identify Author's Purpose

Myths are often created to provide explanations for elements in nature. As you read "Orpheus and Eurydice," remind students to look for the natural element that is being explained in the story.

✔ LITERARY CHECK

Remind students of the meaning of *personification*. You may wish to give them the following example: the trees and stones danced and the rivers stopped flowing and listened to Orpheus's song.

▲ Orpheus leading Eurydice

ORPHEUS AND EURYDICE

In ancient times, no one played more beautiful music or sang more lovely songs than Orpheus. The god Apollo gave Orpheus a lyre made out of a turtle shell. When Orpheus played on the lyre and sang, everyone—gods, humans, and wild creatures—stopped and listened. The trees and stones danced. Even the rivers stopped flowing to listen to his song.

Orpheus was married to a wood nymph named Eurydice. He loved her more than anything else in the world. One day Eurydice was running across a meadow, and failed to notice a poisonous snake. The snake bit her ankle, and she died. Orpheus was left grief-stricken and alone. From that time on, Orpheus played such sad songs that gods, nymphs—anyone

✔ LITERARY CHECK
What examples of personification can you find in the first paragraph?

Apollo, Greek god of the sun, medicine, poetry, music, and prophecy
lyre, musical instrument with strings across a U-shaped frame, used especially in ancient Greece
wood nymph, spirit of nature who, according to ancient Greek and Roman stories, appeared as a young girl living in trees, mountains, and streams
grief-stricken, feeling very sad because of something that has happened

234

TESOL Standards

Goal 2, Standard 2—To use English to achieve academically in all content areas: Students will use English to obtain, process, construct, and provide subject matter information in spoken and written form.
Descriptors—Comparing and contrasting information; Persuading, arguing, negotiating, evaluating, and justifying.

Goal 2, Standard 3—To use English to achieve academically in all content areas: Students will use appropriate learning strategies to construct and apply academic knowledge.
Descriptors—Actively connecting new information to information previously learned.

who heard the music—felt sorry for him. Soon, Orpheus could not bear his grief any longer. He decided to travel to the Underworld to find his beloved Eurydice. The god Hades and his wife Persephone ruled this underground kingdom of the dead.

As Orpheus came near the secret cave that led to the Underworld, he grew hopeful. He whispered to himself, "I will play such lovely songs that maybe Hades himself will return Eurydice to me."

A fierce three-headed guard dog, called Cerberus, stood in front of the entrance to the cave. Orpheus was determined to find Eurydice. He did not turn back. He played on his lyre until Cerberus fell fast asleep, letting him pass. Next, Orpheus came to the river Styx. Here, the boatman Charon ferries dead souls to the Underworld. At first, Charon refused to take Orpheus across the water. But when he heard the lovely music Orpheus made, he was entranced and ferried Orpheus to the other side.

At last, Orpheus entered the Underworld and stood before Hades and Persephone. "I beg you, please, let Eurydice come back with me," Orpheus pleaded. The Lord of the Underworld said, "No. I cannot return her to you."

Bold Orpheus did not give up. He played passionately on his lyre. Hades softened, and Persephone was moved to tears. Suddenly, the Lord of the Underworld understood Orpheus's grief.

"I will let Eurydice go," Hades said, "on one condition. You cannot turn around to look back at her until you reach the light of the living world above."

Orpheus agreed. Eurydice followed Orpheus up the steep path out of the Underworld. They had almost reached the cave entrance, when Orpheus was overwhelmed by a desire to see his wife's face. He glanced back and she cried out. Then Eurydice vanished into the mist. She was caught in the Underworld forever.

Orpheus was desolate and remained so for the rest of his life. When he died, the gods hung his lyre in the night sky. To this day, if you look at the night sky, you can see the constellation called Lyra. It is a reminder of the sad story of Orpheus and Eurydice.

---

ferries, carries a short distance from one place to another in a boat
entranced, focused so much on something that other things go unnoticed
passionately, with very strong feeling
condition, something that is stated in an agreement that must be done
desolate, very sad and lonely
constellation, group of stars that forms a particular pattern and has a name

▲ The body of a lyre was sometimes made out of a turtle shell.

✔ **LITERARY CHECK**

What aspect of nature does the myth of Orpheus explain?

BEFORE YOU GO ON

1 What great skill does Orpheus have?

2 What is the Underworld, and why does Orpheus go there?

💡**On Your Own**
Why is Orpheus desolate at the end of the story?

235

Study Skills: Online Visuals

This myth explains the existence of the constellation Lyra. Have students use a search engine to find images of the constellation.

STEP 5: Monitor Progress

Ask students to check what they have understood in the reading.

Before You Go On

Remind students that these questions will help them monitor their progress. Put students in pairs to answer the questions. Encourage them to share their answers with the class.

ANSWERS

1. Orpheus is a talented musician and singer.
2. The Underworld is where people go when they die. Orpheus goes there to try to bring back his wife.

On Your Own Have students write an answer to the On Your Own question on a separate sheet of paper. Encourage volunteers to share their responses with the class. Then collect student responses to monitor their comprehension, writing skills, and fluency.

✔ **LITERARY CHECK**

Answer: This myth explains the constellation Lyra in the night sky.

Review the Purpose for Reading

Elicit responses to the Set a Purpose for Reading questions at the beginning of this reading. Remind students to relate their responses to the Big Question.

Teach & Apply

STEP 1: Introduce

Speaking Tip

Discuss how tone affects the way words are understood. **SAY:** *I can't believe a tortoise is going to race a hare!* in amused, surprised, and angry tones.

Reader's Theater

Performing by reading aloud is excellent practice for students. It increases fluency and improves oral expression. Have students practice and perform in pairs. **SAY:** *Decide who will play the roles of Hare and Tortoise. Practice your lines individually before you perform the scene with your partner.*

Suggest that students find a quiet corner in which to rehearse.

STEP 2: Practice

Comprehension

Have students work individually, in pairs, or in small groups to answer the questions.

ANSWERS

1. The moral of the fable "The Hare and the Tortoise" is that slow and steady wins the race.
2. In "Orpheus and Eurydice," Orpheus plays a lyre given to him by Apollo.
3. Hare sleeps longer than he plans to because it was hot and he is tired. He is also overconfident.
4. Orpheus plays music to enchant anyone who tries to stop him on his journey.

Teaching Resources

- *Workbook*, p. 115
- CD-ROM/e-book, Reader's Theater, Comprehension, Response to Literature

---

READING 3 — Review and Practice

READER'S THEATER

Act out this scene between Hare and Tortoise.

Hare: Everyone knows that I am the fastest animal in the forest. No one can run as fast as I can. That's why they call me Speedy.

Tortoise: You think you are so fast. You just like to brag.

Hare: Well, how about having a race to prove that I am the fastest animal of all? I can beat anyone. I can certainly beat you. You are such a slowpoke.

Tortoise: Okay, let's race. But I wouldn't be so sure I'd win if I were you. I may not be so fast, but I am steady.

Hare: Ha! Steady doesn't matter at all. Speed is the only important thing in a race.

Tortoise: We'll just see about that. Let's get some friends to watch us and time us.

Hare: I'll ask Mouse to time us. He's good at keeping time because he likes to run up and down clocks.

Tortoise: Here we go! Let the steadiest animal win!

Hare: Yes, here we go! Let the fastest animal win!

▲ Hare and Tortoise at the starting line

> *Speaking TIP*
>
> Speak naturally and with feeling. Try to convey the humor of the situation with your voice.

COMPREHENSION Workbook Page 115

Right There

1. What is the moral of the fable "The Hare and the Tortoise"?
2. What instrument does Orpheus play in the myth "Orpheus and Eurydice"? Who gave it to him?

Think and Search

3. Why does Hare take a nap and sleep longer than he planned to?
4. How does Orpheus use his music to find Eurydice in the Underworld?

236

TESOL Standards

Goal 3, Standard 1—To use English in socially and culturally appropriate ways: Students will use the appropriate language variety, register, and genre according to audience, purpose, and setting.
Descriptors—Using the appropriate degree of formality with different audiences and settings; Determining when it is appropriate to use a language other than English; Determining appropriate topics for interaction.

Goal 3, Standard 2—To use English in socially and culturally appropriate ways: Students will use nonverbal communication appropriate to audience, purpose, and setting.
Descriptors—Interpreting and responding appropriately to nonverbal cues and body language; Using acceptable tone, volume, stress, and intonation, in various social settings; Recognizing and adjusting behavior in response to nonverbal cues.

T236

Author and You

5. Why does Hare lose the race? Why do you think that Aesop created a character like Hare?

6. Why do you think that Orpheus was unable to obey the instructions he received from Hades?

On Your Own

7. Why are fables a good way to teach important lessons?

8. Why do all cultures have myths that try to explain aspects of nature?

DISCUSSION

Discuss in pairs or small groups.

1. How does Aesop use personification in "The Hare and the Tortoise"?

2. What did you learn about loss from reading "Orpheus and Eurydice"?

3. How are the fable and myth you read similar? How are they different?

Q What do we learn through winning and losing? Why do you think that winning and losing are often themes in traditional stories, such as myths and fables? How are winning and losing experiences that everyone can relate to?

Listening TIP

As you listen, write down key points that your classmates make. This will help you recall and participate in the discussion.

RESPONSE TO LITERATURE

Workbook Page 115

Write a brief fable of your own. Use animals as your main characters and give them human traits. Be sure to use dialogue and personification to make your story lively and appealing.

When you are done writing, read your fable to a small group of classmates. Don't read the moral. See whether your friends can identify the moral on their own.

◄ Orpheus and Eurydice with the messenger of the gods, who guided dead souls to the Underworld

237

Differentiated Instruction

Beginning	Have students look at the picture on page 236. Ask them what they think is going on.
Early Intermediate	Have students name two characters that they will include in their fable.
Intermediate	Ask students what the moral or lesson is in their fable.
Greater Challenge	Have students read their fables to the rest of the class.

ANSWERS CONTINUED

5. Hare loses because he thinks he doesn't need any effort to win. Aesop created Hare to teach people that it's more important to be persistent and humble than to be naturally talented.

6. **Possible response:** Orpheus was unable to obey the instructions because he was overcome by temptation.

7. **Possible response:** Fables are a good way to teach important lessons because they present the story in an interesting way that everyone can understand.

8. **Possible response:** All cultures have myths to explain natural events that were not understood at the time.

STEP 3: Extend

Listening Tip

SAY: *If you have a point you want to add, but someone else is talking, write it down and save it for later. That way you will be more able to concentrate on the speaker.*

 Discussion

Before students begin their discussion, decide whether they will work as a class, in small groups, or in pairs. Consider dividing up the questions so each group has a different topic. Set up class norms to make sure that all participants are heard and that ideas are challenged but not discarded. Explain that the purpose is to allow everyone a chance to be heard. Remind students of the vocabulary words they have learned.

Q What do we learn through winning and losing? Guide students to understand that winning and losing are often themes in traditional stories because they are common experiences to all people throughout history. Everyone will win or lose something at some stage in their lives.

STEP 4: Assess

Response to Literature

Help students write a brief fable of their own, using animal characters. They may wish to use one of the morals on page 229 or another moral such as:

● Fair weather friends are not worth much.

● Do not attempt too much at once.

● Necessity is the mother of invention.

Help students create characters for their stories.

STEP 1: Introduce

Adverbs modify verbs in the same way that adjectives modify nouns. Point out to students that using adverbs can help them be more precise in their descriptions.

STEP 2: Teach

Grammar and Writing

Adverbs with *-ly* Read aloud the paragraph and the three example sentences in the box. Be sure students understand the placement of the adverb in each sentence. Now read the words in the Adjective/Adverb chart. As a class, compose three sentences for each adverb, placing it at the beginning, middle, and end. Write the sentences on the board.

STEP 3: Practice

Have students work with a partner to complete the exercise.

ANSWERS

Sample responses:
1. The boy gladly shared his sandwich.
2. Lola easily completed her homework.
3. Charles worked steadily toward his goal.
4. Suddenly the wind began to blow.
5. The man thought about the question and then responded wisely.
6. Julia carefully combed her hair.

Teaching Resources

- *Workbook*, pp. 116–117
- CD-ROM/e-book, Grammar, Writing
- *Transparencies*, Writing Model 38
- *Transparencies, Resources*, Graphic Organizer 6
- *Assessment*, Reading 3 Test, pp. 91–94

Grammar and Writing

GRAMMAR, USAGE, AND MECHANICS

Adverbs with *-ly*

Writers use adverbs to make their writing clear and exact. An adverb usually describes the action of a verb. An adverb can appear at the beginning, middle, or end of a sentence. It can be placed before or after the verb. Place a comma after an adverb when it comes at the beginning of a sentence.

adverb verb
Slowly, the tortoise **moved** along the beach.

verb adverb
The tortoise **moved slowly** along the beach.

adverb verb
The tortoise **slowly moved** along the beach.

▲ A tortoise moves very slowly.

Adding *-ly* to an adjective forms many adverbs.

Adjective	Adverb
happy	happily
quick	quickly
swift	swiftly

Don't confuse adverbs that end with *-ly* with adjectives that end in *-y*.

Adjectives: pretty, merry, sleepy, cloudy, windy, rainy

Practice **Workbook** Page 116

Work with a partner. In your notebook, write sentences for each adverb.

1. gladly   4. suddenly
2. easily   5. wisely
3. steadily   6. carefully

238

WRITING AN EXPOSITORY PARAGRAPH

Write to Compare and Contrast

On this page, you will compare and contrast two things. You'll use a Venn diagram like the one at the right to help you structure your writing. When you compare, you show how two people, places, or things are alike. When you contrast, you show how they are different. To compare and contrast, select two topics that are alike and different in important ways. First, explain how the two items are alike. Then explain how they are different.

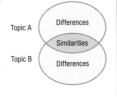

Topic A — Differences
Similarities
Topic B — Differences

Here is a model of how to compare and contrast. Notice how the writer presents similarities in the first paragraph and differences in the second paragraph.

> Wendy Willner
>
> "The Hare and the Tortoise" and "Orpheus and Eurydice"
> The fable by Aesop and the myth of Orpheus have several similarities. First, they are both ancient Greek stories about a series of events that occur between two main characters. In each story, one character acts without thinking. Hare does not think deeply before carelessly napping. Orpheus does not think when he looks back at Eurydice. Both characters suffer a loss because of their mistakes.
>
> There are also differences between the two stories. "The Hare and the Tortoise" is a fable with a moral: Slow and steady wins the race. "Orpheus and Eurydice" is a how-and-why myth that explains how Lyra became a constellation. Each story has a very different ending, too. Hare may have lost the race but can still live happily ever after. Orpheus stays madly in love with Eurydice, so he is sad for the rest of his life.

Practice

Workbook Page 117

Write two paragraphs that compare and contrast two people, places, or things. Choose topics that have points of similarity and difference, such as Orpheus and Hare. Tell how the two things are alike in the first paragraph and how they are different in the second paragraph. List your ideas in a Venn diagram. Be sure to use adverbs that end in -ly correctly.

Writing Checklist

ORGANIZATION:
☑ I explained all the similarities and then all the differences.

WORD CHOICE:
☑ I used specific details and examples to support my comparison and contrast.

239

STEP 1: Introduce

Tell students that comparing and contrasting in writing is a type of expository writing. It gives the writer a structure that helps to organize his or her ideas.

STEP 2: Teach

Writing an Expository Paragraph

Write to Compare and Contrast Draw a Venn diagram on the board (page 239).
SAY: *When comparing and contrasting, it is important to organize your ideas so your reader can see the logic in your paper. One way to organize is to compare in one part and contrast in another.*

Model Writing Skill Have a volunteer read the first sentence of the student model aloud. Then have students describe the function of the first paragraph. (It points out the similarities between the fable and the myth.) Ask students to read the first sentence of the second paragraph. Have them describe the function of the second paragraph. (It points out the differences between them.)

STEP 3: Assess

Have students evaluate their work using the Writing Checklist.

Writing Checklist Note

Organization: Check that students' explained similarities in one paragraph and differences in another.

Word Choice: Check that the words students use clearly explain similarity and difference.

Accelerate Language Development

Common Errors with Adverbs and Adjectives

Distinguishing between adverbs and adjectives seems easy enough, considering one typically modifies a noun, and the other a verb. However, there are a few common difficulties. Some students mistakenly choose adverbs with sensory verbs such as feel, taste or smell. For example, students may say *I feel badly*, which really means *I am not good at feeling*, when actually they should say *I feel bad*, meaning *I feel sad or sick*. The adjective/adverb pair good/well is often misused in these circumstances as well.

STEP 1: Introduce

Objectives

Read aloud the list of objectives in the What You Will Learn section. Tell students that they will be reading two science articles. Have students work in pairs to restate the list of things they will learn.

The Big Question

Before students answer the specific questions about birds, make sure they understand the idiom *die out* (become extinct; no longer exist). Generate a discussion about why some types of birds might die out (loss of habitat as a result of deforestation, chemical pollutants, hunting, disease). Suggest how this might affect other animals and humans (disturbs the balance of nature, loss of a food source, the irreversible loss of a species).

Help students create their two-column charts and brainstorm ideas about what might cause the birds to die out.

Build Background

Read aloud the Build Background text. Invite a volunteer to explain the meaning of the word *extinct*.

STEP 2: Teach

Understanding the Genre:
Informational Text

Tell students that an informational text is a work of nonfiction. Its purpose is to present facts and other information about real people, events, places, and situations. This reading is about animals lost, or nearly lost, to extinction.

Teaching Resources

- CD-ROM/e-book, Key Words
- Audio CD 4, tracks 17–18
- *Workbook*, p. 118

What You Will Learn

Reading
- Vocabulary building: *Context, dictionary skills, word study*
- Reading strategy: *Recognize cause and effect*
- Text type: *Informational text (science)*

Grammar, Usage, and Mechanics
Showing cause and effect: *because, because of,* and *so*

Writing
Write a cause-and-effect explanation

THE BIG QUESTION

What can we learn through winning and losing? You are going to read about three kinds of birds that were lost forever. What might cause a type of bird to die out? How would this affect other animals, including humans?

Think about what you know about birds. Make a two-column chart in your notebook with the headings *Birds* and *Facts*. Work in small groups to list the names of birds you know, such as robins, toucans, penguins, and cardinals. Write any facts you know about each bird; for example, robins eat worms. Then discuss what might happen to cause these birds to die out. Discuss how this would affect other animals.

▲ A toucan

BUILD BACKGROUND

"Going, Going, Gone?" and **"Ivory-Billed Woodpeckers Make Noise"** are science articles. The first article explains why three kinds of birds died out. The second suggests that a type of bird once thought to have died out may actually still exist.

In "Buffalo Dusk" you learned that humans were responsible for killing off most of the buffaloes in North America. If laws had not been passed to protect buffaloes, they would have become extinct, or lost forever. Why do specific kinds of animals become extinct? They may not be able to find the food they need. People or other creatures may destroy their habitats. Disease might wipe them out. In the case of dinosaurs, meteors may have struck Earth and killed off these creatures.

▲ A penguin

▲ A cardinal

240

TESOL Standards

Goal 1, Standard 2—To use English to communicate in social settings: Students will interact in, through, and with spoken and written English for personal expression and enjoyment.
Descriptors—Sharing social and cultural traditions and values; Participating in popular culture.

Goal 3, Standard 1—To use English in socially and culturally appropriate ways: Students will use the appropriate language variety, register, and genre according to audience, purpose, and setting.
Descriptors—Responding to and using slang appropriately; Responding to and using idioms appropriately.

VOCABULARY

Learn Key Words

Read these sentences. Use the context to figure out the meaning of the red words. Use a dictionary to check your answers. Then write each word and its meaning in your notebook.

Key Words

conservationists
destruction
extinct
habitats
ornithology
predator

1. The conservationists at the park protected the lions by keeping them in a safe area.

2. After the destruction of the forest, the animals had nowhere to live. Their homes had been ruined.

3. Dinosaurs have become extinct. They are all gone now.

4. The birds' habitats in the nature preserve look like their original rain forest homes. There is food to eat, and there are trees to live in.

5. The student took a class in ornithology because he wanted to know all about birds.

6. The cat is a predator that likes to attack birds.

Practice Workbook Page 118

Work with a partner to answer these questions. Try to include the red word in your answer. Write the sentences in your notebook.

1. How do conservationists protect animals?

2. What natural disasters might cause destruction in a town?

3. What do you think caused dinosaurs to become extinct?

4. What do you think the habitats of penguins look like?

5. What sort of people would teach classes in ornithology?

6. What animal might be a predator of a cat?

► Serious bird-watchers often read books on ornithology.

241

 Vocabulary

Learn Key Words Play the CD. Have students listen and repeat. If you are not using the CD, read the Key Words aloud. Ask students if any of these words are familiar. **SAY:** *These words are called Key Words because they are words that are important in the text.* Write the following words and definitions on the board.

- **conservationists:** people who work to save natural things
- **destruction:** the process of destroying something
- **extinct:** no longer existing
- **habitats:** places where plants or animals naturally live
- **ornithology:** the study of birds
- **predator:** an animal that kills and eats other animals

Have students copy the definitions and generate sentences for them. Use the Workbook page for extra practice.

STEP 3: Practice

Model answering the first question with the class. Tell students to use words from the questions in their answers. Write the first question on the board, underlining the words as shown: *How do conservationists protect animals?* Now write a possible answer: *Conservationists protect animals by teaching others the importance of animals to humans.*

ANSWERS

1. Conservationists protect animals by teaching others the importance of animals to humans.
2. Earthquakes and hurricanes are natural disasters that might cause destruction in a town.
3. I think some change in the earth caused dinosaurs to become extinct.
4. I think the habitats of penguins are cold and wet.
5. People who study birds would teach classes in ornithology.
6. A coyote might be a predator of a cat.

Differentiated Instruction

Beginning	Have students look at the photos of the birds on page 240, 242, and 244–247. Ask students which look familiar. Where have students seen them before?
Early Intermediate	Have students share the information they came up with for the Big Question exercise on page 240 with the rest of the class.
Intermediate	Ask students to look up the words *destruction* and *predator* in a thesaurus. Tell them to find an antonym for each and to use it in a sentence.
Standard English Learners (CRI)	Have students brainstorm ideas about how this reading will relate to the Big Question. How can the ideas of winning and losing be applied to the animal kingdom?

Teach

CD4 T19–T20

Vocabulary

Learn Academic Words Play the CD. Have students listen and repeat. If you are not using the CD, read the Academic Words aloud.
SAY: *Look at the Academic Words chart. The definition is on the left. On the right, each word is used in a sentence. Write each word, its definition, and the sentence in your notebooks. Then work with a partner to write a new sentence for each Academic Word.*

STEP 2: Practice

Have students work with partners to complete the practice activity. **SAY:** *Take turns reading aloud the sentences with your partner. As you read each sentence, think about the academic word that makes the most sense in that sentence. Once you know which word best completes the sentence, write the sentence in your notebook.*

ANSWERS
1. statistics
2. factors
3. estimate
4. environment

Teaching Resources
- Audio CD 4, tracks 19–20
- *Workbook*, pp. 119–121
- CD-ROM/e-book, Academic Words, Word Study

Learn Academic Words

Study the **red** words and their meanings. You will find these words useful when talking and writing about informational texts. Write each word and its meaning in your notebook. After you read "Going, Going, Gone?" and "Ivory-Billed Woodpeckers Make Noise," try to use these words to respond to the text.

environment = the land, water, and air in which people, animals, and plants live	⇒	Oil spills and other changes in the **environment** had a bad effect on the birds that lived there.
estimate (verb) = judge the value or size of something	⇒	Rico and Li **estimate** that more than 100 birds live in the region. It is a logical guess.
factors = several things that influence or cause a situation	⇒	Many **factors** caused the birds to move to a new area. One reason was the weather.
statistics = a collection of numbers that represents facts or measurements	⇒	The **statistics** show how the number of birds has gone up and down over the years.

Practice **Workbook Page 119**

Write the sentences in your notebook. Choose a **red** word from the box above to complete each sentence. Then take turns reading the sentences aloud with a partner.

1. People gather _____ about the number of animals in a certain place.
2. There are many _____ that help to keep an animal safe.
3. Sometimes it's better to _____ than to count every single item.
4. People and other living creatures need a certain _____ in order to survive.

▶ Gentoo penguins like this one live in the cold environment of Antarctica.

242

Word Study: Homophones

A homophone is a word that sounds the same as another word but has a different meaning and a different spelling, such as *hair* and *hare*. Homophones can be confusing when you read or hear them. To figure out which meaning is being used, check the spelling and use context clues. If you still can't figure out which meaning is correct, look up the word in a dictionary.

▲ The sailor could see the sea.

Homophone	Meaning
one won	number that comes before two simple past of *win*
prey pray	hunt another animal for food speak to a god
sea see	the ocean use your eyes to notice

Practice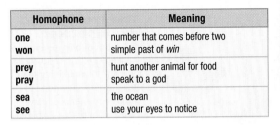

Work with a partner. Define each pair of homophones. Then use each word in a sentence to show its meaning. Check your answers in a dictionary. Write the words and definitions in your notebook.

break/brake	main/mane	tale/tail
hour/our	seen/scene	weather/whether

READING STRATEGY · RECOGNIZE CAUSE AND EFFECT

Recognizing a cause and an effect helps you understand explanations in texts. An effect is "what happened." A cause is "why it happened." To recognize causes and effects, follow the steps in this example:

- Read this sentence: *The bird died because it didn't have food.*
- Look for what happened. (The bird died.) This is the effect.
- Look for the reason why it happened. (It didn't have food.) This is the cause.
- Look for words that signal cause and effect, such as *so*, *because*, *because of*, *therefore*, and *as a result*.

As you read the next two articles, look for the causes and effects. Use a graphic organizer to help you.

243

Linguistic Note

Homophones in Knock-knock Jokes

Homophones are used in puns or jokes playing on the different meanings of words that sound alike. Examples: Why is Cinderella not allowed to play soccer? Because she always runs away from the ball. (*Ball* can refer to *party* or *sports equipment*.) Why do cows have bells? Because their horns don't work. (*Horns* can refer to *an animal's horn* and *a car's horn*.) Point out that many word games using the context of homonyms are based on *false* homonyms, or *oronyms*: words strung together a certain way that only *sound* like homonyms. Example: *I scream* versus *ice cream* or *stuffy nose* versus *stuff he knows*. The popular *knock-knock* jokes or the game *mad gab* make constant use of oronyms. Example:
Knock knock. — Who's there?
Luke. — Luke who?
Look through the keyhole and you'll know. (Oronym: Luke/look)

Reading Summary

The articles in this reading are about several species of birds that have become extinct due to humans.

 The Big Question

Remind students that the Big Question is "What do we learn through winning and losing?" Discuss why it matters if some birds are lost because of extinction. How does this affect humans?

Set a Purpose for Reading

Tell students to copy the purpose for reading into their notebooks and to keep it in mind as they read. Explain that they will have to present details that support their answer to the question and to explain how the reading relates to the Big Question.

Preteaching Highlighted Words

In pairs, have students read aloud the highlighted words and their definitions. Answer any questions students have about the use of a word or its meaning before reading the spread.

CD4 T21–T22 ### Scaffolding: Listen and Read

Have students listen to the Audio CD as they read the selection to themselves. Then have student pairs alternate reading paragraphs from the selection aloud.

Teaching Resources

- *Resources*, Summaries, pp. 153–154
- Audio CD 4, tracks 21–22
- *Reader's Companion Workbook*, pp. 87–93

READING 4

INFORMATIONAL TEXT

SCIENCE

Set a purpose for reading Why did the birds in these paintings become extinct or almost extinct? Read to find out the causes. Do you think that people learned anything from this loss? Analyze the effects.

Going, Going, Gone?

When a species, or kind of animal, becomes extinct, it is lost forever. These online science articles both deal with birds that have become extinct. You will find out the effects that certain events and actions had on the dodo, the passenger pigeon, and the Carolina parakeet. You will also find out why some bird lovers now feel hopeful about a bird that was thought to be extinct. As you read, consider what can be done to prevent other living things from becoming extinct in the future.

More than eighty kinds of birds have died out, or become extinct, in the last 300 years. Some vanished because of natural causes. Humans killed off most of them. They hunted the birds too much and destroyed the birds' habitats. Read on for more details on the search for the ivory-billed woodpecker. (It might not be extinct as once thought.) Then check out the stories behind three extinct birds.

The Ivory-Billed Woodpecker

A team of bird experts is walking through mud and swamps in Louisiana's Pearl River forest. They hope to find the mysterious ivory-billed woodpecker. Experts believed this bird had been extinct for more than fifty years. A college student's sighting of unusual-looking birds sparked hopes that it might still be alive.

Loggers cut down trees in the Pearl River forest during the early 1800s. But some trees have grown back. There are now many old cypress, sweet gum, and oak trees that would serve as a good home for ivory-billed woodpeckers. The birds were known to eat the fat grubs that live under the bark of these trees. The researchers have already found trees with areas of bark that have been chipped off, as if by a large woodpecker. Only time will tell if it is an ivory-billed one.

---

loggers, people whose job it is to cut down trees
grubs, insects when they are in the form of small, soft white worms

Adapted from "Going, Going, Gone?" from *Time for Kids*, January 22, 2002. © 2002 TIME for Kids. Reprinted by permission.

 ## TESOL Standards

Goal 2, Standard 2—To use English to achieve academically in all content areas: Students will use English to obtain, process, construct, and provide subject matter information in spoken and written form.
Descriptors—Comparing and contrasting information; Retelling information; Selecting, connecting, and explaining information; Analyzing, synthesizing, and inferring from information; Understanding and producing technical vocabulary and text features according to content; Formulating and asking questions.

Goal 2, Standard 3—To use English to achieve academically in all content areas: Students will use appropriate learning strategies to construct and apply academic knowledge.
Descriptors—Focusing attention selectively; Using context to construct meaning.

The Dodo

The dodo was the first bird to be wiped out by people during modern times. Dodos were large, flightless birds. They were first seen around 1600 on Mauritius, an island in the Indian Ocean. Less than eighty years later, the dodo was extinct. The dodo's heavy, clumsy body made it an easy target for sailors, who hunted it for food. As forests were destroyed, so was the dodo's food supply. And the cats, rats, pigs, and other predators unleashed by sailors preyed on the dodos. Together these factors led to the dodo's extinction.

The Passenger Pigeon

These pigeons once lived in the eastern United States. They flew across this area in flocks so huge that they darkened the sky. In 1808 a single flock in Kentucky was estimated to contain over 2 billion birds. Today the passenger pigeon is extinct because of human activities. Settlers moving West during the nineteenth century cleared huge numbers of eastern chestnut and oak trees to make room for farms and towns. These trees were the passenger pigeon's main source of food. The birds were seen as a threat to crops, so people killed the birds. They were also hunted for food. All of these factors wiped out the passenger pigeon. The last one, which lived in the Cincinnati Zoological Garden, died on September 1, 1914.

---

preyed on, hunted and ate

The Carolina Parakeet

This colorful bird was the only parrot native to the eastern United States. It had green feathers with a yellow head and orange cheek patches and forehead. The largest Carolina parakeets were 33 centimeters (13 in.) long, including their tail feathers. They once lived throughout the Southeast, as far north as Virginia and as far west as Texas. Parrots are among the smartest of birds. However, farmers thought these fruit-eaters were pests. So they shot them from the skies. The Carolina parakeet became extinct in the 1920s. As a result, all that's left are stuffed examples of this bird in museums.

---

pests, small animals or insects that harm people or destroy things, especially crops or food supplies

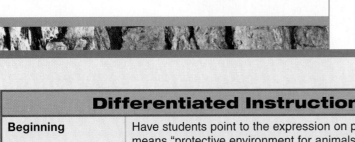

BEFORE YOU GO ON

1. What caused the passenger pigeon to become extinct?

2. Why did farmers kill the Carolina parakeet?

💡 **On Your Own**
Why should we try to prevent species (kinds) of birds from becoming extinct?

STEP 4: Teach

Preteaching Highlighted Words

In pairs, have students read aloud the highlighted words and their definitions. Answer any questions students have about the use of a word or its meaning before reading the spread.

Across the Curriculum:
Math

The American Museum of Natural History in New York reports: "Three species become extinct every hour of every day." If this is true, how many species become extinct each day? (72) How many in a week? (504) In a year? (26,280)

Model the
READING STRATEGY

Recognize Cause and Effect
Remind students of the reading strategy Recognize Cause and Effect
SAY: *What might have caused experts to have doubts that the ivory-billed woodpecker was really extinct?* (blurry videotape). *Why would a recording of the bird's double-rap be so convincing?* (It is a one-of-a-kind noise)

Ivory-Billed Woodpeckers Make Noise

Jill Egan

Bird lovers were chirping back in April of 2005. Why? Scientists from Cornell University announced they'd rediscovered the ivory-billed woodpecker. The rare bird was thought to have been extinct since 1944. It was rediscovered at Cache River National Wildlife Refuge in eastern Arkansas.

Wildlife Refuge, protective environment for animals

In July, a small group of bird experts said that they weren't sure the ivory-billed woodpecker had really been rediscovered. They said a blurry videotape of the bird wasn't enough evidence. Researchers then decided to send them more proof. They shared a sound recording of the ivory-billed woodpecker's one-of-a-kind double-rap.

one-of-a-kind, unique, or very special because there is nothing else like it

Adapted from "Ivory-Billed Woodpeckers Make Some Noise" by Jill Egan, from *Time for Kids*, August 5, 2005. © 2005 TIME for Kids. Reprinted by permission.

The ivory-billed woodpecker ▶

246

TESOL Standards

Goal 3, Standard 3—To use English in socially and culturally appropriate ways: Students will use appropriate learning strategies to extend their sociolinguistic and sociocultural competence.
Descriptors—Experimenting with variations of language in social and academic settings; Seeking information about appropriate language use and behavior; Analyzing the social context to determine appropriate language use.

The unique sounds made believers out of the bird experts. "The thrilling new sound recordings provide clear and convincing evidence that the ivory-billed woodpecker is not extinct," said Richard Prum, a scientist from Yale University.

The ivorybill is the largest woodpecker in the United States. It has a wingspan of about 91 centimeters (3 ft.). The ivorybill began to disappear because loggers cut down forests across the Southeast between 1880 and the 1940s. Soon after the ivorybill was rediscovered, the U.S. government announced a $10 million plan to protect the rare bird.

Conservationists are trying to help the woodpecker by killing trees. Sound strange? The woodpecker feeds on beetle larvae found under the bark of dead trees. When the trees are killed, more beetles will likely be attracted to the trees. With more food for the woodpeckers, the species will have a better chance at recovering.

Only about thirty-five to fifty trees will be cut on four 4-acre sections of land. There are 2,000 to 2,800 trees on each section. In about two or three years, scientists hope the trees will have lots of beetles for the woodpeckers. Then the double-rap of the ivorybill will be a common sound.

---

larvae, young insects with soft, tube-shaped bodies, which will eventually become adult insects with wings

BEFORE YOU GO ON

1. What caused bird lovers to be happy?
2. What effect did loggers have on the ivory-billed woodpecker?

💡 **On Your Own**
How is losing a species different from losing a competition?

247

Study Skills: Reference Book

Bring in bird identification books from your school or local library. In small groups, have students use the index to locate the section on woodpeckers. Have them compare the wingspan of the ivory woodpecker with other species of woodpeckers to help them appreciate its size.

STEP 5: Monitor Progress

Ask students to check what they have understood in the reading.

Before You Go On

Remind students that these questions will help them monitor their progress. Put students in pairs to answer the questions. Encourage them to share their answers with the class.

ANSWERS
1. Bird lovers were happy when they discovered that the ivory-billed woodpecker was not extinct.
2. Loggers cut down forests across the Southeast and destroyed the birds' habitat.

On Your Own Have students write an answer to the On Your Own question on a separate sheet of paper. Encourage volunteers to share their responses with the class. Then, collect student responses to monitor their comprehension, writing skills, and fluency.

Review the Purpose for Reading

Elicit responses to the Set a Purpose for Reading questions at the beginning of this reading. Remind students to relate their responses to the Big Question.

STEP 1: Practice

Comprehension

Have students answer the questions.

ANSWERS

1. The dodo was the first bird to be wiped out by people during modern times.
2. The ivory-billed woodpecker was rediscovered in the Cache River National Wildlife Refuge in Arkansas.
3. Human activities, such as habitat destruction and hunting, contributed to the extinction of the passenger pigeon.
4. Two things that convinced bird experts that the woodpecker was not extinct were a videotape and audio recordings.
5. **Possible response:** Not all of the animals were extinct.
6. **Possible response:** I could have said it's important to leave the parakeets alone; otherwise, there won't be any left in North America.
7. **Possible response:** Some owls may become extinct because of logging. I think that population changes on Earth could be part of the cause.
8. **Possible response:** People can protect animals and plants from extinction through preservation.

(CRI) In Your Own Words

Have students write what they learned in a three-column chart and then use that chart to write a summary. Tell students to read their summaries to each other. Encourage peer feedback.

Speaking Tip

Remind students to use precise words in their explanations to help listeners visualize the main ideas and details.

Teaching Resources

- *Workbook*, p. 122
- CD-ROM/e-book, Comprehension, Extension
- *Reader's Companion Workbook*, pp. 94–98

COMPREHENSION Workbook Page 122

Right There

1. Which bird was the first one to be wiped out by people during modern times?
2. Where was the ivory-billed woodpecker rediscovered?

Think and Search

3. What factors contributed to the extinction of the passenger pigeon?
4. What two things helped to convince bird experts that the ivory-billed woodpecker was not extinct?

Author and You

5. Why does the author use a question mark rather than a period in the title "Going, Going, Gone?"
6. What could you have said to farmers to protect the Carolina parakeet from becoming extinct?

On Your Own

7. Which animals do you know of that are in danger of becoming extinct? Are changes to the animals' environment part of the cause? Explain.
8. How can people help protect animals and plants from extinction?

▲ The green turtle, giant panda, and Bengal tiger are in danger of becoming extinct.

IN YOUR OWN WORDS

Imagine that you are telling a classmate about "Going, Going, Gone?" and "Ivory-Billed Woodpeckers Make Noise." For each article, make a three-column chart with these headings in your notebook: *Section, Main Ideas,* and *Important Details.* Use the charts to organize the information in each article. Then share your summaries with a classmate.

 Speaking TIP

Use words that help your classmate visualize the main ideas and important details.

248

TESOL Standards

Goal 2, Standard 3—To use English to achieve academically in all content areas: Students will use appropriate learning strategies to construct and apply academic knowledge.
Descriptors—Applying self-monitoring and self-corrective strategies to build and expand a knowledge base; Determining and establishing the conditions that help one become an effective learner (e.g., when, where, how to study).

Goal 3, Standard 1—To use English in socially and culturally appropriate ways: Students will use the appropriate language variety, register, and genre according to audience, purpose, and setting.
Descriptors—Responding to and using humor appropriately; Using the appropriate degree of formality with different audiences and settings; Recognizing and using Standard English and vernacular dialects appropriately.

Goal 3, Standard 3—To use English in socially and culturally appropriate ways: Students will use appropriate learning strategies to extend their sociolinguistic and sociocultural competence.
Descriptors—Deciding when use of slang is appropriate.

DISCUSSION

Discuss in pairs or small groups.

1. How are the four kinds of birds in "Going, Going, Gone?" similar and different?

2. Do you believe that the ivory-billed woodpecker is extinct or not? Why?

Q **What do we learn through winning and losing?** Imagine that you could bring back the dodo, passenger pigeon, or Carolina parakeet. Which one would you choose? Why? What lessons would people need to learn to make sure the bird didn't die out again?

READ FOR FLUENCY

It is often easier to read a text if you understand the difficult words and phrases. Work with a partner. Choose a paragraph from the reading. Identify the words and phrases you do not know or have trouble pronouncing. Look up the difficult words in a dictionary.

Take turns pronouncing the words and phrases with your partner. If necessary, ask your teacher to model the correct pronunciation. Then take turns reading the paragraph aloud. Give each other feedback on your reading.

EXTENSION

Endangered species are kinds of animals that are in danger of becoming extinct. Learn more about how people around the world are working to protect endangered species. Use encyclopedias, reference books, and reliable websites. Copy the chart below into your notebook. Use it to organize the information you find. Share your findings with the class.

>))) *Listening* TIP

When people want to persuade you to do something, they often give only arguments that support their position or point of view. As you listen to your classmates' ideas, think about the opposite point of view. Then draw your own conclusions.

▲ Huge flocks of passenger pigeons used to fill the sky.

Ways to Protect Endangered Animals			
Placing Animals in Preserves	Protecting Habitats	Breeding Animals	Passing Protective Laws

249

STEP 2: Extend

Listening Tip

Being able to think about the opposite point of view in a debate is a valuable skill. If you can anticipate someone else's argument you will be better able to address their ideas.

(CRI) Discussion

Place students in appropriate groups to answer the questions.

Q **What do we learn through winning and losing?** Help students consider how winning can lead to losing. **SAY:** *Why might people have felt as though they were "winning" by killing birds like passenger pigeons or Carolina parakeets?* (They got food, eliminated pests.) *How were these ultimately losses?* (These birds no longer exist.) *Can you think of other ways in which winning in one area leads to losing in another?*

STEP 3: Assess

Read for Fluency

Guide students in selecting a paragraph for oral reading. For best results, students should select a paragraph they enjoyed reading silently. Point out that paragraphs with new vocabulary present more challenge.

Extension

There are many endangered species at risk of becoming extinct. Find out how people around the world are working to prevent extinction. Have students copy the chart into their notebooks and then fill in the chart with details about information they've discovered in reference books, encyclopedias, and/or websites. Have them share their findings with the class.

Differentiated Instruction

Beginning	Have students fill in the blank. *One animal that I like that is endangered is the _____.*
Early Intermediate	Ask students if there are animals that they like that are considered endangered. Ask them why they like the animals.
Intermediate	Ask students to name two things they can do to help protect endangered wildlife.
Greater Challenge	Have students research online or in a library about conservation projects in your area.

STEP 1: Introduce

Tell students they will be reviewing different signal words that show cause and effect. Review what cause and effect means, eliciting some example sentences from students.

STEP 2: Teach

Grammar and Writing

Showing Cause and Effect Write the following examples on the board. **SAY:**
Because, because of, and so are specific words that help show cause and effect.

- <u>Because</u> I was sick on Saturday, I didn't play baseball.
- <u>Because of</u> the flu on Saturday, I didn't play baseball.
- I was sick on Saturday, <u>so</u> I didn't play baseball.

STEP 3: Practice

Model and discuss the first sentence with students.

ANSWERS

1. because
2. so
3. because of
4. so
5. because
6. so

Teaching Resources

- *Workbook*, pp. 123–124
- CD-ROM/e-book, Grammar, Writing
- *Transparencies*, Writing Model 39
- *Transparencies*, *Resources*, Graphic Organizer 4
- *Assessment*, Reading 4 Test, pp. 95–98

Grammar and Writing

GRAMMAR, USAGE, AND MECHANICS

Showing Cause and Effect: *because, because of,* and *so*

Writers use expressions such as *because, because of,* and *so* to signal cause and effect. However, these signal words are each used differently in a sentence. *Because* and *so* are followed by a clause. *Because of* is followed by a noun or noun phrase. Look at the examples from "Going, Going, Gone?" and "Ivory-Billed Woodpeckers Make Noise." Notice the difference in structures and punctuation.

because (subordinating conjunction) + clause	The ivorybill began to disappear **because** loggers cut down forests across the Southeast between 1880 and the 1940s.
because of (preposition) + noun or noun phrase	Today the passenger pigeon is extinct **because of** human activities.
so (coordinating conjunction) + clause	The birds were seen as a threat to crops, **so** people killed the birds.

Practice Workbook Page 123

Work with a partner. Copy the sentences into your notebook. Then fill in the blanks with *because, because of,* or *so*.

1. Passenger pigeons were killed _____ they were seen as a threat to crops.
2. Loggers cut down trees in the Pearl River forest, _____ ivory-billed woodpeckers lost their homes.
3. Carolina parakeets are beautiful _____ their colorful feathers.
4. A recording of the ivory-billed woodpecker's sound was sent, _____ bird experts were able to listen to the sound.
5. Dodo birds are extinct _____ their food supply was destroyed.
6. The last passenger pigeon died on September 1, 1914, _____ now passenger pigeons are extinct.

▲ Because of its heavy body, the dodo was an easy target.

TESOL Standards

Goal 1, Standard 1—To use English to communicate in social settings: Students will use English to participate in social interactions.
Descriptors—Sharing and requesting information; Expressing needs, feelings, and ideas.

Goal 1, Standard 2—To use English to communicate in social settings: Students will interact in, through, and with spoken and written English for personal expression and enjoyment.
Descriptors—Describing, reading about, or participating in a favorite activity; Expressing personal needs, feelings, and ideas.

Goal 3, Standard 1—To use English in socially and culturally appropriate ways: Students will use the appropriate language variety, register, and genre according to audience, purpose, and setting.
Descriptors—Using a variety of writing styles appropriate for different audiences, purposes, and settings; Responding to and using idioms appropriately; Responding to and using humor appropriately; Determining when it is appropriate to use a language other than English; Determining appropriate topics for interaction.

WRITING AN EXPOSITORY PARAGRAPH

Write a Cause-and-Effect Explanation

Certain texts are structured according to causes and effects. On this page, you'll write a cause-and-effect paragraph that tells why the ivory-billed woodpecker was nearly wiped out. You'll use a graphic organizer like the one at the right to help you organize your paragraph. To organize your writing by cause and effect:

- Think about why something happened. Use *because* to signal a cause.
- Think about what happened. Use *so* to signal an effect.
- List the chain of causes and effects that led to what happened.

Here is a model of a cause-and-effect paragraph about the passenger pigeon. Notice how the writer presents causes and effects and uses signal words.

Cause | **Effect**

Tamar Honig

What Happened to the Passenger Pigeon?

At one time, passenger pigeons flew in abundance. Now, they can no longer be found because of human actions. These birds, native to the eastern United States, became extinct in the early 1900s. Several factors caused their extinction. The birds lost their habitat because people cleared a great number of oak and eastern chestnut trees to build towns and farms. In doing so, people wiped out the bird's main source of food. The birds were also viewed as a danger to crops, so people killed them. In addition, passenger pigeons were hunted for food. As a result of these causes, their population gradually decreased until fewer and fewer were left. The last passenger pigeon died in the Cincinnati Zoological Garden in 1914.

Practice **Workbook Page 124**

Write a cause-and-effect paragraph that gives reasons why the ivory-billed woodpecker was nearly wiped out. Show how the causes and effects are related to each other. Use a cause-and-effect chart to list your ideas about what happened and why. Include signal words such as *because, because of, so,* and *as a result,* and be sure to use them correctly.

Writing Checklist

SENTENCE FLUENCY:
- [x] I used signal words to show causes and effects.

ORGANIZATION:
- [x] I presented the causes and effects in a logical order.

251

STEP 1: Introduce

Explain to students that effective cause-and-effect writing requires using precise words to indicate exactly how events are related.

STEP 2: Teach

Writing an Expository Paragraph

Write a Cause-and-Effect Explanation
SAY: *When you write a cause-and-effect paragraph, it is important to keep your purpose in mind: to explain what happened and why.* Read the sample paragraph with students.

Model Writing Skill SAY: *Now I will read aloud the model cause-and-effect paragraph. As I read, listen for what happened and what caused it to happen.*

STEP 3: Assess

Have students evaluate their work using the Writing Checklist.

Writing Checklist Note

Sentence fluency: Check that students correctly used signal words to show cause-and-effect relationships.

Organization: Check that students presented their ideas in an order that clearly demonstrates cause and effect.

Linguistic Note

Noticing /z/

Many languages do not have voiced /z/ in their consonantal repertoire. Native speakers of these languages (including Spanish, Cantonese, Filipino, Hmong, Korean, and Mandarin) are unlikely to perceive the difference between voiceless /s/ and voiced /z/. When *s* appears in post-consonantal position, it tends to automatically acquire the voice of the preceding consonant. Therefore, *s* is likely to be pronounced as voiced /z/ in words such as *cabs* and *pigs*; and as voiceless /s/ in words such as *tots* and *caps*.

Unit Wrap-Up

Link the Readings

Critical Thinking Read the directions and have students complete the chart.

ANSWERS

Title of Reading	Purpose	Big Question Link
"Soccer: The World Sport"	to inform	explains how to play and win a soccer match
"Casey at the Bat," "Swift Things Are Beautiful," "Buffalo Dusk"	to entertain	shows how the expectation of winning can be disappointed
"The Hare and the Tortoise," "Orpheus and Eurydice"	to inspire	shows the importance of staying focused on the goal.
"Going, Going, Gone?" "Ivory-billed Woodpeckers Make Noise"	to inform	explains what happens when a species is lost

 Discussion

Have students answer the questions.

ANSWERS

Possible response: The author's purpose in "Soccer: the World Sport" is to inform, but in "The Hare and the Tortoise" it is to teach a lesson

Fluency Check

Encourage students to time themselves as they practice reading. Have partners take turns reading and timing each other.

Teaching Resources

- *Assessment*, Unit 4 Test, pp. 163–172
- CD-ROM/e-book, Fluency Check, Projects

Link the Readings

Critical Thinking

Look back at the readings in this unit. Think about what they all have in common. They all have something to do with winning or losing. Yet they do not all have the same purpose. The purpose of one reading might be to inform, while the purpose of another might be to entertain or persuade. In addition, the content of each reading relates to winning or losing in different ways. Copy the chart into your notebook and complete it.

Title of Reading	Purpose	Big Question Link
"Soccer: The World Sport"		
"Casey at the Bat," "Swift Things Are Beautiful," "Buffalo Dusk"	*to entertain*	
"The Hare and the Tortoise" "Orpheus and Eurydice"		
"Going, Going, Gone?" "Ivory-Billed Woodpeckers Make Noise"		*explains what happens when a species is lost*

Discussion

Discuss in pairs or small groups.

- How does the author's purpose in "Soccer: the World Sport" differ from the author's purpose in "The Hare and the Tortoise"?

 What do we learn through winning and losing? Is it always important to win? What sorts of lessons can you learn from losing? Can you learn as much from winning as you can from losing? Explain.

Fluency Check

Work with a partner. Choose a paragraph from one of the readings. Take turns reading it for one minute. Count the total number of words you read. Practice saying the words you had trouble reading. Take turns reading the paragraph three more times. Did you read more words each time? Copy the chart below into your notebook and record your speeds.

	1st Speed	2nd Speed	3rd Speed	4th Speed
Words Per Minute				

TESOL Standards

Goal 1, Standard 1—To use English to communicate in social settings: Students will use English to participate in social interactions.
Descriptors—Engaging in conversations; Conducting transactions.

Goal 1, Standard 3—To use English to communicate in social settings: Students will use learning strategies to extend their communicative competence.
Descriptors—Seeking support and feedback from others; Using the primary language to ask for clarification; Selecting different media to help understand language.

Goal 2, Standard 2—To use English to achieve academically in all content areas: Students will use English to obtain, process, construct, and provide subject matter information in spoken and written form.
Descriptors—Listening to, speaking, reading, and writing about subject matter information; Gathering information orally and in writing; Selecting, connecting, and explaining information; Analyzing, synthesizing, and inferring from information; Responding to the work of peers and others; Representing information visually and interpreting information presented visually; Understanding and producing technical vocabulary and text features according to content area; Demonstrating knowledge through application in a variety of contexts.

Projects

Work in pairs or small groups. Choose one of these projects.

1 Working with some classmates, define what "winning" and "losing" mean to you. Talk about what character traits it takes to be a real winner.

2 You read about soccer and its popularity around the world. Organize a game of soccer. Invite everyone in the class to play. First, explain the rules and practice a little. Then have fun playing a complete game!

3 Perform "The Hare and the Tortoise" as a play. Work with several classmates. First, rewrite the fable as a script. Then create simple costumes and props. Learn the lines and rehearse the play. When everyone is ready, perform the play for the class.

4 Find out more about buffaloes. Why did they almost become extinct? How did they come back? Research this topic, and write a brief report about buffaloes. Use visuals and present your report to the class. Be sure to mention your sources in your report.

Further Reading

To find out more about the theme of this unit, choose from these reading suggestions.

Moby Dick, Herman Melville
In this Penguin Reader® adaptation of the classic novel, Captain Ahab and his men hunt for Moby Dick, the most dangerous whale in the ocean.

Black Star, Bright Dawn, Scott O'Dell
When her father is injured, Bright Dawn takes his place in the Iditarod, a 1,000-mile dogsled race through Alaska's frozen wilderness. She must learn to keep going despite her fears.

Sasha Cohen: Fire on Ice: Autobiography of a Champion Figure Skater, Sasha Cohen
The much admired skater describes the hard work and challenges she faced that made her a National Champion and an Olympic silver medalist.

253

Home-School Connection

These projects provide students with several ways to practice and apply what they have learned. The projects can be completed independently, with partners, in small groups, in the classroom, or at home.

1. Lead a Discussion Discuss the value of developing character. Suggest including examples of their role models when discussing.

2. Organize a Soccer Game Remind students to explain the rules to and practice plays with those not familiar with the game. Suggest a simple way to identify teams.

3. Perform a Play Help students brainstorm about what steps it will take to perform the play and make suggestions on how to create simple costumes and props.

4. Write a Report Make suggestions on how to research the topic and on the kinds of visuals that might be included.

Further Reading

Each book listed on this page pertains to the Big Question. Encourage students to read them in their free time or for extra credit, if applicable. The first book on the list is easily accessible, the second is accessible, and the third is challenging.

Websites

Log onto www.LongmanKeystone.com for links to related websites.

Differentiated Instruction	
Beginning	Ask students to look back at the four readings. What type of reading did they enjoy most—the poems, myth, fable, or articles. Why?
Early Intermediate	Put students in pairs and ask them to list the types of winning and losing described in each of the readings.
Intermediate	Have students use a graphic organizer to describe someone who won and someone who lost. Ask them to share their list with the class.
Standard English Learners (CRI)	Ask students to think about things they have won and lost. Encourage students to share any experiences and explain how those experiences relate to the Big Question.

Listening & Speaking Workshop

STEP 1: Introduce

 Begin this workshop by reading over with students the checklist on page 255. Use the checklist as a planning guide. Show a recorded example of a TV sports report and then apply the checklist to evaluate what you saw. Make sure the TV sports report is clearly related to the unit theme "winning and losing."

Think About It Read over the instructions with students and brainstorm topic ideas. Suggest that students make a checklist of all the parts of this assignment to be sure they don't miss any.

STEP 2: Teach

Gather and Organize Information Write each of the boldfaced steps on the board. Have students read the directions, and clarify any questions. Remind students that *visuals* may include photos, graphs, posters, primary source documents, drawings, and real objects.

Teaching Resources

- CD-ROM/e-book, Gather and Organize Information

Put It All Together

LISTENING & SPEAKING WORKSHOP
TV Sports Report

You will explain what happened at a sports event as if you were a TV newscaster on the scene.

1 THINK ABOUT IT Think about the baseball game in "Casey at the Bat" and the footrace in "The Hare and the Tortoise." How would a TV sports reporter at the scene tell what happened?

Work in small groups. Discuss what kinds of sports you like to watch in person or on TV. Work together to develop a list of sports events you would like to tell about on TV. For example:
- A championship soccer match
- A World Series baseball game
- An Olympic skating competition

2 GATHER AND ORGANIZE INFORMATION Choose a sports event from your group's list. Write down what you would like to find out about it. Think about how a TV sports reporter would describe it. Watch a TV news show and get ideas from the sports reporters.

Research Go to the library and read newspaper articles about your sports event, or look for information about it on the Internet. If possible, watch the event on TV or in person. Take notes on the information you find. Include details that show why the event was exciting, surprising, or special.

Order Your Notes Arrange your notes in a logical way. For example, you could use a timeline to arrange them in time order, from the beginning of the event to the end. Put extra information, such as descriptive details and quotes from players, in a separate section.

Use Visuals TV sports reporters often show video clips of the events they describe. Make or find posters or other visuals to show during your report, such as drawings of team logos or photographs of the star players. Be sure your visuals can be seen from the back of the room.

Prepare a Script Use your notes to write a script for a TV sports report. Include enough details to explain what happened and to convey the excitement or other emotions felt by people at the event.

254

TESOL Standards

Goal 3, Standard 2—To use English in socially and culturally appropriate ways: Students will use nonverbal communication appropriate to audience, purpose, and setting.
Descriptors—Interpreting and responding appropriately to nonverbal cues and body language; Demonstrating knowledge of acceptable nonverbal classroom behaviors; Using acceptable tone, volume, stress, and intonation, in various social settings; Recognizing and adjusting behavior in response to nonverbal cues.

Goal 3, Standard 3—To use English in socially and culturally appropriate ways: Students will use appropriate learning strategies to extend their sociolinguistic and sociocultural competence.
Descriptors—Experimenting with variations of language in social and academic settings; Seeking information about appropriate language use and behavior; Analyzing the social context to determine appropriate language use; Rehearsing variations of language use in different social and academic settings.

3 **PRACTICE AND PRESENT** Read your
script aloud, over and over, until you know it well.
Practice giving your sports report and showing
your visuals to a friend or family member. Keep
practicing until you can look at the audience while
you talk, glancing at your script only occasionally.

Deliver Your TV Sports Report Speak loudly
enough so that everyone in the class can hear you.
Say each word carefully so that it is clear. Look at
the audience as you speak, and don't hide behind
your script! Hold up your visuals so that everyone
can see them.

4 **EVALUATE THE PRESENTATION**
A good way to improve your speaking and
listening skills is to evaluate each presentation
you give and hear. When you evaluate yourself,
you think about what you did well and what you
can do better. Use this checklist to help you judge
your TV sports report and the sports reports of
your classmates.

- ☑ Did the speaker clearly tell the results and other
  details of the sports event?
- ☑ Did the speaker provide enough description
  to show why the event was exciting, surprising,
  or special?
- ☑ Could you hear the speaker easily?
- ☑ Could you understand the speaker's words?
- ☑ What suggestions do you have for improving
  the presentation?

 Speaking TIPS

Always face the audience (or an
imaginary TV camera) when you
speak. Ask if people can hear
you clearly.

Pronounce names and numbers
carefully. Write these important
details on your visuals so that the
audience can both see them and
hear them.

Listening TIP

Take notes as you listen. Do you
understand who played and what
happened in this sports event? Do
you know why it was exciting or
special? Ask questions after the
report if you need more information.

255

STEP 3: Practice

Practice and Present Read over with
students the information about doing a TV
sports report. As students prepare their
delivery, remind them that although they can
refer to their note cards or outline, they should
practice their TV sports report until they feel
they can speak fluently and confidently. Point
out the Listening and Speaking Tips along the
side of the page to help them.

Speaking Tips

Remind students to speak slowly so that others
can better understand them.

Listening Tips

Remind students that the 5Ws are a good
guide for listening too. If they can answer
the 5Ws after a presentation, they very likely
understood it.

STEP 4: Assess

Evaluate the Presentation Suggest
that students use the checklist on this page
to evaluate the group presentations for the
purpose of giving positive feedback. Giving
specific examples directly from the presentation
is most helpful to the speakers.

Differentiated Instruction

Beginning	Have students take notes as they listen to the presentations. Encourage them to focus on the main idea of each presentation.
Early Intermediate	Have students practice their presentation in front of the mirror. Make sure they check the pronunciation of difficult words before they present.
Intermediate	Encourage students to monitor their understanding of each speaker's presentation. Have them ask for clarification if needed.
Struggling Readers	Ask students to go back to one of the readings and select vocabulary that will help them in their presentation.

Writing Workshop

STEP 1: Introduce

In this workshop, students will practice using the steps of the writing process. They will apply each of the steps, while applying the characteristics of expository writing that they have learned.

STEP 2: Teach

Prewrite SAY: *Let's read together the prewrite instructions on page 256. You will select your essay topic by choosing something that is very interesting to you. Before you outline your topic, you will list key facts, details, and examples. Read the instructions on the page, and work with a partner to complete a graphic organizer like a Venn diagram, T-chart, a 5Ws chart, or three-column chart about the topic you have selected.*

Draft The concept of a rough draft may be new to some students. Explain that a draft is a work in progress. Review the parts of an essay and the meaning of body paragraphs versus a concluding paragraph. Review together the draft of the student essay on pages 257–258 and discuss Tamar's topic.

Teaching Resources

- *Transparencies, Resources,* Graphic Organizer 4, 6, or 8
- *Transparencies,* Writing Model 40, Proofreader's Marks 51
- CD-ROM/e-book, Writing Workshop
- *Workbook,* pp. 125–126

WRITING WORKSHOP
Expository Essay

In this unit, you have been learning the skills of expository writing. Now you will use your skills to write an expository essay. An expository essay is a group of paragraphs that gives information about a specific topic. A good expository essay begins with a paragraph that introduces the writer's topic and focus. Each body paragraph presents a main idea that helps develop the topic. Main ideas are supported by facts and examples. To organize information, the writer uses a method that suits the topic, such as the 5Ws, cause and effect, or comparison and contrast. A conclusion sums up the essay's important ideas in a way that readers will remember.

Your assignment for this workshop is to write a five-paragraph expository essay about a topic that interests you.

1 PREWRITE Brainstorm a list of topics in your notebook. You might focus on some aspect of winning and losing. Winning and losing is relevant to many topics in human life and in the natural world. After selecting a topic, think about your readers. What might they already know about your topic? What would you like them to learn from your essay?

List and Organize Ideas and Details Use a graphic organizer such as a Venn diagram, a 5Ws chart, or a cause-and-effect chart to organize your information. A student named Tamar decided to write about extinct and endangered bird species. Here is her cause-and-effect chart:

Cause	Effect
Passenger Pigeon *1. Food supply destroyed by people* *2. Killed for food and to protect crops*	*Extinct*
Great Auk *1. Climate change* *2. Hunted for its valuable feathers*	*Extinct*
Whooping Crane *1. Wetlands habitat destroyed* *2. Hunted for food and sport*	*Endangered*

2 DRAFT Use the model on page 259 and your graphic organizer to help you write a first draft. Remember to include an introductory paragraph, three body paragraphs, and a concluding paragraph.

256

TESOL Standards

Goal 2, Standard 2—To use English to achieve academically in all content areas: Students will use English to obtain, process, construct, and provide subject matter information in spoken and written form.
Descriptors—Listening to, speaking, reading, and writing about subject matter information; Gathering information orally and in writing; Understanding and producing technical vocabulary and text features according to content area; Demonstrating knowledge through application in a variety of contexts.

3 REVISE Read over your draft. As you do so, ask yourself the questions in the writing checklist. Use the questions to help you revise your essay.

SIX TRAITS OF WRITING CHECKLIST

☑ **IDEAS:** Do I present a main idea in each body paragraph?

☑ **ORGANIZATION:** Do I include an introduction and a conclusion?

☑ **VOICE:** Does my writing show my knowledge of the topic?

☑ **WORD CHOICE:** Do I use words accurately?

☑ **SENTENCE FLUENCY:** Do my sentences begin in different ways?

☑ **CONVENTIONS:** Does my writing follow the rules of grammar, usage, and mechanics?

Here are the changes Tamar plans to make when she revises her first draft:

Extinct and Endangered Birds

It may seem that there are plenty of birds in the world. ∧but Several bird species are endangered, and others already have becomed extinct. It is important to realize that when a bird species dies out, it's gone forever In addition, we're always in danger of losing more birds.

When european explorers first came comed to this continent, passenger pigeons were abundant. Today, this species no longer exists. One reason is that ∧People chopped down forests to build houses, towns, and farms. In doing so, they wiped out the passenger pigeon's food supply. Also, passenger pigeons were shot because ∧They were viewed as a threat to crops. Huge numbers were hunted for food as well. As a result, their population decreased. Eventually, none remained.

257

Revise Point out that the revising step focuses on improving the content and wording of a draft. Revision is not the same as editing. Teach students to give specific and helpful feedback to others. **SAY:** *To revise a draft means to look at it again and make content changes. It can be very difficult to make changes to your own writing, since you know what you meant when you wrote it. That is why getting feedback from other readers is so helpful. We find out what appeals to or confuses the audience so we can change it before publication.*

STEP 3: Assess

Read aloud the Six Traits of Writing Checklist with students, and go over each entry. **SAY:**

Ideas *Check that your topic relates to winning and losing.*

Organization *Check that your essay has a clear introduction and conclusion.*

Voice *Check that your writing reveals your knowledge of the topic in your own words.*

Word Choice *Check that you use accurate words, especially cause-and-effect words such as because, because of, and so.*

Sentence Fluency *Check that you do not start every sentence the same way. Vary your sentence style and structure.*

Conventions *Check that you follow rules of grammar, usage, and mechanics.*

Differentiated Instruction

Beginning	Work with students to brainstorm topic ideas. Write students' suggestions on the board.
Early Intermediate	Have students use a graphic organizer of their choice to organize their information. Put students in pairs and have them compare their charts.
Intermediate	Have students explain why Tamar's decision to move a sentence on page 258 was a good idea.
Special Needs	Explain to students how to use the Copy and Paste tools on a computer. Point out that these tools can save them time when reorganizing their writing.

Writing Workshop

Edit and Proofread Pair English learners with English-proficient students. Review with students the kinds of grammar, word usage, and spelling edits Tamar made on her final draft. (She rearranged sentences, inserted words, added details, corrected verb tenses, and combined sentences.) Discuss why you think Tamar made each edit. Keep dictionaries nearby to check spelling.

Assign the Edit and Proofread Workbook page for extra practice.

Another extinct bird is the great auk, a flightless bird that lived in the North Atlantic. Climate change may have helped cause the great auk's extinction. During a period known as "the little ice age," the climate turned colder. ∧so Many birds died. However, one of the most important causes of the bird's disappearance is that people hunted the great auk for its valuable feathers. They killed as many birds, ∧ and rare eggs and took as many eggs as they could. Mainly because of these human activities, the species did not survive.

The whooping crane, the largest bird in North America, is endangered. It has been hunted for food and also shot for sport. Wetlands, which are its habitat, often have been turned into farmlands and towns. Some of the reasons it is endangered are familiar. Collisions with power lines have killed many birds. Fortunately, the whooping crane, although endangered, still exists.

These three bird species are just a few among the many that are extinct or in danger of becoming so. If people work hard, we may be able to help prevent more birds from becoming extinct. Once a bird species becomes extinct, it has been losed forever. sadly lost

4 EDIT AND PROOFREAD Workbook Page 125

Copy your revised draft onto a clean sheet of paper. Read it again. Correct any errors in grammar, word usage, mechanics, and spelling. Here are the additional changes Tamar plans to make when she prepares her final draft.

258

TESOL Standards

Goal 3, Standard 1—To use English in socially and culturally appropriate ways: Students will use the appropriate language variety, register, and genre according to audience, purpose, and setting.
Descriptors—Using the appropriate degree of formality with different audiences and settings; Recognizing and using Standard English and vernacular dialects appropriately; Using a variety of writing styles appropriate for different audiences, purposes, and settings; Determining appropriate topics for interaction.

Tamar Honig

Extinct and Endangered Birds

It may seem that there are plenty of birds in the world, but several bird species are endangered, and others already have become extinct. It is important to realize that when a bird species dies out, it's gone forever. In addition, we're always in danger of losing more birds.

When european explorers first came to this continent, passenger pigeons were abundant. Today, this species no longer exists. One reason is that people chopped down forests to build houses, towns, and farms. In doing so, they wiped out the passenger pigeon's food supply. Also, passenger pigeons were shot because they were viewed as a threat to crops. Huge numbers were hunted for food as well. As a result, their population decreased. Eventually, none remained.

Another extinct bird is the great auk, a flightless bird that lived in the North Atlantic. Climate change may have helped cause the great auk's extinction. During a period known as "the little ice age," the climate turned colder, so many birds died. However, one of the most important causes of the bird's disappearance is that people hunted the great auk for its valuable feathers and rare eggs. They killed as many birds and took as many eggs as they could. Mainly because of these human activities, the species did not survive.

The whooping crane, the largest bird in North America, is endangered. Some of the reasons it is endangered are familiar. It has been hunted for food and also shot for sport. Wetlands, which are its habitat, often have been turned into farmlands and towns. Collisions with power lines have killed many birds. Fortunately, the whooping crane, although endangered, still exists.

These three bird species are just a few among the many that are extinct or in danger of becoming so. If people work hard, we may be able to help prevent more birds from becoming extinct. Once a bird species becomes extinct, it sadly has been lost forever.

5 PUBLISH Prepare your final draft. Share your essay with your teacher and classmates.

Workbook
Page 126

259

STEP 1: Introduce

Remind students that the Big Question is *What do we learn through winning and losing?* **SAY:** *You have read informational texts, poems, and stories about winning and losing in the natural world as well as the world of sports. There is an old proverb: "It's not whether you win or lose, but how you play the game." What do you think this means? Do you agree? The artists on these pages show that fun and enjoyment are just as important as winning the game.*

STEP 2: Teach

Visual Literacy

Mark Sfirri Explain that a "reject" is something that is not perfect, and is therefore considered inferior and often thrown away. Sfirri, however, has created an artwork out of so-called rejects. By playfully shaping his bats into bat shapes to reveal the textures and patterns of unusual wood, the artist shows that even a "reject" can be a beautiful object.

Have students write a brief story on a note card about a time they played a game (baseball or other game) and really wanted to win but didn't. **ASK:** *Did you learn anything from losing?* Tell them NOT to write their names on the note cards. Then place the cards in a box. Randomly choose the cards and read (or have volunteers read) them to the class. Discuss the issues about winning and losing raised in the stories and what the class can learn about handling both. **ASK:** *Is there actually more to be learned from losing?*

Morris Kantor Explain that in *Baseball at Night*, Kantor plays with perspective to squeeze important elements—the lights, the houses, the crowd, the game—into his painting's frame. Have students experiment with "framing" by creating their own viewfinder and using it to zoom in and out as they look at objects. They will need cardboard squares, a ruler, a pencil, scissors, paperclips, paints, and drawing paper. Using the width of the ruler as a guide, have students trace and cut out two L-shaped pieces from their cardboard squares to create the two halves of a frame. By overlapping the two L-shaped pieces and moving them inwards, they can "tighten" their frame. Paperclips can be used to hold the pieces together.

Teaching Resources

• *Workbook*, pp. 127–128
• CD-ROM/e-book, Smithsonian

BASEBALL IN AMERICA

Americans love to watch and play many different sports. Baseball, basketball, hockey, and football are all very popular. In these games, one team will win and another will lose. Everyone loves a winning team, but we don't always cheer for the winner. Sometimes the losing team has played a great game. Then we might cheer for the loser, too.

Mark Sfirri, *Rejects from the Bat Factory* (1996)

Artist Mark Sfirri's ten-year-old son wanted a new baseball bat. Sfirri agreed to make him one. As he worked, Sfirri realized that he could do a lot with the wood and shape of the bat as an artist. So he made his son a regular bat first. Then he made the five bats hanging in *Rejects from the Bat Factory*.

Sfirri made his bats out of different kinds of unusual wood. A wood called curly maple has a wavy pattern of red and yellow colors in it. Zebrawood has stripes. Sfirri used a method called turning to create the

bats. Turning allows a woodworker to give pieces of wood a rounded shape by rotating them against a cutting tool. The bat on the far left still has a ball "stuck" in it. The bat fourth from the left has a dent!

Sfirri wanted to create a fun set of bats, but he also wanted to show how we often value things that aren't perfect. Sometimes a "loser" can be a real "winner."

◀ Mark Sfirri, *Rejects from the Bat Factory*, 1996, wood, 15⅜ x 36½ in., Smithsonian American Art Museum

260

TESOL Standards

Goal 2, Standard 2—To use English to achieve academically in all content areas: Students will use English to obtain, process, construct, and provide subject matter information in spoken and written form.
Descriptors—Analyzing, synthesizing, and inferring from information; Hypothesizing and predicting; Formulating and asking questions.

Goal 2, Standard 2—To use English to achieve academically in all content areas: Students will use English to obtain, process, construct, and provide subject matter information in spoken and written form.
Descriptors—Representing information visually and interpreting information presented visually.

Goal 2, Standard 3—To use English to achieve academically in all content areas: Students will use appropriate learning strategies to construct and apply academic knowledge.
Descriptors—Focusing attention selectively; Applying basic reading comprehension skills such as skimming, scanning, previewing, and reviewing text; Planning how and when to use cognitive strategies and applying them appropriately to a learning task.

▲ Morris Kantor, *Baseball at Night*, 1934, oil, 37 x 47¼ in.,
Smithsonian American Art Museum

Morris Kantor, *Baseball at Night* (1934)

Morris Kantor captures the charm of a small-town baseball
game in *Baseball at Night*. The crowd fills the stands. The
players in the field are ready for the next play. The pitcher steps
toward the batter, and . . . .

The painting doesn't show what happens next, but you
can use your imagination. Kantor puts all of the important
elements in his painting: the players, the tall umpire dressed
in black, the crowd, the lights that light up the field, and the
warm lights from the house behind the stands. Night lights had
just begun to be added to fields at this time. Now everyone is
out to enjoy the game!

Both of these artists focus on the fun of team sports, where
winning is just one part of a much larger story.

Apply What You Learned

1 How do both of these
artworks show the fun side
of a sport like baseball?

2 What kind of artwork would
you make to capture the
feeling of another sport,
such as basketball
or soccer?

Big Question
What would you show in
a painting to illustrate the
ideas of winning and losing?

Workbook
Pages 127–128

261

Differentiated Instruction

Beginning	Have students identify the artist who painted *Baseball at Night*. (Morris Kantor)
Early Intermediate	Ask students which work of art they prefer, *Rejects from the Bat Factory* or *Baseball at Night*. Ask them to give reasons for their choice.
Intermediate	Have students make a list of adjectives describing either of the works of art on this spread.
Greater Challenge	Have students write a simple paragraph that explains what they think happens after the pitcher throws the ball in the painting on page 261.

Using their viewfinders, have students zoom
in closely on Kantor's painting. **ASK:** *What
do you see?* Now ask them to zoom out so
they see the entire painting. **ASK:** *How does
the new perspective influence how you see
the painting?* Next ask them to look around
the room and use their viewfinders to frame
a scene or object. Have them draw the object
or scene. Encourage them to include as many
details as possible.

Do an oral history project with the class.
Ask students what recollections they have of
either watching on TV, listening on the radio,
or attending in person, a sports event with an
adult they care about. Have students interview
the adult. They can either take notes, or make
an audio or video record of the interview. Ask
students to write up a brief summary of the
sporting event that includes their own memories
as well as the information they recorded from
the adult they interviewed. Encourage them to
write their summary as a story, with dialogue,
scene, and action. Ask for volunteers to share
their stories with the class.

STEP 3: Apply

Apply What You Learned

Have volunteers read the questions aloud,
and be sure students understand the meaning
of difficult words and concepts. Encourage
students to carefully study the artworks, and if
necessary, reread the text to help them.

ANSWERS

1. *Rejects from the Bat Factory* shows the fun
   side of baseball with original-looking bats.
   Baseball at Night shows people having an
   exciting time at a baseball game.
2. **Possible response:** I'd photograph
   a basketball player shooting the ball
   through the hoop in the last seconds of a
   championship game.

Q Possible response: To illustrate the idea
of winning and losing in a painting, I'd show
two teams of football players at the end of a
game. The losing team would be coming off
the field with their heads down and with sad
expressions on their faces. The winning team
would be carrying their quarterback on their
shoulders, and everyone would be laughing.

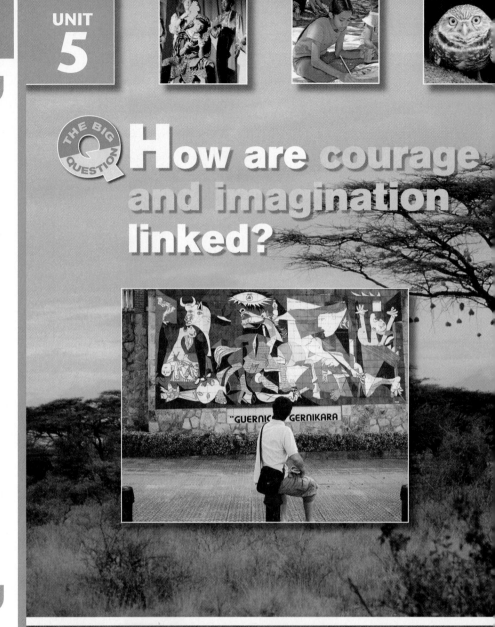

THE BIG QUESTION

How are courage and imagination linked?

"GUERNICA GERNIKARA"

262

STEP 1: Introduce

Unit Content

Tell students that in this unit they will read selections about the ways courage and imagination are linked. Have students look up these words in a dictionary, if necessary. The readings include an adapted play, a photo-essay, a novel excerpt, a biographical article, and a how-to piece. Students will learn new vocabulary and practice reading and comprehension skills, such as analyzing text structure, classifying, summarizing, and more. Throughout, students will use writing and grammar skills, and they will end the unit by writing an expository essay.

The Big Question

Introduce the Big Question "How are courage and imagination linked?" Encourage students to give some potential answers to the question. Express interest in students' answers, and probe their thinking. Emphasize that there is no right or wrong answer to the question. To facilitate class discussion, ask the following questions.

- What have you done that might be considered brave? How did it make you feel?
- What kinds of things have you done that require imagination?
- In what ways do you think courage and imagination can be linked?

STEP 2: Teach

Visual Literacy

Point out that illustrations and photos often accompany a reading so that readers can visualize what is being described. For example, the reading that begins on page 284 is a photo-essay in which the images are as important as the text. Ask students to describe the images in that reading, and then preview images in the other readings.

Teaching Resources

- *Resources*, Unit 5 Lesson Plans, pp. 51–62
- *Transparencies*, Unit 5 Daily Language Practice
- CD-ROM/e-book, Big Question
- Video, Segment 5
- *Resources*, Letters Home, pp. 117–118

🌐 TESOL Standards

Goal 2, Standard 1—To use English to achieve academically in all content areas: Students will use English to interact in the classroom.
Descriptors—Asking and answering questions.

Goal 2, Standard 2—To use English to achieve academically in all content areas: Students will use English to obtain, process, construct, and provide subject matter information in spoken and written form.
Descriptors—Hypothesizing and predicting; Formulating and asking questions.

Goal 2, Standard 3—To use English to achieve academically in all content areas: Students will use appropriate learning strategies to construct and apply academic knowledge.
Descriptors—Actively connecting new information to information previously learned.

This unit is about courage and imagination. You'll read about an orphan who helps a grieving family and about kids who create art in order to promote peace. You'll read about an effort to save burrowing owls from destruction and about a Kenyan woman who created a simple method of improving living conditions in her native country. As you read, you'll practice the literary and academic language you need to use in school.

READING 1: Play

■ *The Secret Garden*
   by Frances Hodgson Burnett,
   adapted by David C. Jones

READING 2: Social Studies Photo-essay

■ "Kids' Guernica"

READING 3: Novel Excerpt

■ From *Hoot* by Carl Hiaasen

READING 4: Science Articles

■ "A Tree Grows in Kenya:
   The Story of Wangari Maathai"
■ "How to Plant a Tree"

Listening and Speaking

At the end of this unit, you'll give a **how-to demonstration** that explains the steps involved in doing something.

Writing

In this unit you'll practice **expository writing**, or writing that explains a topic. You'll write four expository paragraphs and an expository essay.

QuickWrite

Write several sentences about a time when you used courage and imagination to solve a problem.

Visit *LongmanKeystone.com*

263

STEP 3: Practice

QuickWrite

Write the topic *Using Courage and Imagination to Solve a Problem* on the board. Then draw a sequence chart for students to copy and fill in. Help them turn their chain of events into expository writing by filling in their own sequence chart about a time when they used courage and imagination to solve a problem and writing a sentence as an example.

STEP 4: Extend

Have students read aloud the titles of the selections. Point out that most people with courage and imagination are heroes. Ask students to discuss what the word *hero* means to them. Point out that heroes are people who do something brave. It can be a dramatic deed, such as saving someone's life, or it can be a simple act of kindness, such as going out of your way to help someone in need. Ask students:

● to name heroes they have heard or read about in the news
● to identify any heroes they know personally
● to describe heroic things they have done
● to discuss what it takes to be a hero.

Teach

STEP 1: Introduce

Objectives

Read the list in the What You Will Learn section, encouraging students to join in. Tell students that *The Secret Garden* is about an orphaned girl who goes to a new home. Have pairs of students work together to restate the list of things they will learn.

 The Big Question

Remind students that the Big Question is "How are courage and imagination linked?" Have them read the first paragraph on page 264. Answer the question from your own personal experience.

Ask students to share their own experiences or points of view. To segue into the reading selection, **SAY:** *Being imaginative often requires bravery. It means seeing things in new ways or trying to express yourself creatively. In this reading, we will learn about a brave girl who imagines replanting the Secret Garden.*

Build Background

Point out that some flowers traditionally grown in English gardens are columbine, double daisy, roses, heliotrope, lily of the valley, oleander, petunia, verbena, and wild hyacinth. You may want to find pictures of some of these flowers to show the class.

STEP 2: Teach

Understanding the Genre:
Adapted Play

A play is a story that actors usually perform in a theater. Although plays are meant to be performed, actors can also read aloud the written version, or script, and the action can be imagined. *The Secret Garden* is a play based on a novel written in 1911 by Frances Hodgson Burnett.

Teaching Resources

- CD-ROM/e-book, Literary Words
- Audio CD 5, track 1
- *Workbook*, p. 129

What You Will Learn

Reading
- Vocabulary building: *Literary terms, dictionary skills, word study*
- Reading strategy: *Analyze text structure 1*
- Text type: *Literature (play)*

Grammar, Usage, and Mechanics
More adverbs with *-ly*

Writing
Write a formal e-mail

THE BIG QUESTION

How are courage and imagination linked? Why does it take imagination to create a garden? You have to choose which plants to grow and where to plant them. You have to be able to imagine what the garden will look like after it grows and flowers.

Think about what you know about gardens. Maybe you have seen photographs and drawings of gardens in books and magazines, or perhaps you have seen gardens in your own neighborhood. You might even have grown flowers, herbs, or vegetables in your own garden or apartment.

Work with a partner. Talk about what you know about gardens. Use this chart to get you started. Add more columns and rows if you need them. Then share what you know with the class.

Why People Plant Gardens	What Plants I Like

▲ A wild English garden

264

BUILD BACKGROUND

You will read an adapted version of the play ***The Secret Garden***. The play is based on the novel *The Secret Garden*, written by Frances Hodgson Burnett. The book has been popular since it was first published in 1911. The story takes place in the early 1900s in the English countryside.

In the play, the actors tell the story through their dialogue and actions. We get to know the characters by what they say and do. When the play opens, the orphaned girl Mary Lennox has just arrived in England to live with Mr. Craven. Mary had been living in India with her parents. This is a difficult time for Mary because her parents died within days of each other. Mr. Craven was her father's best friend, so he agreed to take care of Mary. Mr. Craven has a very large house with many gardens. Mary is curious about the gardens.

🌐 TESOL Standards

Goal 1, Standard 3—To use English to communicate in social settings: Students will use learning strategies to extend their communicative competence.
Descriptors—Listening to and imitating how others use English; Exploring alternative ways of saying things; Focusing attention selectively.
Goal 2, Standard 1—To use English to achieve academically in all content areas: Students will use English to interact in the classroom.
Descriptors—Requesting and providing clarification; Participating in full-class, group, and pair discussions; Negotiating and managing interaction to accomplish tasks.
Goal 2, Standard 2—To use English to achieve academically in all content areas: Students will use English to obtain, process, construct, and provide subject matter information in spoken and written form.
Descriptors—Selecting, connecting, and explaining information; Understanding and producing technical vocabulary and text features according to content area.

VOCABULARY

Learn Literary Words

Playwrights, or people who write plays, usually begin by setting the scene. They give important details about the time and place of each section of the play. This helps readers and actors to visualize each scene. Study this example from *The Secret Garden.* How has the writer helped you visualize the opening scene?

Literary Words

setting the scene
list of characters
stage directions

> Early 1900s. Bedroom in Misselthwaite Manor, England.
> Bed center; table next to it holds tray of food.

At the beginning of a play, you will also find a list of characters. Below is a list of characters from the *The Secret Garden.*

Characters		
Mary Lennox	Ben Weatherstaff	Mr. Archibald Craven
Martha Sowerby	Dickon Sowerby	Colin Craven

Stage directions are notes included in a play that tell how the play should be performed. These directions are in brackets and set in italics near the character's name. Stage directions tell actors what they should do and how they should look and act. They may also tell about the scenery and costumes. Study the stage directions below. How do they help you understand the characters and what is happening? How do they help you act out the dialogue?

> **Mary:**   [*Puzzled*] How can a garden be locked?
> **Martha:** It can be if there's a high wall around it. [*She exits.*]
> **Mary:**   [*Sighing*] How I wish I were back in India! [*Curtain*]

Practice **Workbook Page 129**

Take turns reading the lines above with a partner. Pay close attention to the stage directions. Act out each line, using the stage directions as your guide. Use a dictionary to look up any words that you don't know.

265

Vocabulary

Learn Literary Words Play the CD. Have students listen and repeat. If you are not using the CD, read the Literary Words aloud. Ask students what comes to mind when they hear each word. Write down student responses.
SAY: *These words are called literary words because in a discussion of literature, they have a unique meaning. Read the paragraph in your book that defines* setting the scene, list of characters, *and* stage directions.

Write the following definitions for *setting the scene, list of characters,* and *stage directions* on the board or on an overhead transparency to reinforce learning.

* **setting the scene:** provides information about the time and place of each section of the play
* **list of characters:** tells who the characters are
* **stage directions:** notes that tell how the play should be performed

Provide examples of the literary words, and ask students to use them in new sentences. Have students use the corresponding Workbook page for extra practice.

STEP 3: Practice

Have students work with partners to complete the practice activity. **SAY:** *Take turns acting the lines with your partner. Pay close attention to the stage directions because they will give you clues as to what your character is thinking and feeling.*

Differentiated Instruction

Beginning	Ask students if they know someone who is courageous.
Early Intermediate	Ask students to name two things that someone with courage does.
Intermediate	Have students describe what it means to be courageous.
Standard English Learners (CRI)	Tell students to find as many alternative words for courage as they can. Encourage students to use a dictionary or a thesaurus if needed.

Teach

STEP 1: Teach

CD5 T2–T3

 Vocabulary

Learn Academic Words Play the CD. Have students listen and repeat. If you are not using the CD, read the Academic Words aloud.

SAY: *Look at the Academic Words chart. The definition for each word is on the left side. On the right side, each word is used in a sentence. Work with a partner to write an additional sentence for each Academic Word. Write each word, its definition, and the sentence in your personal Word Book.*

STEP 2: Practice

Write the first question on the board and underline the words as shown: *How would you* <u>*approach a bird in a garden*</u>?

SAY: *Look at the underlined words in the question on the board. When you are asked a question, try to include words from the question in your answer.*

Write this answer on the board: <u>*I would approach a bird in a garden*</u> *quietly.*

SAY: *Which words from the question are underlined here? This is a good way to answer the question.* Be sure students clearly see the connection.

ANSWERS

Possible responses:
1. I would approach a bird in a garden quietly.
2. Dogs and cats convey their feelings through their tails, the sounds they make, and their behavior.
3. When someone won't cooperate with me, I try to find out why.
4. I like watching a drama because it takes me into another world.

Teaching Resources

- Audio CD 5, tracks 2–3
- *Workbook*, pp. 130–132
- CD-ROM/e-book, Academic Words, Word Study

Learn Academic Words

Study the red words and their meanings. You will find these words useful when talking and writing about literature. Write each word and its meaning in your notebook. After you read *The Secret Garden*, try to use these words to respond to the text.

approach = move closer to someone or something	The girl wanted to **approach** the lamb, but she was afraid of coming too close to the animal.
convey = communicate a message or information, with or without using words	Birds **convey** their fear by flying away. Everyone understands their message.
cooperate = work with someone else to achieve something that you both want	When people **cooperate**, they get the job done faster.
drama = a play for the theater, television, radio, and so forth	The class **drama** was a big success. Everyone enjoyed watching the play.

Practice Workbook Page 130

Work with a partner to answer the questions. Try to include the red word in your answer. Write the sentences in your notebook.

1. How would you **approach** a bird in a garden?
2. How do dogs and cats **convey** their feelings?
3. What happens when someone won't **cooperate** with you? What do you do?
4. What do you like about watching or acting in a **drama**?

Some students love to ▶ study drama and perform.

266

Word Study: Spelling Words with *oo*

In English, the letters *oo* can stand for either a short sound /ŏŏ/ or a long sound /o͞o/. For example, *The Secret Garden* has many words with the short sound of *oo*, such as *book*. It also contains words with the long sound of *oo*, such as *room*. Notice the /ŏŏ/ and /o͞o/ sounds and their spellings in the chart below.

oo as in *book*	*oo* as in *moon*
go**od**-bye	l**oo**se
t**oo**k	n**oo**n
underst**oo**d	ch**oo**se

Practice

Work with a partner. Copy the chart above into your notebook. Say a word from the chart, and ask your partner to spell it aloud. Then have your partner say the next word. Continue until you can spell all of the words correctly. Then work with your partner to spell the following words: *blooming, cook, afternoon, goodness, gloomy, wood, shook,* and *tools*. Add them to the chart under the correct heading.

READING STRATEGY | ANALYZE TEXT STRUCTURE 1

Analyzing text structure can help you understand what kind of text you're reading. It can also help you set a purpose for reading. Different kinds of writing, or genres, have different kinds of text structures. Read these descriptions to help you understand the various types of text structures:

- Stories and novels are written in sentences and paragraphs. Dialogue is enclosed within quotation marks.
- Poems are usually written in lines and groups of lines, called stanzas. The punctuation in poems may not follow the same rules as it does in other kinds of writing.
- Plays are mainly written in dialogue. The characters' names are given, followed by colons (:) and the words the speakers say. Stage directions are usually in brackets ([ ]) and set in italics. Many plays are divided into numbered scenes.

Preview the text structure of *The Secret Garden*. Describe it to a partner.

267

Workbook Page 131

Workbook Page 132

STEP 1: Teach

Word Study

Spelling Words with *oo* SAY: *Some words have a long oo sound and others a short oo sound. Long oo words include* room, food, *and* broom. *Short oo words include* good, look, took, *and* brook. *Let's read the words in the chart on page 267 together. Can you hear how the words are spelled oo but have two different pronunciations?*

STEP 2: Practice

Have students complete the practice exercise.

ANSWERS

Short *oo*	Long *oo*
cook	blooming
goodness	afternoon
wood	gloomy
shook	tools

STEP 3: Teach

Reading Strategy

Analyze Text Structure SAY: *When you analyze text structure, you can figure out what kind of text you are reading. For example, in this text we see the characters' names followed by colons. Then we see dialogue, or words the speakers say. There are also stage directions and numbered scenes. We know that we are reading a play.*

Linguistic Note

The Double *oo* in *Cooperate*

Point out that the double *oo* in *moon* or *book* is part of the same syllable. Sometimes a word is spelled with double *oo*, yet the two *o*'s do not belong to the same syllable. Refer back to the previous discussion of the new academic word *cooperation*. Here two syllables each claim one of the *o*'s: cooperate. Other examples are: *coordinate, cooperation,* and *coordination*. Show the difference with this minimal pair: *co-op/coop*.

Read

STEP 1: Introduce

Reading Summary

This adapted play is about a girl who goes to live with a new family after being orphaned in India. Based on the novel *The Secret Garden*, published in 1911, it takes place in the Yorkshire region of northern England.

 The Big Question

Remind students of the Big Question—"How are courage and imagination linked?" Ask students how being alone in an unfamiliar place might be helped by courage and imagination. (Being or feeling alone can be difficult. You need courage to stay strong. Your imagination can help you find courage by enabling you to see ways to change your situation.) In what ways are courage and imagination linked when you are in a new situation?

STEP 2: Teach

Set a Purpose for Reading

Tell students to copy the purpose for reading into their notebooks and to keep it in mind as they read. Explain that they will have to present details that support their answer to the question and to explain how the reading relates to the Big Question.

Preteaching Highlighted Words

With students, preview the vocabulary on pages 268–269. Write the words on the board, and point out that they are defined at the bottom of each page.

Ask volunteers to read the definitions. Model for students how to use the words in original sentences. For example: *The mansion had twenty-two rooms and six fireplaces.*

CD5 T4 **Scaffolding: Listen and Read**

Have students read along in the text as you play the Audio CD recording. Pause at the end of each page so that you can answer questions.

Teaching Resources

- *Resources*, Summaries, pp. 155–156
- Audio CD 5, track 4

Set a purpose for reading How will certain characters' courage and imagination change life at Misselthwaite Manor? Read the play to find out.

The Secret Garden

Frances Hodgson Burnett,
adapted by David C. Jones

In this classic play, the orphaned girl Mary Lennox comes from India to live at Misselthwaite Manor, England. She finds the place gloomy until she hears about a long-lost garden. Then she has a wonderful idea.

> **CHARACTERS**
> MARY LENNOX
> MARTHA SOWERBY
> BEN WEATHERSTAFF
> DICKON SOWERBY
> MR. ARCHIBALD CRAVEN
> COLIN CRAVEN

Scene 1

Time: Early 1900s.

Setting: Bedroom in Misselthwaite Manor, England. Bed center; table next to it holds tray of food.

At rise: Mary is alone, looking around.

MARY: What a dreary place. I know I'm not going to like it here. [*Martha enters.*]

MARTHA: Good afternoon, miss.

MARY: [*Imperiously*] Good afternoon. Are you going to be my servant?

MARTHA: I'm to do a bit of cleaning up and bring you your food.

MARY: I don't like English food.

MARTHA: [*Sharply*] I've nine little brothers and sisters who would be glad to eat this food in a minute.

MARY: [*Surprised*] My goodness! You have nine brothers and sisters?

---

dreary, very dull and causing sadness
servant, someone paid to clean and cook for someone else

268

 TESOL Standards

Goal 1, Standard 3—To use English to communicate in social settings: Students will use learning strategies to extend their communicative competence.
Descriptors—Using the primary language to ask for clarification; Using context to construct meaning.

Goal 2, Standard 1—To use English to achieve academically in all content areas: Students will use English to interact in the classroom.
Descriptors—Asking and answering questions.

Goal 2, Standard 2—To use English to achieve academically in all content areas: Students will use English to obtain, process, construct, and provide subject matter information in spoken and written form.
Descriptors—Analyzing, synthesizing, and inferring from information; Hypothesizing and predicting; Formulating and asking questions.

MARTHA: Yes. We have to take care of each other since Father died. Thank goodness for Dickon. He's a big help.

MARY: Who's Dickon?

MARTHA: My oldest brother. He's a rare boy. He talks to the animals, and when he plays his pipes, they all stop to listen. Everyone loves him. Well, I must be off now. I have a lot of work to do.

MARY: But what will I do?

MARTHA: You could go play in one of the gardens—except for the one that's locked.

MARY: [Puzzled] How can a garden be locked?

MARTHA: It can be if there's a high wall around it. [She exits.]

MARY: [Sighing] How I wish I were back in India! [Curtain]

Scene 2

Setting: The mansion gardens. There are flowerbeds, bushes, etc., around the stage. Fence covered with ivy, brambles, etc., is upright.

At rise: Ben Weatherstaff is working with a hoe. Mary enters.

BEN: [Looking up] Well, well. You must be Mistress Mary, quite contrary.

MARY: I am not contrary—and who are you?

BEN: I'm Ben Weatherstaff, the gardener. I've worked for Mr. Craven for many, many years.

MARY: And where's this locked garden I've heard about?

BEN: Why, you're standing next to it.

MARY: But where is the entrance?

BEN: Well, the gate is somewhere under all those brambles and ivy that have grown and covered it. It's been locked up so long.

MARY: But why was it ever locked? I never heard of such a thing.

BEN: Well, it was Mr. and Mrs. Craven's favorite spot, and they spent many a happy hour in it, reading and laughing together like two lovebirds. Mrs. Craven used to sit reading on a high branch of one of the big trees, but one day the branch broke and she fell to her death. After that, Mr. Craven had the gate locked, and he hasn't entered the garden since.

---

pipes, tube-shaped musical instruments, such as flutes
mansion, very large house
brambles, wild plants with thorns and berries
upright, straight up
contrary, deliberately doing or saying the opposite of what others want
lovebirds, people who show by their behavior that they love each other very much

✔ **LITERARY CHECK**
*Which two people on the **list of characters** are mentioned in the dialogue but have not yet appeared at the end of page 269?*

BEFORE YOU GO ON

1 What is Mary's first reaction to Misselthwaite Manor?

2 Who is Dickon?

 On Your Own
How do most people feel when they are in an unfamiliar place far from home?

269

Study Skills: Dictionary

Students should write down any unfamiliar words in their Word Books and look up the definitions in a dictionary. Point out that the guide words at the top of each dictionary page show the first and last word on the page, according to alphabetical order.

✔ **LITERARY CHECK**

If students need help remembering the meaning of *list of characters,* refer them to page 265.
Answer: The two people are Dickon and Mr. Craven.

STEP 3: Monitor Progress

Continue reading and listening to the text with your students. Pause the recording at the end of the page and check students' comprehension.

Before You Go On

Remind students that these questions will help them monitor their progress. Put students in pairs to answer the questions. Encourage them to share their answers with the class.

ANSWERS

1. Mary's first reaction to Misselthwaite Manor is that it's dreary.
2. Dickon is Martha's oldest brother.

On Your Own Have students write an answer on a separate sheet of paper. Collect student responses to monitor their comprehension and writing skills.

Differentiated Instruction	
Beginning	Ask students to identify the title of this play and the original author. (The Secret Garden, Frances Hodgson Burnett)
Early Intermediate	Before reading, have students look at only the illustrations. Ask students when they think this play takes place.
Intermediate	Based on the illustrations on pages 268 and 271, have students describe Mary and Colin's appearance.
Greater Challenge	Have students look at the illustrations of pages 268–275. Have students predict what the story will be about. Ask students to share their predictions.

Read

STEP 4: Teach

Preteaching Highlighted Words

Preview the vocabulary by writing on the board the highlighted words from pages 270–271. Make sure students understand each word. Ask students to create original sentences using the words. If necessary, correct students' sentences and read the corrected version aloud.

Across the Curriculum:
Social Studies

The distance between India, where Mary was living, and England, her new home, is over 4,000 miles. At the time Mary was traveling, airplanes had only recently been invented. Mary traveled by carriage and boat to reach England, a journey that took several weeks. Show students a world map to trace Mary's route from India to England.

Model the
READING STRATEGY

Analyze Text Structure

Model for students how to analyze the text structure of this play. **SAY:** *Let's look closely at the text structure of this reading. Which characters are speaking on page 270?* (Mary, Ben, Dickon, and Robin) *How do you know?* (Their names are written followed by a colon.) *Point to any dialogue on the page. How do you know it is dialogue?* (The words are the exact words the characters say.) *How do you know which are the stage directions?* (They're bracketed and in italic type.) *What are some of the stage directions on page 270?* ([Resolutely], [Bleating is heard.], [Scoffing]).

✔ LITERARY CHECK

Point out the Literary Check box, and read the question aloud. Then ask students to look back through the reading to find out how the author sets this scene. Answer: Setting the Scene is important at the beginning of Scene 3 because it emphasizes Colin's isolation. The playwright tells us that there is a room with a bed, a window, and a portrait covered with a sheet. It helps us to see that Mary is in a quiet room that does not have much in it.

MARY: [*Resolutely*] Well, I shall find the entrance and go in there to play.

BEN: You won't be able to go in without the key.

MARY: [*Surprised*] There's a key? Where is it?

BEN: No one knows. Mr. Craven was so heartbroken he took the key one day and threw it as far as he could. No one has ever found it.

MARY: I'll find it. You'll see.

BEN: [*Wryly*] Well, good luck, Mistress Mary. You'll need it. [*Laughs and exits. After a moment, Dickon enters, carrying animals.*]

DICKON: Hello. You must be Miss Mary.

MARY: How did you know my name? And who are you?

DICKON: They call me Dickon. And I know about you because my sister, Martha, told me all about you.

MARY: Is it true you speak to animals?

DICKON: Aye. Say hello to my friends. This is Cert, the crow. [*Cawing sound is heard.*] The fox is Captain, and the lamb, Lady. [*Bleating is heard.*]

MARY: Those are strange names for animals.

DICKON: It's what they asked to be called.

MARY: [*Scoffing*] Animals and birds can't talk.

DICKON: Sure they can. You just have to know how to listen. [*Looks offstage*] Look! Here comes my friend, Robin. [*Robin enters.*]

ROBIN: Hello Dickon, Who is your friend?

MARY: [*Astonished*] Why, he does talk!

DICKON: See? You just have to want to listen to them. [*Curtain*]

Scene 3

Setting: Colin's bedroom. There is a bed center, a large portrait covered with sheet, and a window.

At rise: Colin is in bed, covered completely with blankets. Mary wanders on stage, doesn't notice Colin.

MARY: [*To herself*] I thought that the library was here somewhere. [*Notices bed*] Oh! [*Colin sits up.*]

COLIN: [*Frightened*] Are you a ghost?

MARY: Of course not. Do I look like a ghost? Who are you, and why are you in bed? It's two in the afternoon!

---

resolutely, in a very determined way
bleating, the sound that a sheep or goat makes: "baa"
scoffing, laughing at or talking to in a scornful way
astonished, very surprised

270

✔ LITERARY CHECK

*Why is **setting the scene** important at the beginning of Scene 3? What information does the playwright provide about the place? How does this help you visualize where Mary is now?*

TESOL Standards

Goal 1, Standard 2—To use English to communicate in social settings: Students will interact in, through, and with spoken and written English for personal expression and enjoyment.
Descriptors—Sharing social and cultural traditions and values.

Goal 2, Standard 3—To use English to achieve academically in all content areas: Students will use appropriate learning strategies to construct and apply academic knowledge.
Descriptors—Using context to construct meaning; Applying self-monitoring and self-corrective strategies to build and expand a knowledge base.

COLIN: I'm Colin Craven. My father is the master of this manor.

MARY: Why didn't anyone tell me he had a son?

COLIN: Because no one is allowed to talk about me.

MARY: Why not?

COLIN: Because I'm going to have a hump on my back, just like my father.

MARY: Don't you ever leave this room?

COLIN: No. If people look at me, I get sick.

MARY: That's ridiculous! I'm looking at you and you're not getting sick.

COLIN: Well, I might.

MARY: Save yourself the trouble. I'm leaving.

COLIN: [*Pleading*] No, don't go! Tell me about India. I hear that's where you're from.

MARY: You can read about India in books.

COLIN: Reading gives me a headache.

MARY: Well, if I were your father I'd make you read so you can learn about things.

COLIN: [*Stubbornly*] No one can make me do anything I don't want to do.

MARY: Well, why not?

COLIN: Because I'm sick and I'm dying!

MARY: Well, do you want to live?

COLIN: Not if I have a hump on my back like my father. [*Cries*]

MARY: [*Disgusted*] I'm leaving. You cry too much! [*Mary exits. Quick curtain*]

---

pleading, begging

BEFORE YOU GO ON

1 Who are Dickon's friends?

2 What does Colin beg Mary to do?

 On Your Own
Do you think that animals can communicate with people? Explain.

271

Study Skills: Internet

Students can use the Internet to learn more about the classic children's story *The Secret Garden* and its author, Frances Hodgson Burnett. Suggest that they use a search engine to do a key word search on "The Secret Garden" or "Frances Hodgson Burnett." In the resulting display of links, look for URLs that end in .edu and .org. These will generally be more reliable references than those ending in .com. Students will be able to find a plot summary, major themes of the book, the film and TV program based on the book, and more.

STEP 5: Monitor Progress

Ask students to check what they have understood in the reading. If you are using the Audio CD, pause the recording.

Before You Go On

Remind students that these questions will help them monitor their progress. Put students in pairs to answer the questions. Encourage them to share their answers with the class.

ANSWERS

1. Dickon's friends are a crow, a fox, a lamb, and a robin.
2. Colin wants Mary to tell him about India.

On Your Own Have students write an answer to the On Your Own question on a separate sheet of paper. Ask for volunteers to share their responses with the class. Then collect student responses to monitor their comprehension, writing skills, and fluency.

Preteaching Highlighted Words

Preview the vocabulary by writing on the board the highlighted words from pages 272–273. Make sure students understand each word. Ask students to create original sentences using selected words. When you correct their sentences, focus on correcting usage rather than mechanical errors.

Model the

READING STRATEGY

Analyze Text Structure

Point out another element of the text structure of a play—the scenes. Ask students which scenes take place on page 272. (Scenes 4 and 5) How are the scenes separated in a play? (Each one has its own heading.)

✔ LITERARY CHECK

Have students read the questions in the box before they continue reading. If they need help remembering the meaning of stage directions, go back to page 265. **Answer:** At first, Mary is timid and nervous with Mr. Craven. When she is exploring the grounds with Dickon, she is excited and outgoing.

Scene 4

Setting: Mr. Craven's library, with desk center, and bookshelves on walls.

At rise: Mary enters library where Mr. Craven is sitting.

MARY: [*Timidly*] You sent for me, sir?

MR. CRAVEN: Yes. Come closer, my dear. Don't be afraid. I'm quite harmless.

MARY: [*Boldly*] You don't frighten me.

MR. CRAVEN: [*Kindly*] You look just like your father. He was my best friend, you know, and when he died, and I learned you had no living relatives, I felt it my duty to care for you.

MARY: Yes. And I'm truly thankful, sir.

MR. CRAVEN: I wish I could do more for you, but I have been ill, you know.

MARY: I'm sorry.

MR. CRAVEN: Are you being taken good care of?

MARY: Martha has been very kind to me.

MR. CRAVEN: But are you happy here? Is there anything you need or want?

MARY: I wonder if I could have a place to make a garden? I love gardens so.

MR. CRAVEN: [*Pleased*] You do? [*Distantly*] There was once someone very dear to me who loved gardens, too. Yes, of course. Choose any part of the garden you wish, and I will see that you get all the tools you need. Now, child, leave me—I wish to be alone.

MARY: Thank you, Mr. Craven. [*Nervously*] And . . . and try not to be so sad. [*Runs out. Curtain*]

Scene 5

Setting: Same as Scene 2.

At rise: Mary and Dickon, holding Robin, are looking at fence covered with brambles.

MARY: Oh, Dickon, if only we could find the entrance to this locked garden. Mr. Craven said I could have any garden I wish—and I want this one.

DICKON: But even if we found the door, we'd still need the key.

ROBIN: Key . . . Now, where did I see a key?

DICKON: You saw a key, Robin?

ROBIN: Yes. I was flying around the other day, and I spotted a rusty old key.

---

relatives, members of your family
dear to, much loved by

272

✔ LITERARY CHECK

*Reread Scene 4, paying special attention to the **stage directions**. How does Mary behave at first with Mr. Craven? How does her attitude change?*

TESOL Standards

Goal 1, Standard 3—To use English to communicate in social settings: Students will use learning strategies to extend their communicative competence.
Descriptors—Testing hypotheses about language.

Goal 3, Standard 3—To use English in socially and culturally appropriate ways: Students will use appropriate learning strategies to extend their sociolinguistic and sociocultural competence.
Descriptors—Experimenting with variations of language in social and academic settings.

MARY: [*Excitedly*] Oh, Robin, think—please! Where was it?

ROBIN: [*Thinking*] Over there. Near that bush, I think. [*Mary and Dickon search.*]

DICKON: Look! Here it is! [*Holds up key*] Now if we only knew where the gate was.

ROBIN: Oh, I know that, too.

MARY: Well, why didn't you tell us?

ROBIN: You never asked me.

DICKON: Show us where it is, Robin.

ROBIN: It's over here, behind this ivy. [*They rush over to fence.*]

MARY: [*Finding door*] Yes, yes! Here it is. Quick, Dickon. Try the key!

DICKON: Very well. [*He tries the key.*] It's turning . . . but very slowly. It's very rusty. There! I think I've got it. Now, we'll just give a little push, and—[*Curtain goes up, revealing a dead garden.*]

MARY: [*Excited*] This is it! The locked garden! [*Disappointed*] Oh, but look! Nothing is growing. Everything is dead.

DICKON: It just needs some care, and lots of water. [*Gestures*] See, these rose bushes are alive. Soon they'll be blooming. [*Curtain*]

Scene 6

Setting: *Same as Scene 3.*

At rise: *Colin is in bed. Mary and Dickon enter, holding animals.*

MARY: Hello, Colin. This is my friend, Dickon. He brought his animals to show you.

COLIN: Where were you, Mary? I've missed you. Hello, Dickon. I've heard all about you.

DICKON: Hello! Want to hold Lady? She's a nice and gentle lamb. [*Baaing is heard.*]

COLIN: Oh, yes, thank you. [*Holds lamb*] I'm glad you came. I have so few visitors—only Mary and Martha. Not even Father comes to see me.

DICKON: Why not?

COLIN: Because he doesn't want to see the hump on my back.

MARY: Let me see. [*Looks at Colin's back*] Why, there's no hump there, Colin. Only a knobby spine like mine.

---

knobby spine, backbone with hard parts that stick out from under the surface

---

BEFORE YOU GO ON

1 Why does Mr. Craven decide to take care of Mary?

2 Who helps Mary and Dickon find the key to the garden?

On Your Own
What do you think Mary and Dickon will do next?

273

Study Skills: Index

Point out that you can find information more quickly and efficiently if you use the index of a reference book. For example, to learn more about life in rural England in the early 1900s, students would first find a reference book on the history of England in a library. Then, before reading the book, they could turn to the index, an alphabetical list of topics found at the back of the book, to see if the information they are looking for is included.

Explain that some indexes have listings under a main topic, such as twentieth century. Students should read the listings, note which ones are useful, and go to those pages.

STEP 7: Monitor Progress

Ask students to check what they have understood in the reading. If you are using the Audio CD, pause the recording.

Before You Go On

Remind students that these questions will help them monitor their progress. Put students in pairs to answer the questions. Encourage them to share their answers with the class.

ANSWERS

1. Mr. Craven decides to take care of Mary because her father was his best friend.
2. Robin helps Mary and Dickon find the key.

On Your Own Have students write an answer to the On Your Own question on a separate sheet of paper. Encourage volunteers to share their responses with the class. Then collect student responses to monitor their comprehension, writing skills, and fluency.

Read

Preteaching Highlighted Words

Preview the vocabulary by writing on the board the highlighted words from pages 274–275. Make sure students understand each highlighted word. Ask students to say original sentences using the highlighted words. When you correct their sentences, focus on correcting usage of the highlighted word rather than other errors. Model the right usage and grammar by repeating the correct version of the student's sentence.

Across the Curriculum:
Science

Point out that photosynthesis is the process by which plants make food out of light, carbon dioxide (which is in the air), and water. Without photosynthesis, plants would not grow and flowers would not bloom. Explain that the word *photosynthesis* is made up of the prefix *photo-* (light) and the root word *synthesis* (putting parts together).

COLIN: [*Amazed*] You mean I don't have a hump, and I'm not dying?

MARY: Of course not! It's all in your mind.

DICKON: Roses won't grow where there are only thistles.

COLIN: What does that mean?

MARY: It means that you can't have happy thoughts if you always have gloomy ones.

COLIN: You're right. I must find something to do to keep me happy.

MARY: Dickon and I have a secret. I'll tell you if you promise not to tell anyone else!

COLIN: I promise.

MARY: We have found the garden that your mother and father used to love so much, and we're going to make it beautiful again—just the way it used to be.

COLIN: [*Excited*] Really? Oh, I wish I could help, but I can't walk.

DICKON: I could take you out into the garden in your wheelchair. You could sit on the ground and plant seeds and pull weeds.

COLIN: Do you really think I could?

MARY: Of course you could! In fact, you shall! We'll start tomorrow.

COLIN: [*Delighted*] That's wonderful!

MARY: We have to go now. We'll see you tomorrow. [*Dickon and Mary exit.*]

COLIN: [*Calling off*] Good-bye! Thanks for coming. [*He looks at the picture.*] Oh, Mother. Forgive me for covering you up. [*He gets out of bed and tries to walk toward the picture, but falls.*] If only I could walk . . . I will walk. I'll practice a little bit each day, and when Father comes home I'll show him I'm not an invalid anymore! [*Curtain*]

Scene 7

Time: Two months later.

Setting: The mansion gardens. There are flowerbeds, bushes, etc., around the stage. Fence covered with ivy, brambles, etc., is upright.

At rise: Mr. Craven is on stage alone.

BEN: [*Entering*] Mr. Craven! Welcome home. Mary wants to see you right away. She's in the locked garden, sir.

MR. CRAVEN: [*Amazed*] The garden? How is that? I thought the key was lost forever.

---

thistles, wild plants with purple flowers and leaves that have sharp points
gloomy, sad and hopeless

274

BEN: Come, I'll show you. The entrance is this way. [*Curtain goes up, reveals a beautiful garden. Mary, pushing Colin in a wheelchair, enters, followed by Dickon.*]

MARY AND COLIN: Surprise!

MR. CRAVEN: Why, it's beautiful! You've planted my favorite flowers!

BEN: Just the way it was when your wife was alive, sir. The children worked very hard.

MARY: Ben helped, too. He told us how it used to look and pruned all the dead wood.

MR. CRAVEN: And Colin! You have color in your cheeks, and you've gained weight.

COLIN: And that's not all, Father. [*He gets out of the wheelchair.*] I . . . can walk. [*He walks with difficulty to Mr. Craven, and they embrace. Ben and Dickon watch happily.*]

MR. CRAVEN: My son! [*Mary embraces them, too.*] My children. You have made me very happy! And you have brought love back into our garden.

COLIN: Our secret garden!

MARY: Yes, but now it needn't be a secret any longer. [*Curtain*]

---

pruned, cut back some of the branches of a tree or bush to make it grow better
embrace, hug; put their arms around each other in a caring way

ABOUT THE **AUTHOR** AND **PLAYWRIGHT**

Frances Hodgson Burnett was born in England in 1849. Her family moved to Knoxville, Tennessee, after her father's death. To help support her siblings, she began to write short stories for magazines. Later, she wrote many novels and children's books, including *Little Lord Fauntleroy* and *A Little Princess*.

David C. Jones has written more than a dozen plays for *PLAYS Magazine* with fellow-writer Lewis Mahlmann. He and Mahlmann also published several books through *PLAYS Magazine*, including *Puppet Plays from Favorite Stories* and *Folk Tales for Puppets*.

BEFORE YOU GO ON

1 What does Mary help Colin understand about his back?

2 What makes Mr. Craven happy at the end of the play?

On Your Own
Do you agree with Dickon that "roses won't grow where there are only thistles"? Why or why not?

275

Ask students to check what they have understood in the reading.

Before You Go On

Remind students that these questions will help them monitor their progress. Put students in pairs to answer the questions. Encourage them to share their answers with the class.

ANSWERS

1. Mary helps Colin understand that he doesn't have a hump.
2. At the end of the play, Mr. Craven is happy because his son is healthy and happy, and they have restored his garden.

On Your Own Have students write an answer to the On Your Own question on a separate sheet of paper. Encourage volunteers to share their responses with the class. Then, collect student responses to monitor their comprehension, writing skills, and fluency.

Review the Purpose for Reading

Elicit responses to the Set a Purpose for Reading question at the beginning of this reading. Remind students to relate their responses to the Big Question.

Teach & Apply

STEP 1: Introduce

Speaking Tip

Tell students that varying the volume of their voice makes their performance more interesting. When a person is excited, their voice may rise in volume, or they may talk more quickly than normal. When they are sad, their voice might be quieter and slower.

Reader's Theater

Performing by reading aloud is excellent practice for students. It gives them a reason to rehearse their reading, increase fluency, and improve expression and intonation. Divide students into groups of three to practice and perform.

Have students decide who will play the roles of Mary, Colin, and Mr. Craven. Suggest that they think about how their character feels at this point in the story. Students should find a quiet corner in which to rehearse. When they are ready, ask volunteers to perform before the class.

STEP 2: Practice

Comprehension

Have students work independently, with partners, or in small groups to write their responses. Encourage students to answer in complete sentences.

ANSWERS

1. Mary is not allowed to go into the garden that is locked.
2. Dickon names the animals because those are the names they asked to be called.
3. Mr. Craven tosses away the key to the garden because his wife died in the garden.
4. To fix the garden, the children plant flowers and pull up weeds.
5. **Possible response:** The garden is called "a secret garden" because no one is allowed to go there.
6. **Possible response:** At the beginning of the play, Colin feels hopeless and different from others. At the end of the play he feels happy and like the other children.
7. **Possible response:** If I could talk to animals, I would choose to talk to my dog because I would like to know what he thinks.
8. **Possible response:** I think planting a beautiful garden can improve life because it makes the world a more beautiful place to live in.

Teaching Resources

- *Workbook*, p. 133
- CD-ROM/e-book, Reader's Theater, Comprehension, Response to Literature

---

READER'S THEATER

Speaking TIP
Vary the volume of your voice to keep your audience interested.

Act out the following scene between Colin, Mary, and Mr. Craven.

Mary: Mr. Craven, Colin has a big surprise for you. [*Colin stands.*]

Mr. Craven: Colin, my boy! You are standing on your own!

Colin: Yes, I am, Father. It feels great to finally get out of my room and into the fresh air of this garden.

Mr. Craven: But how did you build your strength?

Colin: Mary and Dickon took me out to the garden. I practiced walking a little bit each day. I couldn't have done it without their help.

Mr. Craven: I'm so proud of you, son. [*Colin and Mr. Craven hug each other.*]

Mary: Congratulations, Colin. You worked very hard. I always knew you could do it.

COMPREHENSION

Right There

1. Which garden is the only one Mary is told that she can't play in?
2. Why does Dickon name the animals?

Think and Search

3. What causes Mr. Craven to toss away the key to the garden?
4. What do the children do to fix the garden?

Author and You

5. Why is the garden called "a secret garden"?
6. What are Colin's feelings about life in the beginning of the play? How do they change by the end?

276

TESOL Standards

Goal 1, Standard 1—To use English to communicate in social settings: Students will use English to participate in social interactions.
Descriptors—Sharing and requesting information; Engaging in conversations.

Goal 1, Standard 2—To use English to communicate in social settings: Students will interact in, through, and with spoken and written English for personal expression and enjoyment.
Descriptors—Participating in popular culture.

7. Other authors write stories about characters who talk to animals. If you could talk to animals, which ones would you choose? Why?

8. Do you think that planting a beautiful garden can improve life in a city or town? Explain.

DISCUSSION

Listening TIP

Look at each speaker as he or she speaks to show that you are interested.

Discuss in pairs or small groups.

1. What part of *The Secret Garden* did you like best? Why?

2. Do you think the children should have restored the garden or left it as it was in memory of Mrs. Craven? Why?

3. This play is called *The Secret Garden*. What would be another good title for this drama? Why?

Q How are courage and imagination linked? Which character in *The Secret Garden* has the most imagination? Which character has the most courage? How does each character affect the other people in the play? How do the characters work together?

RESPONSE TO LITERATURE

Workbook Page 133

Imagine that you are Mary Lennox. What was your life like in India? How do you feel about moving to England? Write a diary entry in which you describe your feelings about the changes in your life. You may want to use a graphic organizer like this one:

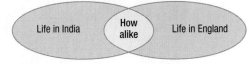

Life in India — How alike — Life in England

When you are done writing, share your diary entry with a classmate. Talk about the details in the play that helped you understand Mary's feelings.

277

Differentiated Instruction

Beginning	Ask students to list some words that describe the secret garden before the children brought it back to life.
Early Intermediate	Have students explain why Mary is living with Mr. Craven at Miselthwaite Manor.
Intermediate	Have students summarize the action of the play in their own words.
Struggling Readers	Ask students to identify the boy in the illustration on page 276.

STEP 3: Extend

Listening Tip

Tell students that it's important to look at someone when he or she is speaking. It shows respect for the speaker and helps you stay focused.

(CRI) Discussion

Congratulate students on successfully completing the reading. **SAY:** *We've learned a lot about how courage and imagination are linked. Now let's discuss a few questions about the reading.* Have students answer the Discussion questions on page 277.

Q How are courage and imagination linked? Ask students to find specific examples in the reading to support their choice of the most courageous and the most imaginative of the characters.

STEP 4: Assess

Response to Literature

Encourage students to review the reading for ideas about how Mary felt about India and how she feels about moving to England.

The Venn diagram could possibly look like the one below. To evaluate diary entries, look to see if the student included information from the reading. Encourage students to use their imaginations to go beyond the information they have at hand.

Life in India   **Life in England**

colorful, not dreary / good food — lots of nature and animals — dreary / bad food

Teach & Apply

STEP 1: Introduce

Tell students that they will be reviewing how to use adverbs that end in -ly with verbs.

STEP 2: Teach

Grammar and Writing

More Adverbs with -ly Adverbs describe verbs, or action words. They usually follow the verb in a sentence. **SAY:** *Look at the chart. Notice the words in bold. These adverbs all end in -ly. Not all words that end in -ly are adverbs. Adverbs may describe verbs, adjectives, or other adverbs. Adverbs that end in -ly describe actions (verbs).*

Draw the chart below on the board and ask students to fill in the missing adverbs.

She spoke _____ to him.	Possible response: angrily
"I would love to see Egypt!" he said _____.	Possible response: excitedly
"I am so tired," he responded _____.	Possible response: wearily

STEP 3: Practice

Ask students to create sentences using the adverbs in the box.

ANSWERS

Possible responses:
1. I worked happily in the garden.
2. She spoke nervously in front of the teacher.
3. He wandered sadly down the garden path.
4. "I don't need any help," she responded stubbornly.
5. After a long pause, he spoke thoughtfully.
6. He smiled wryly as he listened to her plans, which he thought were much too ambitious.

Teaching Resources

- *Workbook*, pp. 134–135
- CD-ROM/e-book, Grammar, Writing
- *Transparencies*, Writing Model 41
- *Transparencies, Resources*, Graphic Organizer 4
- *Assessment*, Reading 1 Test, pp. 99–102

Grammar and Writing

GRAMMAR, USAGE, AND MECHANICS

More Adverbs with -ly

An adverb usually describes the action of a verb. Many adverbs end with -ly. An adverb often answers the question *How?*

Question	Answer
How did Mary speak?	Mary spoke **imperiously**.
How did Martha answer?	Martha answered **sharply**.
How did Colin walk?	Colin walked **carefully**.

Stage directions may include adverbs with -ly to help an actor read his or her lines correctly.

Mary: [*Excitedly*] Oh, Robin, think—please! Where was it?
Mary: [*Timidly*] You sent for me, sir?
Mr. Craven: [*Kindly*] You look just like your father.

Practice

Workbook Page 134

Work with a partner. Use your imagination to write a sentence for each of the adverbs in the box below. Look up any words you don't know in a dictionary. Write the sentences in your notebook. Then take turns reading your sentences to your partner. Compare your sentences.

| happily | sadly | thoughtfully |
| nervously | stubbornly | wryly |

278

TESOL Standards

Goal 2, Standard 1—To use English to achieve academically in all content areas: Students will use English to interact in the classroom.
Descriptors—Following oral and written directions, implicit and explicit; Elaborating and extending other people's ideas and words.

Goal 2, Standard 2—To use English to achieve academically in all content areas: Students will use English to obtain, process, construct, and provide subject matter information in spoken and written form.
Descriptors—Listening to, speaking, reading, and writing about subject matter information; Gathering information orally and in writing; Responding to the work of peers and others.

Goal 3, Standard 1—To use English in socially and culturally appropriate ways: Students will use the appropriate language variety, register, and genre according to audience, purpose, and setting.
Descriptors—Using a variety of writing styles appropriate for different audiences, purposes, and settings.

WRITING AN EXPOSITORY PARAGRAPH

Write a Formal E-mail

On this page, you'll write an expository paragraph that states a problem and presents a solution. The paragraph will be part of a formal e-mail. You'll use a graphic organizer like the one at the right to list the problem and solution.

Problem	Solution

To develop and structure a problem-and-solution paragraph, first, clearly state what is happening and why it is a problem. Then give one or more suggestions about how to solve the problem. Also, explain why your solution will work.

Here is a model of an e-mail about a problem. Notice how the writer first states the problem and then presents a solution.

From: Angelina Xing <axing@coldmail.com>
Date: Tue, 6 Oct 2009 10:29:31
To: Mayor's Office <mayor@briarcliff.gov>
Subject: Law Park in Briarcliff Manor

Dear Mayor:

I am writing to you to address a problem I see with Law Park in Briarcliff Manor. The park's main feature is a monument dedicated to the memory of soldiers who served our country in World War II. However, the bare surroundings don't express the importance of the monument. My suggestion is to start a community garden in Law Park to make a beautiful setting for the monument. The community could work independently on creating the garden. If only one percent of the population actively works on this project, there will be more than enough people to keep the garden alive all year long. The whole town could benefit from improving this special place. Thank you very much for taking the time to consider my idea.

Sincerely,
Angelina Xing

Practice

Workbook Page 135

Write a formal e-mail to your community's mayor about a problem you want to solve in your neighborhood. Use a problem-solution chart to list your ideas. Be sure to use adverbs correctly.

Writing Checklist

IDEAS:
- ☑ I clearly stated the problem and solution.

VOICE:
- ☑ I used the correct type of language and format for a formal e-mail.

279

Linguistic Note

Language Register in E-mail

Tell students that it is important to use the correct register, or subset of language, when writing e-mails. In an informal e-mail, it is acceptable to use non-standard spelling (r u here?), smilies (:) or ☺), and abbreviations (LOL for *laughing out loud*). In a formal e-mail, it is important to use standard spelling and punctuation. Tell students to write a meaningful subject line and to keep the body of the e-mail focused and readable. Also, tell students not to type in all capital letters.

Remind students that expository paragraphs are used to explain something to the reader. Examples of expository writing include informational texts, how-to articles, letters, and essays.

STEP 2: Teach

Writing an Expository Paragraph

Write a Formal E-mail Remind students that a good way to approach expository writing is to write a problem and a solution. Have students use a T-chart for their own ideas.
SAY: *When you select a topic for your letter, try to choose something that really matters to you. This will help make your writing more interesting.* Explain the difference between a formal and informal letter or e-mail. A formal letter is a letter written to a business, professional organization, or college to apply for a job, make a complaint, etc. An informal letter is a letter written to family or friends. Informal letters can use familiar terms such as "kids," "guys," "cool," and abbreviations.

Model Writing Skill Read the model e-mail on page 279 aloud. Encourage students to reread the model e-mail before they write. When students are finished writing, have them read their e-mail to a partner.

STEP 3: Assess

Have students evaluate their e-mails using the Writing Checklist.

Writing Checklist Note

Have students evaluate their work using the Writing Checklist.

Ideas: Check that students stated their problem clearly and explained why their solution will work well.

Voice: Check that students used the correct language register for formal writing.

Teach

STEP 1: Introduce

Objectives

Read the list in the What You Will Learn section, encouraging students to join in. Tell students that "Kids' Guernica" will be about a project in which people use both courage and imagination to promote peace. Have pairs of students work together to restate the list of things they will learn.

The Big Question

Remind students that the Big Question is "How are courage and imagination linked?" Have them read the first paragraph on page 280. Answer one of the questions from your own personal experience. Ask students to share their own experiences or points of view. To provide a segue into the reading selection, **SAY:** *"Kids' Guernica" is inspired by a painting in which an artist named Pablo Picasso used his imagination to protest war.*

Build Background

Picasso painted *Guernica* with shapes that were stylized and symbolic. At that time, people were not used to seeing paintings like this. Critics said that it looked like a young child could have painted it. Picasso, however, chose the forms he did because he felt that they had more power than realistic imagery. Over time, people began to appreciate the self-destruction of war that *Guernica* plainly shows. Today, it is recognized as a masterpiece with a powerful anti-war message.

STEP 2: Teach

Understanding the Genre:
Informational Text

An informational text is a nonfiction text. Its purpose is to present facts and other information about real people, events, places, and situations. This reading is a social studies article about young people who use art to inspire others and promote peace.

Teaching Resources

- CD-ROM/e-book, Key Words
- Audio CD 5, tracks 5–6
- *Workbook*, p. 136

T280

What You Will Learn

Reading
- Vocabulary building: *Context, dictionary skills, word study*
- Reading strategy: *Classify*
- Text type: *Informational text (social studies/art)*

Grammar, Usage, and Mechanics
More uses of the present perfect

Writing
Write a paragraph that classifies something

THE BIG QUESTION

How are courage and imagination linked? Think of some situations in which a person needs to have imagination to do something. These can be situations at school or at home, with your family or friends, or when you are by yourself. Do you think it sometimes takes courage to have imagination? If so, why? Discuss with a partner.

BUILD BACKGROUND

"Kids' Guernica" is a photo-essay about a mural project that began in 1995. It explains how one person's imagination and courage led him to organize an international art project for peace. The title of the project and the ideas for it were based on Picasso's painting *Guernica*. Picasso painted *Guernica* in 1937 during the Spanish Civil War (1936–1939).

In 1936, General Francisco Franco led a revolt against the Spanish Republic. Franco's side received help from the Nazi dictator Adolf Hitler, the leader of Germany. After much chaos and violence, Franco's side won, and he became the dictator of Spain until 1975. As you will read, one of Franco's violent actions during the Spanish Civil War inspired Picasso to create *Guernica*.

The figures on this wall in New York City imitate those in Picasso's *Guernica*. ▶

280

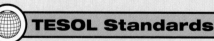 TESOL Standards

Goal 2, Standard 2—To use English to achieve academically in all content areas: Students will use English to obtain, process, construct, and provide subject matter information in spoken and written form.
Descriptors—Demonstrating knowledge through application in a variety of contexts.

Goal 3, Standard 1—To use English in socially and culturally appropriate ways: Students will use the appropriate language variety, register, and genre according to audience, purpose, and setting.
Descriptors—Using a variety of writing styles appropriate for different audiences, purposes, and settings.

Goal 3, Standard 3—To use English in socially and culturally appropriate ways: Students will use appropriate learning strategies to extend their sociolinguistic and sociocultural competence.
Descriptors—Observing and modeling how others speak and behave in a particular situation or setting; Rehearsing variations of language use in different social and academic settings.

VOCABULARY

Learn Key Words

Read the sentences. Use the context to figure out the meaning of the red words. Use a dictionary to check your answers. Then write each word and its meaning in your notebook.

1. People honor the anniversary of World War II. Every year they hold a ceremony on the date the war ended.

2. The atomic bomb is very destructive. It releases energy in a powerful explosion.

3. Many artists paint on canvases. These strong, heavy pieces of cloth are stretched on wooden frames.

4. War causes great chaos. In the confusion, it is difficult for people to live normal lives.

5. Reading about great acts can be an inspiration to do great things yourself.

6. The artist made a mural. The huge painting covered a whole wall.

Key Words

anniversary
atomic bomb
canvases
chaos
inspiration
mural

Practice

Write the sentences in your notebook. Choose a red word from the box above to complete each sentence. Then take turns reading the sentences aloud with a partner.

1. The children painted a _____ on the wall of the playground.

   a. chaos   b. mural   c. anniversary

2. The soldiers celebrated the _____ of the end of the war.

   a. chaos   b. inspiration   c. anniversary

3. The woman got her _____ to become a writer from a novel she read when she was young.

   a. inspiration   b. canvases   c. chaos

4. The fear and violence of war created _____ in the capital city.

   a. chaos   b. mural   c. atomic bomb

5. The art museum was filled with _____ painted by Pablo Picasso.

   a. canvases   b. chaos   c. anniversary

6. The _____ is a powerful explosive weapon that causes enormous damage.

   a. chaos   b. mural   c. atomic bomb

▲ An oil painting on canvas by Picasso

281

 Vocabulary

Learn Key Words Play the CD. Have students listen and repeat. If you are not using the CD, read the Key Words aloud.

SAY: *These words are called key words because they are words that are important in the text we are reading.* On the board or an overhead transparency, write the Key Words and their definitions.

- **anniversary:** a date on which something important happened in an earlier year
- **atomic bomb:** a very powerful bomb that splits atoms to cause an extremely large explosion
- **canvases:** strong, heavy cloths on which artworks are painted
- **chaos:** a situation in which everything is confused
- **inspiration:** something that encourages you to do something good
- **mural:** an artwork that is painted on a wall

Have students copy the definitions into their notebooks and generate original sentences with them.

STEP 3: Practice

Have students work with partners to complete the practice activity. As they work, remind them to think about the key word that makes the most sense in that sentence.

ANSWERS

1. b. mural
2. c. anniversary
3. a. inspiration
4. a. chaos
5. a. canvases
6. c. atomic bomb

Differentiated Instruction

Beginning	Ask students to identify when the Spanish Civil War took place. (1936–1939)
Early Intermediate	Ask students to identify what conflict was taking place when Picasso painted *Guernica*. (Spanish Civil War)
Intermediate	Have students point out similarities and differences between the wall mural on page 280 and Picasso's *Guernica* on page 284–285.
Standard English Learners (CRI)	Have students present an artist of their choice to the rest of the class.

STEP 1: Teach

CD5 T7–T8

 Vocabulary

Learn Academic Words Play the CD. Have students listen and repeat. If you are not using the CD, read the Academic Words aloud. **SAY:** *Look at the Academic Words in the box at the top of the page. Now look at the chart below it. The Academic Words and their definitions are on the left. Sentences containing the words are on the right. What other sentences can we create with the word* react? *(Possible response: How would you react if you saw someone laughing at someone else?)* Pair students and have them add another sentence for each Academic Word. They should write each word, its definition, and the sentence in their Word Books.

STEP 2: Practice

To model the practice exercise, write the following question on the board, and underline the words, as shown: *Under what circumstances would you* <u>want to join a club</u>? **SAY:** *When you are asked a question, try to include words from the question in your answer. Look at the question on the board. What words are underlined?*

Then write this answer on the board: <u>*I would want to join a club if it were an art club.*</u> Be sure to underline the words as shown so students clearly see the connection between words in the question and the answer.

ANSWERS
Possible responses:
1. I would want to join a club if it were an art club.
2. Before they construct a work of art, sculptors decide how they want it to look.
3. I react to surprises by blushing.
4. During winter, the weather in my region of the country is cold.

Teaching Resources
- Audio CD 5, tracks 7–8
- *Workbook*, pp. 137–139
- CD-ROM/e-book, Academic Words, Word Study

Learn Academic Words

Study the red words and their meanings. You will find these words useful when talking and writing about informational texts. Write each word and its meaning in your notebook. After you read "Kids' Guernica," try to use these words to respond to the text.

Academic Words
circumstances
construct
react
region

circumstances = the facts or conditions that affect a situation, action, or event	⇒	The meeting had to be canceled because of difficult **circumstances**. The streets were covered with deep snow.
construct = build something large such as a building, bridge, or sculpture	⇒	Chris and Luz plan to **construct** a class peace project. They will build it with sticks and paper.
react = behave in a particular way because of what someone has done or said to you	⇒	The students usually **react** to one another's speeches by clapping loudly.
region = a fairly large area of a state, country, and so on	⇒	The travelers visited the whole **region** even though it was a large area to travel through.

Practice Workbook Page 137

Work with a partner to answer these questions. Try to include the red word in your answer. Write the sentences in your notebook.

1. Under what circumstances would you want to join a club?
2. What do sculptors do before they construct a work of art?
3. How do you react to surprises?
4. What is the weather like in your region during winter?

Alexander Calder used red metal ▶ arches to contruct this sculpture.

282

Word Study: Spelling Words with *ea*

Two vowels can work as a team to stand for one vowel sound. The vowel team *ea* often stands for the long vowel sound /ē/. The vowel team *ea* can also stand for the short vowel sound /e/. In a few words, *ea* stands for the long vowel sound /ā/. Study the chart.

Single- and Multisyllabic Words with *ea*		
/ē/ spelled *ea*	/e/ spelled *ea*	/ā/ spelled *ea*
peace	spread	steak
be-neath	wealth-y	great-est

In multisyllabic words, or words with more than one syllable, the letters *ea* can also stand for two separate sounds because the letter *e* is part of one syllable and the letter *a* is part of another.

ar-**e-a**	cre-**ate**	i-de-**a**	Ko-re-**a**

Practice

Work with a partner. Copy the chart above into your notebook. Say a word from the chart, and ask your partner to spell it aloud. Then have your partner say the next word. Continue until you can spell all of the words correctly. Now practice spelling these words with your partner: *neat, dead, daybreak, breath,* and *breathe.* Add them to the chart under the correct headings.

READING STRATEGY | CLASSIFY

Classifying helps you understand, organize, and remember what you read. When you classify, you arrange things into groups with common characteristics. For example, you could classify the texts in this book into these categories: articles, stories, poems, photo-essays, and so on. Classifying words is a good way to learn and remember their meanings. To classify words in a text, follow the steps in this example:

- As you read, think of categories that many words fall into. In "Kids' Guernica," many words relate to the categories "war" and "art."
- Ask yourself: "Which words relate to these categories?" Group the words according to category.

As you read "Kids' Guernica," find words that relate to "war" and "art."

283

Accelerate Language Development

Digraphs

A digraph usually stands for a specific sound that is not represented by the individual letters. For example, the individual *t* or *h* in *th* would not be pronounced as /ð/ or /θ/. English has quite a few of them: *th* (the, through), *ph* (photograph), *gh* (rough, night), *ng* (dancing) and more. There are a number of English digraphs that no longer hold a specific pronunciation: *wh* (what), or *rh* (rhinoceros). In some languages, digraphs have such specific sounds that they are part of the alphabet. Example: The Spanish *ll*. In some languages, digraphs have become so distinct that they received their own letter over time. Example: The German *ß*, representing a double *ss*, or the Scandinavian *å*, representing a specific double *aa*.

Reading Summary

This reading is about an international art project for peace begun in Kyoto, Japan, in 1995 by Yasuda Tadashi.

 The Big Question

SAY: *What would make you want to participate in an international project? Are there certain activities that bring out your desire to help make the world a better place?*

Set a Purpose for Reading

Tell students to copy the purpose for reading into their notebooks and to keep it in mind as they read. Explain that they will have to present details that support their answer to the question and to explain how the reading relates to the Big Question.

Preteaching Highlighted Words

With students, preview the highlighted vocabulary on pages 284–285. Write the words on the board, and point out that they are defined at the bottom of each page. Have students record new vocabulary in their personal Word Books.

CD5 T9 ### Scaffolding:
Listen and Read

Have students read along as you play the Audio CD recording of the reading. Pause the recording at the end of each page to ask and answer questions students may have.

Teaching Resources

- *Resources*, Summaries, pp. 157–158
- Audio CD 5, track 9
- *Reader's Companion Workbook*, pp. 99–103

Set a purpose for reading How can one person's courage and imagination inspire other people to work for peace? Read this photo-essay to find out how and why young people around the world are creating works of art to encourage world peace.

Kids' Guernica

In Kyoto, Japan, in 1995, Yasuda Tadashi started an international art project for peace. Its name was Kids' Guernica. Using the Internet, Tadashi organized schools around the world to participate. The goal was to have children in different parts of the world create peace paintings on huge canvases. The model for the project was one of the most famous paintings of the twentieth century.

Spanish artist Pablo Picasso (1881–1973) had painted *Guernica* in 1937 to protest the brutal bombing of a town in Northern Spain during the Spanish Civil War (1936–1939). Guernica had been an independent and democratic town. Around 7,000 people lived there. On April 26, 1937, Spanish dictator Francisco Franco ordered Nazi planes to bomb the town. It was

4:00 P.M. on a busy market day. About 1,650 innocent people were killed, and 889 were injured. Picasso was shocked by the black-and-white photographs he saw in the newspapers. He quickly sketched the first images for a mural. His final painting shows the horror and chaos of war.

participate, do a particular activity
brutal, very cruel and violent
independent, free and not controlled by another country
democratic, controlled by leaders who are elected by the people of a country
Nazi planes, planes flown by members of the National Socialist Party of Adolf Hitler, which controlled Germany from 1938 to 1945

284

TESOL Standards

Goal 1, Standard 2—To use English to communicate in social settings: Students will interact in, through, and with spoken and written English for personal expression and enjoyment.
Descriptors—Expressing personal needs, feelings, and ideas.

Goal 2, Standard 3—To use English to achieve academically in all content areas: Students will use appropriate learning strategies to construct and apply academic knowledge.
Descriptors—Taking notes to record important information and aid one's own learning; Actively connecting new information to information previously learned.

▲ Children created this mural for the Kids' Guernica project in Nepal.

Pablo Picasso painted *Guernica* in 1937. The mural makes a powerful statement about war. ▼

Picasso's symbols

bull = the brutality of war

horse = the people

electric light = an all-seeing God

flower = hope

BEFORE YOU GO ON

1 Who started the Kids' Guernica project?

2 What did Francisco Franco do to the people of Guernica?

💡 **On Your Own** Do you think that works of art can stop violence and war? Explain.

285

Study Skills: World Map

SAY: *A world map is an excellent reference, whether you are studying science, English, math, or social studies. Countries all across the globe, including Israel, Korea, Kuwait, Greece, Chile, India, Canada, Italy, and China, contributed to Kid's Guernica. (See page 287.)* Have students look up the many countries that participated on a world map. Then discuss the advantages to using art as a means of communication around the world.

STEP 3: Monitor Progress

Ask students to check what they have understood in the reading. If you are using the Audio CD, pause the recording.

Before You Go On

Remind students that these questions will help them monitor their progress. Put students in pairs to answer the questions. Encourage them to share their answers with the class.

ANSWERS

1. Yasuda Tadashi started the Kids' Guernica project.
2. Francisco Franco ordered Nazi planes to bomb the town of Guernica.

On Your Own Have students write an answer to the On Your Own question on a separate sheet of paper. Encourage volunteers to share their responses with the class. Then collect student responses to monitor their comprehension, writing skills, and fluency.

Differentiated Instruction	
Beginning	Ask students when the Kids' Guernica international art project was started. (1995)
Early Intermediate	Ask students who founded the Kids' Guernica project, and where. (Yasuda Tadashi, Kyoto, Japan)
Intermediate	Have students describe the purpose of the Kids' Guernica art project in their own words.
Special Needs	Ask students closed questions about the text as they read. Closed questions help students focus their attention, while open questions promote critical thinking skills, which students may not be ready for.

STEP 4: Teach

Model the
READING STRATEGY

Classify

SAY: *Now that we have read some of the text, let's apply the reading strategy. We are classifying the information from the reading into two categories: war and art. At the beginning of the article we read about the Spanish Civil War. We also read about Picasso's Guernica. How are these two topics connected? Can you think of any other information about war or art that we have read about so far? Remember to keep classifying any new information as you finish reading the text.*

▲ *Hiroshima*, by students participating in Kids' Guernica. The mural shows a bombed building in Hiroshima now known as the Atomic Bomb Dome.

Tadashi was inspired by Picasso's painting. Since 1995, he has organized children throughout the world to paint murals for peace that are the same size as the painting *Guernica*. The original painting is 3.5 × 7.8 meters (11.5 × 25.5 ft.).

The ruins known as the Atomic Bomb Dome ▼

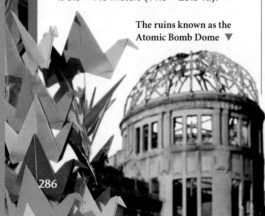

286

Children participate in workshops in their schools and create their own paintings.

The Kids' Guernica project often takes place in areas that have been torn apart by war. Hiroshima, Japan, is one example. In 1945, the United States dropped an atomic bomb on Hiroshima, ending World War II. The city was completely destroyed. In 1999, forty-one students from four elementary schools in Hiroshima participated in the Kids' Guernica art project. These schools are all located in the area where the bomb exploded. The students created their mural in memory of the 140,000 people who died. Their mural also expresses hope for peace in the future.

🌐 TESOL Standards

Goal 1, Standard 1—To use English to communicate in social settings: Students will use English to participate in social interactions.
Descriptors—Expressing needs, feelings, and ideas.

Goal 1, Standard 3—To use English to communicate in social settings: Students will use learning strategies to extend their communicative competence.
Descriptors—Using the primary language to ask for clarification; Using context to construct meaning.

Goal 2, Standard 1—To use English to achieve academically in all content areas: Students will use English to interact in the classroom.
Descriptors—Requesting information and assistance.

▲ Girls creating a mural for the Kids' Guernica project in Bali

The Kids' Guernica project has traveled all over the world. Children across the globe have used art to express their messages of peace. They have made murals in places such as Israel, Palestine, Afghanistan, Korea, and Kuwait. They have tried to spread peace on every continent. In 2004, children involved in the project made a mural for the United Nations building in Geneva, Switzerland. In 2005, the Kids' Guernica project celebrated its tenth anniversary with an art show in Bali, Indonesia. And in 2006 and 2007, participants in the project created murals in Kastelli, Crete, and Chios, Greece. So far, more than 500 children from schools in Cambodia, Sri Lanka, Chile, Nepal, India, Algeria, Germany, the United States, Australia, China, Canada, France, Italy, and other countries have participated.

The people involved in the Kids' Guernica project hope that their paintings will make the world a better place. They want to spread their powerful message around the globe. They say that the project will go on until there is world peace.

BEFORE YOU GO ON

1 What happened in Hiroshima in 1945?

2 When will the Kids' Guernica project end?

💡**On Your Own**
In your opinion, does it take courage and imagination to be part of the Kids' Guernica project? Why?

287

Study Skills: Internet

SAY: *The Internet is an excellent source of information, whether you are studying science, English, math, or social studies.* Have students research Yasuda Tadashi and the Kid's Guernica project. Put students into pairs or small groups and ask them to search the Internet to find another mural created for Kid's Guernica. Ask students to show the mural to the class and to explain how they think it promotes peace.

STEP 5: Monitor Progress

Ask students to check what they have understood in the reading.

Before You Go On

Have students read and answer the questions. Explain that the On Your Own question asks for their opinion. Any thoughtful answer is correct.

ANSWERS
1. In 1945, the United States dropped an atomic bomb on Hiroshima, Japan.
2. The Kids' Guernica project will go on until there is world peace.

On Your Own Have students write an answer to the On Your Own question on a separate sheet of paper. Encourage volunteers to share their responses with the class. Then collect student responses to monitor their comprehension, writing skills, and fluency.

Review the Purpose for Reading

Elicit responses to the Set a Purpose for Reading questions at the beginning of this reading. Remind students to relate their responses to the Big Question.

STEP 1: Practice

Comprehension

Ask students to complete the questions in the Comprehension section either independently or in groups. They can respond orally or in writing.

ANSWERS

1. Yasuda Tadashi began his art project in Kyoto, Japan, in 1995.
2. More than 500 children have participated.
3. Picasso painted *Guernica* to protest the brutal bombing of a town in Spain during the Spanish Civil War.
4. Children from many countries, including Japan, Cambodia, Sri Lanka, Nepal, Chile, India, Algeria, Germany, the United States, Australia, China, France, Italy, and Canada have participated in Kids' Guernica.
5. Possible response: Picasso wanted to show what war is really like for the people affected by it.
6. Possible response: The art expresses the memories and hopes for peace of many children.
7. Possible response: People can create other works of art, such as music, about peace.
8. Possible response: If I participated in the Kids' Guernica project, I would paint images of doves because they symbolize peace.

(CRI) In Your Own Words

Have students work with a partner to summarize what they learned, using the chart on page 288 as their guide.

Speaking Tip

SAY: *Take time to review your chart before you share it with your classmates. Make sure you have organized your ideas and expressed your opinions clearly so you can answer any questions your classmates might have.*

Teaching Resources

- *Workbook*, p. 140
- CD-ROM/e-book, Comprehension, Extension
- *Reader's Companion Workbook*, pp. 104–108

COMPREHENSION Workbook Page 140

Speaking TIP
Be ready to answer questions and share your opinions with your classmates.

Right There

1. When and where did Yasuda Tadashi start an international art project for peace?
2. About how many children have participated in Kids' Guernica?

Think and Search

3. Why did Picasso paint *Guernica*?
4. Which countries have had children participate in Kids' Guernica?

Author and You

5. Why do you think that Picasso wanted to show the chaos and horror of war in his mural?
6. Why do you think that the text of "Kids' Guernica" is illustrated with so many photographs and works of art?

On Your Own

7. In what ways can people around the world use their imagination to work for peace?
8. If you were participating in the Kids' Guernica project, what would you paint on your mural? Why?

IN YOUR OWN WORDS

Imagine that you are telling a classmate about "Kids' Guernica." You want to include all the main ideas and important details in the photo-essay. Complete the chart below to help you organize your ideas. Then share your summary with a classmate.

Section	Main Idea	Important Details
Introduction (first paragraph)		
Picasso paints *Guernica* in protest		
Kids' Guernica project since 1995		
Conclusion (last paragraph)		

288

🌐 TESOL Standards

Goal 1, Standard 1—To use English to communicate in social settings: Students will use English to participate in social interactions.
Descriptors—Using nonverbal communication in social interactions; Conducting transactions.

Goal 1, Standard 3—To use English to communicate in social settings: Students will use learning strategies to extend their communicative competence.
Descriptors—Selecting different media to help understand language.

Goal 2, Standard 3—To use English to achieve academically in all content areas: Students will use appropriate learning strategies to construct and apply academic knowledge.
Descriptors—Determining and establishing the conditions that help one become an effective learner (e.g., when, where, how to study); Recognizing the need for and seeking assistance appropriately from others (e.g., teachers, peers, specialists, community members); Knowing when to use native language resources (human and material) to promote understanding.

DISCUSSION

Discuss in pairs or small groups.

Listening TIP

Do not interrupt your classmates when they are speaking. Save your questions until a speaker is finished.

1. How did the bombing of Guernica affect Picasso? Why do you think he reacted this way?

2. Name some places around the world where the Kids' Guernica project has traveled. How are these places alike? How are they different?

3. What places do you think the Kids' Guernica project should visit in the future? Why?

Q How are courage and imagination linked? Think of other courageous and imaginative projects that might help to spread world peace. What would the projects be? Would the projects use art or something else imaginative? Explain.

READ FOR FLUENCY

Reading with feeling helps make what you read more interesting. Work with a partner. Choose a paragraph from the reading. Read the paragraph to yourselves. Ask each other how you felt after reading the paragraph. Did you feel happy or sad?

Take turns reading the paragraph aloud to each other with a tone of voice that represents how you felt when you read it the first time. Give each other feedback.

EXTENSION Workbook Page 140

In "Kids' Guernica," you read about people who make art to bring about peace. Picasso created his mural *Guernica* during the Spanish Civil War. Find out more about the Spanish Civil War. Use encyclopedias, reference books, and reliable websites. Share your findings with the class.

▲ A painting of poet Antonio Machado during the Spanish Civil War

289

STEP 2: Extend

Listening Tip

Remind students that they can take notes about any questions they have. Then, when their peers have finished speaking, they will have the chance to ask their questions.

(CRI) Discussion

Before students begin their discussion, decide if they will work as a whole group, in small teams, or as partners.

Q How are courage and imagination linked? Ask students to work in small groups and think of a project to promote peace. Have each group describe why they think their project is creative and why they think it is courageous. Ask students to share their ideas with the class.

STEP 3: Assess

Read for Fluency

SAY: *When reading aloud, pay attention to how you felt after reading the paragraph. What does the tone of your voice say about your feelings? Take turns reading and giving each other feedback.*

Extension

Have students create a timeline of the Spanish Civil War, using the information they've discovered in reference books, encyclopedias, and websites. Have them share their findings with the class.

Differentiated Instruction

Beginning	Remind students to let each student speak without interruption as they complete the Discussion activity.
Early Intermediate	Have students describe the original *Guernica* by Pablo Picasso.
Intermediate	Have students explain why Pablo Picasso painted *Guernica*.
Struggling Readers	Ask students if they have seen other murals in their neighborhood. Ask them to describe the mural to the class.

Teach & Apply

STEP 1: Introduce

Remind students that the present perfect is often used to talk about the past. Ask them to look at page 290 and tell them you will be reviewing uses of the present perfect.

STEP 2: Teach

Grammar and Writing

Present Perfect The present perfect is formed with the verb *have* plus the past participle. Write the following examples on the board. **SAY:** *These examples all contain the present perfect. In the first two examples, the action began at some time in the past. Using the present perfect with* for *or* since *tells us that the action continues into the present. In the third example, we don't know when the action occurred. In this case, the use of the present perfect describes an action that happened at an indefinite time in the past.*

- Children have made murals since 1995.
- She has lived in Alaska for ten years.
- It looks like he has left the room.

STEP 3: Practice

Have students work with partners to complete the sentences in the practice activity. Tell students to read each sentence aloud with the verb choices and to give a reason for their choice.

ANSWERS

1. have participated
2. was
3. have worked
4. has been/was
5. painted
6. created

Teaching Resources

- *Workbook*, pp. 141–142
- CD-ROM/e-book, Grammar, Writing
- *Transparencies*, Writing Model 42
- *Transparencies*, *Resources*, Graphic Organizer 5
- *Assessment*, Reading 2 Test, pp. 103–106

GRAMMAR, USAGE, and MECHANICS

More Uses of the Present Perfect

Sometimes when you write, you will use the present perfect to talk about the past. The present perfect refers to an action that happened at an indefinite time in the past. The present perfect also is used to describe an action that started in the past and continues into the present. In addition, you can use the present perfect to ask questions with the word *ever*.

Use of the Present Perfect	Example
Actions that happened at an indefinite time	Children in different places **have made** murals.
Actions that started in the past and continue into the present (with *for* or *since*)	He **has organized** children to paint murals for peace since 1995.
Actions with *ever* to ask if the person has done something "at any time" or "in your entire life"	**Have** you **ever visited** Hiroshima, Japan?

Practice  Workbook Page 141

Work with a partner. Copy the sentences below into your notebook. Choose the correct verb to complete each sentence. Then take turns reading the sentences aloud with a partner.

1. The students at my school (participated / have participated) in an art project since 2005.
2. My teacher (was / has been) in charge of one event on May 3.
3. We (worked / have worked) on many special projects since the fall.
4. The art club (was / has been) the most popular club for many years.
5. The children (painted / have painted) murals outdoors in June.
6. Picasso (created / has created) these paintings on plates during the 1940s and 1950s.

290

TESOL Standards

Goal 2, Standard 1—To use English to achieve academically in all content areas: Students will use English to interact in the classroom.
Descriptors—Following oral and written directions, implicit and explicit.

Goal 2, Standard 2—To use English to achieve academically in all content areas: Students will use English to obtain, process, construct, and provide subject matter information in spoken and written form.
Descriptors—Gathering information orally and in writing; Representing information visually and interpreting information presented visually; Demonstrating knowledge through application in a variety of contexts.

Goal 2, Standard 3—To use English to achieve academically in all content areas: Students will use appropriate learning strategies to construct and apply academic knowledge.
Descriptors—Evaluating one's own success in a completed learning task.

WRITING AN EXPOSITORY PARAGRAPH

Write a Paragraph That Classifies Something

Grouping information by category is an effective way to organize ideas and details. On this page, you'll use categories to organize a paragraph. You'll use a graphic organizer like the one on the right to classify your ideas and details. Suppose you want to write a paragraph about Picasso's artwork. You could categorize the information by subject, style, or the materials used. Choose the categories that best suit your purpose. Then describe the features of each category.

Paintings	Plates	Sculptures

Here is a model of an expository paragraph that discusses three categories of work by Picasso. Notice how the writer presents the three categories first. Then he discusses each type of art one at a time.

Koji Mori

Picasso's Paintings, Plates, and Sculptures
I have seen and enjoyed three types of artwork by Picasso: his paintings, plates, and sculptures. His paintings on canvas are his most well-known works. Like all paintings, they are two dimensional. Picasso's come in a wide range of styles including realistic portraits and abstract works. Picasso did a second type of artwork that I like very much: paintings and sculpted designs on three-dimensional objects such as plates. The subjects of these paintings include images of people and birds. The third type of artwork, and my own personal favorite, are Picasso's sculptures. These three-dimensional artworks were made from all kinds of materials. Picasso used wood, clay, metal, stone, or a combination of materials. His sculptures exhibit a wide range of subjects, from realistic figures of people, animals, and birds to abstract works.

Practice **Workbook Page 142**

Write a paragraph about three types of art that you enjoy. List your categories on a chart. Explain the features of each category. Tell why you like each type of art. Be sure to use the present perfect correctly.

> **Writing Checklist**
>
> **ORGANIZATION:**
> ☑ I presented each category one at a time.
>
> **WORD CHOICE:**
> ☑ I chose words carefully to explain the features of each category.

291

STEP 1: Introduce

Tell students that classifying, or grouping things by category, is a way to organize expository writing.

STEP 2: Teach

Writing an Expository Paragraph

Write a Paragraph That Classifies Something Draw a graphic organizer on the board (page 291). **SAY:** *When writing a paragraph that classifies something, begin by deciding the categories you want to use. Then complete the graphic organizer with details you wish to include. Finally, decide in what order you wish to discuss the categories.*

Model Writing Skill SAY: *As I read the model paragraph aloud, listen for the three types of Picasso's artwork the author discusses. Notice the details that describe the features of the artwork in each category. Did the author's organization make it easy to understand what he was writing about?*

STEP 3: Assess

Have students evaluate their work using the Writing Checklist.

Writing Checklist Note

Organization: Check that students' paragraphs are presented in an orderly way, with each category being presented in a different body paragraph.

Word Choice: Check that the words students used in their paragraphs help us understand their categories.

Accelerate Language Development

Since and For

When the present perfect is used to describe an action or event that started in the past and continues in the present, the time adverbs *since* and *for* are often used. Language learners may have difficulty deciding which one to use. Point out that *since* is used to express that something has happened *after* a specific point in time. Example: I've lived here <u>since 2006</u>. We've been working on this <u>since two in the afternoon</u>. *For* is used to express that something has happened over a period of time. Example: I've lived here <u>for 10 years</u>. We've been working on this <u>for two hours</u>.

Teach

STEP 1: Introduce

Objectives
Tell students that this reading will be about using courage and imagination to help the natural world around us. Have pairs of students work together to restate the list of things they will learn.

The Big Question
Have students think about part of the natural world that they love. To what lengths would they go to protect it? Would they risk being arrested?

Build Background
Read this section of the student book aloud. Explain that *Hoot* is set in present-day America. Even though *Hoot* is a work of fiction, many students can relate to the desire to protect our natural resources. Ask students if they've ever thought about what animals used to live where they live now.

STEP 2: Teach

Understanding the Genre: Novel Excerpt
Point out that a novel is a long work of fiction. Novels contain elements such as characters, plot, setting, and conflict. *Hoot* is a comic novel. Remind students that an excerpt is an episode, or part, of a novel. Point out that a comic novel is amusing and makes you want to laugh.

Teaching Resources
- CD-ROM/e-book, Literary Words
- Audio CD 5, track 10
- *Workbook*, p. 143

What You Will Learn

Reading
- Vocabulary building: *Literary terms, dictionary skills, word study*
- Reading strategy: *Summarize*
- Text type: *Literature (novel excerpt)*

Grammar, Usage, and Mechanics
Quoted versus reported speech

Writing
Write a plot summary

THE BIG QUESTION

How are courage and imagination linked? Why might people care enough about birds and animals to take risks to protect them? Why might courage and imagination be necessary to convince people that birds and animals have rights, too? Discuss with a partner.

The next reading involves efforts to save a unique type of owl. Explore with your partner what you know about owls. Where do they live? What do they eat? Why might it be important to protect their habitats? In your notebook, copy and fill in the first two columns of the K-W-L-H chart below.

K What do I **know**?	W What do I **want** to know?	L What did I **learn**?	H **How** did I learn it?

As you read the excerpt from *Hoot* and complete the activities after the reading, fill out the rest of the K-W-L-H chart with your partner.

▲ Burrowing owls live in holes in the ground.

292

BUILD BACKGROUND

In the comic novel ***Hoot***, burrowing owls play an important role. These tiny owls with big yellow eyes are quite different from most owls. Burrowing owls are very small, only 23 centimeters (9 in.) tall. They hunt throughout the day, not just at night, and they don't live in trees. They make their nests in underground holes, or burrows. They often use burrows made by prairie dogs or other animals. Burrowing owls eat mice, like other owls do, but they also eat beetles, moths, grasshoppers, frogs, and lizards. They even eat scorpions.

TESOL Standards

Goal 1, Standard 3—To use English to communicate in social settings: Students will use learning strategies to extend their communicative competence.
Descriptors—Selecting different media to help understand language; Using context to construct meaning.

Goal 2, Standard 3—To use English to achieve academically in all content areas: Students will use appropriate learning strategies to construct and apply academic knowledge.
Descriptors—Focusing attention selectively; Applying basic reading comprehension skills such as skimming, scanning, previewing, and reviewing text; Using context to construct meaning.

VOCABULARY

Learn Literary Words

Everyone likes a funny story! **Humor** is anything that amuses people or makes them laugh. Writers create humor with the words they choose and the images these words create.

Sometimes writers exaggerate a scene or a character's traits to make something seem funny. Read these examples from *Hoot*. What is humorous about each sentence?

Literary Words

humor
colorful language

> Mr. Muckle's cheeks turned purple.
> The chamber-of-commerce guy looked like he'd swallowed a bar of soap.

Writers often use **colorful language**, such as idioms, hyperbole, and slang, to make their stories humorous. Slang is very informal language that certain people use. Colorful expressions can be used to create a silly character or to make the dialogue between characters amusing. Here are some examples of colorful language that you will read in *Hoot*.

> *dorky*: silly-looking or strange-looking
> *hotshot*: someone who is very successful and confident
> *twerp*: an annoying or stupid person
> *noggin*: head or brain

Practice
 **Workbook** Page 143

Write a funny paragraph about a "hotshot" who tries to convince a "dorky" friend of his to do something silly. You may want to use some of the words above in your paragraph and add some colorful expressions of your own. Share your paragraph with a partner.

293

Vocabulary

Learn Literary Words Play the CD. Have students listen and repeat. If you are not using the CD, read the Literary Words aloud. Ask students what comes to mind when they hear each word. Write down student responses.
SAY: *These words are called literary words because in a discussion of literature, they have a unique meaning. Read the paragraphs in your book that define* humor *and* colorful language.

Write the following definitions for *humor* and *colorful language* on the board or an overhead transparency to reinforce learning.

- **humor:** anything that makes people laugh or amuses people
- **colorful language:** idioms, hyperbole, and slang to make stories humorous

Provide examples of humor and colorful language. Ask students to use the words *humor* and *colorful language* in new sentences. Have students use the corresponding Workbook page for extra practice.

STEP 3: Practice

Have students work with partners. Explain that "hotshot" means someone who is very successful and over-confident and that "dorky" means someone who you think is or looks foolish. Invite volunteers to read their story aloud or write their paragraphs on the board.

Differentiated Instruction

Beginning	Ask students to share some facts that they know about owls.
Early Intermediate	Have students look at the illustrations for the story. Ask them how they can tell that this is a literature selection and not a nonfiction article.
Intermediate	Have students write a sentence that has humor and a sentence that has colorful language.
Standard English Learners (CRI)	Have students write and present a brief paragraph that contains both humor and colorful language.

Teach

CD5 T11–T12

Vocabulary

Learn Academic Words Play the CD. Have students listen and repeat. If you are not using the CD, read the Academic Words aloud.
SAY: *Look at the Academic Words chart. The definition for each word is on the left side. On the right side, each word is used in a sentence. Work with a partner to write an additional sentence for each academic word. Write each word, its definition, and the sentences in your Word Book.*

STEP 2: Practice

Have students work with partners to complete the practice activity. **SAY:** *Take turns reading aloud the sentences with your partner. As you read each sentence, think about the key word that makes the most sense in that sentence. If you are uncertain which word fits a sentence, skip it and complete the others. Then return to the sentence and see which words remain on the list. This is a good test-taking strategy as well.*

ANSWERS
1. a. site
2. b. deny
3. b. image
4. a. demonstrate

Teaching Resources

- Audio CD 5, tracks 11–12
- *Workbook*, pp. 144–146
- CD-ROM/e-book, Academic Words, Word Study

Learn Academic Words

Study the red words and their meanings. You will find these words useful when talking and writing about literature. Write each word and its meaning in your notebook. After you read the excerpt from *Hoot*, try to use these words to respond to the text.

Academic Words
demonstrate
deny
image
site

demonstrate = protest or support something in public with a lot of other people	The students decided to **demonstrate** against the builders who were destroying the owls' habitat.
deny = say that something is not true	The builders will **deny** that the burrowing owls live here. However, we know they're lying.
image = a picture that you can see through a camera, on television, or in a mirror; a picture that you have in your mind	The protester drew the **image** of a burrowing owl on her poster. The picture looked real.
site = a place where something is being built or will be built	The protest took place at the construction **site**, where the owls lived.

Practice Workbook Page 144

Write the sentences in your notebook. Choose a red word from the box above to complete each sentence. Then take turns reading the sentences aloud with a partner.

1. What possible motive could the company have for constructing a restaurant on this _____?
   a. site   b. image

2. The boy is afraid of admitting the truth, so he will _____ what he did.
   a. demonstrate   b. deny

3. Roy's _____ of the owls was blurry.
   a. site   b. image

4. Many people plan to _____ against the new law, because they think that it is unfair.
   a. demonstrate   b. deny

▲ People demonstrate on Earth Day to protect our planet.

294

TESOL Standards

Goal 1, Standard 3—To use English to communicate in social settings: Students will use learning strategies to extend their communicative competence.
Descriptors—Listening to and imitating how others use English; Exploring alternative ways of saying things.

Goal 2, Standard 1—To use English to achieve academically in all content areas: Students will use English to interact in the classroom.
Descriptors—Participating in full-class, group, and pair discussions; Negotiating and managing interaction to accomplish tasks.

Goal 3, Standard 1—To use English in socially and culturally appropriate ways: Students will use the appropriate language variety, register, and genre according to audience, purpose, and setting.
Descriptors—Recognizing and using Standard English and vernacular dialects appropriately.

Word Study: Prefixes *mega-*, *tele-*, *re-*

A prefix is a word part added to the beginning of a word that changes the word's meaning. Knowing the meanings of prefixes can help you figure out the meaning of many unfamiliar words. Study the chart.

Prefix	+ Base Word	= New Word
mega- (large; one million)	ton	megaton ("1 million tons")
tele- (distance; distant)	communication	telecommunication ("communication over a large distance by electronic means")
re- (again; backward)	capture	recapture ("capture again")

Practice

Work with a partner. Use what you have learned about prefixes to figure out the meanings of the words below. Copy the items below into your notebook. Write your own definitions for each word. Then check the meanings in a dictionary. Discuss how learning about prefixes can expand your vocabulary.

1. mega- + phone = _____
2. tele- + scope = _____
3. re- + viewing = _____

▲ A telescope

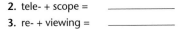

READING STRATEGY | **SUMMARIZE**

Summarizing helps you remember and understand a text. When you summarize fiction, you write a few sentences about what happened. You tell the goals of the characters, how they tried to reach their goals, and whether they succeeded. When you summarize nonfiction, you write a few sentences about the main ideas. To summarize, follow these steps:

- As you read, stop from time to time to summarize parts of the text.
- Write a sentence or two about the most important event or idea in that section. Leave out unimportant events, ideas, and details.
- After reading, summarize the most important points of the whole text.

As you read the excerpt from "Hoot," stop to summarize the plot. When you finish reading, summarize the entire excerpt in a short paragraph.

295

Linguistic Note

Quantity

The prefix *mega* is one among a whole list of prefixes used to describe quantities. Examples are: *kilo*, *giga*, and *nano*. While *kilo*, meaning one thousand, has always been a common measurement in words such as *kilometer* and *kilogram*, the other prefixes have entered everyday language through the growing importance of telecommunications and computers. Words such as *megabyte* or *gigabyte* are common usage by now. *Mega* means one million; *giga* means one thousand million. *Nano*, from the Greek word meaning *dwarf*, denotes a very small quantity: one billionth of a meter. Sometimes called *prefix multipliers*, these prefixes are frequently used in electronics and physics.

Read

Reading Summary

This reading is a comic novel about some kids trying to prevent building on lands inhabited by burrowing owls.

 The Big Question

SAY: *As you read, keep the Big Question in mind. Ask yourself which of the characters' actions require courage. Which require imagination? Are there any that require both?*

STEP 2: Teach

Set a Purpose for Reading

Tell students to copy the purpose for reading into their notebooks and to keep it in mind as they read. Explain that they will have to present details that support their answer to the question and to explain how the reading relates to the Big Question.

Preteaching Highlighted Words

In pairs, have students read aloud the highlighted words and their definitions. Answer any questions students have about the use of a word or its meaning before reading the spread.

 CD5 T13 Scaffolding:
Listen and Read

Have students read along as you play the Audio CD recording of the reading. Pause the recording at the end of each page to ask and answer questions students may have.

✔ **LITERARY CHECK**

Read the Literary Check question aloud. To review the meaning of *colorful language,* see page 293. (snooty-looking, dorky, hot snot)

Teaching Resources

- *Resources,* Summaries, pp. 159–160
- Audio CD 5, track 13

READING 3 | **LITERATURE** | **NOVEL**

Set a purpose for reading What will happen when the Mother Paula Company starts to build a restaurant on lands inhabited by burrowing owls? Read to find out whether anyone will have the courage and imagination to help save the owls and their habitat.

from

HOOT
Carl Hiaasen

Chuck E. Muckle plans to build a new Mother Paula's restaurant on lands that are home to burrowing owls. The special groundbreaking ceremony is about to begin, and many people have gathered for the occasion. Three kids, Roy, Mullet Fingers, and his stepsister, Beatrice, are also on the scene. They are determined to save the tiny owls from the developers.

At a quarter past twelve, the door of the construction trailer swung open. First to emerge was a policeman whom Roy recognized as Officer Delinko; then the bald construction foreman with the rotten temper; then a snooty-looking guy with silver hair and dorky sunglasses.

The last to come out was the woman who played Mother Paula on the TV commercials. She wore a shiny gray wig, wire-rimmed glasses, and a calico apron. A few people clapped in recognition, and she waved halfheartedly.

The group marched to a rectangular clearing that had been roped off in the center of the construction site. A megaphone was handed to the silvery-haired guy, who said his name was Chuck E. Muckle, a vice-president from Mother Paula's company headquarters. He really thought he was hot snot, Roy could tell.

✔ **LITERARY CHECK**
What colorful language does the author use to describe Chuck E. Muckle?

---

temper, tendency to become suddenly angry
commercials, advertisements
calico, light cotton cloth with a small pattern
halfheartedly, without interest or enthusiasm

296

 TESOL Standards

Goal 1, Standard 1—To use English to communicate in social settings: Students will use English to participate in social interactions.
Descriptors—Sharing and requesting information; Expressing needs, feelings, and ideas.

Goal 2, Standard 1—To use English to achieve academically in all content areas: Students will use English to interact in the classroom.
Descriptors—Asking and answering questions; Requesting information and assistance.

Ignoring the foreman and the police officer, Mr. Muckle proceeded with great enthusiasm to introduce some local big shots—the mayor, a city councilman, and the head of the chamber of commerce.

"I can't tell you how proud and delighted we are to make Coconut Cove the home of our 469th family-style restaurant," Mr. Muckle said. "Mr. Mayor, Councilman Grandy, all of you terrific folks who've come out on this gorgeous Florida day . . . I'm here to promise you that Mother Paula will be a good citizen, a good friend, and a good neighbor to everybody!"

"Unless you're an owl," Roy said.

Mr. Muckle didn't hear it. . . . He snickered nervously. "Mother Paula, dearest, I think it's time. Shall we do the deed?"

They all posed side by side—the company V.P., the mayor, Mother Paula, Councilman Grandy, and the boss of the chamber of commerce—for the television crew and the news photographer.

Gold-painted shovels were handed out, and on Mr. Muckle's signal all the dignitaries smiled, leaned over, and dug up a scoopful of sand. . . .

As soon as the photo pose ended, Mr. Muckle tossed down his gold shovel and snatched up the megaphone. "Before the bulldozers and backhoes get rolling," he said, "Mother Paula herself wants to say a few words."

Mother Paula didn't look overjoyed to have the megaphone shoved in her hand. "You've got a real nice town," she said. "I'll see you next spring at the grand opening—"

"Oh no, you won't!"

This time the words came out of Roy's mouth as a shout, and nobody was more stunned than he. A tremor rippled through the audience and Beatrice edged closer, half expecting somebody to come after him.

The actress playing Mother Paula seemed miffed, peering over her cheap wire-rimmed glasses into the crowd.

"Now, who said that?"

Roy found himself raising his right arm. "I did, Mother Paula," he called out. "If you hurt a single one of our owls, I'm not eating any more of your stupid pancakes."

"What're you talking about? What owls?"

---

foreman, person who is in charge of a group of workers
proceeded, continued
snickered, laughed quietly in a way that is not nice at something that is not supposed to be funny
deed, action
dignitaries, people who have important official positions
backhoes, large digging machines
tremor, tense feeling or shudder

BEFORE YOU GO ON

1 Which characters pose for the television crew and news photographer?

2 Who is playing Mother Paula at the ceremony?

On Your Own Summarize the main events in the story so far.

297

Study Skills: Thesaurus

Have students work with a partner to find synonyms for *laugh* (*chuckle, giggle, snicker, hoot, cackle*). Have students create short dialogues to demonstrate the differences between each type of laughter.

STEP 3: Monitor Progress

Ask students to check what they have understood in the reading. If you are using the Audio CD, pause the recording.

Before You Go On

Have students read and answer the questions. Explain that the On Your Own question asks for an opinion. Any thoughtful answer is correct.

ANSWERS

1. The company V.P., the mayor, Mother Paula, Councilman Grandy, and the boss of the local Chamber of Commerce pose for the TV crew and the news photographer.
2. An actress is playing Mother Paula at the ceremony.

On Your Own Have students write an answer to the On Your Own question on a separate sheet of paper. Encourage volunteers to share their responses with the class. Then, collect student responses to monitor their comprehension, writing skills, and fluency.

Differentiated Instruction	
Beginning	Ask students what the term "buttermilk" refers to. (pancakes)
Early Intermediate	Ask students why they think the novel is named Hoot.
Intermediate	Have students explain the expression "bury the buttermilks" that appears on a sign in the illustration on page 298.
Struggling Readers	Have students identify Chuck E. Muckle and Mother Paula in the illustrations.

Preteaching Highlighted Words

In pairs, have students read aloud the highlighted words and their definitions. Answer any questions students have about the use of a word or its meaning before reading the spread.

Across the Curriculum:
Science

Burrowing owls can be found in North and South America. The burrows that they make serve as a place to keep their eggs before they hatch, as well as a place to protect their young before they are ready to fly. Burrowing owls will often reuse their burrows year after year.

✔ LITERARY CHECK

Read the question in the Literary Check box aloud. If students need to review the meaning of humor, see page 293. Answer: A possible answer is that both of these phrases use a play on words, combining two different meanings or connotations of the same word. "Chuckie Cheeseball" is a reference to a popular pizza chain, and "doesn't give a hoot" is an idiom meaning "doesn't care."

Chuck Muckle lunged for the megaphone, but Mother Paula threw an elbow and caught him square in the gut. "Back off, Chuckie Cheeseball," she huffed.

"Go on, check it out for yourself," Roy said, gesturing around. "Wherever you see one of those holes, there's an owl den underneath. It's where they build their nests and lay their eggs. It's their home."

Mr. Muckle's cheeks turned purple. The mayor looked lost, Councilman Grandy looked like he was going to faint, and the chamber-of-commerce guy looked like he'd swallowed a bar of soap.

By now, the parents in the crowd were talking loudly and pointing at the den holes. A few of the schoolkids started chanting in support of Roy, and Beatrice's soccer teammates began waving their hand-lettered signs.

One said: MOTHER PAULA DOESN'T GIVE A HOOT ABOUT OWLS!

Another read: BIRD KILLERS GO HOME!

And still a third sign said: SAVE THE OWLS, BURY THE BUTTERMILKS!

As the news photographer snapped pictures of the protesters, Mother Paula pleaded, "But I don't want to hurt your owls! Really, I wouldn't hurt a flea!"

Chuck Muckle finally recaptured the megaphone and boomed a harsh scolding at Roy: "Young fellow, you'd better get your facts straight before making such outrageous and slanderous charges. There are no owls here, not one! Those old burrows have been abandoned for years."

 LITERARY CHECK

How do these sentences—"Back off, Chuckie Cheeseball" and "Mother Paula doesn't give a hoot about owls"—add to the **humor** *of the story?*

---

lunged for, made a sudden forceful movement toward
threw an elbow, stuck out an elbow to stop someone
give a hoot, care
scolding, statement that someone has done something wrong
slanderous, untrue
abandoned, not used or taken care of

298

"Yeah?" Roy reached into his backpack and whipped out his mother's camera. "I've got proof!" he shouted. "Right here."

The kids in the crowd hooted and hurrahed. Chuck Muckle's face went gray and slack. He held out his arms and lurched toward Roy. "Lemme see that!"

Scooting out of reach, Roy switched on the digital camera and held his breath. He had no idea what he was about to see.

He pressed the button to display the first photograph that Mullet Fingers had taken. The instant that the blurred, crooked image appeared in the viewfinder, Roy knew he was in trouble.

It was a picture of a finger.

Anxiously he clicked to the second frame, what he saw was no less discouraging: a dirty bare foot. It appeared to be a boy's foot, and Roy knew whose it was.

Beatrice's stepbrother had many special talents, but nature photography obviously wasn't one of them. . . .

Roy was crushed—the pictures taken by Beatrice's stepbrother were worthless. The authorities in charge of protecting the burrowing owls would never block the construction of the pancake house based on such fuzzy evidence. . . .

Then a young voice rose up: "Wait, it ain't over! Not by a mile it ain't."

This time it wasn't Roy.

"Uh-oh," said Beatrice, lifting her eyes.

A girl in the rear of the crowd let out a shriek, and everybody wheeled at once to look. At first glance the object on the ground could have been mistaken for a kickball, but it was actually . . . a boy's head.

His matted hair was blond, his face was caramel-brown, and his eyes were wide and unblinking. A kite string led from his pursed lips to the handle of a large tin bucket a few feet away.

The big shots came hurrying out of the crowd, with Beatrice and Roy at their heels. They all stopped to gape at the head on the ground.

"What now?" moaned the construction foreman.

Chuck Muckle thundered: "Is this somebody's idea of a sick joke?"

"Good heavens," cried the mayor, "is he dead?"

The boy wasn't the least bit dead. He smiled up at his stepsister and winked slyly at Roy. Somehow he'd fit his entire skinny body down the opening of an owl burrow, so that only his noggin stuck out.

"Yo, Mother Paula," he said.

---

scooting, moving quickly
authorities, people or organization
gape, look at something for a long time, with their mouths open because they are shocked
thundered, yelled in a loud voice

✔ LITERARY CHECK

*What is **humorous** about this scene in the story?*

BEFORE YOU GO ON

 1 Who are the people demonstrating against Mother Paula's?

2 Where is Mullet Fingers and what does he have in his mouth?

💡**On Your Own**
Summarize the most important events on pages 298–299.

299

✔ LITERARY CHECK

If students need help remembering the meaning of *humorous*, refer them to page 293. Possible answer: There is no photograph to show or there is a boy in the owl burrow.

STEP 5: Monitor Progress

Ask students to check what they have understood in the reading. If you are using the Audio CD, pause the recording.

Before You Go On

Remind students that these questions will help them monitor their progress. Put students in pairs to answer the questions. Encourage them to share their answers with the class.

ANSWERS
1. schoolchildren
2. Mullet Fingers is in an owl burrow, and he has a kite string in his mouth.

On Your Own Have students write an answer to the On Your Own question. Explain that this question asks for your opinion. Any thoughtful answer is correct.

Preteaching Highlighted Words

In pairs, have students read aloud the highlighted words and their definitions. Answer any questions students have about the use of a word or its meaning before reading the spread.

Model the
READING STRATEGY

Summarize

SAY: *The reading strategy is summarize, so let's restate the main points of the story in the order in which they occur. Where did the story begin? What happened first? Then what happened? What is happening now?*

The actress stepped forward hesitantly. Her wig looked slightly crooked and her makeup was beginning to melt in the humidity.

"What is it?" she asked uneasily.

"You bury those birds," Mullet Fingers said, "you gotta bury me, too."

"But no, I love birds! All birds!"

"Officer Delinko? Where are you!" Chuck Muckle motioned for the policeman to come forward. "Arrest this impertinent little creep right now."

"For what?"

"Trespassing, obviously."

"But your company advertised this event as open to the public," Officer Delinko pointed out. "If I arrest the boy, I'll have to arrest everyone else on the property, too."

Roy watched as a vein in Mr. Muckle's neck swelled up and began to pulse like a garden hose. "I'll be speaking to Chief Deacon about you first thing tomorrow," Mr. Muckle hissed under his breath at the patrolman. "That gives you one whole night to work on your sorry excuse for a résumé."

Next he turned his withering gaze upon the forlorn foreman. "Mr. Branitt, please uproot this . . . this stringy *weed*."

"Wouldn't try that," Beatrice's stepbrother warned though clenched jaws.

"Really. And why not?" Chuck Muckle said.

The boy smiled. "Roy, do me a favor. Check out what's in the bucket."

Roy was happy to oblige.

"What do you see?" the boy asked.

"Cottonmouth moccasins," Roy replied.

"How many?"

"Nine or ten."

"They look happy, Roy?"

"Not really."

"What do you think's gonna happen if I tip that thing over?" With his tongue Mullet Fingers displayed the string that connected him to the bucket.

"Somebody could get hurt pretty bad," Roy said, playing along. He had been mildly surprised (though relieved) to see that the reptiles in the bucket were made of rubber.

---

motioned, gave directions using his hand(s)
impertinent, impolite, disrespectful
sorry excuse, worthless or poor excuse
withering gaze, look that makes someone feel stupid
　　or embarrassed
forlorn, sad and lonely
oblige, do what he asked
cottonmouth moccasins, venomous water snakes
　　that live in the southeastern United States

300

🌐 TESOL Standards

Goal 1, Standard 1—To use English to communicate in social settings: Students will use English to participate in social interactions.
Descriptors—Expressing needs, feelings, and ideas; Engaging in conversations.

Goal 3, Standard 3—To use English in socially and culturally appropriate ways: Students will use appropriate learning strategies to extend their sociolinguistic and sociocultural competence.
Descriptors—Self-monitoring and self-evaluating language use according to setting and audience.

Mr. Muckle stewed. "This is ridiculous—Branitt, do what I told you. Get that kid outta my sight!"

The foreman backed away. "Not me. I don't much care for snakes."

"Really? Then you're fired." Once again the vice-president turned to confront Officer Delinko. "Make yourself useful. Shoot the damn things."

"No, sir, not around all these people. Too dangerous."

The policeman approached the boy and dropped to one knee.

"How'd you get here?" he asked.

"Hopped the fence last night. Then I hid under the backhoe," the boy said. . . . "Man, you don't understand. The owls got no chance against those machines."

"I do understand. I honestly do," Officer Delinko said. "One more question: You serious about the cottonmouths?"

"Serious as a heart attack."

"Can I have a look inside the bucket?"

The boy's eyes flickered. "It's your funeral," he said.

Roy whispered to Beatrice: "We've gotta do something quick. Those snakes aren't real."

"Oh, great."

As the policeman approached the tin bucket, Beatrice shouted, "Don't do it! You might get bit—"

Officer Delinko didn't flinch. He peeked over the rim for what seemed to Roy and Beatrice like an eternity.

Jig's up, Roy thought glumly. No way he won't notice they're fake.

Yet the patrolman didn't say a word as he backed away from the bucket.

"Well?" Mr. Muckle demanded. "What do we do?"

"Kid's for real. If I were you, I'd negotiate," said Officer Delinko.

"Ha! I don't negotiate with juvenile delinquents." With a snarl, Chuck Muckle snatched the gold-painted shovel from Councilman Grandy's hands and charged toward the bucket.

"Don't!" hollered the boy in the owl hole, spitting the string.

But the man from Mother Paula's was unstoppable. With a wild swing of the shovel he knocked over the bucket, and commenced flailing and hacking at the snakes in a blind, slobbering fury. He didn't stop until they were in pieces.

Little rubber pieces.

---

stewed, became angry because something bad has just happened
glumly, unhappily
negotiate, discuss something in order to reach an agreement
snarl, angry growl like an animal
flailing, waving his arms and legs in a fast but uncontrolled way
slobbering fury, state of extreme anger

BEFORE YOU GO ON

1 What does Chuck E. Muckle ask Officer Delinko to do to Mullet Fingers?

2 Why doesn't Officer Delinko flinch when he looks in the bucket?

On Your Own
What do you think will happen next?

301

Study Skills: Dictionary

The highlighted words are defined at the bottom of the reading pages, but there may be other words that students are unfamiliar with. Have students look through the story to find any additional words they don't know. Have them look these up in the dictionary and write the words and the definitions in their Word Books.

STEP 7: Monitor Progress

Ask students to check what they have understood in the reading. If you are using the Audio CD, pause the recording.

Before You Go On

Have students read and answer the questions. Explain that the On Your Own question asks for your opinion. Any thoughtful answer is correct.

ANSWERS
1. Chuck E. Muckle asks Officer Delinko to arrest Mullet Fingers.
2. Officer Delinko doesn't flinch because he sees that the snakes aren't real.

On Your Own Have students write an answer to the On Your Own question on a separate sheet of paper. Encourage volunteers to share their responses with the class. Then collect student responses to monitor their comprehension, writing skills, and fluency.

Read

Preteaching Highlighted Words

In pairs, have students read aloud the highlighted words and their definitions. Answer any questions students have about the use of a word or its meaning before reading the spread.

Across the Curriculum:
Social Studies

In this story, the kids are participating in an active demonstration against the new construction. There are many different types of protests. Some examples are strikes, sit-ins, marches, meetings, and vigils. **SAY:** *People organize protests when they feel strongly about an issue. Protests aim to change or prevent something from happening, and protesters aim to bring their opinion to the attention of a wider audience. What protests have you heard of, seen, or participated in? What were the issues being protested? Were the protests successful?*

Exhausted, Chuck Muckle leaned over and squinted at the mutilated toy snakes. His expression reflected both disbelief and humiliation. . . .

"Hey, them snakes're fake!" Curly piped. "They ain't even real."

Roy leaned toward Beatrice and whispered, "Another Einstein."

Chuck Muckle pivoted in slow motion. Ominously he pointed the blade of the shovel at the boy in the owl burrow.

"You!" he bellowed, stalking forward.

Roy jumped in front of him.

"Outta my way, kid," Chuck Muckle said. "I don't have time for any more of your nonsense. Move it *now*!"

It was clear that the Mother Paula's bigshot had totally lost his cool, and possibly his marbles.

"What're you doing?" Roy asked, knowing he probably wouldn't get a calm, patient answer.

"I said, *Get outta my way*! I'm gonna dig that little twerp out of the ground myself."

Beatrice Leep darted forward and stood next to Roy, taking his right hand. An anxious murmur swept through the crowd.

"Aw, that's real cute. Just like Romeo and Juliet," Chuck Muckle taunted. He dropped his voice and said, "Game over, kiddies. On the count of three, I'm going to start using this shovel—or better yet, how about I get Baldy over here to crank up the bulldozer?"

The foreman scowled. "Thought you said I was fired." . . .

Roy turned to see that Beatrice had been joined by the entire soccer team, linking arms in a silent chain. They were tall, strong girls who weren't the least bit intimidated by Chuck Muckle's blustery threats.

Chuck Muckle realized it, too. "Stop this foolishness right now!" he begged. "There's no need for an ugly mob scene."

Roy watched in wonderment as more and more kids slipped out of the crowd and began joining hands, forming a human barricade around Beatrice's self-buried stepbrother. None of the parents made a move to stop them.

The TV cameraman announced that the demonstration was being broadcast live on the noon news, while the photographer from the paper swooped in for a close-up of Mr. Muckle, looking drained, defeated, and suddenly very old. He braced himself on the ceremonial shovel as if it were a cane.

---

mutilated, severely damaged
bellowed, shouted loudly in a deep voice
Romeo and Juliet, two young lovers in a Shakespeare play
taunted, joked to anger or upset someone
blustery, loud and bullying
swooped in, moved in very quickly

302

TESOL Standards

Goal 2, Standard 2—To use English to achieve academically in all content areas: Students will use English to obtain, process, construct, and provide subject matter information in spoken and written form.
Descriptors—Comparing and contrasting information; Persuading, arguing, negotiating, evaluating, and justifying.

"Didn't any of you people hear me?" he rasped. "This event is over! Done! You can all go home now." . . .

Roy was in an eerie yet tranquil daze.

Some girl started singing a famous old folk song called "This Land Is Your Land." It was Beatrice, of all people, and her voice was surprisingly lovely and soft. Before long, the other kids were singing along, too. Roy shut his eyes and felt like he was floating on the sunny slope of a cloud.

"Excuse me, hotshot. Got room for one more?"

Roy blinked open his eyes and broke into a grin.

"Yes, ma'am," he said.

Mother Paula stepped between him and Garrett to join the circle. Her voice was gravelly, but she could carry a tune just fine. . . .

Overhead, a small dusky-colored bird was flying in marvelous daring corkscrews. Roy and Beatrice watched in delight as it banked lower and lower, finishing with a radical dive toward the burrow at the center of the circle.

Everybody whirled to see where the bird had landed. All of a sudden the singing stopped.

There was Mullet Fingers, trying not to giggle, the daredevil owl perched calmly on the crown of his head.

"Don't worry, little guy," the boy said. "You're safe for now."

---

rasped, spoke in a rough, unpleasant way
tranquil, pleasantly calm
banked, sloped to one side while turning
radical, wonderful
daredevil, bold and not caring about danger

ABOUT THE **AUTHOR**

Carl Hiaasen is a best-selling author of young adult novels and a proud lifelong resident of Florida. After graduating from the University of Florida, Hiaasen began working at the *Miami Herald* as a reporter. He still contributes a weekly column to the paper today, in addition to writing novels. *Hoot*, one of Hiaasen's most popular novels, was a Newbery Honor book. It was so successful that it was made into a movie.

BEFORE YOU GO ON

1 What do Roy, Beatrice, and the other demonstrators do to protect Mullet Fingers?

2 How does Chuck E. Muckle look at the end?

☀ **On Your Own**
How do Roy, Mullet Fingers, and Beatrice show courage and imagination?

303

Study Skills: Internet

SAY: *The Internet is an excellent resource for information, whether you are studying science, English, math, or social studies.* Ask students to research Carl Hiaasen, the author of *Hoot*, on the internet. Have students create a timeline of his life with the information they find.

STEP 9: Monitor Progress

Ask students to check what they have understood in the reading.

Before You Go On

Have students read and answer the questions. Explain that the On Your Own question asks for your opinion. Any thoughtful answer is correct.

ANSWERS

1. Roy, Beatrice, and the other demonstrators form a human barricade around Mullet Fingers to protect him.
2. Chuck E. Muckle looks drained, defeated, and very old at the end.

On Your Own Have students write an answer to the On Your Own question on a separate sheet of paper. Encourage volunteers to share their responses with the class. Then collect student responses to monitor their comprehension, writing skills, and fluency.

Review the Purpose for Reading

Elicit responses to the Set a Purpose for Reading question at the beginning of this reading. Remind students to relate their responses to the Big Question.

Teach & Apply

STEP 1: Introduce

Speaking Tip

Remind students that only a small percent of what we say is understood by words alone. To communicate more fully they should also practice their tone of voice and body language.

Reader's Theater

Performing by reading aloud is excellent practice for students. It gives them a reason to rehearse their reading several times, increase fluency, and improve expression and intonation.

Have students begin the Reader's Theater. Students should find a quiet corner in which to rehearse. When they are ready, ask volunteers to perform before the class.

STEP 2: Practice

Comprehension

These questions help students review and extend what they have read. Have students work in small groups and write their responses.

ANSWERS

1. Chuck E. Muckle is the vice-president of Mother Paula's company.
2. Roy says that cottonmouth moccasins are in the bucket.
3. Roy has photographs, but they show a finger and a foot rather than the owls.
4. Mullet Fingers uses rubber snakes. His plan works because Chuck E. Muckle gets angry and tries to kill them. He totally loses his cool and appears ridiculous.
5. Possible response: I think the author agrees with Roy and Mullet Fingers because they are the heroes of the story.
6. Possible response: Perhaps Mother Paula decides to demonstrate because she doesn't want to hurt animals.
7. Possible response: Humans should help protect wildlife from people who want to develop land where they live because all creatures are important in some way to the environment.
8. Possible response: Yes, I demonstrated at a rally to clean up the harbor because it was polluted.

Teaching Resources

- *Workbook*, p. 147
- CD-ROM/e-book, Reader's Theater, Comprehension, Response to Literature

---

READER'S THEATER

Act out the following scene between Roy and Beatrice.

Roy: Bea, did you hear what just happened? Mother Paula's decided to build a new restaurant in our town!

Beatrice: Oh, that's cool.

Roy: No, it's not! They want to build it where the burrowing owls live over by Coconut Cove! They've got the mayor and the city council on their side.

Beatrice: Those poor little owls! We have to do something!

Roy: What can we do? They start building next week.

Beatrice: Hmm . . . I know! We have to get out and tell people. Once they know about the owls, they definitely won't want the restaurant there.

Roy: But how can we tell the whole town?

Beatrice: We'll bring signs and posters to the groundbreaking ceremony. The whole town will show up, and then we'll let them know what's *really* going on!

Speaking TIP

Use realistic voices and facial expressions to communicate different emotions.

COMPREHENSION

Workbook Page 147

Right There

1. Who is Chuck E. Muckle?
2. What kind of snakes does Roy say are in the bucket?

Think and Search

3. Roy wants to show that the owls still live in their burrows. What proof does he have? Why isn't it any good?
4. What kind of snakes does Mullet Fingers use to stop Chuck Muckle from breaking ground for the new restaurant? Why does this plan work?

304

 TESOL Standards

Goal 3, Standard 1—To use English in socially and culturally appropriate ways: Students will use the appropriate language variety, register, and genre according to audience, purpose, and setting.
Descriptors—Using the appropriate degree of formality with different audiences and settings; Determining when it is appropriate to use a language other than English; Determining appropriate topics for interaction.

Goal 3, Standard 2—To use English in socially and culturally appropriate ways: Students will use nonverbal communication appropriate to audience, purpose, and setting.
Descriptors—Interpreting and responding appropriately to nonverbal cues and body language; Using acceptable tone, volume, stress, and intonation, in various social settings; Recognizing and adjusting behavior in response to nonverbal cues.

Author and You

5. Do you think that the author agrees with Roy and Mullet Fingers or with Chuck Muckle? What makes you think so?

6. Why does Mother Paula decide to demonstrate with the kids and other community members at the end of the excerpt?

On Your Own

7. Is it a good idea for human beings to try to take care of wildlife? Why?

8. Have you or someone close to you ever felt so strongly about an issue that you decided to demonstrate about it? Explain.

DISCUSSION

Discuss in pairs or small groups.

1. Which part of the excerpt from *Hoot* did you find the most humorous? Why?

2. In what ways can writers add humor to a story? Give some examples of humorous stories, television shows, and movies.

3. In what ways can builders be more careful when preparing to build on sites where birds and animals live?

Q How are courage and imagination linked? Do you think that it is important to fight for animals' rights? Would you be willing to work to preserve animals and their habitats? If so, how could you use your imagination to come up with ways to help animals?

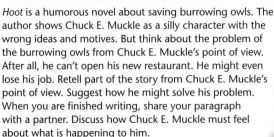

Listening TIP

When listening to your classmates, pay attention to the examples they use to illustrate their ideas. Think about how these ideas are similar to or different from your own.

RESPONSE TO LITERATURE

Workbook Page 147

Hoot is a humorous novel about saving burrowing owls. The author shows Chuck E. Muckle as a silly character with the wrong ideas and motives. But think about the problem of the burrowing owls from Chuck E. Muckle's point of view. After all, he can't open his new restaurant. He might even lose his job. Retell part of the story from Chuck E. Muckle's point of view. Suggest how he might solve his problem. When you are finished writing, share your paragraph with a partner. Discuss how Chuck E. Muckle must feel about what is happening to him.

A burrowing owl ▶

305

Listening Tip

SAY: *Pay close attention to others while they are speaking. How do they support their opinions? Are their opinions the same as your own? Are their reasons the same?*

CRI Discussion

Before students begin their discussion, decide if they will work as a whole group, in small teams, or as partners. Consider dividing up the questions so each group has a different topic.

Q How are courage and imagination linked? Encourage students to express their opinions, give specific examples, and use their imaginations.

Response to Literature

Having read the story *Hoot*, help students rewrite part of the story from Chuck E. Muckle's point of view. **SAY:** *In your notebook, rewrite Hoot from Chuck E. Muckle's point of view. Remember, he can't open his new restaurant, and he might lose his job. Things are probably not so funny from his perspective. Think about how he might solve his problem.*

Differentiated Instruction	
Beginning	Ask students if they think Chuck E. Muckle should have handled the situation differently.
Early Intermediate	Ask students who they side with in the story, the Beatrice, Roy, and Mullet Fingers, or Chuck. E. Muckle.
Intermediate	Have students explain some recommendations they have for Chuck E. Muckle on how to approach the situation differently.
Greater Challenge	Have students put themselves in Roy, Beatrice, and Mullet Fingers' place. Have them explain to the class another way they could have gone about saving the owls.

Teach & Apply

STEP 1: Introduce

Tell students that authors often use quoted speech as well as reported speech in their stories. Tell students that you will be reviewing how to distinguish between them.

STEP 2: Teach

Grammar and Writing

Quoted vs. Reported Speech Quoted speech reports exactly what someone says, surrounded by quotation marks. Reported speech, on the other hand, is used to report what someone said without repeating the exact words. Read aloud the samples in the text box on page 306, so students will hear the difference between the two.

SAY: *Read the text in the box on page 306 as I read it aloud. Notice that the sentences provide the same information. However, one is written using quoted speech, and the other uses reported speech. Remember that quoted speech uses quotation marks around the exact words someone has said.*

STEP 3: Practice

Have students work with a partner to determine whether the sentences use quoted or reported speech.

ANSWERS

1. quoted; want–present
2. reported; wanted–past
3. reported; was–past
4. quoted; is–present
5. quoted; need–present
6. reported; needed–past

Teaching Resources

- *Workbook*, pp. 148–149
- CD-ROM/e-book, Grammar, Writing
- *Transparencies*, Writing Model 43
- *Assessment*, Reading 3 Test, pp. 107–110

GRAMMAR, USAGE, AND MECHANICS

Quoted versus Reported Speech

Quoted speech is used to state exactly what someone said. A writer uses quotation marks around the speaker's words. Reported speech is used to tell another person what someone said without using his or her exact words. A writer does not use quotation marks in reported speech.

Notice that the verb changes from present to past in reported speech. The word *that* is often added to reported speech.

Quoted speech: "I **love** birds," Mother Paula said.
Reported speech: Mother Paula said that she **loved** birds.

Quoted speech: "This event **is** over," Mr. Muckle said.
Reported speech: Mr. Muckle said that the event **was** over.

Quoted speech: "You **have** a real nice town," she said.
Reported speech: She said that you **had** a real nice town.

Quoted speech: Roy said, "I **want** those pictures."
Reported speech: He said that he **wanted** those pictures.

Practice

Work with a partner. Write each sentence in your notebook. Label each sentence *quoted speech* or *reported speech*. Underline the present verb in the quoted speech and the past verb in the reported speech.

1. Roy said, "I want to save the owls." _____
2. Roy said that he wanted to save the owls. _____
3. The policeman said that everything was ready. _____
4. The policeman said, "Everything is ready." _____
5. Mr. Muckle said, "I need the gold shovel." _____
6. Mr. Muckle said that he needed the gold shovel. _____

306

WRITING AN EXPOSITORY PARAGRAPH

Write a Plot Summary

On this page, you will write a plot summary. You'll use a graphic organizer like the one at the right to organize your ideas. As you know, a plot is what happens in a story. It includes a problem or conflict and the outcome. When you summarize a plot, you say in a few sentences what happened. You introduce the main characters and the setting. You tell the goals of the characters, how they tried to reach them, and whether they succeeded.

Below is a plot summary of the excerpt you just read from *Hoot*. Notice that the writer describes the setting and the main characters in the first two sentences. Then he presents the main events in chronological order. He ends by telling the outcome.

Main characters and setting:
Characters' goals:
Main events: 1. 2. 3.
Outcome:

Brandon Saiz

Hoot: A Summary of the Excerpt

Hoot is a funny novel set in Coconut Cove, Florida. The main characters are three teenagers: Roy, Beatrice, and her stepbrother, Mullet Fingers. They want to stop Mother Paula's, a pancake chain, from building a new restaurant on land that is home to burrowing owls. The excerpt begins at the groundbreaking ceremony for the new restaurant. Everyone in town is there, including the vice president of the restaurant chain, Chuck E. Muckle. First, Roy tries to stop the builders by speaking out. Mr. Muckle tries to shut Roy up, by saying that he'd better get his facts straight. Next, Roy tries to convince the crowd by showing photos of the owls, but the photos are unclear. Finally, Mullet Fingers appears. He has buried his body in an owl burrow. He and Roy play a prank on Mr. Muckle that involves a bucket of snakes. The snakes turn out to be fake, and Muckle ends up looking foolish. Through their courage and creativity, the main characters save the burrowing owls.

Practice
Workbook Page 149

Write a paragraph that summarizes the plot of a story, novel, movie, or television show. Use a plot-summary chart to list information about the plot. Then write your summary. Be sure to use reported and quoted speech correctly.

Writing Checklist

IDEAS:
☑ I included only the most important events in my plot summary.

ORGANIZATION:
☑ I first introduced the characters and setting. Then I presented the main events in time order.

307

STEP 1: Introduce

A good expository paragraph presents information in a clear, logical way. Remind students that it's important to use only the most important details when writing a summary.

STEP 2: Teach

Writing an Expository Paragraph

Write a Plot Summary Draw the plot summary chart on the board (page 307). **SAY:** *When writing a plot summary, remember you say in a few sentences what happened in a story. Details such as the main characters and setting, the goals of the characters, how they tried to reach them, and whether or not they succeeded are all important.*

Model Writing Skill SAY: *As I read the student model aloud, listen for the details that the writer included in his summary. What are some of the story details he left out? How did he organize his ideas?*

STEP 3: Assess

Have students evaluate their work using the Writing Checklist.

Writing Checklist Note

Ideas: Check that students used only the main events in their summary.

Organization: Check students' essays include an introduction that the information the present in the body of their essay is clear and written in chronological order.

Accelerate Language Development

Changing Tense in Reported Speech

Point out that the tense in the reported speech only changes if the reporting verb (he said/she said) is in a past tense. If, on the other hand, the reporting verb is in a present tense (he says/she says), the tense of the reported speech is retained. Compare: *Mother said, "I love birds."* becomes *Mother said (that) she loved birds.* But: *Mother says, "She loves birds."* becomes *Mother says (that) she loves birds.* Mention that the latter is more common in spoken English. The tense of the reported speech is also retained when you report a general truth. Example: *He said that elephants can't fly.*

Teach

STEP 1: Introduce

Objectives

Read aloud the list of objectives in the What You Will Learn section. Tell students that this reading will be about growing trees in Kenya. Have students work in pairs to restate the list of things they will learn.

The Big Question

Read aloud the Build Background section. To help students understand, explain the meaning of *environmentalist*. **SAY:** *An environmentalist is someone who is concerned about protecting the environment. Do you know anyone who is an environmentalist? Not everyone agrees on the effects of pollution on the environment. How does an environmentalist need to show imagination or courage?*

Build Background

SAY: *What do you know about how trees benefit the environment in general? They help by absorbing carbon dioxide and giving off oxygen. They are an integral part of the natural atmospheric exchange cycle here on Earth. However, there are too few of them to counter the increases in carbon dioxide caused by automobile traffic, manufacturing, and other human activities. Did you know that a single tree will absorb approximately one ton of carbon dioxide during its lifetime?*

STEP 2: Teach

Understanding the Genre:
Informational Text

Tell students that an informational text is a work of nonfiction. Its purpose is to present factual information about real people, events, places, and situations. This informational text is a science article that looks at courageous and imaginative ways to solve the problem of deforestation in Kenya.

Teaching Resources

- CD-ROM/e-book, Key Words
- Audio CD 5, tracks 14–15
- *Workbook*, p. 150

READING 4 — Prepare to Read

What You Will Learn

Reading
- Vocabulary building: *Context, dictionary skills, word study*
- Reading strategy: *Follow steps in a process*
- Text type: *Informational texts (science) (instructions)*

Grammar, Usage, and Mechanics
Imperatives

Writing
Write how-to instructions

THE BIG QUESTION

How are courage and imagination linked? Why might courage and imagination be needed to improve our environment? Do you think that one person really can make a difference? How might planting trees make a big difference to people throughout a country? Discuss with a partner.

BUILD BACKGROUND

▲ A beech tree forest

"A Tree Grows in Kenya: The Story of Wangari Maathai" is a biographical science article about an environmentalist from Kenya. An environmentalist is someone who works to protect the natural world. The woman you will be reading about, Wangari Maathai, has done a lot to improve the environment of Kenya, her home country. You will see how she used her imagination and courage to change the land around her.

Kenya is a country in eastern Africa. The southeastern part of the country borders the Indian Ocean. Kenya was once a colony ruled by the British. In 1963, Kenya won its independence from Britain. In 1964, Kenya became an independent republic.

Today Kenya is a popular place for travelers to visit. It has wildlife parks, mountains, sophisticated cities, and beaches. Imagine going on a safari and seeing lions, elephants, zebras, and wildebeests.

308

TESOL Standards

Goal 1, Standard 2—To use English to communicate in social settings: Students will interact in, through, and with spoken and written English for personal expression and enjoyment.
Descriptors—Sharing social and cultural traditions and values; Participating in popular culture.

Goal 3, Standard 1—To use English in socially and culturally appropriate ways: Students will use the appropriate language variety, register, and genre according to audience, purpose, and setting.
Descriptors—Responding to and using slang appropriately; Responding to and using idioms appropriately.

VOCABULARY

Learn Key Words

Read the sentences. Use the context to figure out the meaning of the red words. Use a dictionary to check your answers. Then write each word and its meaning in your notebook.

Key Words

campaign
committee
continent
democratic
natural
nutrition

1. The campaign to save the forest was successful. The series of actions helped to save the forest.

2. The committee has six members. The group is preparing a report on Kenya.

3. North America is a continent, one of the seven main areas of land in the world.

4. A democratic government is controlled by leaders who are elected by the people of the country.

5. Wood is a natural material. It is not man-made.

6. Fruit gives us the nutrition we need. It has many of the vitamins and minerals we need to stay healthy.

Practice
Workbook Page 150

Write the sentences in your notebook. Choose a red word from the box above to complete each sentence. Then take turns reading the sentences aloud with a partner.

1. If you live in a _____ country, you elect leaders by voting for them.

2. Water is one important _____ resource. Others are minerals and land.

3. Trees get the _____ they need to grow from water, sun, and soil.

4. The girl started a _____ to save trees. She planned six events.

5. The planting _____ is in charge of planting trees.

6. Kenya and the United States are not located on the same _____.

309

 ## Vocabulary

Learn Key Words Play the CD. Have students listen and repeat. If you are not using the CD, read the Key Words aloud. **SAY:** *These words are important to the subject matter of the text we are reading.* **Write the following words and their definitions on the board.**

- **campaign:** a series of public actions to achieve a particular result
- **committee:** a group of people chosen to do a particular job or make decisions
- **continent:** one of the main areas of land on the earth
- **democratic:** a system in which everyone has the same right to vote and speak
- **natural:** coming from nature; not made by people
- **nutrition:** the process of getting the right food for good health and growth

Have students copy the Key Words and the definitions into their notebooks and create an original sentence using each.

STEP 3: Practice

Have students work with partners to complete the activity.

ANSWERS
1. democratic
2. natural
3. nutrition
4. campaign
5. committee
6. continent

Differentiated Instruction

Beginning	Have students point out the zebras and wildebeests in the photo on page 308.
Early Intermediate	Ask students what year Kenya became an independent republic. (1964)
Intermediate	Ask students to describe where Kenya is located. Have students point out Kenya on a map if one is available.
Standard English Learners (CRI)	Have students briefly research Kenya. Have them prepare and present a short report to the class in which they state five facts about the country.

Teach

STEP 1: Teach

CD5 T16–T17

 Vocabulary

Learn Academic Words Play the CD. Have students listen and repeat. If you are not using the CD, read the Academic Words aloud. **SAY:** *Look at the Academic Words list. Now look at the chart below it. Notice that the words and their definitions are on the left. Sentences containing the words are on the right. What other sentence can we create with the word aspect?* (Possible response: One aspect of her plan to find water was to scout the whole area around the campsite.)

Have partners work together to add an original sentence for each word. Suggest that students write each word, its definition, and the sentence in their notebook.

STEP 2: Practice

Write the following question on the board and underline the words as shown: *What aspect of nature would you like to photograph?* **SAY:** *When you are asked a question, try to include words from the question in your answer. Look at the question on the board.*

Then write this answer on the board: *The aspect of nature I would like to photograph is the trees.* Be sure to underline the words as shown, so students can clearly see the connection.

ANSWERS
Possible responses:
1. The aspect of nature I would like to photograph is the trees.
2. I might finance a campaign to save a forest by holding a bake sale at school.
3. Oil is a valuable resource because it is needed for so many things: transportation, heating, manufacturing, etc.
4. Forests help sustain life by releasing oxygen into the atmosphere.
5. Computers and cell phones are types of technology used to communicate across continents.
6. A diet rich in fruits and vegetables is good for people's welfare because it is rich in nutrients and fiber.

Teaching Resources
- Audio CD 5, tracks 16–17
- *Workbook*, pp. 151–153
- CD-ROM/e-book, Academic Words, Word Study

T310

Learn Academic Words

Study the red words and their meanings. You will find these words useful when talking and writing about informational texts. Write each word and its meaning in your notebook. After you read "A Tree Grows in Kenya: The Story of Wangari Maathai," try to use these words to respond to the text.

Academic Words
aspect
finance
resource
sustain
technology
welfare

aspect = one of the parts or features of a situation, idea, or problem	➡	People try to think of every **aspect** of a problem and try to solve each part.
finance = provide money for something	➡	The club needed to **finance** a trip, so they raised money with a bake sale.
resource = something such as land, minerals, or natural energy that exists in a country and can be used in order to increase its wealth	➡	A waterfall is a natural **resource**. It makes power that can be turned into electricity.
sustain = make it possible for someone or something to continue to exist over time	➡	Trees **sustain** life for many animals. They make life for these animals possible.
technology = a combination of all the knowledge, equipment, or methods used in scientific or industrial work	➡	Computers and cars are examples of modern **technology**. We use these machines daily.
welfare = health, comfort, and happiness	➡	Trees are good for our **welfare**. They add to our health and happiness.

Practice Workbook Page 151

Work with a partner to answer the questions. Try to include the red word in your answer. Write the sentences in your notebook.

1. What **aspect** of nature would you like to photograph?
2. How might you **finance** a campaign to save a forest?
3. Which **resource** do you think helps a country become wealthier—gold or oil? Why?
4. How do forests help to **sustain** life?
5. What types of **technology** are used to communicate across continents?
6. How is a diet rich in fresh fruits and vegetables good for people's **welfare**?

310

Forests help to sustain life in many ways. ▶

 TESOL Standards

Goal 1, Standard 3—To use English to communicate in social settings: Students will use learning strategies to extend their communicative competence.
Descriptors—Testing hypotheses about language.

Goal 2, Standard 2—To use English to achieve academically in all content areas: Students will use English to obtain, process, construct, and provide subject matter information in spoken and written form.
Descriptors—Hypothesizing and predicting; Formulating and asking questions.

Goal 2, Standard 3—To use English to achieve academically in all content areas: Students will use appropriate learning strategies to construct and apply academic knowledge.
Descriptors—Applying basic reading comprehension skills such as skimming, scanning, previewing, and reviewing text.

Word Analysis: Suffixes *-ic, -ist, -able*

A suffix is a letter or group of letters placed at the end of a base word. It can change a word's part of speech and its meaning. If you know the meaning of a suffix, it can help you understand the meaning of the new word. Study the examples in the chart below. If a base word ends in *e*, remember to drop the *e* before adding the suffix.

Word	Suffix	New Word (Part of Speech and Meaning)
democrat (noun)	*-ic*	democratic (adjective) (having the characteristics of a democrat)
environmental (adjective)	*-ist*	environmentalist (noun) (person who works for the environment)
sustain (verb)	*-able*	sustainable (adjective) (capable of being sustained)

▲ Wind energy is a sustainable resource.

Practice **Workbook Page 152**

Copy the chart above into your notebook. Work with a partner. Add these words and the suffixes to the chart to create new words:

poet + ic	art + ist	understand + able

Identify each new word's part of speech. Then define each word using what you know about suffixes. Check the dictionary to make sure that your answers are correct.

READING STRATEGY | FOLLOW STEPS IN A PROCESS

Learning how to follow steps in a process will help you read and understand instructions. The steps are usually arranged in chronological order, from first to last. The author often numbers the steps to make them easier to follow. When you read instructions, follow these steps:

- Look for numbers.
- Look for time-order words such as *first, second, then, next,* and *last.*
- Read the steps from first to last.
- Restate the steps to make sure that you can follow them in the correct order.

As you read "How to Plant a Tree," follow the steps above to understand the steps in the process.

 Workbook Page 153

311

STEP 1: Teach

Word Study

Suffixes *-ic, -ist, -able* **SAY:** *The words in the chart on page 311 have suffixes that change their meaning and part of speech. With a partner, use each of these words in a sentence. Consult your dictionaries for help. Can you add any more examples to the chart?*

STEP 2: Practice

Have students work with a partner to do the activity. Check definitions in a dictionary.

ANSWERS

Word	Suffix	New Word: Part of Speech & Meaning
poet	poetic	Adjective; having qualities of deep feeling or graceful expression
art	artist	Noun; someone who produces art
understand	understandable	Adjective; easy to understand; reasonable

STEP 3: Teach

Reading Strategy

Follow Steps in a Process Model for students how to follow the order of events as a way of remembering what is read. **SAY:** *Stop reading from time to time and look for numbers or time-order words to help you remember what you've read.*

Linguistic Note

New Words in English

Point out that English is a living language and therefore continuously creates new words and phrases. New words may come about by adding prefixes and suffixes to words that already exist. The suffixes *-ic, -ist, -able* are still productive, as are the prefixes *tele-, mega-* and *re-*. Point out that words such as *sustainable* or *environmentalist* entered the language only recently with the ecological movement at the end of the 20th century. Other new advances, such as telecommunications, have and may still create new words. For example, the prefix *tele-* has turned the word *commute,* meaning *drive to and from work,* into *telecommute,* meaning *work from home and commute electronically.* It is quite possible that the new word *email,* for example, will create an even newer word such as *emailable.* Ask your students for other examples they may know.

Read

Reading Summary

This reading is about a woman who was awarded the Nobel Peace Prize in 2004 for her work connecting environmentalism and peace. The final page is a how-to guide to planting a tree.

The Big Question

SAY: *How does planting trees make a difference in our lives? Think about what trees provide—food, shelter, beauty, and soil protection. Now think about what those things mean for everyday life: wood to build houses and heat homes, wood for paper, protection from pollution, habitats for animals, and so on. By planting trees, we ensure that future generations will enjoy the resources trees provide. How do trees make your life better?*

STEP 2: Teach

Set a Purpose for Reading

Tell students to copy the purpose for reading into their notebooks and to keep it in mind as they read. Explain that they will have to present details that support their answer to the question and to explain how the reading relates to the Big Question.

Preteaching Highlighted Words

With students, preview the highlighted vocabulary on pages 312–313. Write the words on the board, and point out that they are defined at the bottom of each page. Model using the words in original sentences and ask students to do the same.

CD5 T18–T19 ### Scaffolding:
Listen and Read

Have students read along as you play the Audio CD recording of the reading. Pause the recording at the end of each page to ask and answer questions students may have.

Teaching Resources

- *Resources*, Summaries, pp. 161–162
- Audio CD 5, tracks 18–19
- *Reader's Companion Workbook*, pp. 109–117

READING
4
INFORMATIONAL TEXT
SCIENCE

Set a purpose for reading Why might something as simple as planting a tree require courage and imagination? As you read this article, think about how a simple action can have a big effect. Then find out how to plant a tree yourself.

A Tree Grows in Kenya:
The Story of Wangari Maathai

In October 2004, Wangari Maathai (wan-GAH-ree mah-DHEYE), an environmentalist from Kenya, Africa, received an unexpected phone call. The person on the phone told her that she had won the Nobel Peace Prize. Each year, the Nobel committee chooses someone whose work for peace is judged to be the most important to the world. This was an incredible honor and an enormous surprise for Maathai. She was very excited. In an interview with *Time* magazine, she said, "I think what the Nobel committee is doing is going beyond war and looking at what humanity can do to prevent war. Sustainable management of our natural resources will promote peace." She was pleased that the judges had recognized the deep connection between environmentalism and peace. "If we conserved our resources better," she said, "fighting would not occur."

humanity, people in general

Maathai's love of the environment began when she was very young. She was born in the highland village of Nyeri in Kenya in 1940. As a child she enjoyed the lush, green forests around her. Her parents were farmers, so she grew up close to the natural world. In her Nobel prize speech, she said:

I would visit a stream next to our home to fetch water for my mother. I would drink water straight from the stream. Playing among the arrowroot leaves, I tried in vain to pick up the strands of frogs' eggs, believing they were beads. But every time I put my little fingers under them they would break. Later, I saw thousands of tadpoles: black, energetic, and wriggling through the clear water against the background of the brown earth. This is the world I inherited from my parents.

---

highland, mountain
tadpoles, small creatures with long tails that live in water and grow into frogs or toads
inherited, received

312

Maathai was an excellent student. She won a scholarship to attend a college in the United States. She studied hard and received a degree in biology. Then she worked toward more advanced degrees at the University of Pittsburgh and University of Nairobi in Kenya. In 1971, she earned a doctoral degree. She was honored to be the first woman in East and Central Africa to earn such an advanced degree.

At first, Maathai taught at the University of Nairobi. Soon she wanted to do more than teach. While in the United States, she had been deeply impressed by the democratic freedom that people enjoyed. She wanted the Kenyan people to enjoy similar freedom and a better quality of life.

Maathai was concerned that the luxuriant forests of her childhood were rapidly disappearing because of excessive logging and other practices. She wanted the people of her village, especially the women, to have more of a voice in government. Maathai decided that it was time for a change.

It is said that "a journey of a thousand miles begins with a single step." Maathai took one step to change the world around her: She planted nine trees in her backyard. With this simple act, she planted the seed of her campaign to save the forests of Africa!

In 1976, Maathai interviewed many farmers in the Kenyan countryside.

scholarship, money given to help pay for a person's education
luxuriant, healthy, thick, and strong
excessive, much more than reasonable or necessary

Most of them were women, and they often had the same concerns. They needed more firewood, which was their main source of energy. They needed clean water for drinking, cooking, and bathing. They needed to be able to grow their own food. In addition, they needed to be able to make more money so that they could become self-sufficient.

Maathai knew that the destruction of the forests was at the root of these problems. She decided to put her knowledge and creativity to work. Trees were needed to stop soil erosion. They were also important sources of firewood for cooking. Why not encourage farmers in Kenya to plant as many trees as possible? This would be a simple way to improve the farmers' living conditions. And this method wouldn't require expensive tools or large sums of money.

In 1977, Maathai founded the Green Belt Movement. A greenbelt is a band of farmland or parks surrounding a village. Maathai hoped to see belts of green trees again throughout Kenya. The goals of the Green Belt Movement were to encourage Kenyan farmers to plant trees and to conserve the environment. This, in turn, would help farmers, and women in particular, to improve their living conditions.

self-sufficient, able to provide for themselves
erosion, destruction and wearing away because of wind and rain

BEFORE YOU GO ON

1 Where in Kenya did Wangari Maathai grow up?

2 What did Maathai study in college?

On Your Own
Have you ever thought of a simple solution to a big problem? Explain.

313

Study Skills: Globe

A globe is an excellent resource for students, whether they are studying science, English, math, or social studies. Have students use a globe to locate Kenya. What countries border Kenya? What are the major bodies of water?

STEP 3: Monitor Progress

Ask students to check what they have understood in the reading. If you are using the Audio CD, pause the recording.

Before You Go On

Remind students that these questions will help them monitor their progress. Put students in pairs to answer the questions. Encourage them to share their answers with the class.

ANSWERS

1. Wangari Maathai grew up in the village of Nyeri.
2. In college, Maathai studied biology.

On Your Own Have students write an answer to the On Your Own question on a separate sheet of paper. Encourage volunteers to share their responses with the class. Then, collect student responses to monitor their comprehension, writing skills, and fluency.

Differentiated Instruction	
Beginning	Have students fill in the blank. A word that means "mountain" is _____.
Early Intermediate	Have students identify the name of the highland village Wangari Maathai comes from. (Nyeri)
Intermediate	Have students describe the landscape in your area.
Special Needs	Ask students to assign themselves a task, e.g. to read the first or last paragraphs only, in order to empower them and promote self-advocacy.

Read

Preteaching Highlighted Words

With students, preview the highlighted vocabulary on pages 314–315. Write the words on the board, and point out that they are defined at the bottom of each page.

Ask volunteers to find and read the definitions. Model how to use the words in sentences. For example: *I usually speak my mind, and that is why people call me outspoken.* Then ask volunteers to do the same.

Across the Curriculum:
Science

Tell students that there are hundreds of species of trees all around the world. All trees, no matter how large or small they may be, are able to help the environment by producing oxygen and absorbing carbon dioxide. Ask students to name several types of trees that they know about. What trees are indigenous to the area you are in?

At first, her idea wasn't very popular. As Maathai said, "It took me a lot of days and nights to convince people that women could improve their environment without much technology or . . . financial resources." Although it took a long time, the movement achieved its goal. Within thirty years, the women of Kenya had planted 30 million trees. The Green Belt Movement did other things to improve the quality of Kenyan life. Members also promoted better education and nutrition throughout the country.

When Maathai started her campaign to plant trees, she was working at the grass-roots level. This means that she worked directly with the local people. Sometimes, she also worked directly with the government to bring about change. For example, in the 1980s, Kenyan President Daniel arap Moi planned to build a sixty-two-story skyscraper. This plan would have destroyed Uhuru Park, a beautiful park in Nairobi, the nation's capital. Maathai had visited Uhuru Park many times. It was one of the only green spaces available in the city for public use. Families often went there on weekends to relax, play, and enjoy time together. To save this precious

---

financial resources, money or access to money
skyscraper, very tall building
precious, valuable and important

green space, she led protests against the government. President Moi called her "a threat to the order and security of the country." Maathai was arrested by the police and treated badly, but she never gave up the fight. Because of her courage and persistence, she eventually succeeded in preserving the park.

Wangari Maathai strongly believes that solutions to most of the world's problems will come from the people themselves. She is now a national hero in Kenya. If young Kenyan girls are strong-willed and outspoken, people say they are "like Wangari." "Like Wangari" has become an expression of admiration and affection.

Today, Wangari Maathai and the members of the Green Belt Movement continue to plant trees throughout many countries in Africa, as well as in Haiti and the United States. They have educated thousands of people along the way. As the Nobel committee said, "Maathai is a strong voice speaking for the best forces in Africa to promote peace and good living conditions on the continent. She thinks globally and acts locally."

---

persistence, determination
strong-willed, determined to achieve goals
outspoken, expressing opinions honestly and directly
admiration, approval and respect

▼ Uhuru Park

314

 TESOL Standards

Goal 3, Standard 3—To use English in socially and culturally appropriate ways: Students will use appropriate learning strategies to extend their sociolinguistic and sociocultural competence.
Descriptors—Experimenting with variations of language in social and academic settings; Seeking information about appropriate language use and behavior; Analyzing the social context to determine appropriate language use.

How to Plant a Tree

What You Need

- Something to dig with, like a shovel or spade.
- A tree! You can buy a tree at a garden center. In some places, state or community foresters have trees that they'll give to anyone who wants to plant them. When you buy your tree, you'll notice that all of its roots are wrapped up with fabric in a little ball. This is called the rootball.
- A watering can and some water.

What to Do

1. First, choose a site. Pick a place that gets enough sun, where your tree will be happy. Don't plant close to power or telephone wires.
2. Dig a hole as deep as the rootball and three times as wide.
3. Unwrap the rootball and spread out the roots. If they're tangled up, straighten them out.
4. Put the tree in the hole. The soil should come up as high on the tree as it was before you got it. Usually this will be to the top of the rootball. Be sure that the tree is straight.
5. Fill in the space around the rootball gently but firmly with soil. Pack down the soil with your hands and feet. Be sure that there are no air pockets.
6. Make a little dam around the base of the tree about as wide as the hole. This will keep the water close to the tree.
7. After it's planted, your tree will be very thirsty, so give it lots of water.
8. If you need more help, call your local garden store or contact a community park or forest agency.

Some Tips to Keep in Mind

- If you want to plant your tree in a park or other public place, make sure you ask for permission. Some places may have rules about what kind of trees can be planted there.
- Your tree is just a baby, and like any baby, you need to take care of it. You should water it every week. Most trees need 7.5 to 11 liters (2–3 gal.) of water per week.

BEFORE YOU GO ON

1 What did the Green Belt Movement promote besides planting trees?

2 What park did Maathai help to save in Kenya?

On Your Own
What do you think of Wangari Maathai? How did she show courage and imagination?

315

Study Skills: Almanac

An almanac is an interesting and useful source of information for many different subjects, including math, science, English and social studies. Have students use an almanac, either in print or online, to determine which types of trees and other plants are appropriate for their specific area. One of the most famous American almanacs, *The Old Farmers' Almanac* has been published continuously since the late eighteenth century.

STEP 5: Monitor Progress

Ask students to check what they have understood in the reading.

Before You Go On

Remind students that these questions will help them monitor their progress. Put students in pairs to answer the questions. Encourage them to share their answers with the class.

ANSWERS

1. The Green Belt Movement promoted better education and nutrition throughout Kenya.
2. Maathai helped save Uhuru Park in Kenya.

On Your Own Have students write an answer to the On Your Own question on a separate sheet of paper. Encourage volunteers to share their responses with the class. Then, collect student responses to monitor their comprehension, writing skills, and fluency.

Review the Purpose for Reading

Elicit responses to the Set a Purpose for Reading questions at the beginning of this reading. Remind students to relate their responses to the Big Question.

Teach & Apply

STEP 1: Practice

Comprehension

Ask students to complete the questions in the Comprehension section.

ANSWERS

1. The first step Wangari Maathai took to change the world was planting nine trees in her backyard.
2. The Green Belt Movement's goals are to encourage Kenyan farmers to plant trees and conserve the environment
3. Maathai studied biology and earned a degree in it. She also earned advanced degrees, including a doctoral degree.
4. The women farmers of Kenya needed more firewood, clean water, and the ability to grow their own food. They also needed to be able to make enough money to be self-sufficient.
5. Possible response: Wangari always loved nature and felt connected to it, so she wanted to conserve the environment.
6. Possible response: Wangari was awarded the Nobel Peace Prize because her work in sustaining resources helps to promote peace.
7. Possible response: I would give the Nobel Prize to people who do work that helps others, like conserving the environment, saving children, and helping the poor.
8. Possible response: City parks give people in cities some of the natural world to enjoy.

 ### In Your Own Words

Have students work in groups to fill in the chart with details and then write a summary using that information.

Speaking Tip

SAY: *We can show our classmates that we are interested in what we are saying by speaking with enthusiasm and trying to begin a discussion about the questions.*

Teaching Resources

- *Workbook,* p. 154
- CD-ROM/e-book, Comprehension, Extension
- *Reader's Companion Workbook,* pp. 118–122

COMPREHENSION
Workbook Page 154

Right There

1. What was the first step Wangari Maatthai took to change the world?
2. What are the goals of the Green Belt Movement?

Think and Search

3. What education did Maathai receive? What degrees did she earn?
4. What concerns did the women farmers of Kenya have?

Author and You

5. How did Wangari's childhood affect the way she thought when she was growing up?
6. Why did the Nobel committee award her the peace prize?

On Your Own

7. Suppose that you could award the Nobel Prize. To whom would you give the prize and why?
8. Why are city parks important to people who live near them?

IN YOUR OWN WORDS

Imagine that you are telling a small group of friends about this biographical article. Tell your friends three facts about Maathai's life and work. Use the chart below to help you list your facts and write a brief summary of the article's main points. Then share your summary with a classmate. Compare and contrast your summaries.

> **Speaking TIP**
> Communicate your interest in what you are saying so that your partner will be interested, too.

A Tree Grows in Kenya: The Story of Wangari Maathai
Fact 1:
Fact 2:
Fact 3:
Overall summary:

316

TESOL Standards

Goal 2, Standard 3—To use English to achieve academically in all content areas: Students will use appropriate learning strategies to construct and apply academic knowledge.
Descriptors—Applying self-monitoring and self-corrective strategies to build and expand a knowledge base; Determining and establishing the conditions that help one become an effective learner (e.g., when, where, how to study).

Goal 3, Standard 1—To use English in socially and culturally appropriate ways: Students will use the appropriate language variety, register, and genre according to audience, purpose, and setting.
Descriptors—Responding to and using humor appropriately; Using the appropriate degree of formality with different audiences and settings; Recognizing and using Standard English and vernacular dialects appropriately.

Goal 3, Standard 3—To use English in socially and culturally appropriate ways: Students will use appropriate learning strategies to extend their sociolinguistic and sociocultural competence.
Descriptors—Deciding when use of slang is appropriate.

DISCUSSION

Discuss in pairs or small groups.

1. In what ways is Wangari Maathai an admirable person?
2. Maathai spent time living and studying in the United States. How do you think this affected her life and her goals?
3. A Nobel Prize winner receives more than $1 million. How would you have advised Maathai to spend the money?

Q How are courage and imagination linked? What is the meaning of the saying, "A journey of a thousand miles begins with a single step"? What role does courage play in that journey? What role does imagination play?

READ FOR FLUENCY

When we read aloud to communicate meaning, we group words into phrases, pause or slow down to make important points, and emphasize important words. Pause for a short time when you reach a comma and for a longer time when you reach a period. Pay attention to rising and falling intonation at the end of sentences.

Work with a partner. Choose a paragraph from the reading. Discuss which words seem important for communicating meaning. Practice pronouncing difficult words. Give each other feedback.

EXTENSION Workbook Page 154

Learn more about other Nobel Peace Prize winners. Choose one recent winner and report on his or her life and accomplishments. Here are some Nobel winners to choose from: Muhammad Yunus, Shirin Ebadi, Kim Dae Jung, Jody Williams, Nelson Mandela, F. W. de Klerk, Aung San Suu Kyi, and Elie Wiesel. Use encyclopedias, reference books, and reliable websites. Copy and complete the following diagram to organize your ideas. Report your findings to the class.

Winner's Name — year prize won — reason for winning — life story — accomplishments then and since

▲ Elie Wiesel

▲ Nelson Mandela

317

Listening Tip

SAY: *When listening to others in class, it can be helpful to know the reasons for their answers. If you do not hear any supporting details for a certain answer, politely ask your partner what details he or she was thinking of when answering the question.*

(CRI) Discussion

Before students begin their discussion, decide if they will work as a whole group, in small teams, or as partners.

Q How are courage and imagination linked? If necessary, explain that the saying "A journey of a thousand miles begins with a single step" means that every long journey or large project must start somewhere. Sometimes it takes courage to start something we know will be difficult, but once we start, it often gets easier. Problems encountered along the way can often be solved in imaginative and creative ways. Encourage students to think of examples of how courage and imagination can help along life's journey.

STEP 3: Assess

Read for Fluency

SAY: *Remember to stop at the end of each sentence as you read, and pause at each comma. This will help your reader know when you have finished an idea. Try to read the rest of the sentence as fluently as possible. Take turns practicing the reading and giving each other feedback.*

Extension

Have students select another Nobel Peace Prize winner about whom whey would like to learn more. Have students display their findings on a bulletin board.

Differentiated Instruction

Beginning	Ask students if they think planting trees made a difference to the people in Kenya.
Early Intermediate	Ask students to state the name of the group that Wangari Maathai founded. (Green Belt Movement)
Intermediate	Have students identify what they think are the most important steps when planting a tree.
Standard English Learners (CRI)	Have students come up with a plan to plant trees in your area. Ask them to identify where they would plant, how they'd get permission, how they'd get others to help, etc.

STEP 1: Introduce

As students review the information on page 318, tell them that imperatives are used to give instructions or commands. Give some examples, e.g. *stand up*, *sit down*, *read*, *listen*.

STEP 2: Teach

Grammar and Writing

Imperatives Read aloud with students the information on the student page. The imperative or command form is used to give someone directions. "How to Plant a Tree" (page 315) provides instructions about tree planting. Each of the steps in the instructions uses the imperative (or command) form of the verb. **SAY:** *The imperative is used for giving an instruction, a direction, or an order. The subject is understood to be "you." Use the imperative in your how-to writing assignment on page 319.*

STEP 3: Practice

Model the first sentence, and discuss with students how to rewrite the practice sentences as imperatives.

ANSWERS

1. Pick a place that gets enough sun.
2. Plant far from any power or telephone lines.
3. Straighten the roots if they are tangled.
4. Make sure that the tree is straight.
5. Be sure that there are no air pockets.
6. Give the tree lots of water after it is planted.

Teaching Resources

- *Workbook*, pp. 155–156
- CD-ROM/e-book, Grammar, Writing
- *Transparencies*, Writing Model 44
- *Transparencies*, *Resources*, Graphic Organizer 7
- *Assessment*, Reading 4 Test, pp. 111–114

Grammar and Writing

GRAMMAR, USAGE, AND MECHANICS

Imperatives

An imperative is the form of a verb used for giving instructions. An imperative sentence ends with a period or an exclamation mark.

Use imperatives to make your how-to instructions direct and clear. Study these examples from "How to Plant a Tree."

> **Dig** a hole as deep as the rootball.
> **Pack** down the soil with your hands and feet.
> **Put** the tree in the hole.

Practice Workbook Page 155

Work with a partner. Copy the sentences into your notebook. Rewrite them as imperatives. Do not state the subject.

1. You will pick a place that gets enough sun.
2. You will plant far from any power or telephone lines.
3. You can straighten the roots if they are tangled.
4. You will make sure that the tree is straight.
5. You should be sure that there are no air pockets.
6. You can give the tree lots of water after it is planted.

Notice the beautiful palm trees.

318

WRITING AN EXPOSITORY PARAGRAPH

Write How-to Instructions

On this page, you will write a paragraph on how to do something step by step. When you wrote a plot summary, you presented events in a chronological sequence. You can organize your "how-to" paragraph in the same way. You can use a graphic organizer like the one at the right to put the steps in a process in a clear order.

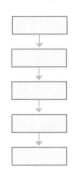

Sometimes you will need to explain how to do something by writing instructions. To make your instructions clear and easy to follow:

- Present the steps in order from first to last.
- Use words that signal time order, such as *first, later,* and *last.*
- Use imperatives to make your instructions clear and direct.

Below is a model of how-to instructions for taking care of a young tree. Notice how the student has put the steps in chronological order and used time-order words and imperatives.

Danielle Christian

Caring for a Newly Planted Tree

After planting a new tree, the first thing you need to do is water it. Water the tree where the roots are located, just under the tree. Make sure that you widen the watering area as the tree grows. It is better to give regular deep soakings rather than water the tree lightly every day. Never water too little or too much! Next, make sure you place mulch, or decaying leaves, around the tree. Do not put a protective covering around the tree; that will prevent water and air from reaching the roots. Don't fertilize the tree unless it is lacking in nutrients. Finally, keep checking the tree to make sure that it is healthy and growing well. Check for any diseases or insects that might hurt the tree. If you think there are any problems, call a professional to come and check the tree out immediately.

Practice

Workbook Page 156

Give step-by-step instructions that explain how to do something, such as how to build a tree house or create a family recipe book. List your ideas in a steps-in-a-process chart. Be sure to use imperatives to make your instructions easy to follow.

Writing Checklist

ORGANIZATION:
☑ I organized my instructions in chronological order.

SENTENCE FLUENCY:
☑ I used imperatives to make each step clear.

319

Accelerate Language Development

Softened Imperatives

Imperatives are used in every language—for instructions, requests, orders and suggestions. They are also used in public signs and announcements, such as "Keep out." Point out that the English imperative is characterized by NOT using the personal pronoun *you* in the imperative. This might be unusual for speakers of languages such as Japanese and Chinese, which have an elaborate system of honorifics to politely address another person. Speakers from language backgrounds with such a degree of politeness might have difficulty using the imperative for cultural reasons. Point out that the English imperative can be softened by adding *please*, or tag lines such as *will you, would you* or *won't you.* Examples: *Give me a hand, would you? Open the door, please. Be careful, won't you?*

Unit Wrap-Up

Link the Readings

Critical Thinking SAY: *What do the readings in this unit have in common?* **Allow students time to answer. SAY:** *They all tell about courage and imagination, yet they do not all have the same purpose. The fiction pieces are designed to entertain and provoke thought. The nonfiction pieces provide information.*

ANSWERS

Title of Reading	Purpose	Big Question Link
From *The Secret Garden*	To entertain	Tells the story of a girl sent to live in England after her parents have died.
"Kids' Guernica"	To inform	Tells about the artworks kids around the world are creating to promote peace.
From *Hoot*	To entertain	Tells a funny story about what happens when a restaurant chain tries to build a restaurant where owls live.
"A Tree Grows in Kenya"	To inform	tells the story of an environmentalist who won the Nobel Peace Prize
"How to Plant a Tree"	To inform	gives step-by-step instructions on how to plant a tree

 Discussion

Preview the discussion questions and assign groups to work together. Remind students to refer to the charts they created to find information for their discussion.

Q How are courage and imagination linked? SAY: *What happens in each of these readings when courage and imagination are linked? Can you make a general statement about the result of using both your courage and your imagination?*

STEP 2: Assess

Fluency Check

Emphasize that precise timing is needed to get comparable scores. Remind students that reading quickly is important, but understanding what they are reading is more important.

Teaching Resources

- *Assessment*, Unit 5 Test, pp. 173–182
- CD-ROM/e-book, Fluency Check, Projects

Link the Readings

Critical Thinking

Look back at the readings in this unit. Think about what they all have in common. They all have something to do with courage and imagination. Yet they do not all have the same purpose. The purpose of one reading might be to inform, while the purpose of another might be to entertain or persuade. In addition, the content of each reading relates to courage and imagination in different ways. Now copy the chart below into your notebook and complete it.

Title of Reading	Purpose	Big Question Link
From *The Secret Garden*	to entertain	
"Kids' Guernica"		
From *Hoot*		
"A Tree Grows in Kenya"	to inform	tells the story of an environmentalist who won the Nobel Peace Prize
"How to Plant a Tree"		

Discussion

Discuss in pairs or small groups.

- What conclusion can you draw about the imagination and courage of the people and characters in the readings? Do the real people and fictional characters share certain traits? Explain.

Q How are courage and imagination linked? Think about the readings. In what ways do you think courage and imagination are linked? How do the people and situations in the readings demonstrate the link between the two traits?

Fluency Check

Work with a partner. Choose a paragraph from one of the readings. Take turns reading it for one minute. Count the total number of words you read. Practice saying the words you had trouble reading. Take turns reading the paragraph three more times. Did you read more words each time? Copy the chart below into your notebook and record your speeds.

	1st Speed	2nd Speed	3rd Speed	4th Speed
Words Per Minute				

 TESOL Standards

Goal 1, Standard 1—To use English to communicate in social settings: Students will use English to participate in social interactions.
Descriptors—Engaging in conversations; Conducting transactions.

Goal 1, Standard 3—To use English to communicate in social settings: Students will use learning strategies to extend their communicative competence.
Descriptors—Seeking support and feedback from others; Using the primary language to ask for clarification; Selecting different media to help understand language.

Goal 2, Standard 2—To use English to achieve academically in all content areas: Students will use English to obtain, process, construct, and provide subject matter information in spoken and written form.
Descriptors—Listening to, speaking, reading, and writing about subject matter information; Gathering information orally and in writing; Selecting, connecting, and explaining information; Analyzing, synthesizing, and inferring from information; Responding to the work of peers and others; Representing information visually and interpreting information presented visually; Understanding and producing technical vocabulary and text features according to content area; Demonstrating knowledge through application in a variety of contexts.

Projects

Work in pairs or small groups. Choose one of these projects.

1 Mary Lennox in *The Secret Garden* was born and raised in India. When her parents die, she moves to England. Create a poster showing all the countries controlled by Great Britain in the early 1900s when the story was written.

2 "A Tree Grows in Kenya: The Story of Wangari Maathai" is about the country of Kenya. Find out more about this country's history. Make a fact file about Kenya with interesting facts about the country. Share your file with a partner.

3 Create a painting or other artwork that could be part of the Kids' Guernica project. Display your art in the classroom. Tell your classmates how your artwork stands for peace.

4 You read only one chapter of *Hoot*. What do you think happens at the end of the novel? Write a plot summary of the ending. Then read the book to see if your prediction is correct.

5 You learned how to plant a tree. Now, grow some seeds. Save the seeds from the fruits you eat, such as apples and avocados. Plant different kinds of seeds in different containers. Write down when each type of seed starts to grow and how fast it grows.

Further Reading

To find out more about the theme of this unit, choose from these reading suggestions.

The Gift of the Magi and Other Stories, O. Henry
This Penguin Reader® adaptation includes the classic story of a poor couple who use their imaginations to buy each other a special holiday gift.

The Lotus Seed, Sherry Garland
Fleeing her war-torn country, a Vietnamese girl takes a lotus seed to remind her of her homeland. Later, when her grandson plants the seed, a pink lotus blossom grows.

Flash, Carl Hiaasen
This book, by the author of *Hoot*, also tackles environmental issues with a touch of humor.

 Home-School Connection

These projects provide students with several ways to practice and apply what they have learned in this unit. The projects can be completed independently, with partners, or in small groups. Students can complete the projects either in the classroom or at home.

Tell students that they are going work on a project with a partner or in a small group. **SAY:** *Read along in your student book as I describe each project.*

Help students organize their chosen project by brainstorming lists of supplies they will need, as well as answering any questions they may have about the projects. Encourage students to choose a project which challenges them.

Further Reading

Each book listed on this page pertains to the Big Question. Encourage students to peruse them in their free time or read them for extra-credit book reports. The first book on the list is easily accessible, the second is accessible, and the third is challenging.

Websites

Log onto www.LongmanKeystone.com for links to other interesting websites about people with courage and imagination.

Differentiated Instruction

Beginning	Ask students to state their favorite reading from the unit and why it was their favorite.
Early Intermediate	Ask students which genre seen in this unit they prefer— plays, articles, or novels. Encourage them to say why.
Intermediate	Put students in pairs and ask them to list how courage and imagination are demonstrated in each reading.
Standard English Learners	Ask students to write the words *courage* and *imagination* in a personal thesaurus. Tell them to find two synonyms for each word.

Listening & Speaking Workshop

STEP 1: Introduce

 Begin this workshop by reading over with students the checklist on page 323. Use the checklist as a planning guide. If possible, show a recorded example of a how-to demonstration, and then apply the checklist to evaluate what you saw. Show students how to change the questions into directions by changing the beginning of the sentence. For example: *Was the how-to demonstration clearly related to the unit theme of courage and imagination?* becomes *Make sure the how-to demonstration is clearly related to the unit theme courage and imagination.*

Think About It Read over the instructions with students, and brainstorm topic ideas. Suggest that students make a checklist of all the parts of this assignment to be sure they don't miss any.

STEP 2: Teach

Gather and Organize Information Write each of the boldfaced steps on the board. Have students read the directions, and clarify any questions. The word *visuals* is used to describe a category of visual portrayals including photos, graphs, posters, primary source documents, drawings, and real objects to aid comprehension. Step-by-step visuals are especially helpful in how-to demonstrations.

Teaching Resources

- CD-ROM/e-book, Gather and Organize Information

Put It All Together

LISTENING & SPEAKING WORKSHOP

How-To Demonstration

With a group, you will tell and show the class how to do something.

1 THINK ABOUT IT Reread "A Tree Grows in Kenya: The Story of Wangari Maathai" and "How to Plant a Tree."

In small groups, discuss how Wangari Maathai helped the environment and the people of Kenya. Review the steps involved in planting a tree. Practice listing the steps you follow to perform another simple activity, such as making a sandwich or brushing your teeth.

Work together to develop a list of ideas for a how-to demonstration. Think of interesting activities your group could show the class, using props or pictures. For example:

- How to play the flute
- How to make an origami flower
- How to build a birdhouse
- How to wash a car

2 GATHER AND ORGANIZE INFORMATION As a group, choose a topic from your list. Write down what you already know about how to do the activity. Try to write step-by-step instructions. Also write down any questions you have.

Research Go to the library, search the Internet, or ask an adult for more information about how to perform the activity. Look for answers to your questions. Take notes on what you find.

Order Your Notes Organize your notes, using a sequence-of-events chart to show the order of the steps in your activity. Decide which step(s) each group member will present. Assign one person to give a short introduction that tells what activity your group will demonstrate.

Use Visuals Find or make props that you can use to show the key steps in the process that you will demonstrate. You may also want to create posters, models, or other visuals to help you explain the steps.

322

TESOL Standards

Goal 3, Standard 2—To use English in socially and culturally appropriate ways: Students will use nonverbal communication appropriate to audience, purpose, and setting.
Descriptors—Interpreting and responding appropriately to nonverbal cues and body language; Demonstrating knowledge of acceptable nonverbal classroom behaviors; Using acceptable tone, volume, stress, and intonation, in various social settings; Recognizing and adjusting behavior in response to nonverbal cues.

Goal 3, Standard 3—To use English in socially and culturally appropriate ways: Students will use appropriate learning strategies to extend their sociolinguistic and sociocultural competence.
Descriptors—Experimenting with variations of language in social and academic settings; Seeking information about appropriate language use and behavior; Analyzing the social context to determine appropriate language use; Rehearsing variations of language use in different social and academic settings.

3 **PRACTICE AND PRESENT** Use your sequence-of-events chart as an outline for your how-to demonstration. As a group, practice your demonstration several times. Use your visuals to help explain each step in the activity. When possible, act out the steps with props. Work on making smooth transitions between speakers. If possible, ask a classmate or friend to listen and give your group feedback. Or you can tape-record your presentation and listen for parts that need more work.

Deliver Your How-to Demonstration Speak loudly enough so that everyone in the class can hear you. Make eye contact with people as you speak. Emphasize important points by changing your tone of voice, slowing down, and using actions or visuals to help show your meaning. At the end of the demonstration, give your audience a chance to ask questions.

4 **EVALUATE THE PRESENTATION**
A good way to improve your speaking and listening skills is to evaluate each presentation you give and hear. When you evaluate yourself, you think about what you did well and what you can do better. Use this checklist to help you judge your group's how-to demonstration and the demonstrations of your classmates.

- ☑ Did the group present each step in the how-to demonstration clearly?
- ☑ Were the steps presented in a logical order?
- ☑ Did the demonstration give you enough information to do the activity on your own?
- ☑ Did the group members use props and other visuals effectively?
- ☑ What suggestions do you have for improving the demonstration?

〽️ *Speaking* TIPS

Make note cards to remind yourself of important ideas and details in the step(s) you are presenting. Add words or symbols that tell you when to speak and what props or visuals to use.

To show order and to help with transitions, use numbers and time-order words such as *first*, *then*, and *next*.

👂 *Listening* TIPS

Watch and listen carefully. Give the speakers your full attention.

Think about what you are hearing. Does it make sense? Would you be able to explain the steps to someone else? Write down questions and ask them at the end of the demonstration.

323

STEP 3: Practice

Practice and Present Read over with students the information about doing a how-to demonstration. As students prepare their delivery, remind them that although they can refer to their note cards or outline, they should practice their how-to demonstration until they feel they can speak smoothly and confidently. Point out the listening and speaking tips which are along the side of the page to help them.

STEP 4: Assess

Evaluate the Presentation Suggest that students use the checklist on this page to evaluate the group presentations for the purpose of giving positive feedback. Giving specific examples directly from the presentation is most helpful to the speakers.

Teaching the Tips

Speaking Tips SAY: *You should not read your entire presentation from your notes. Think of your notes as cue cards. Use symbols, numbers, and short words to help you remember what you want to say and when you should say it.*

Listening Tips SAY: *These presentations are a great chance for you to learn how to do something new. Listen carefully when your classmates are speaking, and take notes if you wish. Do you understand the instructions? If not, ask your classmates to clarify the process.*

Writing Workshop

STEP 1: Introduce

In this workshop, students learn the steps of the writing process. They will apply each of the steps from prewriting to publication, while applying the characteristics of expository paragraphs they have learned.

STEP 2: Teach

Prewrite Review the writing process with students: prewrite, draft, revise, edit and proofread, and publish. Point out that these steps will make the job of writing their expository essays easier and more orderly. Review with students the structure of an essay, reminding them that an essay usually includes an introduction, body paragraphs, and a conclusion. **SAY:** *Let's read the prewrite instructions on page 324. I am going to select my essay topic by choosing something that is very interesting to me. Before I outline my topic, I will list key facts, details, and examples on the board.*

SAY: *Read the instructions on the page, and work with a partner to complete a graphic organizer such as a problem-solution chart about the topic you have selected.*

Draft Explain that a draft is a work in progress. Review together the draft of the student essay on page 325, and discuss Danielle's topic. Notice how each of Danielle's body paragraphs is about a different way to attract birds to an area.

Teaching Resources

- *Transparencies, Resources,* Graphic Organizer 4
- *Transparencies,* Writing Model 45, Proofreader's Marks 51
- CD-ROM/e-book, Writing Workshop
- *Workbook,* pp. 157–158

WRITING WORKSHOP
Expository Essay

You have learned that an expository essay gives readers information about a topic. One type of expository essay explains how to solve a problem or how to do an activity. In this type of expository essay, the writer organizes information by using a problem-solution method or by including step-by-step instructions. The writer begins with a paragraph that states the essay's purpose and topic. Body paragraphs develop the topic with facts, details, and examples. This information explains solutions to the problem or instructions for the activity. The essay concludes with a summary of what the writer has explained.

Your assignment for this workshop is to write an expository essay that presents a problem and explains how it was solved.

1 PREWRITE Brainstorm a list of topics for your essay in your notebook. Think about something you accomplished that made you really happy or proud. Maybe it was a problem that took imagination to solve. Maybe it was a problem that took courage and daring to solve. Maybe you discovered a solution that will help readers solve a similar problem in their own lives. Choose a topic that you can write about with enthusiasm.

List and Organize Ideas and Details Use a graphic organizer such as a problem-solution chart to gather ideas and facts for your essay. A student named Danielle wanted to attract more wildlife to her backyard. Here is the problem-solution chart she prepared.

Problem	Solution
Wanted to attract more wildlife to my yard	Figured out what lives in area, like butterflies and hummingbirds Found out facts about things they need for food and shelter Asked permission to add things like feeders Stopped doing things that might scare wildlife away Now, see hummingbirds in my yard

2 DRAFT Use the model on page 327 and your graphic organizer to help you write a first draft. Remember to use time-order words such as *first, then,* and *next* to explain the sequence of events. Time-order words can help readers better understand the steps involved in solving the problem.

324

TESOL Standards

Goal 2, Standard 2—To use English to achieve academically in all content areas: Students will use English to obtain, process, construct, and provide subject matter information in spoken and written form.
Descriptors—Listening to, speaking, reading, and writing about subject matter information; Gathering information orally and in writing; Understanding and producing technical vocabulary and text features according to content area; Demonstrating knowledge through application in a variety of contexts.

3 REVISE Read over your draft. As you do so, ask yourself the questions in the writing checklist. Use the questions to help you revise your essay.

SIX TRAITS OF WRITING CHECKLIST

- ☑ **IDEAS:** Do my explanations, details, and examples tell how a problem was solved?
- ☑ **ORGANIZATION:** Do I present information in a logical order?
- ☑ **VOICE:** Does my writing express my personality?
- ☑ **WORD CHOICE:** Do I use words that tell the time order of events?
- ☑ **SENTENCE FLUENCY:** Do I use the imperative correctly?
- ☑ **CONVENTIONS:** Does my writing follow the rules of grammar, usage, and mechanics?

Here are the changes Danielle plans to make when she revises her first draft:

Wildlife Report

Last year, my friend ~~digged~~ dug a hole in her backyard to plant a

flower. Out of the hole jumped a big toad! When she excited ly told

that a toad lived in her garden

me, I decided to try to attract more birds and other animals to my

did

yard. I ~~done~~ it and you can do it, too.

First

You need to know what appeals to the wildlife in your region. Which

nearby?   Books and websites can tell you these facts.

birds and animals can be found. What food and shelter do they like?

Then ask permission to add some of these things to your yard. Once

For example

you have permission, you can create a little habitat. Hummingbirds

visit my area every summer. I learned that they love nectar plants,

so I planted a red hibiscus. A hummingbird feeder works, too.

Birdbaths provide many birds with water and a place to splash and

325

Revise Revising is not the same as editing. The revising step focuses on improving the content and wording of the draft. Point out that word processing on a computer allows us to copy, cut and paste, and move text easily from one place in the draft to another. **SAY:** *To revise a draft means to look at it again and make changes in content or wording. It can be very difficult to make changes to your own writing, since you know what you meant when you wrote it. That is why getting feedback from other readers is so helpful. We find out what appeals to or confuses the audience so we can change it before publication.*

STEP 3: Assess

Writing Checklist Note

SAY: *Review the writing checklist, then look over your draft and answer each question. When we give feedback to others about their writing, we are helping them to improve their writing. Remember to give specific feedback about what you liked and to give positive suggestions to the writer. When you receive feedback, remember that the person helping you is part of your reading audience and their reactions are likely to be similar to those of other readers of your published work. If your reviewer does not understand something, chances are that others will misunderstand too. Decide which suggestions to include in your writing. Then make changes to your draft. A rough draft is not expected to be perfect. Use a pencil so that you can make changes easily.*

Differentiated Instruction	
Beginning	Before students start writing, brainstorm ideas with the class. Write a list of problems and possible solutions on the board.
Early Intermediate	Refer students to the writing handbook at the end of their books for additional help in writing their first draft.
Intermediate	Have students explain why Danielle's decision to move a sentence on page 326 was a good idea.
Special Needs	Tell students that many word processing applications have a grammar checking tool. Explain that they may use this to help them check their draft and final versions.

Writing Workshop

Edit and Proofread Form small editing teams by pairing English Learners with English proficient students. Remind students of the kind of edits Danielle made on her final draft. (She added commas, added an adjective, and capitalized a letter.) Discuss why you think each edit was made. Have students look at their own first draft and discuss the edits they should make. Keep dictionaries nearby to check spelling.

play. Some creatures are very private, so you can build hiding places for them with piles of dirt brush, or rocks.

There are some other general tips for attracting wildlife. Try not to use chemical pesticides. Don't place nests where barking dogs may scare the birds away. Don't put lots of food in bird feeders all at once. Instead, put in only a small amount of food every day. Predators may come and eat the leftovers.

Finally ₍ ₎ You don't need to live in the country to attract wildlife. I have a little backyard in a town. If you don't have a yard, you may be able to volunteer at a neighborhood park or community garden. you may have a window large enough for a bird feeder. Maybe your schoolyard can

Remember to ask permission.

be turned into a garden!

Right now I'm looking at a yellow butterfly on a green bush. Have

ever

you ₍ ₎ wanted to invite wildlife to visit you? If you learn the facts and do some work, you will probably see lots of wildlife!

4 EDIT AND PROOFREAD Workbook Page 157

Copy your revised essay onto a clean sheet of paper. Read it again. Correct any errors in grammar, word usage, mechanics, and spelling. Here are the additional changes Danielle plans to make when she prepares her final draft.

326

TESOL Standards

Goal 3, Standard 1—To use English in socially and culturally appropriate ways: Students will use the appropriate language variety, register, and genre according to audience, purpose, and setting.
Descriptors—Using the appropriate degree of formality with different audiences and settings; Recognizing and using Standard English and vernacular dialects appropriately; Using a variety of writing styles appropriate for different audiences, purposes, and settings; Determining appropriate topics for interaction.

Danielle Christian

Wildlife Report

Last year, my friend dug a hole in her backyard to plant a flower. Out of the hole jumped a big toad! When she excitedly told me that a toad lived in her garden, I decided to try to attract more birds and other animals to my yard. I did it and you can do it, too.

First, you need to know what appeals to the wildlife in your region. Which birds and animals can be found nearby? What food and shelter do they like? Books and websites can tell you these facts. Then ask permission to add some of these things to your yard. Once you have permission, you can create a little habitat. For example, hummingbirds visit my area every summer. I learned that they love brightly colored nectar plants, so I planted a red hibiscus. A hummingbird feeder works, too. Birdbaths provide many birds with water and a place to splash and play. Some creatures are very private, so you can build hiding places for them with piles of dirt, brush, or rocks

There are some other general tips for attracting wildlife. Try not to use chemical pesticides. Don't place nests where barking dogs may scare the birds away. Don't put lots of food in bird feeders all at once. Predators may come and eat the leftovers. Instead, put in only a small amount of food every day.

Finally, you don't need to live in the country to attract wildlife. I have a little backyard in a town. If you don't have a yard, you may be able to volunteer at a neighborhood park or community garden. you may have a window large enough for a bird feeder. Maybe your schoolyard can be turned into a garden! Remember to ask permission.

Right now I'm looking at a yellow butterfly on a green bush. Have you ever wanted to invite wildlife to visit you? If you learn the facts and do some work, you will probably see lots of wildlife!

5 PUBLISH Prepare your final draft. Share your essay with your teacher and classmates.

Workbook
Page 158

327

Career Connection:
Aboriculturist

Horticulture is the practice or science of growing flowers, fruit, and vegetables. Horticulture involves six areas of study, one of which is called aboriculture. Aboriculture is specific to the selection, planting, and care of trees, shrubs, and so on. This is different from forestry, which is the commercial production and use of tree products for making lumber, paper products, and so forth. Students interested in planting trees as a way to encourage both economic and environmental growth might consider aboriculture for a career.

Accelerate Language Development

Simple Past and Present Perfect

Review the uses of the simple past and the present perfect with your students. English learners often have difficulty choosing which tense to use. Even in languages that have both of these tenses, such as Spanish and French, there is a tendency to neutralize them. The time marker (today, yesterday, last year) is the most reliable clue to determine which tense to use.

STEP 1: Introduce

Remind students that the Big Question is *How are courage and imagination linked?* **SAY:** *You have read about various ways people have used courage and imagination to influence the world around them, to promote peace, and to protect the environment. The great scientist Albert Einstein once said: "Imagination is more important than knowledge. For knowledge is limited to all we now know and understand, while imagination embraces the entire world, and all there ever will be to know and understand." Do you agree?*

Artists must have an active imagination to create great artworks, as well as courage to pursue their art, despite obstacles such as economic hardship.

STEP 2: Teach

Visual Literacy

James Hampton Explain that Hampton made an artwork out of things he found in his everyday life. Have students make their own wearable headdresses. They will need newspapers, a stapler, scissors, aluminum foil, tape or glue, paint, and small "found objects" such as buttons, leaves, beads etc.. Each student will need five sheets of newspaper. Make the headdress as follows:

- Twist one piece of newspaper into a rope that is long enough to place around the student's head, and then staple the ends together.

- Center the four sheets of newspaper on the top of the student's head and then use the newspaper rope to make a headband.

- Let the edges of the four sheets hang down over the headband, which should be snug.

- Roll the excess newspaper into the headband, starting at the back and working forward, constantly tucking and rolling.

Now students are ready to decorate their headdress with the foil, paint, and found objects. They can use glue to attach the foil and objects.

Young people are often the most avid collectors. Go to the Smithsonian Education website at www.LongmanKeystone.com for classroom activities on starting collections. Poll students to see who collects what and why.

Teaching Resources

- *Workbook,* pp. 159–160
- CD-ROM/e-book, Smithsonian

Learn about Art with the
Smithsonian American Art Museum

Dignity Through Art

*I*t takes courage to follow your imagination. You can't worry about what other people think. You have to follow where your imagination takes you. Some artists become famous because they follow their imaginations. They do things that most other people would not think about doing.

James Hampton, *The Throne of the Third Heaven of the Nations' Millennium General Assembly* (about 1950–64)

Gold and silver foil cover every object in James Hampton's *The Throne of the Third Heaven of the Nations' Millennium General Assembly*. When the light hits it, you feel as though you are looking at something from another world. This sculpture once filled an empty garage which became the artist's studio behind his small apartment in Washington, D.C. Art experts believe that Hampton started the piece in 1950 and worked on it for hours nearly every day for fourteen years. When Hampton finished it, the sculpture comprised dozens of parts, including a central unit that rose as high as 4.6 meters (15 ft.) and was 8.2 meters (27 ft.) across. The sculpture contains about 180 separate glittering objects!

Hampton had little money and was not trained as an artist. He could not afford to make a throne out of real gold and silver. But he wanted to celebrate his deep religious beliefs. He worked as a janitor at night. At his job, he picked up objects that he would later turn into parts of his artwork. He collected old lightbulbs, wood furniture, jelly glasses, pieces of a mirror, and many other objects. He carefully wrapped every single object in foil.

A throne that is 2.13 meters (7 ft.) high sits at the center of the sculpture. At the top of the throne, Hampton made a sign with the words FEAR NOT in foil. He added to his religious ideas by making altars and tablets with writings from the Bible. He also included many angels' wings. He made the wings from paper and cardboard covered with foil.

328

▲ James Hampton, *The Throne of the Third Heaven of the Nations'*
Millennium General Assembly, about 1950–64, mixed media,
10½ x 27 x 14½ ft., Smithsonian American Art Museum

Hampton's artwork was virtually unknown until shortly
after his death. However, he left behind a lot of his own writing
in journals. He wrote in a code that only he understood, so no
one knows what it says. Perhaps it's best that his feelings are
kept private.

Hampton had the courage to follow his own artistic ideas,
even though he was poor and had few resources to work with.

Apply What You Learned

1 Why did James Hampton use
found objects to make his
artwork?

2 Why do you think that James
Hampton used a secret code
in his journals?

 Big Question
How did James Hampton
show courage, imagination,
and dignity through his
artwork?

 Workbook
Pages 159–160

329

Create a chart that tallies each type of item
(such as stamps, coins, sports cards, DVDs).
Once you have a full tally, ask students to pick
an object from the chart and imagine a way
they might use that object in an artwork. Have
students create a sketch of their artwork and
write a brief written description of why they
chose the particular object and what inspired
the idea for their artwork.

James Hampton put the words FEAR NOT at
the center top of his artwork. Explain that these
words encourage viewers not to be afraid of
anything, to have courage. **ASK:** *What scares
you?* Have students use everyday objects,
pencils, scrap and colored paper, scissors, glue
and tape, markers and stencils to create an
artwork with the words FEAR NOT at the
center. Have them explore how their artwork
might help them confront and perhaps
overcome their fears.

Explain that Hampton chose to work with
aluminum and gold foil for his artwork, partly
because the foil was inexpensive and shiny.
However, there was a time when aluminum
was more expensive than gold. Go to the
Smithsonian National Museum of Natural
History website feature "The Dynamic Earth" at
www.LongmanKeystone.com to learn more
about why aluminum was once so rare. Ask
students to brainstorm some of the ways that
we use aluminum today (cars, trucks, soda
cans, windows and doors, cooking utensils,
pots and pans).

STEP 3: Apply

Apply What You Learned

Have volunteers read the questions aloud,
and be sure students understand the
meaning of difficult words and concepts.
Encourage students to carefully study the
artworks, and if necessary, reread the text to
help them.

ANSWERS

1. Hampton used found objects to make his
work of art because he could collect them
while working as a janitor and recycle them
into an artwork.
2. Hampton used a secret code in his journal
because he didn't want anyone to know his
personal feelings.

Q Possible response: Hampton showed
courage, imagination, and dignity through his
artwork by following his own artistic ideas,
working hard collecting objects over many
years for his project, and completing an
imaginative sculpture representing his great
respect for religion.

STEP 1: Introduce

Unit Content

Tell students that they will read fiction and nonfiction selections about advances in science and life in the future. Point out that this unit includes an excerpt from a science fiction novel, poetry, an interview, and a science and a social studies article. Students will practice reading strategies, such as taking notes, analyzing text structure, and making generalizations. They will write research reports and practice word analysis skills, such as using Greek and Latin roots.

 The Big Question

Introduce the Big Question, "What is your vision of life in the future?" **SAY:** *Wondering about the future requires imagination. We know that changes will occur in so many aspects of our lives.*

Ask students to brainstorm ideas about how life may change 100 years from now and to keep these ideas in mind as they read this unit. Use the following questions to stimulate discussion:

* *What do you think schooling will be like in the future? How do you think students will learn their subjects?*

* *How will we communicate with each other? What is already happening in communication that will help answer this question?*

* *How will forms of entertainment be different?*

STEP 2: Teach

Visual Literacy

Have students work in groups to brainstorm ideas of what might happen in the future based on the images they see in the unit. Discuss images, such as the photos of machines of the future, on pages 336, 339, and 340; space travel on pages 354 and 368; and DNA fingerprinting on pages 382–383. Explain how the images help you predict what the readings will be about.

Teaching Resources

* *Resources*, Unit 6 Lesson Plans, pp. 63–74
* *Transparencies*, Unit 6 Daily Language Practice
* CD-ROM/e-book, Big Question
* Video, Segment 6
* *Resources*, Letters Home, pp. 119–120

 What is your vision of life in the future?

330

TESOL Standards

Goal 2, Standard 1—To use English to achieve academically in all content areas: Students will use English to interact in the classroom.
Descriptors—Asking and answering questions.

Goal 2, Standard 2—To use English to achieve academically in all content areas: Students will use English to obtain, process, construct, and provide subject matter information in spoken and written form.
Descriptors—Hypothesizing and predicting; Formulating and asking questions.

Goal 2, Standard 3—To use English to achieve academically in all content areas: Students will use appropriate learning strategies to construct and apply academic knowledge.
Descriptors—Actively connecting new information to information previously learned.

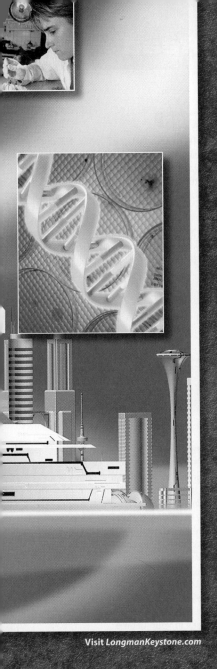

This unit is about life in the future. You will explore life in the years to come. You will read about how Earth and space look to an astronaut and how Earth might look to a visitor. You will read about a group of friends who travel to the year 2095 and about scientists who are unlocking the secrets of DNA. As you read, you will practice the literary and academic language you need to use in school.

READING 1: Social Studies Article

■ "Life in the Future"

READING 2: Poetry and Interview

■ "Southbound on the Freeway" and "Cardinal Ideograms" by May Swenson

■ "Interview with an Astronaut: Dan Bursch"

READING 3: Novel Excerpt

■ From *The Time Warp Trio: 2095* by Jon Scieszka

READING 4: Science Article

■ "Genetic Fingerprints"

Listening and Speaking

At the end of this unit, you will give a **speech** on life in the future.

Writing

In this unit you will practice writing parts of a **research report** (a special kind of expository writing). You will choose a topic, do research, and write about it. At the end of the unit, you will develop one of your topics into a research report.

QuickWrite

Write several sentences about a prediction you made in the past.

Visit *LongmanKeystone.com*

331

STEP 3: Practice

QuickWrite

To help students begin writing, create a two-column chart on the board. Label the first column *What I Predicted* and the second *What Happened.* Ask a volunteer to offer an answer and write it on the chart for students to use as a model. Then have students create their own charts and use the information they fill in to write their sentences. Example: *I predicted that by the time I was a teenager, I would be able to play the trumpet in the school band. I was right.*

STEP 4: Extend

Preview the titles of the readings, and ask students to predict how each might relate to life in the future. **SAY:** *Let's look at the titles of the selections in this unit and see how each relates to the Big Question. "Life in the Future" is an article. What might an article about life in the future tell us?* (It might be about new gadgets and how people will live.)

Continue this discussion for the rest of readings. Ask students to offer examples of books or articles they have read that helped them understand what the future might be like. Encourage them to discuss both fiction and nonfiction.

Teach

STEP 1: Introduce

Objectives

Read the list of objectives in the What You Will Learn section. Tell students that this reading will be about population growth, living in cities, and new technology. Have students work in pairs to restate the list of things they will learn.

The Big Question

Remind students of the Big Question for the unit: "What is your vision of life in the future?" Offer your own predictions for the future. **SAY:** *I think the future will provide people with opportunities unheard of today. They'll take vacations to resorts on the moon and Mars and spend time in flying vehicles from their hotels. Perhaps the reading will confirm some of these predictions for life in the future.*

Build Background

Read aloud the Build Background section. Talk about how people have always been interested in what life might be like in the future. Mention H.G. Wells's classic novel *The War of the Worlds*, which is about Martians invading Earth. Tell students about Orson Welles's radio broadcast of the novel in 1938. **SAY:** *This radio broadcast was so realistic that listeners thought Earth was actually being invaded by aliens.* Encourage students to talk about whether they think people are more excited or anxious about what might happen in the future.

STEP 2: Teach

Understanding the Genre:
Informational Text

An informational text is a work of nonfiction. Its purpose is to present factual information about real people, events, places, and situations. This reading uses facts based on research to speculate about life in the future.

Teaching Resources

- CD-ROM/e-book, Key Words
- Audio CD 6, tracks 1–2
- *Workbook*, p. 161

What You Will Learn

Reading
- Vocabulary building: *Context, dictionary skills, word study*
- Reading strategy: *Take notes*
- Text type: *Informational text (social studies)*

Grammar, Usage, and Mechanics
Different ways of expressing predictions

Writing
Write an introductory paragraph

THE BIG QUESTION

What is your vision of life in the future? What will our world be like one hundred years from now? What will travel, home life, medicine, and technology be like? Work in small groups. Study the picture below. Then create a word web with your ideas about life in the future. Share your ideas with other groups. Find out what your classmates think.

▲ *Exploration of Mars* by Chesley Bonestell

BUILD BACKGROUND

"Life in the Future" is a nonfiction article that explores what life might be like ten, twenty, thirty, or more years from now. The article uses facts to describe inventions and advances that people are developing for the future. People have always tried to predict what will happen in the future. We sometimes call people who try to predict what will happen in years to come "futurists." In Italy, there was a futurist movement in the early 1900s. It inspired new forms of art, architecture, and writing. In the United States, organizations were formed to "think about" the future during the 1940s. As you read the selection, think about why people are fascinated by a time that hasn't come yet. Think also about the inventions you would like to see in your lifetime.

▲ A futurist sculpture by Umberto Boccioni

332

TESOL Standards

Goal 1, Standard 3—To use English to communicate in social settings: Students will use learning strategies to extend their communicative competence.
Descriptors—Listening to and imitating how others use English; Exploring alternative ways of saying things; Focusing attention selectively.

Goal 2, Standard 1—To use English to achieve academically in all content areas: Students will use English to interact in the classroom.
Descriptors—Requesting and providing clarification; Participating in full-class, group, and pair discussions; Negotiating and managing interaction to accomplish tasks.

Goal 2, Standard 2—To use English to achieve academically in all content areas: Students will use English to obtain, process, construct, and provide subject matter information in spoken and written form.
Descriptors—Selecting, connecting, and explaining information; Understanding and producing technical vocabulary and text features according to content area.

VOCABULARY

Learn Key Words

Read the sentences. Use the context to figure out the meaning of the red words. Use a dictionary to check your answers. Then write each word and its meaning in your notebook.

Key Words

- artificial
- canyons
- frontier
- mass-produced
- robots
- volcanoes

1. In the future, doctors will use more **artificial** body parts to replace real body parts.

2. The airplane flew into the deep **canyons**. The pilot had to steer away from the steep cliffs surrounding the plane.

3. Space is called a **frontier** because it is far away from Earth. We have explored Earth but we are just beginning to explore space.

4. Now many cars at a time are made in factories. They are **mass-produced**. The first cars were produced one at a time.

5. In the future, dangerous work will be done by machines called **robots**.

6. Scientists study active **volcanoes** and watch as they send out red-hot lava.

Practice

▲ Mount Etna is an active volcano in Sicily.

Write the sentences in your notebook. Choose a **red** word from the box above to complete each sentence. Then take turns reading the sentences aloud with a partner.

1. The power of the erupting _____ surprised the movie audience.

2. In the United States in the 1800s, the area beyond the Appalachian Mountains was called the _____.

3. Car parts are _____ at factories.

4. Some people would like to have _____ do their housework.

5. Real plants need sunshine and water, but _____ plants do not.

6. The planet Mars has many deep _____ with steep rocky cliffs.

333

Vocabulary

Learn Key Words Play the CD. Have students listen and repeat. If you are not using the CD, read the Key Words aloud. **SAY:** *These words are important to the subject matter of the text we are reading.* On the board or an overhead transparency, write the words below and their definitions.

- **artificial:** not real or natural, but made by people
- **canyons:** deep valleys with very steep sides
- **frontier:** the area beyond the places people know well
- **mass-produced:** produced in large numbers using machinery so that each object is the same and can be sold cheaply
- **robots:** machines that move and can do some of the work of human beings.
- **volcanoes:** mountains with a large hole on top, out of which lava, rock, and ashes sometimes explode

Have students copy the definitions into their Word Books and generate original sentences for them. For extra practice, assign the corresponding Workbook page.

STEP 3: Practice

Have students work with partners to complete the activity. **SAY:** *As you read each sentence, think about the word that makes the most sense in that sentence.*

ANSWERS
1. volcanoes
2. frontier
3. mass-produced
4. robots
5. artificial
6. canyons

Differentiated Instruction

Beginning	Have students name something that they think will be different in 100 years.
Early Intermediate	Write on the board: *When I was younger, _____. When I am older, _____.* Complete the sentences for students, identifying events that occurred in the past and future. For example: *When I was younger, I used only pens to write. When I am older, all my friends will have their own computers.* Ask each student to use the same sentence frame to form his or her own sentence and share it orally.
Intermediate	Have students use each vocabulary word in a new sentence.
Struggling Readers	Have students work with a partner to use an online or traditional thesaurus. Ask students to make a word web for each of the Key Words and list synonyms for the words on the branches. Then have students use the vocabulary words in sentences of their own.

STEP 1: Teach

CD6 T3–T4

 Vocabulary

Learn Academic Words Play the CD. Have students listen and repeat. If you are not using the CD, read the academic words aloud. **SAY:** *These words will help you discuss the reading.* Have students work with a partner to write additional sentences for each academic word. Encourage them to share their sentences with the class.

STEP 2: Practice

Write the questions from the Practice section on the board. **SAY:** *Use the context of the sentences to remember the meanings of the academic word. Underline the words surrounding the academic words. What do they tell you about the word's meaning?* Have students work in pairs to write answers to the questions.

ANSWERS
Possible responses:
1. A computer has many functions now, such as allowing people to access the Internet. In the future, it might help solve global problems such as hunger and pollution.
2. Twenty years from now I would like my occupation to be something to do with health care.
3. To research a topic like future inventions, I would use the Internet. I would use sources on inventions, like the website of the U.S. Patent Office.
4. The trend I predict for schools in the future is that students will study online. I think this would be a good development because it might allow more people to become educated.

Teaching Resources
- Audio CD 6, tracks 3–4
- *Workbook*, pp. 162–164
- CD-ROM/e-book, Academic Words, Word Study

Learn Academic Words

Study the red words and their meanings. You will find these words useful when talking and writing about informational texts. Write each word and its meaning in your notebook. After you read "Life in the Future," try to use these words to respond to the text.

Academic Words
function
occupation
research
trend

function = the usual purpose of a thing, or the job that someone usually does	⇒	The **function** of a brake is to stop a car. That's the brake's purpose.
occupation = job or profession	⇒	An astronaut's **occupation** is exploring space.
research = serious study of a subject that is intended to discover new facts about it	⇒	Scientists do **research** to predict the future. They study many books to gather information.
trend = the way a situation is generally developing or changing	⇒	The **trend** is toward smaller cars. People want cars that use less gas.

Practice **Workbook** Page 162

Work with a partner to answer the questions. Try to include the red word in your answer. Write the sentences in your notebook.

1. What is a computer's function now? What might its purpose be in the future?
2. What occupation would you like to have twenty years from now? Why?
3. How would you research a topic like future inventions? What sources would you use to find factual information?
4. What trend do you predict for schools in the future? Would this be a good development or not?

▲ Using computers to design cars is the current trend in the automotive world.

334

Goal 1, Standard 3—To use English to communicate in social settings: Students will use learning strategies to extend their communicative competence.
Descriptors—Self-monitoring and self-evaluating language development; Learning and using language "chunks"; Practicing new language.

Goal 2, Standard 3—To use English to achieve academically in all content areas: Students will use appropriate learning strategies to construct and apply academic knowledge.
Descriptors—Focusing attention selectively; Applying basic reading comprehension skills such as skimming, scanning, previewing, and reviewing text; Planning how and when to use cognitive strategies and applying them appropriately to a learning task.

Goal 3, Standard 3—To use English in socially and culturally appropriate ways: Students will use appropriate learning strategies to extend their sociolinguistic and sociocultural competence.
Descriptors— Analyzing the social context to determine appropriate language use.

Word Study: Spelling the Diphthongs /oi/ and /ou/

Some English words, such as *boil* and *round* contain two vowel sounds that are said quickly so that the sounds glide into one another. Together the two sounds form a vowel sound called a diphthong. In the word *boil*, the letters *oi* stand for the diphthong /oi/. In the word *round*, the letters *ou* stand for the diphthong /ou/.

Below are some examples of words with the diphthongs /oi/ and /ou/. As you read each word, say it aloud. Listen to how the two vowel sounds glide into one another in one syllable.

/oi/ as in *coin*	/oi/ as in *boy*	/ou/ as in *ground*	/ou/ as in *how*
boil	joy	found	now
voice	enjoy	shout	down
points	toy	our	downstage

Practice

Workbook Page 163

Work with a partner. Copy the chart above into your notebook. Say a word from the chart, and ask your partner to spell it aloud. Then have your partner say the next word. Continue until you can spell all of the words correctly. Now work with your partner to spell these words: *house, soil, destroy, mountain, royal, cow, noise, how, loyal, toil, brown, sound*. Add them to the chart under the correct headings.

READING STRATEGY | TAKE NOTES

Taking notes keeps you focused on what you are reading, and it helps you organize and remember new information. Notes are also a useful tool to refer back to when answering questions about a reading selection. To take notes, follow these steps:

- In your notebook, make two columns, one for main ideas and one for details.
- Think about your purpose for reading the text.
- Look for key dates, names, places, and events.
- Write short notes about the most important facts and details you may need to know.

As you read "Life in the Future," think about the information you want to remember. Take notes while you read. Review your notes and check that they are correct.

Workbook Page 164

335

Linguistic Note

Homophones

Students may be confused by the fact that the letter combination *ow* not only stands for the diphthong /au/ as in *now* or *cow*, but also for the long /ou/ as in *tow* (a car) or *sow* (seeds). Remind your students that English is not a perfectly phonetic language. Therefore several sounds can be produced by the same letter combination, and several different letter combinations can produce one sound (homophones). The latter is somewhat rare with diphthongs. However, *ou* creates a rather troublesome homophone, which is mixed up by English speakers and English learners: flour/flower. Ask your students which one is used for baking, and which one smells good.

Word Study

Spelling the Diphthongs /oi/ and /ou/
SAY: *In English, two vowel sounds that are said quickly so that the sounds glide into one another are called diphthongs. For example, in the word* boil, *the two vowels* oi *stand for the diphthong* /ɔɪ/. *In the word* round, *the two vowels* ou *stand for the diphthong* /aʊ/. *Read aloud the words in the chart on page 335 together.*

Have students take turns reading the words in the activity aloud with a partner.

ANSWERS

oi coin	*oi* boy	*ou* ground	*ow* how
soil	destroy	house	cow
noise	royal	mountain	how
toil	loyal	ground	brown

Reading Strategy

Take Notes Read aloud the text in the box.
SAY: *Taking notes as you read means writing down the important facts and details that you want to remember.* Demonstrate the steps to note-taking given in the student book. Explain to students that note-taking is a valuable transferable skill. Not only is it useful when reading, it can also be used while listening, and in preparation for written assignments and oral presentations. The more students get used to taking notes, the easier they will find it. Encourage students to practice good note-taking skills, by focusing on the information they need to remember rather than the details.

Reading Summary

This article is about life in the future. It discusses how populated our planet will become and how we will live and travel on Earth and in outer space.

The Big Question

Remind students of the Big Question for the unit: "What is your vision of life in the future?"
SAY: *Imagine it is twenty-five years from now. You've read a lot about going to Mars. Would you consider going there? If so, how long would it take you to get there and what kinds of things would you need to pack? Think about these questions as you read.*

Set a Purpose for Reading

Tell students to copy the purpose for reading into their notebooks and to keep it in mind as they read. Explain that they will have to present details that support their answers to the questions and to explain how the reading relates to the Big Question.

Preteaching Highlighted Words

In pairs, have students read aloud the highlighted words and their definitions. Answer any questions students have about the use of a word or its meaning before reading the spread.

CD6 T3 Scaffolding:

Listen and Read

Ask students to read "Life in the Future" as you play the CD. Encourage students to take notes while they read. Pause the CD at the end of each page so they have time to write.

Teaching Resources

- *Resources*, Summaries, pp. 163–164
- Audio CD 6, track 3
- *Reader's Companion Workbook*, pp. 123–131

Set a purpose for reading What will cities, travel, medicine, and other aspects of life be like in the future? As you read, contrast the writer's vision of the future with your own. Do you think that the writer's description of the future is accurate? Why?

Life in the Future

Imagine traveling in a time machine into the future. What do you think life will be like? This timeline shows some predictions about the future.

A robot ▶

2012	fire-fighting robots that can find and rescue people
2013	clothes that become cooler or warmer depending on the temperature
2014	robotic pets
2015	telephone calls between speakers of different languages translated in real time
2020	humans traveling to Mars; cars that drive themselves on automated highways; artificial lungs, kidneys, and brain cells
2025	underground cities
2030	more robots than people in some countries
2035	fully functioning artificial eyes and legs; people cured of 98 percent of all cancers

▲ A robotic dog

◀ An artificial leg

▼ A robotic bug

cured, healed; restored to health

336

TESOL Standards

Goal 1, Standard 3—To use English to communicate in social settings: Students will use learning strategies to extend their communicative competence.
Descriptors— Using the primary language to ask for clarification; Using context to construct meaning.

Goal 2, Standard 1—To use English to achieve academically in all content areas: Students will use English to interact in the classroom.
Descriptors—Asking and answering questions.

Goal 2, Standard 2— To use English to achieve academically in all content areas: Students will use English to obtain, process, construct, and provide subject matter information in spoken and written form.
Descriptors—Analyzing, synthesizing, and inferring from information; Hypothesizing and predicting; Formulating and asking questions.

The Growing World

The world's population is growing very fast. In 1800, the population was about 1 billion. Now it is over 6.5 billion. One reason for this fast growth is that the birthrate is higher than the death rate. That is, there are more people being born than there are people dying. Also, medical advances and better living conditions help people live longer. Scientists predict that in the year 2100, the population will be 11 billion.

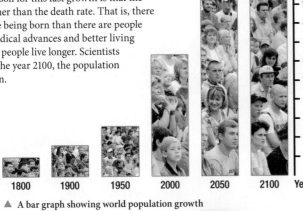

Population in billions

	11
	10
	9
	8
	7
	6
	5
	4
	3
	2
	1

1800 1900 1950 2000 2050 2100 Year

▲ A bar graph showing world population growth

Future Cities

As the population grows, it will be necessary to rebuild existing cities and build new ones. Some apartment buildings will be like small cities. Architects have created a model for an apartment building in Tokyo. It will be 840 meters (2,750 ft.) high and will have 180 floors. A population of 60,000 will be able to live there. High-speed elevators will carry sixty people at a time. The building will have stores, restaurants, and cinemas. People won't ever have to leave!

---

elevators, machines in a building that carry people from one floor to another

A model for an apartment building in Tokyo ▶

BEFORE YOU GO ON

1 What new inventions do experts predict will be used in the future?

2 How large do experts think the population will be in 2100?

💡 **On Your Own**
Do you think that life in the future will be more fun than it is today? Why?

337

Read

Preteaching Highlighted Words

In pairs, have students read aloud the highlighted words and their definitions. Answer any questions students have about the use of a word or its meaning before reading the spread. In case students have trouble understanding the correct usage, provide them with an example: *Architects make small prototypes, or simple models, of buildings before actually building them.*

Across the Curriculum:
Social Studies

Draw students' attention to the photo of an apartment building in Tokyo on page 337. Ask students to use their geography and history skills to predict what other cities might serve as models for how future cities should be. **SAY:** *Think of cities that have been centers of progress in the past. Rome and Athens are two examples that come to my mind.*

Model the
READING STRATEGY

Take Notes

Remind students of the reading strategy taking notes. **SAY:** *What notes have you taken so far? What are the most important points in the reading?* Encourage students to share their notes, perhaps writing them on the board. **SAY:** *If you were to write the main point of the section entitled "Hypersonic Planes," what would you write?*

▲ The X-43A will reach hypersonic speeds using an air-breathing engine.

Hypersonic Planes

The National Aeronautics and Space Administration (NASA) is developing a hypersonic plane that will be able to fly at least ten times faster than the speed of sound. It will be able to fly to outer space. NASA has produced a $230 million prototype plane, but it doesn't expect to use it for space travel until about 2020.

The X-43A prototype plane looks like a flying surfboard. It is thin and has a wingspan of 1.5 meters (5 ft.). It is 3.6 meters (12 ft.) long and weighs 1,270 kilograms (2,800 lbs.). This plane set a new world speed record by flying at nearly ten times the speed of sound. A fully functioning version of the X-43A will be about 60 meters (200 ft.) long.

prototype, model

338

 TESOL Standards

Goal 1, Standard 2—To use English to communicate in social settings: Students will interact in, through, and with spoken and written English for personal expression and enjoyment.
Descriptors—Sharing social and cultural traditions and values.

Goal 2, Standard 3—To use English to achieve academically in all content areas: Students will use appropriate learning strategies to construct and apply academic knowledge.
Descriptors—Using context to construct meaning; Applying self-monitoring and self-corrective strategies to build and expand a knowledge base.

Goal 3, Standard 3—To use English in socially and culturally appropriate ways: Students will use appropriate learning strategies to extend their sociolinguistic and sociocultural competence.
Descriptors— Experimenting with variations of language in social and academic settings.

Cars of the Future

As more people own cars, the roads become more crowded. This causes more traffic jams and more accidents. The cost of traffic jams in the United States is about $78 billion per year—4.5 billion hours of travel time plus 26 billion liters (7 billion gal.) of fuel wasted sitting in traffic.

Car manufacturers are always looking for ways to make cars safer, faster, and more convenient. In the future, there may be automated highways. On these highways, cars will steer themselves. They will go faster and brake by themselves. Cars will have computers that pick up signals from magnets in the road.

▲ A model of a futuristic car

Jetpacks

People have always dreamed of flying. In the fifteenth century, the Italian artist Leonardo da Vinci drew many designs of flying machines. But a personal flying machine—or jetpack—has proved to be one of the most difficult inventions.

---

steer, guide
magnets, pieces of iron that attract other pieces of iron

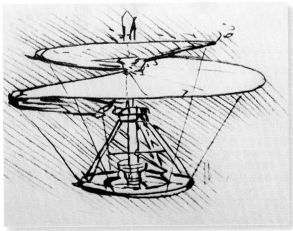
▲ One of Leonardo da Vinci's drawings of a flying machine

BEFORE YOU GO ON

1 What is a hypersonic plane?

2 Who is Leonardo da Vinci, and what kind of machines did he draw?

On Your Own
Would you like to fly in a personal flying machine? Why or why not?

339

Study Skills: Encyclopedia

Tell students that encyclopedias are very useful tools when what you want is a general overview of a subject. Point out that sometimes students will find just a paragraph on a given topic, other times there may be a long article available. Encourage students to think critically about the information they find in an encyclopedia—is it really useful? Is it what they need for their assignment? Remind students also that a print encyclopedia in a library may or may not be fully up-to-date. Show them how to check the publication date and explain that for certain purposes, an encyclopedia does not need to be up-to-date. For example, information about ancient Greece may not have changed all that much; however, if students were looking for information about Internet banking, another source would be more useful.

STEP 5: Monitor Progress

Ask students to check what they have understood in the reading. If you are using the Audio CD, pause the recording.

Before You Go On

Remind students that these questions will help them monitor their progress. Put students in pairs to answer the questions. Encourage them to share their answers with the class.

ANSWERS

1. A hypersonic plane is an aircraft that will be able to fly at least ten times faster than the speed of sound. It will be able to fly to outer space.
2. Leonardo da Vinci was an Italian artist who lived during the fifteenth century. He drew many designs of flying machines.

On Your Own Ask students to take out a separate sheet of paper and write an answer to the On Your Own question. Encourage volunteers to share their responses. Then collect responses to monitor student comprehension, writing skills, and fluency.

Preteaching Highlighted Words

In pairs, have students read aloud the highlighted words and their definitions. Answer any questions students have about the use of a word or its meaning before reading the spread. In case students have trouble understanding the correct usage, give them an example: **SAY:** *On page 341, the reading says that "In the future, perhaps we will colonize other planets." Some of the first towns in the United States were founded by Europeans sent to colonize the country. These towns eventually became parts of areas called colonies.*

Across the Curriculum:
Science

Draw students' attention to the information about Mars. **SAY:** *Instead of using more scientific names, the planets are named after Roman gods. Mars is named for the Roman god of war because of its red, bloodlike color.* Introduce the names of other planets and elicit students' comments.

Model the
READING STRATEGY

Take Notes

Remind students of the reading strategy taking notes. **SAY:** *Now that we have read more about predictions for the future, what notes have you added in your notebooks? What main points and details are important to your understanding of the reading? Ask students to tell you why skimming a text is a useful skill. Refer them back to page 365 if they need a reminder.*

▲ The Trek Aerospace Exoskeleton Flying Vehicle (EFV-4A)

Jetpacks have appeared in such movies as *The Rocketeer*, *Spy Kids*, and *Minority Report*. A "rocket man" flew into the opening ceremony of the 1984 summer Olympics in Los Angeles. Jetpacks today can fly for only a short time. In the future, they will fly longer and go faster.

One of the most successful jetpacks is the Trek Aerospace Exoskeleton Flying Vehicle (EFV-4A). The EFV uses propellers to lift you off the ground. Once in the air, you can zip over treetops at 181 kilometers (113 mi.) per hour for 296 kilometers (184 mi.) before refueling.

---

zip, move very fast
refueling, refilling with gasoline, oil, or some other fuel

340

▲ An artist's idea of a colony on Mars

New Frontiers

Throughout history, humans have loved to explore. Today, we have explored most of our planet. There are few new lands to explore, but there are new worlds, new planets, and new galaxies.

In the future, perhaps we will colonize other planets. The most likely planet will be Mars. NASA scientists have already sent probes—spacecraft without people—to explore Mars. But when will people be able to go there? Astronauts could travel to Mars by about 2020. However, it will be a difficult task! It will take six months to reach the red planet. (It takes only three days to reach the moon.) And Mars is not a friendly environment. Mars probably once had liquid water, but now it is a cold, rocky desert. It has the largest volcano in the solar system and the deepest canyons. Dust storms can cover the whole planet. There is no breathable oxygen.

For people to live on Mars, the cities will have to be protected from the poisonous air. Giant domes will have to be built to control the atmosphere. All food will have to be grown inside the domed cities.

---

galaxies, very large groups of stars
colonize, set up human communities on
oxygen, gas in the air that all plants and animals need in order to live
poisonous, deadly
domes, round roofs

Earth-Mars Comparison

	Earth	Mars
Average distance from sun	150 million kilometers (93 million mi.)	228 million kilometers (142 million mi.)
Length of year	365.25 days	687 Earth days
Length of day	23 hours, 56 minutes	24 hours, 37 minutes
Temperature	average 14°C (57°F)	average −63°C (−81°F)
Atmosphere	nitrogen, oxygen, argon, others	mostly carbon dioxide, some water vapor
Number of moons	1	2

BEFORE YOU GO ON

1 What is an example of a new frontier that humans can explore?

2 Look at the Earth-Mars comparison chart. Which planet is farther away from the sun?

On Your Own
What other frontiers do you think will become important in the future?

341

Study Skills: Atlas

Encourage students to use an atlas to learn more about Earth in comparison to other planets. **SAY:** *The more you know about the makeup of Earth, the more you will understand how different it is from other planets as you learn more about them.* Explain that atlases not only give lots of useful facts about geography, but they also provide photos and sometimes satellite pictures of Earth.

STEP 7: Monitor Progress

Ask students to check what they have understood in the reading.

Before You Go On

Remind students that these questions will help them monitor their progress. Put students in pairs to answer the questions. Encourage them to share their answers with the class.

ANSWERS
1. New frontiers that humans can explore include other planets.
2. Mars is farther from the sun than Earth is.

On Your Own Have students write an answer to the On Your Own question on a separate sheet of paper. Encourage volunteers to share their responses with the class. Then collect student responses to monitor their comprehension, writing skills, and fluency.

Review the Purpose for Reading

Elicit responses to the Set a Purpose for Reading questions at the beginning of this reading. Remind students to relate their responses to the Big Question.

Teach & Apply

Comprehension

Ask students to complete the questions either independently, in pairs, or in groups. They can respond orally or in writing. Model answering the first question with the class.

ANSWERS

1. $78 billion
2. 2016
3. In the future, cars will be able to steer, accelerate, and brake themselves. They will run on computers.
4. Jetpacks will serve as personal flying machines.
5. Some advantages of having everything in the building where you live would be that you could save time and wouldn't have to go out in bad weather.
6. Answers will vary.
7. Answers will vary.
8. Answers will vary.

Speaking Tip

Ask a student to read aloud the Speaking Tip. **SAY:** *A listener will always be more interested in what you are saying if you use colorful language.* Encourage students to include vivid verbs and adjectives in their summaries.

In Your Own Words

Have students work in pairs. **SAY:** *Use your note-taking skills to complete this exercise.* Have students copy the chart on page 342 into their notebooks. **SAY:** *Using the chart as your guide, summarize each section. Work with your partner to identify the important details.* Complete the first item in the chart with the class.

Teaching Resources

- *Workbook*, p. 165
- CD-ROM/e-book, Comprehension, Extension
- *Reader's Companion Workbook*, pp. 132–136

Review and Practice

COMPREHENSION

Workbook Page 165

Right There

1. What is the cost of traffic jams in the United States per year?
2. According to the timeline, when will humans travel to Mars?

Think and Search

3. According to the article, what will cars be like in the future?
4. What will be the function of jetpacks?

Author and You

5. What would be the advantages of having everything you need in the building where you live?
6. What advantages does a hypersonic plane have over a rocket?

On Your Own

7. What trends do you think will be popular fifty years from now?
8. Would you rather live 100 years in the past or 100 years in the future? Explain your reasons.

An artist's idea of future travel ▼

IN YOUR OWN WORDS

Imagine that a friend asked you to summarize the article "Life in the Future." You need to include the main ideas and important details in your summary. Use the chart below to help you organize your ideas. Then share your summary of the article with a classmate.

 Speaking TIP

Use active, colorful verbs and adjectives to summarize "Life in the Future."

Section	Main Idea	Important Details
The Growing World		
Future Cities		
Hypersonic Planes		
Cars of the Future		
Jetpacks		
New Frontiers		

342

🌐 TESOL Standards

Goal 1, Standard 1—To use English to communicate in social settings: Students will use English to participate in social interactions.
Descriptors—Sharing and requesting information; Engaging in conversations.

Goal 1, Standard 2—To use English to communicate in social settings: Students will interact in, through, and with spoken and written English for personal expression and enjoyment.
Descriptors—Participating in popular culture.

DISCUSSION

Discuss in pairs or small groups.

1. Does the article present a positive or negative view of the future? Give examples to support your conclusion.

2. Why is Mars the most likely planet to colonize? What would you need to live on Mars?

3. How are hypersonic planes and jetpacks similar? How are they different?

Q What is your vision of life in the future? How do you see life in twenty years? Fifty years? A hundred years?

 Listening TIP

Give each speaker your attention. Make eye contact with the speaker.

READ FOR FLUENCY

It is often easier to read a text if you understand the difficult words and phrases. Work with a partner. Choose a paragraph from the reading. Identify the words and phrases you do not know or have trouble pronouncing. Look up the difficult words in a dictionary.

Take turns pronouncing the words and phrases with your partner. If necessary, ask your teacher to model the correct pronunciation. Then take turns reading the paragraph aloud. Give each other feedback on your reading.

EXTENSION

Workbook Page 165

In "Life in the Future," you read about trends the author thinks we might see in the future. Pretend that you live in the future. Write a paragraph about a typical day in your life. Where do you live? How do you travel? What kinds of clothing do you wear? What foods do you eat? You can use some of the inventions and trends described in "Life in the Future," or you can create your own inventions and trends. Share your paragraph with a classmate.

▲ An artist's idea of a future space colony

343

STEP 2: Extend

Listening Tip

Direct students to the Listening Tip at the top of the page. **SAY:** *Making eye contact with the speaker shows that you're listening attentively and respectfully to his or her ideas.*

(CRI) Discussion

Before students begin their discussion, decide whether they will work as a class, in small groups, or in pairs. Consider dividing up the questions so each group has a different topic. Set up class norms to make sure that all participants are heard and that ideas are challenged but not discarded. Explain that the purpose is to allow everyone a chance to be heard. Remind students of the new vocabulary they have learned.

Q What is your vision of life in the future? Ask the class how they would answer the question, *what is your vision of life in the future?*, in light of the reading they've completed. Encourage them to talk about the future within the span of their lives and beyond.

STEP 3: Assess

Read for Fluency

Read aloud this section and have students work with a partner to select a paragraph and practice reading it aloud.

Extension

Suggest that students use the photos and illustrations that accompany the text of this reading as springboards for story ideas.

Differentiated Instruction	
Beginning	Help students find three main ideas in the Future Cities section. Write the ideas on the board, and discuss them. Have students decide which one best summarizes the section.
Early Intermediate	Ask students which aspect of life in the future would they like to see most—future cities, future transportation, or new frontiers. Have them present their ideas to the class.
Intermediate	Have students create a poster showing an invention for a futuristic item they think the world needs. Then have students present the poster to the class.
Struggling Readers	Have students design and illustrate a car of the future. Ask them to label the features of the car. Then have students develop a sales pitch or commercial to sell the car. Encourage students to present their commercials to classmates.

Teach & Apply

STEP 1: Introduce

Tell students that different ways of expressing predictions are often used in writings about the future. Ask them to look at page 344 and read the text at the top of the page aloud.

STEP 2: Teach

Grammar and Writing

Different Ways of Expressing Predictions Draw students' attention to the charts on page 344. **SAY:** *The charts show different ways to express predictions. In the first chart, the writer is certain about what will happen in the future. The helping verb* will *is used. The other examples express uncertainty about what will happen in the future. Although some of these also use the helping verb* will, *they express uncertainty by modifying* will *with* probably, maybe, *or* perhaps.

Ask students to copy the chart below into their notebooks, giving them only the helping verbs. Encourage them to write sentences offering predictions about the year 2040.

Helping Verbs	Sentences
will	People will use jetpacks in 2040.
could	I could own my own plane in 2040.
may	There may be cures for more diseases in 2040.
perhaps . . . will	Perhaps I will have a house on Mars in 2040.

STEP 3: Practice

Have students work with partners to complete the activity. Invite students to share their sentences.

ANSWERS

Answers will vary.

Teaching Resources

- *Workbook*, pp. 166–167
- CD-ROM/e-book, Grammar, Writing
- *Transparencies*, Writing Model 46
- *Transparencies*, *Resources*, Graphic Organizer 12
- *Assessment*, Reading 1 Test, pp. 115–118

Grammar and Writing

GRAMMAR, USAGE, AND MECHANICS

Different Ways of Expressing Predictions

You have just read an article that predicts what the future might be like. In English, there are different ways to express predictions. Knowing each way will help you choose the words to express your meaning most clearly. This will help your readers understand what you are writing.

You may make predictions about things that you are certain will happen. Or you may make predictions about things that you are not certain will happen. Study the charts below.

Showing Certainty	Example
will	People **will** study Mars.

Showing Uncertainty	Example
may/might	People **may/might** travel to Mars.
could	People **could** travel to Mars.
probably will	People **probably will** travel to Mars.
maybe . . . will	**Maybe** people **will** travel to Mars.
perhaps . . . will	**Perhaps** people **will** travel to Mars.

Practice Workbook Page 166

Work with a partner. Take turns making predictions about each topic listed below. Listen to your partner's predictions, and write them in your notebook. Identify how the statement expresses the prediction. Is the speaker certain or not? Identify the words your partner used to express each prediction with certainty or uncertainty.

1. Robotic pets
2. Cars that drive themselves
3. Artificial organs
4. Cured diseases
5. Underground cities

344

TESOL Standards

Goal 2, Standard 1—To use English to achieve academically in all content areas: Students will use English to interact in the classroom.
Descriptors—Following oral and written directions, implicit and explicit; Elaborating and extending other people's ideas and words.

Goal 2, Standard 2—To use English to achieve academically in all content areas: Students will use English to obtain, process, construct, and provide subject matter information in spoken and written form.
Descriptors—Listening to, speaking, reading, and writing about subject matter information; Gathering information orally and in writing; Responding to the work of peers and others.

Goal 3, Standard 1—To use English in socially and culturally appropriate ways: Students will use the appropriate language variety, register, and genre according to audience, purpose, and setting.
Descriptors—Using a variety of writing styles appropriate for different audiences, purposes, and settings.

Write an Introductory Paragraph

On this page, you'll practice writing an introductory paragraph to a research report. You'll narrow a topic using a graphic organizer like the one at the right. Suppose you have to write a report about the future. First, you narrow the topic to something more specific, such as flying machines. Next, you ask a question to narrow your topic more and guide your research. You might ask: *Who designed early flying machines?* Then you can choose appropriate resources and do research. After doing research and organizing your ideas, you can write an introductory paragraph that introduces your topic in an interesting way with an exciting question, quote, or fact.

| Broad topic |
| Narrower topic |
| Specific topic |

Here is a model introductory paragraph about da Vinci's flying machines. Notice how the writer introduces the topic and presents her research question and the results of her research.

Anna Espínola

Leonardo da Vinci's Flying Machines

Why have humans always been fascinated with flight? The reason may be that flight has been beyond our reach for most of human history. Leonardo da Vinci, an artist, scientist, and engineer, wanted to create a way for humans to achieve flight. He observed birds and studied how they flew. Then using his observations and scientific knowledge, he began to design flying machines for humans. Many of da Vinci's concepts and designs are used in today's flying machines, such as helicopters and gliders. Other inventions that da Vinci envisioned and dreamed of may one day develop into new technology that will advance the human race and allow us to fly with the birds.

Practice

Workbook Page 167

Select and narrow a topic related to life in the future. Use an inverted pyramid like the one above to narrow your topic. Then ask a question to guide your research. After doing research, write an introductory paragraph for a research report on the topic. Be sure to express certainty and uncertainty correctly.

Writing Checklist

IDEAS:
- ☑ I introduced my topic in an interesting way and presented the question that guided my research.

SENTENCE FLUENCY:
- ☑ I used a variety of sentence types to make my writing style engaging.

345

Tell students that research reports offer facts about a topic. Explain that it is very important to cite sources when writing a research report. Elicit from students other features of research reports, e.g. narrowing the focus and engaging the reader's attention. Make a special point of telling students that they need to narrow the topic down to one question that will guide their research.

Writing a Research Report

Write an Introductory Paragraph Read aloud this section to the students. Draw the inverted pyramid on page 345 on the board. **SAY:** *Now I will read aloud the model introductory paragraph. As I read, listen for the details that tell you how the author narrowed his topic: Leonardo da Vinci's flying machines, from the broad to the specific.*

Model Writing Skill Help students select a topic and then narrow it down so that it is not too broad for a single paragraph. Have students ask the 5Ws about their topic to begin the narrowing process.

Have students evaluate their work, using the Writing Checklist.

Writing Checklist Note

Ideas: Check that students introduced their topic in an interesting way and presented the question that guided their research.

Sentence Fluency: Check that students used a variety of sentence types to make their writing engaging.

Accelerate Language Development

Minimalist Writing

Point out to students that English writing is very succinct. While it is important to present the main idea and give supporting details, good writers go back over their writing to delete words and phrases that are not necessary. Remind students that wordiness can obscure the writer's point.

STEP 1: Introduce

Objectives

Read the list of objectives in the What You Will Learn section, encouraging students to join in. Tell students that this reading consists of two poems and an interview. Have students work in pairs to restate the list of things they will learn.

The Big Question

Remind students that the Big Question is "What is your vision of life in the future?" Elicit answers to the questions in the Student Book.

Build Background

Read aloud this section from the Student Book. Be sure students understand the word *freeway*. Ask students what they know about astronauts. Have they ever read about what it is like to live in space?

STEP 2: Teach

Understanding the Genre:
Poetry and an Interview

Remind students that a poem is a piece of writing that expresses ideas, experiences, and emotions. The written lines of a poem are often short. Groups of these lines are called stanzas or verses. Sometimes words in poems rhyme.

An interview tells us about the personal experience of the person being asked the questions.

Teaching Resources

- CD-ROM/e-book, Literary Words
- Audio CD 6, track 6
- *Workbook*, p. 168

What You Will Learn

Reading
- Vocabulary building: *Literary terms, dictionary skills, word study*
- Reading strategy: *Analyze text structure 2*
- Text type: *Literature (poetry and interview)*

Grammar, Usage, and Mechanics
Different ways of asking questions

Writing
Support a main idea with examples

▲ Astronaut Bruce McCandless II "space walking"

346

THE BIG QUESTION

What is your vision of life in the future? Why are people fascinated by places beyond Earth? Work with a partner to explore the marvels and riddles of our universe. Discuss what Earth must look like from space. Talk about whether it is likely that humans will be able to travel to other planets or galaxies someday. Explore whether there might be life on other planets or in other galaxies. If so, how would it be different than life on Earth?

BUILD BACKGROUND

You will read two poems about the universe: **"Southbound on the Freeway"** and **"Cardinal Ideograms."** They come from *Poems to Solve* by May Swenson. Swenson says that solving a poem can be like unwrapping a mysterious package. In a few short lines, a poem can express big ideas.

   "Interview with an Astronaut: Dan Bursch" follows the poems. Bursch answers questions about his three flights into space and his time spent living on the International Space Station. U.S. astronauts train at NASA (National Aeronautics and Space Administration). The first astronauts were all pilots. Today, scientists and other people can travel in space along with the astronauts who are trained to fly the aircraft.

The Andromeda Galaxy is the nearest galaxy to our own. ▶

TESOL Standards

Goal 2, Standard 2— To use English to achieve academically in all content areas: Students will use English to obtain, process, construct, and provide subject matter information in spoken and written form.
Descriptors—Demonstrating knowledge through application in a variety of contexts.

Goal 3, Standard 1—To use English in socially and culturally appropriate ways: Students will use the appropriate language variety, register, and genre according to audience, purpose, and setting.
Descriptors—Using a variety of writing styles appropriate for different audiences, purposes, and settings.

Goal 3, Standard 3—To use English in socially and culturally appropriate ways: Students will use appropriate learning strategies to extend their sociolinguistic and sociocultural competence.
Descriptors—Observing and modeling how others speak and behave in a particular situation or setting; Rehearsing variations of language use in different social and academic settings.

VOCABULARY

Learn Literary Words

Poets often make imaginative comparisons to help you experience something ordinary in an extraordinary way. If a poet uses the word *like* or *as* to make the comparison, it is called a simile. May Swenson uses a simile in "Southbound on the Freeway" to describe the way cars on the highway might look from above to a visitor from outer space. What does she compare the cars to?

> They all hiss as they glide, like inches, down the marked tapes.

The everyday expressions "*sly as a fox*" or "*fast as lightning*" are also similes, but they no longer call up an image in our minds. They are used too often. Poetic similes invent a new way of looking at something.

Sometimes a poet compares two things in a bolder way, without using the words *like* or *as*. For example, a poet might say that dreams are birds or the sea is a singer. A comparison like this is called a metaphor. In the poem "Cardinal Ideograms," Swenson uses metaphors that make you look at the cardinal numbers (1, 2, 3, etc.) in an unusual way. What does she compare the cardinal number 1 to?

> 1 A grass blade or a cut.
> 2 A question seated. And a proud bird's neck.

Many poems are divided into groups of lines called stanzas. "Southbound on the Freeway" is divided into two-line stanzas called couplets. "Cardinal Ideograms" has stanzas of varying lengths.

Practice

Workbook Page 168

Take turns reading the metaphor and simile below aloud with a partner. Identify the two things that are being compared.

All the world's a stage . . . —William Shakespeare	Mars glowed like a lone fire in the dark galaxy.

Create a metaphor and a simile of your own. You might compare time or a feeling to something in nature or space. Write your metaphor and simile in your notebook. Share them with a classmate.

Literary Words

simile
metaphor
stanzas

▲ Mars is known as the red planet.

347

 Vocabulary

Learn Literary Words Play the CD. Have students listen and repeat. If you are not using the CD, read the Literary Words aloud. Write down the following key points on the board or on an overhead transparency in order to reinforce learning.

- **simile:** a comparison of two things, using the word *as* or *like*
- **metaphor:** a comparison of two unrelated things, without using the word *as* or *like*
- **stanzas:** groups of lines in a poem

Choose an object in the room or in nature, and offer a metaphor or simile about it. For example, *[A student's shirt] is as blue as the sky.* Encourage students to offer their own metaphors or similes of objects in the room or outside. Ask students to turn to page 350 so they have a visual image of a stanza. **SAY:** *Stanzas can be of various lengths.*

STEP 3: Practice

Have students work with partners. Tell them to identify the two things being compared. (stage/world and Mars/fire) Then have them create a simile and metaphor of their own. **SAY:** *Have an object in mind. Think about its color, taste, or smell. Think of other things that have those qualities. Then build a metaphor or simile comparing those two things.*

ANSWERS

Possible responses:
- An hour is like a leaf on a tree, just part of an entire day.
- The stars are pieces of silver thrown into the sky.

Differentiated Instruction

Beginning	Ask students to write one sentence using a simile and one sentence using a metaphor. For additional support, provide a sentence starter.
Early Intermediate	Direct students' attention to the photo of the astronaut on page 346. Have them name any famous astronauts they may have heard about.
Intermediate	Ask students to identify the simile and metaphor in the Practice section on page 347. Have them explain how they could tell which was which.
Standard English Learners	Have students write a short poem about something in nature or space that includes similes and metaphors. Have them share it with the class.

STEP 1: Teach

CD6 T7–T8

🔘 Vocabulary

Learn Academic Words Play the CD. Have students listen and repeat. If you are not using the CD, read the Academic Words aloud.
SAY: *These words will come up in our reading. If we try to understand them now, it will help us enjoy and better understand the reading. They will also come up in other things you read. Building your vocabulary will enhance your reading experience.* Have students work with partners to write additional sentences for each academic word. Encourage them to share the sentences with the class. If a sentence has an incorrect usage, **SAY:** *That is good, but a more accurate usage would be ____.*

STEP 2: Practice

Write the questions from the practice section on the board. **SAY:** *Use the context of the sentences to remember the meanings of the academic word. Underline the words surrounding the academic words. What do they tell you about the word's meaning?* Have students work in pairs to write answers to the questions. Encourage them to share their answers. Gently correct their usage if necessary.

ANSWERS
Possible responses:
1. In the future, I think there will be complex cars that steer themselves.
2. My interpretation of a poem may differ from my friend's because we have different ideas about the subject.
3. If I could have a book published, I would write about horses.
4. A bookstore might put up a sign saying "Ages 3 to 5" in the children's section.

Teaching Resources
- Audio CD 6, tracks 7–8
- *Workbook*, pp. 169–171
- CD-ROM/e-book, Academic Words, Word Study

T348

Learn Academic Words

Study the red words and their meanings. You will find these words useful when talking and writing about literature. Write each word and its meaning in your notebook. After you read "Southbound on the Freeway," "Cardinal Ideograms," and "Interview with an Astronaut: Dan Bursch," try to use these words to respond to the text.

Academic Words

complex
interpretation
published
section

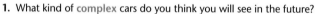

complex = complicated	➡	A computer is a **complex** tool because it is made of many parts. A wrench is a simple tool.
interpretation = an explanation	➡	Everyone had a different **interpretation** of the poem. Each of us had a different reaction to the poet's metaphors.
published = printed and sold	➡	A new book of poems was **published**. The poet was happy to see her poems in print in the bookstore.
section = a part of something	➡	I looked in the nonfiction **section** of the library for a book about our space program.

Practice 📖 **Workbook Page 169**

Work with a partner to answer the questions. Try to include the red word in your answer. Write the sentences in your notebook.

1. What kind of complex cars do you think you will see in the future?
2. Why might your interpretation of a poem be different from your friend's ideas?
3. What subject would you write about if you could have a book published?
4. In what section might a bookstore put up this sign: *Ages 3 to 5*?

▲ A wrench is a simple tool.

A race car is a complex machine. ▶

348

Word Study: Greek and Latin Roots

As you have learned, many English words come from Greek and Latin word parts called roots. Sometimes knowing the meaning of a root word can help you figure out the meaning of a new word. Knowing the meaning of a prefix can help, too.

Take, for example, the word *cycle*. It contains the root *cycl*, meaning "round." What happens when you add the following prefixes to *cycle*?

▲ A unicycle

The prefix *uni-* means one.	A unicycle has **one** round wheel.
The prefix *bi-* means two.	A bicycle has **two** round wheels.
The prefix *tri-* means three.	A tricycle has **three** round wheels.

Practice

Workbook Page 170

Work with a partner. Copy the chart below into your notebook. Talk about meanings of the word parts, and discuss what the new word means. Use a dictionary to check the meanings. List other words you know of that contain the roots *spec* and *verse* in your notebook. Add them to the chart.

Prefix	+ Root	= New Word
re- ("again")	spec ("see")	respect
uni- ("one")	verse ("turn")	universe

READING STRATEGY | **ANALYZE TEXT STRUCTURE 2**

Analyzing text structure can help you identify what kind of text you're reading. Poems and interviews each have a special text structure.

To analyze the text structure of a poem, follow these steps:

- Look for rhyming patterns and stanzas.
- Look for punctuation that shows you where to pause, such as commas, periods, dashes, or line breaks.

To analyze the text structure of an interview, follow these steps:

- Find speakers' names; they will be bold and followed by a colon (:).
- Look for name changes that signal different speakers.

Preview the text structures of the poems and interview. Discuss them with a partner.

Workbook Page 171

349

Linguistic Note

Helpful Hints to Decode Roots

Most European languages have Latin or Greek roots. To students from non-European language backgrounds, studying these roots may seem like studying another language. Here are a few helpful hints. Remind your students that entire word groups, such as the numerals, show clusters of Latin and Greek roots. Point out that the spelling of a word may indicate the original language of a word root. Words with *ph* are often taken from Greek. Example: *telephone*, *pharmacy*, *philosophy*. A *y* in the middle of a word may indicate Greek origin as well. Example: *physics*, *rhythm*, *hygiene*.

Read

Reading Summary

The poem "Southbound on the Freeway" explores what a tourist from outer space might think about Earthlings. The poem "Cardinal Ideograms" is a unique look at cardinal numbers. "Interview with an Astronaut: Dan Bursch" is an online interview with an American astronaut before he lived on the International Space Station in 2001.

 The Big Question

Remind students that the Big Question is "What is your vision of life in the future?" **SAY:** *What careers having to do with space or future technology might be available to you when you are older?*

STEP 2: Teach

Set a Purpose for Reading

Tell students to copy the purpose for reading into their notebooks and to keep it in mind as they read. Explain that they will have to present details that support their answers to the questions and to explain how the reading relates to the Big Question.

Preteaching Highlighted Words

In pairs, have students read aloud the highlighted words and their definitions. Answer any questions students have about the use of a word or its meaning before reading the spread.

CD6 T9

Scaffolding: Listen and Read

Ask students to follow along in the text as you play the CD recording of it. Pause after each page, so you can answer students' questions.

Teaching Resources

- *Resources*, Summaries, pp. 165–166
- Audio CD 6, track 9

READING 2

LITERATURE

POETRY AND INTERVIEW

Set a purpose for reading How does Earth look to a tourist from Orbitville or an astronaut on a space flight? In what ways does the number 8 seem like a model for the universe? Think about how the poems and interview affect your vision of time, space, and the future.

Southbound on the Freeway

May Swenson

A tourist came in from Orbitville,
parked in the air, and said:

The creatures of this star
are made of metal and glass.

Through the transparent parts
you can see their guts.

Their feet are round and roll
on diagrams—or long

measuring tapes—dark
with white lines.

They have four eyes.
The two in the back are red.

transparent, clear and easy to
see through

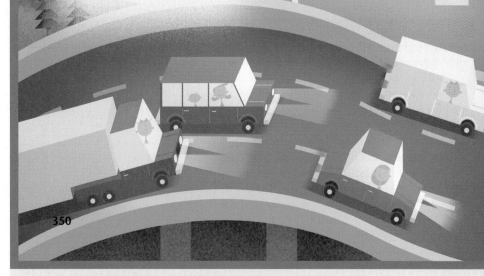

350

TESOL Standards

Goal 1, Standard 2—To use English to communicate in social settings: Students will interact in, through, and with spoken and written English for personal expression and enjoyment.
Descriptors—Expressing personal needs, feelings, and ideas.

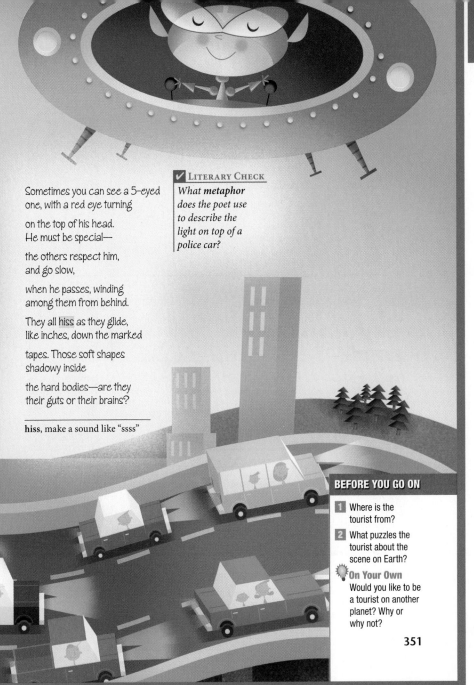

Sometimes you can see a 5-eyed
one, with a red eye turning

on the top of his head.
He must be special—

the others respect him,
and go slow,

when he passes, winding
among them from behind.

They all hiss as they glide,
like inches, down the marked

tapes. Those soft shapes
shadowy inside

the hard bodies—are they
their guts or their brains?

hiss, make a sound like "ssss"

✔ **LITERARY CHECK**

*What metaphor
does the poet use
to describe the
light on top of a
police car?*

BEFORE YOU GO ON

1. Where is the
tourist from?

2. What puzzles the
tourist about the
scene on Earth?

💡 **On Your Own**
Would you like to be
a tourist on another
planet? Why or
why not?

351

Study Skills: Dictionary

Encourage students to use dictionaries when
reading poetry. Remind them to look for the
guide words at the top of each page to find
a word quickly. **SAY:** *Poems use words in a
creative way, sometimes using a meaning of
a word that you may not be familiar with. It is
always a good idea to look up a word you think
you know but are unsure of.*

✔ LITERARY CHECK

Read the question aloud. If students need help
remembering the meaning of *metaphor,* go
back to page 347. Answer: The metaphor that
the poet uses to describe a police car is a five-
eyed creature with a red eye turning on top of
its head.

STEP 3: Monitor Progress

Ask students to check what they have
understood in the reading. If you are using the
Audio CD, pause the recording.

Before You Go On

Remind students that these questions will help
them monitor their progress. Put students in
pairs to answer the questions. Encourage them
to share their answers with the class.

ANSWERS

1. The tourist is from Orbitville.
2. The tourist is puzzled about the soft shapes
   inside the creatures of metal and glass. The
   tourist isn't sure if they're guts or brains.

On Your Own Ask students to take out a
separate sheet of paper and write an answer
to the On Your Own question. Encourage
volunteers to share their responses. Then
collect responses to monitor student
comprehension, writing skills, and fluency.

Differentiated Instruction

Beginning	Ask students to point to the second stanza. Ask a volunteer to read it aloud.
Early Intermediate	Ask students to find two metaphors in "Southbound on the Freeway." Ask them to identify what the poet is referring to.
Intermediate	Direct students' attention to the question that the poet poses in the last two stanzas on page 351. Ask them to say what the poet is describing.
Special Needs	Check students' power of recall by asking them to tell you three things they remember about the text. Monitor students' responses and encourage them to look back at the text when necessary.

Read

Preteaching Highlighted Words

In pairs, have students read aloud the highlighted words and their definitions. Answer any questions students have about the use of a word or its meaning before reading the spread. Make sure that students understand each highlighted word. If appropriate, ask students to generate original sentences using the highlighted words. Give them an example, such as *Many things that happen in nature are enigmatic unless we understand the science behind why they happen.*

Across the Curriculum: Math

Explain to students that math is important in the formation of a stanza of poetry. Some older forms of poetry have very strict rules about how many lines are in a stanza and how many stresses, or beats, are in a line. Point out that some poets use a certain number of lines or beats in order to repeat a rhythm over and over again. Ask students to clap the beats in a nursery rhyme, such as "Mary Had a Little Lamb." They will see that the rhythm, 4 beats, 3 beats, 4 beats, 3 beats, keeps repeating.

Model the
READING STRATEGY

Analyze Text Structure

Ask students to study the text structure of "Cardinal Ideograms" and decide what makes it a poem. (Each number gets its own stanza. There are many periods to show you where to pause.) If students need further help, review the steps to analyzing text structure on page 349.

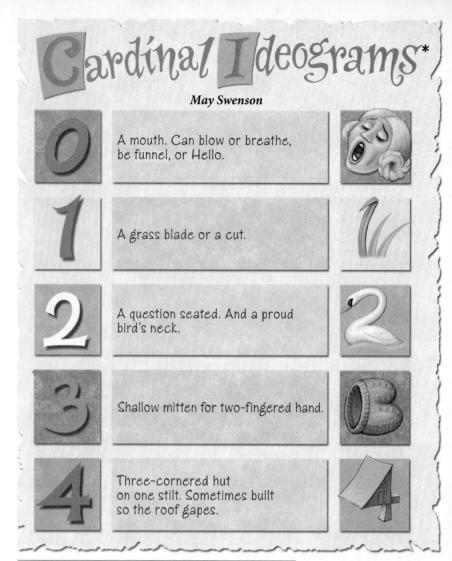

Cardinal Ideograms*

May Swenson

0 A mouth. Can blow or breathe, be funnel, or Hello.

1 A grass blade or a cut.

2 A question seated. And a proud bird's neck.

3 Shallow mitten for two-fingered hand.

4 Three-cornered hut on one stilt. Sometimes built so the roof gapes.

---

funnel, a tube with a wide top used for pouring things

* This excerpt from "Cardinal Ideograms" contains eight of the ten stanzas from the original poem. Cardinal numbers are any of the numbers 0, 1, 2, 3, and so on. Ideograms are written signs that stand for an idea or thing.

352

5
A policeman. Polite.
Wearing visored cap.

6
O unrolling,
tape of ambiguous length
on which is written the mystery
of everything curly.

7
A step,
detached from its stair.

8
The universe in diagram:
A cosmic hourglass.
(Note enigmatic shape,
absence of any valve of origin,
how end overlaps beginning.)
Unknotted like a shoelace
and whipped back and forth,
can serve as a model of time.

✔ LITERARY CHECK
*Which stanza
contains a simile?*

---

ambiguous, uncertain or hard to understand
enigmatic, mysterious and hard to explain
valve, part of a pipe that opens and closes to control the flow of liquid,
    air, or gas passing through it

ABOUT THE **POET**

May Swenson (1913–1989) was born in Utah.
She came from a very large family and was the
oldest of ten children. English was her second
language; Swedish was spoken at home. She
attended Utah State University and later taught
poetry there. Swenson also worked as an editor
and was the Chancellor of the Academy of
American Poets. Her poetry won many awards, including
the Bollingen Prize and the Shelley Memorial Award.

BEFORE YOU GO ON

1 What does the poem
compare the cardinal
number 3 to?

2 What reasons does
the poem give for
calling the cardinal
number 8 enigmatic,
or mysterious?

On Your Own
What does the
number 9 look like
to you? Create
your own cardinal
ideogram.

353

Study Skills: Thesaurus

Encourage students to write alternative
stanzas for "Cardinal Ideograms" by using a
thesaurus. Point out that a thesaurus is a book
of synonyms. Like a dictionary, the entry words
are listed in alphabetical order, and guide words
at the top of each page help in quickly locating
words. Ask students to replace words from the
poem, such as *visored, ambiguous,* and *cosmic*
with new words of similar meaning.

STEP 5: Monitor Progress

Ask students to check what they have
understood in the reading. If you are using the
Audio CD, pause the recording.

Before You Go On

Tell students that the answers to these
questions can be found in the poem itself. In
addition to providing the answer, ask students
to point out where in the poem they found the
answers to the questions.

ANSWERS

1. The cardinal number 3 is likened to a shallow
   mitten for a two-fingered hand.
2. The cardinal number 8 is called enigmatic
   because of the absence of any valve of
   origin. The end overlaps the beginning.

On Your Own Have students write their
answers to On Your Own on a separate
sheet of paper. Ask them to share their
responses, and collect the papers to monitor
comprehension, writing skills, and fluency.

Read

Preteaching Highlighted Words

In pairs, have students read aloud the highlighted words and their definitions. Answer any questions students have about the use of a word or its meaning before reading the spread. In case students have trouble understanding the correct usage, give them an example: *My best friend and I chatted on the phone last weekend.*

Across the Curriculum:
Social Studies

Tell students that there is a rich history to the NASA program and the International Space Station. Trips to the International Space Station have been occurring since 2000. The first crew consisted of three astronauts: Sergei Krikalev, Bill Shepherd, and Yuri Gidzenko. It launched October 31, 2000, from Kazakhstan and landed March 21, 2001. The trip lasted 136 days.

Model the
READING STRATEGY

Analyze Text Structure
Ask students to point out how the text structure of this selection is different from the two poems they just read. Have students find the speakers' names in boldface type and notice their exact words. Where do the speakers' words begin? (after the colon) If necessary, have students use their Analyzing Text Structure checklist on page 349 to figure out the components of an interview.

▲ The International Space Station

Interview with an Astronaut:
Dan Bursch

Dan Bursch has made three space flights and has been in space for 746 hours. He lived on the International Space Station from December 5, 2001, until June 19, 2002. Before this expedition, he chatted online with some students on www.discovery.com.

Dan Bursch: I would just like to say welcome to everyone tonight. Thank you for spending your Sunday evening with me. . . .

Cody: I am ten years old, and I would like to know what the food is like. I would also like for you to trade me just one day in the space station and you can go to my school.

---

chatted, talked informally

354

 TESOL Standards

Goal 1, Standard 1—To use English to communicate in social settings: Students will use English to participate in social interactions.
Descriptors—Expressing needs, feelings, and ideas.

▲ Astronaut Dan Bursch works in the weightless environment of space.

Dan Bursch: Food is very important for us up in space, as it is here on Earth. In fact, one of the things that I will be starting tomorrow . . . is food tasting. We are selecting our menu for the four- to six-month flight that I will have in space. What is different about my next mission on the space station is that we will have a mixture of American and Russian food, so that will certainly make it different. . . . Perhaps I can come to your school someday and perhaps in fifteen years or so you can go to space!

Gary TX: What kind of work do you do when you are at the space station?

Dan Bursch: We have a crew of three—myself, Carl Walz (another American astronaut), and Yuri. He is a Russian cosmonaut. He will be our commander. We divide up the work because there is a lot of work to be done. . . .

---

selecting, choosing
cosmonaut, Russian astronaut
commander, leader

BEFORE YOU GO ON

1 Who are the people interviewing Dan Bursch?

2 What is different about the menu on this trip?

On Your Own
Would you like to spend a day on the space station? Why or why not?

355

Study Skills: Internet

Tell students that the Internet offers many interesting websites about space travel. The NASA site often has live feed from space stations or U.S. space expeditions. There are also many facts about the space program. If a computer is available, show students the website, and find answers to some of their questions about the space program.

STEP 7: Monitor Progress

Ask students to check what they have understood in the reading. If you are using the Audio CD, pause the recording.

Before You Go On

SAY: *Answering questions about a text before you go on to the next page in the text can help make sure you understand what the text is about. It can also help you to predict what may happen next.* Elicit answers to the questions from the students. Ask them to point out where they found the answer.

ANSWERS
1. Students are interviewing Dan Bursch.
2. The menu on this trip is a mixture of American and Russian food.

On Your Own Have students write their answers to the On Your Own question on a separate sheet of paper. Ask them to share their responses, and then collect the papers to monitor comprehension, writing skills, and fluency.

Read

STEP 8: Teach

Preteaching Highlighted Words

In pairs, have students read aloud the highlighted words and their definitions. Answer any questions students have about the use of a word or its meaning before reading the spread. If necessary, review the words in a dictionary. Encourage volunteers to use them in sentences. If students have trouble understanding the correct usage, give them an example: *There is nothing quite as spectacular as a fireworks show on the Fourth of July.*

Across the Curriculum: Math

Explain to students that the basis of space travel is mathematics. Astronautics is a type of engineering that is specifically for machines designed to leave Earth's atmosphere. It is a fairly new field that began in the mid-twentieth century. But the foundations of space travel can be found as far back as in the math equations of the famous seventeenth-century mathematician Sir Isaac Newton.

Model the READING STRATEGY

Analyze Text Structure

Ask students to continue analyzing the text structure. **SAY:** *Why do you think an interview structure lists the questions and answers in the way that it does and does not describe the interview in a prose paragraph?* (It is more fact-based this way. You know exactly what was said and who said it.)

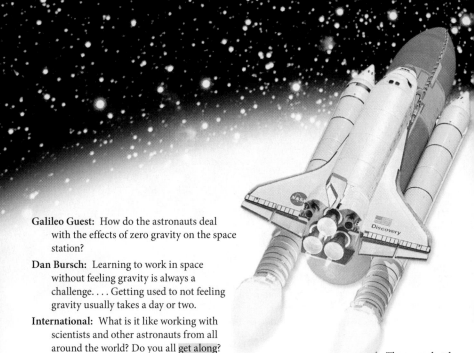

Galileo Guest: How do the astronauts deal with the effects of zero gravity on the space station?

Dan Bursch: Learning to work in space without feeling gravity is always a challenge. . . . Getting used to not feeling gravity usually takes a day or two.

International: What is it like working with scientists and other astronauts from all around the world? Do you all get along? Do you have fun?

Dan Bursch: This job is particularly interesting just because of that fact. . . . In the astronaut office, the range of different kinds of people is pretty wide. . . . But we all share one common goal, and that is to fly and live and work in space. . . .

Hollifield: Can you see the lights of the world's cities from space?

Dan Bursch: Yes. We spend half of our time while in orbit on the dark side of the planet. If there is a thin cloud layer, you see kind of a glow like from a lampshade that dampens the light a little bit. But when it is clear—when there are no clouds—the lights are spectacular. . . .

Venus: What is the first time you go into space like? Is it hard to learn to use the tools or get used to things floating around?

Dan Bursch: I remember my first flight in 1993 on [the space shuttle]

▲ The space shuttle *Discovery* blasts off into space.

get along, act friendly
in orbit, circling around Earth
spectacular, wonderful and exciting to see
floating around, moving around freely in the air

356

TESOL Standards

Goal 2, Standard 1—To use English to achieve academically in all content areas: Students will use English to interact in the classroom.
Descriptors—Requesting information and assistance.

T356

Discovery. . . . At lift-off, there is a lot of vibration and a lot of noise, and eight-and-a-half minutes later you are in orbit. When the engines turn off, instantly everything floats. . . . You have to make sure that you either strap something down or use Velcro because you will probably lose it otherwise.

AstroBob: Do you think that at some point ordinary people will get to go to the space station? Or will it always be reserved for scientists?

Dan Bursch: I think that is certainly a goal that we should try to reach. If it will be in my lifetime, I don't know. . . . When airplanes first came out, they were reserved at first for just the very daring or risk takers. And now anybody can fly on an airplane. So, I don't think it is a question of IF the opportunity will come . . . it is simply a matter of WHEN.

Sandy Fay: What kinds of things do they hope the space station will be good for once it is completed?

Dan Bursch: . . . I see the biggest challenge and the biggest thing that we are learning is two former enemies learning how to work together and build such a large and complex structure in space. And not just two former enemies, but all of the over one dozen countries that are working together . . .

Discovery.com: Thank you, Dan, for chatting with us tonight.

Velcro, a material that can stick to itself to fasten things together
reserved for, set aside for
daring, brave

▲ **Planet Earth, as seen from space**

BEFORE YOU GO ON

1 How do astronauts make sure that none of their things float away while in space?

2 For Dan Bursch, what is the biggest challenge of the space station?

💡 **On Your Own** What question would you like to ask Dan Bursch about the future?

357

Study Skills: Internet

Ask students to identify when the interview with Astronaut Dan Bursch was conducted. (before December 19, 2001). Direct students to use the Internet to research how the International Space Station has developed since then. Has it been completed? What is different? What is the same? Remind students that it is critical to look at the date that information online was posted or updated.

STEP 9: Monitor Progress

Ask students to check what they have understood in the reading.

Before You Go On

Remind students that these questions will help them monitor their progress. Put students in pairs to answer the questions. Encourage them to share their answers with the class.

ANSWERS
1. They strap things down or use Velcro.
2. For Dan Bursch, the biggest challenge of the space station is two former enemies learning to work together and build such a large and complex structure.

On Your Own Have students write an answer to the question. Encourage volunteers to share their responses with the class. Then collect student responses to monitor their comprehension, writing skills, and fluency.

Review the Purpose for Reading

Elicit responses to the Set a Purpose for Reading questions at the beginning of this reading. Remind students to relate their responses to the Big Question.

STEP 1: Introduce

Speaking Tip

Remind students to speak in a clear voice, facing the class.

Dramatic Reading

Memorizing a poem gives students the opportunity to understand the emotional impact of the poem's cadence, rhythm, and content much better than simply reading or listening to it. Help students organize into groups of six. Encourage them to memorize the portion of the poem that they feel most strongly about and to try to allow that emotion to color their reading.

Have groups rehearse reciting the poem. When they are ready, ask each group to perform before the class.

STEP 2: Practice

Comprehension

Have students write answers to the questions.

ANSWERS

1. The tourist is from Orbitville.
2. It takes one to two days.
3. She compares the number 2 to a question seated and a proud bird's neck.
4. If there's a cloud layer, the Earth appears to have a kind of glow, like that from a lampshade. When it is clear, the lights from the cities are spectacular.
5. The tourist thinks the people on Earth look like cars. Answers will vary.
6. One reason it's important for astronauts to cooperate in space is that there's a lot of work that must get done.
7. Answers will vary.
8. Answers will vary.

Teaching Resources

- *Workbook*, p. 172
- CD-ROM/e-book, Comprehension, Response to Literature

DRAMATIC READING

One of the best ways to understand a poem is to memorize it, or learn it by heart. Work in groups of six to reread, discuss, and interpret "Southbound on the Freeway." Describe what you visualize as you read the poem line by line. Identify any metaphors, similes, or vivid sensory words you find. Work together to interpret any difficult words or phrasing. Use a dictionary or ask your teacher for help if necessary.

After your group has reread and examined the poem carefully, have each member of your group memorize one or two of the poem's stanzas. Then recite the entire poem, with each student reciting the stanzas that he or she memorized. Comment on one another's oral reading and make helpful suggestions for improvements. Practice reciting the poem with your group. Then hold a "poetry slam" with the whole class in which each group competes for the best oral reading.

🔊 Speaking TIP

Face the audience when you say your lines. Speak clearly and loudly. If you turn away from the audience too much, people may not be able to hear or understand you.

COMPREHENSION

 Workbook Page 172

Right There

1. Where does the tourist come from in "Southbound on the Freeway"?
2. How long does it take astronaut Dan Bursch to get used to not feeling gravity?

Think and Search

3. What two things does the poet compare to the number 2 in "Cardinal Ideograms"?
4. What does Earth look like from space according to Dan Bursch?

Author and You

5. What does the tourist think the people on Earth look like in "Southbound on the Freeway"? What is the tourist's interpretation of Earth's complex people?
6. Why would it be important for astronauts to cooperate with each other while they are in space?

▲ Astronauts cooperate with each other to repair the International Space Station.

358

TESOL Standards

Goal 1, Standard 1—To use English to communicate in social settings: Students will use English to participate in social interactions.
Descriptors—Using nonverbal communication in social interactions; Conducting transactions.

Goal 1, Standard 3—To use English to communicate in social settings: Students will use learning strategies to extend their communicative competence.
Descriptors—Selecting different media to help understand language

Goal 2, Standard 3—To use English to achieve academically in all content areas: Students will use appropriate learning strategies to construct and apply academic knowledge.
Descriptors—Determining and establishing the conditions that help one become an effective learner (e.g., when, where, how to study); Recognizing the need for and seeking assistance appropriately from others (e.g., teachers, peers, specialists, community members); Knowing when to use native language resources (human and material) to promote understanding.

On Your Own

7. What do you think the number 8 looks like? Compare the number 8 to different things.

8. What kinds of food would you choose for a six-month journey into space? Explain your reasons.

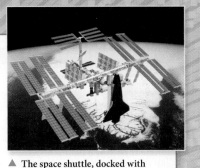

▲ The space shuttle, docked with the International Space Station

DISCUSSION

Discuss in pairs or small groups.

1. How are "Southbound on the Freeway" and "Cardinal Ideograms" similar? How are they different?

2. Which of the metaphors in "Cardinal Ideograms" did you think was most interesting or accurate? Why?

3. Dan Bursch talks about the challenges of living on the space station, such as dealing with gravity and working with others. What would be your biggest challenge on the space station? Why?

Q **What is your vision of life in the future?** Imagine that you are going to the space station at some point in the future. What would you take with you? What do you think you would see?

> **Listening TIP**
>
> Listen to the verbs and adjectives your classmates use when they speak. Try to visualize, or picture in your mind, what each speaker is describing.

RESPONSE TO LITERATURE

Workbook Page 172

If you were a tourist from Orbitville visiting Earth, what aspects of Earth would you find most confusing? What aspects would you find most amazing? Write an e-mail to send to your home planet telling what strange and interesting things you discovered on Earth. When you have finished your e-mail, share it with a classmate.

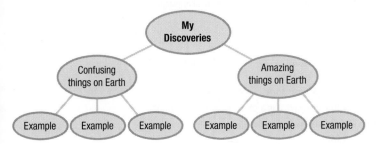

359

Listening Tip

Demonstrate for students how visualizing active verbs and adjectives can help a listener better understand what the speaker is describing.

CRI Discussion

Model a discussion starter for each question. For example, for the first question, **SAY:** *One similarity I see between "Cardinal Ideograms" and "Southbound on the Freeway" is that they both look at familiar objects in a new way. A swan's neck is the number two and a car is a person."*

Q **What is your vision of life in the future?** Guide students in a discussion about going to the space station in the future. Brainstorm things they might take with them. Suggestions might include good books, music, favorite food, souvenirs from home. You might see the beauty of Earth from space, other spacecrafts, aliens from other worlds.

Response to Literature

Invite students to imagine that they are tourists from Orbitville visiting Earth. Reread "Southbound on the Freeway" as a class. Draw the graphic organizer on page 359 on the board, and ask students to offer examples of things that they found confusing and amazing about Earth. Then have students write emails "home," describing their discoveries.

Differentiated Instruction	
Beginning	Ask students which description of a number they like best from "Cardinal Ideograms." Why?
Early Intermediate	Ask students to give you an alternative caption for the photo on page 355.
Intermediate	Have students write a list of three things they learned from reading the *Interview with an Astronaut: Dan Bursch*.
Struggling Readers	Give students extra support as they complete the Comprehension section by modeling your thinking and guiding them to the correct answer.

Grammar and Writing

STEP 1: Introduce

Tell students you will be reviewing different ways of asking questions in English. Elicit some question words from volunteers. Then ask other students to form a question.

STEP 2: Teach

Grammar and Writing

Different Ways of Asking Questions

Read aloud and discuss the opening paragraph. Write each of the 5Ws (*Who, What, Where, When, Why*) and *how* on the board. Ask students to describe the type of information that a question beginning with each word would reveal. Model some *yes/no* questions for students so that they see the difference between using an auxiliary verb and a question word. Tell them that question words require a detailed answer, whereas a question with *can* or *do* does not.

Tell students that there are other ways of asking questions, for example in statement form, but ask them to focus on using question words and questions with *can* and *do.*

STEP 3: Practice

Have students write a question for each answer.

ANSWERS

1. **Possible response:** <u>Where</u> did the interview with Dan Bursch take place?
2. <u>What</u> is a challenge for astronauts?
3. **Possible response:** <u>How</u> would you describe the lights from the planet?
4. **Possible response:** <u>Who</u> is Yuri?
5. **Possible response:** <u>When</u> might everyone visit a space station?

Teaching Resources

- *Workbook*, pp. 173–174
- CD-ROM/e-book, Grammar, Writing
- *Transparencies*, Writing Model 47
- *Transparencies*, *Resources*, Graphic Organizer 2 or 16
- *Assessment*, Reading 2 Test, pp. 119–122

GRAMMAR, USAGE, AND MECHANICS

Different Ways of Asking Questions

In English, there are different ways of asking questions. Knowing the different ways will help you get the information you need. In each case, use the method that best helps you get the facts, details, and opinions that you are looking for. You can ask questions using the 5Ws: *Who? Where? When? What? Why?* You can also ask questions that start with *How?*

- **Who** were the first astronauts?
- **Where** do you want to travel in space?
- **When** did you decide to become an astronaut?
- **What** is it like working with scientists and astronauts from all around the world?
- **Why** is it important that we travel into space?
- **How** long does it take to become an astronaut?

You can also ask *yes/no* questions using the words *can* and *do.*

- **Can** you see the lights of the world's cities from space?
- **Do** you all get along?
- **Do** you have fun?

In addition, you can ask a question in statement form.

- I would like to know if astronaut training is difficult.
- I want to ask you whether you think people will ever live on other planets.

Practice
Workbook
Page 173

Work with a partner. Write a question for each of the answers. Try to use different ways of asking questions.

1. The interview with Dan Bursch took place online.
2. Learning to work without gravity is a challenge for astronauts.
3. The lights from the planet look spectacular.
4. Yuri is a Russian cosmonaut.
5. Someday maybe everyone will visit a space station.

360

TESOL Standards

Goal 2, Standard 1—To use English to achieve academically in all content areas: Students will use English to interact in the classroom.
Descriptors—Following oral and written directions, implicit and explicit.

Goal 2, Standard 2— To use English to achieve academically in all content areas: Students will use English to obtain, process, construct, and provide subject matter information in spoken and written form.
Descriptors—Gathering information orally and in writing; Representing information visually and interpreting information presented visually; Demonstrating knowledge through application in a variety of contexts.

Goal 2, Standard 3—To use English to achieve academically in all content areas: Students will use appropriate learning strategies to construct and apply academic knowledge.
Descriptors—Evaluating one's own success in a completed learning task.

WRITING A RESEARCH REPORT

Support a Main Idea with Examples

Using examples is often the best way to explain an idea clearly. Examples are bits of information that explain or describe a point. They can include facts, dates, numbers, and descriptions of events. On this page, you will support a main idea with examples, using a graphic organizer like the one at the right.

To find examples, you can do research and take notes. Suppose that your main idea is the following: *Astronauts must go through difficult training before going into space.* In your research, you might find specific examples to support this idea. For example, an astronaut must spend 1,000 hours flying in a jet aircraft and take a class in aircraft safety.

Here is a model of a paragraph that uses examples to support a main idea. Notice the different kinds of examples the writer uses.

Koji Mori

Mars

What do scientists know about the red planet? Mars is the fourth planet from the sun and the seventh largest planet in our solar system. It has two moons, Deimos and Phobos. Temperatures on Mars can get extremely cold because of the planet's thin atmosphere. The temperature can drop to -133 degrees Celsius (-207 degrees Fahrenheit). Huge dust storms also take place on the planet. Despite the extreme weather, Mars is more like Earth than any other planet in our solar system. In fact, scientists think that there is frozen water at the poles on Mars, especially at the south polar region. There may be enough ice to cover the entire planet.

Practice Workbook Page 174

Write a paragraph about space missions or astronauts in which your main idea is supported by three short examples. List your ideas in a main idea/examples web. Try to begin your paragraph with an interesting question that is connected to your main idea.

Writing Checklist

IDEAS:
☑ I chose specific examples that explain and support my main idea.

CONVENTIONS:
☑ I corrected all errors in spelling, capitalization, and punctuation.

361

Teach

STEP 1: Introduce

Objectives

Read the list of objectives in the What You Will Learn section, encouraging students to join in. Tell students that this reading will be about what it would be like to travel into the future. Have pairs of students work together to restate the list of things they will learn.

The Big Question

Remind students that the Big Question for the unit is "What is your vision of life in the future?" Ask students whether they believe the future will be positive or negative or both, and why.

Build Background

Locate New York City on a map. If possible show students a picture of the American Museum of Natural History and the statue of Theodore Roosevelt that stands outside it.

STEP 2: Teach

Understanding the Genre:
Novel Excerpt

Tell students that a novel is a long work of fiction. An excerpt is part of a novel. Ask students to name a novel they have read. What do they think the features of a novel are? (Plot, setting, characterization, etc.)

Teaching Resources

- CD-ROM/e-book, Literary Words
- Audio CD 6, track 11
- *Workbook*, p. 175

What You Will Learn

Reading
- Vocabulary building: *Literary terms, dictionary skills, word study*
- Reading strategy: *Skim*
- Text type: *Literature (novel excerpt)*

Grammar, Usage, and Mechanics
Using punctuation

Writing
Include quotations and citations

THE BIG QUESTION

What is your vision of life in the future? Some people think the future will be wonderful, thanks to machines that will save us time and effort. They think that there will be new ways to communicate and connect people all over the world. Others think that the future will not be so bright. They predict the world will be overcrowded and that wars will be fought over natural resources.

Work with a partner. Debate whether the future will be positive or negative. Decide whether the future holds great things or not-so-great things, or a combination of both. Put all of your ideas together and write a statement about the future. Share your statement with other pairs.

▲ An artist's idea of two future cities, with protective domes

BUILD BACKGROUND

The Time Warp Trio: 2095 is a science fiction novel about traveling into the future. The novel takes place at two different times: 1995 and 2095. To create this science fiction story, author Jon Scieszka combined real things with imaginary, or fantastic, things. He made up the characters and their adventures. One part of the setting is real: the American Museum of Natural History. This famous museum is located in New York City opposite Central Park. And a statue of Theodore Roosevelt, the twenty-sixth president of the United States, really does stand outside the museum. Roosevelt loved nature and was a great friend of the museum. He was a strong believer in preserving the environment.

362

TESOL Standards

Goal 1, Standard 3—To use English to communicate in social settings: Students will use learning strategies to extend their communicative competence.
Descriptors—Selecting different media to help understand language; Using context to construct meaning.

Goal 2, Standard 3—To use English to achieve academically in all content areas: Students will use appropriate learning strategies to construct and apply academic knowledge.
Descriptors—Focusing attention selectively; Applying basic reading comprehension skills such as skimming, scanning, previewing, and reviewing text; Using context to construct meaning.

VOCABULARY

Learn Literary Words

Writers of science fiction often imagine what life in the future might be like. They base their plots on ideas and predictions about science and technology. Science fiction usually takes place in the future or involves time travel. It may be about an ideal society or fantastic creatures, inventions, and places. For example, in *The War of the Worlds*, author H. G. Wells tells a story about visitors from Mars.

Setting is the time and place when an event or story occurs. Sometimes writers tell you the setting. Other times, you have to figure it out from clues such as the characters' speech, clothing, or ways of traveling.

Read this excerpt from *The Best New Thing*, by Isaac Asimov. How do you know that this selection is science fiction? Which paragraph reveals the setting?

> Rada lived on a little world, far out in space. Her father and her mother and her brother, Jonathan, lived there too. So did other men and women.
> Rada was the only little girl on the little world. Jonny was the only little boy. They had lived there all their lives. Rada's father and other men worked on the spaceships. They made sure everything was all right before the spaceships went on their way back to Earth or to other planets.

Practice **Workbook** Page 175

With a partner, take turns reading aloud the descriptions below. Do you think that each is a setting for a science fiction novel? Explain your reasoning to your partner.

1. The story takes place on Mars in the year 2891. Humans live in a big dome. Martians live on the surface of the planet. The Martians and humans get along well but do not interact much.

2. The year is 1850. The place is Austin, Texas. The novel tells the real life story of a ranching family whose members are close and loving.

In your notebook, write a paragraph describing the setting for a science fiction story of your own. Share it with a partner.

▲ *The War of the Worlds* is a classic science fiction novel about visitors from space.

363

 Vocabulary

Learn Literary Words Play the CD. Have students listen and repeat. If you are not using the CD, direct students to the Literary Words at the top of the page, and read them aloud. **SAY:** *These words are called Literary Words because in a discussion of literature, they have a unique meaning.* Write the following definitions of *science fiction* and *setting* on the board or on an overhead transparency to reinforce learning.

- **science fiction:** stories about life in the future based on imaginary developments in science and technology

- **setting:** the time and place when an event or story occurs

Ask students to provide examples of *science fiction* and *setting*.

STEP 3: Practice

Have students work with partners to complete the practice activity.

ANSWERS

Possible responses:

1. This is a setting for a science fiction novel because it takes place in the future, and it has creatures from Mars.

2. This is not a setting for a science fiction novel, because it takes place in the past in a real place—Austin, Texas.

Differentiated Instruction

Beginning	Ask students when the science fiction story on page 366 takes place; the past, present, or future. Tell them to look at the title of the story to find out.
Early Intermediate	Ask students to list other works of science fiction they may have read, watched on TV, or seen in the movies.
Intermediate	Have students look at the illustrations on pages 366 and 368. Ask them how they can tell that this story is science fiction.
Struggling Readers	To help students understand *setting*, ask them to describe the setting of the classroom or school.

STEP 1: Teach

CD6 T12–T13

Vocabulary

Learn Academic Words Play the CD. Have students listen and repeat. If you are not using the CD, read the Academic Words at the top of the page aloud and discuss their possible meanings. **SAY:** *Look at the Academic Word chart. The definition for each word is on the left side. On the right side, each word is used in a sentence. Work with a partner to write an additional sentence for each academic word. Write each word, its definition, and the sentence in your personal word book.*

STEP 2: Practice

Write the first question on the board, underlining the word as shown: *Do you think we will see a shift in how we use natural resources in the future?* **SAY:** *Look at the question on the board and notice the underlined words. When you answer a question, try to include words from the question in your answer.*

ANSWERS

Answers will vary.

Teaching Resources

- Audio CD 6, tracks 12–13
- *Workbook*, pp. 176–178
- CD-ROM/e-book, Academic Words, Word Study

Learn Academic Words

Study the red words and their meanings. You will find these words useful when talking and writing about literature. Write each word and its meaning in your notebook. After you read the excerpt from *The Time Warp Trio: 2095,* try to use these words to respond to the text.

shift = a change in the way most people think about something, or in the way something is done	➡	There was a huge **shift** in their ideas about nature after their visit to the natural history museum.
specific = detailed and exact	➡	Tell me more about your trip. You told me some general things, but I'd like to hear some **specific** details.
strategies = sets of plans and skills used in order to gain success or achieve an aim	➡	Her **strategies** for preparing for an exam are to study with friends and get a good night's sleep.
techniques = special methods of doing something	➡	There are many **techniques** that science fiction writers use to create believable stories.

Practice   **Workbook Page 176**

Work with a partner to answer these questions. Try to include the red word in your answer. Write the sentences in your notebook.

1. Do you think that we will see a shift in how we use natural resources in the future? Explain.
2. What specific facts about the future would you like to know?
3. What strategies do you use to help you remember new words?
4. What techniques do you use to help you take good photographs?

▲ A popular study strategy is to have a friend quiz you on facts.

364

TESOL Standards

Goal 1, Standard 3—To use English to communicate in social settings: Students will use learning strategies to extend their communicative competence.
Descriptors—Listening to and imitating how others use English; Exploring alternative ways of saying things.

Goal 2, Standard 1—To use English to achieve academically in all content areas: Students will use English to interact in the classroom.
Descriptors—Participating in full-class, group, and pair discussions; Negotiating and managing interaction to accomplish tasks.

Goal 3, Standard 1—To use English in socially and culturally appropriate ways: Students will use the appropriate language variety, register, and genre according to audience, purpose, and setting.
Descriptors—Recognizing and using Standard English and vernacular dialects appropriately.

Word Study: Schwa spelled *a, e, i, o, u*

In many English words, the letters *a, e, i, o,* and *u* can stand for the sound you hear when you say "uh." The "uh" sound is called a schwa. The symbol for the schwa is the letter *e* turned upside down /ə/. In multisyllabic words, the schwa occurs only in an unstressed syllable. Recognizing and pronouncing /ə/ will help you spell many words correctly. Study the chart. Notice that the schwa occurs only in an unstressed syllable.

/ə/ spelled *a*	/ə/ spelled *e*	/ə/ spelled *i*	/ə/ spelled *o*	/ə/ spelled *u*
a-'maze	'tak-**en**	'an-**i**-mal	'les-s**on**	'care-f**ul**
'so-f**a**	'trav-**el**	ex-'per-**i**-ment	'com-m**on**	'Ve-n**us**

Practice Workbook Page 177

Work with a partner to spell these words: *alike, museum, uniforms, lion, happen.* Write five headings in your notebook: *a, e, i, o, u.* Say a word from the list slowly and clearly, syllable by syllable. Listen for the schwa. Ask your partner to spell the word aloud. Then have your partner say the next word. Continue until you can spell all of the words correctly. Write the words under the correct headings in your notebook. If you have trouble finding the schwa, check the word's pronunciation in a dictionary.

READING STRATEGY | SKIM

Skimming helps you get an idea of what a text is about. Skimming will also help you make and confirm predictions and become an active reader. To skim a text, follow these steps:

- Glance at the title, text, and illustrations to see what the plot, characters, and setting will be like.
- Read through the first page quickly.
- Make predictions about what you think will happen in the selection.

Skim the excerpt from *The Time Warp Trio: 2095* and make predictions. Then read the selection carefully. Confirm or revise your predictions.

 Workbook Page 178

365

Linguistic Note

Schwa

The word *schwa* comes from a Hebrew word meaning *nought,* or *zero.* Originally the word referred only to specific nipped sounds in the Hebrew alphabet, but soon was used for unstressed vowel sounds in other languages as well. Point out that in English any and all vowels can be pronounced as a schwa if in an unstressed syllable. Mention that this shows the tendency of spoken language towards simplification. In some regional varieties of English (Northeastern US) entire syllables may even be *merged* into the schwa. A two-syllable word such as *mirror* may become a homophone with a one-syllable word such as *mere.* Other examples: *terror/tear, error/air/heir.*

STEP 1: Teach

Word Study

Schwa spelled *a, e, i, o, u* Tell students there are several ways to spell the sound you hear when you say "uh." This sound is called a *schwa* and it can be spelled with a, e, i, o, or u. Draw the table on page 365 on the board, and read the words in them aloud. **SAY:** *Notice that the schwa always occurs in an unstressed syllable.*

STEP 2: Practice

Have students work with a partner to write each word under the correct heading in the chart.

ANSWERS

a	e	i	o	u
alike	happen	uniforms	lion	museum

STEP 3: Teach

Reading Strategy

Skim Read aloud the instructions for skimming in the Reading Strategy box. Demonstrate each step as you skim the excerpt from *The Time Warp Trio: 2095*. Impress on students that skimming is not the same as reading. Point out that they probably already skim things far more than they actually realize—billboards, bus tickets, menus, and TV listings. Tell students that skimming is a fast, efficient way of separating out what they really need to read from what they don't. Remind them that all the reading strategies they are learning to use are transferable to other areas of the curriculum. Skimming will be a strategy they can use in social studies and science classes as well as language arts.

Read

Reading Summary

Tell students that in this novel excerpt, three friends suddenly find themselves transported 100 years into the future, to 2095.

 The Big Question

Remind students that the Big Question is "What is your vision of life in the future?"
SAY: *Imagine that you were transported 100 years into the future. What do you think you would see?*

STEP 2: Teach

Set a Purpose for Reading

Tell students to copy the purpose for reading into their notebooks and to keep it in mind as they read. Explain that they will have to present details that support their answers to the questions and to explain how the reading relates to the Big Question.

Preteaching Highlighted Words

In pairs, have students read aloud the highlighted words and their definitions. Answer any questions students have about the use of a word or its meaning before reading the spread.

CD6 T14 **Scaffolding:**
Listen and Read

Have students listen to the Audio CD as they read the selection to themselves. Then have student pairs alternate reading aloud paragraphs from the selection.

Teaching Resources

- *Resources*, Summaries, pp. 167–168
- Audio CD 6, track 14

READING 3 LITERATURE NOVEL

Set a purpose for reading What would it be like to travel into the future? Read to find out how Sam, Fred, and Joe travel to the year 2095. How did they get there? How will they get back home?

from

THE TIME WARP TRIO: 2095

Jon Scieszka

 TESOL Standards

Goal 1, Standard 1—To use English to communicate in social settings: Students will use English to participate in social interactions.
Descriptors—Sharing and requesting information; Expressing needs, feelings, and ideas.

Goal 2, Standard 1—To use English to achieve academically in all content areas: Students will use English to interact in the classroom.
Descriptors—Asking and answering questions; Requesting information and assistance.

Goal 2, Standard 2—To use English to achieve academically in all content areas: Students will use English to obtain, process, construct, and provide subject matter information in spoken and written form.
Descriptors—Selecting, connecting, and explaining information; Analyzing, synthesizing, and inferring from information.

Sam, Fred, and Joe are three friends. They are visiting the American Museum of Natural History in New York City in the year 1995. Joe, the narrator, has The Book, a time-travel guide given to him by his uncle, who is also named Joe. Without meaning to, Joe does something that transports him and his two friends into the year 2095. As this excerpt begins, the trio of friends is running away from a security robot called a Sellbot.

We jumped over the twitching Sellbot and ran down a flight of stairs. We had almost made it to the lobby, when the sound of a buzzer filled the halls.

The museum doors opened. A tidal wave of people came flooding in, and we were right in its path.

We dodged the first bunch of teenagers. They had corkscrew, spike, and Mohawk hair in every color you can think of. But the most amazing thing was that no one was touching the ground.

"They're flying. People in the future have figured out how to fly," said Sam.

A solid river of people flowed past us. An old man in an aluminum suit. A woman with leopard-patterned skin. A class in shiny school uniforms. Everyone was floating about a foot above the floor.

"How do they do that?" I said.

"Look closely," said Sam. "Everyone has a small disk with a green triangle and a red square."

"Hey, you're right," I said.

"I'm always right," said Sam. "That is obviously the antigravity disk that kid was talking about. Now let's get out of here before another Sellbot tracks us down."

Fred grabbed my belt. Sam grabbed Fred's belt. And we fought our way outside. We stopped at the statue of Teddy Roosevelt sitting on his horse looking out over Central Park. We stood and looked out with him.

"Wow," said Fred. "I see it but I don't believe it."

The sidewalk was full of floating people of every shape and color. There were people with green skin, blue skin, purple skin, orange, striped, plaid, dotted, and you-name-it skin. The street was packed three high and three deep with floating bullet-shaped things that must have been antigravity cars. And all around the trees of Central Park, towering buildings spread up and out like gigantic mechanical trees taller than the clouds.

---

flight of stairs, group of steps from one floor to the next
tidal wave of people, large crowd of people
antigravity disk, small item that fights the force of gravity, allowing one to float above the ground
tracks us down, finds us
you-name-it skin, every kind of skin

✔ **LITERARY CHECK**

*What details confirm that this is a **science fiction** selection?*

BEFORE YOU GO ON

1. What do the people of the future look like?

2. What is the most amazing thing about people in the future?

💡 **On Your Own**
Imagine that you could travel to any time period. Which one would you choose?

367

Study Skills: Dictionary

Ask students to use the dictionary to define what an idiom is and to pick out the examples of idioms in the text. Ask pairs of students to come up with their own examples of idioms and share them with the class.

✔ **LITERARY CHECK**

Have students answer the question in the Literary Check box. **Answer:** Details in the story that confirm this is a science fiction selection are people flying and floating in the air, and antigravity disks.

STEP 3: Monitor Progress

Ask students to check what they have understood in the reading. If you are using the Audio CD, pause the recording.

Before You Go On

Remind students that these questions will help them monitor their progress. Put students in pairs to answer the questions. Encourage them to share their answers with the class.

ANSWERS

1. They come in every shape and color.
2. They don't touch the ground.

On Your Own Ask students to take out a separate sheet of paper and write an answer to the On Your Own question. Encourage volunteers to share their responses. Then collect responses to monitor student comprehension, writing skills, and fluency.

Differentiated Instruction

Beginning	As students read or listen to the story, have them identify the character seen in the illustration on page 371. (Uncle Joe)
Early Intermediate	After they finish the story, have students tell the class in their own words what they enjoyed most about the story.
Intermediate	Have students look at the illustrations on pages 366 and 368 and describe the characters.
Standard English Learners	Have students write a brief story involving time travel. Suggest that the setting of their story be their neighborhood. Tell them to include details about what will be the same and what will change. Have them share their stories with the class.

Preteaching Highlighted Words

Write the highlighted vocabulary words on pages 368–369 on the board and ask volunteers to read the definitions in the glosses at the bottom of the pages. Make sure students understand the difference between the idioms and those words which represent imaginary objects in the future. Model using each "real" word or expression in an original sentence and then ask students to do the same.

Across the Curriculum: Math

Joe says he and his friends were transported to a room that must have been five miles above New York City in five seconds. Ask students how many miles per second the friends traveled (one mile per second). Then ask students to research how many feet there are in a mile (5,280 feet). Today's fastest elevators travel about 2,000 feet in a *minute*. Ask students to roughly compare the two speeds. (Today it takes 60 times longer to go less than half the distance that Joe and his friends did!)

Layers and layers of antigravity cars and lines of people snaked around a hundred stories above us. New York was bigger, busier, and noisier than ever. . . .

Now wearing antigravity disks, the boys fly through the streets of New York, still chased by the Sellbot and three futuristic girls who look strangely familiar. Joe's uncle has appeared out of nowhere to help. The girls catch up, and Joe is surprised to see that one of the girls looks very much like his sister.

"Come on," said the girl who looked like my sister. "Follow us."

Sam looked at Fred. Fred looked at me. I looked at Uncle Joe.

"Do we have any choice?" I asked.

We took off and followed the girls around the buildings, over crowds of crazily colored people, past streamlined pods and more talking, blinking, singing 3-D ads, until I had no idea where we were.

We finally stopped in front of a building too tall to believe.

"Here's my house," said the lead girl.

Fred, Sam, and I looked up and up and up at the building that disappeared in the clouds.

The girl led us through a triangle door that opened at her voice. She put her hand over a blinking red handprint on the wall. And in five seconds we were all transported to a room that must have been five miles above New York City.

The girls flopped down on cushions. "This is my room," said the girl who looked like my sister.

We stood nervously in one corner.

"So you're not killer time cops?" I said.

---

took off, left quickly
pods, long vehicles
lead girl, girl at the front of the others
killer time cops, secret police who catch time travelers

368

The three girls looked at me like I was crazy.

"Of course not," said one.

"Whatever gave you that idea?" said another.

Then we all started asking questions.

"Who are you guys?"

"How did you know we'd be at the museum?"

"Do you have anything to eat?"

The girls laughed. The one who led us there pushed a green dot on a small table. A bowl of something looking like dried green dog food appeared with a pile of liquid filled plastic balls.

"Here's some Vitagorp and Unicola," said the girl who looked like my sister. "Now let me try to explain things from the beginning."

We copied the girls and sucked on the plastic ball things the same way they did. Fred ate a handful of the green dog food.

"I'm Joanie. This is Samantha. That's Frieda."

"But everybody calls me Freddi," said the girl with the baseball hat.

"And we have these names," Joanie continued, "because we were named after our great-grandfathers—Joe, Sam, and Fred."

"Or in other words—you," said Samantha.

Everything suddenly made sense. That's why they looked so much like us.

"Of course," said Uncle Joe, dusting off his top hat. "Your great-grandkids have to make sure you get back to 1995. Otherwise you won't have kids. Then your kids won't have kids. Then your kids' kids won't have—"

"Us," said Samantha. "Your great-grandkids. And we knew you would be at the museum because you wrote us a note." Samantha handed me a yellowed sheet of paper that had been sealed in plastic. It was our Museum Worksheet from 1995. On the back was a note in my handwriting that said:

Girls,
Meet us under Teddy Roosevelt's statue at the Museum of Natural History, September 28, 2095.
Sincerely,
Joe, Sam, Fred

"How did you get our worksheet from 1995?" asked Sam.

"I got it from my mom," said Joanie. "And she got it from her mom."

"But we didn't write that," I said.

"You will," said Samantha, "if we can get you back to 1995."

Vitagorp and Unicola, imaginary food and drink of the future
top hat, tall black hat

BEFORE YOU GO ON

1 Who are the three girls?

2 How do the girls know the boys will be at the museum?

On Your Own
Imagine that you are Joe. How do you feel at this point in the story?

369

Study Skills: Map

Have students look at a map of New York City to get a sense of where the action of the story takes place. Have them find the location of the American Museum of Natural History (81st Street and Central Park West) and Central Park. Point out that the museum is across the street from Central Park, which Joe mentions when the boys exit the museum. If possible, look at a satellite map of the area online so students can see the museum and the towering buildings that surround the park today.

STEP 5: Monitor Progress

Ask students to check what they have understood in the reading. If you are using the Audio CD, pause the recording.

Before You Go On

Remind students that these questions will help them monitor their progress. Put students in pairs to answer the questions. Encourage them to share their answers with the class.

ANSWERS

1. The three girls are Joanie, Samantha, and Frieda (Freddi). They are Joe, Sam, and Fred's great-grandkids.
2. A museum worksheet that the boys will fill out has been passed down to them.

On Your Own Have students write their answers on a separate sheet of paper, then collect them to monitor their comprehension, writing skills, and fluency.

Read

STEP 6: Teach

Preteaching Highlighted Words

Write the highlighted vocabulary words on pages 370–371 on the board and ask volunteers to read the definitions in the gloss at the bottom of the pages. Make sure students understand the difference between the idioms and expressions that are used in conversational English and those words which represent imaginary objects from the future that the author has invented. Model using each "real" word or expression in an original sentence and then ask students to do the same.

Model the
READING STRATEGY

Skim

SAY: *What predictions that you made while skimming the* Time Warp Trio 2095 *turned out to be true on this page? Did any turn out to be not true?* Remind students that skimming a text allows you to predict several things, including the genre of the text, the setting, and some aspects of the plot.

"Saved by our own great-grandkids with a note we haven't written yet?" said Sam. "I told you something like this was going to happen. Now we're probably going to blow up."

"Wow," said Fred, eating more Vitagorp. "Our own great-grandkids. So what team is that on your hat? I've never seen that logo."

"That's the Yankees," said Freddi. "They changed it when Grandma was pitching."

"Your grandma? Fred's daughter?" I said. "A pitcher for the Yankees?"

"Not just a pitcher. She was a great pitcher," said Freddi. "2.79 lifetime ERA, 275 wins, 3 no-hitters, and the Cy Young award in '37."

"Forget your granny's stats," said Sam. "We could be genius inventors back in 1995 if we could reconstruct these levitation devices."

"What did he just say?" asked Freddi.

"He wants to know how the antigravity disks work," said Samantha. "A truly amazing discovery. More surprising than Charles Goodyear's accidental discovery of vulcanized rubber. More revolutionary than Alexander Graham Bell's first telephone. But all I can tell you is that the antigravity power comes from the chemical BHT. And it was discovered in a breakfast accident."

"What's a breakfast accident?" said Sam. "A head-on collision with a bowl of cornflakes? And who found out BHT could make things fly?"

"You did," said Samantha. "That's why we can't tell you more. You know the Time Warp Info-Speed Limit posted in *The Book*. Anyone traveling through time with too much information from another time blows up."

Sam's eyes nearly bugged out of his head. "I knew it. Don't tell me another word."

"Hey, wait a minute," I said. "Where did you say that info-speed limit was?"

Samantha looked at me like I was an insect.

"In *The Book*, of course."

"How do you know about *The Book*?"

"I got it for my birthday last year," said Joanie.

---

blow up, explode
logo, brand name or label
granny's stats, Grandma's *statistics*—facts about how well Grandma played
levitation devices, machines that let you float off the ground
head-on collision, violent crash
bugged out, popped out

370

"And since then we've been all over time," said Freddi. "We've met cavewomen, Ann the Pirate, Calamity Jane...."

"And don't forget Cleopatra and the underground cities of Venus," said Samantha.

"But if you have *The Book*, that means we're saved," said Sam.

Samantha gave Sam her look. "If you remember the Time Warpers' Tips, you know nothing can be in two places at once. Of course our *Book* disappeared as soon as your *Book* appeared."

"So now we have to help you get *The Book* back to the past," said Freddi, "so we can have it in the future."

"Of course," said Sam.

"We knew that," said Fred.

"Uh, right . . ." I said, trying to talk my way out of this mess. "We knew that would happen, but we uh . . ." I looked around at Sam, Fred, Samantha, Freddi, and Joanie. Then I spotted Uncle Joe. "We thought we could really learn some tricks about finding *The Book* from Uncle Joe!"

Uncle Joe looked up from something he was fiddling with in his lap. "*The Book*? Oh, I never could get it to work the way your mother did. That's why I gave it to you for your birthday."

"Oh, great," said Sam. "We're *doomed*."

"But that's also why I put this together." Uncle Joe held up the thing he had been fiddling with in his lap. It was an old-fashioned pocket watch. "My Time Warp Watch."

"We're saved!" yelled Sam.

Calamity Jane, an American frontier woman from the 1800s famous for her unconventional behavior and courage
Cleopatra, an ancient Egyptian queen
spotted, saw
fiddling with, playing with
doomed, in a hopeless situation

ABOUT THE **AUTHOR**

Jon Scieszka has written many books for kids. Other books in the Time Warp Trio series include *The Good, the Bad, and the Goofy; Knights of the Kitchen Table; The Not-So-Jolly Roger;* and *Your Mother Was a Neanderthal.*

BEFORE YOU GO ON

1 Which character discovers the antigravity disk but doesn't know it?

2 What will happen to the boys if they learn too much information while visiting the future?

On Your Own
Do you think that any of the inventions described in this selection will really exist in the future? Explain.

371

Study Skills: Biographical Dictionary

Have students use a biographical dictionary to find out more information about Calamity Jane and Cleopatra.

STEP 7: Monitor Progress

Ask students to check what they have understood in the reading.

Before You Go On

Preview these questions with students before they read the page so they know what to look for. When it comes time to answer the questions, remind them that they can go back to the text to find the answer if necessary.

Put students into pairs. Have them choose one of the questions and answer it together. Encourage them to share their answers with another pair.

ANSWERS

1. Sam discovers the antigravity disk but doesn't know it.
2. If they learn too much information while visiting the future, the boys will blow up.

On Your Own Remind students that there is no right answer to this question. Have students write their answers on a separate sheet of paper. Encourage volunteers to share their responses with the class. Then collect student responses to monitor their comprehension, writing skills, and fluency.

Review the Purpose for Reading

Elicit responses to the Set a Purpose for Reading questions at the beginning of this reading. Remind students to relate their responses to the Big Question.

Teach & Apply

Speaking Tip

Encourage students to use gestures and intonation to emphasize a character's emotions. **SAY:** *What gestures and intonations might Joe use to indicate he thinks it's strange that Joanie looks so much like his sister?*

 Reader's Theater

Put students into pairs. Ask them to read the dialogue quietly to themselves. Have partners decide who will play the roles of Joe and Joanie.

After students have rehearsed, ask for volunteers to perform in front of the class.

STEP 2: Practice

Comprehension

Have groups of students write their responses to the questions.

ANSWERS

1. The boys meet the girls under Teddy Roosevelt's statue.
2. Antigravity power comes from the small disk with a green triangle and a red square.
3. The girls have visited cavewomen, Ann the Pirate, Calamity Jane, and Cleopatra.
4. Sellbots are security robots.
5. Answers may vary, but will probably include "funny."
6. Answers will vary, but will probably include "positive."
7. Answers will vary.
8. Answers will vary.

Teaching Resources

- *Workbook*, p. 179
- CD-ROM/e-book, Reader's Theater, Comprehension, Response to Literature

---

READER'S THEATER

Speaking TIP

Speak clearly and slowly. Use gestures to emphasize your character's emotions.

Act out the following scene between Joe and Joanie.

Joe: You look so much like my sister. This is very strange, Joanie.

Joanie: Well, I was named after my great-grandfather Joe. Samantha, Frieda, and I were named after our great-grandfathers.

Joe: Well, that explains why you look like you are part of my family. You are! I am your great-grandfather!

Joanie: This means that all three of you—Sam, Fred, and you, Joe—must get back to your own time, 1995.

Joe: Why does that matter so much?

Joanie: If you don't get back, you won't be able to have kids when you grow up. Then your kids won't have kids, and . . .

Joe: I understand now! If we don't get back, you, Samantha, and Frieda won't be born. If we don't get back, we will change the future.

Joanie: We must find a way to get all of you back to 1995—and fast!

COMPREHENSION Workbook Page 179

Right There

1. Under what statue do the boys meet the girls at the American Museum of Natural History?
2. Where does the antigravity power come from?

Think and Search

3. Who are some of the people the girls have visited?
4. What are the Sellbots?

Author and You

5. Describe the tone of this story. For example, is it serious or funny?
6. Do you think the author's view of the future is positive or negative? Expain.

TESOL Standards

Goal 3, Standard 1—To use English in socially and culturally appropriate ways: Students will use the appropriate language variety, register, and genre according to audience, purpose, and setting.
Descriptors—Using the appropriate degree of formality with different audiences and settings; Determining when it is appropriate to use a language other than English; Determining appropriate topics for interaction.

Goal 3, Standard 2—To use English in socially and culturally appropriate ways: Students will use nonverbal communication appropriate to audience, purpose, and setting.
Descriptors—Interpreting and responding appropriately to nonverbal cues and body language; Using acceptable tone, volume, stress, and intonation, in various social settings; Recognizing and adjusting behavior in response to nonverbal cues.

7. What specific strategies would you use to write a believable story about the future? How would you make your story realistic and futuristic at the same time?

8. Imagine that you could travel in time. Would you go ahead to the future or back to the past? Why?

DISCUSSION

Discuss in pairs or small groups.

1. Why do the girls—Frieda, Joanie, and Samantha—help the boys?

2. How is the year 2095 different from the year 1995? How is it similar?

3. Describe the skin of people in the future. Why do you think the author included this detail in the novel?

Q What is your vision of life in the future? Is Jon Scieszka's vision of the future realistic and believable? Why or why not?

Listening TIP

When your classmates speak, listen for supporting details and reasons. Ask yourself, "Did the speaker explain why these ideas are important?"

RESPONSE TO LITERATURE

Workbook Page 179

The Book has directions for time travel. But nothing can be in two places at the same time. As a result, the girls' copy of *The Book* disappeared as soon as the boys' copy of *The Book* appeared. Help the boys get back to 1995. Write directions for time travel. When you have finished writing, share your instructions with a classmate. Talk about the steps in the process.

373

STEP 3: Extend

Listening Tip

Remind students to listen for the details and reasons a speaker gives to support the point he or she is trying to make, and to ask themselves whether the speaker explained why those details were important.

(CRI) Discussion

Model a discussion starter for each question. For example, for the first one, **SAY:** *For the first question, why do you think the girls helped the three boys? What if they had not been the boys' great-granddaughters? Would they have even been able to help the boys?*

Q **What is your vision of life in the future?** **SAY:** *Does each person have a different vision about life in the future? Why or why not? What kinds of things can influence your vision of the future?* Make sure students support their answers with reasons.

STEP 4: Assess

Response to Literature

Have students write directions for the boys that will allow them to travel back in time to 1995. Remind them that the boys don't have *The Book* because it can only be in one place at a time. Then invite students to share their directions with the class.

Differentiated Instruction

Beginning	As students prepare for the Reader's Theater, remind them to ask for help pronouncing the words when necessary.
Early Intermediate	Remind students to jot down notes as they participate in the Discussion. Tell them that this will help them remember each speaker's ideas.
Intermediate	Have students read aloud their instructions for time travel to the class.
Greater Challenge	Ask students if they could travel in time, to what time period would they travel and why. Ask them what they would do once they got there.

STEP 1: Introduce

Tell students that proper punctuation helps readers understand what they're expressing. Ask students to name some punctuation marks that they already know, e.g. period, comma. Ask them to describe the function of each punctuation mark if possible.

STEP 2: Teach

Grammar and Writing

Using Punctuation Explain the type of sentence each end mark is used for. Then read the sentences in the student book aloud, demonstrating how end marks influence how we read or say something. Explain that commas are used to separate words or phrases in a sentence, and indicate that the reader or speaker should pause briefly.

STEP 3: Practice

Have pairs of students complete the practice activity.

ANSWERS

1. The museum doors opened.
2. "I'm always right," said Sam.
3. Do we have any choice?
4. That's amazing!

Teaching Resources

- *Workbook*, pp. 180–181
- CD-ROM/e-book, Grammar, Writing
- *Transparencies*, Writing Model 48
- *Transparencies*, *Resources*, Graphic Organizer 2
- *Assessment*, Reading 3 Test, pp. 123–126

Grammar and Writing

GRAMMAR, USAGE, AND MECHANICS

Using Punctuation

Good writers use proper punctuation. It's important to punctuate your writing correctly so that readers understand what you want to say.

End marks are punctuation marks that come at the end of sentences. There are three kinds of end marks: periods, question marks, and exclamation points.

Use a period to end a statement or to end an imperative.

The girls flopped down on cushions.	Look closely.

Use a question mark to end a question.

What do you know about wormholes, or space-time warps?

Use an exclamation point to end a sentence that expresses strong feeling.

We're saved!

▲ This computer art shows how a wormhole might look.

A comma separates, or sets off, parts of a sentence, for instance, certain words or phrases. Use commas to separate nouns or phrases in a series, to separate introductory words and phrases, and to set off a speaker's quoted words in a sentence.

I looked around at Sam, Fred, Samantha, Freddi, and Joanie. Hey, wait a minute. "Of course not," said one.

Practice **Workbook Page 180**

Copy the sentences below into your notebook. Add proper punctuation to each. Then compare your sentences with a partner's.

1. The museum doors opened
2. "I'm always right" said Sam
3. Do we have any choice
4. That's amazing

374

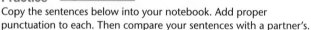

🌐 TESOL Standards

Goal 1, Standard 2—To use English to communicate in social settings: Students will interact in, through, and with spoken and written English for personal expression and enjoyment.
Descriptors—Describing, reading about, or participating in a favorite activity.

Goal 3, Standard 1—To use English in socially and culturally appropriate ways: Students will use the appropriate language variety, register, and genre according to audience, purpose, and setting.
Descriptors—Responding to and using slang appropriately; Responding to and using idioms appropriately.

Goal 3, Standard 3—To use English in socially and culturally appropriate ways: Students will use appropriate learning strategies to extend their sociolinguistic and sociocultural competence.
Descriptors—Experimenting with variations of language in social and academic settings.

WRITING A RESEARCH REPORT

Include Quotations and Citations

An effective research report should include what other people have said or researched about your topic. On this page, you'll practice using quotations to support an idea or explain a topic in a research report. Use a graphic organizer like the one at the right to help you.

Whenever you copy material word for word from another person's writing or speech, you must acknowledge the person by placing his or her words within quotation marks. After the quotation, you must also provide a citation, that is, information about the source of the quote. (See pages 455–456 for how to create citations for various sources.)

Here is a model of a paragraph with a quotation and a citation. The writer uses a quotation to support his main idea.

Andrew C. Dubin

Wormholes and Black Holes

Time travel is a popular topic in science fiction. Authors sometimes have their characters use wormholes as a way to travel through time. Wormholes are two black holes that are connected. Researchers say that wormholes "are more science fiction than they are science fact" (NASA). Wormholes are popular in science fiction, but there is no proof that they even exist. Researchers can prove that black holes exist, though. A black hole is the last stage in the life of a star. The force of gravity in black holes is very strong. Black holes and wormholes are related, but black holes are science fact, and wormholes are science fiction.

Works Consulted List

"Black Holes." *NASA Goddard Space Flight Center.* September 2006.
28 March 2009 <http://imagine.gsfc.nasa.gov/docs/science/know_12/black_holes.html>.

Practice **Workbook** Page 181

Write a paragraph about time travel or science fiction. List your ideas in a main idea/details web like the one above. Be sure to use quotations, citations, and punctuation correctly.

Writing Checklist

SENTENCE FLUENCY:
- ☑ I introduced my quotations and made sure that they flowed smoothly within my paragraph.

CONVENTIONS:
- ☑ I punctuated my citations correctly.

375

STEP 1: Introduce

Tell students that citing other people's research can make their report more compelling and convincing, but remind them that other people's words must be put into quotation marks.

STEP 2: Teach

Writing a Research Report

Include Quotations and Citations On the board, write examples of material that should be put in quotation marks. Demonstrate where the quotation marks and citations should go.

Model Writing Skill Show the model paragraph from the student book on an overhead projector. Ask students to identify the quote and citation.

Read the practice exercise aloud. Ask students to copy and fill in the main idea/details web in their notebooks before they begin writing.

STEP 3: Assess

Have students evaluate their work using the Writing Checklist.

Writing Checklist Note

Sentence fluency: Check that students introduced quotations and made sure they flowed smoothly within their paragraph.

Conventions: Check that students punctuated their citations correctly.

Accelerate Language Development

The Importance of Punctuation

Point out that in speaking, tone of voice, pausing, and stress or emphasis can all determine the meaning of a sentence. In writing, punctuation marks take over this role, and the way they are used can determine the meaning of a sentence. Write the following words on the board without any punctuation marks: *You have fun* Ask volunteers to add punctuation. Here are the two possible versions: *You have fun!* versus *You have fun?*

STEP 1: Introduce

Objectives

Read the list of objectives in the What You Will Learn section, encouraging students to join in. Tell students that this reading will be about DNA and DNA fingerprinting. Have pairs of students work together to restate the list of things they will learn.

The Big Question

Read aloud the Big Question. **SAY:** *What are some physical traits that children inherit from their parents?*

Build Background

Read aloud the Build Background section from the student text. Be sure students understand the meaning of *genes*.

STEP 2: Teach

Understanding the Genre:
Informational Text

Tell students that an informational text is a nonfiction text. It presents facts and other information about real things.

Teaching Resources

- CD-ROM/e-book, Key Words
- Audio CD 6, tracks 15–16
- *Workbook*, p. 182

What You Will Learn

Reading
- Vocabulary building: *Context, dictionary skills, word study*
- Reading strategy: *Make generalizations*
- Text type: *Informational text (science)*

Grammar, Usage, and Mechanics
Using quotation marks

Writing
Include paraphrases and citations

THE BIG QUESTION

What is your vision of life in the future? Do you ever imagine what your great-grandkids will look and be like? Think about Sam, Fred, and Joe from the last reading. They figured out that the futuristic girls who looked "strangely familiar" were their great-grandkids because the girls looked like them. The girls had inherited some of their great-grandparents' genetic traits. Certain physical traits, such as eye and hair color, straight or curly hair, and the shape of a person's face, are passed on from one generation to the next.

What physical or character traits do you want to pass on to future generations? Why do you think that these traits would be helpful to people in the future? Discuss with a partner.

BUILD BACKGROUND

"Genetic Fingerprints" is a science article that explains facts about DNA—the chemical instructions that tell a plant or animal what it needs to grow and work.

People have long wondered how certain traits are passed down from person to person, from animal to animal, and from plant to plant. Why do children look like their parents? Why are some horses faster than others?

In 1865, a monk named Gregor Mendel discovered that traits are passed down through tiny bits of material he called "genes." He studied pea plants and learned that certain traits were passed down from one plant to the next. It wasn't until 1953, however, that two scientists, James Watson and Francis Crick, figured out the structure of DNA and linked it to how traits are passed down. Some people have called this the biggest scientific discovery of all time.

 Gregor Mendel discovered the laws of heredity by studying pea plants.

376

TESOL Standards

Goal 1, Standard 2—To use English to communicate in social settings: Students will interact in, through, and with spoken and written English for personal expression and enjoyment.
Descriptors—Sharing social and cultural traditions and values; Participating in popular culture.

Goal 3, Standard 1—To use English in socially and culturally appropriate ways: Students will use the appropriate language variety, register, and genre according to audience, purpose, and setting.
Descriptors—Responding to and using slang appropriately; Responding to and using idioms appropriately.

Learn Key Words

Read the sentences. Use the context to figure out the meaning of the red words. Use a dictionary to check your answers. Then write each word and its meaning in your notebook.

1. **Cells** are the smallest living things. Scientists use microscopes to study cells.

2. The **defendant** was charged with a crime. The jury had to decide whether he was guilty or not guilty.

3. The **forensic** evidence was used in court. Fingerprints were one of many pieces of evidence used.

4. **Genes** carry traits, such as eye and hair color, that are passed down from one generation to the next.

5. People **inherit** qualities from both parents. A girl may be tall like her mother and have curly hair like her father.

6. Fingerprints have **whorls** that look like circles and swirls. Each person has a different pattern of whorls.

Practice

Workbook Page 182

Write the sentences in your notebook. Complete each sentence using the red word. Then take turns reading the sentences aloud with a partner.

1. The researcher was studying . . . (**cells**)

2. A lawyer was hired to help . . . (**defendant**)

3. At the trial, different kinds of . . . (**forensic**)

4. The baby developed an illness because . . . (**genes**)

5. Some children . . . (**inherit**)

6. The police matched one set of fingerprints to the . . . (**whorls**)

Case # 05-01234

◀ A fingerprint whorl comparison

Latent Print
Inside of bathroom window

John Smith
Finger #7

377

CD6 T15–T16

 Vocabulary

Learn Key Words Play the CD. Have students listen and repeat. If you are not using the CD, read the key words aloud.

- **cells:** the smallest living things
- **defendant:** the person in a court of law who has been accused of doing something illegal
- **forensic:** ways to find out about a crime
- **genes:** parts of a cell in a living thing that control how it develops
- **inherit:** to get a quality, way of acting, physical feature, and so on from one of your parents
- **whorls:** shapes that curl or swirl

STEP 3: Practice

Have students complete the practice activity.
SAY: *As you read each sentence, think about the key word that makes the most sense in each sentence.*

ANSWERS
Possible responses include:
1. The researcher was studying human cells.
2. A lawyer was hired to help the defendant get a fair trial.
3. At the trial, different kinds of forensic evidence were presented.
4. The baby developed an illness because of some inherited genes.
5. Some children inherit their mother's eye color.
6. The police matched one set of fingerprints to the whorls on another.

Differentiated Instruction

Beginning	Use each vocabulary word in a new sentence for students. Have them clap their hands when they hear the vocabulary word.
Early Intermediate	Remind students that *context clues* can help them determine the meaning of an unknown word. Context clues are the words that come before or after an unknown word or phrase.
Intermediate	Have students work in pairs to write each key word in an original sentence. Have them share one or two sentences with the group.
Standard English Learners	Encourage students to make a family tree of their immediate family. Ask them to write one sentence about each family member that compares similar traits.

Teach

CD6 T17–T18

 Vocabulary

Learn Academic Words Play the CD. Have students listen and repeat. If you are not using the CD, read the Academic Words aloud.
SAY: *Look at the academic words chart. The definition is on the left. On the right, each word is used in a sentence. Work with a partner to write an additional sentence for each academic word. Write each word, its definition, and the sentence in your notebook.*

STEP 2: Practice

Write the first question on the board. Then write this answer on the board: Six people <u>in my generation</u> are my four brothers and two cousins. Be sure to underline the words as shown so students clearly see the connection.
SAY: *When you are asked a question, try to include words from the question in your answer.*

ANSWERS

Answers will vary. Make sure students include the academic words in their answers.

Teaching Resources

- Audio CD 6, tracks 17–18
- *Workbook,* pp. 183–185
- CD-ROM/e-book, Academic Words, Word Study

Learn Academic Words

Study the **red** words and their meanings. You will find these words useful when talking and writing about informational texts. Write each word and its meaning in your notebook. After you read "Genetic Fingerprints," try to use these words to respond to the text.

Academic Words
- generation
- legislation
- medical
- policy
- procedure

generation = all the people who are about the same age, especially in a family	My grandfather's **generation** believed in the value of hard work.
legislation = a law or set of laws	New **legislation** has been passed about DNA. These laws allow DNA evidence to be used in court.
medical = relating to medicine and the treatment of disease or injury	**Medical** people work to prevent some diseases and treat other ones.
policy = a way of doing things that has been officially agreed upon and chosen by a political party or an organization	The lab has a firm **policy** about DNA testing. The rules can be found in the lab's guidebook.
procedure = the correct or normal way of doing something	Lawyers follow a careful **procedure** during a trial.

Practice Workbook Page 183

Work with a partner to answer the questions. Try to include the **red** word in your answer. Write the sentences in your notebook.

1. Who is in your **generation**? Name six people.
2. What type of **legislation** do you think is important to young people?
3. What job in the **medical** field would you like to have?
4. What **policy** does your school have to keep students and teachers safe?
5. What **procedure** do you follow when you begin to write a story? What things do you do first?

▲ Three generations of a family

378

 TESOL Standards

Goal 1, Standard 3—To use English to communicate in social settings: Students will use learning strategies to extend their communicative competence.
Descriptors—Testing hypotheses about language.

Goal 2, Standard 2— To use English to achieve academically in all content areas: Students will use English to obtain, process, construct, and provide subject matter information in spoken and written form.
Descriptors—Hypothesizing and predicting; Formulating and asking questions.

Goal 2, Standard 3—To use English to achieve academically in all content areas: Students will use appropriate learning strategies to construct and apply academic knowledge.
Descriptors—Applying basic reading comprehension skills such as skimming, scanning, previewing, and reviewing text.

Word Study: Multiple-Meaning Words

You have learned that many English words have multiple meanings. To figure out which meaning fits, look at the context in which you found the word. Are there any clues in the words and sentences surrounding the word? See which meaning makes most sense in the sentence. Also, identify the word's part of speech. It may be an important clue. If necessary, look up the word in a dictionary.

Word and Meaning	Part of Speech	Sentence
matches: two or more things or people that go well together	Verb	The tie **matches** the shirt.
matches: pieces of wood or cardboard with a flammable tip used to start a fire	Noun	The campers used **matches** to start the campfire.
matches: games or contests	Noun	We played two tennis **matches**.

▲ A book of matches

Practice

Work with a partner to explore the different meanings of these words: *tissue, tests, code, suspect, serve,* and *commit*. Start by looking up each word in a dictionary. Then use each word in two sentences to show two of the word's meanings. Write the sentences in your notebook.

READING STRATEGY | MAKE GENERALIZATIONS

Making generalizations helps you apply what you read to other situations. A generalization is a statement or rule that applies to most examples and can be supported by facts. Suppose you read this sentence: *Baby polar bears, baby elephants, and baby giraffes look like their mothers, only smaller.* The following would be a good generalization:

Generalization: <u>Many</u> baby animals look like their parents.
Be careful not to make a false generalization—one that cannot be supported by facts. Why is the following generalization false?

False Generalization: <u>All</u> baby animals look like their parents.

Make generalizations when you read "Genetic Fingerprints." Combine facts from the text with what you already know to make a generalization. Be sure that you can support the generalization with facts.

379

Word Study

Multiple-Meaning Words Read aloud the text on the student book page and go over the examples in the chart. **SAY:** *There are many words with more than one meaning in English. Noticing whether the word is used as a noun or a verb can help you figure out the correct meaning.*

STEP 2: Practice

Have students work with a partner to complete the practice activity. Monitor their progress, checking that they have fully understood the meaning of each word.

ANSWERS
Answers will vary.

STEP 3: Teach

Reading Strategy

Make Generalizations Help students understand that making a generalization is drawing a conclusion based on what you know. Caution them against making false generalizations, or drawing conclusions that are not based on facts.

Linguistic Note

Homographs

Words that are spelled the same but pronounced differently are called homographs, as opposed to homophones, which are spelled differently but pronounced the same. Point out that there are quite a few examples: The <u>dove</u> <u>dove</u> into the bushes. Demonstrate the difference between the noun *dove* /dʌv/ and the verb *dove* /doʊv/. Write example sentences on the board. Ask volunteers to circle the homographs. Examples: *The farmers <u>produce</u> <u>produce</u>. It was time to <u>present</u> the <u>present</u>.*

Read

Reading Summary

This reading is about the discovery and uses of DNA fingerprinting.

 The Big Question

Remind students that the Big Question is "What is your vision of life in the future?" **SAY:** *How might scientists' knowledge of DNA affect your life in the future?*

STEP 2: Teach

Set a Purpose for Reading

Tell students to copy the purpose for reading into their notebooks and to keep it in mind as they read. Explain that they will have to present details that support their answers to the questions and to explain how the reading relates to the Big Question.

Preteaching Highlighted Words

In pairs, have students read aloud the highlighted word and its definition. Answer any questions students have about the use of this word or its meaning before reading the spread.

CD6 T19  **Scaffolding:**
Listen and Read

Have students listen to the Audio CD as they read the selection to themselves. Then have student pairs alternate reading aloud paragraphs from the selection.

Teaching Resources

- *Resources*, Summaries, pp. 169–170
- Audio CD 6, track 19
- *Reader's Companion Workbook*, pp. 137–141

Set a purpose for reading What surprising discoveries have been made about DNA and DNA fingerprinting? How might these discoveries affect the future? Read the article to find out.

Genetic Fingerprints

Your fingerprints are unlike anyone else's. They have a pattern of ridges and whorls that is unique to you. The same is true of your DNA "fingerprints." You can't see them with the naked eye, but they have a pattern that is unique to you. Your DNA fingerprint exists in every cell of your body, and it is yours and yours alone.

The Wonders of DNA

Within the cells of your body, there is a chemical set of instructions, called DNA (deoxyribonucleic acid). These instructions tell a plant's or animal's body what it needs to grow and work.

You inherit about 80,000 genes from your parents. All 80,000 genes are present in each individual cell of your body. These genes contain the instructions that make you human.

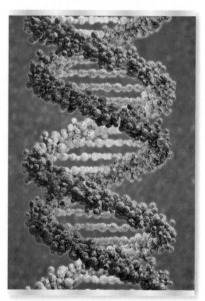

▲ A DNA double helix

380

 TESOL Standards

Goal 2, Standard 2— To use English to achieve academically in all content areas: Students will use English to obtain, process, construct, and provide subject matter information in spoken and written form.
Descriptors—Comparing and contrasting information; Retelling information; Selecting, connecting, and explaining information; Analyzing, synthesizing, and inferring from information; Understanding and producing technical vocabulary and text features according to content; Formulating and asking questions.

Goal 2, Standard 3—To use English to achieve academically in all content areas: Students will use appropriate learning strategies to construct and apply academic knowledge.
Descriptors—Focusing attention selectively; Using context to construct meaning.

Discovery of the DNA Fingerprint

In 1984, Sir Alec Jeffreys discovered how to make a DNA fingerprint. It happened by accident. He had been studying the differences in human DNA.

DNA is like a long, twisted ladder. The rungs of the ladder have a unique pattern of genes for each person. This unique arrangement of genes is what makes human beings different from one another.

Jeffreys took pieces of DNA. He marked them with a radioactive substance. Then he made images of these DNA fragments on X-ray film. When he developed the pictures, he was surprised at what he saw.

Instead of a few isolated images . . . [he] saw long strings of images arranged in patterns. Dark bands—some thick, some thin—were stacked in patterns that looked a great deal like the bar codes found on products in the supermarkets (Fridell 18).

---

fragments, small pieces of something

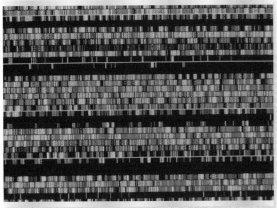

◀ This human DNA sequence is displayed as a series of colored bands.

Here in visual form was a code that could be used to identify every living thing. This DNA "fingerprint" was a picture of a person's unique genetic code. Now scientists had solid evidence that they could use to uniquely identify people through their genes. Your DNA fingerprint, Alec Jeffreys said, "does not belong to anyone on the face of the planet who ever has been or ever will be."

▲ A scientist examines a DNA sequence.

BEFORE YOU GO ON

1. Where does DNA exist?
2. What did Sir Alec Jeffreys see when he developed pictures of DNA on X-ray film?

💡 **On Your Own**
What do you find most interesting about DNA so far?

381

Preteaching Highlighted Words

In pairs, have students read aloud the highlighted words and their definitions. Answer any questions students have about the use of a word or its meaning before reading the spread.

Across the Curriculum:
Science

Sir Alec Jeffreys is not the only scientist who has made a life-changing discovery by accident. In 1928, Alexander Fleming, a Scottish researcher, returned home from vacation to discover that he had forgotten to clean some lab dishes in which he had been growing bacteria before he left. The dishes were contaminated with a fungus. He was about to disinfect them when he noticed that the fungus had stopped the bacteria from growing. That discovery led him to develop penicillin, one of the first antibiotics, or medicines that kill bacteria.

◀ A man walks out of court after his conviction is overturned because of DNA evidence.

DNA and Justice

Once DNA fingerprinting was discovered, it was used to identify people. Forensic scientists study crimes by looking at evidence. They use various scientific tests. Since the 1980s, they have used DNA fingerprints to investigate and solve crimes. They take a sample of blood, hair, or other body tissue found at the scene of a crime. This tissue contains DNA. The scientists check to see whether the DNA from a crime scene matches a sample of the suspect's DNA. This way they can figure out whether the suspect could have possibly committed a crime.

In recent years, many people have been released from prison after DNA tests proved that they were "wholly innocent." These people had not committed any crime at all.

---

investigate, look into, research
tissue, material, such as skin and muscle
committed a crime, done something wrong or illegal
innocent, not guilty

In 1992, the Innocence Project was founded. It serves defendants who could be proved innocent through DNA testing. Since that time, innocence organizations have spread throughout the United States.

Law students at the Wisconsin Innocence Project investigate about twenty to thirty criminal cases at a time. In 2001, the project was responsible for the release of a Texas prisoner, Chris Ochoa. He was serving a life sentence for a 1988 murder. DNA tests on samples found on the victim proved that Ochoa did not commit the crime. He was innocent. Chris Ochoa had spent twelve years in prison for a crime he didn't commit. He is not alone. As of 2008, more than 200 people previously convicted of serious crimes have been found innocent because of DNA testing.

DNA testing is now a very important tool in criminal investigation. It is going to be more important in the future. More forensic scientists are going to use DNA tests to help make sure the right people are punished for their crimes.

382

Other Uses of DNA Fingerprints

DNA is also being used in many other ways. For example, in India, chefs were having trouble identifying the type of rice they were cooking. Each type had to be soaked and cooked differently. So a rice producer used DNA fingerprinting to identify specific types. Now the chefs know how to cook each type correctly. Medical researchers have used DNA tests to identify and fight bacteria that cause food-related illnesses. DNA has also been used to investigate objects from the past. For instance, archaeologists have used DNA to help piece together the remains of the Dead Sea Scrolls. DNA fingerprinting has been used to identify family members who have been separated from one another because of wars or natural disasters. As DNA fingerprinting becomes increasingly popular, it will be used for many other purposes in the future.

---

bacteria, very small living things, some of which cause illness or disease

Dead Sea Scrolls, ancient texts, approximately 2,000 years old, discovered in caves near the Dead Sea

Work Cited
Fridell, Ron. *DNA Fingerprinting: The Ultimate Identity.* New York: Franklin Watts, 2001.

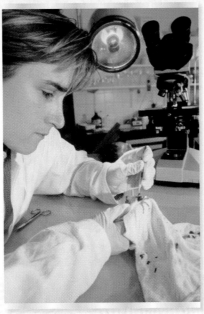
▲ A forensic scientist extracts DNA evidence from a piece of clothing.

Scientists clean fragments of the Dead Sea Scrolls. ▼

BEFORE YOU GO ON

1 What can scientists test to find DNA?

2 What group of people does the Innocence Project serve?

On Your Own
What uses would you like to see for DNA fingerprints in the future?

383

Study Skills: Atlas

Have students use an atlas to find out where India is located as well as facts about the country. Students should also use the atlas to find out where the Dead Sea is located.

STEP 5: Monitor Progress

Ask students to check what they have understood in the reading.

Before You Go On

Ask students to answer the questions and to point out where in the text they found the answers.

ANSWERS
1. Scientists can test blood, hair, and other body tissues to find DNA.
2. The Innocence Project serves defendants who could be proved innocent of crimes they've been convicted of through DNA testing.

On Your Own Have students write an answer to the On Your Own question on a separate sheet of paper. Encourage volunteers to share their responses with the class. Then collect student responses to monitor their comprehension, writing skills, and fluency.

Review the Purpose for Reading

Elicit responses to the Set a Purpose for Reading questions at the beginning of this reading. Remind students to relate their responses to the Big Question.

Teach & Apply

STEP 1: Practice

Comprehension

Ask students to complete the questions either independently, in pairs, or in a group.

ANSWERS

1. DNA is a chemical set of instructions that tell a plant or animal's body what it needs to know in order to grow and work.
2. You inherit about 80,000 genes from your parents.
3. He marked pieces of DNA with a radioactive substance, made images of the DNA fragments on X-ray film, and developed them.
4. One way DNA is being used in India is to identify different types of rice.
5. DNA proves that each person is unique because no two people's DNA fingerprints are the same.
6. Answers will vary.
7. Answers will vary.
8. Answers will vary.

Speaking Tip

Encourage students to ask their listeners if they have any questions. Tell students that answering questions can help you clarify your point.

In Your Own Words

Have students fill in the chart with main ideas and details then write a summary of that information to share with classmates.

Teaching Resources

- *Workbook*, p. 186
- CD-ROM/e-book, Comprehension, Extension
- *Reader's Companion Workbook*, pp. 142–146

Review and Practice

COMPREHENSION
Workbook Page 186

Right There

1. What is DNA?
2. About how many genes do you inherit from your parents?

Think and Search

3. What procedure did Sir Alec Jeffreys use to make a DNA fingerprint?
4. What is one way that DNA is being used in India?

Author and You

5. In what ways does DNA prove that each person is unique?
6. How do you think people reacted to Jeffreys's discovery of the DNA fingerprint?

On Your Own

7. Would you want to work for the Innocence Project? Why or why not?
8. Do you think that DNA will have a greater effect on scientists or lawyers? Explain your opinion.

▲ Each person has a unique fingerprint.

IN YOUR OWN WORDS

Summarize "Genetic Fingerprints" for a friend. Include all the main ideas and important details in your summary. Make your summary interesting so that your friend will want to read the article. Use the following chart to help you organize your ideas. Then share your summary of the article with a classmate.

Speaking TIP

Ask your friend whether he or she has any questions about your summary. Receiving feedback will help you improve.

Section	Main Idea	Important Details
The Wonders of DNA		
Discovery of DNA Fingerprints		
DNA and Justice		
Other Uses of DNA Fingerprints		

384

🌐 TESOL Standards

Goal 2, Standard 3—To use English to achieve academically in all content areas: Students will use appropriate learning strategies to construct and apply academic knowledge.
Descriptors— Applying self-monitoring and self-corrective strategies to build and expand a knowledge base; Determining and establishing the conditions that help one become an effective learner (e.g., when, where, how to study).

Goal 3, Standard 1—To use English in socially and culturally appropriate ways: Students will use the appropriate language variety, register, and genre according to audience, purpose, and setting.
Descriptors—Responding to and using humor appropriately; Using the appropriate degree of formality with different audiences and settings; Recognizing and using Standard English and vernacular dialects appropriately.

Goal 3, Standard 3—To use English in socially and culturally appropriate ways: Students will use appropriate learning strategies to extend their sociolinguistic and sociocultural competence.
Descriptors—Deciding when use of slang is appropriate.

DISCUSSION

Discuss in pairs or small groups.

1. Why was the discovery of DNA so important?

2. How has DNA changed the legal field?

Q **What is your vision of life in the future?** What are some other ways that people might use DNA in the future? Could there be some negative uses? Explain.

 Listening TIP

Listen carefully to other people's ideas so that you understand what they're saying.

READ FOR FLUENCY

When we read aloud to communicate meaning, we group words into phrases, pause or slow down to make important points, and emphasize important words. Pause for a short time when you reach a comma and for a longer time when you reach a period. Pay attention to rising and falling intonation at the end of sentences.

Work with a partner. Choose a paragraph from the reading. Discuss which words seem important for communicating meaning. Practice pronouncing difficult words. Take turns reading the paragraph aloud and give each other feedback.

EXTENSION **Workbook Page 186**

You read about Sir Alec Jeffreys's important contribution to DNA research. Many other scientists contributed to our current understanding of DNA as well. Make a timeline showing at least five people who made important discoveries about DNA and heredity. Use encyclopedias, reference books, and reliable websites. Copy the following timeline into your notebook. Use it to help you organize your ideas.

▲ Scientists James Watson and Francis Crick discovered the structure of DNA.

History of DNA Research

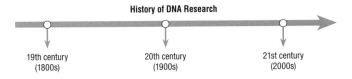

| 19th century (1800s) | 20th century (1900s) | 21st century (2000s) |

385

Listening Tip

Remind students to listen carefully to other people's ideas.

CRI ## Discussion

Have students work in pairs or small groups to answer the questions.

Q **What is your vision of life in the future?** Guide students in a discussion about DNA. What have they learned about DNA so far? What good uses are there for DNA? **SAY:** *Are there any negative ways DNA fingerprinting might be used in the future?*

STEP 3: Assess

Read for Fluency

Read the section in the Student Book aloud. **SAY:** *When you read aloud, your voice can communicate things to your listener beyond the words you say. For example, try to pause or slow down when making important points, and emphasize important words. With a partner, select a paragraph from the reading and practice reading it aloud.*

Extension

Have students copy the timeline in their notebooks and do research in order to add other important discoveries about DNA and heredity to it.

Differentiated Instruction

Beginning	Remind students to ask for clarification if necessary as they participate in the Discussion.
Early Intermediate	Based on the reading, have students fill in the blank. One use of DNA is _____.
Intermediate	Have students present the timeline they made in the extension activity to the class. Invite other class members to give feedback.
Greater Challenge	Help students practice the listening tip by reading aloud a recipe. Read slowly and clearly, pausing to give students time to think about what you said. Then have students describe in their notebooks how to make the food item. Invite students to discuss how using the listening tip helped them remember what they heard.

Teach & Apply

STEP 1: Introduce

Tell students that using quotation marks correctly is a hallmark of good writing. Review with students what dialogue is. When and where is dialogue used in writing? Why do they think it needs special punctuation?

STEP 2: Teach

Grammar and Writing

Using Quotation Marks Learning to punctuate quoted speech can be challenging for students. Read aloud the explanation in the student book. Write the examples from the student book on the board and ask the class to provide others.

STEP 3: Practice

Have students work with a partner to complete the practice activity.

ANSWERS

1. "I have read about DNA before," he said.
2. I read a short story called "A Family History."
3. The word *legislation* means "a law or set of laws."
4. The student said, "Learning about DNA is exciting."
5. The scientist felt that the tests were "useless."
6. He's written an article called "DNA for Beginners."

Teaching Resources

- *Workbook*, pp. 187–188
- CD-ROM/e-book, Grammar, Writing
- *Transparencies*, Writing Model 49
- *Transparencies, Resources*, Graphic Organizer 2
- *Assessment*, Reading 4 Test, pp. 127–130

Grammar and Writing

GRAMMAR, USAGE, AND MECHANICS

Using Quotation Marks

Knowing how to use quotation marks correctly will help you write stories, essays, and research reports. In dialogue in narratives, enclose a character's exact words or thoughts in quotation marks. In expository writing, place quotation marks around a person's exact words. For long quotations of more than five lines, indent and single-space the quotes, and do not use quotation marks.

> "I'm hungry," Fred said.
> "Your DNA fingerprint," Jeffreys said, "does not belong to anyone on the face of the planet who ever has been or ever will be."

In addition, use quotation marks to enclose special or technical terms, unfamiliar slang, and any other unusual expressions. Also, use quotation marks to set off a word or phrase that defines another word and to set off the titles of short written works such as articles, poems, and short stories.

> DNA tests proved they were "wholly innocent."
> *Generation* means "all the people who are about the same age."
> "Genetic Fingerprints"
> "Mending Wall" by Robert Frost

Practice Workbook Page 187

Copy the sentences below into your notebook. Add quotation marks where they are needed.

1. I have read about DNA before, he said.
2. I read a short story called A Family History.
3. The word *legislation* means a law or set of laws.
4. The student said, Learning about DNA is exciting.
5. The scientist felt that the tests were useless.
6. He's written an article called DNA for Beginners.

386

 TESOL Standards

Goal 1, Standard 1—To use English to communicate in social settings: Students will use English to participate in social interactions.
Descriptors—Sharing and requesting information; Expressing needs, feelings, and ideas.

Goal 1, Standard 2—To use English to communicate in social settings: Students will interact in, through, and with spoken and written English for personal expression and enjoyment.
Descriptors—Describing, reading about, or participating in a favorite activity; Expressing personal needs, feelings, and ideas.

Goal 3, Standard 1—To use English in socially and culturally appropriate ways: Students will use the appropriate language variety, register, and genre according to audience, purpose, and setting.
Descriptors—Using a variety of writing styles appropriate for different audiences, purposes, and settings; Responding to and using idioms appropriately; Responding to and using humor appropriately; Determining when it is appropriate to use a language other than English; Determining appropriate topics for interaction.

Include Paraphrases and Citations

To support your own ideas in a research report, you can quote information directly from a source, or you can put the information into your own words. When you put other people's ideas into your own words, you are paraphrasing. On this page, you will learn how to paraphrase information from other sources. You will use a graphic organizer like the one at the right to organize your information.

To paraphrase, read a source several times, then put it away. Write what you learned in your own words. Check your paraphrase against the original source for accuracy. When you write research reports, you should include more paraphrases than quotations. Whether you quote or paraphrase, provide a citation.

Here is a model paragraph in which the writer paraphrases information and includes a citation.

> Angelina Xing
>
> *Fraternal and Identical Twins*
>
> There are two types of twins, identical and fraternal. The word _identical_ means "exactly the same." Identical twins have the same DNA and look almost exactly alike. Identical twins are also always the same sex. Giving birth to identical twins occurs less frequently than giving birth to fraternal twins. According to doctors, approximately two-thirds of twin pregnancies are fraternal (Iannelli). Fraternal twins are actually quite different from each other. Most of the time, they don't look alike at all. Fraternal twins are sometimes the same sex, and other times, they're not. They also have different blood types and different DNA.
>
> *Works Consulted List*
>
> Iannelli, Vincent. "Facts about Twins." _Keep Kids Healthy._ May 2003. 15 March 2009 <http://www.keepkidshealthy.com/twins/expecting_twins.html>.

Practice **Workbook** Page 188

Write a paragraph about DNA that includes a paraphrase and a citation. Use reliable sources and a main idea/details web to organize the information. Use quotation marks if and when they are needed.

Writing Checklist

IDEAS:
- ☑ I used paraphrases that clearly support my main idea.

ORGANIZATION:
- ☑ I included a citation within and at the end of my paragraph.

387

Tell students that using quotations and paraphrasing information from a source can support their own ideas in a research report.

Writing a Research Report

Include Paraphrases and Citations

SAY: *When you include a person's exact words in your writing, enclose the words in quotation marks and provide a citation. If you restate the information in your <u>own</u> words, do not enclose the words in quotation marks, but still provide a citation.*

Model Writing Skill Show the sample paragraph on the overhead projector and read it aloud. Ask students to identify the instances where the author used quotation marks and paraphrasing.

Have students complete the practice activity.

Writing Checklist Note

Ideas: Check if students used paraphrases that clearly support their main idea.

Organization: Check if students included citations within and at the end of their paragraphs.

Accelerate Language Development

Punctuation with Quotation Marks

The placement of punctuation with quotation marks creates difficulties. Here's a rule of thumb: Place question marks and exclamation points within the quotation marks only if the punctuation applies to the quotation itself. Example: *I asked, "Do you need this book?"* Place the punctuation outside the quotation marks if the punctuation applies to the whole sentence. Example: *Does your mother always tell you, "You must listen more closely"?* If the question mark applies to both the quotation and the sentence, use only one quotation mark inside the quotation. Example: *Did she ask, "Where is he?"* Point out that periods and commas always go inside the quotation marks, whether they apply to the quotation only, or to the whole sentence.

Unit Wrap-Up

Link the Readings

Critical Thinking Have students copy the chart in the student book and fill it in.

ANSWERS

Title of Reading	Purpose	Big Question Link
"Life in the Future"	To inform	Tells about how everyday life will be different in the future.
"Southbound on the Freeway" "Cardinal Ideograms" "Interview with Dan Bursch"	To entertain and inform	Tells about different ways of looking at things and about being an astronaut.
From *Time Warp Trio: 2095*	To entertain	Tells about the unexpected experiences of three boys in the future.
Genetic Fingerprints	To inform	Tells about practical applications of our knowledge of DNA in the future.

 Discussion

Have students discuss the questions in pairs or small groups.

Q What is your vision of life in the future?
As a discussion starter, **SAY:** *Now that you have read the entire unit, how do the readings affect the way you would answer the Big Question? As a result of the readings, is your vision positive, negative, or both?*

STEP 2: Assess

Fluency Check

Have students draw the fluency check chart in their notebooks. Review with students how to use a stopwatch or read a clock's second hand. Emphasize that precise timing is important to get comparable scores.

Teaching Resources

- *Assessment*, Unit 6 Test, pp. 183–192
- CD-ROM/e-book, Fluency Check, Projects

Link the Readings

Critical Thinking

Look back at the readings in this unit. Think about what they all have in common. They all tell about the future. Yet they do not all have the same purpose. The purpose of one reading might be to inform, while the purpose of another might be to entertain or persuade. In addition, the content of each reading relates to the future in different ways. Now copy the chart below into your notebook and complete it.

Title of Reading	Purpose	Big Question Link
"Life in the Future"		
"Southbound on the Freeway" "Cardinal Ideograms" "Interview with Dan Bursch"		
From *The Time Warp Trio: 2095*	*to entertain*	
"Genetic Fingerprints"		*tells about how our knowledge of DNA will help fight disease in the future*

Discussion

Discuss in pairs or small groups.

- How does the purpose of "Life in the Future" differ from the purpose of *The Time Warp Trio: 2095*?

Q What is your vision of life in the future? Think about the readings in this unit. What picture of the future does each one show? Is the picture positive or negative? What's your opinion? Does life in the future look positive, negative, or both? Explain.

Fluency Check

Work with a partner. Choose a paragraph from one of the readings. Take turns reading it for one minute. Count the total number of words you read. Practice saying the words you had trouble reading. Take turns reading the paragraph three more times. Did you read more words each time? Copy the chart below into your notebook and record your speeds.

	1st Speed	2nd Speed	3rd Speed	4th Speed
Words Per Minute				

 TESOL Standards

Goal 1, Standard 1—To use English to communicate in social settings: Students will use English to participate in social interactions.
Descriptors—Engaging in conversations; Conducting transactions.

Goal 1, Standard 3—To use English to communicate in social settings: Students will use learning strategies to extend their communicative competence.
Descriptors—Seeking support and feedback from others; Using the primary language to ask for clarification; Selecting different media to help understand language.

Goal 2, Standard 2—To use English to achieve academically in all content areas: Students will use English to obtain, process, construct, and provide subject matter information in spoken and written form.
Descriptors—Listening to, speaking, reading, and writing about subject matter information; Gathering information orally and in writing; Selecting, connecting, and explaining information; Analyzing, synthesizing, and inferring from information; Responding to the work of peers and others; Representing information visually and interpreting information presented visually; Understanding and producing technical vocabulary and text features according to content area; Demonstrating knowledge through application in a variety of contexts.

Projects

1 You have read a lot about the future. What do you think the future will look like? Paint a picture of your town or city 100 years from now.

2 You read an interview with an astronaut. What training do astronauts need? Go to the NASA website to find out the requirements for being a U.S. astronaut. Share your findings in an oral report. Include handouts or other visuals.

3 *The Time Warp Trio: 2095* is part of a series of books about the travels of Sam, Fred, and Joe. Read another book in the series, such as *Tut Tut* or *It's All Greek to Me*. Then give a brief book report to the class. You might want to read the entire series!

4 Make a model of the DNA double helix. You may use any material you like, such as marshmallows and sticks or Styrofoam and clay. Label each part of the model. Present your model to the class.

5 Working with some classmates, adapt *The Time Warp Trio: 2095* as a brief play. Choose any part of the novel you like, rewrite it as a script, and act it out for the class. Include some costumes and simple props, too.

Further Reading

To find out more about the theme of this unit, choose from these reading suggestions.

Hulk, Based on the Motion Picture Story by James Schamus
In this Penguin Reader® adaptation, Bruce knows he's different. When he gets angry, his body changes. It grows and turns green. But where did he come from?

Tomorrowland: Ten Stories About the Future, Michael Cart
This collection of short stories, written by current writers, explores many aspects of life in the future.

Tuck Everlasting, Natalie Babbitt
The Tuck family discovers a spring with "unusual" properties. A conflict arises when others learn the spring's secret.

389

 ## Home-School Connection

These projects provide students several ways to practice and apply what they have learned in this unit. The projects can be completed independently, with partners, or in small groups. Students can complete the projects either in the classroom or at home.

Further Reading

Each book listed on this page pertains to the Big Question. Encourage students to peruse them in their free time or read them for extra-credit book reports. The first book on the list is easily accessible, the second is accessible, and the third is challenging.

Websites

Log onto www.LongmanKeystone.com for links to other interesting websites about life in the future.

Differentiated Instruction	
Beginning	Ask students to identify which readings were fiction and which were nonfiction.
Early Intermediate	Have students explain if they enjoyed learning about DNA. Why or why not?
Intermediate	Remind students to ask for clarification of another student's point or idea if necessary as they do the Discussion activity.
Struggling Readers	Ask students to tell you which reading they enjoyed the most. Ask them why they enjoyed it.

Listening & Speaking Workshop

STEP 1: Introduce

 Begin this workshop by encouraging groups of students to list several areas of daily life that they believe will be considerably different in the future than they are today. Tell students to discuss the examples given in the student book and add others to the list.

Think About It Help students brainstorm suitable topics for a speech. Encourage them to select topics that are of personal interest to them. Explain that the more genuinely interested they are in a topic, the more compelling their speech will be.

STEP 2: Teach

Gather and Organize Information Read over the instructions and ask students to select one topic from their group's list to be the focus of their speech. Suggest students choose as their topic an aspect of life in the future that excites them, because it's easier to prepare and give a speech if you're enthusiastic about the topic.

Teaching Resources

- CD-ROM/e-book, Gather and Organize Information

Put It All Together

LISTENING & SPEAKING WORKSHOP
Speech

You will give a speech that expresses your vision of life in the future.

1 THINK ABOUT IT In small groups, discuss the texts you read in this unit. Did any influence your vision of life in the future? Discuss your own predictions about life in the future. For instance, discuss what you think future schools will be like. Work together to develop a list of topics for a speech about the future. Here are some examples:
- space tourism
- new technology for communications
- homes of the future
- environmental issues in the future

2 GATHER AND ORGANIZE INFORMATION Choose a topic from your group's list. Write down what you already know about the topic. Look at an encyclopedia or a website to find out more about it. Decide what the focus of your speech will be.

Research Use the library or the Internet to find more information about your topic. Look for interesting facts, examples, and details that support your main idea or prediction about the topic. Take notes on what you find. Be sure to write down the sources of the information you wish to include.

Order Your Notes Decide on the main idea or prediction for your speech; for example: *In the future, people will live in "smart houses." Computers will turn the lights on and off, lock the doors, and water the plants.* Arrange your note cards in logical order and prepare an outline for your speech. Your outline should include your main idea and the facts, examples, and details that you will use to support it. Think of an interesting way to begin your speech. Plan a conclusion that summarizes your findings.

Prepare a Script Use your outline and note cards to write a script for your speech.

Use Visuals To make your speech more interesting and effective, find or make visuals such as posters and models that illustrate your ideas and predictions. Your visuals should be big enough for everyone to see easily. Decide when to show your visuals, and mark reminders in your speech.

390

TESOL Standards

Goal 3, Standard 2—To use English in socially and culturally appropriate ways: Students will use nonverbal communication appropriate to audience, purpose, and setting.
Descriptors—Interpreting and responding appropriately to nonverbal cues and body language; Demonstrating knowledge of acceptable nonverbal classroom behaviors; Using acceptable tone, volume, stress, and intonation in various social settings; Recognizing and adjusting behavior in response to nonverbal cues.

Goal 3, Standard 3—To use English in socially and culturally appropriate ways: Students will use appropriate learning strategies to extend their sociolinguistic and sociocultural competence.
Descriptors—Experimenting with variations of language in social and academic settings; Seeking information about appropriate language use and behavior; Analyzing the social context to determine appropriate language use; Rehearsing variations of language use in different social and academic settings.

3 **PRACTICE AND PRESENT** Practice reading your speech aloud until you know it very well. Keep practicing until you can speak smoothly, looking just occasionally at your script. Have a friend or family member listen as you practice giving your speech. Ask whether your words and ideas are understandable. Keep practicing until you feel comfortable and confident saying your speech while looking at your audience.

Deliver Your Speech Speak clearly and loudly enough so that everyone in the class can hear you. Glance at your script as needed, but remember to look up and make eye contact with your listeners. Be careful not to hide behind your visuals or turn away from the audience while speaking. At the end of your speech, ask the audience members whether they have any questions.

4 **EVALUATE THE PRESENTATION**
A good way to improve your speaking and listening skills is by evaluating each presentation you give and hear. Use this checklist to help you judge your speech and the speeches of your classmates.

- ☑ Was the speaker's main idea or prediction clear?
- ☑ Do you agree with the speaker's main idea or prediction? Why or why not?
- ☑ Was the speaker easy to hear and understand?
- ☑ Did you enjoy listening to the speech? Why or why not?
- ☑ What suggestions do you have for improving the speech?

🔊 *Speaking* TIPS

Use words such as *may, might, will, could, would, perhaps,* and *probably* to explain your predictions for the future.

Make sure your voice and body language show your enthusiasm for your topic. If you're having fun, your audience will enjoy the speech, too.

🔊 *Listening* TIPS

Try to visualize, or picture in your mind, what the speaker is describing.

Think about the speaker's reasons for his or her prediction. Do they seem logical and possible? Are they supported by research?

391

Practice and Present Read this section aloud. Remind students that while they can refer to note cards or an outline when giving their speech, they should practice it until they can deliver it smoothly and confidently, without reading directly from their notes.

Speaking Tips

Remind students that when talking about the future it's important to use words and structures that are associated with uncertain predictions, including modal verbs, as no one knows for sure what is going to happen. But emphasize that this doesn't have to diminish their enthusiasm for their predictions!

Listening Tips

Tell students that when they listen to their classmates' speeches, they should try to picture in their mind what is being said, and to think carefully about the reasons the speaker gives to support his or her prediction.

Evaluate the Presentation Suggest that students use the checklist to evaluate their classmates' speeches for the purpose of giving positive feedback. Tell students that citing specific examples from the speeches is most helpful to the speakers.

Differentiated Instruction

Beginning	Ask students to listen to each speech and make notes about it. What information did they get from the speeches they heard?
Early Intermediate	Have students explain why visuals are a useful tool when making a speech.
Intermediate	Have students brainstorm ways of asking for feedback. Ask them to model some feedback for the class.
Struggling Readers	Ask students to name someone who might give a speech, for example, the President, an actor, writer, etc.

Writing Workshop

STEP 1: Introduce

SAY: *A research report explains a topic you have studied in depth. It includes a paragraph that introduces the main idea, several paragraphs that develop the idea, and a concluding paragraph that sums up what the report says.*

STEP 2: Teach

Prewrite Together with students read the prewrite instructions. **SAY:** *When taking notes, remember to write down the source of the information report. You will need to cite all your sources at the end of your report. If you copy down information exactly as it appears in a source, be sure to put quotation marks around the words.*

Go over the sample outline in the student book. Emphasize that although creating an outline may seem like extra work, it will make it easier to write their report and make it better, too.

Teaching Resources

- *Transparencies, Resources,* Graphic Organizer 20
- *Transparencies,* Writing Model 50, Proofreader's Marks 51
- CD-ROM/e-book, Writing Workshop
- *Workbook,* pp. 189–190

WRITING WORKSHOP
Research Report

In a research report, you explain a topic you have studied in depth. You include research gathered from several different sources. If you use an exact quotation from a source, you put the words in quotation marks and include a citation. You list all your sources at the end of your report. A good research report begins with a paragraph that introduces the writer's topic and states a controlling idea or focus. Each body paragraph presents a main idea that develops the topic. Main ideas are supported by facts, details, and examples. A concluding paragraph sums up what the writer has explained.

Your assignment for this workshop is to write a five-paragraph research report about a topic related to life in the future.

 PREWRITE Select a topic that interests you. You might write about medicine, education, transportation, architecture, or any other area of human life that will probably be different in the future from the way it is now. Then ask yourself, "What do I want to know about my topic?" Use this question to guide your research. Consult sources such as books, magazines, encyclopedias, and websites. Take notes on note cards.

List and Organize Ideas and Details Create an outline to organize your ideas. A student named Brandon decided to write about future transportation. Here is the outline he prepared.

> I. Introduction
>   A. Huge advances made in the last 200 years
>   B. More advances coming in the future
> II. Hybrid cars
>   A. Already have better gas mileage than before
>   B. Stronger batteries needed to become main energy source
> III. Faster and more fuel-efficient airplane
>   A. Flying wing
>   B. Shaped like triangle
> IV. Other flying vehicles
>   A. SoloTrek EFV
>   B. Urban Aeronautics X-Hawk
> V. Safer, faster, more fuel-efficient modern vehicles
>   A. Will be even better in the future
>   B. Designed for environment-friendly society

392

TESOL Standards

Goal 2, Standard 2—To use English to achieve academically in all content areas: Students will use English to obtain, process, construct, and provide subject matter information in spoken and written form.
Descriptors—Listening to, speaking, reading, and writing about subject matter information; Gathering information orally and in writing; Understanding and producing technical vocabulary and text features according to content area; Demonstrating knowledge through application in a variety of contexts.

2 DRAFT Use the model on pages 396–397 and your outline to help you write a draft of your report. Be sure to use your own words when you write your report. If you use exact words from a source, make sure to use quotation marks correctly. List all of your sources accurately at the end of your report.

Citing Sources Look at the style, punctuation, and order of information in the following sources. Use these examples as models.

Book
Stanchak, John. <u>Civil War</u>. New York: Dorling Kindersley, 2000.

Magazine article
Kirn, Walter. "Lewis and Clark: The Journey That Changed America Forever." <u>Time</u> 8 July 2002: 36–41.

Internet website
Smith, Gene. "The Structure of the Milky Way." <u>Gene Smith's Astronomy Tutorial</u>. 28 April 1999. Center for Astrophysics & Space Sciences, University of California, San Diego. 20 July 2009 <http://casswww.ucsd.edu/public/tutorial/MW.html>.

Encyclopedia article
Siple, Paul A. "Antarctica." <u>World Book Encyclopedia</u>. 1991 ed.

---

3 REVISE Read over your draft. As you do so, ask yourself the questions in the writing checklist. Use the questions to help you revise your report.

SIX TRAITS OF WRITING CHECKLIST

- ☑ **IDEAS:** Does my first paragraph introduce my topic and focus?
- ☑ **ORGANIZATION:** Do facts, examples, and details support the main idea in each paragraph?
- ☑ **VOICE:** Is my tone serious and suited to the topic?
- ☑ **WORD CHOICE:** Do I use words that clearly express my meaning?
- ☑ **SENTENCE FLUENCY:** Do my sentences vary in length and type?
- ☑ **CONVENTIONS:** Does my writing follow the rules of grammar, usage, and mechanics?

393

Draft Review with students the draft on pages 396–397. Emphasize that any time they use someone else's words, they must put quotation marks around them.

Revise
SAY: *To revise a draft means to look at it again and make changes in content or wording that make the draft better.*

STEP 3: Assess

Writing Checklist

Read aloud the Writing Checklist in the student book and have students ask themselves each question as they review their drafts.
SAY: *If you answer "no" to any of the questions, revise your draft until you can answer the question "yes."*

Ideas: *Does your first paragraph introduce your topic and focus?*

Organization: *Do facts, examples, and details support the main idea in each paragraph?*

Voice: *Is your tone serious and suited to the topic?*

Word Choice: *Do you use words that clearly express your meaning?*

Sentence Fluency: *Do your sentences vary in length and type?*

Conventions: *Does your writing follow the rules of grammar, usage, and mechanics?*

Differentiated Instruction

Beginning	Work with students individually or in small groups to help them choose and narrow their topic.
Early Intermediate	Have students read the Citing Sources box so they know how to structure their sources. Refer them to pages 455–456 for additional information on citing sources.
Intermediate	Have students explain the reason for Brandon's edits to his second paragraph (page 394). How is this paragraph improved by his changes?
Special Needs	Show students a reliable search engine on the Internet. Explain how to conduct a keyword search to speed up their research. More information is available in the Handbook at the back of their books.

Writing Workshop

Avoiding Plagiarism

Many students do not understand what plagiarism is or how serious an offense it is. Explain that plagiarism occurs when you present someone else's ideas or words as your own. This can be done either by copying a sentence, a paragraph, or more from a source without acknowledging it, or when you use ideas you found in a source without acknowledging it, even if you express the ideas in your own words.

SAY: *To avoid plagiarism, check the following points in your research report:*

Acknowledge sources *Check that you have acknowledged all text and ideas that are not your own by including citations for all quotations and paraphrased material.*

Use your own language *Check that you have used your own language to paraphrase text that is not your own.*

Use quotation marks *Check that you have included quotation marks at the beginning and end of all text that you have copied from a source.*

Make sure citations are accurate *Check that your list of works consulted is complete and that each citation is accurate.*

Here are the changes Brandon plans to make when he revises his first draft:

Transportation of the Future

In the last 200 years, transportation technology has made ^astonishing^ advances. Steamships replaced sailing ships. Railroads were created. ⊙ ^Automobiles were invented^ The Wright brothers made the first airplane flight. Astronauts traveled to the moon! What ^will^ can transportation be like in the future ^?^ Transportation technology ^will^ may continue to advance, perhaps more than we can imagine today. We will see improvements in hybrid and electric cars, airplanes, and personal jetpacks.

Car companies are already making hybrid or fuel efficient cars that have improved gas mileage. ^However,^ Batteries must become stronger and cheaper in order to become the main energy source for cars. electric cars today (must use gasoline power as a backup.) They can go only 50 to 100 miles between charges. ^so they^ According to scientist Joshua Cunningham, "Gasoline will remain a dominant fuel until at least 2050" (Layton, Nice).

Many airlines are trying to make their jets faster and more fuel efficient. ^A group called^ Greener By design predicts that a new kind of plane, the flying wing, will be carrying passengers by 2025. These planes ^made of plastic and^ will be shaped like a triangle. Passengers will sit in rows of up to 40 seats across.

394

 ## TESOL Standards

Goal 3, Standard 1—To use English in socially and culturally appropriate ways: Students will use the appropriate language variety, register, and genre according to audience, purpose, and setting.
Descriptors—Using the appropriate degree of formality with different audiences and settings; Recognizing and using Standard English and vernacular dialects appropriately.

Several new flying vehicles ~~will~~ *may* be in the sky *in the next few decades*. Inventors are close

to creating a jetpack that can go as high as a plane and maneuver

better than a helicopter. The SoloTrek EFV is one example. According

to its inventor, Michael Moshier, it ~~one day~~ will "fly at altitudes of

nearly 8,000 feet . . . and reach speeds of up to 80 mph" (Sieberg). An

emergency vehicle by Urban Aeronautics, known as the X-Hawk, will

go places that cannot be reached by helicopters *or other emergency vehicles*.

Modern vehicles are becoming safer, faster, and more fuel-efficient.

In the future, people will have access to even better transportation.

This new technology will be specially designed to work in a

environment-friendly fast-paced society.

Works Consulted List

"Future Planes Might Be 'Flying Wings'." <u>Future Planes</u>. 5 April 2007. 23 March

2009 <http://futureplanes.blogspot.com/>.

Layton, Julia, and Karim Nice. "How Hybrid Cars Work." <u>How Stuff Works</u>.

23 March 2009 <http://auto.howstuffworks.com/hybrid-car.htm>.

Sieberg, Daniel. "Personal 'Jetpack' Gets off the Ground." <u>CNN Sci-Tech</u>.

6 February 2002. 24 March 2009 <http://archives.cnn.com/2002/TECH/

ptech/02/06/solotrek.jetpack/index.html>.

Stearns, Peter N., general editor. "The Modern Period: Transportation and

Communication." <u>The Encyclopedia of World History</u>. 2001 ed.

Citing Sources

Explain to students that they should start preparing their list of works consulted at the very beginning of their research. It's important to do this because it is very difficult or even impossible to reconstruct sources and page references when finalizing a report. Many students do not understand this because the list of works consulted appears at the end of the research report.

Make sure students understand the different format for in-text citations and works consulted. Find the in-text citations in the student model. Explain that the list of works consulted must contain complete information for each source.

Have students examine each source in the list of works consulted. Discuss the format of each one.

Linguistic Note

Word Order

As students write their first draft, remind them that word order in English is more rigid than in some other languages. Native speakers of languages like Spanish have difficulty understanding that English does not allow for much flexibility. In addition, English sentences require a stated subject. In Spanish, the verb ending implies the subject. Point out that in the simple present most English verbs change their spelling only in the third-person singular, and therefore the subject needs to be explicitly stated.

Edit and Proofread Review with students the changes Brandon made to the first draft of his research report entitled "Transportation of the Future." List the differences between his first draft and his revised draft. What changed from draft to draft? (Brandon added more details, moved around text, changed verbs that express predictions, added a transition and a conjunction, and corrected punctuation.)

Then review with students the additional edits Brandon plans to make when he prepares his final version of his report. Discuss why you think each edit was made. Keep dictionaries nearby to check spelling.

Copy your revised report onto a clean sheet of paper. Read it again. Correct any errors in grammar, word usage, mechanics, and spelling. Here are the additional changes Brandon plans to make when he prepares his final draft.

Brandon Saiz

Transportation of the Future

In the last 200 years, transportation technology has made astonishing advances. Steamships replaced sailing ships. Railroads were created. Automobiles were invented. The Wright brothers made the first airplane flight. Astronauts traveled to the moon! What will transportation be like in the future? Transportation technology will continue to advance, perhaps more than we can imagine today. We will see improvements in hybrid and electric cars, airplanes, and personal jetpacks.

Car companies are already making hybrid or fuel efficient cars that have improved gas mileage. However, batteries must become stronger and cheaper in order to become the main energy source for cars. electric cars today can go only 50 to 100 miles between charges, so they must use gasoline power as a backup. According to scientist Joshua Cunningham, "Gasoline will remain a dominant fuel until at least 2050" (Layton, Nice).

Many airlines are trying to make their jets faster and more fuel efficient. A group called Greener By design predicts that a new kind of plane, the flying wing, will be carrying passengers by 2025. These planes will be made of plastic and shaped like a triangle. Passengers will sit in rows of up to 40 seats across.

TESOL Standards

Goal 3, Standard 1—To use English in socially and culturally appropriate ways: Students will use the appropriate language variety, register, and genre according to audience, purpose, and setting.
Descriptors—Using a variety of writing styles appropriate for different audiences, purposes, and settings; Determining appropriate topics for interaction.

Several new flying vehicles may be in the sky in the next few decades. Inventors are close to creating a jetpack that can go as high as a plane and maneuver better than a helicopter. The SoloTrek EFV is one example. According to its inventor, Michael Moshier, one day it will "fly at altitudes of nearly 8,000 feet . . . and reach speeds of up to 80 mph" (Sieberg). An emergency vehicle by Urban Aeronautics, known as the X-Hawk, will go places that cannot be reached by helicopters or other emergency vehicles.

Modern vehicles are becoming safer, faster, and more fuel-efficient. In the future, people will have access to even better transportation. This new technology will be specially designed to work in a fast-paced, environment-friendly society.

Works Consulted List

"Future Planes Might Be 'Flying Wings'." Future Planes. 5 April 2007. 23 March 2009 <http://futureplanes.blogspot.com/>.

Layton, Julia, and Karim Nice. "How Hybrid Cars Work." How Stuff Works. 23 March 2009 <http://auto.howstuffworks.com/hybrid-car.htm>.

Sieberg, Daniel. "Personal 'Jetpack' Gets off the Ground." CNN Sci-Tech. 6 February 2002. 24 March 2009 <http://archives.cnn.com/2002/TECH/ptech/02/06/solotrek.jetpack/index.html>.

Stearns, Peter N., general editor. "The Modern Period: Transportation and Communication." The Encyclopedia of World History. 2001 ed.

5 **PUBLISH** Prepare your final draft. Share your research report with your teacher and classmates.

Workbook
Page 190

Publish Now have students look over their final drafts and discuss their options for publishing them. **SAY:** *To publish means to make public. When you share your writing, you make it public. Think about how best to publish your piece of writing. Does your report need illustrations? Graphs or data displays? Diagrams? Before you copy your final changes, plan how you will showcase your writing.*

Career Connection

Engineer Engineers are people who use sequential, logical planning skills to design, build, and repair roads, bridges, and large buildings. However, that's not all engineers do. Today's engineers do everything from designing roller coasters to inventing timesaving gadgets to working behind the scenes on space missions. Among the many engineering specialties are mechanical engineers, who design the engines on ships and aircraft, chemical engineers, who are involved with the design and maintenance of chemical processes for large-scale manufacture, and genetic engineers, who are involved in the science of changing the genetic structures of animals, plants, and/or people for the purpose of making them healthier or stronger.

STEP 1: Introduce

Remind students that the Big Question is *What is your vision of life in the future?* **SAY:** *The artist Andy Warhol once said that in the future, everyone will be famous for fifteen minutes. If you could be famous for fifteen minutes in the future, what would you do?*

Have students send a postcard from the future. Using 4 x 6 inch pieces of poster board and colored pencils or paints, have them design the image on the front. On the back, they should divide their postcard into two sections. They should put a name and address on the right side and describe the reason for their fifteen minutes of fame on the left side. Have them "mail" their postcards in a box and then read them to the class.

STEP 2: Teach

Visual Literacy

Alexander A. Maldonado Explain that in *San Francisco to New York in One Hour*, Maldonado imagines a transportation system that can carry people across the country at amazing speeds. Spaceship designer Burt Rutan imagined privately built and run spacecrafts flying average citizens into outer space. He realized his dream with *SpaceShipOne,* the first privately run spaceship, which a pilot successfully flew into space in 2004. The spaceship is on view at the Smithsonian National Air and Space Museum. Go to "SpaceShipOne Joins the Icons of Light on Display at Smithsonian's National Air and Space Museum" (www.LongmanKeystone.com) for more information about Rutan's successful and inexpensive design.

Divide the class into two groups to debate whether or not students think average citizens should be able to travel into space.

Harry Bertoia Read a quotation by Bertoia about his work *Sculpture Group Symbolizing World's Communication in the Atomic Age* in the Smithsonian American Art Museum website feature "Collections & Exhibitions" (www.LongmanKeystone.com) and watch the slide show. Bertoia talks about living in a time "dominated by these invisible forces" and "giving sculptural shape and form" to the electronic age. While students may not be able to understand the meaning of his words, it does raise the interesting question of how to create

Teaching Resources

- *Workbook*, pp. 191–192
- CD-ROM/e-book, Smithsonian

IMAGINING THE FUTURE

N*o one can see into the future, but most of us can imagine it. Artists often show the future in their work. Sometimes they show people zooming around in flying jackets across strange-looking cities. Other times, they just try to capture a futuristic mood.*

Alexander A. Maldonado, *San Francisco to New York in One Hour* (1969)

In Alexander A. Maldonado's vision of the future, people are able to travel thousands of miles quickly. In *San Francisco to New York in One Hour*, vehicles zip through underground tubes. The tops of these tunnels are round. The overall image looks like a big stadium with a parking lot packed with cars and buses. The artist surrounded his brightly colored painting with a wooden frame. This makes you feel as though you are looking through a window into the future.

A Mexican American who lived in California for most of his adult life, Maldonado continued to have strong ties to his native Mexico. One of the tunnel stations in the painting travels from the United States to Mexico (notice the Mexican flag on the upper right building), a speedy route between the artist's past as a child and where he built his future.

▲ Alexander A. Maldonado, *San Francisco to New York in One Hour*, 1969, oil, 18 x 24 in., Smithsonian American Art Museum

398

▲ Harry Bertoia, *Sculpture Group Symbolizing World's Communication in the Atomic Age*, 1959, brass and bronze, 142¼ x 231¼ x 81 in., Smithsonian American Art Museum

Harry Bertoia, *Sculpture Group Symbolizing World's Communication in the Atomic Age* (1959)

Harry Bertoia's *Sculpture Group Symbolizing World's Communication in the Atomic Age* is made up of one large 2.4-meter (8-ft.) sculpture and three smaller sculptures. Bertoia worked with metals such as brass and copper. Then he added light so that the objects seem to glow like the planets and stars. In the larger piece to the left, he put together squares of metal attached to poles, which formed a circle shaped like the sun.

Even though Bertoia lived at a time when computers and television were new, he felt that electronics and atomic energy already dominated American culture. When you look at his bright sculpture, it's easy to imagine that you're in outer space or inside a TV.

Any future that someone can imagine is always based on what we find in our present. Both of these artists used images we understand today to imagine a different world tomorrow.

Apply What You Learned

1 What is similar in the way each of these artists views the future? In what way are their artworks different?

2 What do you think Alexander Maldonado wanted to express in his painting?

Big Question
If you were asked to imagine the future in an artwork, what would you create?

Workbook
Pages 191–192

399

---

symbols or art to represent things we still don't fully know or understand. Point out to students that Bertoia created his work of art for a major electronics company at a time (1959) when most American homes had few electronic items. He had to imagine a world that did not yet exist. Ask students what symbols they would use to depict the way we communicate today. What symbols would they use to depict the way we might communicate in 2100? Have them sketch their ideas on paper and share them with the class.

Explain that most inventions begin with a sketch. Even Alexander Graham Bell, inventor of the telephone and many other amazing inventions, started with pen and paper. Students can see Bell's sketches and then draw their own "inventions" online by going to the Smithsonian National Museum of American History's Lemelson Center for the Study of Invention and Innovation website (www.LongmanKeystone.com). First click on "Alexander G. Bell's Sketch" to see his sketches for the first telephone. Then click on "Inventor's Sketchbook" where students can draw some ideas for inventions of their own.

STEP 3: Apply

Apply What You Learned

Have volunteers read the questions aloud, and be sure students understand the meaning of difficult words and concepts. Encourage students to carefully study the artworks, and if necessary, reread the text to help them.

ANSWERS

1. Both artworks are similar in that they are based on what we find in our present: cars and perhaps a solar system. They are different because one is a painting and one is a sculpture.

2. **Possible response:** On one level, Maldonado wanted to express the speedy road he traveled from his childhood in Mexico to his adult life in the United States. On another level, Maldonado also wanted to create a view of the future, in which he thought we'll all be able to travel extremely fast.

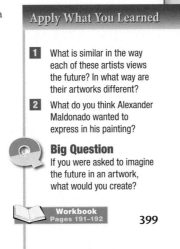 **Possible response:** I would create an oil painting of the inside of a very comfortable spaceship, in which passengers would be enjoying their ride. A flight attendant would be standing in the aisle, talking about all the planets the passengers would be seeing outside their windows.

Contents
Handbooks and Resources

Using the Handbook

This handbook contains valuable information about the study skills and language learning skills students need to succeed in school. It covers the following topics: how to learn language; how to build vocabulary; how to use reference books; how to take tests; and study skills and learning strategies.

To introduce the handbook, walk your students through the pages and, together, note the information found under major headings and subheadings. Direct teaching of the handbook for brief periods will help students learn how to find information and understand content. Point out to students that they may consult the handbook on their own to find information, such as how to use a dictionary.

HOW TO LEARN LANGUAGE

Read the introduction as students follow along in the text. Explain that listening, speaking, reading, and writing are the four key skills of learning a language.

Listening

Read aloud the four tips as students follow along. Discuss each item and ask students for examples. **ASK:** *What does it mean to listen with a purpose, and what are some examples? What do you do when you listen actively? When is active listening important? How does taking notes help you listen? How can you use the radio, TV, and Internet to help you listen and learn language?*

Speaking

Read aloud the four tips as students follow along. Discuss each item and ask students for examples. Write a question and an answer on the board. **ASK:** *How is the order of words different? What are some situations when it's good to think before you speak?* Discuss the importance of speaking your new language at school, at home, in stores, at the doctor's office, and other places. Reassure students that we all make mistakes as part of the learning process, whether it's learning to ride a bike or speak a new language.

Study Skills and Language Learning

HOW TO LEARN LANGUAGE

Learning a language takes time, but, just like learning to swim, it can be fun. Whether you're learning English for the first time or adding to your knowledge of English by learning academic or content-area words, you're giving yourself a better chance of success in your studies and in your everyday life.

Learning any language is a skill that requires you to be active. You listen, speak, read, and write when you learn a language. Here are some tips that will help you learn English more actively and efficiently.

Listening
1. Set a purpose for listening. Think about what you hope to learn from today's class. Listen for these things as your teacher and classmates speak.
2. Listen actively. You can think faster than others can speak. This is useful because it allows you to anticipate what will be said next. Take notes as you listen. Write down only what is most important, and keep your notes short.
3. If you find something difficult to understand, listen more carefully. Do not give up and stop listening. Write down questions to ask afterward.
4. The more you listen, the faster you will learn. Use the radio, television, and Internet to practice your listening skills.

Speaking
1. Pay attention to sentence structure as you speak. Are you saying the words in the correct order?
2. Think about what you are saying. Don't worry about speaking fast. It's more important to communicate what you mean.
3. Practice speaking as much as you can, both in class and in your free time. Consider reading aloud to improve your pronunciation. If possible, record yourself speaking.
4. Do not be afraid of making mistakes. Everyone makes mistakes!

Reading

1. Read every day. Read as many different things as possible: Books, magazines, newspapers, and websites will all help you improve your comprehension and increase your vocabulary.

2. Try to understand what you are reading as a whole, rather than focusing on individual words. If you find a word you do not know, see if you can figure out its meaning from the context of the sentence before you look it up in a dictionary. Make a list of new vocabulary words and review it regularly.

3. Read texts more than once. Often your comprehension of a passage will improve if you read it twice or three times.

4. Try reading literature, poems, and plays aloud. This will help you understand them. It will also give you practice pronouncing new words.

Writing

1. Write something every day to improve your writing fluency. You can write about anything that interests you. Consider keeping a diary or a journal so that you can monitor your progress as time passes.

2. Plan your writing before you begin. Use graphic organizers to help you organize your ideas.

3. Be aware of sentence structure and grammar. Always write a first draft. Then go back and check for errors before you write your final version.

Reading

Read aloud the four tips as students follow along. **ASK:** *How can you make reading part of your day? How do visuals (pictures, photos, diagrams) help you figure out what words mean? How does rereading help you understand better?* **Explain what** *literature* **is. Discuss why reading different kinds of literature improves reading skills.**

Writing

Read aloud the three tips as students follow along. Discuss the value of writing everyday. **ASK:** *Why is it important to plan your writing before you start?* **Discuss the importance of checking spelling and grammar before turning in work.**

HOW TO BUILD VOCABULARY

Discuss the meaning of the word *vocabulary*. Tell students that building a strong vocabulary is essential for learning a language.

1. Improving Your Vocabulary

Explain that the most common ways to increase vocabulary are through listening, reading, and taking part in conversation.

Listening and Speaking Note the importance of listening for new words in conversation or on the radio or television. Urge students to ask the meaning of any new words they hear. Alternatively, suggest that students use clues to figure out a word's meaning or look up the meaning in a dictionary. Invite students to use new words as often as is appropriate in conversation. **ASK:** *Why is it important to use your new words in conversation?* Have students provide examples of new words they've recently heard in conversation or on the radio or television. List the words on the board. Ask volunteers to use these words in sentences.

Reading Aloud Encourage students to listen to audio books. Explain that audio books can help individuals hear how specific words are pronounced and used. Urge students to read a copy of the book as they listen.

Scaffolding

Choose an audio book and play a segment aloud for students. Afterwards, ask students to share examples of any new words they heard. Write the words on the board. Have students discuss the pronunciation and meaning of the new words. Then have volunteers use these words in sentences.

Reading Often Emphasize that the more students read, the more new words they will find. Ask students to name any new words they recently found in their reading. Write these new words on the board. Have volunteers read aloud the dictionary definition of each word.

2. Figuring Out What a Word Means

Explain that students may often be able to use clues to figure out a word's meaning from its context. Discuss the meaning of *context*.

Using Context Clues Read aloud the four tips as students follow along. **ASK:** *Why is it important to look up a new word in the dictionary after you have figured out its possible meaning?* (Students should recognize the need for checking accuracy.)

1. Improving Your Vocabulary
Listening and Speaking
The most common ways to increase your vocabulary are listening, reading, and taking part in conversations. One of the most important skills in language learning is listening. Listen for new words when talking with others, joining in discussions, listening to the radio or audio books, or watching television.

You can find out the meanings of the words by asking, listening for clues, and looking up the words in a dictionary. Don't be embarrassed about asking what a word means. It shows that you are listening and that you want to learn. Whenever you can, use the new words you learn in conversation.

Reading Aloud
Listening to texts read aloud is another good way to build your vocabulary. There are many audio books available, and most libraries have a collection of them. When you listen to an audio book, you hear how new words are pronounced and how they are used. If you have a printed copy of the book, read along as you listen so that you can both see and hear new words.

Reading Often
Usually, people use a larger variety of words when they write than when they speak. The more you read, the more new words you'll find. When you see new words over and over again, they will become familiar to you and you'll begin to use them. Read from different sources—books, newspapers, magazines, Internet websites—in order to find a wide variety of words.

2. Figuring Out What a Word Means
Using Context Clues
When you come across a new word, you may not always need to use a dictionary. You might be able to figure out its meaning using the context, or the words in the sentence or paragraph in which you found it. Sometimes the surrounding words contain clues to tell you what the new word means.
Here are some tips for using context clues:
- Read the sentence, leaving out the word you don't know.
- Find clues in the sentence to figure out the new word's meaning.
- Read the sentence again, but replace the word you don't know with another possible meaning.
- Check your possible meaning by looking up the word in the dictionary. Write the word and its definition in your vocabulary notebook.

3. Practicing Your New Words

To make a word part of your vocabulary, study its definition, use it in your writing and speaking, and review it to make sure that you really understand its meaning.

Use one or more of these ways to remember the meanings of new words.

Keep a Vocabulary Notebook

Keep a notebook for vocabulary words. Divide your pages into three columns: the new words; hint words that help you remember their meanings; and their definitions. Test yourself by covering either the second or third column.

Word	Hint	Definition
zoology	zoo	study of animals
fortunate	fortune	lucky
quizzical	quiz	questioning

Make Flashcards

On the front of an index card, write a word you want to remember. On the back, write the meaning. You can also write a sentence that uses the word in context. Test yourself by flipping through the cards. Enter any hard words in your vocabulary notebook. As you learn the meanings, remove these cards and add new ones.

Say the Word Aloud

A useful strategy for building vocabulary is to say the new word aloud. Do not worry that there is no one to say the word to. Just say the word loud and clear several times. This will make you feel more confident and help you to use the word in conversation.

Record Yourself

Record your vocabulary words. Leave a ten-second space after each word, and then say the meaning and a sentence using the word. Play the recording. Fill in the blank space with the meaning and a sentence. Replay the recording until you memorize the word.

---

3. Practicing Your New Words

Explain to students that integrating a new word into their vocabulary involves studying the word's definition, using it in speaking and writing, and reviewing it. Note that there are useful techniques for remembering new words.

Keep a Vocabulary Notebook Read aloud this suggestion as students follow along. Tell students to keep a running list of new words and definitions, using the suggested format.

Make Flashcards Read aloud this suggestion as students follow along. Show sample flashcards to students. You may wish to give students blank index cards and dictionaries to make their own flashcards. Some students may benefit from drawing a picture to help them remember the meaning of a word.

Cooperative Grouping

You may want to have pairs of students use their flashcards to test each other on new vocabulary words.

Say the Words Aloud Read aloud this suggestion as students follow along. Discuss why saying and repeating words aloud helps students learn new words.

Scaffolding

Write several key words from a unit in the student book on the board. Say each word aloud and have students repeat. Encourage students to listen to themselves to make sure they are saying the words correctly.

Record Yourself Read aloud this suggestion as students follow along in the text. Remind students to check that their pronunciation of a word is correct before recording it.

Metacognition

To help students understand how building vocabulary is already a part of their learning process, **ASK:** *What new word did you learn recently? How did you learn it? Can you use it in a sentence? How can you teach the word to a friend or someone in your family?*

Tell students that knowing how to use reference books will help them improve their reading and writing skills.

The Dictionary

Read the introduction to using a dictionary aloud as students follow along in the text. Discuss the information given in a sample entry—the pronunciation, syllables, and stress marks; the part of speech; and the definitions and example sentences. Point out that there are two different definitions for the word *handle*.

Students may ask how to look up a word that they don't know how to spell. Write the word *cloud* on the board. **ASK:** *How would you look up the word* cloud *if you didn't know how to spell it? What letter or letters have a k sound?* (c, k, ch) *What letter or letters have an ow sound?* (ow, ou) Explain to students that, in a situation where a word may have more than one possible spelling, they may have to look up various possible spellings before they find the right one.

Metacognition

To help students monitor their comprehension, ask, *Who has seen a dictionary page that looks like this? When have you used a dictionary?*

Scaffolding

You may want to hand out dictionaries to students to practice looking up words. Point out guide words at the top of dictionary pages to help students find words. Write a set of key words from the student book on the board. Ask students to look up these words in the dictionary, write down at least one definition for each word, and write a sentence using the word. Depending on students' dictionary skills, you may wish to repeat this exercise on a daily or weekly basis. Also, make sure students use a dictionary every day as they do their reading lessons. Bilingual dictionaries may help some students.

The Dictionary

When you look up a word in the dictionary, you find the word and information about it. The word and the information about it are called a dictionary entry. Each entry tells you the word's spelling, pronunciation, part of speech, and meaning. Many English words have more than one meaning. Some words, such as *handle*, can be both a noun and a verb. For such words, the meanings, or definitions, are numbered. Sometimes example sentences are given in italics to help you understand how the word is used.

Here is part of a dictionary page with its important features labeled.

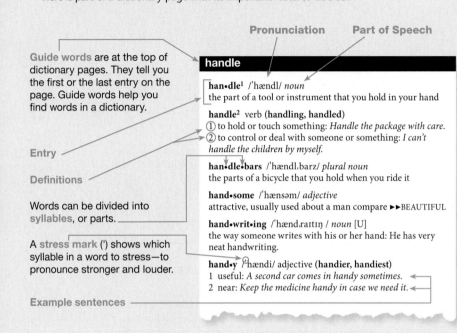

Guide words are at the top of dictionary pages. They tell you the first or the last entry on the page. Guide words help you find words in a dictionary.

Entry

Definitions

Words can be divided into **syllables**, or parts.

A **stress mark** (') shows which syllable in a word to stress—to pronounce stronger and louder.

Example sentences

Pronunciation   **Part of Speech**

handle

han·dle[1] /ˈhændl/ *noun*
the part of a tool or instrument that you hold in your hand

handle[2] verb (**handling, handled**)
① to hold or touch something: *Handle the package with care.*
② to control or deal with someone or something: *I can't handle the children by myself.*

han·dle·bars /ˈhændlˌbarz/ *plural noun*
the parts of a bicycle that you hold when you ride it

hand·some /ˈhænsəm/ *adjective*
attractive, usually used about a man compare ▶▶BEAUTIFUL

hand·writ·ing /ˈhændˌraɪtɪŋ / *noun* [U]
the way someone writes with his or her hand: *He has very neat handwriting.*

hand·y /ˈhændi/ adjective (**handier, handiest**)
1 useful: *A second car comes in handy sometimes.*
2 near: *Keep the medicine handy in case we need it.*

406

T406

The Thesaurus

A thesaurus is a kind of dictionary. It is a specialized dictionary that lists synonyms, or words with similar meanings, for words. You can use a print thesaurus (a book) or an online thesaurus on the Internet.

A thesaurus is a useful writing tool because it can help you avoid repeating the same word. It can also help you choose more precise words. Using a thesaurus regularly can help build your vocabulary by increasing the number of words you know that are related by an idea or concept.

In a thesaurus, words may either be arranged alphabetically or be grouped by theme. When the arrangement is by theme, you first have to look up the word in the index to find out in which grouping its synonyms will appear. When the thesaurus is arranged alphabetically, you simply look up the word as you would in a dictionary.

The entry below is from a thesaurus that is arranged alphabetically.

> **sad** *adjective* Tending to cause sadness or low spirits : blue, cheerless, depressed, depressing, dismal, dispiriting, downcast, gloomy, heartbreaking, joyless, melancholy, miserable, poignant, sorrowful, unhappy. See **happy** (antonym) in index.
> —See also **depressed, sorrowful**.

Choose synonyms carefully. You can see from the thesaurus entry above that there are many synonyms for the word *sad*. However, not all of these words may be the ones you want to use. For example, *depressed* can mean that you have an illness called depression, but it can also mean that you feel sad. If you are not sure what a word means, look it up in a dictionary to check that it is, in fact, the word you want to use.

The Thesaurus

Read the introduction to using a thesaurus aloud as students follow along. Read aloud the sample entry for *sad*. Discuss the information—the part of speech, definition, synonyms, and antonym.

Scaffolding

Tell students that they can replace the word *sad* with the synonyms in the thesaurus sample. Write an example of a sentence on the board using the word *sad*, e.g., *He was sad when his best friend moved away.* Then write the same sentence using a synonym for *sad*, e.g., *He was depressed when his best friend moved away.* Discuss the different shades of meaning among the synonyms. Have students write their own sentences using *sad* and then replace *sad* with a synonym. Ask volunteers to share their sentences with the class.

Metacognition

To help students monitor their comprehension, **ASK:** *Why is it useful to know synonyms for words? Why is a thesaurus a better source than an ordinary dictionary for finding synonyms?*

Suggest that students refer to the tips in this section whenever they take a test.

1. Taking Tests

Read aloud the definition of *objective test* as students follow along. Discuss the difference between *objective* and *subjective*. Stress that the most effective way to prepare for most tests is to study the material that the test covers.

Preview the Test Point out the importance of reading or listening carefully to instructions before beginning to take a test. Suggest that students ask questions if they do not understand the instructions. Then read aloud the five tips as students follow along in the text. **ASK:** *Why is it useful to look a test over to get an idea of the kinds of questions it contains?* (Among other reasons, previewing can help them gauge their time.)

Answer the Questions Read aloud and discuss the five tips with students. Address any concerns they may have about taking tests. Tell students that these tips will help them approach tests in an efficient way. Urge students to read each question twice before answering it.

Proofread Your Answers Ask a volunteer to define *proofread*. Remind students that one aspect of proofreading is to review directions. Students should make sure they have followed instructions carefully and completely. Tell students that if they misunderstand the instructions, they may give an incorrect answer even when they know the right answer.

2. Answering Different Kinds of Questions

To introduce this section, walk students through the subheads. Have volunteers read aloud the definitions of the types of questions.

True or False Questions Read aloud the four tips as students follow along. You may want to provide examples of each tip. For example, have students read a statement and then add the word *not* to change the meaning. Ensure that students understand the meanings of words such *as true, false, all, always, never, no, none, only, generally, much, many, most, often, sometimes,* and *usually.*

In this section, you will learn some ways to improve your test-taking skills.

1. Taking Tests
Objective tests are tests in which each question has only one correct answer. To prepare for these tests, you should study the material that the test covers.

Preview the Test
1. Write your name on each sheet of paper you will hand in.
2. Look over the test to get an idea of the kinds of questions being asked.
3. Find out whether you lose points for incorrect answers. If you do, do not guess at answers.
4. Decide how much time you need to spend on each section of the test.
5. Use the time well. Give the most time to questions that are hardest or worth the most points.

Answer the Questions
1. Answer the easy questions first. Put a check next to harder questions and come back to them later.
2. If permitted, use scratch paper to write down your ideas.
3. Read each question at least twice before answering.
4. Answer all questions on the test (unless guessing can cost you points).
5. Do not change your first answer without a good reason.

Proofread Your Answers
1. Check that you followed the directions completely.
2. Reread questions and answers. Make sure you answered all the questions.

2. Answering Different Kinds of Questions
This section tells you about different kinds of test questions and gives you specific strategies for answering them.

True-or-False Questions
True-or-false questions ask you to decide whether or not a statement is true.
1. If a statement seems true, make sure that it is *all* true.
2. Pay special attention to the word *not*. It often changes the meaning of a statement entirely.
3. Pay attention to words that have a general meaning, such as *all, always, never, no, none,* and *only.* They often make a statement false.
4. Pay attention to words that qualify, such as *generally, much, many, most, often, sometimes,* and *usually.* They often make a statement true.

408

Multiple-Choice Questions

This kind of question asks you to choose from four or five possible answers.

1. Try to answer the question before reading the choices. If your answer is one of the choices, choose that answer.
2. Eliminate answers you know are wrong. Cross them out if you are allowed to write on the test paper.

Matching Questions

Matching questions ask you to match items in one group with items in another group.

1. Count each group to see whether any items will be left over.
2. Read all the items before you start matching.
3. Match the items you know first, and then match the others. If you can write on the paper, cross out items as you use them.

Fill-In Questions

A fill-in question asks you to give an answer in your own words.

1. Read the question or exercise carefully.
2. If you are completing a sentence, look for clues in the sentence that might help you figure out the answer. If the word *an* is right before the missing word, this means that the missing word begins with a vowel sound.

Short-Answer Questions

Short-answer questions ask you to write one or more sentences in which you give certain information.

1. Scan the question for key words, such as *explain*, *compare*, and *identify*.
2. When you answer the question, give only the information asked for.
3. Answer the question as clearly as possible.

Essay Questions

On many tests, you will have to write one or more essays. Sometimes you are given a choice of questions that you can answer.

1. Look for key words in the question or questions to find out exactly what information you should give.
2. Take a few minutes to think about facts, examples, and other types of information you can put in your essay.
3. Spend most of your time writing your essay so that it is well planned.
4. Leave time at the end of the test to proofread and correct your work.

409

Multiple-Choice Questions Read aloud tips as students follow along. You may want to provide examples. Ensure that students understand the process of logical elimination.

Matching Questions Read aloud tips as students follow along. You may want to provide examples. Tell students they should match the items they know for sure first.

Fill-In Questions Read aloud tips as students follow along. You may want to provide examples. Help students find clues to figure out answers.

Short-Answer Questions and Essay Questions Read aloud tips as students follow along. You may want to provide sample short-answer questions and essay topics. The process described in the Writing Handbook will also help students in writing essays.

Scaffolding

To help students practice test-taking skills, you may want to find existing sample practice tests for recent standardized examinations. Make copies of tests which include different types of test items. Review test tips, and guide students through each type of item.

Metacognition

To help students monitor their comprehension, **ASK:** *Which types of questions have you seen on tests? Which types of questions are easy for you, and which types are hard? Why? How do you get better at taking tests?*

1. Understanding the Parts of a Book

Have students look through the student book. Point out the different sections, such as the title page and table of contents. Ask students what information each section provides. Make sure students understand the uses of a glossary, index, and bibliography. Note that nonfiction books often include a glossary, index, and bibliography, while fiction books usually do not.

Select a fiction and nonfiction book from your classroom library and give each book to a volunteer. Invite the volunteer to look through his or her book and state whether the book is fiction or nonfiction; tell the class the information on the book's title page and table of contents; note whether the book includes headings, a glossary, index, or bibliography; and suggest what the book will be about, based on these facts.

2. Using the Library

Discuss with students the importance of libraries throughout history and today. Explain that libraries were repositories of knowledge in the past, when only a few handwritten copies of any single work existed. Point out that today the nation's public libraries are also great democratic institutions that allow everyone equal access to a vast array of resources. Help students recognize that most public and school libraries permit individuals to borrow books and also provide Internet access for those who may not have it at home. Point out that many specialized libraries give researchers access to rare books and manuscripts and also link with other libraries to create electronic networks of valuable shared information.

The Card Catalog Review the definition of *call number* and make sure students understand how to use the card catalog. Explain how to find a book by title, author, or subject.

The Online Library Catalog Review how to find a book using a computer. Point out that many libraries permit individuals to use their online catalogs from home. Note that not every book in a library may be listed on the computer. Tell students to check the card catalog if they do not find a book online or if computers are busy or not operating.

---

1. Understanding the Parts of a Book
The Title Page
Every book has a **title page** that states the title, author, and publisher.

The Table of Contents and Headings
Many books have a **table of contents**. The table of contents can be found in the front of the book. It lists the chapters or units in the book. Beside each chapter or unit is the number of the page on which it begins. A **heading** at the top of the first page of each section tells you what that section is about.

The Glossary
While you read, you can look up unfamiliar words in the **glossary** at the back of the book. It lists words alphabetically and gives definitions.

The Index
To find out whether a book includes particular information, use the **index** at the back of the book. It is an alphabetical listing of names, places, and subjects in the book. Page numbers are listed beside each item.

The Bibliography
The **bibliography** is at the end of a nonfiction book or article. It tells you the other books or sources where an author got information to write the book. The sources are listed alphabetically by author. The bibliography is also a good way to find more articles or information about the same subject.

2. Using the Library
The Card Catalog
To find a book in a library, use the **card catalog**—an alphabetical list of authors, subjects, and titles. Each book has a **call number**, which tells you where to find a book on the shelf. Author cards, title cards, and subject cards all give information about a book. Use the **author card** when you want to find a book by an author but do not know the title. The **title card** is useful if you know the title of a book but not the author. When you want to find a book about a particular subject, use the **subject card**.

The Online Library Catalog
The **online library catalog** is a fast way to find a book using a computer. Books can be looked up by author, subject, or title. The online catalog will give you information on the book, as well as its call number.

Strategy	Description and Examples
Organizational Planning	Setting a learning goal; planning how to carry out a project, write a story, or solve a problem
Predicting	Using parts of a text (such as illustrations or titles) or a real-life situation and your own knowledge to anticipate what will occur next
Self-Management	Seeking or arranging the conditions that help you learn
Using Your Knowledge and Experience	Using knowledge and experience to learn something new, brainstorm, make associations, or write or tell what you know
Monitoring Comprehension	Being aware of how well a task is going, how well you understand what you are hearing or reading, or how well you are conveying ideas
Using/Making Rules	Applying a rule (phonics, decoding, grammar, linguistic, mathematical, scientific, and so on) to understand a text or complete a task; figuring out rules or patterns from examples
Taking Notes	Writing down key information in verbal, graphic, or numerical form, often as concept maps, word webs, timelines, or other graphic organizers
Visualizing	Creating mental pictures and using them to understand and appreciate descriptive writing
Cooperation	Working with classmates to complete a task or project, demonstrate a process or product, share knowledge, solve problems, give and receive feedback, and develop social skills
Making Inferences	Using the context of a text and your own knowledge to guess meanings of unfamiliar words or ideas
Substitution	Using a synonym or paraphrasing when you want to express an idea and do not know the word(s)
Using Resources	Using reference materials (books, dictionaries, encyclopedias, videos, computer programs, the Internet) to find information or complete a task
Classification	Grouping words, ideas, objects, or numbers according to their attributes; constructing graphic organizers to show classifications
Asking Questions	Negotiating meaning by asking for clarification, confirmation, rephrasing, or examples
Summarizing	Making a summary of something you listened to or read; retelling a text in your own words
Self-evaluation	After completing a task, judging how well you did, whether you reached your goal, and how effective your problem-solving procedures were

411

3. Learning Strategies

Tell students that this chart lists various strategies that can help them understand, use, and remember information. Suggest that students refer to this chart whenever they need clarification of information or have a special assignment or project to complete.

Cooperation Point to the strategy *Cooperation* listed in the chart. Read the description and examples of cooperation aloud as students follow along in the text. Paraphrase and elaborate on the description. For example, **SAY:** *Whenever I ask you to work in pairs or groups and to prepare a project together or share input with your partners, I am asking you to cooperate.* Give a specific instance of cooperation. For example, **SAY:** *When I asked you to work in pairs last week to prepare and deliver an oral report, I wanted you to cooperate.* Discuss with students why cooperation is an effective learning strategy. Ask them to provide examples of information they learned or tasks they completed by cooperating with others. Answer questions students may have about this strategy.

Cooperative Grouping Tell students that they are going to use the learning strategy *cooperation* to help one another review each of the other fifteen learning strategies listed on the chart.

Have students work in pairs. Assign each pair a learning strategy. Have partners develop a brief presentation that explains their assigned strategy. Tell students to use the presentation you made about cooperation as a model. Suggest that partners be prepared to read aloud the description of their learning strategy; paraphrase the information in their own words; provide a concrete example of the strategy; discuss with the class the effectiveness of the strategy; ask the class for additional examples of the strategy; and answer any questions the class may have about the learning strategy.

Ask all student pairs to read aloud the description of their assigned learning strategy to the class. Have selected pairs give their full presentations.

This handbook contains a concise summary of English grammar, sentence structure, and punctuation and covers these topics: parts of speech, clauses, sentences, and mechanics.

To introduce this handbook, walk your students through the pages and note the kind of information that can be found under each major heading and subheading. Tell students they may use the handbook in the classroom or on their own for grammar questions and review.

THE PARTS OF SPEECH

List the eight parts of speech on the board and say each one aloud with your students.

Nouns

Read aloud the definition of a noun as students follow along in their books. Help students differentiate between the two types of nouns—common and proper nouns. Write the categories *people, places*, and *things* on the board. Call on volunteers to name nouns that fit into the categories, and write the words on the board. Then read the definition of a compound noun aloud. Call on volunteers to read aloud the compound nouns in the box.

Scaffolding

Draw two webs on the board. Write *Common Nouns* in the center of the first web and write *Proper Nouns* in the second web. List the following nouns outside the web. Then ask students to write each noun in the correct web.

Common Nouns: desk, garden, boy, month, baseball, pizza, nurse, house

Proper Nouns: Glen, Mexico, October, Liza, Tuesday, Yankees, California, American

Articles

Read aloud and discuss the definition of an article. Focus on the indefinite articles *a* and *an* and give examples of how they are used.

Next, focus on the definite article *the*. **SAY:** *The definite article the is used to talk about one or more specific person, place, or thing.*

Scaffolding

Write a list of nouns preceded by definite articles on the board. Next write the same nouns preceded by indefinite articles. Then have students take turns using each article and noun in a sentence.

Grammar Handbook

THE PARTS OF SPEECH

In English there are eight **parts of speech**: nouns, pronouns, adjectives, verbs, adverbs, prepositions, conjunctions, and interjections.

Nouns

Nouns name people, places, or things. There are two kinds of nouns: **common nouns** and **proper nouns**.

A **common noun** is a general person, place, or thing.

person	thing	place

The **student** brings a **notebook** to **class**.

A **proper noun** is a specific person, place, or thing. Proper nouns start with a capital letter.

person	place	thing

Joseph went to **Paris** and saw the **Eiffel Tower**.

A noun that is made up of two words is called a **compound noun**. A compound noun can be one word or two words. Some compound nouns have hyphens.

One word: **newspaper, bathroom**
Two words: **vice president, pet shop**
Hyphens: **sister-in-law, grown-up**

Articles identify nouns. *A, an*, and *the* are articles.

A and *an* are called **indefinite articles**. Use the article *a* or *an* to talk about one general person, place, or thing.

Use *an* before a word that begins with a vowel sound.

I have **an** idea.

Use *a* before a word that begins with a consonant sound.

May I borrow **a** pen?

The is called a **definite article**. Use *the* to talk about one or more specific people, places, or things.

Please bring me **the** box from your room. **The** books are in my backpack.

Pronouns

Pronouns are words that take the place of nouns or proper nouns. In this example, the pronoun *she* replaces, or refers to, the proper noun *Angela*.

proper noun   pronoun
Angela is not home. **She** is babysitting.

Pronouns can be subjects or objects. They can be singular or plural.

	Subject Pronouns	**Object Pronouns**
Singular	I, you, he, she, it	me, you, him, her, it
Plural	we, you, they	us, you, them

A **subject pronoun** replaces a noun or proper noun that is the subject of a sentence. A **subject** is who or what a sentence is about. In these sentences, *He* replaces *Daniel*.

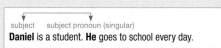

subject   subject pronoun (singular)
Daniel is a student. **He** goes to school every day.

In these sentences, *We* replaces *Heather* and *I*.

subject   subject pronoun (singular)
Heather and **I** like this movie. **We** think it's great.

413

Pronouns

Read aloud the definition of a pronoun with students. Write the list of singular and plural subject and object pronouns on the board.

Subject Pronouns Explain that pronouns can take the place of the subject of a sentence. Have a volunteer read aloud the definition of a subject pronoun. Call students' attention to the singular and plural subject pronouns on the board and read the words aloud.

Scaffolding

Write the following sentences on the board. Have students take turns completing the second sentence in each pair with a subject pronoun that can take the place of the underlined noun or proper noun in the first sentence.

1. *Mark is playing ball. _____ is in the field.*
2. *Ted and I play tennis. _____ play tennis after school.*
3. *These books are for Jen. _____ are about lions.*
4. *The boys are here. _____ are here.*
5. *This school is very clean. _____ has a fresh coat of paint on the walls.*

Metacognition

Point out to students how the headings and boldface type in this handbook can be helpful when students want to learn about the eight parts of speech.

Object Pronouns Read aloud the definition of an object pronoun with students. Point out the object pronoun *him* that takes the place of *Ed* in the example. Then write these sentences on the board:

Lauren gave <u>Ed</u> the notes.
Lauren gave <u>him</u> the notes.

Have students take turns replacing the name *Ed* in the first sentence with other names and then using the correct object pronoun *him*, *her*, or *them* to complete the second sentence.

Present and practice using pronouns that are objects of a preposition in the same way: Write the sentences in the second box on the board. Then ask students to replace the proper names with the correct object pronoun *him, her,* or *them.*

Possessive Pronouns Read aloud the definition of a possessive pronoun with students as well as the examples in the box. Then write the following on the board:

<u>Kyoko</u> put on <u>her</u> coat.

Have students take turns replacing the name *Kyoko* with other names and then using the correct possessive pronoun in the sentence.

Scaffolding

To give students practice with possessive pronouns, have them place items they own, such as a book, a pen, or a box of markers, on a table. Have students say sentences about the items using possessive pronouns. For instance:

This is his pen.
These are their markers.
This is my book.

Metacognition

To help students understand how they learn, **ASK:** *What worked better for helping you understand pronouns—changing the subjects and pronouns in the sentences or just reading about pronouns?*

An **object pronoun** replaces a noun or proper noun that is the object of a verb. A verb tells the action in a sentence. An **object** receives the action of a verb.

In these sentences the verb is *gave*. *Him* replaces *Ed*, which is the object of the verb.

Lauren gave **Ed** the notes. Lauren gave **him** the notes.

An object pronoun can also replace a noun or proper noun that is the **object of a preposition**. Prepositions are words like *for, to,* or *with*. In these sentences, the preposition is *with*. *Them* replaces *José* and *Yolanda*, which is the object of the preposition.

I went to the mall with **José and Yolanda**. I went to the mall with **them**.

Pronouns can also be possessive. A **possessive pronoun** replaces a noun or proper noun. It shows who owns something.

	Possessive Pronouns
Singular	mine, yours, hers, his
Plural	ours, yours, theirs

In these sentences, *hers* replaces the words *Kyoko's coat*. It shows that Kyoko owns the coat.

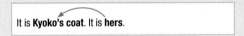

It is **Kyoko's coat**. It is **hers**.

Adjectives

Adjectives describe nouns. An adjective usually comes before the noun it describes.

tall grass	**big** truck	**two** kittens

An adjective can also come *after* the noun it describes.

The bag is **heavy**. The books are **new**.

Do not add -s to adjectives that describe plural nouns.

the **red** houses	the **funny** jokes	the **smart** teachers

Verbs

Verbs express an action or a state of being.

subject   verb   subject   verb
Jackie **walks** to school. The school **is** near her house.

An **action verb** tells what someone or something does or did. You cannot always see the action of an action verb.

Verbs That Tell Actions You Can See		Verbs That Tell Actions You Cannot See	
dance	swim	know	sense
play	talk	remember	name
sit	write	think	understand

A **linking verb** shows no action. It links the subject with another word that describes the subject.

Linking Verbs		
look	is	appear
smell	are	seem
sound	am	become
taste	were	
feel		

415

Adjectives

Remind students that nouns are words that name people, places, and things. Then show a crayon. Ask students to suggest words that describe the crayon and list them on the board. Explain that words that describe nouns are called adjectives.

Point out that an adjective usually comes <u>before</u> the noun. Call on a volunteer to read the examples in the first box on the page. Next, discuss adjectives that come <u>after</u> nouns. Read aloud the examples in the second box.

Scaffolding

Write two lists on the board. <u>Nouns:</u> *weather, sky, person, day, beach, paper, child, dog;* <u>Adjectives:</u> *silly, beautiful, stormy, wonderful, clear, kind, happy, funny.* Have students take turns choosing a noun and an adjective to describe it. Then have students write sentences using at least three nouns and adjectives. Call on volunteers to read their sentences.

Verbs

Call on a volunteer to act out verbs that you whisper. Ask the other students to say what the student is doing and record it on the board. For example, *Johnny jumps.* Explain that words that name actions or states are called *verbs.*

Action Verbs Read aloud the definition and examples of action verbs with students. Help them distinguish between the action verbs you can see and those you cannot see.

Scaffolding

Print each action verb from the lists in the student book on a card. Have students take turns choosing a card, reading the verb, and using the verb in a sentence.

Linking Verbs Ask a volunteer to explain the function of a linking verb. Emphasize that linking verbs *themselves* do not show action. Read aloud the examples of linking verbs in the box. Ask students for sentences using linking verbs, and write them on the board.

Cooperative Grouping Have students work in pairs. Write these incomplete sentences on the board. Ask students to complete each sentence by adding a word after each linking verb.

1. *I look _____.*
2. *He seems _____.*
3. *They appear _____.*
4. *The flower smells _____.*
5. *We are _____.*

T415

Helping Verbs Read the definition of a helping verb aloud with students, and note the examples in the box. Ask students for examples of sentences using helping verbs and write them on the board.

Cooperative Grouping Have students work in pairs. Write the following incomplete sentences on the board. Ask students to add an action verb after each helping verb and complete each sentence.

1. *I am _____.*
2. *He did _____.*
3. *She has _____.*
4. *We can _____.*
5. *They should _____.*

Then ask student pairs to write five additional sentences using helping verbs.

Have students compare the differences among action, helping, and linking verbs.

In this sentence, the adjective *tired* tells something about the subject, *dog*. *Seems* is the linking verb.

Our dog **seems** tired.

In this sentence, the noun *friend* tells something about the subject, *brother*. *Is* is the linking verb.

Your brother **is** my friend.

A **helping verb** comes before the main verb. It adds to the main verb's meaning. Helping verbs can be forms of the verbs *be, do,* or *have.*

	Helping Verbs
Forms of *be*	am, was, is, were, are
Forms of *do*	do, did, does
Forms of *have*	have, had, has
Other helping verbs	can, must, could, have (to), should, may, will, would

In this sentence, *am* is the helping verb; *walking* is the action verb.

helping action
verb   verb
I **am walking** to my science class.

In this sentence, *has* is the helping verb; *completed* is the action verb.

helping action
verb   verb
He **has completed** his essay.

In questions, the subject comes between a helping verb and a main verb.

person
Did Liang **give** you the CD?

416

Adverbs

Adverbs describe the action of verbs. They tell *how* an action happens. Adverbs answer the question *Where? When? How? How much?* or *How often?*

Many adverbs end in *-ly.*

easily	slowly	carefully

Some adverbs do not end in *-ly.*

seldom	fast	very

In this sentence, the adverb *everywhere* modifies the verb *looked*. It answers the question *Where?*

>   verb   adverb
> Nicole looked **everywhere** for her cell phone.

In this sentence, the adverb *quickly* modifies the verb *walked*. It answers the question *How?*

>   verb   adverb
> They walked home **quickly**.

Adverbs also modify adjectives. They answer the question *How much?* or *How little?*

In this sentence, the adjective *dangerous* modifies the noun *road*. The adverb *very* modifies the adjective *dangerous*.

>   adverb adjective noun
> This is a **very** dangerous road.

Adverbs can also modify other adverbs. In this sentence, the adverb *fast* modifies the verb *runs*. The adverb *quite* modifies the adverb *fast*.

>   verb adverb adverb
> John runs **quite** fast.

417

Adverbs

Read the definition of adverbs aloud with students. Then review the examples on the page. Ask volunteers to use the adverbs in the first two boxes in a sentence. Write each sentence on the board. Ask students to say if the adverb in each sentence answers the question *Where? When? How? How much?* or *How often?*

Scaffolding

Write the following words in lists on the board. Have students take turns choosing a verb and an adverb to describe it. *Verbs: run, eat, study, dance, think, play, draw, look; Adverbs: beautifully, wildly, quickly, slowly, well, seldom, fast, everywhere. For each pair of verb and adverb, ask students which question the adverb answers (Where? When? How? How much? or How often?). Also, explain that though many adverbs come* <u>after</u> *a verb (run quickly), some adverbs are used* <u>before</u> *a verb (seldom study).*

Metacognition

To help students understand how they learn, **SAY:** *How do you remember the difference between adverbs and adjectives when you read?*

Websites For more information, log on to www.LongmanKeystone.com for links to other interesting websites about adverbs.

Prepositions

Read aloud the definition of a preposition with students. Emphasize that a preposition answers the questions *When? Where?* and *In what direction?*

Choose a volunteer to hold a marker and then model giving directions. Use prepositions from the *Place* list to tell the student where to place the marker. *(under the table, below the chair)*

Ask another volunteer to follow instructions as students use prepositions from the *Direction* list to tell him or her in which direction to walk. *(across the room, to the window)*

Have a third volunteer follow instructions as students use prepositions from the *Time* list to tell the student when to jump three times. *(after counting to two, before you clap)*

Scaffolding

Remind students that a preposition shows time, place, or direction, and that it answers the questions *When? Where?* and *In what direction?* Write the following prepositions on the board: *after, above, across, before, below, to.* Invite volunteers to use each preposition in a sentence.

Prepositional Phrases Call attention to the definition of a *prepositional phrase.* Help students locate the preposition that begins the prepositional phrase *(near)* and the noun that ends the phrase *(school).* Tell students that the noun is the object of the preposition. Remind students that a pronoun can also be the object of a preposition. Give examples *(near her, above it, after us, below them).*

Conjunctions

Introduce the word *conjunction* and explain that conjunctions are used to join words, groups of words, and whole sentences together. Read aloud the examples that show how a conjunction may be used. Point out that an independent clause is a sentence that can stand alone, forming a complete sentence.

Prepositions

Prepositions can show time, place, and direction.

Time	Place	Direction
after	above	across
before	below	down
during	in	into
since	near	to
until	under	up

In this sentence, the preposition *above* shows where the bird flew. It shows place.

preposition
A bird flew **above** my head.

In this sentence, the preposition *across* shows direction.

preposition
The children walked **across** the street.

A **prepositional phrase** starts with a preposition and ends with a noun or pronoun.

In this sentence, the preposition is *near* and the noun is *school.*

prepositional phrase
The library is **near the new school**.

Conjunctions

A **conjunction** joins words, groups of words, and whole sentences.

Conjunctions			
and	for	or	yet
but	nor	so	

418

In this sentence, the conjunction *and* joins two proper nouns: *Jonah* and *Teresa.*

noun	noun
Jonah **and** Teresa are in school.	

In this sentence, the conjunction *or* joins two prepositional phrases: *to the movies* and *to the mall.*

prepositional phrase · prepositional phrase
They want to go to the movies **or** to the mall.

In this sentence, the conjunction *and* joins two independent clauses: *Amanda baked the cookies,* and *Eric made the lemonade.*

independent clause · independent clause
Amanda baked the cookies, **and** Eric made the lemonade.

Interjections

Interjections are words or phrases that express emotion.

Interjections that express strong emotion are followed by an exclamation point.

Wow! Did you see that catch?
Hey! Watch out for that ball.

Interjections that express mild emotion are followed by a comma.

Gee, I'm sorry that your team lost.
Oh, it's okay. We'll do better next time.

419

Write the following incomplete sentences on the board. Ask students to add a conjunction to complete each sentence:

1. *Leo _____ Joey play baseball.*
2. *On Saturday, the girls want to go to the movies _____ and the park.*
3. *My grandmother wants to make tuna sandwiches _____ chicken soup for lunch.*
4. *Beth wants to buy the red dress, _____ her mother wants her to get the blue one.*

Then ask students to write four additional sentences using conjunctions to join nouns, prepositional phrases, and independent clauses. Ask students to share their sentences.

Interjections

Read the definition and examples of interjections aloud with students. Call attention to the exclamation points in the examples. Then list these interjections on the board.

Hurray!   Surprise!
Wow!   Amazing!
Hey!   Yikes!

Discuss situations in which people might use these interjections. Have students take turns making statements that begin with interjections. Then ask students to pretend they are at a sports event and make up sentences with interjections, using that theme. Write the sentences on the board and read them aloud together.

Discuss the difference between using an exclamation point and a comma after an interjection.

This completes the Parts of Speech section. Once again, encourage students to use the handbook whenever they need to review or learn more about any of the parts of speech.

CLAUSES

Introduce the section on clauses by reviewing the meaning of the terms *subject* and *verb*. Explain that clauses are groups of words with a subject and a verb. Tell students that there are two kinds of clauses, independent and dependent.

Read the definition of clauses aloud with students. Remind them that an independent clause is a complete sentence. Write several independent clauses on the board and help students name the subject and the verb.

Read aloud the definition of dependent clauses. Point out that a dependent clause is not a complete sentence. List the following clauses on the board. Have students determine if the clause is independent or dependent.

After a long time
The puppy likes to play
I fed the puppy
When I was little

SENTENCES

Explain to students that there are different kinds of sentences. **ASK:** *What do all sentences have in common?* Write a list of the attributes of a sentence on the board. Discuss each attribute and have students copy the list to keep as a reference.

1. A sentence has a subject and a verb.

2. A sentence tells at least one complete thought.

3. A sentence always begins with a capital letter.

4. A sentence always ends with a period, question mark, or exclamation point.

Clauses are groups of words with a subject and a verb. Some clauses form complete sentences; they tell a complete thought. Others do not.

This clause is a complete sentence. Clauses that form complete sentences are called **independent clauses**.

> subject verb
> The dog's **tail wagged**.

This clause is not a complete sentence. Clauses that don't form complete sentences are called **dependent clauses**.

> subject verb
> when the **boy patted** him.

Independent clauses can be combined with dependent clauses to form a sentence.

In this sentence, *The dog's tail wagged* is an independent clause. *When the boy patted him* is a dependent clause.

> ┌independent clause┐ ┌dependent clause┐
> The dog's tail wagged when the boy patted him.

SENTENCES

Sentences have a subject and a verb, and tell a complete thought. A sentence always begins with a capital letter. It always ends with a period, question mark, or exclamation point.

420

Simple Sentences and Compound Sentences

Some sentences are called simple sentences. Others are called compound sentences. A **simple sentence** has one independent clause. Here is an example.

> ⌐—— independent clause ——⌐
> The dog barked at the mail carrier.

Compound sentences are made up of two or more simple sentences, or independent clauses. They are joined together by a **conjunction** such as *and* or *but*.

> ⌐— independent clause —⌐   ⌐— independent clause —⌐
> The band has a lead singer, **but** they need a drummer.

Sentence Types

Sentences have different purposes. There are four types of sentences: declarative, interrogative, imperative, and exclamatory.

Declarative sentences are statements. They end with a period.

> We are going to the beach on Saturday.

Interrogative sentences are questions. They end with a question mark.

> Will you come with us?

Imperative sentences are commands. They usually end with a period. If the command is strong, the sentence may end with an exclamation point.

> Put on your life jacket. Now jump into the water!

Exclamatory sentences express strong feeling. They end with an exclamation point.

> I swam all the way from the boat to the shore!

421

Simple Sentences and Compound Sentences

Remind students that an independent clause is a complete sentence. Explain that a simple sentence is a sentence that has one independent clause.

Read aloud the example of a simple sentence. Discuss how this sentence has all the attributes of a sentence. Ask students to give other examples of simple sentences and write them on the board.

Read the description of a compound sentence with students. Emphasize that when two independent clauses are joined to make a compound sentence, it must include a comma and a conjunction.

Write the following compound sentences on the board. Have a volunteer draw a line under the conjunction that links the independent clauses and then read each clause.

1. *We went to the game, but it rained.*
2. *The rain stopped, so we went for a walk.*
3. *We met our friends, and they came home with us.*

Sentence Types

Tell students that there are four types of sentences (*declarative, interrogative, imperative,* and *exclamatory*) and that each type of sentence has a different purpose. Read the definitions and examples together. After students read each example, ask them to create their own sentences and write them on the board. For each sentence, have students identify the sentence attributes described above.

You may wish to have students create a book of different kinds of sentences, using one page for each type. This will give students practice writing the four different kinds of sentences.

Explain that in the Mechanics section of this handbook, students will find information about different kinds of punctuation marks they will see and use.

End Marks

Read the definition of *end marks* aloud with students, noting the three kinds of end marks.

Cooperative Grouping Have students work in pairs. Tell them to copy the following sentences from the board and take turns completing each sentence by adding an end mark. Then have students explain to their partner why that particular mark was used.

1. *Who lives across the street*
2. *That house has yellow shutters*
3. *There are so many things to do on the weekend*
4. *Your writing is so wonderful*
5. *Are you going to visit your aunt*
6. *What fun we had on the picnic*
7. *Be careful not to walk on thin ice*

Periods

Emphasize that periods are not just used at the end of sentences. Read aloud with students the different ways periods are used. For each, write an example on the board of how a period is used.

Write the following on the board. Have students take turns adding a period when necessary and explaining why they added a period.

Mrs Green	*JK Rowling*
Gov Jones	*Avenue*
Blvd	*Rd*
in	*kg*
gal	*cm*
St	*ft*
Ms White	*Mr Todd*

End Marks

End marks come at the end of sentences. There are three kinds of end marks: periods, question marks, and exclamation points.

Use a **period** to end a statement (declarative sentence).

> The spacecraft *Magellan* took pictures of Jupiter.

Use a **period** to end a command or request (imperative sentence) that isn't strong enough to need an exclamation point.

> Please change the channel.

Use a **question mark** to end a sentence that asks a question. (interrogative sentence).

> Where does Mrs. Suarez live?

Use an **exclamation point** to end a sentence that expresses strong feeling (exclamatory sentence).

> That was a great party!
> Look at that huge house!

Use an **exclamation point** to end an imperative sentence that gives an urgent command.

> Get away from the edge of the pool!

Periods are also used after initials and many abbreviations.

Use a **period** after a person's initial or abbreviated title.

Ms. Susan Vargas	Mrs. Fiske	J. D. Salinger
Gov. Lise Crawford	Mr. Vargas	Dr. Sapirstein

Use a **period** after the abbreviation of streets, roads, and so on.

| Avenue | Ave. | Road | Rd. |
| Highway | Hwy. | Street | St. |

Use a **period** after the abbreviation of many units of measurement. Abbreviations for metric measurements do *not* use periods.

inch	in.	centimeter	cm
foot	ft.	meter	m
pound	lb.	kilogram	kg
gallon	gal.	liter	l

Commas

Commas separate, or set off, parts of a sentence, or phrase.

Use a comma to separate two independent clauses linked by a conjunction. In this sentence, the comma goes before the conjunction *but*.

┌─ independent clause ─┐   ┌─ independent clause ─┐
We went to the museum, **but** it is not open on Mondays.

Use commas to separate the parts in a series. A series is a group of three or more words, phrases, or very brief clauses.

Commas in Series	
To separate words	Lucio's bike is red, white, and silver.
To separate phrases	Today, he rode all over the lawn, down the sidewalk, and up the hill.
To separate clauses	Lucio washed the bike, his dad washed the car, and his mom washed the dog.

Use a comma to set off an introductory word, phrase, or clause.

Commas with Introductory Words	
To separate words	Yes, Stacy likes to go swimming.
To set off a phrase	In a month, she may join the swim team again.
To set off a clause	If she joins the swim team, I'll miss her at softball practice.

423

Commas

Tell students that another mark they will see and use often is the comma. Draw a comma on the board. Explain that a comma is used to separate or set off parts of a sentence or a phrase.

Commas in a Series

To help students better understand the uses of the comma, review what they previously learned about clauses and conjunctions. Then read aloud the definition of *series* as students follow along in the text. Read aloud the three examples to model how a reader pauses briefly at commas between items in a series. For each point listed on the chart, write another example on the board to show how a comma is used in series. Ask a volunteer to read the examples on the board, pausing appropriately at the commas.

Commas with Introductory Words

Read aloud the three examples to model how a reader pauses briefly after commas with introductory words. For each point listed on the chart, write another example on the board to show how a comma is used after introductory words. Ask a volunteer to read the examples on the board, pausing appropriately at the commas.

Commas with Interrupting Words Read aloud the three examples to model how a reader pauses briefly at a comma with an interrupting word, phrase, or clause. For each point listed on the chart, write another example on the board to show how a comma is used to set off an interrupting word, phrase, or clause. Ask a volunteer to read the examples on the board, and to pause appropriately at the commas.

Scaffolding

Write the following sentences on the board. Ask students to copy the examples into their notebooks, adding commas as appropriate. Then add commas to the examples you wrote on the board. Have students check the accuracy of their punctuation against the punctuation you added. Ask volunteers to explain why each comma was needed.

1. *We waited for the bus but it never came.*
2. *We got into a cab and the driver asked us where to go.*
3. *Jim's shirt is white green and orange.*
4. *Yes Jenny likes to go swimming. Olga do you like to swim?*
5. *We left the store finally to get something to eat.*
6. *Tony asked "How do I get the hospital from here?"*
7. *Thank you Ming for putting away the dishes.*

Cooperative Grouping Have students work in pairs to write sentences that use commas, similar to the ones given above. When students share their sentences with the class, ask why they used the commas.

Use commas to set off an interrupting word, phrase, or clause.

	Commas with Interrupting Words
To set off a word	We left, finally, to get some fresh air.
To set off a phrase	Carol's dog, a brown pug, shakes when he gets scared.
To set off a clause	The assignment, I'm sorry to say, was too hard for me.

Use a comma to set off a speaker's quoted words in a sentence.

> Jeanne asked, "Where is that book I just had?"
> "I just saw it," said Billy, "on the kitchen counter."

In a direct address, one speaker talks directly to another. Use commas to set off the name of the person being addressed.

> Thank you, Dee, for helping to put away the dishes.
> Phil, why are you late again?

Use a comma between the day and the year.

> My cousin was born on September 9, 2003.

If the date appears in the middle of a sentence, use a comma before and after the year.

> Daria's mother was born on June 8, 1969, in New Jersey.

Use a comma between a city and a state and between a city and a nation.

> My father grew up in Bakersfield, California.
> We are traveling to Acapulco, Mexico.

424

If the names appear in the middle of a sentence, use a comma before *and* after the state or nation.

> My friend Carl went to Mumbai, India, last year.

Use a comma after the greeting in a friendly letter. Use a comma after the closing in both a friendly letter and formal letter. Do this in e-mail letters, too.

> Dear Margaret,   Sincerely,   Yours truly,

Semicolons and Colons

Semicolons can connect two independent clauses. Use them when the clauses are closely related in meaning or structure.

> The team won again; it was their ninth victory.
> Ana usually studies right after school; Rita prefers to study in the evening.

Colons introduce a list of items or important information.

Use a colon after an independent clause to introduce a list of items. (The clause often includes the words *the following, these, those,* or *this*.)

> The following animals live in Costa Rica: monkeys, lemurs, toucans, and jaguars.

Use a colon to introduce important information. If the information is in an independent clause, use a capital letter to begin the first word after the colon.

> There is one main rule: Do not talk to anyone during the test.
> You must remember this: Stay away from the train tracks!

Use a colon to separate hours and minutes when writing the time.

> 1:30   7:45   11:08

425

Semicolons

Say the word *semicolon* and write a semicolon on the board. Read the definition of semicolons aloud with students.

Write these independent clauses on the board: *It was a perfect day for a soccer game. The team was ready to play.* Show students that the two independent clauses can be joined with a comma and the conjunction *and*. Write: *It was a perfect day for a soccer game, and the team was ready to play.* Then explain that these two independent clauses may be joined in another way. Write: *It was a perfect day for a soccer game; the team was ready to play.* Call attention to the semicolon used to join the sentences.

Have students suggest additional pairs of independent clauses. Write them on the board without punctuation. Ask student volunteers to insert semicolons and periods.

Colons

Say the word *colon* and write a colon on the board. Tell students that a colon is different from a semicolon in the way it looks and in the way it is used. Read about the use of colons aloud with students. Then write the following examples on the board:

1. *There are three kinds of end marks: periods, question marks, and exclamation points.*

2. *You must remember this: Always try your best.*

3. *4:30*

Have volunteers locate the colon in each example and tell why it is used there.

Quotation Marks

Read aloud the explanation of when and how to use quotation marks for direct quotations and dialogue. Then ask students to suggest a brief dialogue between two of their favorite characters from a story, movie, or TV show. Write the lines on the board without punctuation. Invite students to suggest where to put quotation marks, commas, periods, question marks, or exclamation points.

Read aloud the information about the use of quotation marks for titles of short works. Tell students that this rule applies to titles of chapters, short stories, articles, songs, single TV episodes, and short poems. Ask students to suggest items for each category and list them on the board. Explain that for all other written work and artwork, titles are underlined or set in *italic type;* this applies to books, magazines, newspapers, plays, movies, TV series, and paintings.

Quotation Marks

Quotation Marks set off direct quotations, dialogue, and some titles. A **direct quotation** is the exact words that somebody said, wrote, or thought.

Commas and periods *always* go inside quotation marks. If a question mark or exclamation point is part of the quotation, it is also placed *inside* the quotation marks.

> "Can you please get ready?" Mom asked.
> My sister shouted, "Look out for that bee!"

If a question mark or exclamation point is *not* part of the quotation, it goes *outside* the quotation marks. In these cases there is no punctuation before the end quotation marks.

> Did you say, "I can't do this"?

Conversation between two or more people is called **dialogue**. Use quotation marks to set off spoken words in dialogue.

> "What a great ride!" Pam said. "Let's go on it again."
> Julio shook his head and said, "No way. I'm feeling sick."

Use quotation marks around the titles of short works of writing or other art forms. The following kinds of titles take quotation marks:

Chapters	"The Railroad in the West"
Short Stories	"The Perfect Cat"
Articles	"California in the 1920s"
Songs	"This Land Is Your Land"
Single TV episodes	"Charlie's New Idea"
Short poems	"The Bat"

Titles of all other written work and artwork are underlined or set in italic type. These include books, magazines, newspapers, plays, movies, TV series, and paintings.

426

T426

Apostrophes

Apostrophes can be used with singular and plural nouns to show ownership or possession. To form the possessive, follow these rules:

For singular nouns, add an apostrophe and an *s*.

Maria's eyes	hamster's cage	the sun's warmth

For singular nouns that end in *s*, add an apostrophe and an *s*.

her boss's office	Carlos's piano	the grass's length

For plural nouns that do not end in *s*, add an apostrophe and an *s*.

women's clothes	men's shoes	children's books

For plural nouns that end in *s*, add an apostrophe.

teachers' lounge	dogs' leashes	kids' playground

Apostrophes are also used in **contractions**. A contraction is a shortened form of two words that have been combined. The apostrophe shows where a letter or letters have been taken away.

I will
I'll be home in one hour.
do not
We **don't** have any milk.

Capitalization

There are five main reasons to use capital letters:

1. To begin a sentence and in a direct quotation
2. To write the word *I*
3. To write a proper noun (the name of a specific person, place, or thing)
4. To write a person's title
5. To write the title of a work (artwork, written work, magazine, newspaper, musical composition, organization)

427

Apostrophes

Read aloud the information on the uses of apostrophes. Discuss using apostrophes to show possession and in contractions. Give examples. Then draw a web on the board. In the center of the web, write *Apostrophes*. Have students suggest ideas for the web by giving examples in which apostrophes are used.

Capitalization

Read aloud the list of reasons for using capital letters. Write each reason on the board and discuss the reasons with students. Ask students for examples, including names of people and places, days and months, holidays, languages, religions, and titles. Write these examples under each reason for capitalization. Have students copy the capitalization rules and examples in their notebooks to use for reference.

Have students refer to the rules governing the use of capital letters. Ask students to write sentences using capital letters where appropriate. Tell students to create at least one separate sentence to illustrate each rule; however, they may use more than one capital letter per sentence.

Invite volunteers to share their sentences with the class. After each reading, **ASK:** *Which letters did you capitalize in that sentence and why?*

Use a capital letter to begin the first word in a sentence.

Cows eat grass. They also eat hay.

Use a capital letter for the first word of a direct quotation. Use the capital letter even if the quotation is in the middle of a sentence.

Carlos said, "We need more lettuce for the sandwiches."

Use a capital letter for the word *I*.

How will I ever learn all these things? I guess I will learn them little by little.

Use a capital letter for a proper noun: the name of a specific person, place, or thing. Capitalize the important words in names.

| Robert E. Lee | Morocco | Tuesday | Tropic of Cancer |

Capital Letters in Place Names	
Streets	Interstate 95, Center Street, Atwood Avenue
City Sections	Greenwich Village, Shaker Heights, East Side
Cities and Towns	Rome, Chicago, Fresno
States	California, North Dakota, Maryland
Regions	Pacific Northwest, Great Plains, Eastern Europe
Nations	China, Dominican Republic, Italy
Continents	North America, Africa, Asia
Mountains	Mount Shasta, Andes Mountains, Rocky Mountains
Deserts	Mojave Desert, Sahara Desert, Gobi Desert
Islands	Fiji Islands, Capri, Virgin Islands
Rivers	Amazon River, Nile River, Mississippi River
Lakes	Lake Superior, Great Bear Lake, Lake Tahoe
Bays	San Francisco Bay, Hudson Bay, Galveston Bay
Seas	Mediterranean Sea, Sea of Japan
Oceans	Pacific Ocean, Atlantic Ocean, Indian Ocean

428

Capital Letters for Specific Things	
Historical Periods, Events	Renaissance, Battle of Bull Run
Historical Texts	Constitution, Bill of Rights
Days and Months	Monday, October
Holidays	Thanksgiving, Labor Day
Organizations, Schools	Greenpeace, Central High School
Government Bodies	Congress, State Department
Political Parties	Republican Party, Democratic Party
Ethnic Groups	Chinese, Latinos
Languages, Nationalities	Spanish, Canadian
Buildings	Empire State Building, City Hall
Monuments	Lincoln Memorial, Washington Monument
Religions	Hinduism, Christianity, Judaism, Islam
Special Events	Boston Marathon, Ohio State Fair

Use a capital letter for a person's title if the title comes before the name. In the second sentence below, a capital letter is not needed because the title does not come before a name.

> I heard Senator Clinton's speech about jobs. The senator may come to our school.

Use a capital letter for the first and last word and all other important words in titles of books, newspapers, magazines, short stories, plays, movies, songs, paintings, and sculptures.

> Lucy wants to read The Lord of the Rings.
> The newspaper my father reads is The New York Times.
> Did you like the painting called Work in the Fields?
> This poem is called "The Birch Tree."

Cooperative Learning Continue helping students learn and review the rules governing the use of capital letters. Have students work in pairs. Choose a brief selection from the student book or distribute a copy of a selection from a newspaper or magazine. Ask partners to read the selection together and take turns identifying the capital letters in the selection, as well as the reason why each capital letter was used.

Metacognition

Help students monitor their comprehension of the use of capital letters in titles. **ASK:** *When would you capitalize the word* president *if you were writing a report about several different presidents of the United States?* (Students should recognize that the word *president* should be capitalized only in front of a specific name.)

This handbook contains valuable information about the skills and strategies students need to become strong and active readers. It covers the following topics:

- What is reading comprehension?
- What are reading strategies?
- How to improve reading fluency

To introduce the handbook, walk your students through the pages and, together, note the information found under the major headings and subheadings. Tell students that they may consult the handbook for tips and suggestions whenever they start a new text or have difficulty understanding a text. Remind students that reading is both an essential skill in everyday life, and also something that can enrich their lives.

WHAT IS READING COMPREHENSION?

Read aloud the introduction as students follow along in the text. Discuss the meaning of *active* versus *passive* with students. Explain that reading comprehension involves more than simply understanding a text. It involves all five of the skills outlined in the introduction.

Understanding What You Are Reading

Remind students that recognizing letters and words is the first step in understanding a text. Stress the importance of figuring out the meaning of new words from their context. **ASK:** *If you cannot figure out a word's meaning from the context, what are some other ways to find the meaning?* (Students might ask someone or use a dictionary.) To highlight the usefulness of rereading difficult material, have students read a challenging passage from their student book. Then have them read the passage a second time. Discuss what they learned and understood from the second reading that may not have fully understood on their first reading.

Engaging with the Text

Point out that writers *want* readers to understand and appreciate their work. Read aloud the first tip as students follow along in the text. **ASK:** *What are some clues that can help you predict what will happen in a story?* (Clues might include what a character says or does or other devices that foreshadow events.) Then read aloud the second and third tips as students follow along. Ask students to brainstorm questions that can help readers clarify the main idea of a paragraph or message of a text. Write students' suggestions on the board.

WHAT IS READING COMPREHENSION?

People often think of reading as a passive activity—that you don't have to do much, you just have to take in words—but that is not true. Good readers are active readers.

Reading comprehension involves these skills:
1. Understanding what you are reading.
2. Being part of what you are reading, or engaging with the text.
3. Evaluating what you are reading.
4. Making connections between what you are reading and what you already know.
5. Thinking about your response to what you have read.

Understanding What You Are Reading
One of the first steps is to recognize letters and words. Remember that it does not matter if you do not recognize all the words. You can figure out their meanings later. Try to figure out the meaning of unfamiliar words from the context of the sentence or paragraph. If you cannot figure out the meaning of a word, look it up in a dictionary. Next, you activate the meaning of words as you read them. That is what you are doing now. If you find parts of a text difficult, stop and read them a second time.

Engaging with the Text
Good readers use many different skills and strategies to help them understand and enjoy the text they are reading. When you read, think of it as a conversation between you and the writer. The writer wants to tell you something, and you want to understand his or her message.

Practice using these tips every time you read:
- Predict what will happen next in a story. Use clues you find in the text.
- Ask yourself questions about the main idea or message of the text.
- Monitor your understanding. Stop reading from time to time and think about what you have learned so far.

430

Evaluating What You Are Reading

The next step is to think about what you are reading. First, think about the author's purpose for writing. What type of text are you reading? If it is an informational text, the author wants to give you information about a subject, for example, about science, social science, or math. If you are reading literature, the author's purpose is probably to entertain you.

When you have decided what the author's purpose is for writing the text, think about what you have learned. Use these questions to help you:

- Is the information useful?
- Have you changed your mind about the subject?
- Did you enjoy the story, poem, or play?

Making Connections

Now connect the events or ideas in a text to your own knowledge or experience. Think about how your knowledge of a subject or your experience of the world can help you understand a text better.

- If the text has sections with headings, notice what these are. Do they give you clues about the main ideas in the text?
- Read the first paragraph. What is the main idea?
- Now read the paragraphs that follow. Make a note of the main ideas.
- Review your notes. How are the ideas connected?

Thinking about Your Response to What You Have Read

You read for a reason, so it is a good idea to think about how the text has helped you. Ask yourself these questions after you read:

- What information have I learned? Can I use it in my other classes?
- How can I connect my own experience or knowledge to the text?
- Did I enjoy reading the text? Why or why not?
- Did I learn any new vocabulary? What was it? How can I use it in conversation or in writing?

WHAT ARE READING STRATEGIES?

Reading strategies are specific things readers do to help them understand texts. Reading is like a conversation between an author and a reader. Authors make decisions about how to effectively communicate through a piece of writing. Readers use specific strategies to help them understand what authors are trying to communicate. Ten of the most common reading strategies are Previewing, Predicting, Skimming, Scanning, Comparing and Contrasting, Identifying Problems and Solutions, Recognizing Cause and Effect, Distinguishing Fact from Opinion, Identifying Main Idea and Details, and Identifying an Author's Purpose.

431

Evaluating What You Are Reading

Emphasize that active readers think about and evaluate what is on the page. Suggest that the first step in evaluating a text is to identify the author's purpose in writing.

Read aloud the three questions that students can use to evaluate what they are reading. Invite volunteers to recommend texts that either provided them with useful information about a subject or changed their ideas on a topic.

Scaffolding

Select a story with which the class is familiar. Write the name of the story and the author on the board. **ASK:** *What is the author's purpose in this story? Has the author fulfilled his or her purpose? Why or why not?* Discuss and evaluate the elements of the story, including the plot, characters, and setting. Explain that evaluations may differ, but that readers should be able to support their ideas with reasons.

Making Connections

Explain that making connections among ideas within a text—and also between a text and the reader's own experience—is an essential aspect of reading comprehension. Read this section aloud as students follow along. Stress that every paragraph in a text has a main idea, and that taking notes on the main ideas can help students better understand, link, and remember the important information in a text.

Thinking about Your Response to What You Have Read

Invite students to brainstorm reasons why people need and want to read. Then read aloud the questions as students follow along. **ASK:** *What new words have you recently learned from your reading?* Write students' new words on the board. With the class, define each new word.

Metacognition

To help students recognize the relationship between reading and their own lives, **ASK:** *How can making connections to your own experience help you better understand a text? How can better understanding a text provide insight into your own life?*

WHAT ARE READING STRATEGIES?

Note that there are specific strategies students can use to improve their reading comprehension. Then read this section aloud as students follow along. Ask them to give specific examples to illustrate the meaning of Comparing and Contrasting; Identifying Problem and Solution; and Recognizing Cause and Effect.

T431

HOW TO IMPROVE READING FLUENCY

1. What Is Reading Fluency?

Read aloud the definition of reading fluency as students follow along. Explain that fluency involves four key areas: accuracy and rate, phrasing, intonation, and expression. Choose a passage from a story or nonfiction text to read aloud. Model reading the passage fluently. Tell students that, whether they are reading silently to themselves or aloud to one another, fluency will enhance their enjoyment of the reading experience and their appreciation of a text.

2. How to Improve Accuracy and Rate

Read aloud the definition of accuracy and rate as students follow along. Note the three key factors that improve accuracy and rate.

3. How to Read with Proper Rate

Point out the necessity of adjusting one's reading rate to match a text. **ASK:** *What types of texts do you usually need to read more slowly?* (Difficult or technical material.) *What types of texts are you usually able to read more quickly?* (Lighter material such as mysteries or stories.)

4. Test Your Accuracy and Rate

Challenge students to practice the suggested activities to improve their accuracy and rate.

Cooperative Grouping

Invite students to work in pairs. Ask partners to take turns reading a selected passage aloud and to share input about one another's reading. Have partners practice together until both are able to read the passage accurately and at an appropriate rate.

5. How to Improve Intonation

Read aloud the definitions of *intonation* and *pitch* and the six steps to achieve proper intonation. Then model proper intonation by reading aloud a passage from a story or nonfiction article. Next, reread the passage, pausing after each sentence to highlight some aspect of your intonation. For example, **SAY:** *Notice how, when I read this sentence, I raise the pitch of my voice to emphasize certain words.*

Cooperative Grouping

Ask partners to take turns reading aloud the same passage that they read together, this time focusing on improving their intonation.

T432

HOW TO IMPROVE READING FLUENCY

1. What Is Reading Fluency?
Reading fluency is the ability to read smoothly and expressively with clear understanding. Fluent readers are better able to understand and enjoy what they read. Use the strategies that follow to build your fluency in these four key areas: accuracy and rate, phrasing, intonation, expression.

2. How to Improve Accuracy and Rate
Accuracy is the correctness of your reading. Rate is the speed of your reading.
- Use correct pronunciation.
- Emphasize correct syllables.
- Recognize most words.

3. How to Read with Proper Rate
- Match your reading speed to what you are reading. For example, if you are reading a mystery story, read slightly faster. If you are reading a science textbook, read slightly slower.
- Recognize and use punctuation.

4. Test Your Accuracy and Rate
- Choose a text you are familiar with, and practice reading it multiple times.
- Keep a dictionary with you while you read, and look up words you do not recognize.
- Use a watch or clock to time yourself while you read a passage.
- Ask a friend or family member to read a passage for you so you know what it should sound like.

5. How to Improve Intonation
Intonation is the rise and fall in the pitch of your voice as you read aloud. Pitch means the highness or lowness of the sound. Follow these steps:
- Change the sound of your voice to match what you are reading.
- Make your voice flow, or sound smooth, while you read.
- Make sure you are pronouncing words correctly.
- Raise the pitch of your voice for words that should be stressed, or emphasized.
- Use proper rhythm and meter.
- Use visual clues.

432

Visual Clue and Meaning	Example	How to Read It
Italics: draw attention to a word to show special importance	He is *serious*.	Emphasize "serious."
Dash: shows a quick break in a sentence	He is—serious.	Pause before saying "serious."
Exclamation point: can represent energy, excitement, or anger	He is serious!	Make your voice louder at the end of the sentence.
All capital letters: can represent strong emphasis or yelling	HE IS SERIOUS.	Emphasize the whole sentence.
Boldfacing: draws attention to a word to show importance	He is **serious**.	Emphasize "serious."
Question mark: shows curiosity or confusion	Is he serious?	Raise the pitch of your voice slightly at the end of the sentence.

6. How to Improve Phrasing

Phrasing is how you group words together. Follow these steps:
- Use correct rhythm and meter by not reading too fast or too slow.
- Pause for key words within the text.
- Make sure your sentences have proper flow and meter, so they sound smooth instead of choppy.
- Make sure you sound like you are reading a sentence instead of a list.
- Use punctuation to tell you when to stop, pause, or emphasize.

7. How to Improve Expression

Expression in reading is how you express feeling. Follow these steps:
- Match the sound of your voice to what you are reading. For example, read louder and faster to show strong feeling. Read slowly and more quietly to show sadness or seriousness.
- Match the sound of your voice to the genre. For example, read a fun, fictional story using a fun, friendly voice. Read an informative, nonfiction article using an even tone and a more serious voice.
- Avoid speaking in monotone, or using only one tone in your voice.
- Pause for emphasis and exaggerate letter sounds to match the mood or theme of what you are reading.

433

Visual Clues and Meaning Point out that the chart shows both how visual clues can shape a reader's intonation, and how a reader's intonation helps reveal the meaning of a text.

Scaffolding

Invite six volunteers to each read a version of the sentence *He is serious*. Ask the class to comment on each volunteer's intonation and to discuss the visual clues that guided that particular reading. After each reading, **ASK:** *What is the meaning of this version of the sentence? How did the reader's intonation help reveal the meaning? What visual clues influenced the reader's intonation?*

Metacognition

To reinforce students' understanding of the way intonation reveals meaning, write this familiar question on the board: *How are you?* Underscore the word *How*. Then write the same sentence again, underscoring the word *are*. Now, write the question a third time, underscoring the word *you*. Have a volunteer read aloud all three versions. Discuss with students the possible differences in meaning created by the different intonations.

6. How to Improve Phrasing

Read aloud the definition of *phrasing* and the five steps readers can take to achieve proper phrasing. Model reading a passage with proper phrasing. Note where and how you used punctuation to guide your phrasing.

7. How to Improve Expression

Read aloud the definition of *expression* and the four steps readers can take to achieve proper expression. **ASK:** *How does someone speak when they have strong feelings about something? How does someone speak when they feel sad about something?* Emphasize the idea that readers, like speakers in ordinary conversation, can adjust their voices to show feeling. Help students recognize that reading with appropriate expression is important whether one is reading silently or aloud.

Scaffolding

Dialogue is an excellent way to demonstrate the importance of reading with expression. Choose a short play and ask volunteers to read the various roles. After the reading, discuss whether the actors read with expression and whether their interpretations suited their particular characters and the play's events.

This handbook contains useful information about ways to view and represent different kinds of information. It covers the following topics:

- How to read maps and diagrams
- How to read graphs
- How to use graphic organizers

To introduce the handbook, walk your students through the pages and, together, note the information found under the major headings and subheadings. Direct teaching of the handbook for brief periods will help students become familiar with finding information and understanding content. Point out to students that they may consult the handbook on their own to review how to read and use visual material such as maps and diagrams.

WHAT ARE VIEWING AND REPRESENTING?

Ask students to brainstorm different types of visuals. Write their suggestions on the board. With students, discuss different purposes visuals can fulfill. Read aloud the definition of *representing* and the examples of possible visuals students can use in their work and presentations.

HOW TO READ MAPS AND DIAGRAMS

Maps

Read aloud the introduction on why maps are useful. Have students describe their own experiences using maps. **ASK:** *Parts of which three countries are shown on this map?* (Mexico, the United States, and Canada)

Point out the compass rose in the upper half of the map. Ask questions such as, *Using the compass rose as a guide, which city do you think is east of Sedalia?* (St. Louis)

Ask students if they are more familiar with kilometers or miles. Ask questions such as, *Using the scale, approximately how many miles do you think there are between San Antonio and Dallas?* (about three hundred)

Tell students to always read map titles and captions to better understand content. **ASK:** *What specific information is this map designed to provide, and how do you know this fact?* (The caption says that the map shows cowboy trails.) **ASK:** *Using the key, which trail do you think went through Dallas?* (the Sedalia Trail)

Viewing and Representing

WHAT ARE VIEWING AND REPRESENTING?

Viewing

Viewing is something you do every day. Much of what you read and watch includes visuals that help you understand information. These visuals can be maps, charts, diagrams, graphs, photographs, illustrations, and so on. They can inform you, explain a topic or an idea, entertain you, or persuade you.

Websites use visuals, too. It is important for you to be able to view visuals critically in order to evaluate what you are seeing or reading.

Representing

Representing is creating a visual to convey an idea. It is important for you to be able to create and use visuals in your own written work and presentations. You can use graphic organizers, diagrams, charts, posters, and artwork to illustrate and explain your ideas. Following are some examples of visuals.

HOW TO READ MAPS AND DIAGRAMS

Maps

Maps help us learn more about our world. They show the location of places such as countries, states, and cities. Some maps show where mountains, rivers, and lakes are located.

Many maps have helpful features. For example, a **compass rose** shows which way is north. A **scale** shows how miles or kilometers are represented on the map. A **key** shows what different colors or symbols represent.

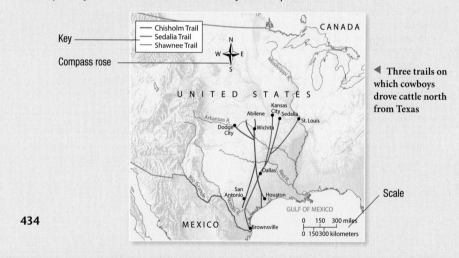

◀ Three trails on which cowboys drove cattle north from Texas

434

Diagrams

Diagrams are drawings or plans used to explain things or show how things work. They are often used in social studies and science books. Some diagrams show pictures of how objects look on the outside or on the inside. Others show the different steps in a process.

This diagram shows what a kernel of corn looks like on the inside.

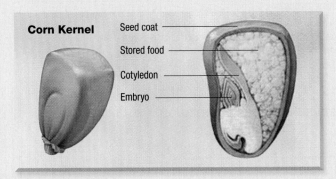

Corn Kernel
Seed coat
Stored food
Cotyledon
Embryo

A **flowchart** is a diagram that uses shapes and arrows to show a step-by-step process. The flowchart below shows the steps involved in baking chicken fingers. Each arrow points to the next step.

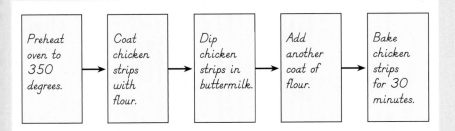

Preheat oven to 350 degrees. → Coat chicken strips with flour. → Dip chicken strips in buttermilk. → Add another coat of flour. → Bake chicken strips for 30 minutes.

Diagrams

Read aloud the introduction that defines diagrams. Invite students to tell about various diagrams they have seen in textbooks, newspapers, and magazines.

Make sure students understand that the diagrams on this page are only two types and that many different kinds of diagrams exist. Have students look at the first diagram. **ASK:** *What does this diagram show?* (It shows the four parts of a corn kernel.) *What do we call the outside of a corn kernel?* (We call it the seed coat.) Then have students look at the second diagram on the page. **ASK:** *What is the third step in the process of baking chicken fingers?* (The third step is dipping the strips in buttermilk.)

Metacognition

To monitor students' comprehension, **ASK:** *What are some examples of diagrams you use in everyday life? Why are they useful? Can you draw a diagram to show someone how to do something?*

Websites For more information on maps and diagrams, log on to www.LongmanKeystone.com for links to other interesting websites.

Read aloud the introduction to graphs as students follow along. Emphasize that graphs organize and explain different kinds of information. **ASK:** *Have you ever used a graph? How do graphs help you? If you've made a graph before, describe how it looked and the kind of information it showed.*

Line Graphs

Look at the line graph. Have a volunteer read aloud the title. **ASK:** *Have you seen or made a graph like this? What do you remember about that graph?* Point out that the information on this graph might be important to someone studying Native-American history or the history of Mexico.

Draw students' attention to the numbers at the bottom of the graph. **SAY:** *These numbers represent years. There are forty years in between the numbers shown.* Call attention to the numbers on the left side of the graph. **SAY:** *These numbers represent the estimated number of people in millions.*

Have students answer the following questions based on the graph. Afterwards, ask students to create additional questions that may be answered by looking at the graph.

1. What was the Native-American population of Central Mexico in 1520? *(It was about 24 million.)*

2. Between 1540 and 1620, by about how much did the Native-American population of Central Mexico decrease? *(It decreased by about 5 million.)*

Graphs organize and explain information. They show how two or more kinds of information are related, or how they are alike. Graphs are often used in math, science, and social studies books. Three common kinds of graphs are **line graphs**, **bar graphs**, and **circle graphs**.

Line Graphs

A line graph shows how information changes over a period of time. This line graph explains how, over a period of about 100 years, the Native-American population of Central Mexico decreased by more than 20 million people. Can you find the population in the year 1540? What was it in 1580?

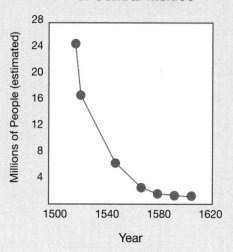

Native-American Population of Central Mexico

Bar Graphs

We use bar graphs to compare information. For example, this bar graph compares the populations of the thirteen United States in 1790. It shows that, in 1790, Virginia had over ten times as many people as Delaware.

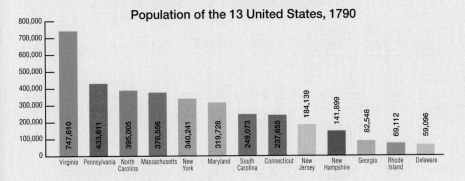

Population of the 13 United States, 1790

Circle Graphs

A circle graph is sometimes called a pie chart because it looks like a pie cut into slices. Circle graphs are used to show how different parts of a whole thing compare to one another. In a circle graph, all the "slices" add up to 100 percent. This circle graph shows that only 29 percent of the earth's surface is covered by land. It also shows that the continent of Asia takes up 30 percent of the earth's land.

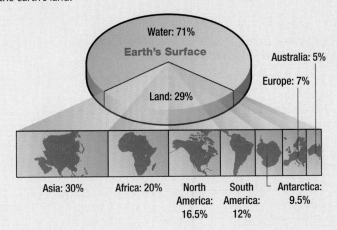

437

Bar Graphs

Read aloud the introduction to bar graphs and the graph title with students. **ASK:** *What information is shown in the graph? What kind of book might have a bar graph like this?* (It might be included in a United States history book, for example.) Have students answer the following questions based on the graph. Afterwards, ask students to create additional questions that could be answered by looking at the graph.

1. What was the population of Maryland in 1790? *(It was 319,728.)*

2. Which state had the biggest population in that year? *(It was Virginia.)*

Circle Graphs

Read the definition and chart title aloud as students follow along. **ASK:** *Has anyone heard the term* pie chart? *Why is this a good name for this chart?* Then **ASK:** *What two things does this pie chart show?* (It shows land and water.) Call attention to the information about the continents. **ASK:** *Which continent takes up 12 percent of the earth's land?* (South America) *Which takes up 20 percent?* (Africa)

HOW TO USE GRAPHIC ORGANIZERS

Read aloud the definition of a graphic organizer as students follow along in the text. Stress that graphic organizers show how ideas are related.

Venn Diagrams

Read aloud the definition of a Venn diagram, and note that Venn diagrams consist of two overlapping circles. Have students examine the diagram. **ASK:** *In what ways are oranges and bananas similar? How are they different?* (Students should recognize, for example, that both are fruit and then identify differences in shape and color.)

Word Webs

Read aloud the definition of a word web as students follow along in the text. With students, discuss the meaning of the term *sensory details*. Point out that each detail about popcorn on the word web appeals to one of the reader's five senses.

Scaffolding

Write the word *onion* in the center of a word web on the board. In the circles around *onion*, write the name of each of the five senses. Ask students to brainstorm sensory details that describe an onion, including what one looks, smells, tastes, feels, and even—as it is peeled or chewed—sounds like. Write students' ideas on the board. Next, create a word web with students to describe the word *carrot*. Finally, work with students to use the information listed in the two word webs to create a Venn diagram that compares and contrasts onions and carrots. Write the Venn diagram on the board.

HOW TO USE GRAPHIC ORGANIZERS

A graphic organizer is a diagram that helps you organize information and show relationships among ideas. Because the information is organized visually, a graphic organizer tells you—in a quick snapshot—how ideas are related. Before you make a graphic organizer, think about the information you want to organize. How are the ideas or details related? Choose a format that will show those relationships clearly.

Venn diagrams and **word webs** are commonly used graphic organizers. Here is an example of each.

Venn Diagrams

A Venn diagram shows how two thing are alike and different. The diagram below compares oranges and bananas.

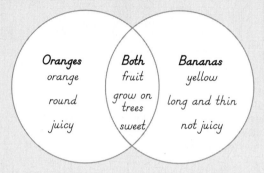

Word Webs

A word web is often used to help a writer describe something. The word web below lists five sensory details that describe popcorn.

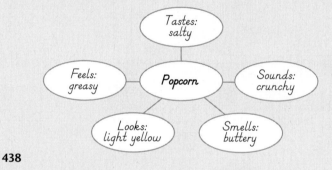

438

Writing Handbook

Narration

When writers tell a story, they use narration. There are many kinds of narration. Most include characters, a setting, and a sequence of events. Here are some types of narration.

A **short story** is a short, creative narrative. Most short stories have one or more characters, a setting, and a plot. A few types of short stories are realistic stories, fantasy stories, science-fiction stories, and adventure stories.

Autobiographical writing is a factual story of a writer's own life, told by the writer, usually in the first-person point of view. An autobiography may tell about the person's whole life or only a part of it.

Biographical writing is a factual story of a person's life told by another person. Most biographies are written about famous or admirable people.

Description

Description, or descriptive writing, is writing that gives the reader a mental picture of whatever is being described. To do this, writers choose their words carefully. They use figurative language and include vivid sensory details.

Persuasion

Writers use persuasion to try to persuade people to think or act in a certain way. Forms of persuasive writing include advertisements, essays, letters, editorials, speeches, and public-service announcements.

Exposition

Exposition, or expository writing, is writing that gives information or explains something. The information that writers include in expository writing is factual. Here are some types of expository writing.

A **compare-and-contrast essay** analyzes the similarities and differences between or among things.

A **cause-and-effect essay** explains causes or effects of an event. For example, a writer might examine several causes of a single effect or several effects of a single cause.

439

Using the Handbook

This handbook contains an overview of writing modes and the writing process. The handbook is divided into several different sections, including:

- Modes of writing
- The writing process
- Rubrics for writing

To introduce the handbook, walk your students through the pages and, together, note the information found under the major headings and subheadings. Point out that students may consult the handbook on their own whenever they have a writing assignment to complete.

MODES OF WRITING

Tell students there are many different modes, or forms, of writing. You may wish to identify books or find chapters in the student book to show examples of each mode.

Narration

Ask students to recall autobiographies, biographies, or short stories they have read. **ASK:** *If someone wanted to learn the story of your life, what would be some differences between reading an autobiography and a biography?* (the writer, how information is collected, what facts are included, etc.)

Description

Ask students to find examples of descriptive writing. Call on volunteers to read aloud brief passages. **ASK:** *What makes these descriptions vivid or clear?* (sensory details, precise words, etc.)

Persuasion

Read aloud the definition of *persuasion* as a mode of writing. Ask students for examples of situations in which they tried to persuade someone else to think or act in a certain way.

Exposition

Read aloud the definition of *exposition*. Introduce the following types of expository writing:

- **Compare and contrast** Ensure that students understand the difference between *compare* and *contrast*.
- **Cause and effect** Make a two-column chart on the board for *Cause* and *Effect*. Ask students for ideas to write on the chart.

Scaffolding

Ask students to write a persuasive letter to an adult for permission to do something special.

- **Problem-and-Solution Essay** Make a
two-column chart on the board for *Problem*
and *Solution*. Ask students for ideas to write
in the chart. Remind them there could be
more than one solution to a problem. Select
one example, and discuss how students
might expand on these ideas to write an
expository piece.

- **How-to Essay** Ask students for examples
of tasks or actions they know how to do well,
e.g., take care of a pet, play a game, or cook
a favorite dish. Select one example, and ask
students to provide each step to complete the
task. Discuss how to use these ideas to write
a how-to essay.

- **Summary** Ask each student to read a brief
selection from the student book and then
to write a summary of the main ideas in the
selection. Ask volunteers to read aloud their
summaries. Have the class discuss whether
each volunteer's summary accurately and
concisely reflected the selection's main ideas.

Research Writing

Stress the point that *research* means using
several different resources to investigate a
topic thoroughly. Review with students different
sources they can use for their reports, ranging
from encyclopedias to interviews. Highlight
the differences among research reports,
biographical reports, and multimedia reports.

Responses to Literature

Remind students that being an active reader
means being able to evaluate a text. Explain
that writers are often called upon to put their
evaluations and responses to literature in
writing. Read aloud the definition of *literary
essay* as students follow along. Be sure that
students understand the terms *literary criticism*
and *critique*.

Creative Writing

Ask students to brainstorm ideas about the
meaning and different forms of creative writing.
Ask them to name works of creative writing that
they particularly enjoyed and to tell why they
liked them.

Writers use a **problem-and-solution essay** to describe a problem and offer
one or more solutions to it.

A **how-to essay** explains how to do or make something. The process is
broken down into steps, which are explained in order.

A **summary** is a brief statement that gives the main ideas of an event or a
piece of writing. One way to write a summary is to read a text and then reread
each paragraph or section. Next put the text aside and write the main ideas in
your own words in a sentence or two.

Research Writing

Writers often use research to gather information about topics, including
people, places, and things. Good research writing does not simply repeat
information. It guides the readers through a topic, showing them why each
fact matters and creating a complete picture of the topic. Here are some types
of research writing.

Research report A research report presents information gathered from
reference books, interviews, or other sources.

Biographical report A biographical report includes dates, details, and
main events in a person's life. It can also include information about the time in
which the person lived.

Multimedia report A multimedia report presents information through a
variety of media, including text, slides, photographs, prerecorded music and
sound effects, and digital imaging.

Responses to Literature

A **literary essay** is one type of response to literature. In a literary essay, a writer
discusses and interprets what is important in a book, short story, essay, article,
or poem.

Literary criticism is another type of response to literature. Literary criticism
is the result of a careful examination of one or more literary works. The writer
makes a judgment by looking carefully and critically at various important
elements in the work.

A book **critique** gives readers a summary of a book, encouraging the
reader either to read it or to avoid reading it. A movie critique gives readers a
summary of a movie, tells if the writer enjoyed the movie, and then explains
the reasons why or why not.

A **comparison of works** compares the features of two or more works.

Creative Writing

Creative writing blends imagination, ideas, and emotions, and allows the
writer to present a unique view of the world. Poems, plays, short stories,
dramas, and even some cartoons are examples of creative writing.

440

Practical and Technical Documents

Practical writing is fact-based writing that people do in the workplace or in their day-to-day lives. A business letter, memo, school form, job application, and a letter of inquiry are a few examples of practical writing.

Technical documents are fact-based documents that identify a sequence of activities needed to design a system, operate machinery, follow a procedure, or explain the rules of an organization. You read technical writing every time you read a manual or a set of instructions.

In the following descriptions, you'll find tips for tackling several types of practical and technical writing.

Business letters are formal letters that follow one of several specific formats.

News releases, also called press releases, announce factual information about upcoming events. A writer might send a news release to a local newspaper, local radio station, TV station, or other media that will publicize the information.

Guidelines give information about how people should act or how to do something.

Process explanations are step-by-step explanations of how to do something. The explanation should be clear and specific and can include diagrams or other illustrations. Below is an example.

KEYSTONE
CD-ROM

Usage Instructions
1. Insert the *Keystone* CD-ROM into your CD drive.
2. Open "My Computer."
3. Double-click on your CD-ROM disk drive.
4. Click on the *Keystone* icon. This will launch the program.

Practical and Technical Documents

Ask students to name examples of practical and technical documents that they have read or had to write in their own lives. They may cite instruction manuals, applications, or even lists of information. Emphasize the importance of learning to communicate practical information clearly in writing.

Scaffolding

Examine with students the document at the bottom of their student book page. **ASK:** *Why is this document a successful example of practical writing?* (Students should recognize, for example, that it is clearly labeled, that instructions are numbered in order, and that directions are complete.) With students, draft a document on the board providing clear directions to someone planning to walk from a well-known landmark to your school. Elicit students' suggestions for each step in the directions. Help them elaborate on their ideas by asking questions such as, *Do you think the directions are in the right order? Have we given enough details to enable someone to recognize when and where to turn?*

Read aloud the definition of the *writing process* with students. Tell students they will use the writing process to write in a variety of forms and to share their work with others.

Step 1: Prewrite

Explain that writers use this step to brainstorm ideas, select a topic, plan their writing, and gather information.

Brainstorm Topic Ideas Read aloud the definition of *brainstorming* with students. Help students understand the concept by writing some ideas for topics on the board and asking for suggestions. Encourage students to think freely and be creative during this process. Then ask students to brainstorm on their own and write a list of topics in their notebooks.

Choose a Topic After students have created a list of ideas, call on volunteers to share their topics. With students, discuss whether or not these topics would be interesting subjects to write and to read about. Tell students that, when they are asked to write something, they should choose a topic that they like, that would interest readers, and that fulfills the assignment.

Plan Your Writing Help students understand that, if they haven't been assigned a writing form, they should decide on the writing form that best suits their topic. Point out the importance of identifying audience and purpose before starting to write.

Gather Information Explain that writers often use graphic organizers to gather their ideas and plan their writing. Call students' attention to Becca's web in their student book. Explain that it shows the writer's main idea and supporting details.

Scaffolding

Remind students that they learned about Venn diagrams and word webs. Discuss some other common graphic organizers, including T-charts and sequence of events charts. Ask a volunteer to tell what he or she did between waking up and coming to class. List these activities, such as eating breakfast, saying goodbye to parents, walking to school, or taking a social studies test, on a sequence of events chart.

The **writing process** is a series of steps that can help you write effectively.

Step 1: Prewrite
During **prewriting**, you collect topic ideas, choose a topic, plan your writing, and gather information.

A good way to get ideas for a topic is to **brainstorm**. Brainstorming means writing a list of all the topic ideas you can think of.

Look at your list of topic ideas. Choose the one that is the most interesting to you. This is your **topic**, the subject you will write about.

Plan your writing by following these steps:
- First, decide on the **type** of writing that works best with your topic. For example, you may want to write a description, a story, or an essay.
- The type of writing is called the **form** of writing.
- Then think about your **audience**. Identifying your audience will help you decide whether to write formally or informally.
- Finally, decide what your reason for writing is. This is your **purpose**. Is your purpose to inform your audience? To entertain them?

How you gather information depends on what you are writing. For example, for a report, you need to do research. For a description, you might list your ideas in a graphic organizer. A student named Becca listed her ideas for a description of her week at art camp in the graphic organizer below.

442

T442

Step 2: Draft

In this step, you start writing. Don't worry too much about spelling and punctuation. Just put your ideas into sentences.

Here is the first paragraph that Becca wrote for her first draft.

> I saw an art contest advertised in the newspaper last spring. I entered my best drawing. I have always loved art. The prize was a week at an art camp in June with 9 other kids. I was very happy when I won.

Step 3: Revise

Now it's time to revise, or make changes. Ask yourself these questions:

- Are my ideas presented in the order that makes the most sense?
- Does my draft have a beginning, a middle, and an end?
- Does each paragraph have a main idea and supporting details?

If you answered *no* to any of these questions, you need to revise. Revising can mean changing the order of paragraphs or sentences. It can mean changing general words for specific words. It can mean correcting errors.

Once you decide what to change, you can mark the corrections on your draft using editing marks. Here's how Becca marked up her first paragraph.

> When I saw an art contest advertised in the newspaper last spring. I entered my best drawing. (I have always loved art.) The prize was a week at an art camp in June with nine 9 other kids. I was very excited happy when I won.

443

Step 2: Draft

Explain to students that they should use their graphic organizers to write a first draft. Point out that writing a draft is part of the thinking process. Make sure students understand that the purpose of a draft is to get ideas down on paper, not to have perfect spelling, grammar, and punctuation. Perfection will come later. As students follow along, read aloud the first paragraph of Becca's first draft.

Step 3: Revise

Stress the importance of revision. Explain that writers reread their first drafts and, as they do so, they mark changes—or revisions—they plan to make to improve their work.

Have students turn to the student book page that discusses editing marks, and review it with them. Ensure that students understand what each mark means and how to use it.

Have students turn back to the page that explains how to revise an essay. Ask them to follow along in the text as you read aloud the three questions writers need to ask themselves as they revise. Then ask students to look at the first paragraph of Becca's draft. **ASK:** *What sentence is circled? Why is it circled? What does the arrow mean?* (It means that Becca plans to move the sentence *I have always loved art* to make it first.) *Why does Becca plan to make this revision?* (It is a lively way to begin.) *What other revisions does Becca plan to make? Why?* (She plans to combine two short, choppy sentences to make a longer one, to change *9* to *nine*, and to substitute a more precise word for a general one.)

Cooperative Grouping Prior to class, make an overhead transparency of a first draft written by a student volunteer. Show the transparency to the class. Model a peer review session with the student author. Demonstrate how to ask questions about the first draft and give positive, constructive criticism on ways to improve the writing.

If students have already started a writing project, have them work in pairs to read first drafts to each other. They can conduct a peer review by using the bulleted questions and sharing constructive criticism to improve first drafts.

After the peer review, have students work individually to revise their drafts.

Step 4: Edit

Explain that, in a second draft, the writer makes all the revisions he or she marked on the first draft. Point out that, in editing the work and creating a second draft, the writer may also add details or include changes that he or she has thought of since marking up the first draft. Note that, once a writer has prepared a second draft, it needs to be proofread. Explain that *proofreading* means rereading work for errors and marking final corrections.

Tell students to use the checklist in their student book as a guide for proofreading their work. Remind them to refer to the Grammar Handbook for answers to questions about grammar, usage, and mechanics.

Call students' attention to Becca's editing marks. **ASK:** *Why are there three lines under the* m *and a* in *museum of art?* (The lines show that the letters need to be capitalized.) *What other proofreading corrections has Becca marked?* (Among others, she corrected a verb tense and inserted commas.)

Scaffolding

Review editing marks with students. Since students may be unfamiliar with some or all of the marks, write each mark on the board. Have students come to the chalkboard and recreate the marks.

You may also want to give students a variety of sentences with mistakes on which they can practice using the editing marks to make corrections. Another way to practice is to give students sentences with editing marks, and then have them rewrite the sentences correctly.

In this step, you make a second draft that includes the changes you marked on your first draft. You can also add details you may have thought of since writing your first draft. Now you're ready to **proofread**, or check your work for errors and make final corrections.

Here's Becca's first draft after she finished proofreading.

My Week at Art Camp

I have always loved art. When I saw an art contest advertised in the newspaper last spring, I entered my best drawing. The prize was a week at an art camp in June with nine other students. I was very excited when I won.

The camp was located at the Everson museum of art. On the first day, we looked at paintings by different artists. My favorite was by a painter named Monet. He painted colorful land scapes of boats and gardens. On the second day, we began our own paintings. I choose to paint a picture of the duck pond on the campus. I worked hard on my painting because we were going to have an art show of all our work at the end of the week.

I learned alot about painting at camp. I especially liked learning to use watercolors. For example, I found out that you can make interesting designs by sprinkling salt on a wet watercolor painting.

I had a great time at art camp. The show at the end of the week was a big success, and I made some new friends. I hope to go again next year.

444

Step 5: Publish

Prepare a final copy of your writing to **publish**, or share with your audience. Here are some publishing tips.

- Photocopy and hand out your work to your classmates.
- Attach it to an e-mail and send it to friends.
- Send it to a school newspaper or magazine for possible publication.

Here is the final version of Becca's paper.

My Week at Art Camp

I have always loved art. When I saw an art contest advertised in the newspaper last spring, I entered my best drawing. The prize was a week at an art camp in June with nine other students. I was very excited when I won.

The camp was located at the Everson Museum of Art. On the first day, we looked at paintings by different artists. My favorite was by a painter named Monet. He painted colorful landscapes of boats and gardens. On the second day, we began our own paintings. I chose to paint a picture of the duck pond on the campus. I worked hard on my painting because we were going to have an art show of all our work at the end of the week.

I learned a lot about painting at camp. I especially liked learning to use watercolors. For example, I found out that you can make interesting designs by sprinkling salt on a wet watercolor painting.

I had a great time at art camp. The show at the end of the week was a big success, and I made some new friends. I hope to go again next year.

Once you have shared your work with others, you may want to keep it in a **portfolio**, a folder or envelope with your other writing. Each time you write something, add it to your portfolio. Compare recent work with earlier work. See how your writing is improving.

Step 5: Publish

Explain that, in this fifth and final step, students prepare a final copy of their writing and share their work with others.

Have a volunteer read aloud Becca's final version. Point out that she made all the changes she marked on her second draft.

Read the bulleted publishing ideas aloud with students. Invite students to think of other ways they can publish their work. You may wish to explore having a class web page where students can post their work.

Have students place their work in their assessment portfolios for comparison with past and future assignments. Sometimes it is helpful for students to keep all their drafts and revisions together with their final published work. This provides evidence of growth, improvement, and learning through use of the writing process.

Metacognition

To help students monitor their comprehension, **ASK:** *What do you think of Becca's final version? What, if anything, would you have done differently?*

Websites For more information on the writing process, log on to www.LongmanKeystone.com for links to other interesting websites.

Tell students that a *rubric* is a tool or set of guidelines used to assess quality. Point out that a rubric is often presented in the form of a chart or grid. Check to see what students already know about rubrics. **ASK:** *Have you seen rubrics to grade or score your work before? How do rubrics work?*

How Are Rubrics Structured?

Read aloud the five ways rubrics can be structured as students follow along. Address any questions students may have about rubrics.

How Will a Rubric Help Me?

Stress the fact that rubrics not only help a teacher to assess students' work, but that they can also help students to assess their own work. Tell students that understanding rubrics can help them understand the basis for the grades you give or comments you make on their writing. Note that using rubrics can help students improve their writing by giving them clear point-by-point guidelines for appraising their own work.

What Are the Types of Rubrics?

Read aloud the definitions of *holistic rubric* and *analytic rubric* as students follow along in the text.

What Is a Rubric?

A **rubric** is a tool, often in the form of a chart or a grid, that helps you assess your work. Rubrics are helpful for writing and speaking assignments.

To help you or others assess your work, a rubric offers several specific criteria to be applied to your work. Then the rubric helps you indicate your range of success or failure according to those specific criteria. Rubrics are often used to evaluate writing for standardized tests.

Using a rubric will save you time, focus your learning, and improve your work. When you know the rubric beforehand, you can keep the specific criteria for the writing in your mind as you write. As you evaluate the essay before giving it to your teacher, you can focus on the specific criteria that your teacher wants you to master—or on areas that you know present challenges for you. Instead of searching through your work randomly for any way to improve or correct it, you will have a clear and helpful focus.

How Are Rubrics Structured?

Rubrics can be structured in several different ways:

1. Your teacher may assign a rubric for a specific assignment.
2. Your teacher may direct you to a rubric in your textbook.
3. Your teacher and your class may structure a rubric for a particular assignment together.
4. You and your classmates may structure a rubric together.
5. You can create your own rubric with your own specific criteria.

How Will a Rubric Help Me?

A rubric will help you assess your work on a scale. Scales vary from rubric to rubric but usually range from 6 to 1, 5 to 1, or 4 to 1, with 6, 5, or 4 being the highest score and 1 being the lowest. If someone else is using the rubric to assess your work, the rubric will give your evaluator a clear range within which to place your work. If you are using the rubric yourself, it will help you improve your work.

What Are the Types of Rubrics?

A **holistic rubric** has general criteria that can apply to a variety of assignments. An **analytic rubric** is specific to a particular assignment. The criteria for evaluation address the specific issues important in that assignment. The following pages show examples of both types of rubrics.

446

T446

Holistic Rubrics

Holistic rubrics such as this one are sometimes used to assess writing assignments on standardized tests. Notice that the criteria for evaluation are focus, organization, support, and use of conventions.

Points	Criteria
6 Points	• The writing is focused and shows fresh insight into the writing task. • The writing is marked by a sense of completeness and coherence and is organized with a logical progression of ideas. • A main idea is fully developed, and support is specific and substantial. • A mature command of the language is evident. • Sentence structure is varied, and writing is free of fragments. • Virtually no errors in writing conventions appear.
5 Points	• The writing is focused on the task. • The writing is organized and has a logical progression of ideas, though there may be occasional lapses. • A main idea is well developed and supported with relevant detail. • Sentence structure is varied, and the writing is free of fragments. • Writing conventions are followed correctly.
4 Points	• The writing is focused on the task, but unrelated material may intrude. • Clear organizational pattern is present, though lapses occur. • A main idea is adequately supported, but development may be uneven. • Sentence structure is generally fragment free but shows little variation. • Writing conventions are generally followed correctly.
3 Points	• Writing is focused on the task, but unrelated material intrudes. • Organization is evident, but writing may lack a logical progression of ideas. • Support for the main idea is present but is sometimes illogical. • Sentence structure is free of fragments, but there is almost no variation. • The work demonstrates a knowledge of conventions, with misspellings.
2 Points	• The writing is related to the task but generally lacks focus. • There is little evidence of an organizational pattern. • Support for the main idea is generally inadequate, illogical, or absent. • Sentence structure is unvaried, and serious errors may occur. • Errors in writing conventions and spellings are frequent.
1 Point	• The writing may have little connection to the task. • There has been little attempt at organization or development. • The paper seems fragmented, with no clear main idea. • Sentence structure is unvaried, and serious errors appear. • Poor diction and poor command of the language obscure meaning. • Errors in writing conventions and spelling are frequent.
Unscorable	• The response is unrelated to the task or is simply a rewording of the prompt. • The response has been copied from a published work. • The student did not write a response. • The response is illegible. • The words in the response are arranged with no meaning. • There is an insufficient amount of writing to score.

447

Holistic Rubrics

Review with students the definition of holistic rubrics. Note that rubrics such as the one presented in their student book are sometimes used to assess writing assignments on standardized tests. Have students notice the criteria for evaluation. Point out that the scoring system ranges from a high of *6* to a low of *unscorable*.

Should you decide to use this rubric to score your students' writing, you may wish to have writing conferences to explain how the rubric was applied and provide specific suggestions to improve writing. You may want to give students an opportunity to revise or edit their writing so they can meet the criteria set by the rubric.

Scaffolding

Read aloud the rubric items for each score level as students follow along in the text. Pause to explain each item. Make sure students understand why a score of 4 differs from a 2 or 3.

If you have samples of student writing that illustrate the different score levels, review these samples with students. (Organizations that create and publish standardized writing tests often provide scored student writing samples.)

Analytic Rubrics

Review with students the definition of analytic rubrics. Note that the analytic rubric in their student book is specifically designed to assess a persuasive essay. Have students notice the criteria for evaluation. Point out that the scoring system ranges from a high of *6* to a low of *1*.

Scaffolding

Read aloud the rubric items for each score level as students follow along in the text. Pause to explain each item. Make sure students understand why a score of 4 differs from a 2 or 3.

If you have samples of student persuasive essays that illustrate the different score levels, review these samples with students. (Organizations that create and publish standardized writing tests often provide scored student writing samples.)

Analytic Rubrics

This analytic rubric is an example of a rubric to assess a persuasive essay. It will help you assess presentation, position, evidence, and arguments.

Presentation	Position	Evidence	Arguments
6 Points Essay clearly and effectively addresses an issue with more than one side.	Essay clearly states a supportable position on the issue.	All evidence is logically organized, well presented, and supports the position.	All reader concerns and counterarguments are effectively addressed.
5 Points Most of essay addresses an issue that has more than one side.	Essay clearly states a position on the issue.	Most evidence is logically organized, well presented, and supports the position.	Most reader concerns and counterarguments are effectively addressed.
4 Points Essay adequately addresses issue that has more than one side.	Essay adequately states a position on the issue.	Many parts of evidence support the position; some evidence is out of order.	Many reader concerns and counterarguments are adequately addressed.
3 Points Essay addresses issue with two sides but does not present second side clearly.	Essay states a position on the issue, but the position is difficult to support.	Some evidence supports the position, but some evidence is out of order.	Some reader concerns and counterarguments are addressed.
2 Points Essay addresses issue with two sides but does not present second side.	Essay states a position on the issue, but the position is not supportable.	Not much evidence supports the position, and what is included is out of order.	A few reader concerns and counterarguments are addressed.
1 Point Essay does not address issue with more than one side.	Essay does not state a position on the issue.	No evidence supports the position.	No reader concerns or counterarguments are addressed.

Friendly Letters

A friendly letter is less formal than a business letter. It is a letter to a friend, a family member, or anyone with whom the writer wants to communicate in a personal, friendly way. Most friendly letters are made up of five parts: the **date**, the **greeting** (or salutation), the **body**, the **closing**, and the **signature**. The greeting is followed by a comma, and the paragraphs in the body are indented.

The purpose of a friendly letter is usually to share personal news and feelings, to send or to answer an invitation, or to express thanks.

In this letter, Maité tells her friend Julio about her new home.

Greeting   **Date**

March 2, 2009

Dear Julio,

   I was so happy to receive your letter today. I am feeling much better. My mom and I finally finished decorating my room. We painted the walls green and the ceiling pink. At first, my mom was nervous to paint the ceiling something other than white, but I knew it would look good. Now that my bedroom is finished, Manhattan is starting to feel more like home.

   Over the weekend I went to the Museum of Natural History. The whale exhibit made me think of back home and how you and I would spend hours at the beach. I am starting to adjust to city life, but I miss the smell of salt in the air and collecting sea glass on the shore.

   My parents said I can spend the summer with my grandparents at their beach house. They said I could invite you for a couple of weeks. We'll go swimming every day. I can't wait!

Body

Your friend,   **Closing**

Maité   **Signature**

449

Remind students that writing letters is an important way to communicate with others. With students, discuss why someone might want to send a letter via the mail rather than sending an e-mail. Note that some people may not have access to a computer or may simply prefer to write, receive, or read a letter sent by regular mail.

Friendly Letters

Point out the five parts of the friendly letter and the punctuation used in the date, greeting, and closing. Discuss with students the meaning of the word *tone*. **ASK:** *What is usually the purpose of a friendly letter?* (The purpose, among other possibilities, may be to send personal news or share feelings.) *What kind of tone do writers usually use in a friendly letter?* (They usually use an informal, friendly tone.)

Scaffolding

Work with students to identify some similarities and differences between friendly letters and friendly e-mails. Note that the purpose of the two may be the same. Note that some elements of the form may be different. For example, the date is automatically included in an e-mail. Also note differences in content. For example, a friendly letter may be more detailed and better written than an e-mail, with greater attention paid to grammar, spelling, and usage. Friendly e-mails may be written more on the spur of the moment than friendly letters and may rely on a kind of shorthand that has evolved specifically for use in text messaging. Remind students that informal conventions used in text messaging should not influence their other writing habits.

Business Letters

Have students read the business letter in their student book. Explain that business letters may be written in block or modified block format. Point out the six parts of the business letter, along with the punctuation used in the date, inside address, greeting, and closing. Note that a writer both signs a business letter *and* types his or her name beneath the signature.

With students, discuss the differences in purpose, tone, and audience between a business letter and a friendly letter. Stress the importance of carefully editing and proofreading a business letter before mailing it.

Tell students that they should send a business letter by regular mail unless they are sure that the intended recipient prefers to receive business letters via e-mail.

Scaffolding

Provide students with practice writing business letters. Ask a volunteer to name the six parts of a business letter. Write the six parts on the board. With students, invent the name and address of a company and an executive within that company. Write the information on the board. Then ask students each to write a business letter to that executive requesting an interview for the school paper. Tell students to be sure that the body of their letter explains why they want to interview the executive and that the form of their letter is correct.

Cooperative Grouping Have students work in pairs to critique one another's business letters. Remind partners to provide constructive criticism.

Metacognition

To help students monitor their comprehension, **ASK:** *What are some reasons for writing a friendly letter? What are some reasons for writing a business letter?*

Business Letters

Business letters follow one of several formats. In **block format**, each part of the letter begins at the left margin. A double space is used between paragraphs. In **modified block format**, some parts of the letter are indented to the center of the page. No matter which format is used, all letters in business format have a date, an inside address, a greeting (or salutation), a body, a closing, and a signature. These parts are shown on the model business letter below, formatted in block style.

June 11, 2009 ←——————————— **Date**

Edward Sykes, Vice President
Animal Rights Group ←——————— **Inside Address**
154 Denver Street
Syosset, NY 11791

Dear Mr. Sykes: ←————————— **Greeting**

Many students at Bellevue High School would like to learn about animal rights for a project we're starting next fall. We've read about your program on your website and would like to know more about your activities.

Would you send us some information about your organization? We're specifically interested in learning what we as students can do to help protect animals. About 75 students have expressed interest so far—I think we'll have the people power to make the project a success and have an impact.

← **Body**

Please help us get started. Thank you for your time and consideration.

Sincerely, ←———— **Closing**

Pedro Rodriguez ←———— **Signature**

Pedro Rodriguez

The **inside address** shows where the letter will be sent. The **greeting** is punctuated with a colon. The **body** of the letter states the writer's purpose. The **closing** "Sincerely" is common, but "Yours truly" or "Respectfully yours" are also acceptable. The writer types his or her name and writes a **signature**.

Forms are preprinted documents with spaces for the user to enter specific information. Some include directions; others assume that users will follow the labels and common conventions. Two common forms in the workplace are fax cover sheets and applications. When you fill out forms, it is important to do the following:

- Fill them out accurately and completely.
- Write neatly in blue or black ink.
- Include only information that is asked for on the form.

Forms usually have limited space in which to write. Because space is limited, you can use standard symbols and abbreviations, such as *$10/hr.* to mean "10 dollars per hour."

FAX COVER SHEET

To: *Mr. Robert Thompson*   **From:** *Laura Rivas*

Fax: *(001) 921-9833*   **Pages:** *2 (including cover sheet)*

Date: *12/04/09*

Re: *Job Application*

Message:

Dear Mr. Thompson:

Thank you for meeting with me today about the sales associate position at Story Land Bookshop. The following page is my completed application form.

Sincerely,

Laura Rivas

451

Read aloud the three bulleted tips for filling in forms as students follow along. Tell students that fax cover sheets and applications are two common types of forms they may encounter. Ask whether or not students have had experience faxing material. Discuss why it is extremely important to include a fax cover sheet with any material that is faxed.

Review the FAX COVER SHEET with students. Point to each preprinted item, such as *To:* and *Fax:* and **ASK:** *Why is it important to fill in this information? How is this information useful to the person who receives the fax?*

Scaffolding

To give students practice, you may want to distribute and have them fill in blank fax cover sheets. Ask students to imagine that they are Pedro Rodriquez and that they are going to fax the business letter written by Pedro that appears in their student book. Ask students to complete a fax cover sheet for Pedro's letter, leaving out only the fax number.

Filling in an Application for Employment

Help students recognize that filling in applications is an important activity that almost everyone has to do at some point in life. Stress the importance of reading instructions thoroughly and filling in all applications completely.

With students, read the application for employment at the Story Land Bookshop. Be sure that students understand what each item is or means. For example, **ASK:** *What is the meaning of* Equal Opportunity Employer? *What is a* Social Security Number? *What or who is a* former employer?

Scaffolding

To give students practice filling in job application forms, distribute a blank copy of the Story Land Bookshop application or another application for employment. If a student lacks work experience, suggest that he or she fill in a volunteer activity under the category *Former Employers*, noting *volunteer* under the category *Salary*. Alternatively, suggest that the student leave those categories blank. Answer any questions or concerns students may have as they fill in their practice applications. Collect and review students' practice applications, providing feedback on whether students have completed the information in a neat and thorough manner. If necessary, suggest ways for students to improve their future applications.

Story Land Bookshop

PRE-EMPLOYMENT QUESTIONNAIRE
EQUAL OPPORTUNITY EMPLOYER
Date: 12/04/2009

PERSONAL INFORMATION

Name (last name first)
Rivas, Laura

Social Security No.
145-53-6211

Present Address	**City**	**State**	**Zip Code**
351 Middleton Road	Osborne	TX	78357

Permanent Address	**City**	**State**	**Zip Code**
Same			

Phone No.
(001) 661-1567

Referred by
Josh Logan

EMPLOYMENT DESIRED

Position	**Start Date**	**Salary Desired**
Sales associate	Immediately	$10/hr.

Are you presently employed? ☐ Yes ☑ No
May we contact your former employer? ☑ Yes ☐ No
Were you ever employed by this company? ☐ Yes ☑ No

EDUCATION

Name and Location of School	**Yrs Attended**	**Did you graduate?**
Osborne High School, Osborne, TX	3	Expect to graduate 2010

FORMER EMPLOYERS

Name and Address of Employer	**Salary**	**Position**
Blue River Summer Camp	$195 per week	Junior camp
127 Horse Lane		counselor
Millwood, TX 78721		

Date Month and Year
6/20/09 to 9/20/09

Reason for Leaving
Summer ended

452

T452

Proofreading and Preparing Manuscript

Before preparing a final copy, proofread your manuscript.

- Choose a standard, easy-to-read font.
- Type or print on one side of unlined 8 1/2" x 11" paper.
- Set the margins for the side, top, and bottom of your paper at approximately one inch. Most word-processing programs have a default setting that is appropriate.
- Double-space the document.
- Indent the first line of each paragraph.
- Number the pages in the upper right corner.

Follow your teacher's directions for formatting formal research papers. Most papers will have the following features: Title page, Table of Contents or Outline, Works Consulted List.

Crediting Sources

When you credit a source, you acknowledge where you found your information and you give your readers the details necessary for locating the source themselves. Within the body of the paper, you provide a short citation, a footnote number linked to a footnote, or an endnote number linked to an endnote reference. These brief references show the page numbers on which you found the information. Prepare a reference list at the end of the paper to provide full bibliographic information on your sources. These are two common types of reference lists:

A **bibliography** provides a listing of all the resources you consulted during your research. A **works consulted list** lists the works you have referenced in your paper.

The chart on the next page shows the Modern Language Association format for crediting sources. This is the most common format for papers written in the content areas in middle school and high school. Unless instructed otherwise by your teacher, use this format for crediting sources.

Before you discuss this section with students, identify a strong example of a student research report that includes a bibliography or a works consulted list. You will use this manuscript as a model.

Proofreading and Preparing Manuscript

Distribute copies of the research report you identified or show it on an overhead transparency. Using this example, walk students through the requirements for preparing a final manuscript, including using a standard font and double-spacing. Have students notice the model report's Title Page, Table of Contents, and Bibliography or Works Consulted List.

Crediting Sources

Read aloud the material on crediting sources as students follow along in the text. Note the information that needs to be included in footnotes or endnotes. Help students distinguish between a bibliography and a works consulted list. Show students examples of bibliographies and works consulted lists in research papers written by other students.

ASK: *Why is it important to cite sources when you write a research paper?* **Possible answers are listed below:**

- To give credit to people for their ideas and writing.
- To show that various different sources were used.
- To enable others to find more information on a topic.

MLA Style for Listing Sources

Tell students that the Modern Language Association (MLA) is an organization for language teachers and professors. Explain that the MLA has made a special set of rules for writing and using words.

You may want to mention that when students do research, they may see works cited in a style that differs a little from the MLA. That's because some writers use other style guidelines.

Read aloud the citation for each type of source as students follow along in their books. Explain the specific information provided in each type of citation. For example, for "Book," you may want to offer an explanation, as follows:

Pyles, Thomas	(author of the book)
The Origins and Development of the English language	(book title)
2nd ed.	(second edition)
New York	(place it was published)
Harcourt Brace Jovanovich, Inc.	(publishing company)
1971	(year it was published)

Since many students will start their research using encyclopedias, you may want to show them how to cite this type of source by writing an example on the board.

Scaffolding

To help students better understand the kind of information that is included in each type of citation, you may wish to have them look at a magazine and fill in the following information:

Magazine citation
Author (last name, first name):
Title of magazine article (in quotation marks):
Name of magazine (in italics or underlined):
Date of magazine:
Volume number:

Next, ask students to write the full magazine citation, following the MLA format.

Cooperative Learning You may want to repeat this exercise for different types of sources, such as books, encyclopedias, and Internet. Provide source materials to students and have them work in pairs to create correct citations using the MLA format.

MLA Style for Listing Sources

Book with one author	Pyles, Thomas. *The Origins and Development of the English Language.* 2nd ed. New York: Harcourt Brace Jovanovich, Inc., 1971.
Book with two or three authors	McCrum, Robert, William Cran, and Robert MacNeil. *The Story of English.* New York: Penguin Books, 1987.
Book with an editor	Truth, Sojourner. *Narrative of Sojourner Truth.* Ed. Margaret Washington. New York: Vintage Books, 1993.
Book with more than three authors or editors	Donald, Robert B., et al. *Writing Clear Essays.* Upper Saddle River, NJ: Prentice Hall, Inc., 1996.
Single work from an anthology	Hawthorne, Nathaniel. "Young Goodman Brown." *Literature: An Introduction to Reading and Writing.* Ed. Edgar V. Roberts and Henry E. Jacobs. Upper Saddle River, NJ: Prentice-Hall, Inc., 1998. 376–385. [Indicate pages for the entire selection.]
Introduction in a published edition	Washington, Margaret. Introduction. *Narrative of Sojourner Truth.* By Sojourner Truth. New York: Vintage Books, 1993, pp. v–xi.
Signed article in a weekly magazine	Wallace, Charles. "A Vodacious Deal." *Time* 14 Feb. 2000: 63.
Signed article in a monthly magazine	Gustaitis, Joseph. "The Sticky History of Chewing Gum." *American History* Oct. 1998: 30–38.
Unsigned editorial or story	"Selective Silence." Editorial. *Wall Street Journal* 11 Feb. 2000: A14. [If the editorial or story is signed, begin with the author's name.]
Signed pamphlet or brochure	[Treat the pamphlet as though it were a book.]
Pamphlet with no author, publisher, or date	*Are You at Risk of Heart Attack?* n.p. n.d. ["n.p. n.d." indicates that there is no known publisher or date.]
Filmstrips, slide programs, videocassettes, DVDs, and other audiovisual media	*The Diary of Anne Frank.* Dir. George Stevens. Perf. Millie Perkins, Shelly Winters, Joseph Schildkraut, Lou Jacobi, and Richard Beymer. Twentieth Century Fox, 1959.
Radio or television program transcript	"Nobel for Literature." Narr. Rick Karr. *All Things Considered.* National Public Radio. WNYC, New York. 10 Oct. 2002. Transcript.
Internet	*National Association of Chewing Gum Manufacturers.* 19 Dec. 1999 <http://www.nacgm.org/consumer/funfacts.html> [Indicate the date you accessed the information. Content and addresses at websites change frequently.]
Newspaper	Thurow, Roger. "South Africans Who Fought for Sanctions Now Scrap for Investors." *Wall Street Journal* 11 Feb. 2000: A1+ [For a multipage article, write only the first page number on which it appears, followed by a plus sign.]
Personal interview	Smith, Jane. Personal interview. 10 Feb. 2000.
CD (with multiple publishers)	Simms, James, ed. *Romeo and Juliet.* By William Shakespeare. CD-ROM. Oxford: Attica Cybernetics Ltd.; London: BBC Education; London: HarperCollins Publishers, 1995.
Signed article from an encyclopedia	Askeland, Donald R. "Welding." *World Book Encyclopedia.* 1991 ed.

Technology Handbook

Technology is a combination of resources that can help you do research, find information, and write. Good sources for research include the Internet and your local library. The library contains databases where you can find many forms of print and nonprint resources, including audio and video recordings.

The Internet

The Internet is an international network, or connection, of computers that share information with each other. It is a popular source for research and finding information for academic, professional, and personal reasons. The World Wide Web is a part of the Internet that allows you to find, read, and organize information. Using the Web is a fast way to get the most current information about many topics.

Words or phrases can be typed into the "search" section of a search engine, and websites that contain those words will be listed for you to explore. You can then search a website for the information you need.

Information Media

Media is all the organizations, such as television, radio, and newspapers that provide news and information for the public. Knowing the characteristics of various kinds of media will help you to spot them during your research. The following chart describes several forms of information media.

Types of Information Media	
Television News Program	• Covers current news events • Gives information objectively
Documentary	• Focuses on one topic of social interest • Sometimes expresses controversial opinions
Television Newsmagazine	• Covers a variety of topics • Entertains and informs
Commercial	• Presents products, people, or ideas • Persuades people to buy or take action

Other Sources of Information

There are many other reliable print and nonprint sources of information to use in your research. For example: magazines, newspapers, professional or academic journal articles, experts, political speeches, press conferences.

Most of the information from these sources is also available on the Internet. Try to evaluate the information you find from various media sources. Be careful to choose the most reliable sources for this information.

457

Using the Handbook

This handbook contains valuable information about the skills students need to successfully use technology. It covers the following topics:

- What is technology?
- How to use technology for research
- How to evaluate the quality of information
- How to use technology in writing

To introduce the handbook, walk your students through the pages and, together, note the information found under major headings and subheadings. Direct teaching of the handbook for brief periods will help students become familiar with finding information and understanding content. Point out to students that they may consult the handbook on their own to find information whenever they have a question about using technology.

WHAT IS TECHNOLOGY?

Read aloud the introduction as students follow along. Emphasize the point that the library is an excellent place to find a wide variety of print and non-print resources.

The Internet

With students, discuss the meaning of the terms *Internet*, *World Wide Web*, *website*, and *search engine*. Ask volunteers to share different ways in which they have used the Internet for research.

Information Media

Information media is an important part of our lives. Read aloud and discuss each type of information media presented in the box.

- **Television news program. ASK:** *What are some news programs currently on TV? What are some recent news stories you learned about?*
- **Documentary. ASK:** *What are some topics presented by documentaries?*
- **Television newsmagazine. ASK:** *What have you learned from TV newsmagazines?*
- **Commercial. ASK:** *What commercials have you seen lately? How do commercials try to sell you products?*

Other Sources of Information

Have students brainstorm other reliable sources of print and nonprint information that they can use for research.

The Internet has become a significant source of research for students and professionals. It is important for students to understand how to use the Internet effectively. This portion of the Handbook provides some useful suggestions.

Review the definitions of *Internet* and *World Wide Web*. Point out that the abbreviation for "World Wide Web" is part of most website addresses, such as *www.weather.com.* Give examples of popular search engines and those that are particularly useful for research.

Keyword Search

Read aloud the information and tips on keywords as students follow along in the text. Emphasize that spelling keywords correctly is essential for productive Internet searches.

How to Narrow Your Search

Remind students that research on the Internet can produce a huge list of possible websites to explore. Suggest that, if necessary, students refine their list of keywords to include only the most important ones. Explain how to use search connectors between keywords.

Scaffolding

Ask students to brainstorm some topics for Internet research. Write their ideas on the board. For each idea, ask students to think of important keywords to help them do Internet research. Discuss which keywords are the most important and why.

Good Search Tips

Read aloud the four search tips as students follow along in the text. Although students generally should first open the top links on the list produced by the search engine, they sometimes might want to read through the list before deciding which links to open. They may find a link further down on the list that is exactly what they are looking for.

Metacognition

To monitor students' comprehension of the importance of keywords, **ASK:** *What is the role of keywords in doing research on the Internet? How can you focus an Internet search to make it as productive as possible?*

Keyword Search

Before you begin a search, narrow your subject to a keyword or a group of **keywords**. These are your search terms, and they should be as specific as possible. For example, if you are looking for information about your favorite musical group, you might use the band's name as a keyword. You might locate such information as band member biographies, the group's history, fan reviews of concerts, and hundreds of sites with related names containing information that is irrelevant to your search. Depending on your research needs, you might need to narrow your search.

How to Narrow Your Search

If you have a large group of keywords and still don't know which ones to use, write out a list of all the words you are considering. Then, delete the words that are least important to your search, and highlight those that are most important.

Use search connectors to fine-tune your search:

AND: narrows a search by retrieving documents that include both terms.
  For example: *trumpets AND jazz*
OR: broadens a search by retrieving documents including any of the terms.
  For example: *jazz OR music*
NOT: narrows a search by excluding documents containing certain words.
  For example: *trumpets NOT drums*

Good Search Tips

1. Search engines can be case-sensitive. If your first try at searching fails, check your search terms for misspellings and search again.
2. Use the most important keyword first, followed by the less important ones.
3. Do not open the link to every single page in your results list. Search engines show pages in order of how close it is to your keyword. The most useful pages will be located at the top of the list.
4. Some search engines provide helpful tips for narrowing your search.

Respecting Copyrighted Material

The Internet is growing every day. Sometimes you are not allowed to access or reprint material you find on the Internet. For some text, photographs, music, and fine art, you must first get permission from the author or copyright owner. Also, be careful not to plagiarize while writing and researching. Plagiarism is presenting someone else's words, ideas, or work as your own. If the idea or words are not yours, be sure to give credit by citing the source in your work.

HOW TO EVALUATE THE QUALITY OF INFORMATION

Since the media presents large amounts of information, it is important to learn how to analyze this information critically. Analyzing critically means you can evaluate the information for content, quality, and importance.

How to Evaluate Information from Various Media

Sometimes the media tries to make you think a certain way instead of giving all the facts. These techniques will help you figure out if you can rely on information from the media.

- ☑ Ask yourself if you can trust the source, or if the information you find shows any bias. Is the information being given in a one-sided way?

- ☑ Discuss the information you find from different media with your classmates or teachers to figure out its reliability.

- ☑ Sort out facts from opinions. Make sure that any opinions given are backed up with facts. A fact is a statement that can be proved true. An opinion is a viewpoint that cannot be proved true.

- ☑ Be aware of any loaded language or images. Loaded language and images are emotional words and visuals used to persuade you.

- ☑ Check surprising or questionable information in other sources. Are there instances of faulty reasoning? Is the information adequately supported?

- ☑ Be aware of the kind of media you are watching. If it's a program, is it a documentary? A commercial? What is its purpose? Is it correct?

- ☑ Read the entire article or watch the whole program before reaching a conclusion. Then develop your own views on the issues, people, and information presented.

459

Respecting Copyrighted Material

Tell students that it is sometimes necessary to obtain permission from the author or copyright holder before using material found on the Internet.

Read aloud the definition of *plagiarism* as students follow along. Discuss why plagiarism is considered a serious offense. Tell students the rules in your school regarding plagiarism. Review the following ways to avoid plagiarizing on a research paper:

- Read the research, think about it, and write down the ideas <u>in your own words</u>.

- Do not copy exact sentences from research sources, unless you are going to quote a source.

- Avoid depending on one or two people's ideas for your paper. Make sure you use several different sources of information.

- When you are done writing your paper, read it aloud. Do the words sound like your own words, or do they sound like someone else wrote it?

HOW TO EVALUATE THE QUALITY OF INFORMATION

Students are presented with oceans of information every day. It's important for them to be able to analyze this information and discern fact from opinion, truth from fantasy, and objectivity from bias.

How to Evaluate Information from Various Media

Read aloud the introduction as students follow along in their books. Then read aloud and discuss each checklist item. When possible, provide examples, or ask students for examples to illustrate each point on the checklist.

Scaffolding

You may want to help students practice evaluating media. Find a documentary approved by your school district in your school library about a controversial topic. Preview it and note examples of fact versus opinion and bias. Introduce the documentary to your students. Ask them to follow along on the media checklist as they watch and to take notes if they spot examples of facts/opinions and bias. You may wish to stop the documentary from time to time to point out examples from the checklist.

At the end of the documentary, discuss what students have learned.

T459

How to Evaluate Information from the Internet

The Internet provides vast amounts of information. Discuss why information on the Internet is sometimes incorrect or not to be trusted. **ASK:** *Why is the information you find on the Internet sometimes different from what you read in printed matter?* (Discuss how people publish information on the Internet.)

Internet Research Checklist Review of this section will be most effective if you can use a computer that is connected to a projector to enable students to see examples of the tips. Ideally, students should also have access to computers in the classroom or in a computer lab.

Read aloud each point on the checklist. If you have Internet access, provide appropriate examples of each point.

Explain to students that URL stands for *Uniform Resource Locator* and refers to the web address for a particular site. In addition to ".edu" and ".gov," there are URLs that end in ".org" (for non-profit organizations) and ".com" or ".net" (for businesses).

Cooperative Learning You may want students to practice their Internet research skills in the computer lab.

- Reserve time for your students in your school's computer lab.
- Create a list of research topics with your students, along with important keywords and a list of appropriate search engines.
- In the computer lab, have students work in pairs. Each pair should select one research topic. They can type keywords into the suggested search engines to find research sources.
- Have students look at the information on websites and evaluate each source by using the checklist. Students should write down the URL for each source and the reasons why the source seems trustworthy or not.
- At the end of class, discuss what sources the students found and how they evaluated them.

Metacognition

To monitor students' ability to evaluate and compare source materials, **ASK:** *Where can you find better research materials—the Internet or published books and magazines? How can you judge research materials?*

How to Evaluate Information from the Internet

There is so much information available on the Internet that it can be hard to understand. It is important to be sure that the information you use as support or evidence is reliable and can be trusted. Use the following checklist to decide if a Web page you are reading is reliable and a credible source.

- ☑ The information is from a well-known and trusted website. For example, websites that end in **.edu** are part of an educational institution and usually can be trusted. Other cues for reliable websites are sites that end in **.org** for "organization" or **.gov** for "government." Sites with a **.com** ending are either owned by businesses or individuals.
- ☑ The people who write or are quoted on the website are experts, not just everyday people telling their ideas or opinions.
- ☑ The website gives facts, not just opinions.
- ☑ The website is free of grammatical and spelling errors. This is often a hint that the site was carefully made and will not have factual mistakes.
- ☑ The website is not trying to sell a product or persuade people. It is simply trying to give correct information.
- ☑ If you are not sure about using a website as a source, ask your teacher for advice. Once you become more aware of the different sites, you will become better at knowing which sources to trust.

460

Personal Computers

A personal computer can be an excellent writing tool. It enables a writer to create, change, and save documents. The cut, copy, and paste features are especially useful when writing and revising.

Organizing Information

Create a system to organize the research information you find from various forms of media, such as newspapers, books, and the Internet.

Using a computer and printer can help you in the writing process. You can change your drafts, see your changes clearly, and keep copies of all your work. Also, consider keeping an electronic portfolio. This way you can store and organize copies of your writing in several subject areas. You can review the works you have completed and see your improvement as a writer.

It is easy to organize electronic files on a computer. The desktop is the main screen, and holds folders that the user names. For example, a folder labeled "Writing Projects September" might contain all of the writing you do during that month. This will help you find your work quickly.

As you use your portfolio, you might think of better ways to organize it. You might find you have several drafts of a paper you wrote, and want to create a separate folder for these. Every month, take time to clean up your files.

Computer Tips

1. Rename each of your revised drafts using the SAVE AS function. For example, if your first file is "essay," name the first revision "essay2" and the next one "essay3."
2. If you share your computer with others, label a folder with your name and keep your files separate by putting them there.
3. Always back up your portfolio on a server or a CD.

Screen

Keyboard

Mouse

Personal computer ▶

461

This section provides some useful tips to students on how to use computers for writing. You may find a wide range of computer skills among your students, depending on prior training and access to computers at home and at school.

Review of this section would be more effective if you could use a computer that is connected to a projector to enable students to see examples of the tips. Ideally, students should also have access to computers in the classroom or in a computer lab.

Personal Computers

Read aloud the introduction as students follow along in the text. If you are using a computer and a projector, demonstrate how to save documents and revise by using *cut*, *copy*, and *paste* commands.

You may also want to show students how to use the grammar and spell check functions. Point out that students need to use their own grammar and spelling skills when they write and should not depend on these software functions to correct their work. Also, the grammar and spell check functions are not always correct.

Organizing Information

You may want to create a simple, logical folder system for students to use for saving documents. Give them naming protocols, and advise which documents should go into the folders.

Computer Tips

In addition to saving drafts by using the SAVE AS function, it may also be helpful to show students how file manager functions show the date and time of their most recent work.

You should emphasize the importance of saving and backing up as part of the computer writing process. Discuss the consequences of failing to do this. At the end of each computer writing session, have students save and back up their work before they leave the class.

Glossary

accurate correct or exact

achieve succeed in doing or getting something as a result of your actions

affect to do something that produces a change in someone or something; influence

alter change in some way

ancient very old

anniversary a day when you remember something special or important that happened on the same date in an earlier year

approach to move closer to someone or something

appropriate suitable for a particular time, situation, or purpose

archaeologist someone who studies very old things and buildings made by people who lived a long time ago

architecture the shape and style of buildings

arrangement a plan or agreement that something will happen

artificial not natural, but made by people

aspect one of the parts or features of a situation, idea, or problem

assassinated murdered, especially for political reasons

assist to help someone do something

athletes people who are good at sports and take part in sports competitions

atomic bomb a very powerful bomb that splits atoms to cause an extremely large explosion

attitude the opinions and feelings that you usually have about someone or something

author someone who writes a book, story, article, play, etc.

average calculated by adding several amounts together and dividing by the total number of amounts

aware realizing that something is true, exists, or is happening

benefit something that gives you an advantage, that helps you, or that has a good effect

bond a feeling or interest that unites two or more people or groups

boundaries lines that divide two places

brief continuing for a short time

campaign a series of actions done to get a result, especially in business or politics

canvases strong cloths that are painted on

canyons deep valleys with very steep sides

category a group of people or things that have related characteristics

cells the smallest living things

ceremony a group of special actions done and special words spoken at an important public or religious event

chaos a state of no order or no control

character traits special qualities or features that someone or something has that make that person or thing different from others

characters people or animals in a novel, story, movie, or play

circumstances the facts or conditions that affect a situation, action, or event

462

citizen a person who lives in a particular country or city and has special rights there

classical belonging to the culture of ancient Greece or ancient Rome

clues things that help you find the answer to a difficult problem

colorful language words an author uses to make a story, play, or movie sound and look more fun

comment a stated opinion made about someone or something

committee a group of people chosen to do something, make decisions, etc.

communicate express your thoughts and feelings so that others understand them

complex complicated

concept an idea of how something is or how something should be done

conflict disagreement

conservationists people who protect natural things such as animals, plants, or forests

consist to be made up of or contain particular things or people

constant happening regularly or all the time

construct build something large such as a building, bridge, or sculpture

continent one of the large areas of land on earth, such as Africa, Europe, Australia, etc.

conversion the art or process of changing from one form, purpose, or system to a different one

convey communicate a message or information, with or without using words

cooperate to work together with someone else to achieve something that you both want

create make something exist

creature an animal or insect

cultural relating to a particular society and its way of life

damage harm that has been done to something

defendant the person in a court of law who has been accused of doing something illegal

define show or describe what something is or means

democratic organized by a system in which everyone has the same right to vote, speak, etc.

demonstrate protest or support something in public with a lot of other people

deny say that something is not true

destruction the act of breaking or damaging something completely

device a way of achieving a particular purpose or effect

dialect a form of language that is spoken in one area in a different way than it is in another area

dialogue a conversation by two or more characters in a book, play, or movie

disappeared was lost or stopped existing

drama a play for the theater, television, radio, etc.

education teaching and learning

effect a result or a reaction to something or someone

463

element part of a plan, system, piece of writing, etc.

enormous extremely large in size or amount

environment the land, water, and air in which people, animals, and plants live

establish create

estimate judge the value or size of something

evidence facts, objects, or signs that make you believe that something exists or is true

extinct no longer existing or living

extraordinary very special

fable a story that teaches a lesson

factors several things that influence or cause a situation

fantasy an imagined situation or thing that is not real

feature quality, element, or characteristic of something that seems important, interesting, or typical

figure of speech a word or expression that is used in a different way from the usual one, to give you a picture in your mind

final last in a series of actions, events, or parts of something

finance provide money for something

focus attention to a particular person or thing

forensic relating to methods for finding out about a crime

founders people who establish a business, organization, school, etc.

frontier the area where people are just beginning to explore or live

function the usual purpose of a thing, or the job that someone usually does

generation all the people who are about the same age, especially in a family

genes parts of a cell that decide what traits you will have

gigantic very big

gradual happening or changing slowly

habitats the natural environments in which plants or animals live

height how tall or how far from the ground something is

humor something that amuses people or makes them laugh

hyperbole a way of describing something by saying that it is much bigger, smaller, heavier, etc., than it really is

identify recognize and name someone or something

idioms groups of words that have special meaning when they are used together

illustrate explain or make something clear by giving examples

image a picture that you can see through a camera, on television, or in a mirror; a picture that you have in your mind

impact the effect that something or someone has on someone or something

individual a person, not a group

infinity a space or distance without limits or an end

inherit to get a quality, type of behavior, appearance, etc., from one your parents

464

inspiration someone or something that encourages you to do or produce something good

instruct to teach someone or show him or her how to do something

intelligent having a high ability to learn, understand, and think about things

interpretation an explanation

intruder someone or something that enters a building or area where they are not supposed to be

legislation a law or set of laws

length the distance from one end of something to the other; how long something is

list of characters a set of names that identify the characters of a play to the reader

mass-produced produced in large numbers using machinery so that each object is the same and can be sold cheaply

medical relating to medicine and the treatment of disease or injury

metaphor a way of describing something by comparing it to something else that has similar qualities, without using the words *like* or *as*. "A river of tears" is a metaphor.

method a planned way of doing something

mood the way that a place, book, movie, etc., makes you feel

moral a lesson about what is right and wrong that you learn from a story or an event

motive the reason that makes someone do something, especially when this reason is kept hidden

mural a very large painting that is painted or placed directly on a wall

myth an ancient story, especially one that explains cultural beliefs or a natural or historic event

narrator someone who tells the story in a movie, book, etc.

natural found in nature, not made by people or machines

numerals written signs that represent numbers

nutrition the process of giving or getting the right kinds of food in order to be healthy

objective something that you are working hard to achieve

occupation job or profession

occur happen

ornithology the scientific study of birds

percent equal to a particular amount in every hundred

period a particular length of time in history or in a person's life

personification a literary device in which nonhuman characters are given human traits

perspective a way of thinking about something that is influenced by the type of person you are or by what you do

philosophy the study of what it means to exist, what good and evil are, what knowledge is, or how people should live

physical relating to the body or to other things you can see, touch, smell, feel, or taste

465

plot the main events that make up the story of a book, movie, or play

point of view the perspective from which a story is written or told

policy a way of doing things that has been officially agreed upon and chosen by a political party or an organization

positive good or useful

precise exact and correct in every detail

predator an animal that kills and eats other animals

procedure the correct or normal way of way of doing something

process a series of actions that someone does in order to achieve a particular result

professional relating to a job for which you need special education or training

published printed and sold

puns amusing uses of a word or phrase that has two meanings, or of words with the same sound but different meanings

pursue chase or follow someone or something to catch him, her, or it

rate the number of times or the speed at which something happens

react to behave in a particular way because of what someone has done or said to you

region a fairly large area of a state, country, etc.

rely on to trust or depend on someone or something

repetition the act of doing or saying something again

require need something

research serious study of a subject that is intended to discover new facts about it

resistance refusal to give in to someone or something

resource something such as land, minerals, or natural energy that exists in a country and can be used in order to increase wealth

respond to react to something that has been said or done

responsibilities things that you have a duty to do or take care of

rhyme scheme a pattern of end rhymes in poems or song lyrics

rhythm a regular pattern of sounds or beats

rights what things are or should be allowed by the law

rituals ceremonies or sets of actions that are always done in the same way

robots machines that can move and do some of the work

role the position, job, or function someone or something has in a particular situation or activity

sacred relating to a god or religion; extremely important and greatly respected

sacrifice to not do something so that you can do something more important

science fiction a type of writing that describes imaginary future developments in science and their effect on life, for example, time travel

section a part of something

sequence a series of related events, actions, or numbers that have a particular order setting where and when a story or real-life event takes place

setting the scene an author's details about the time and place in a book or play

shift a change in the way people think about something or in the way something is done

simile an expression in which you compare two things using the words *like* or *as*, for example, "Her face was as pale as the moon."

site a place where something is being built or will be built

specific detailed and exact

sphere something in the shape of a ball

spirals shapes that go around and around as they go up

stage directions notes in a play that tell actors what they should do and how they should act

stanzas groups of lines that form part of a poem

statistics a collection of numbers that represents facts or measurements

steep having a slope that is high and difficult to go up

strategies sets of plans and skills used in order to gain success or achieve an aim

stress continuous feelings of worry caused by difficulties in your life

structure the way in which the parts of something connect with each other to form a whole

style a way of doing, making, or painting, something that is typical of a particular period

superintendent a person who is responsible for a place, job, activity, etc.

survive continue to live or exist

suspense a feeling of not knowing what is going to happen next

sustain to make it possible for someone or something to continue to exist over time

techniques special methods of doing something

technology a combination of all the knowledge, equipment, or methods used in scientific or industrial work

theory an explanation that may or may not be true

tolerance willingness to allow people to do, say, or believe what they want

trend the way that a situation is generally developing or changing

tsunami a very large, forceful wave that causes a lot of damage when it hits the land

uniforms particular types of clothing that members of an organization wear to work

unique the only one of its type

volcanoes mountains with holes at the top through which burning rock and fire sometimes rise into the air

weight how heavy something is

welfare health, comfort, and happiness

whorls patterns made out of lines that curl in circles that get bigger and bigger

467

Index of Skills

Further Reading, 59, 125, 189, 253, 321, 389

Grammar, Usage, and Mechanics
Active voice, 42
Adjectives
  comparative, 28, 110
  placement of, 174
Adverbs
  with -ly, 238, 278
Asking questions, 360
Cause-and-effect structures, 250
Comparison structures
  -er than, 28, 110
  as...as and not as...as, 28, 110
  more than and less than, 110
Conjunctions, coordinating, 82
Expressing predictions, 344
Imperatives, 318
Indefinite pronouns, 56
Parts of speech, 16
Prepositions
  of location, 186
  of time, 160
Punctuation, 374
  apostrophe, 139
  quotation marks, 386
Quoted versus reported speech, 306
Sentences
  simple and compound, 148
Subject-verb agreement, 56
Transitions, 82
Verbs
  imperatives, 318
  non-action, 96
  passive voice, 42
  present perfect, 212, 290
  regular and irregular, 122, 226
  simple past, 122, 226

Language Development
Language functions
  comprehension, 14, 26, 40, 54, 80, 94, 108, 120, 146, 158, 172, 184, 210, 224, 236, 248, 276, 288, 304, 316, 342, 358, 372, 384

Language learning strategies
  dramatic reading, 224, 358
  listening and speaking workshop, 60–61, 126–127, 190–191, 254–255, 322–323, 390–391
  reader's theater, 14, 54, 94, 108, 146, 172, 236, 276, 304, 372

Listening and Speaking
Dramatic reading, 224, 358
Gathering and organizing information, 60, 126, 190, 254, 322, 390
Listening and speaking workshop
  description guessing game, 60–61
  how-to demonstration, 322–323
  skit, 126–127
  speech, 390–391
  TV sports report, 254–255
  TV talk show, 190–191
Reader's theater, 14, 54, 94, 108, 146, 172, 236, 276, 304, 372

Literary Analysis
Genre
  art text, 284–287
  diary excerpt, 166–171
  fable, 232–233
  folk tale, 118–119
  interview, 354–357
  math text, 22–25
  myth, 234–236
  novel excerpt, 8–13, 88–93, 102–107, 140–145, 296–303, 366–371
  play, 268–275
  poetry, 218–221, 222, 223, 350–353
  science text, 22–25, 116–117, 180–183, 244–247, 312–315, 380–383
  short story, 48–53
  social studies text, 34–39, 74–79, 154–157, 204–209, 284–287, 336–341

Literary response and evaluation
  analyzing text, 27, 210
  creating timelines, 385
  describing objects, 15
  identifying cause and effect, 248
  summarizing, 26, 80, 120, 158, 173, 184, 210, 248, 288, 316, 342, 384
  writing about the future, 343, 373
  writing e-mail, 359
  writing fables, 237
  writing from another point of view, 305
  writing journal entries, 109, 147, 277
  writing new endings, 55, 109
  writing poetry, 225
  writing travel brochures, 95
Literary terms
  character traits, 5
  characters, 5
  colorful language, 293
  dialect, 137
  dialogue, 85
  fable, 229
  figure of speech, 163
  humor, 293
  hyperbole, 163
  idioms, 45
  list of characters, 265
  metaphor, 347
  mood, 137
  moral, 229
  myth, 229
  narrator, 99
  personification, 229
  plot, 99
  point of view, 99
  puns, 45
  repetition, 215
  rhyme scheme, 215
  rhythm, 215
  science fiction, 363
  setting, 85, 363
  setting the scene, 265
  simile, 347
  stage directions, 265
  stanzas, 347

469

Index of Authors, Titles, Art, and Artists

Acknowledgments

UNIT 1

Excerpts from *Chasing Vermeer* by Blue Balliett. Scholastic Inc./Scholastic Press. Copyright © 2004 by Elizabeth Balliett Klein. Used by permission of Scholastic Inc.

Excerpt from *G Is for Googol: A Math Alphabet Book* by David M. Schwartz. Copyright © 1998 by David M. Schwartz, Tricycle Press, Berkeley, CA, www.tenspeed.com. Reprinted with permission.

"Fact or Fiction?" Copyright © Pearson Longman, 10 Bank Street, White Plains, NY 10606.

Teenage Detectives: "The Case of the Defaced Sidewalk" by Carol Farley and "The Case of the Disappearing Signs" by Hy Conrad. Originally appeared on MysteryNet.com. Copyright © 1998, 2005 by Newfront Productions, Inc. Reprinted by permission.

UNIT 2

"Ancient Kids." Copyright © Pearson Longman, 10 Bank Street, White Plains, NY 10606.

"A Cry of Hounds" and "Soap Carving" from *Becoming Naomi León* by Pam Muñoz Ryan. Copyright © 2004 by Pam Muñoz Ryan. Reprinted by permission of Scholastic Inc.

Excerpt from *Later, Gator* by Laurence Yep. Copyright © 1995 by Laurence Yep. Reprinted with permission of Hyperion Books for Children. All rights reserved.

"Amazing Growth Facts." Adapted from *Incredible Comparisons* by Russell Ash, Dorling Kindersley.

"The Old Grandfather and His Little Grandson," an adapted folktale by Leo Tolstoy. Public domain.

UNIT 3

Excerpt from *Run Away Home* by Patricia C. McKissack. Scholastic Inc./Scholastic Press. Copyright © 1997 by Patricia C. McKissack. Reprinted by permission.

"Extraordinary People: Serving Others." Copyright © Pearson Longman, 10 Bank Street, White Plains, NY 10606.

Excerpt from *Zlata's Diary: A Child's Life in Sarajevo* by Zlata Filipović, translated by Christina Pribichevich-Zoric. Translation copyright © 1994 Editions Robert Laffont/Fixot. Used by permission of Viking Penguin, a Division of Penguin Group (U.S.A.) Inc. First published in France as *Le Journal de Zlata* by Fixot et Editions Robert Laffont 1993. Copyright © Fixot et Editions Robert Laffont, 1993. Reproduced by permission of Penguin Books Ltd. and by permission of Editions Robert Laffont.

"Friendships and Cooperation in the Animal Kingdom." Copyright © Pearson Longman, 10 Bank Street, White Plains, NY 10606.

UNIT 4

"Soccer: The World Sport" by Jane Schwartz. Copyright © Pearson Longman, 10 Bank Street, White Plains, NY 10606.

"Casey at the Bat" by Ernest Lawrence Thayer, 1888. Public domain.

"Swift Things Are Beautiful" from *Away Goes Sally* by Elizabeth Coatsworth. Copyright © 1934 by Macmillan Publishing Company, renewed 1962 by Elizabeth Coatsworth Beston. By permission of Paterson Marsh Ltd on behalf of the Estate of Elizabeth Coatsworth.

"Buffalo Dusk" from *Smoke and Steel* by Carl Sandburg. Copyright © 1920 by Harcourt, Inc. and renewed 1948 by Carl Sandburg. Reprinted by permission of the publisher.

"The Hare and the Tortoise" by Aesop. Public domain.

"Going, Going, Gone?" Adapted from *Time for Kids*, January 22, 2002. © 2002 Time for Kids. Reprinted by permission.

"Ivory-Billed Woodpeckers Make Some Noise" by Jill Egan. Adapted from *Time for Kids*, August 5, 2005. © 2005 Time for Kids. Reprinted by permission.

UNIT 5

Excerpt from *The Secret Garden* by Frances Hodgson Burnett and adapted by David C. Jones, from *Plays, The Drama Magazine for Young People*, © 2005. Reprinted with the permission of the publisher PLAYS/Sterling Partners, Inc., PO Box 600160, Newton, MA 02460.

"Kids' Guernica." Copyright © Pearson Longman, 10 Bank Street, White Plains, NY 10606.

Excerpt from *Hoot* by Carl Hiaasen. Copyright © 2002 by Carl Hiaasen. Used by permission of Alfred A. Knopf, an imprint of Random House Children's Books, a Division of Random House, Inc., and by permission of the author c/o Rogers, Coleridge & White Ltd., 20 Powis Mews, London, W11 1JN.

"A Tree Grows in Kenya: The Story of Wangari Maathai" and "How to Plant a Tree." Copyright © Pearson Longman, 10 Bank Street, White Plains, NY 10606.

UNIT 6

"Life in the Future." Copyright © Pearson Longman, 10 Bank Street, White Plains, NY 10606.

"Southbound on the Freeway" and "Cardinal Ideograms" from *The Complete Poems to Solve* by May Swenson. Copyright © 1993. Used with permission of The Literary Estate of May Swenson.

"Interview with an Astronaut: Dan Bursch." Copyright © 2000 Discovery Communications, Inc. All rights reserved. Reprinted by permission of Discovery Kids.

Excerpt from *The Best New Thing* by Isaac Asimov. Copyright © The World Publishing Company, New York, 1971.

Excerpt from *2095: Time Warp Trio* by Jon Scieszka. Copyright © 1995 by Jon Scieszka. Used by permission of Viking Penguin, a Division of Penguin Young Readers Group, a member of Penguin Group (U.S.A.) Inc., 345 Hudson Street, New York, NY 10014. All rights reserved.

"Genetic Fingerprints." Copyright © Pearson Longman, 10 Bank Street, White Plains, NY 10606.

Credits

Smithsonian American Art Museum
List of Artworks

UNIT 1 Solving the Puzzle of Letters and Numbers
Page 66
Mike Wilkins
Preamble, 1987
painted metal on vinyl and wood
96 x 96 in.
Smithsonian American Art Museum, Gift of Nissan Motor Corporation in U.S.A.
© 1987 Mike Wilkins

Page 67
Robert Indiana
Five, 1984
wood and metal
69⅛ x 26¾ x 18½ in.
Smithsonian American Art Museum, Gift of the artist
© 1984 Robert Indiana

UNIT 2 Capturing Childhood
Page 132
Albert Bisbee
Child on a Rocking Horse, about 1855
daguerreotype
4¼ x 4½ in.
Smithsonian American Art Museum, Museum purchase from the Charles Isaacs Collection
made possible in part by the Luisita L. and Franz H. Denghausen Endowment

Page 133
William Holbrook Beard
The Lost Balloon, 1882
oil on canvas
47¾ x 33¾ in.
Smithsonian American Art Museum, Museum purchase

UNIT 3 Respect
Page 196
Jesse Treviño
Mis Hermanos, 1976
acrylic on canvas
48 x 70 in.
Smithsonian American Art Museum, Gift of Lionel Sosa, Ernest Bromley,
Adolfo Aguilar of Sosa, Bromley, Aguilar and Associates
© Smithsonian American Art Museum

Page 197
Jacob Lawrence
"Men exist for the sake of one another. Teach them then or bear with them."—Marcus Aurelius
Antoninus, Meditations, VIII: 59. From the series Great Ideas of Western Man., 1958
oil on fiberboard
20¾ x 16¾ in.
Smithsonian American Art Museum, Gift of Container Corporation of America

477

UNIT 4 Baseball in America
Page 260
Mark Sfirri
Rejects from the Bat Factory, 1996
various woods
15⅜ x 36½ in.
Smithsonian American Art Museum, Gift of Fleur and Charles Bresler in honor of
Kenneth R. Trapp, curator-in-charge of the Renwick Gallery (1995–2003)
© 1996 Mark Sfirri

Page 261
Morris Kantor
Baseball at Night, 1934
oil on linen
37 x 47¼ in.
Smithsonian American Art Museum, Gift of Mrs. Morris Kantor

UNIT 5 Dignity Through Art
Page 329
James Hampton
The Throne of the Third Heaven of the Nations' Millennium General Assembly, about 1950–64
gold and silver aluminum foil, Kraft paper, and plastic
180 pieces: 10½ x 27 x 14½ ft.
Smithsonian American Art Museum, Gift of anonymous donors

UNIT 6 Imaging the Future
Page 398
Harry Bertoia
Sculpture Group Symbolizing World's Communication in the Atomic Age, 1959
braised and welded brass and bronze
142¼ x 231¼ x 81 in.
Smithsonian American Art Museum, Gift of the Zenith Corporation

Page 399
Alexander A. Maldonado
San Francisco to New York in One Hour, 1969
oil on canvas and wood
18 x 24 in.
Smithsonian American Art Museum, Gift of Herbert Waide Hemphill Jr.
and museum purchase made possible by Ralph Cross Johnson
© Smithsonian American Art Museum

478